2^2

Members of the
Mathematics in Action Group
associated with this book:

D. Brown
R.D. Howat
E.C.K. Mullan
R. Murray
K. Nisbet
D. Thomas
J. Thomson

T

Published in 2003 by:
Nelson Thornes Ltd
Delta Place
27 Bath Road
CHELTENHAM
GL53 7TH
United Kingdom

08 09 / 10 9 8 7 6 5

A catalogue record of this book is available from the British Library

ISBN 978 0 7487 6520 1

Illustrations by Ian Foulis, Oxford Designers and Illustrators, Peters and Zabransky
Page make-up by Tech-Set Ltd

Printed and bound in India by Replika Press Pvt. Ltd.

Acknowledgements
The publishers thank the following for permission to reproduce copyright material. British Museum: 277; Columbia University: 224 (Rare Book and Manuscript Library); Corel (NT): 125L, 366; Corel 84 (NT): 244 left; Corel 85 (NT): 141; Corel 281 (NT): 396; Corel 565 (NT): 344; Corel 584 (NT): 125 right, 137; Corel 658 (NT): 240 right; Diamar 5 (NT): 240 left; Digital Vision 6 (NT): 57; Digital Vision 7 (NT): 149 right; Digital Vision 15 (NT): 170; Fotomas Index: 149L; Greek Postal Service: 214 (TRIPOD); JSC: 381; Lucent Archives: 177 (R L Dietzold); NASA: 377; Photodisc 54 (NT): 244 right, 317; Public Record Office: 101 (Crown Copyright); Science Photolibrary: 236 (Pekka Parviainen); Stockscotland: 11; T Clayton: 31; University of Massachusetts: 59 (Lowell Gallery); University of Toledo: 80; Yale University: 253 (Centre for Earth Observation, Frank Hole).
The publishers have made every effort to contact copyright holders but apologise if any have been overlooked.

Contents

Introduction

The principal aim of this resource is to provide a comprehensive coverage of Level E attainment targets as defined in the 5-14 National Guidelines. This includes materials not mentioned explicitly in section 2 of these Guidelines, but which the authors feel are essential, indispensable aspects for the proper development and understanding of mathematics. As suggested by the Guidelines, natural opportunities are taken to introduce new content and depth. Common vocabulary associated with each topic is emphasised and tools to assist in communication, e.g. notation and conventions, are promoted. Opportunities to exercise mental agility and non-calculator skills are provided, especially in chapters developing the attainment outcome Number, Money, Measurement. Problem solving and Enquiry is catered for throughout the resource through *Challenges, Brainstormers* and *Investigations*.

An opportunity to develop the mathematics to level F is provided in each chapter. Here, unless it is essential, technical vocabulary is not included. Problem solving, investigation and abstraction are also kept to a minimum. All targets are visited to the standard required by the National assessments. Where a student regularly completes this standard of level F, Book S2^3 may offer a more appropriate learning curve.

Each chapter follows the same structure.

> *Looking Back* – establishes the knowledge and skills required to proceed with the topic. Questions in this section may examine a lower level or an essential topic at the same level.
> *Level E Exercises* – comprehensive and graded.
> *Level F Exercises* – establish the basic mathematical skills required at this level.
> *Check-Up* – provides a diagnostic test ensuring that all attainment targets are known before progression to the next topic. Level F questions are indicated by purple question numbers.

Contexts have been chosen to show students the variety of places where maths may be applied. *Brainstormers*, *Challenges, Puzzles* and *Investigations* appear throughout the text, providing stimulating and motivating opportunities to enrich mathematical experience.

A Teacher Resource Pack providing material for homework, extension and preparation for assessment is available. The pack also contains a section that examines problems exemplifying the strategies listed on page 13 of the National Guidelines.

1 Whole numbers and integers

'The ingenious method of expressing every possible number using a set of ten symbols emerged in India. The idea seems so simple nowadays that its significance and importance is no longer appreciated. Its simplicity lies in the way it made calculation easy and placed arithmetic foremost amongst useful inventions.'

This was said by the French mathematician Laplace at the end of the eighteenth century.

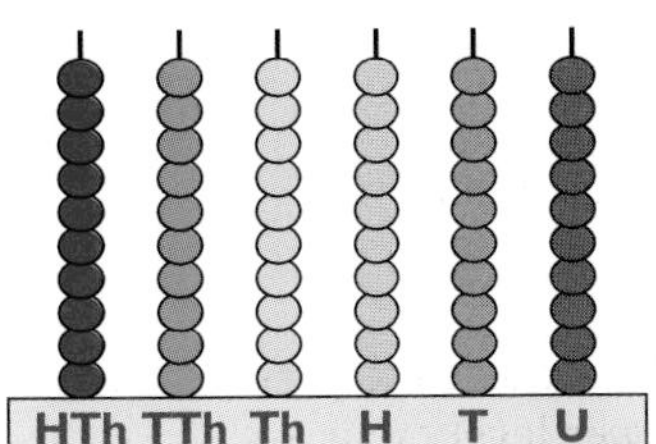

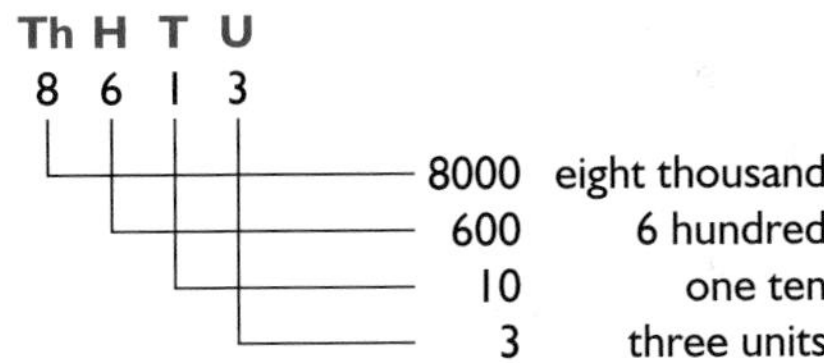

1 Looking back

Exercise 1.1

Do the first eight questions without written working.

1 **a** The number of households in Glasgow in 1996 was estimated as 271 900. Write this estimate in words.

b Last year, Scottish residents made four hundred and ninety-eight thousand, six hundred and fifty holiday trips to Spain. Write this number in figures.

2 Tom, Rana and Sal played the computer game 'Spider Kong'. Here are their scores:

Tom 28 905 Rana 29 065 Sal 30 825

a Who had the highest score?

b Who had the lowest score?

c Write the three scores in words.

3 The votes received by four candidates during an election were:

M. Tee	nineteen thousand, eight hundred and seven
T. Pott	thirty-seven thousand and twenty-three
B. Still	forty-two thousand, one hundred and fifty-one
C. Shore	twenty-seven thousand, nine hundred and eighty.

a Who received the most votes?

b Who was second?

c Write each candidate's number of votes in figures.

4 To the number 86 745:

a add 100 **b** subtract 10 **c** add 1000 **d** take away 6.

5 **a** Add 67 and 89. **b** Subtract 38 from 93.

c Multiply 7500 by 6. **d** Divide 920 by 5.

6 Greg's taxi fare is £12·40. What change should he be given from £20?

7 **a** A holiday for ten friends costs £2350 altogether. How much does it cost each friend?

b Last year's holiday cost each of the ten friends £195. What was the total cost of last year's holiday?

100 centimetres = 1 metre

8 **a** Change 2650 m to centimetres. **b** Change 35 000 cm to metres.

9

6 oranges	£1·92
1 melon	£2·35
Basket of fruit	£9·50

What is the change if Jill pays for everything with a £20 note?

10 **a** How many more people live in Carrick than in Kyle?

b What is the combined population of the two towns?

11 **a** How many complete weeks are in 1000 days?

b How many days are left over?

12 Last month an aircraft flew six times between London and Tokyo. How many miles is that altogether?

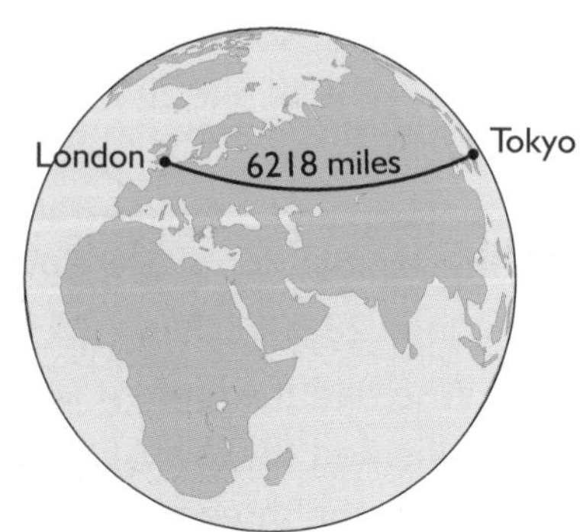

13 a A dining-hall table can seat eight pupils.
How many of the tables are needed to seat 298 pupils?

b A box of eggs can hold six eggs.
How many boxes of eggs can be filled if there are 106 eggs?

14 What is the cost of:

a seven CDs at £11·99 each

b nine packs of golf balls at £18·90 per pack?

15 a Add 8365 and 7648.
b Subtract 2658 from 8305.
c Multiply 7694 by 12.
d Divide 7618 by 26.

16 Round your answers to question **15** to the nearest **a** 10 **b** 100.

17 Gina's annual salary is £8762.
How much is she paid

a per month
b per week?

Round your answers to the nearest pound (£).

2 Take smaller steps

Many calculations can be made easier by breaking the problem down into simple problems.

Example 1

$$130 \times 20 = 130 \times 10 \times 2 = 1300 \times 2 = 2600$$

Example 2

$$8400 \div 60 = 8400 \div 10 \div 6 = 840 \div 6 = 140$$

Example 3

$$265 \times 300 = 265 \times 100 \times 3 = 26\,500 \times 3 = 79\,500$$

Example 4

$$17\,600 \div 400 = 17\,600 \div 100 \div 4 = 176 \div 4 = 44$$

Example 5 Calculate the cost of 18 tickets at £37 each.
Method: Find the cost of 20 tickets and subtract the cost of 2 tickets.

- Find the cost of 20: $37 \times 20 = 37 \times 10 \times 2 = 740$
- Find the cost of 2: $37 \times 2 = 74$

18 tickets cost £740 − £74 = £666

Example 6 Calculate the cost of 41 pens at 85p each.
Method: Find the cost of 40 pens and add on the cost of 1 pen.

- Find the cost of 40: $85 \times 40 = 85 \times 10 \times 4 = 850 \times 4 = 3400$
- Find the cost of 1: $85 \times 1 = 85$

41 pens cost 3400p + 85p = 3485p = £34·85

1

Exercise 2.1

1 Calculate:

a 12×20 **b** 25×20 **c** 25×30 **d** 240×40 **e** 365×50
f 35×200 **g** 48×300 **h** 92×500 **i** 87×400 **j** 234×300

2 Calculate:

a $150 \div 30$ **b** $640 \div 40$ **c** $7200 \div 60$ **d** $8250 \div 50$
e $72\,000 \div 30$ **f** $3000 \div 200$ **g** $7800 \div 300$ **h** $54\,000 \div 400$
i $25\,500 \div 300$ **j** $123\,000 \div 500$

3 Find the value of:

a 42×19 **b** 27×29 **c** 65×99 **d** 53×99 **e** 24×18
f 33×28 **g** 28×21 **h** 36×41 **i** 15×32 **j** 72×101
k 34×102 **l** 460×51

4 Calculate the cost for a person having a Happy Holidays break for:

a three weeks in April
b the whole of February
c the whole of March.

HAPPY HOLIDAYS
Special offers for 2005:

3-week stay	£48 per day
February	£43 per day
March	£47 per day

5 500 washers weigh 2000 grams.
Calculate the weight of one washer.

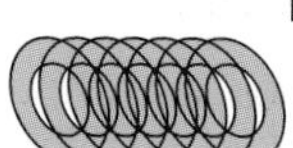

6 A pile of 400 similar sheets of metal is 3600 mm high.
What is the thickness of each sheet of metal?

7 A total of £1950 was paid for the 30 front row seats at the Popstars concert.
What was the price of each seat?

E

3 Mental calculations

You are to attempt Exercises 3.1 and 3.2 without written working.

Exercise 3.1

Selection A Pretty easy

1 Add 36 and 28
2 Subtract 19 from 42
3 Add 250 and 370
4 Take 160 from 220

Selection B Not so easy

1 Add 85 and 85
2 Subtract 78 from 200
3 Add 550 and 650
4 Take 170 from 310

Selection C Not easy

1 Add 87 and 76
2 Subtract 26 from 73
3 Add 480 and 650
4 Take 470 from 840

5 98 times 9

6 Divide 464 by 8

7 Divide 123 by 5

8 Multiply 175 by 30

9 Divide 8400 by 60

10 Multiply 2000 by 1000

11 Divide 750 000 by 1000

12 1 + 2 + 3 + 4 + 5 + 6 + 7 + 8 + 9 + 10

5 Multiply 780 by 6

6 Divide 702 by 9

7 Divide 152 by 6

8 Multiply 880 by 20

9 Divide 6800 by 80

10 Multiply 30 000 by 1000

11 Divide 1 million by 1000

12 2 + 4 + 6 + 8 + 10 + 12 + 14 + 16 + 18 + 20

5 Multiply 278 by 7

6 Divide 1000 by 8

7 Divide 527 by 6

8 Multiply 365 by 40

9 Divide 245 000 by 700

10 Multiply 72 500 by 1000

11 Divide 12 million by 1000

12 1 + 3 + 5 + 7 + 9 + 11 + 13 + 15 + 17 + 19

Exercise 3.2

E

1 If 18 out of 81 students are left-handed, how many are right-handed?

2 58 km by bus. 75 km by train. How many kilometres altogether?

3 Sam drove 250 miles on Monday and 380 miles on Tuesday. How many miles did he drive altogether?

4 Tara delivered 330 leaflets. Anwar delivered 160 leaflets. How many more leaflets did Tara deliver?

5 23 600 people each paid £8 to see a pay-as-you-view football match. How much money was paid altogether?

6 How many weeks are there in 546 days?

7 £335 is shared equally among 9 people.

  a How many whole pounds (£) does each person receive?

  b How many pounds are left over?

8 185 passengers each pay £50 for an air ticket. How much is paid altogether?

9 A car used 40 litres of petrol to travel 760 km. How many kilometres did it travel per litre?

10 An ounce of gold is worth 300 dollars. How much is 100 ounces of gold worth?

11 One thousand paper clips weigh one million milligrams. What is the weight of one paperclip?

12 A bolt is 80 mm long. What is the total length of 1000 of the bolts? Give your answer in metres.

A puzzle to help your mental agility!

1	3	5	7
9	11	13	15
17	19	21	23
25	27	29	31
33	35	37	39
41	43	45	47
49	51	53	55
57	59	61	63

2	3	6	7
10	11	14	15
18	19	22	23
26	27	30	31
34	35	38	39
42	43	46	47
50	51	54	55
58	59	62	63

4	5	6	7
12	13	14	15
20	21	22	23
28	29	30	31
36	37	38	39
44	45	46	47
52	53	54	55
60	61	62	63

8	9	10	11
12	13	14	15
24	25	26	27
28	29	30	31
40	41	42	43
44	45	46	47
56	57	58	59
60	61	62	63

Meg found these six cards in her Christmas cracker. The instructions told her how to use them in a trick.

First she asked a friend to think of a number from 1 to 64.

Then, showing him one card at a time she asked, 'Is it on this card?'

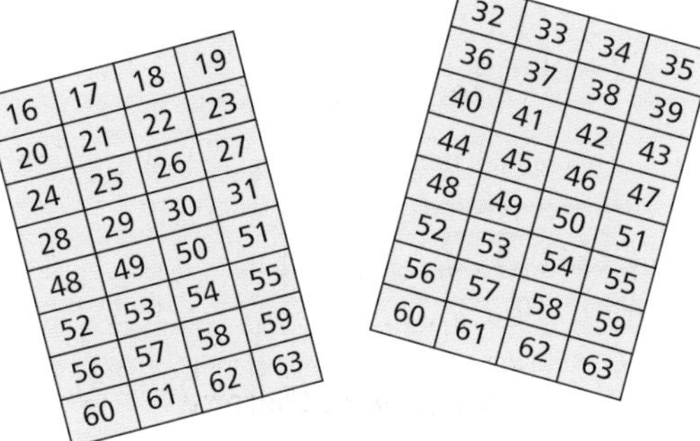

16 17 18 19
20 21 22 23
24 25 26 27
28 29 30 31
48 49 50 51
52 53 54 55
56 57 58 59
60 61 62 63
32 33 34 35
36 37 38 39
40 41 42 43
44 45 46 47
48 49 50 51
52 53 54 55
56 57 58 59
60 61 62 63

As soon as he answered yes or no for the last card she could instantly tell him his chosen number.

Remembering that it is a card trick to help improve your mental skills, how did she do it?

E

4 Going big with numbers

'*Notation* is the expressing of a number in figures.
Numeration is the expressing of a number in words.'

Walkingame's Arithmetic book, 1844.

856 372 is read as '*eight hundred and fifty-six thousand, three hundred and seventy-two*'.
68 075 402 is read as '*sixty-eight million, seventy-five thousand, four hundred and two*'.

Exercise 4.1

1 **a** Write the number 370 145 in words.

b From 370 145:

i subtract 5 **ii** subtract 40 **iii** subtract 100 **iv** subtract 1000.

2 **a** Write the number *five hundred and six thousand, two hundred and seventy-eight* in figures.

b What do you need to subtract from this number to get:
i 506 078 **ii** 505 278 **iii** 6278 **iv** 506 168?

3 

a Write the number in words.

b **i** Add 1 **ii** Add 10 **iii** Add 100 **iv** Add 1000

4 The total number of vehicles licensed in Scotland at the beginning of 1998 was *two million, twenty-two thousand and six hundred*. Write this number in figures.

5 The number of vehicles that crossed the Forth Road Bridge in 1997 was 17 560 500.
The money taken from them in tolls totalled £8 824 750.
Write both of these numbers in words.

6 The number of households in Fife is 145 600. Last year there were 900 fewer. How many households in Fife were there last year?

7 The number of visitors to Stirling Castle last year was four hundred and twenty-three thousand, two hundred and fifty, which was just 500 more than two years ago.
How many visitors were there two years ago?

8 Put these numbers in order, smallest first:
201 687, 110 380, 98 362, 109 712, 200 989.

9 The table shows the number of pupils enrolled in Scottish Secondary schools over a five-year period.

Year	1994	1995	1996	1997	1998
Number of pupils	311 833	315 500	316 883	316 574	314 916

a In which year was the number of pupils greatest?

b Write the numbers of pupils in order, starting with the smallest.

c What is the difference between the largest and the smallest numbers?

d The figure for 1999 was 100 higher than the figure for 1998.
How many pupils were there in Scottish Secondary schools in 1999?

5 Making numbers work

Exercise 5.1

1 **a** Add 4739 and 7682 **b** Subtract 3857 from 9204.

c Multiply 6328 by 7. **d** Divide 5888 by 8.

2 **a** How many more people live in Craig?

b What is the total population of the two towns?

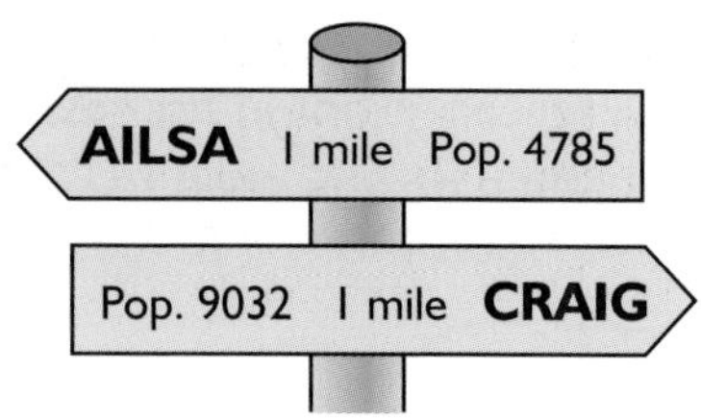

3 The table shows the number of letters delivered by a postman each day for a week.

	Mon	Tue	Wed	Thu	Fri	Sat
No. of letters	2577	3724	3372	5413	6073	4138

a How many more letters were delivered on Thursday than on Tuesday?

b How many more were there on Friday than on Monday?

c What was the total number of letters delivered in the week?

4 The table shows the number of people who saw the pantomime at the Palace Theatre and the prices of the tickets.

	Stalls	**Circle**	**Gallery**
Adults	6563	3704	1897
Children	9312	5043	3675
	Adults £9 Children £7	Adults £8 Children £6	Adults £5 Children £4

a How many people sat in the stalls?

b How many adults went to the pantomime?

c How many children went?

d How much money was collected from the sale of
i adult tickets for the stalls **ii** children's tickets for the circle
iii all the gallery tickets?

e How much money was collected altogether from the sale of tickets?

5 **a** Find all the single-digit numbers that divide evenly into 3780.

b What is the remainder when 9 is divided into
i 1000 **ii** 2000 **iii** 3000 **iv** 7000?

6 Which is bigger? **a** 8888×9 or 9999×8 **b** 6666×8 or 8888×6

7 A lorry can safely carry 256 cases of Tingle, the fizzy health drink.
Each case holds nine cans of Tingle.

a How many cans of Tingle can a lorry hold?

b In a normal day a lorry can make five deliveries and the lorries are in use six days a week.
How many cans of Tingle can be delivered in
i a day **ii** a week?

8 A school spends £2592 on books.
Half of the money is spent on history books costing £9 each.
One third of the money is spent on geography books costing £8 each.
The rest of the money is spent on maths books costing £6 each.
How many of each kind of book were bought?

9 Calculate the number of days you have lived.
Remember that some years have 365 days and others have 366 days.

Brainstormer

Mattie wins £7560 on the lottery.

She spends one ninth on a computer, one eighth on clothes, one seventh on furnishing her room, one sixth on a holiday, one fifth on a jet-ski and one quarter on jewellery. She saves the remainder of the money.

How much money does Mattie save?

6 Counting on the calculator

When using a calculator, remember to *estimate, calculate* and *check*.

Example 1 19 520 × 112

- *Estimate:* $20\,000 \times 100 = 2\,000\,000$
- *Calculate:* $19\,520 \times 112 = 2\,186\,240$
- *Check:* ✓ Estimate and calculation are close.

For addition, subtraction and multiplication, looking at the last digit is also a good safeguard against error.

$19\,520 \times 112 = 2\,186\,240 \ldots$

the fact that $0 \times 2 = 0$ adds confidence to the answer.

Example 2 $\dfrac{15\,789 + 12\,561}{63}$

- *Estimate:* $(16\,000 + 13\,000) \div 60 = 29\,000 \div 60 \approx 30\,000 \div 60 = 500$
- *Calculate:* $(15\,789 + 12\,561) \div 63 = 28\,350 \div 63 = 450$
- *Check:* $450 \approx 500$ ✓

1

Exercise 6.1

1 Copy and complete the table:

	Problem	Estimate	Calculation	Check
a	12 350 + 9245	10 000 + 10 000 = 20 000	21 595	✓
b	21 642 − 14 758	20 000 − 15 000 =		
c	894 × 47			
d	31 044 ÷ 52			
e	78 244 + 19 895			
f	67 475 − 31 658			
g	7165 × 82			
h	23 725 ÷ 365			

2 Find the value of each of these:

a 27 731 + 89 089

b 109 034 − 87 458

c 39 850 × 380

d 9765 ÷ 465

e $\dfrac{31\,708 + 12\,926}{86}$

f $\dfrac{36\,267 - 17\,443}{26}$

g $\dfrac{576\,088}{247 + 609}$

h $\dfrac{527\,356 + 155\,340}{14\,761 - 5409}$

3 Sean bought a second-hand car. The reading on its mileometer was 27 452.
After he had driven it for a year, the reading was 36 068.
How many miles did the car travel in the year?

4 The table shows the number of males and females aged between 10 and 19 living in Ayrshire and Lanarkshire in 1999.

Age 10–19	Ayrshire	Lanarkshire
males	25 045	38 435
females	23 769	36 799

a How many more males than females aged 10–19 lived in
i Ayrshire **ii** Lanarkshire?

b How many in this age range lived in
i Ayrshire **ii** Lanarkshire?

c How many more of them lived in Lanarkshire than in Ayrshire?

E

5 This table shows the number of visitors to two tourist attractions in the west of Scotland over a three-year period.

	Year 1	Year 2	Year 3
Brodick Castle	58 047	63 525	68 136
Culzean Castle	195 659	202 132	193 000

a How many more people visited Culzean Castle than Brodick Castle in Year 3?

b Calculate the total number of visitors over the three years to each castle.

c How many more visitors did Culzean have than Brodick over the three years?

6 In 1996, the first full year in which the Skye Bridge was open, 612 000 vehicles crossed the bridge.
A total of £3 178 000 was paid in tolls.
Divide the money received by the number of vehicles to find the average toll paid per vehicle.
Give your answer in pence, rounded to the nearest penny.

7 Wimple Homes built 284 houses last year.
116 of them were detached villas, each costing £53 750 to build.
The rest were semi-detached houses, each costing £37 450 to build.
The detached villas were sold at £62 850 each and the semi-detached houses at £41 250 each.
Calculate the profit made by Wimple Homes last year.

Challenge

Top secret!
Work out the message which has been sent in code.

After each calculation turn the calculator upside down to read the word.
Words are separated by /.

/ 9845 + 21 728 / 16 575 ÷ 325 / 75 558 ÷ 98 /.

/ 13 012 − 12 667 / $\frac{264\,354 + 173\,116}{82}$ / $\frac{29\,046}{47}$ / $\frac{4\,211\,844}{42 \times 13}$ /.

/ 929 × 342 / 13 721 − 7916 /. / 577 720 ÷ 715 / 14 501 × 216 + 12 400 × 181 /.

E

1

7 What's left?

When a calculator is used to divide, the remainder is not always given in the form that we want.

Example 1 How many weeks are there in 200 days?
How many days are left over?

Step 1 Using a calculator, 200 ÷ 7 = 28·571 429 …
There are 28 weeks, but how many days are left over?

Step 2 Reverse the process using the whole number answer 28.
28 weeks = 28 × 7 = 196 days

Step 3 Subtract this from the given number of days.
200 − 196 = 4
So 200 ÷ 7 = 28 remainder 4
or 200 days = 28 weeks and 4 days left over

Example 2 Find the remainder when 8460 is divided by 52.
8460 ÷ 52 = 162·692 31…
162 × 52 = 8424
so the remainder = 8460 − 8424 = 36

E

Exercise 7.1

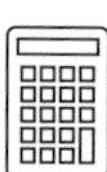

1 Find the answer and the remainder for each division.

a 467 ÷ 18 **b** 2085 ÷ 26 **c** 19 382 ÷ 105 **d** 27 500 ÷ 87

2 Express each of the following in years and months.

a 162 months **b** 215 months

3 Share £1654 equally among 15 people so that they each get a whole number of pounds.
How many pounds are left over?

4 A lorry-load of gravel weighs 18 tonnes. How many lorry-loads are there in 350 tonnes?
How many tonnes of gravel are left over?

5 There are 28 lights in a set of Christmas tree lights.

a How many sets can be made from 1000 lights?

b How many lights are left over?

6 A maths book costs £13. Calculate:

a how many of the books can be bought for £1500

b how much money remains.

7 a There are 36 bricks in a child's toy set.
  i How many toy sets can be made from 500 bricks?
  ii How many bricks are left unused?

  b Another toy set needs 48 bricks.
  i How many fewer of these toy sets can be made from 500 bricks?
  ii How many bricks would be left over in this case?

Brainstormer

A local council needs £23 525 000 to provide all its services. The money is to be collected in taxes from every one of its 36 450 households. Everyone pays the same amount. The calculation is done and the amount each household is asked to pay is rounded to the nearest £1.

a By how much is the local authority short of the required amount?

b If every household is charged £1 more, how much extra money will the local authority have?

8 Factors and prime numbers

When one whole number divides another, *without a remainder*, the first is called a **factor** of the second.

Example 1 1, 2, 4 and 8 divide 8, without remainder, so 1, 2, 4 and 8 are the factors of 8.

Factors of 8							
1	2	3	4	5	6	7	8
✓	✓	✗	✓	✗	✗	✗	✓

Example 2 1, 2, 3, 6, 9 and 18 are the factors of 18.

When a number has only two factors, namely the number itself and 1, then it is said to be a **prime number**.

Example 3 13 is a prime number because 1 and 13 are the only factors of 13.

Example 4 21 is not prime because it can be divided by 3.

Example 5 1 is not prime because it does not have two factors.

Exercise 8.1

1 List all the factors of:

a 6 **b** 10 **c** 12 **d** 15 **e** 16 **f** 17
g 20 **h** 24 **i** 26 **j** 30 **k** 35 **l** 36.

2 **a** 72 has twelve factors. 1, 2, 3, 4, 6 and 8 are six of them. Find the other six factors of 72. (Hint: find how many times 1, 2, 3, 4, 6 and 8 divide into 72.)

b Four of the factors of 56 are 1, 2, 4 and 7. Find the other four factors of 56.

c Six of the factors of 84 are 1, 2, 3, 4, 6 and 7. Find the other six factors of 84.

3 Find all the factors of: **a** 45 **b** 60 **c** 90 **d** 100.

4 **a** Find three numbers which have 2 and 3 as two of their factors.

b Find three numbers which have 2, 3 and 4 as three of their factors.

c Find three numbers which have 2, 3 and 5 as three of their factors.

5 Write down the numbers less than 20 that have exactly two factors. These are the **prime numbers** less than 20. You should have found eight of them.

6 Which of the following numbers are prime numbers?
Give a reason for your answer.

a 25 **b** 29 **c** 31 **d** 51 **e** 59

7 Write down all the even numbers that are prime.

8 The first three whole numbers ending in 3 are prime numbers. They are 3, 13 and 23. Which of the next seven whole numbers ending in 3 are prime numbers?

9 **Sieve of Eratosthenes**
A Greek mathematician called Eratosthenes, who lived over 2000 years ago, made up a way to find prime numbers.
He used a '100 square'.

~~1~~	(2)	(3)	~~4~~	(5)	~~6~~	7	~~8~~	~~9~~	~~10~~
11	~~12~~	13	~~14~~	~~15~~	~~16~~	17	~~18~~	19	~~20~~
~~21~~	~~22~~	23	~~24~~	~~25~~	~~26~~	~~27~~	~~28~~	29	~~30~~
31	~~32~~	~~33~~	~~34~~	~~35~~	~~36~~	37	~~38~~	~~39~~	~~40~~
41	~~42~~	43	~~44~~	~~45~~	~~46~~	47	~~48~~	49	~~50~~
~~51~~	~~52~~	53	~~54~~	~~55~~	~~56~~	~~57~~	~~58~~	59	~~60~~
61	~~62~~	~~63~~	~~64~~	~~65~~	~~66~~	67	~~68~~	~~69~~	~~70~~
71	~~72~~	73	~~74~~	~~75~~	~~76~~	77	~~78~~	79	~~80~~
~~81~~	~~82~~	83	~~84~~	~~85~~	~~86~~	~~87~~	~~88~~	89	~~90~~
91	~~92~~	~~93~~	~~94~~	~~95~~	~~96~~	97	~~98~~	~~99~~	~~100~~

Step 1 Make a 100 square as shown.

Step 2 Score out 1.
It is not prime as it doesn't have two factors.

Step 3 Circle the first number not scored out (2) and then score out every number that can be divided by 2.

Step 4 Circle the first number not scored out (3) and then score out every number that can be divided by 3.

Step 5 Circle the first number not scored out (5) and then score out every number that can be divided by 5.

Step 6 Keep going until you run out of numbers.
You will have circled all the prime numbers between 1 and 100.

9 Some expressions

A prime factor is a factor that is a prime number.
Every whole number has at least one prime factor.

Example 1 The factors of 18 are 1, 2, 3, 6, 9 and 18.

2 and 3 are prime numbers, so 2 and 3 are the prime factors of 18.

Example 2 Express 660 as the product of its prime factors.

Perform repeated divisions by the smallest prime possible:

2	660
2	330
3	165
5	55
11	11
	1

Thus $660 = 2 \times 2 \times 3 \times 5 \times 11$

The **sum** is what you get when you **add** numbers together.
The **difference** between two numbers is found by **subtracting** one number from the other.
The **product** is what you get when numbers are **multiplied** together.
The **quotient** is what you get when one number is **divided** by another.

Example 3 The sum of 3, 5 and 9 is 17.

Example 4 The difference between 23 and 19 is 4.

Example 5 The product of 2, 4 and 5 is 40.

Example 6 The quotient when 20 is divided by 4 is 5.

Exercise 9.1

1 Find the prime factors of: **a** 6 **b** 8 **c** 12 **d** 14 **e** 23 **f** 24 **g** 28 **h** 30 **i** 32

2 Write down four whole numbers that have only one prime factor.

3 Find the sum of:
a 6 and 5 **b** 3 and 998 **c** 795 and 20 **d** 4769 and 7856

4 Find the difference between:
a 24 and 16 **b** 101 and 89 **c** 10 000 and 1
d 10 000 and 10 **e** 9347 and 3574

5 Find the product of:

a 6 and 9 b 25 and 8 c 345 and 30 d 3864 and 5

6 Find the quotient:

a $35 \div 7$ b $2688 \div 7$ c $1000 \div 100$ d $3950 \div 50$

7 Express these numbers as a product of their prime factors:

a 42 b 18 c 40 d 48 e 50

8 Which is bigger and by how much?

a The product of 1, 2 and 3 or the sum of 1, 2 and 3?

b The sum of the first four odd numbers or the sum of the first four prime numbers?

9 The **proper factors** of a number are all its factors not including itself.
The proper factors of 12 are 1, 2, 3, 4 and 6.
When a number equals the sum of its proper factors the number is said to be **perfect**.
When the sum is bigger, the number is called **abundant**.
When the sum is smaller, the number is called **deficient**.
List the numbers 1 to 30 and decide whether they are perfect, abundant or deficient.

F

Brainstormers

1 What is the difference between the sum of 17 and 19 and the product of 6 and 3?

2 What is the quotient when the difference between 33 and 17 is divided by the product of 4 and 2?

3 Find two numbers greater than 40 that have 2 and 3 as their only prime factors.

4 What is the smallest number to have three prime factors?

5 220 and 284 are called amicable numbers.
It was once thought that if one person wore a badge with 220 on it and another person wore a badge with 284 on it then their fates would be linked.

a Calculate the sum of the proper factors of i 220 ii 284.

b Why are they called amicable?

c Which of the following pairs are amicable pairs?
i 1184, 1210 ii 360, 813 iii 2620, 2924

10 Squares, cubes and square roots

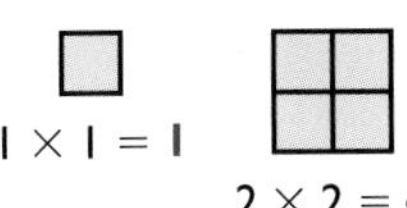
$1 \times 1 = 1$

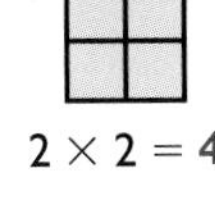
$2 \times 2 = 4$

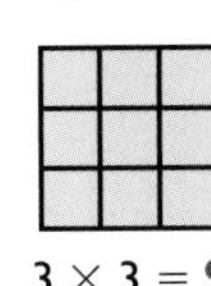
$3 \times 3 = 9$

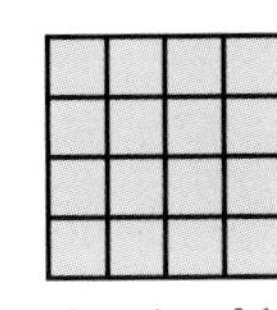
$4 \times 4 = 16$

The numbers 1, 4, 9, 16, … are called **square numbers**. Can you see why?

What are the next four square numbers?

When we multiply a number by itself, we are said to **square** the number.

Example 1 Square 9.

$9^2 = 9 \times 9 = 81$ … we say '9 **squared** equals 81'.

Example 2 Square 20.

$20^2 = 20 \times 20 = 400$ … '20 **squared** equals 400'.

The small number is called the **power** or **index**.

We can say 9^2 is '9 **to the power** 2' and 20^2 is '20 **to the power** 2'.

For any number a, $a^2 = a \times a$

Similarly, $a^3 = a \times a \times a$

a^3 is read as 'a **cubed**' or 'a to the power of 3'.

Example 3 $2^3 = 2 \times 2 \times 2 = 8$

Example 4 $5^3 = 5 \times 5 \times 5 = 125$

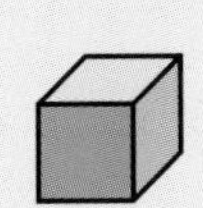
$1^3 = 1 \times 1 \times 1 = 1$

$2^3 = 2 \times 2 \times 2 = 8$

$3^3 = 3 \times 3 \times 3 = 27$

Exercise 10.1

Do not use a calculator unless the question asks you to use one.

1 Calculate:

a 8^2 **b** 10^2 **c** 1^2 **d** 1^3 **e** 4^3

f 6^3 **g** 10^3 **h** $3^3 - 3^2$ **i** $5^2 - 4^2$ **j** $(6^2 + 8^2)^2$

2 Find the value of each of these when $a = 3$ and $b = 5$.

a a^2 **b** b^3 **c** $(b - a)^3$ **d** $a^2 + b^2$ **e** $(a + b)^2$

f $b^3 - a^3$ **g** a^3 **h** $2a^3$ **i** b^2 **j** $4b^2$

Using a calculator:

to square a number, e.g. 9^2  9 x^2 = gives **81**

… or 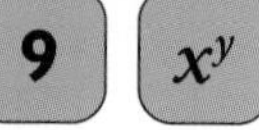 9 x^y  2 = gives **81**

to cube a number, e.g. 5^3  5  x^y 3  = gives **125**

3 Use a calculator to find the value of:

a 3^2 **b** 6^2 **c** 10^2 **d** 2^3
e 4^3 **f** 10^3 **g** 12^2 **h** 15^2
i 20^3 **j** 25^3 **k** 50^2 **l** 13^2
m 11^3 **n** $5^2 + 12^2$ **o** $8^3 - 7^3$ **p** $20^2 - 19^2$

4 **a** Calculate the sum of:
i the first two odd numbers **ii** the first three odd numbers
iii the first four odd numbers.
b What rule seems to be in action?
c Test your rule for each sum up to ten odd numbers.

F

5 **a** 1, 2 and 3 are three consecutive numbers. Calculate their product.
b Calculate the product of the consecutive numbers:
i 2, 3, 4 **ii** 3, 4, 5 **iii** 4, 5, 6 **iv** 5, 6, 7.
c Can you spot a connection between your answers and the cubic numbers?

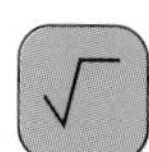 $\sqrt{\ }$ 25  = will give the value 5, so $5^2 = 25$

 $\sqrt{\ }$ 196 = will give the value 14, so $14^2 = 196$

We say the **square root** of 25 is 5 because $5^2 = 25$. We write $\sqrt{25} = 5$.
The square root of 196 is 14 because $14^2 = 196$. We write $\sqrt{196} = 14$.

6 Use a calculator to find the square root of:

a 121 **b** 256 **c** 529
d 2116 **e** 5625 **f** 1 000 000

7 Without using a calculator, write down the value of:

a $\sqrt{1}$ **b** $\sqrt{4}$ **c** $\sqrt{9}$
d $\sqrt{36}$ **e** $\sqrt{64}$ **f** $\sqrt{81}$
g $\sqrt{100}$ **h** $\sqrt{400}$ (Hint: think 4×100) **i** $\sqrt{900}$
j $\sqrt{3600}$ **k** $\sqrt{10\,000}$

8

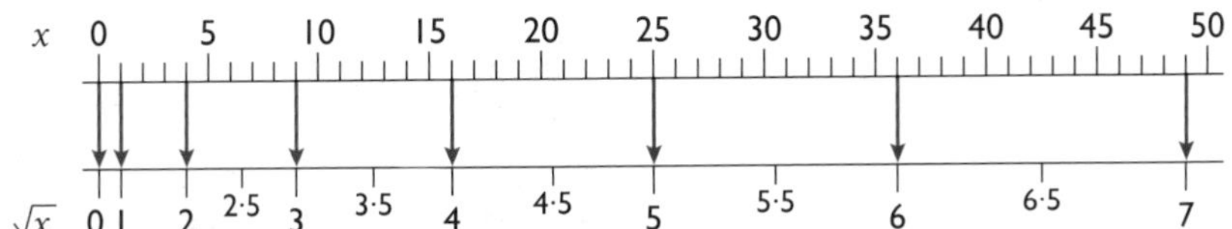

Use the number lines above to give estimates for:

a $\sqrt{3}$ **b** $\sqrt{6}$ **c** $\sqrt{10}$ **d** $\sqrt{12}$ **e** $\sqrt{14}$

f $\sqrt{20}$ **g** $\sqrt{28}$ **h** $\sqrt{33}$ **i** $\sqrt{42}$ **j** $\sqrt{50}$

9 $\sqrt{60}$ lies between 7 and 8 since it is bigger than $\sqrt{49}$ but less than $\sqrt{64}$. Make similar statements about:

a $\sqrt{90}$ **b** $\sqrt{110}$ **c** $\sqrt{72}$ **d** $\sqrt{66}$

11 Integers – being negative

When we measure things we invent a scale which suits our needs.
We pick our own units and decide where to set zero.
Sometimes numbers below zero are needed.

Example 1 Water freezes to ice at zero degrees Celsius (0 °C).
On a really cold day the temperature can fall below zero.
Four degrees below zero is written as −4 °C
We read −4 °C as '**negative** 4 °C' or '4 degrees **below** zero'.
The temperatures at the North and South Poles have fallen as low as −88 °C.

Example 2 The height of an object on earth is measured from sea level.
The top of Mount Everest is 8848 m above sea level.
The floor of the Marianas Trench is 10 900 m below sea level.
We can write this as −10 900 m.
The depth to which a diver dives is given as his or her depth below sea level.
A diver 80 metres below sea level is at −80 m.

Example 3 A business can make a profit or a loss.
A loss of £5000 can be considered to be a profit of −£5000.

Positive and negative whole numbers are called **integers**.

They can be represented on a number line:

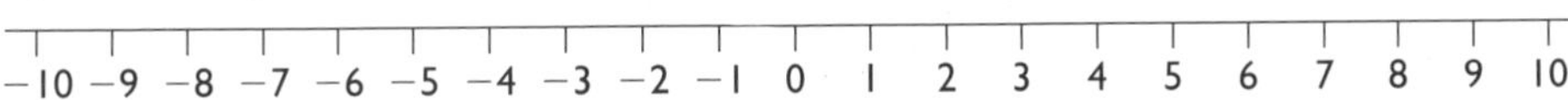

F

Adding integers using a number line

Treat the addition as a set of instructions.

> Start at the first number and do what the second number tells you, where 3 means 'go 3 to the right', and −3 means 'go 3 to the left'.)

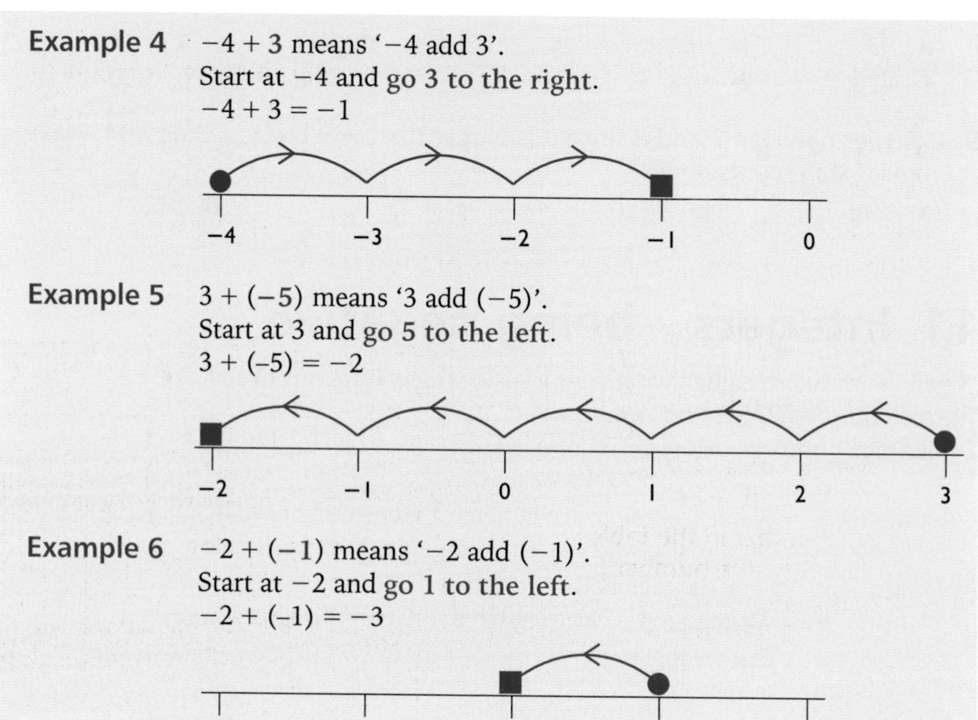

Example 4
−4 + 3 means '−4 add 3'.
Start at −4 and go 3 to the right.
−4 + 3 = −1
−4
−3
−2
−1
0
Example 5
3 + (−5) means '3 add (−5)'.
Start at 3 and go 5 to the left.
3 + (−5) = −2
−2
−1
0
1
2
3
Example 6
−2 + (−1) means '−2 add (−1)'.
Start at −2 and go 1 to the left.
−2 + (−1) = −3
−5
−4
−3
−2
−1

Exercise 11.1

A number line may be useful to help you find the value of the following.

1 $-3+2$	**2** $-4+1$	**3** $-5+2$	**4** $-6+4$	**5** $-1+6$
6 $-2+3$	**7** $-3+5$	**8** $-7+9$	**9** $-4+4$	**10** $-8+2$
11 $4+(-6)$	**12** $3+(-4)$	**13** $1+(-5)$	**14** $0+(-2)$	**15** $7+(-3)$
16 $6+(-2)$	**17** $4+(-1)$	**18** $3+(-3)$	**19** $2+(-6)$	**20** $9+(-5)$
21 $-1+(-3)$	**22** $-2+(-4)$	**23** $-5+(-1)$	**24** $-1+(-4)$	**25** $-3+(-2)$
26 $-2+(-6)$	**27** $0+(-5)$	**28** $-1+(-1)$	**29** $-4+(-5)$	**30** $-5+(-4)$

31 Here are some number patterns created by adding a fixed amount each time. Continue each pattern for three more terms.

a 1, 4, 7, ..., ..., ...
b −9, −5, −1, ..., ..., ...
c −3, 2, 7, ..., ..., ...
d 10, 7, 4, ..., ..., ... (adding −3)
e −3, −7, −11, ..., ..., ...
f −3, −2, −1, ..., ..., ...
g −6, −4, −2, ..., ..., ...

32 Calculate each of these pairs. A number line may help you with the addition part.

a **i** $6-2$ **ii** $6+(-2)$
b **i** $4-3$ **ii** $4+(-3)$
c **i** $5-4$ **ii** $5+(-4)$
d **i** $7-1$ **ii** $7+(-1)$
e **i** $3-1$ **ii** $3+(-1)$
f **i** $4-4$ **ii** $4+(-4)$

What do you notice about each pair of answers?

33 **a** Copy and complete this addition table.

b Each number in the table is 1 more than the number to its left.
What is 1 more than
i −4 **ii** −2?

c Each number in the table is 1 less than the number to its right.
What is 1 less than
i −2 **ii** −1?

d What is
i 2 less than −3
ii 3 less than 1?

Second number (columns); First number (rows)

+	−4	−3	−2	−1	0	1	2	3	4
4	0	1	2	3	4	5	6	7	8
3	−1	0	1	2	3	4	5	6	7
2	−2	−1	0	1	2	3	4	5	6
1	−3	−2	−1	0	1	2	3	4	5
0									
−1									
−2									
−3									
−4									

12 Subtracting integers

Here we have a subtraction table partially completed.

We know that $x - x = 0$, hence the diagonal of zeros:

$-4 - (-4) = 0$; $-3 - (-3) = 0$;
$-2 - (-2) = 0$; and so on.

We know $x - 0 = x$, which allows us to fill in the column headed '0'.

By filling in the subtractions we know, we see that as we move to the right each number is 1 less than the number before it.

Second number (columns); First number (rows)

−	−4	−3	−2	−1	0	1	2	3	4
4					4	3	2	1	0
3					3	2	1	0	−1
2					2	1	0	−1	−2
1					1	0	−1	−2	−3
0					0				
−1				0	−1				
−2			0		−2				
−3		0			−3				
−4	0				−4				

1

Exercise 12.1

1 **a** We see from the table that as we move to the left each number is 1 bigger than the one before it. Copy the subtraction table on page 21 and use the pattern to complete the top four rows.

b We see that as we move down the table each number is 1 less than the number above it. Use this pattern to complete the bottom five rows.

2 From your completed table write down the answers to:

a $4-(-2)$ **b** $4-(-1)$ **c** $3-(-4)$
d $1-(-1)$ **e** $3-4$ **f** $2-4$
g $1-4$ **h** $-1-4$ **i** $-2-2$
j $-3-4$ **k** $-3-(-2)$ **l** $-4-(-3)$

3 Perform each pair of calculations.

a **i** $1-3$ **ii** $1+(-3)$ **b** **i** $2-3$ **ii** $2+(-3)$
c **i** $-2-1$ **ii** $-2+(-1)$ **d** **i** $-4-3$ **ii** $-4+(-3)$
e **i** $-2-(-3)$ **ii** $-2+3$ **f** **i** $-3-(-1)$ **ii** $-3+1$

From questions **1**, **2** and **3**, we see that:

Instead of **subtracting** an integer, we can **add its negative.**

$$a-b=a+(-b)$$

Example 1 $3-4 \quad =3+(-4) \quad =-1$

Example 2 $5-(-2) \quad =5+2 \quad =7$

Once the subtraction has been expressed as an addition, the number line can be used as before.

Exercise 12.2

1 Use a number line to help you with these calculations:

a $4-5$ **b** $1-4$ **c** $0-3$
d $2-6$ **e** $4-7$ **f** $3-6$
g $-1-2$ **h** $-3-5$ **i** $-4-7$
j $-8-1$ **k** $5-(-5)$ **l** $4-(-3)$
m $1-(-4)$ **n** $6-(-3)$ **o** $4-(-7)$
p $-1-(-3)$ **q** $-3-(-5)$ **r** $-7-(-6)$

2 Find the value of:

a $2-7$ **b** $-3+8$ **c** $-9+4$

d $-7-1$ **e** $-1+1$ **f** $-7-8$

g $-2-(-2)$ **h** $-5-(-2)$ **i** $-3+(-7)$

j $-4-(-7)$ **k** $-38-16$ **l** $-43-(-62)$

m $2500-4400$ **n** $-1570+8000$ **o** $-7584+2386$

p $-6724-2865$ **q** $4635-5825$ **r** $-7256-(-4305)$

3 Portia was born in May, 3 BC and died in June, AD 77. How old was Portia when she died?

4 Brutus was born on the 1st of March, 45 BC and died on his 78th birthday. In which year did he die?

5 A diver is at −75 metres. A helicopter is directly overhead at a height of 85 metres. What is their distance apart?

6 Julius Caesar invaded Britain in 55 BC.
How many years ago was that?

F

7 Find the next three numbers in each pattern of numbers:

a 9, 6, 3, 0, −3, _, _, _, … **b** 7, 5, 3, 1, _, _, _, …

c 7, 3, −1, _, _, _, … **d** 11, 6, 1, _, _, _, …

e −13, −7, −1, _, _, _, … **f** 12, 5, −2, _, _, _, …

8 When one number is to the right of another on the number line then it is the bigger number.
Which of these temperatures is the higher temperature?

a 3 °C or 7 °C **b** 5 °C or −2 °C **c** −8 °C or 3 °C

d −1 °C or −3 °C **e** −10 °C or −5 °C

9 Put these groups of numbers in order, smallest first:

a 6, 1, −3 **b** −2, 5, −6

c 0, −3, −1 **d** 4, −5, −3

10 Which integer is:

a just bigger than

i 3·6 **ii** −2·8 **iii** −0·9?

b just smaller than

i 2·7 **ii** −3·4 **iii** −0·5?

1

13 Multiplying integers

×	−5	−4	−3	−2	−1	0	1	2	3	4	5
5						0	5	10	15	20	25
4						0	4	8	12	16	20
3						0	3	6	9	12	15
2						0	2	4	6	8	10
1	−5	−4	−3	−2	−1	0	1	2	3	4	5
0	0	0	0	0	0	0	0	0	0	0	0
−1						0	−1				
−2						0	−2				
−3						0	−3				
−4						0	−4				
−5						0	−5				

Here is a partially completed multiplication table.

$0 \times x = 0$ … hence the row of zeros.
$x \times 0 = 0$ … hence the column of zeros.
$1 \times x = x$ … hence the row beginning 1 is complete.
$x \times 1 = x$ … hence the column beginning 1 is complete.

Exercise 13.1

F

1 **a** Copy the table.

b 3×4 = three fours $= 4 + 4 + 4 = 12$.
Similarly $3 \times (-4)$ = three negative fours $= (-4) + (-4) + (-4) = -12$.
Use this idea to fill in the top part of the table.

c $3 \times 4 = 12 = 4 \times 3$. Similarly $(-4) \times 3 = 3 \times (-4) = -12$.
Use this idea to fill in the lower right section of the table.

d Complete the table by pattern spotting.

2 Use your completed table to find the value of:

a $3 \times (-4)$ **b** $2 \times (-5)$ **c** -1×4 **d** -3×3
e -5×3 **f** $-1 \times (-1)$ **g** $-2 \times (-3)$ **h** $-5 \times (-4)$

3 Imagine the table extended to find the value of:

a $7 \times (-4)$ **b** $6 \times (-5)$ **c** -6×4 **d** -8×3
e -6×7 **f** $-7 \times (-7)$ **g** $-7 \times (-10)$ **h** $-8 \times (-9)$

The product of two numbers with the **same** sign is **positive**.
The product of two numbers with **opposite** signs is **negative**.

Example 1 $6 \times 5 = 30$ **Example 2** $-4 \times (-2) = 8$

Example 3 $2 \times (-3) = -6$ **Example 4** $-1 \times 7 = -7$

4 Use this set of rules to help you calculate these.

a 8×7 **b** $-5 \times (-6)$ **c** $4 \times (-8)$
d -3×6 **e** 6×9 **f** $-1 \times (-6)$
g $-6 \times (-2)$ **h** -4×8 **i** $7 \times (-4)$
j -10×9 **k** -8×0 **l** $0 \times (-7)$
m $6 \times (-6)$ **n** $-1 \times (-1)$ **o** $3 \times (-10)$
p -8×1 **q** $-4 \times (-9)$ **r** $8 \times (-8)$

5 **a** Calculate: **i** 3^2 **ii** $(-3)^2$ **iii** 4^2 **iv** $(-4)^2$
b Using a calculator evaluate **i** -5^2 **ii** $(-5)^2$.
Are they the same? Explain.
c Explain the reaction of the calculator to $\sqrt{(-1)}$.

6 Calculate:
a 3^3 **b** $(-3)^3$ **c** 4^3 **d** $(-4)^3$

14 Dividing integers

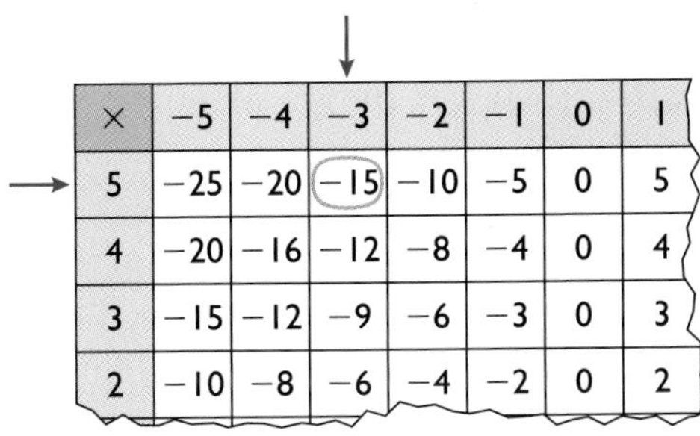

×	−5	−4	−3	−2	−1	0	1
5	−25	−20	−15	−10	−5	0	5
4	−20	−16	−12	−8	−4	0	4
3	−15	−12	−9	−6	−3	0	3
2	−10	−8	−6	−4	−2	0	2

Any multiplication that does not involve zero leads to two equivalent divisions, e.g.

$3 \times 5 = 15$ gives $15 \div 5 = 3$ and $15 \div 3 = 5$.

We can see this from the multiplication table.

Example 1

$5 \times (-3) = -15$ from the table.
So $-15 \div 5 = -3$
and $-15 \div (-3) = 5$

Example 2

$3 \times (-4) = -12$
So $-12 \div 3 = -4$
and $-12 \div (-4) = 3$

When we divide two numbers,

- if both numbers have the **same** sign, the quotient is **positive**
- if the numbers have **opposite** signs, the quotient is **negative**.

Example 3

$6 \div 2 = 3$ and $-8 \div (-4) = 2$

Example 4

$10 \div (-2) = -5$ and $-12 \div 3 = -4$

1

Exercise 14.1

1 Write down the answers to these calculations:

a $20 \div 5$

b $-20 \div 5$

c $-16 \div 4$

d $-3 \div (-1)$

e $14 \div (-2)$

f $-5 \div (-5)$

g $8 \div (-8)$

h $24 \div (-6)$

i $-28 \div 7$

j $0 \div (-2)$

k $-50 \div 10$

l $30 \div (-6)$

m $-40 \div (-8)$

n $-27 \div (-9)$

o $-36 \div 3$

2 What number belongs in the OUT circle of each machine?

a

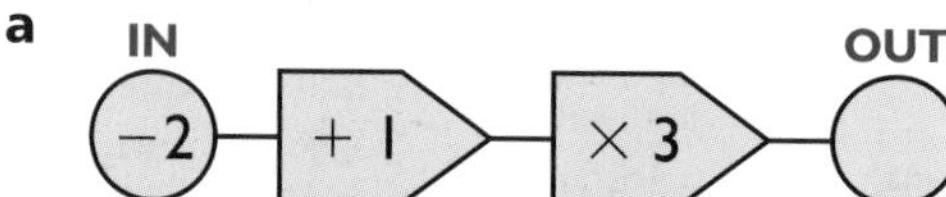

b

IN −6 → ÷ 3 → + 2 → OUT

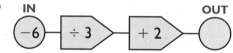

c

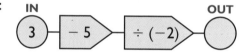

IN 3 → − 5 → ÷ (−2) → OUT

F

3 These are the temperatures taken at noon for one week at a weather station:

−8 °C, −2 °C, 0 °C, 2 °C, −6 °C, −4 °C, −3 °C.

Add the temperatures and divide by 7 to get the average noon temperature.

4 At the end of each month Jack noted his bank balance. −£5 means he is overdrawn by £5.

Here are his recordings for the first 6 months of the year:

£20, −£30, −£15, −£45, £24, £10.

a What is his average monthly balance?

b Over the last 6 months of the year his balance was:

£36, −£10, −£35, −£12, £2, −£5.

Is this a better or worse average?

15 More mental calculations

Exercise 15.1 

No written working is allowed in this exercise.

Selection A

1. What are the factors of 54?
2. Write down the prime factors of 42.
3. What is the value of $\sqrt{1600}$?
4. Write down the value of 20^2.
5. What is the value of 9^3?
6. Write down a number that has 2, 3 and 5 as three of its factors.
7. What is $-480 \div 8$?
8. Calculate $24 + (-30)$.
9. Evaluate $-8 - (-21)$.
10. Subtract 29 from 18.
11. Divide the product of 9 and 6 by 3.
12. Calculate $9^2 - 4^2$.

Selection B

1. What are the factors of 92?
2. Write down the prime factors of 85.
3. What is the value of $\sqrt{3600}$?
4. Write down the value of 90^2.
5. What is the value of 20^3?
6. Write down a number that has 3, 4 and 9 as three of its factors.
7. What is $270 \div (-9)$?
8. Calculate $40 + (-60)$.
9. Write down the value of $-10 - (-10)$.
10. Subtract 38 from 25.
11. Sum 16 with the difference of 36 and 12.
12. What is the sum of $\sqrt{81}$ and 4^3?

F

Challenge

In a magic square the numbers in any row, column or diagonal sum to the same total.
Copy and complete each of these magic squares.

a

4	−1	0
		−2

b

3		
	0	4
		−3

c

		0
	−1	1
−2		

CHECK-UP

1 Write down the answer to:

a 65 + 76 **b** 93 − 56 **c** 280 + 350

d 720 − 430 **e** 87 × 6 **f** 424 ÷ 8

g 526 ÷ 7 **h** 3462 × 1000 **i** 280 000 ÷ 1000 **j** 56 000 ÷ 100

2 Write down the answer to:

a 36 × 20 **b** 855 × 30 **c** 365 × 400

d 350 ÷ 50 **e** 75 600 ÷ 600

3 A straight pathway through a playpark is 40 000 cm long.
It is made up of 1000 slabs laid end to end. What is the length of each slab?

4 The length of a fence panel is 180 cm. What is the total length in centimetres of 100 of the panels?

5 **a** It has been estimated that the population of Scotland in the year 2014 will be 5 082 084.
Write this population figure in words.

b If the population is 10 000 less than this, what will it be?

6 The number of people under five years of age in Scotland in 1998 was *three hundred thousand, eight hundred and fifty*. Write this number in figures.

7 Calculate the following:

a 7518 + 3694 **b** 8020 − 5743 **c** 6294 × 8 **d** 4938 ÷ 6

8 What is the remainder when 7 is divided into 9274?

9 Last year there were 7315 complaints received about noise pollution. 5035 of them were investigated and 1759 of those investigated were found to be valid complaints.

a How many complaints were not investigated?

b How many complaints investigated were not valid complaints?

10 The population of Adamton is 9072. A ninth of the population is left-handed, an eighth have red hair and a seventh are teenagers.
How many people in Adamton:

a are left-handed

b have red hair

c are teenagers?

11 A factory makes jugs, bowls and vases. The number of each it makes in a week is shown in the table.

jugs	bowls	vases
5492	8350	6725

a What is the total number of items made in the week?

b How many more bowls were made than jugs?

c The jugs sell for £7 each, the bowls for £8 each and the vases for £9 each.

How much money is made altogether if all the items are sold?

12 Find the value of each of these:

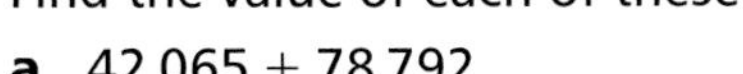

a 42 065 + 78 792 **b** 63 526 − 27 952

c 38 750 × 365 **d** 44 044 ÷ 52

13 The number of overseas visitors to Scotland in each of the last three years is shown in the table.

Year 1	Year 2	Year 3
1 772 000	1 959 000	2 018 000

a How many more visitors were there in Year 3 than in Year 1?

b What was the total number of visitors over the three years?

14 A school has £6000 to spend on textbooks. The following are bought: 165 geography books at £11 each, 128 history books at £12 each and 135 maths books at £13 each. How much of the £6000 is left?

15 £135 838 is raised from selling tickets for a pop concert. The tickets were £23 each. How many tickets were sold?

16 Seventeen canes are needed to make the frame of a child's playhouse.

a How many frames can be made with 1000 canes?

b How many canes are left over?

17 List all the factors of: **a** 18 **b** 28 **c** 40.

18 a Find a number that has 3, 4 and 7 as three of its factors.

b Write down all the prime numbers between 40 and 50.

c Explain how you know 161 is not a prime number.

d Find the prime factors of 70.

19 Express these numbers as a product of their prime factors:

a 210 **b** 98.

20 Calculate:

a the product of 16 and 8 **b** the sum of 12 and 4

c the quotient on dividing 36 by 9

d the difference between 84 and 21.

21 Write down:

a the square of 9 **b** the cube of 4 **c** the square root of 16.

22 Use a calculator to calculate: **a** $\sqrt{625}$ **b** 21^2 **c** 12^3

23 Write down the answers to:

a $-6 + 1$ **b** $7 + (-3)$ **c** $-5 + (-4)$ **d** $3 - 8$
e $-6 - 1$ **f** $2 - (-5)$ **g** $-3 - (-3)$ **h** $-1 - (-4)$
i $9 \times (-2)$ **j** $-4 \times (-3)$ **k** -6×4 **l** $-8 \div 2$
m $6 \div (-3)$ **n** $-10 \div (-2)$ **o** $0 \div (-6)$

24 Calculate:

a $-236 + 418$ **b** $5318 - 6435$
c $-6145 - 2641$ **d** $-4583 - (-2098)$

F

2 Decimals

The penny has existed since the eighth century. It was made from $\frac{1}{240}$th of a pound (weight) of silver, so there were 240 pennies to the pound. 12 pennies were worth 1 shilling and 20 shillings made £1. Pounds, shillings and pence (£. s. d.) continued until decimalisation in 1971 when the new penny was introduced. 1 new penny = 2·4 old pennies. £1 became equal to 100 new pence. One shilling became 5p.

1 Looking back

Exercise 1.1

1 In the number 41·6 the purple digit is in the tens column.

a Which column is the purple digit in these numbers?

i 106 **ii** 103·5 **iii** 95·28 **iv** 97·3

b Arrange the numbers in **a** in order, smallest first.

2 Calculate:

a 6·8 + 9·3 **b** 7·41 + 45·62 **c** 28·78 + 9·4

d 40·6 − 24·3 **e** 50 − 6·2 **f** 71·3 − 6·84

3 Ursula buys new kitchen floor material for £53·99. Delivery and fitting costs £18·75.

a Calculate the total cost.

b How much change is there from £80?

4 Calculate:

a $6{\cdot}23 \times 10$ **b** $4{\cdot}052 \times 100$ **c** $2{\cdot}79 \div 10$
d $37{\cdot}5 \div 100$ **e** $24{\cdot}52 \times 7$ **f** $36{\cdot}16 \div 8$

5 In a test drive, a new car travels 132·5 km on 10 litres of petrol.
How far will the car go on **a** 1 litre **b** 100 litres of petrol?

6 Flora pays £73·95 to hire a motor boat for 5 hours.

a Calculate the cost for each hour.
b Calculate the cost for 6 hours' hire at the same rate.

7 Round each of the following to the nearest whole number.

a 6·4 **b** 3·7 **c** 42·5 **d** 609·9

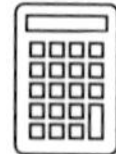

8 Three classes collect money for charity. Hannah's class raise £36·27.
Kevin's class get £80·25 and Lara's collect £28·94.

a What is the total amount collected?
b How much more have Kevin's class collected than the other two classes added together?

◀◀ E

9 Calculate the total cost of 25 rose bushes at £12·49 each and 18 shrubs at £9·99 each.

10 Forty-five identical bottles are filled with olive oil from a tank containing 56·25 litres.
How much does each bottle hold?

2 Adding and subtracting without a calculator

So far we've used tenths and hundredths. $26{\cdot}73 = 26 + \frac{7}{10} + \frac{3}{100} = 26\frac{73}{100}$
Now we are going to include thousandths. $26{\cdot}735 = 26 + \frac{7}{10} + \frac{3}{100} + \frac{5}{1000} = 26\frac{735}{1000}$

When adding or subtracting, keep the decimal points in a line.

Example 1 $5{\cdot}137 + 2{\cdot}348$

$$\begin{array}{r} 5{\cdot}137 \\ +\,2{\cdot}348 \\ \hline 7{\cdot}485 \\ \hline \end{array}$$

Example 2 $9{\cdot}604 - 4{\cdot}153$

$$\begin{array}{r} 9{\cdot}604 \\ -\,4{\cdot}153 \\ \hline 5{\cdot}451 \\ \hline \end{array}$$

Exercise 2.1

1 What is the column value of the purple digit in these numbers?

a 6·685 b 9·271 c 4·287 d 6·032

2 Calculate:

a 4·341 + 3·252 b 1·038 + 2·459 c 3·659 + 4·758 d 7·637 + 0·999

3 Calculate:

a 8·696 − 3·241 b 7·065 − 1·831 c 9·143 − 5·753 d 5·003 − 0·879

4 Before a radiator is turned on, the temperature in a room is 8·5 °C.
With the radiator on the temperature rises by 7·9 °C.
What is the new temperature?

5 In the long jump Yvonne jumps 5·63 m.
In the high jump she clears 1·84 m.
Calculate the difference in these two jumps.

6 For a trip to the beach Paul buys a parasol for £16·99, sun cream for £4·49 and a magazine which costs 85p Calculate:

a the total cost

b the change from two £20 notes.

7 a How much longer is the rectangle than it is wide?

b The length of the diagonal is 24·77 m. How much shorter is the diagonal PQ than the sum of the two edges?

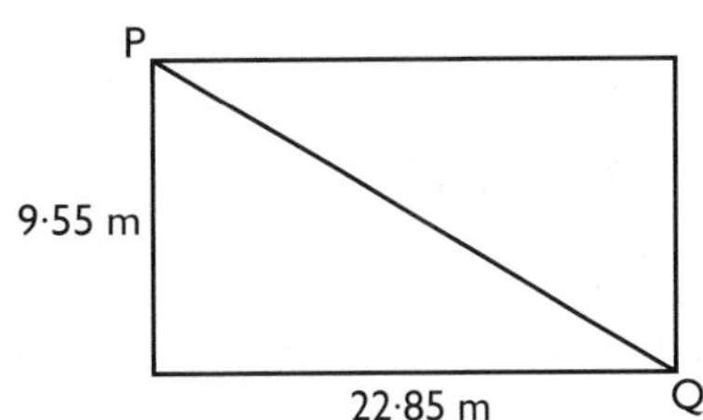

8 Ruth's phone bill lists calls of over 40p separately.
Calculate the total cost of these two calls: £4·689 and £2·895.

9 a A copper rod is 1·498 m long. In a science experiment it is heated and expands by 0·007 m. Calculate its length after heating.

b A brass rod measures 1·695 m. It is heated and expands to 1·704 m. Calculate the increase in length.

E

10 The table shows Baby Robbie's weight. Calculate the weight gained in the

a first

b second month.

Month	Weight (kg)
at birth	3·635
1	4·065
2	5·870

In these examples, trailing zeros have been added, giving both numbers the same number of decimal places.

Example 3 4·7 + 2·372

$$\begin{array}{r} 4{\cdot}700 \\ +\,2{\cdot}372 \\ \hline 7{\cdot}072 \end{array}$$

Example 4 6·7 − 2·421

$$\begin{array}{r} 6{\cdot}700 \\ -\,2{\cdot}421 \\ \hline 4{\cdot}279 \end{array}$$

Exercise 2.2

E

1 Place these lengths in order of size, greatest first. (Hint: add trailing zeros.)
3·099 m 3·19 m 3·2 m

2 Calculate:

a 6·25 + 3·148 **b** 4·349 + 1·37 **c** 2·7 + 6·801 **d** 0·975 + 8·145

3 Calculate:

a 9·863 − 6·72 **b** 8·057 − 5·2 **c** 7·5 − 6·473 **d** 8·0 − 4·269

4 A truck weighs 4·875 tonnes. It is loaded with sand weighing 3·65 tonnes. What is the total weight of the truck and sand?

5 The engine size of George's van is given as approximately 2·4 litres.
The exact size is 2·384 litres.
Calculate the difference between these two numbers.

6 Trisha's phone bill lists these charges.

Premium rate £3·874
National rate £4·432
Lo-call £1·528

Calculate the total of these charges.

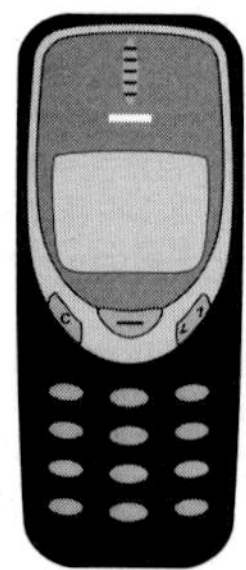

7 In one year Cosmic Computers have an income of £7·15 million.
The cost of running the business is £5·098 million.
Calculate the profit for the year.

8 The perimeter of the triangle is 8·5 m.

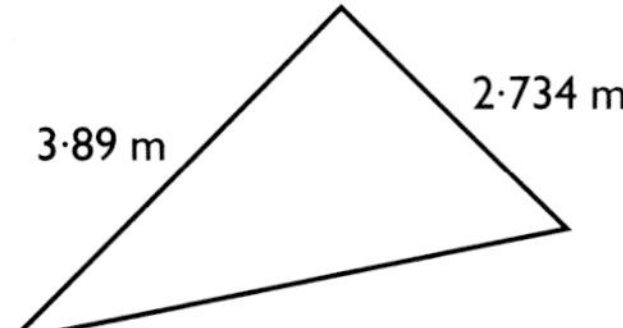

Calculate the length of the third side.

9 $\frac{1}{8} = 0{\cdot}125$; $\frac{1}{2} = 0{\cdot}5$; $\frac{3}{8} = 0{\cdot}375$.
Add the three decimal numbers to find the sum of $\frac{1}{8} + \frac{1}{2} + \frac{3}{8}$.

3 Adding and subtracting on the calculator

Most calculators will allow you to FIX the number of decimal places that appear on the display.
When working with money, fix to 2 decimal places, then the result of a calculation such as £5 ÷ 2 is displayed as 2·50 rather than 2·5.

Often with weights, volumes, etc., we use 3 decimal places.

Exercise 3.1

1 1 UK gallon = 4·546 litres. 1 US gallon = 3·785 litres.
Calculate the difference, in litres, between 1 UK and 1 US gallon.

2 Louise's holiday flight costs £194·75. Her hotel costs £227·85.

a Calculate the total cost for her hotel and flight.

b Her budget for the holiday is £600.
How much has she left after paying for the flight and hotel?

3 Hilda uses 0·25 of a litre of milk from the carton to make pancakes.

a How much is left in the carton?

b Then she pours 0·5 of a litre into a jug.
How much milk is now in the carton?

4 The Mighty Mauler weighs 72·275 kg and Tyrone the Tank weighs 71·84 kg.

a Calculate the difference in their weights.

b In boxing the minimum weight for a middleweight is 73 kg.
How much weight does each boxer need to gain to become a middleweight?

5 Peter the plumber is self-employed.
The table shows his earnings for one week.
Calculate:

a his total earnings

b the difference between his best and worst day.

Day	Earnings
Mon	£96·38
Tue	£139·50
Wed	£150·25
Thu	£126·80
Fri	£129·25

Example Monica buys a DVD recorder for £247·25 and a digital TV for £382·99.
Round each number to the nearest £10 and estimate the total cost.

Answer: £247·25 = £250 (to nearest £10)
£382·99 = £380 (to nearest £10)
Estimated total = £630

E

Exercise 3.2

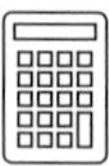

1 Anita and Olga compare their personal bests in field events.

a Who is better at each event, and by how much?

b For each athlete add the three distances.
Who has the greater total and by how much?

Event	Anita	Olga
Shot	12·57 m	13·04 m
Discus	45·38 m	43·97 m
Javelin	42·95 m	43·86 m

2 Stella looks at prices in a computer store.

Classic Computers	
Laptops	£1259·49
PCs	£1424·95
Digital Camera	£359·89
Printer	£169·99

a **i** Round the prices of the laptop and printer to the nearest £100 and estimate their total price.

ii Calculate the actual total price.

b **i** By rounding each price to the nearest £100 estimate the total cost of the PC, printer and digital camera.

ii How much less than £2000 is this?

c Calculate the exact answers to **bi** and **ii**.

3 To complete 1500 m, Freddie runs three full laps of the track and then part of a lap. His times for the first three laps are: 63·68 s, 59·36 s and 61·42 s.

a **i** Round each time to the nearest whole second and estimate the total time for the three laps.

ii Calculate the exact time for the three laps.

b His best time for 1500 m is 223·41 s.

i Use your answer to **ai** to estimate how fast he has to run the last part to equal this time.

ii Calculate the exact time needed.

4 **a** Opposite are a triangle and a rectangle. Round the length of each side to the nearest whole number.

b Estimate the perimeter of each shape.

c Which shape has the greater estimated perimeter? By how much?

d Calculate the exact answer.

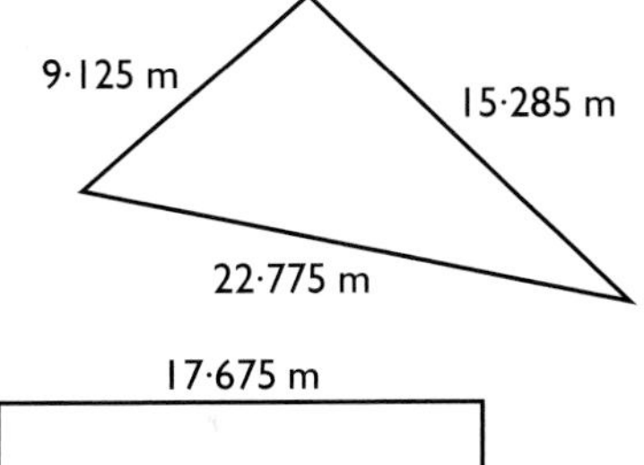

17·675 m

6·855 m

Brainstormer

This is some of Kevin's homework. Can you spot what he's done wrong?

E

4 Rounding to 1 decimal place

Example 1 Round each number to 1 decimal place:

a 0·17 b 0·32 c 0·45

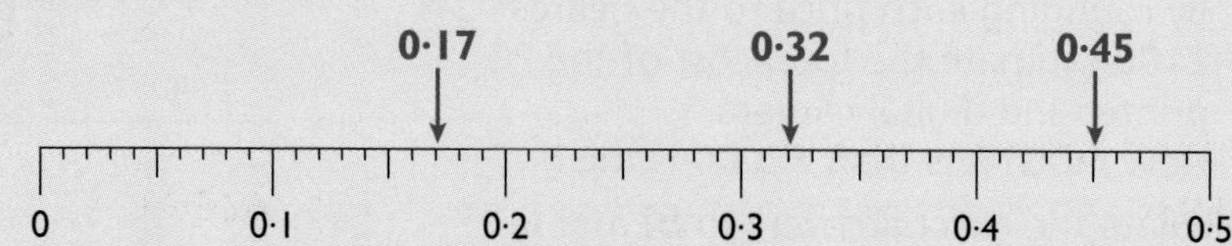

a 0·17 lies between 0·1 and 0·2. It is closer to 0·2. 0·17 = 0·2 (to 1 d.p.)

b 0·32 lies between 0·3 and 0·4. It is closer to 0·3. 0·32 = 0·3 (to 1 d.p.)

c 0·45 lies midway between 0·4 and 0·5. The rule is *always round up*. 0·45 = 0·5 (to 1 d.p.)

Example 2 Round each of these numbers to 1 decimal place:

a 6·372 b 38·649 c 9·9522

a The second decimal place is 7 (more than 4 so round up) 6·372 = 6·4 (to 1 d.p.)

b The second decimal place is 4 (not more than 4 so round down) 38·649 = 38·6 (to 1 d.p.)

c The second decimal place is 5 (more than 4 so round up) 9·9522 = 10·0 (to 1 d.p.)

E

Exercise 4.1

1 Round to 1 decimal place:

a 7·04 **b** 7·15 **c** 7·28 **d** 7·39

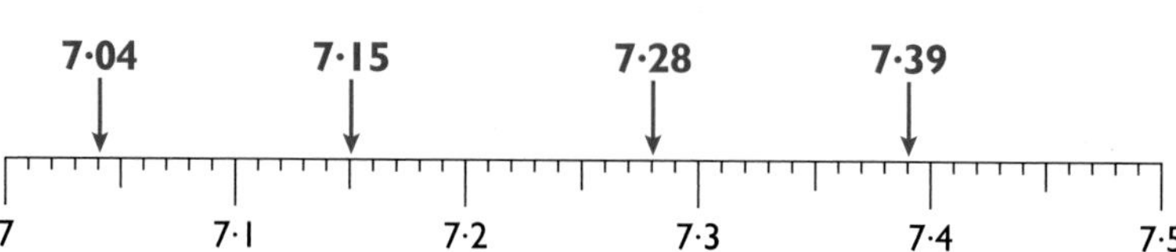

2 Round to 1 decimal place:

a 0·74

b 3·19

c 7·15

d 26·84

e 72·95

3 These were world record times in 2002.
Round each of them to 1 decimal place.

a men's 100 m → 9·79 s

b women's 100 m → 10·49 s

c men's 200 m → 19·32 s

d women's 200 m → 21·34 s

4 Round to 1 decimal place:

a 0·583 **b** 4·758 **c** 62·333

d 40·3751 **e** 79·9099

5 Round these conversion factors to 1 decimal place.

a 1 cm = 0·3937 inch **b** 1 hectare = 2·471 acres

c 1 tonne = 0·9842 ton **d** 1 mile = 1·6093 km

e 1 ounce = 28·3495 g **f** 1 pound = 0·4536 kg

Example 3 Round each number to 1 decimal place to make an estimate for each calculation.

a 6·94 + 8·29 → 6·9 + 8·3 = 15·2

b 25·71 − 17·35 → 25·7 − 17·4 = 8·3

E

Exercise 4.2

1 Round each number to 1 decimal place to make an estimate for:

a 2·49 + 5·84 **b** 7·35 + 4·81 **c** 15·18 + 24·04

d 3·616 + 1·493 **e** 4·855 + 2·129 **f** 5·052 + 3·909

2 Similarly, make an estimate for these:

a 6·72 − 3·51 **b** 7·36 − 1·75 **c** 25·78 − 16·04

d 9·243 − 5·785 **e** 8·093 − 7·806 **f** 7·848 − 4·992

3 Two parts of a flag pole measure 3·28 m and 2·84 m.

a Round each length to 1 decimal place.

b Use your answers to estimate

i the sum **ii** the difference of the parts.

4 In the 200 m sprint Maurice's time is 24·23 s and Chris's is 22·65 s.

a Round each time to 1 decimal place.

b Use your answers to estimate the difference in time.

5 The bill shows what Mel had for lunch.

a Round each price to 1 decimal place (nearest 10p).

b Estimate the total cost.

c Roughly how much change should she expect from £10?

Salad	£2·29
Pizza	£3·79
Coffee	£1·14

6 A metallurgist makes brass from copper and zinc. He uses 3·485 kg of copper and 2·625 kg of zinc.

a Round each weight to 1 decimal place.

b Use your answers to estimate
  i the total weight
  ii how much more copper than zinc is used.

Brainstormer

The table shows the prices of the items Bert buys at the supermarket and the prices after he's rounded them to 1 decimal place.
He estimates the total to be £4·90 and hands over a £5 note. The cashier tells him he's wrong.
Can you spot the problem?

Item	Price	Rounded to 1 d.p.
Chicken	£2·64	£2·60
Butter	£1·33	£1·30
Salt	£0·23	£0·20
Vegetable	£0·84	£0·80

E

5 Multiplying and dividing by 1000

Example 1 $98{\cdot}765 \times 1000 = 98{\cdot}765 \times 10 \times 10 \times 10 = 98\,765{\cdot}0$
Multiplying by 1000, the point seems to jump *3 places to the right*.

Example 2 $345{\cdot}0 \div 1000 = 345 \div 10 \div 10 \div 10 = 0{\cdot}345$
Dividing by 1000, the point seems to jump *3 places to the left*.

Exercise 5.1

1 Calculate:

a $0{\cdot}642 \times 1000$
b $5{\cdot}7 \times 1000$
c $26{\cdot}3 \times 1000$
d $0{\cdot}3 \times 1000$
e $0{\cdot}017 \times 1000$
f $69{\cdot}3 \times 1000$
g $0{\cdot}06 \times 1000$
h $0{\cdot}0007 \times 1000$

2 Calculate:

a 864·0 ÷ 1000 **b** 48·0 ÷ 1000

c 5·9 ÷ 1000 **d** 40·0 ÷ 1000

e 7·0 ÷ 1000 **f** 630 ÷ 1000

g 36·5 ÷ 1000 **h** 19 ÷ 1000

3 1 mile ≈ 1·6 km (≈ means 'approximately equal to')
Convert 1000 miles to kilometres.

4 Joan collects points when she spends money at the supermarket.
For 1000 points she gets a voucher worth £1.
Calculate the value of 1 point, in pence.

5 One house brick weighs 2·75 kg. Jim buys 1000 of them.
Calculate the total weight.

6 Wayne checks the price of gold. It is trading at $9850 for 1000 g (1 kg).
What is the price for

a 1 g

b 10 g

c 100 g?

7 In 1000 years a stalagmite grows 45 cm.
At that rate, how much does it grow in

a 1 year **b** 100 years?

8 100 ml of perfume costs £38·75.
Calculate the cost of

a 1 ml **b** 1000 ml.

6 Multiplying and dividing a decimal by a whole number

Example 1 Estimate the value of 428·3 × 7.

428·3 rounded to the nearest 100 is 400.
428·3 × 7 ≈ 400 × 7 = 2800

Example 2 Estimate the value of 287·9 ÷ 7.

287·9 rounded to the nearest 100 is 300.
287·9 ÷ 7 ≈ 300 ÷ 7 = 42·8 which is approximately 40
(We could use 280 ÷ 7 = 40 because 28 ÷ 7 is a whole number.)

2

Exercise 6.1

1 Calculate:

a $56{\cdot}24 \times 7$ **b** $328{\cdot}6 \times 5$ **c** $80{\cdot}95 \times 8$ **d** $99{\cdot}9 \times 9$

e $783{\cdot}5 \div 5$ **f** $946{\cdot}4 \div 7$ **g** $78{\cdot}88 \div 8$ **h** $79{\cdot}11 \div 9$

2 Natalie earns £13·98 an hour.

a She works 8 hours on a Monday. How much does she earn?

b She gets a pay rise of 85p per hour.
What is her pay for a Monday now?

3 At Venture Valley Holiday Resort a 5-day ski pass costs $99·75.
A 3-day pass costs $71·61.
How much is saved per day by buying a 5-day pass?

E

4 Estimate these calculations:

a $53{\cdot}85 \times 4$ **b** $893{\cdot}6 \times 6$ **c** $9{\cdot}743 \times 8$ **d** $438{\cdot}9 \times 9$

e $218{\cdot}3 \div 5$ **f** $84{\cdot}88 \div 8$ **g** $324{\cdot}8 \div 6$ **h** $823{\cdot}7 \div 9$

5 A lorry's full load is 28·75 tonnes.

a Estimate the total weight carried in eight trips.

b Calculate the actual weight carried in eight trips.

6 Theresa buys a three-piece suite priced £735.
She arranges to make six equal monthly payments.

a Estimate the monthly payment.

b Calculate the actual monthly payment.

7 A carton of orange juice contains 2·25 litres.

a Round this volume to 1 decimal place.

b Use your answer to estimate the volume of six cartons.

c Calculate the actual volume.

8 Bob the builder hires a cement mixer for 5 days. It costs him £73·56.

a Estimate the cost **i** per day **ii** per hour assuming it's used 8 hours each day.

b Calculate the actual cost **i** per day **ii** per hour, to the nearest 10p.

Often the context of a problem will demand practical answers.

Example 3 One tin of paint will cover 6 m^2. How many tins are needed to cover 53·5 m^2?

$$\begin{array}{r} 8\cdot9\,1\,6\,6\ldots \\ 6\overline{)\,5\,3\cdot{}^{5}5\,{}^{1}0\,{}^{4}0\,{}^{4}0\ldots} \end{array}$$

$53{\cdot}5 \div 6 = 8{\cdot}916$

So nine tins are needed.

Exercise 6.2

1 Calculate, giving your answers to 1 decimal place:

a $32{\cdot}6 \times 4$ **b** $75{\cdot}8 \times 7$ **c** $60{\cdot}49 \times 6$ **d** $89{\cdot}25 \times 9$

e $17{\cdot}43 \div 3$ **f** $80{\cdot}67 \div 6$ **g** $645{\cdot}8 \div 7$ **h** $523{\cdot}9 \div 8$

2 One tin of paint covers 7 m^2.

a Calculate $40 \div 7$, correct to 1 decimal place.

b How many tins are needed for 40 m^2?

3 At Direct DIY, rolls of wallpaper are sold in 8 m lengths. Pasha calculates he needs 52·85 m to decorate his lounge.

a **i** Calculate $52{\cdot}85 \div 8$, correct to 1 decimal place.
ii How many rolls should he buy?

b **i** Estimate the cost at £12·49 per roll. (Round £12·49 to 1 decimal place.)
ii Calculate the exact cost.

4 Fencing panels are made in 2 metre lengths. Linda needs 17·5 m of fencing.

a **i** Calculate $17{\cdot}5 \div 2$. **ii** How many panels must she buy?

b Panels cost £17·29.
i Round this to 1 decimal place and estimate the total cost.
ii Calculate the exact cost.

5 Six friends hire a limousine to go to a party. It costs £81·81.

a Calculate £81·81 ÷ 6, correct to 1 decimal place.

b They all pay an equal amount. What is the least amount, correct to the nearest 10 pence, each should pay?

6 Mal wants to buy new floor covering. He measures his floor. The material is sold in whole square metres.

a Calculate the exact area of the floor.

b How many square metres should be buy?

c Estimate the cost at £19·85 per square metre.

E

7 Graham compares the holiday prices of two companies.
   a Estimate the price per day for each.
   b Calculate the actual price per day, correct to the nearest 10p.

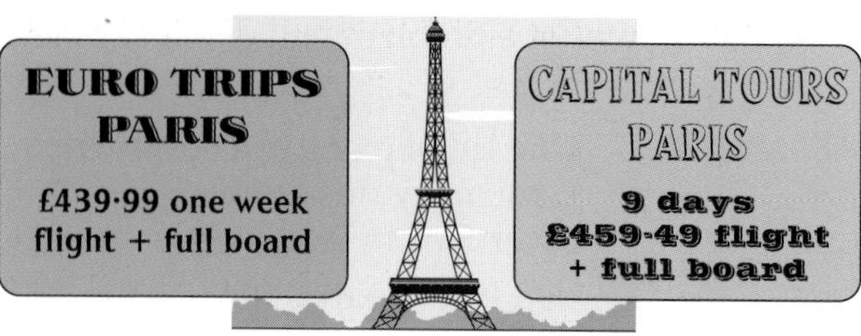

7 Multiplying and dividing on the calculator

Remember to **estimate, calculate and check.**

Example Find the cost of 47·3 litres of fuel at 78·9p per litre.

Estimate: 47·3 = 50 (to nearest 10) 78·9p = 80 (to nearest 10p)
$50 \times 80\text{p} = 4000\text{p} = £40$

Calculate: $47{\cdot}3 \times 78{\cdot}9 = 3731{\cdot}97$ pence = £37·32 (to nearest penny)

Check: $£37{\cdot}32 \approx £40$

E

Exercise 7.1

1 Ian earns £10·28 an hour. He works 7·5 hours a day and 5 days each week.
   a Estimate his wages for **i** 1 day **ii** 1 week **iii** 1 year.
   b Calculate the exact answers to **a**.

2 Moonlight Alure perfume is sold in 0·125 litre bottles.
   a **i** Estimate the total volume in 380 bottles. (Round 0·125 to 1 decimal place.)
   ii Calculate the exact volume.
   b **i** How many bottles can be filled from a 100 litre container?
   ii How much perfume is left?

3 **a** Estimate the total of this butcher's bill:
   b Calculate the actual total.

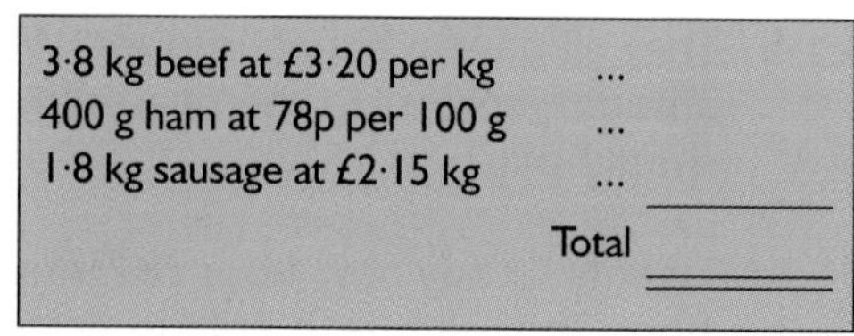

3·8 kg beef at £3·20 per kg	...
400 g ham at 78p per 100 g	...
1·8 kg sausage at £2·15 kg	...
Total	

4 Donna's car averages 12·7 km to 1 litre of fuel.
   a Estimate the distance it should go on **i** 18 litres **ii** a full tank of 68·5 litres.
   b Calculate the exact answers to **a**.

5 **a** Calculate the cost for one exposure for each.
b Which is the better value? By how much?

> **SPEEDY PHOTOS**
> **processing charges**
> **24 exposures for £3·48**
> **36 exposures for £4·50**

6 The rate of Value Added Tax (VAT) on most goods is 17·5%.
It can be calculated by multiplying by 0·175.
Use the constant facility on your calculator to find the tax, to the nearest 10 pence, on these items of furniture:

a table £85·70 **b** set of chairs £253·80 **c** bed £472·99
d fitted kitchen £2499·99 **e** bathroom suite £1099·49

7 Copy and complete this gas bill:

1100 units of gas at 1·73p per unit	£...·...
5180 units of gas at 1·25p per unit	£...·...
Total	£...·...

8 One euro buys $0·913.
On holiday Michelle changes 480 euros into dollars.
a **i** Round 0·913 to 1 decimal place and estimate how many dollars she gets.
ii Calculate the exact amount.
b After her holiday she has $24 left which she changes back into euros at the same rate. How much does she receive, correct to the nearest 10 cents?

9 1 pint = 0·568 litre.
a **i** Estimate how many litres there are in 27 pints.
ii Calculate the exact answer.
b How many 0·568 litre containers can be filled from a tank holding 200 litres?

EF

8 Further addition and subtraction

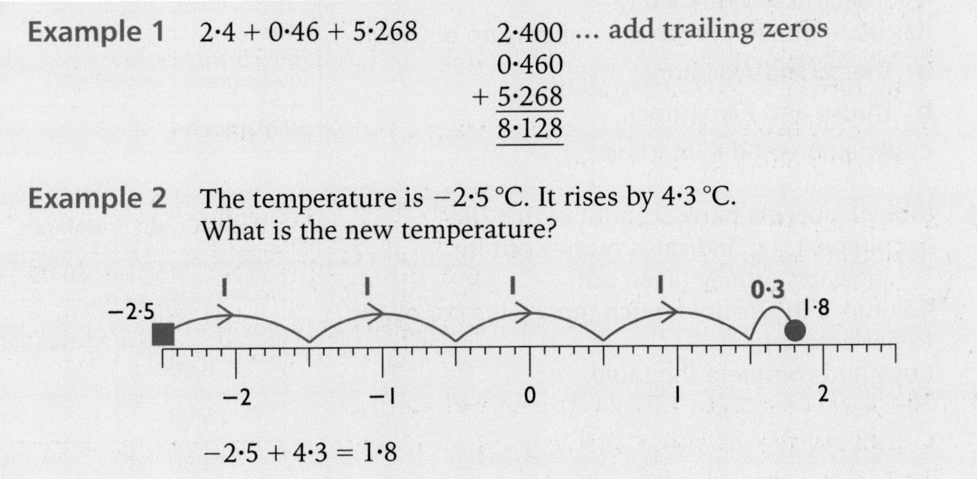

Example 1 2·4 + 0·46 + 5·268
2·400 ... add trailing zeros
0·460
+ 5·268
8·128
Example 2 The temperature is −2·5 °C. It rises by 4·3 °C.
What is the new temperature?
−2·5
1
1
1
1
0·3
1·8
−2
−1
0
1
2
−2·5 + 4·3 = 1·8

2

Exercise 8.1 

1 Calculate:

a 1·5 + 2·37 + 3·219 **b** 0·53 + 5·183 + 7·2 **c** 0·065 + 6·8 + 7·95
d 7·4 − 2·56 + 3·296 **e** 8·41 + 5·9 − 7·043 **f** 9·6 − 0·42 − 5·391

2 Two ladders measure 3·2 m and 2·85 m. When fitted together they overlap by 0·325 m. Calculate their length when fastened together.

F

3 Flora's time for the 100 m is recorded at 12·42 s.
The stopwatch may have an error of up to 0·005 s too slow or too fast.
This means the slowest possible time is 12·425 s.
Calculate the fastest possible time.

4 The evening temperature is 4·2 °C. By midnight it has fallen 5·7 °C.

a What is the temperature at midnight?

b By morning it has risen 2·8 °C.
What is the morning temperature?

5 The table shows the minimum temperatures recorded on a winter's day.
Calculate the difference in temperature between:

a Thurso and Aviemore

b Thurso and Kilmarnock

c Aviemore and Kilmarnock.

Place	Temperature
Thurso	−4·0 °C
Aviemore	−9·5 °C
Kilmarnock	3·5 °C

6 Monica opens a bank account with £20.
In column 1, '+' indicates money put in;
'−' indicates money taken out.
Column 2 shows how much money is in or owing to her account.
Copy and complete the table.

Debit/Credit	Balance
	20·00
−12·50	
+8·00	
−25·00	
+15·50	

Check how to enter negative numbers into your calculator.

 or +/− means 'negative' but  means 'minus'.

Example 3 Calculate −3·5 − 5·7. **'negative 3·5 minus 5·7'**

(−) 3·5 − 5·7 = −9·2

Exercise 8.2

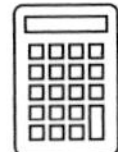

1 Calculate:

a −3·7 + 6·2 **b** −8·1 + 3·8 **c** −5·3 − 6·2 **d** −2·4 − 6·9

2 Calculate:

a −4·8 + (−3·9) **b** −12·6 + (−16·7) **c** −6·5 − (−8·9) **d** −35·6 − (−46·3)

3 The table shows the temperature at midnight. What is the difference in temperature between

a Brodick and Stornoway

b Brodick and Lerwick

c Stornoway and Lerwick?

Town	**Temperature (°C)**
Brodick	−6·2
Stornoway	−4·9
Lerwick	2·7

4 The table shows the profits (+) and losses (−) of Intergalactic Traders Plc. over 6 months. Calculate the overall profit or loss for the 6-month period.

Month	Jan	Feb	Mar	Apr	May	Jun
Profit/Loss (£million)	−3·626	+2·674	−1·846	−0·593	+6·508	−3·073

9 Rounding to a given number of decimal places

Example An important number which you will meet later is 3·141 59 …
Rounding this number to:

- 1 decimal place = 3·1 (second place digit is not greater than 4 … 3·141 59 …)
- 2 decimal places = 3·14 (third place digit is not greater than 4 … 3·141 59 …)
- 3 decimal places = 3·142 (fourth place digit is greater than 4 … 3·141 59 …)
- 4 decimal places = 3·1416 (fifth place digit is greater than 4 … 3·141 59 …)

F

Exercise 9.1

1 Round these numbers to 2 decimal places:

a 6·374 **b** 5·128 **c** 7·465 **d** 9·593 **e** 2·299

2 Round these numbers to 3 decimal places:

a 5·1849 **b** 8·9461 **c** 1·8435 **d** 3·0797 **e** 4·7092

3 Round 0·6666 to:

a 2 **b** 3 decimal places.

4 The exchange rate for 1 euro is given in the table. Round each number to

a 2

b 3 decimal places

Country	Amount
Canada	1·4109 dollars
India	44·2628 rupees
S. Africa	9·54935 rand
Switzerland	1·45373 francs

F

5 Carry out these calculations and round your answers to 2 decimal places.

a $6{\cdot}3 \times 2{\cdot}67$ **b** $2{\cdot}18 \times 7{\cdot}9$ **c** $7{\cdot}508 \times 12$

d $5{\cdot}962 \times 6{\cdot}28$ **e** $7{\cdot}46 \times 6{\cdot}704$

6 Carry out these calculations and round your answers to 3 decimal places.

a $2 \div 7$ **b** $1 \div 3$ **c** $6 \div 11$

d $7{\cdot}4 \div 25{\cdot}8$ **e** $3{\cdot}7 \div 352$

10 Further multiplication and division

There are lots of shortcuts when you do not have a calculator.

Example 1 $2{\cdot}4 \times 400 = 2{\cdot}4 \times 100 \times 4 = 240 \times 4 = 960$

Example 2 $32 \div 8000 = 32 \div 8 \div 1000 = 4 \div 1000 = 0{\cdot}004$

Example 3 $18 \div 0{\cdot}03 = 1800 \div 3$ (× both numbers by 100) $= 600$

Example 4 $0{\cdot}6 \times 0{\cdot}007$
We know that $6 \times 7 = 42$. There are four digits after a decimal point in the question. There should be four after the decimal point in the answer, so the answer is 0·0042.

Exercise 10.1

1 Calculate:

a $0{\cdot}3 \times 2$ **b** $0{\cdot}3 \times 20$ **c** $0{\cdot}3 \times 200$
d $0{\cdot}3 \times 2000$ **e** $0{\cdot}4 \times 3$ **f** $0{\cdot}4 \times 30$
g $0{\cdot}4 \times 300$ **h** $0{\cdot}4 \times 3000$ **i** $0{\cdot}6 \times 40$
j $0{\cdot}8 \times 600$ **k** $0{\cdot}004 \times 40$ **l** $0{\cdot}7 \times 5000$
m $0{\cdot}009 \times 20$ **n** $0{\cdot}05 \times 8000$ **o** $0{\cdot}007 \times 900$

2 Calculate:

a $0{\cdot}6 \times 0{\cdot}3$ **b** $0{\cdot}06 \times 0{\cdot}3$ **c** $0{\cdot}6 \times 0{\cdot}03$
d $0{\cdot}06 \times 0{\cdot}03$ **e** $0{\cdot}02 \times 0{\cdot}7$ **f** $0{\cdot}5 \times 0{\cdot}09$
g $0{\cdot}007 \times 0{\cdot}3$ **h** $0{\cdot}09 \times 0{\cdot}08$ **i** $0{\cdot}004 \times 0{\cdot}05$
j $0{\cdot}008 \times 0{\cdot}007$

3 Calculate:

a $8 \div 4$ **b** $8 \div 0{\cdot}4$ **c** $8 \div 0{\cdot}04$
d $8 \div 0{\cdot}004$ **e** $15 \div 5$ **f** $15 \div 0{\cdot}5$
g $15 \div 0{\cdot}05$ **h** $15 \div 0{\cdot}005$ **i** $9 \div 0{\cdot}3$
j $20 \div 0{\cdot}4$ **k** $40 \div 0{\cdot}08$ **l** $30 \div 0{\cdot}06$
m $12 \div 20$ **n** $35 \div 70$ **o** $24 \div 600$

4 Calculate:

a $14 \div 0{\cdot}7$ **b** $1{\cdot}4 \div 0{\cdot}7$ **c** $0{\cdot}14 \div 0{\cdot}7$
d $0{\cdot}014 \div 0{\cdot}7$ **e** $0{\cdot}014 \div 0{\cdot}007$ **f** $0{\cdot}9 \div 0{\cdot}3$
g $0{\cdot}21 \div 0{\cdot}7$ **h** $0{\cdot}036 \div 0{\cdot}9$ **i** $0{\cdot}54 \div 0{\cdot}006$
j $0{\cdot}008 \div 0{\cdot}4$

5 A bag of crisps weighs 0·03 kg.
What is the weight of:

a 5 **b** 50 **c** 500 bags?

6 A bottle of shampoo holds 0·2 litre.
How many bottles can be filled from a drum holding:

a 6 litres **b** 60 litres **c** 600 litres?

7 A piece of wood is 4·5 m long.
How many pieces 0·05 m long can be cut from it?

F

8 A rectangular strip of cloth measures 0·8 m by 0·04 m.
Calculate its area in m^2.
(Area = length × breadth)

When using your calculator keys remember:

- the +/− key for negative number problems
- the constant facility for repeated use of one number and operation
- FIX to work correct to a given number of decimal places.

Example 5 Set your calculator to work to 2 decimal places and set the constant facility to **×0·175** to calculate the tax on a meal costing

a £24·67 b £18·00 c £45·50.

Answer:

a 24·67 × 0·175 = £4·32 (to the nearest penny)

b tax on £18 = £3·15 (calculator remembers × 0·175 if using constant facility)

c tax on £45·50 = £7·96 (to the nearest penny)

Exercise 10.2

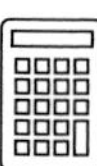

1 Calculate:

a −3·8 × 4	**b** 2·7 × (−6)	**c** −4·9 × (−5)	**d** −3·5 × (−9)
e −7·5 ÷ 5	**f** 4·8 ÷ (−3)	**g** −8·4 ÷ (−7)	**h** −7·2 ÷ (−8)

2 Calculate the area of each rectangle, correct to 2 decimal places.

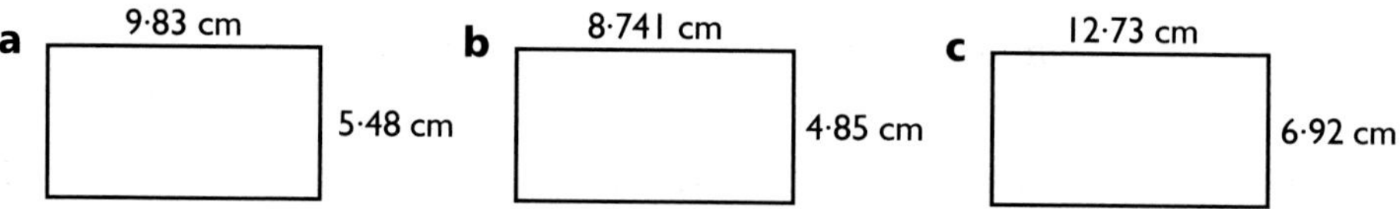

3 Calculate the tax on each of these items, correct to the nearest penny.

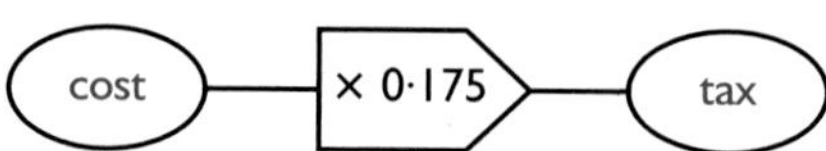

a a meal costing £52·29
b a garage bill of £153·63
c a TV priced at £265·49
d a car priced at £19 999·99

4 Use an exchange rate of £1 = €1·604 93 to change these amounts:

a **i** £60
ii £727
iii £1820 to euro (€), correct to 2 decimal places

b **i** €5
ii €834
iii €7492 to pounds (£), correct to the nearest penny.

Investigation

1 a Does multiplying by a number which is greater than 1 have an increasing or decreasing effect?

b Does multiplying by a number which is less than 1 have an increasing or decreasing effect?

c Are there any exceptions?

2 What effect does dividing by a number

a greater than 1

b less than 1 but not zero have?

3 What happens when you try to divide by zero on your calculator?

11 Significant figures

A digit or figure in a number is **significant** if it gives an idea of **i** quantity or
ii accuracy.

The label on a shampoo bottle says it contains 8·8 fluid ounces/250 ml of liquid.
8·8 has 2 significant figures.
250 also has only 2 significant figures as the quantity is measured to the nearest 10 ml.
The trailing zero is not significant.

However, the 10 on the ten pence coin has 2 significant figures, the ten being an accurate description of the amount of pence it is worth.

When dealing with whole numbers with trailing zeros, we generally must be told to what accuracy the number is being given before we can specify the significant figures.

②

Examples

850 measured to the nearest ten has 2 significant figures
42 000 measured to the nearest thousand has 2 significant figures
42 000 measured to the nearest hundred has 3 significant figures (think '420 hundreds')
18 400 measured to the nearest hundred has 3 significant figures
18 400 measured to the nearest ten has 4 significant figures (think '1840 tens'

304 has 3 significant figures	The 0 here is always significant.
3·04 has 3 significant figures	
0·304 has 3 significant figures	The leading zero is only positioning the decimal point.
0·0304 has 3 significant figures	The leading zeros are only positioning the decimal point.
0·030 40 has 4 significant figures	The trailing zero is telling you that the measurement is more accurate than 0·0304.

Here is another example.
The population of a village is 4597.
Rounded to the nearest thousand, or to 1 significant figure: 4597 = 5000 (1 s.f.)
Rounded to the nearest hundred, or to 2 significant figures: 4597 = 4600 (2 s.f.)
Rounded to the nearest ten, or to 3 significant figures: 4597 = 4600 (3 s.f.)

F

Exercise 11.1

1 Choose which answer is correct for each of these.

a 4738 rounded to 1 s.f.	**i** 4000	**ii** 5000
b 62 184 rounded to 1 s.f.	**i** 60 000	**ii** 62 000
c 0·052 rounded to 1 s.f.	**i** 0·05	**ii** 0·06
d 0·0039 rounded to 1 s.f.	**i** 0·004	**ii** 0·04

2 **a** Round each number to 1 significant figure:

i 413 (nearest 100)
ii 7827 (nearest 1000)
iii 64 791 (nearest 10 000)
iv 852
v 9183
vi 29 483
vii 0·062 (nearest hundredth)
viii 0·0029 (nearest thousandth)
ix 0·58 (nearest tenth)
x 0·026
xi 0·0073
xii 0·91

b Round each number to 2 significant figures:
- **i** 839 (nearest 10)
- **ii** 2618 (nearest 100)
- **iii** 75 837 (nearest 1000)
- **iv** 506
- **v** 8239
- **vi** 28 470
- **vii** 0·0437 (nearest thousandth)
- **viii** 0·892 (nearest hundredth)
- **ix** 0·0819
- **x** 0·465

3 In each statement, round the number to **i** 1 significant figure **ii** 2 significant figures.

a There are 8163 spectators at an athletic event.

b Ruth scores 78 388 points at a computer game.

c Riverside High School has 928 pupils.

d The longest river in the world is the River Nile at 6695 km.

e A piece of paper is 0·0384 mm thick.

f A bottle holds 0·845 litre.

4 Say how many significant figures are involved in each of the following statements.

a There are 30 days in September.

b There are 30 days in a month.

c There are 90° in a right angle.

d There is 90 ml of liquid in a mug of tea.

e The gap in the car's spark plug was set to 0·006 mm.

f The gap in the car's spark plug was set to 0·020 inch.

5 You buy a bottle of cola and the label says 'contents: 500 ml'.

a Would you take it back to the shop if you found that it was
i 100 ml short **ii** 10 ml short **iii** 1 ml short?

b To how many significant figures is the label probably giving the contents?

Investigation

A book contains 83 leaves. Its thickness has been measured as 12 mm (2 s.f.).

a Talking about accuracy, what is the basic difference between the figures 83 and 12 in this storyline?

b To find the thickness of one leaf of the book, James divides 12 by 83. His calculator gives 0·144 578 313 253 mm as an answer. To how many significant figures should James give his answer?

F

12 Scientific notation

Scientists often have to work with very large and very small numbers. They use a system called **scientific notation** or **standard form**.

Example 1 The earth is 4 500 000 000 years old.

A scientist would write $4{\cdot}5 \times 10^9$ years.
which means $4{\cdot}5 \times 10 \times 10 \times 10 \times 10 \times 10 \times 10 \times 10 \times 10 \times 10$

We move the point 9 places to the right to get the normal way of writing it: 4 500 000 000·

Note that the 4 and 5 are the significant figures.

Example 2 A film of oil is 0·000 000 65 mm thick.

A scientist would write $6{\cdot}5 \times 10^{-7}$ mm.
which means $6{\cdot}5 \times \frac{1}{10} \times \frac{1}{10} \times \frac{1}{10} \times \frac{1}{10} \times \frac{1}{10} \times \frac{1}{10} \times \frac{1}{10}$
or $6{\cdot}5 \div 10 \div 10 \div 10 \div 10 \div 10 \div 10 \div 10$

We move the point 7 places to the left to get the normal way of writing it: 0·000 000 65

F

To write a number in scientific notation, we:

- write down the significant figures
- put the decimal point after the first figure (the most significant)
- write '×10'
- give the 10 an index which tells you how many places to move the point to get the normal form of the number.

Exercise 12.1

1 Express each of these numbers in the normal way of writing numbers:

a $3{\cdot}8 \times 10^3$ **b** $8{\cdot}3 \times 10^5$ **c** $9{\cdot}1 \times 10^4$ **d** $2{\cdot}7 \times 10^6$
e $5{\cdot}0 \times 10^1$ **f** $7{\cdot}0 \times 10^0$ **g** $4{\cdot}58 \times 10^5$ **h** $8{\cdot}93 \times 10^4$

2 Express each of these numbers in scientific notation:

a 6100 **b** 84 000 **c** 9000 **d** 30 000
e 4 000 000 **f** 753 000 **g** 502 **h** 92 700

3 Express each of these numbers in the normal way of writing numbers:

a $6{\cdot}2 \times 10^{-3}$ **b** $9{\cdot}5 \times 10^{-2}$ **c** $8{\cdot}0 \times 10^{-5}$ **d** $4{\cdot}0 \times 10^{-4}$
e $7{\cdot}31 \times 10^{-6}$ **f** $3{\cdot}27 \times 10^{-1}$ **g** $1{\cdot}0 \times 10^{-6}$ **h** $9{\cdot}6 \times 10^{-8}$

4 Express each of these numbers in scientific notation:

a 0·025 **b** 0·004 **c** 0·000 57 **d** 0·28

e 0·3 **f** 0·000 369 **g** 0·0063 **h** 0·000 014

5 Rewrite the following sentences, changing between normal and standard form.

a The average distance between the moon and the earth is 382 000 km.

b The speed of light is $2{\cdot}998 \times 10^8$ m/s.

c Sound takes 3×10^{-3} s to travel 1 metre.

d For action photographs a shutter speed of 0·0005 s may be used.

Brainstormer

1 The mass of an electron is $9{\cdot}11 \times 10^{-31}$. How many zeros are between the decimal point and the 9 when the number is written in the normal way?

2 The earth weighs $5{\cdot}97 \times 10^{24}$ kg. How many zeros are there between the 7 and the decimal point when the number is written in the normal way?

CHECK-UP

1 Calculate:

a $5{\cdot}963 + 2{\cdot}208$ **b** $8{\cdot}604 - 4{\cdot}275$

c $4{\cdot}6 + 7{\cdot}539$ **d** $8{\cdot}6 - 6{\cdot}802$

2 Kate's tent is 1·735 m high and 2·14 m long.
By how much is the length greater than the height?

3 In a 200 m race Ron runs the first 100 m in 11·83 s and the second 100 m in 10·49 s.

a Round each time to 1 decimal place.

b Use the answers to **a** to estimate his time for the race.

4 Calculate:

a $0{\cdot}45 \times 1000$ **b** $2{\cdot}01 \times 1000$ **c** $5{\cdot}78 \div 1000$ **d** $64 \div 1000$

5 Calculate and round your answers to 1 decimal place:

a $73{\cdot}87 \times 5$ **b** $98{\cdot}97 \times 8$ **c** $51{\cdot}32 \div 4$ **d** $12{\cdot}53 \div 7$

6 To hire a mountain bike costs £62·75 for 5 days.

a **i** Estimate the cost per day. **ii** Estimate the cost for 7 days' hire.

b Calculate the exact cost for **i** 1 day **ii** 7 days at the same rate.

7 The exchange rate is £1 = \$1·423.

a Change:
i £60
ii £4500 into dollars, correct to the nearest whole dollar.

b Change:
i \$56
ii \$11 000 into pounds, correct to the nearest 10p.

8 The temperature at the foot of Ben Nevis is 3 °C. The temperature at the summit is −5·5 °C.

a What is the difference in temperature?

b The temperature at both the summit and foot of the mountain falls by 3·5 °C.
Calculate the new temperatures.

9 Round these numbers to **i** 2 **ii** 3 decimal places.

a 4·7029 **b** 6·49251

10 Perform these calculations and round your answers to 3 decimal places:

a $3·142 \times 8·27$ **b** $6 \div 3·142$

11 Calculate:

a $0·02 \times 7000$ **b** $0·004 \times 0·09$ **c** $42 \div 0·007$ **d** $0·0027 \div 0·09$

12 Round each number to 2 significant figures:

a 562 **b** 47 520 **c** 0·0526

13 Express in scientific notation:

a 7000 **b** 84 300 000 **c** 0·000 06 **d** 0·000 528

14 Express in normal form:

a 8×10^1 **b** $9·2 \times 10^6$ **c** 3×10^{-4} **d** $7·52 \times 10^{-6}$

E
F

3 Angles

Measuring and making angles are important skills.

When the space shuttle returns to earth, for example, the angle at which it re-enters the atmosphere is critically important:

- too steep and the craft burns up
- too shallow and it will bounce back into space.

1 Looking back

Exercise 1.1

1 What kind of angle (acute, right, obtuse or straight) is each of the following?

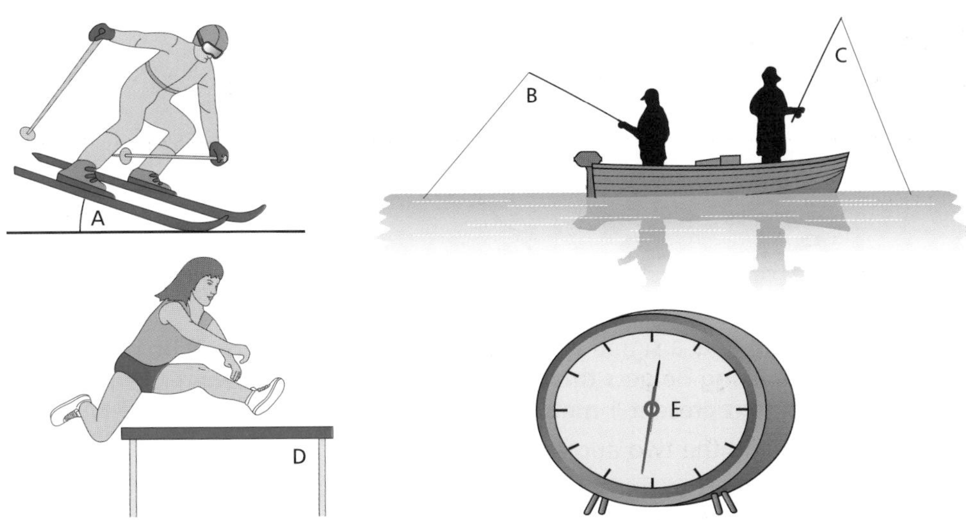

2 State the size of each angle. Choose your answer from: 30°, 70°, 90°, 100°, 130°.

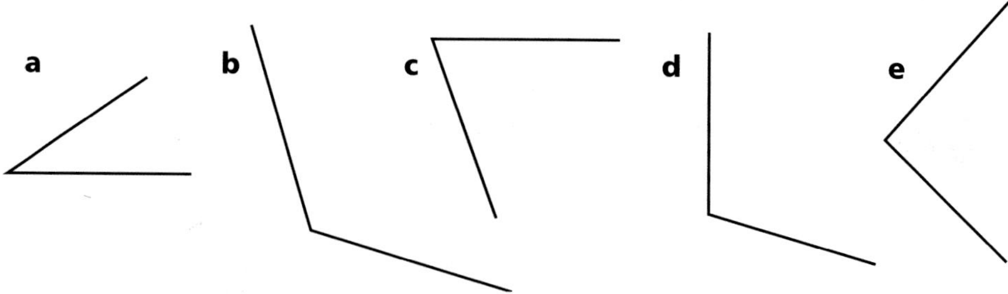

3

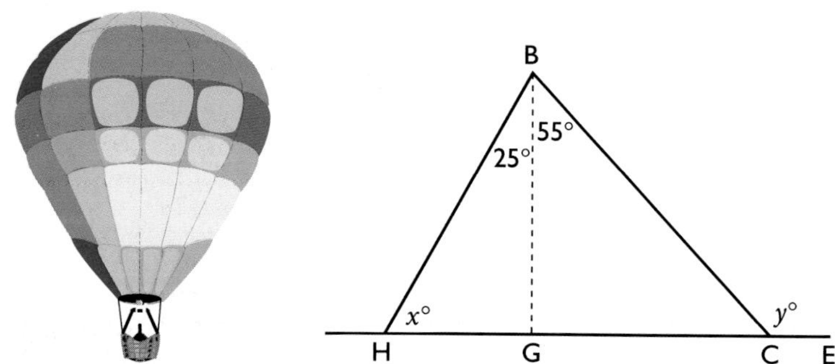

A balloonist at B spots a house at H and a bridge at C.
G is a point directly below him.
He measures ∠GBH as 25° and ∠GBC as 55°.

a Make an accurate diagram of the situation using a 5 cm line to represent BG.

b Measure

i ∠BHG **ii** ∠BCE.

4

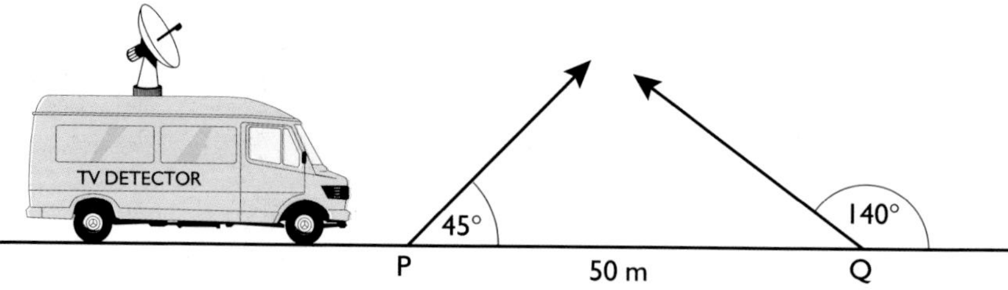

A detector van gets a signal at P in a direction 45° to the road he is on.
50 m further along he gets the same signal at 140° to the road as shown.
Using 1 mm to represent 1 metre we can let a 50 mm line represent PQ.

a Draw PQ and the two angles.

b Extend the lines to find the source of the signal.
How far from the road is it?

2 Some relations

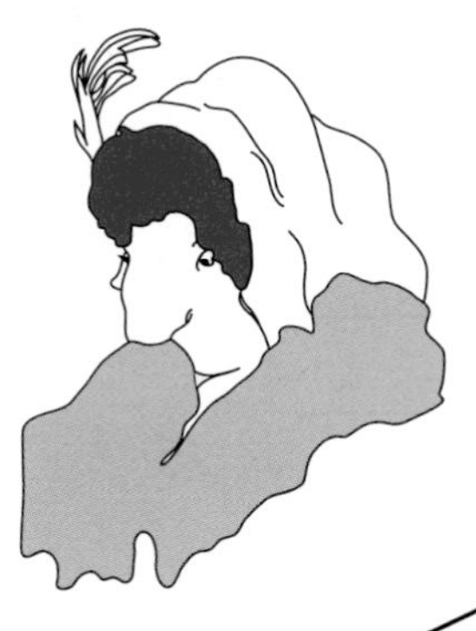

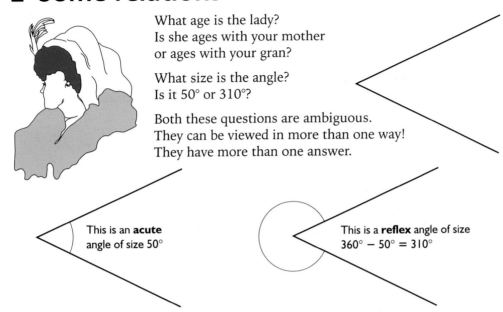

What age is the lady?
Is she ages with your mother
or ages with your gran?

What size is the angle?
Is it 50° or 310°?

Both these questions are ambiguous.
They can be viewed in more than one way!
They have more than one answer.

This is an **acute** angle of size 50°

This is a **reflex** angle of size 360° − 50° = 310°

A reflex angle is an angle whose size is greater than 180°.

If it is not a straight line then every angle you draw contains:

- an angle of size $x°$ which might be acute, right or obtuse
- an angle of size $(360 - x)°$ which is reflex.

Complementary angles

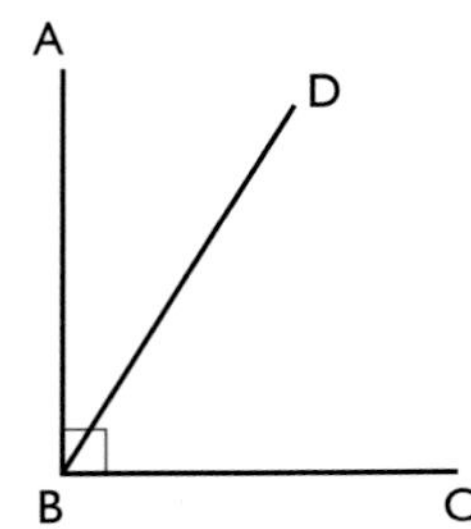

∠ABC = 90°

So ∠ABD + ∠DBC = 90°

When two angles add to make 90° then they are said to be **complementary**.

∠ABD is the complement of ∠DBC.

∠DBC is the complement of ∠ABD.

40° is the complement of 50°.

Supplementary angles

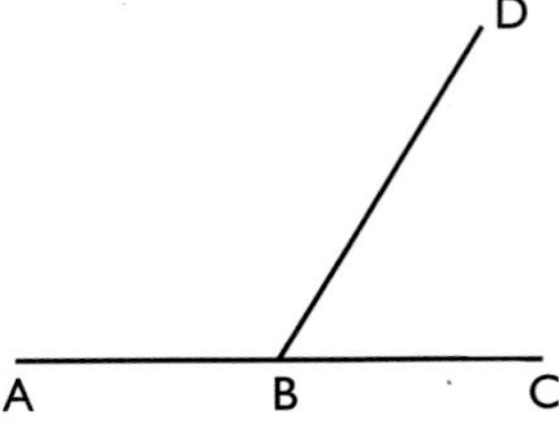

∠ABC = 180°

So ∠ABD + ∠DBC = 180°

When two angles add to make 180° then they are said to be **supplementary**.

∠ABD is the supplement of ∠DBC.

∠DBC is the supplement of ∠ABD.

40° is the supplement of 140°.

Exercise 2.1

1 Calculate the size of the reflex angle in each case.

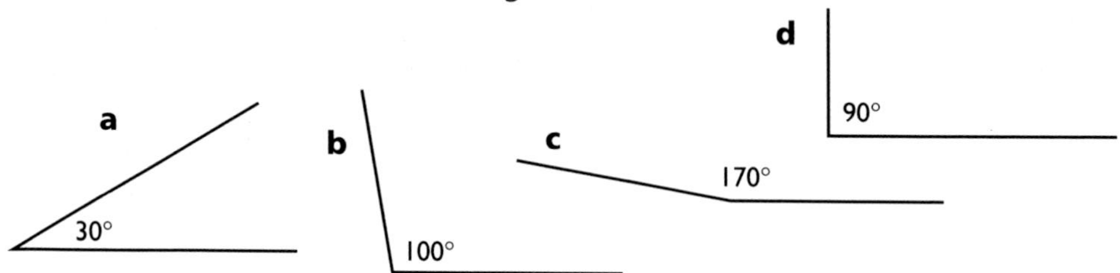

2 Draw each reflex angle by drawing the related acute or obtuse angle.

a 320° **b** 190°

c 260° **d** 345°

3 Here are some V-kites. Measure the size of the reflex angle in each.

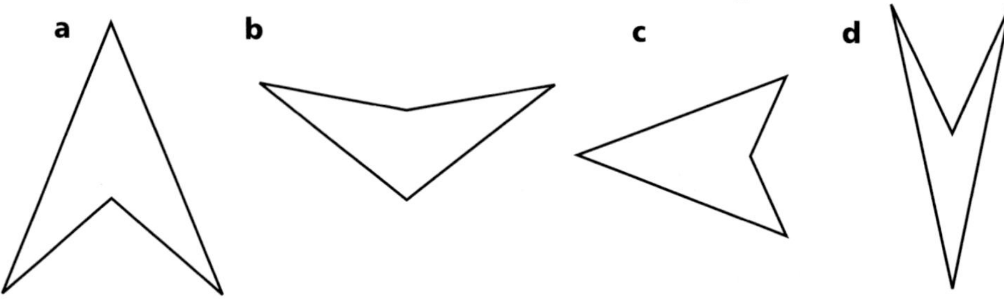

4

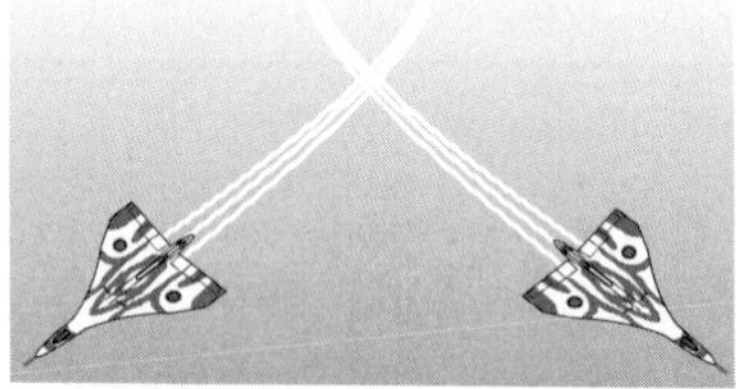

When the jets fly-by at the air show they leave contrails AD, BE and CF.
Calculate the size of these reflex angles:

a ∠AGB **b** ∠BGD

c ∠CGD **d** ∠DGF

5 State the complement of:

a 25° **b** 72° **c** 40°

d 89° **e** 90°.

6 Which angle is its own complement?

7 Peter's knife has many gadgets. When extended, the corkscrew, CD, is at 90° to the body of the knife.
The pencil sharpener, DP, also extends the same way.
Calculate the size of ∠BDP when ∠PDC is:

a 20°

b 14°

c 38°.

8 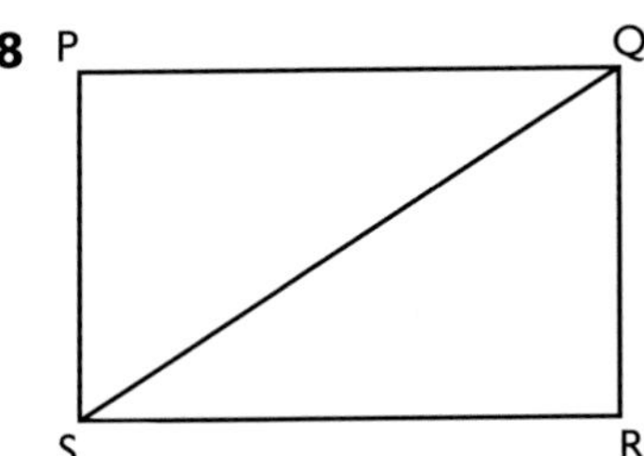

PQRS is a rectangle. QS is one of its diagonals.

a What is the size of ∠PSR?

b What size is ∠PSQ when ∠QSR =

i 74° **ii** 80° **iii** 5°?

c What size is ∠PQS when ∠SQR =

i 16° **ii** 34° **iii** 62°?

9 State the supplement of:

a 35° **b** 125° **c** 66° **d** 89° **e** 167°.

10 Which angle is its own supplement?

11 The nail clippers on Peter's knife open out as shown. They turn through 180° to open out.
Calculate the size of ∠CBD when ∠ABC is:

a 70°

b 126°

c 145°.

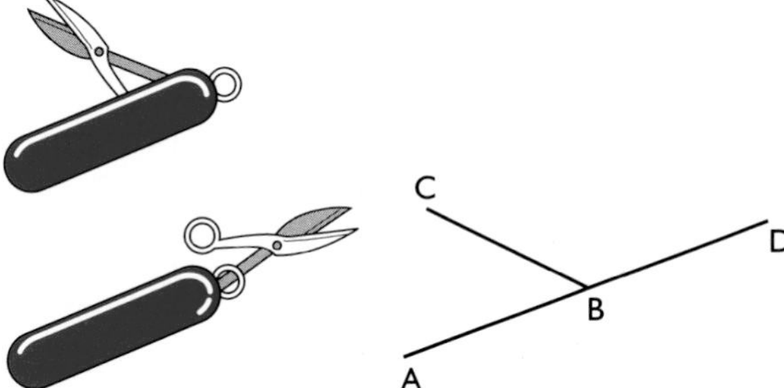

12 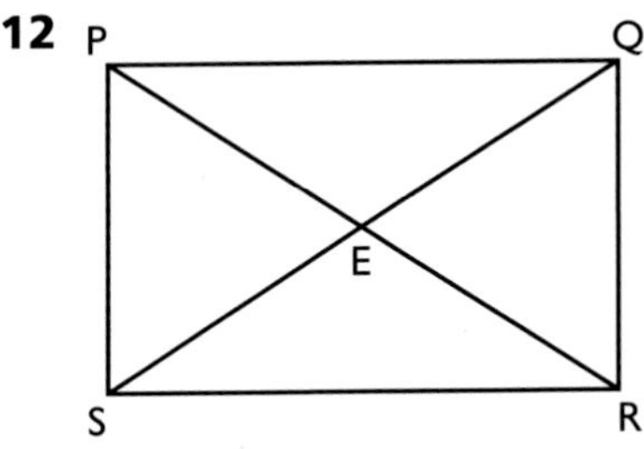

The diagonals of the rectangle PQRS intersect at E.

a Name four pairs of supplementary angles.

b What size is ∠PES when ∠PEQ =

i 100° **ii** 144° **iii** 25°?

c Find the size of each angle round E when ∠SER = 112°.

d What is the size of the reflex angle QER when ∠PES = 30°?

Exercise 2.2

1 **a** A Christmas cake has had a piece cut out.
If $x°$ has been cut out and $3x°$ remains, what kind of angle is
i $x°$ **ii** $3x°$?

b If, instead, an angle of $4y°$ remains and is reflex,
i what is the largest that y can be?
ii what is the smallest that y can be?

c If $a°$ is removed, write down an expression for the amount that remains.

2 A plane flies parallel to the ground watched by Michael at J.
K is the point where the plane will be immediately above Michael.

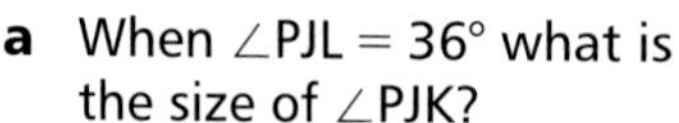

a When $\angle PJL = 36°$ what is the size of $\angle PJK$?

b When $\angle PJL = x°$, $\angle PJK$ is $3x°$. What is the value of x?

c When $\angle PJL = k + 10°$, $\angle PJK$ is $k + 30°$. What is the value of k?

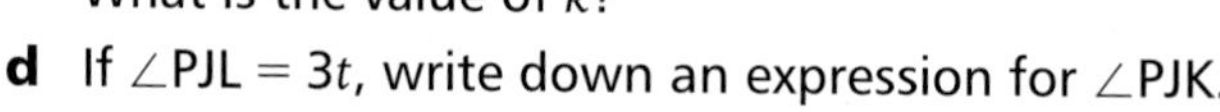

d If $\angle PJL = 3t$, write down an expression for $\angle PJK$.

3 Find the value of x in each of the following diagrams.

a

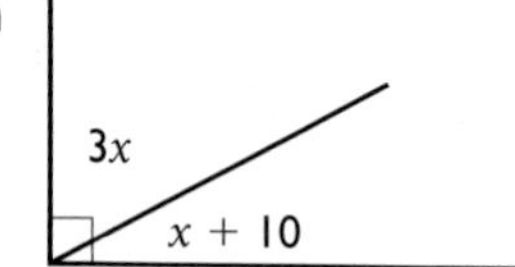

b

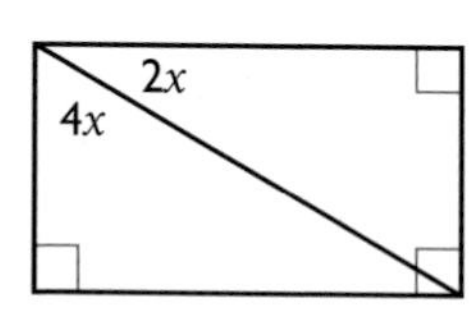

c

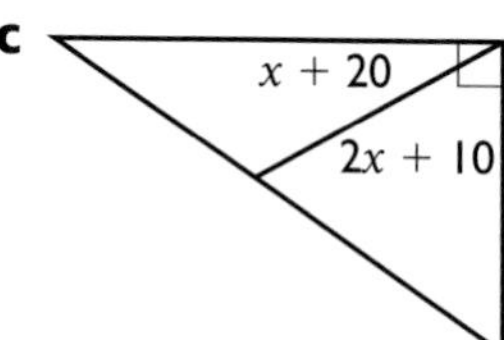

4 The angle of the cutting edge of the plane is quite important.

a Calculate $\angle ABD$ when $\angle ABC$ is
i 124°
ii 150°
iii $x°$.

b Find the value of a when $\angle ABC = 2a°$ and $\angle ABD = (a + 30)°$.

c Write down an expression for $\angle ABD$ when $\angle ABC = (y + 60)°$.

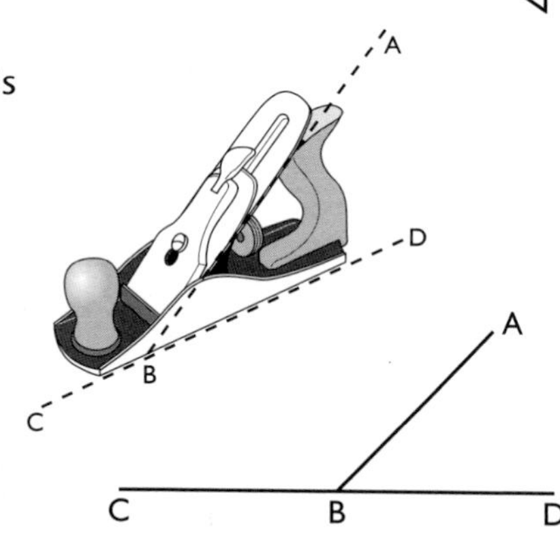

5 Find the value of x in each case.

a

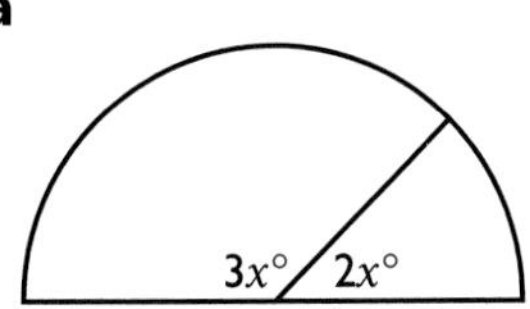

b

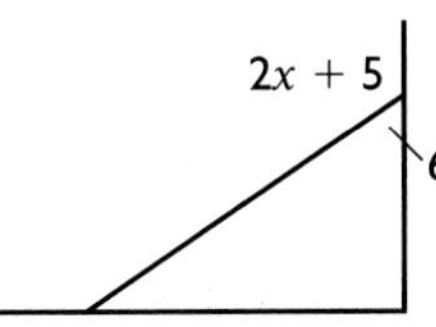

c

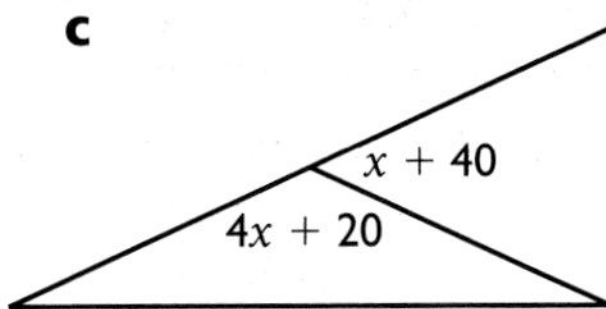

6 **a** Express x in terms of y.
b Express z in terms of y.
c What can you say about x and z?

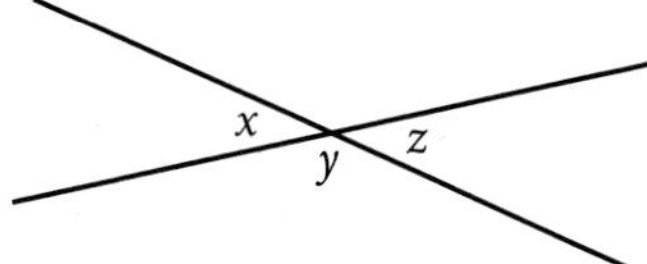

3 Vertically opposite angles

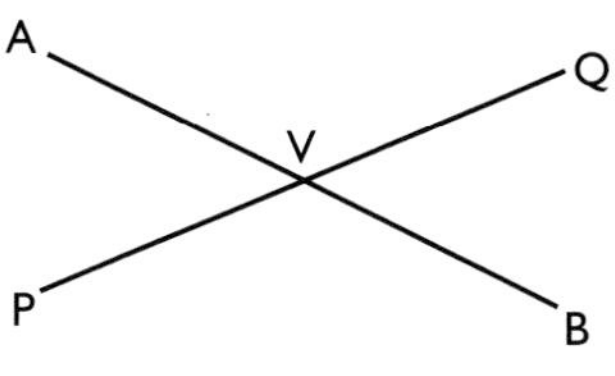

AB and PQ are straight lines intersecting at the vertex V.
∠AVP = 180 − ∠PVB (supplementary angles … AB straight)
∠QVB = 180 − ∠PVB (supplementary angles … PQ straight)
So ∠AVP = ∠QVB (both equal to 180 − ∠PVB).

When two straight lines intersect, the angles opposite each other across the vertex are called **vertically opposite angles**.

Vertically opposite angles are equal.

Example The diagonals of the quadrilateral EFGH intersect at K. ∠FKE = 70°. Calculate the sizes of the other angles round K.

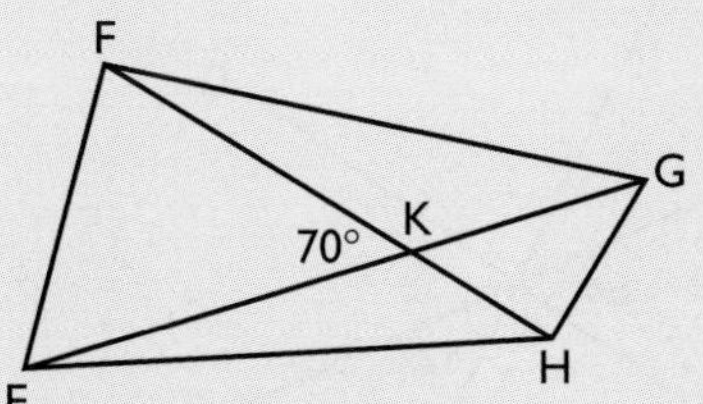

Answer:
∠EKH = 180° − 70° = 110° (supplementary angles)
∠HKG = 70° (vertically opposite ∠FKE)
∠FKG = 110° (vertically opposite ∠EKH)

Exercise 3.1

1 Calculate the sizes of the angles round each vertex.

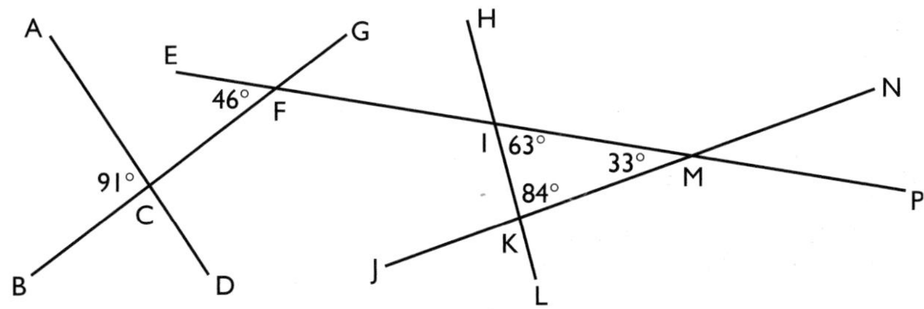

2 This diagram contains six pairs of vertically opposite angles.
Can you find them all?

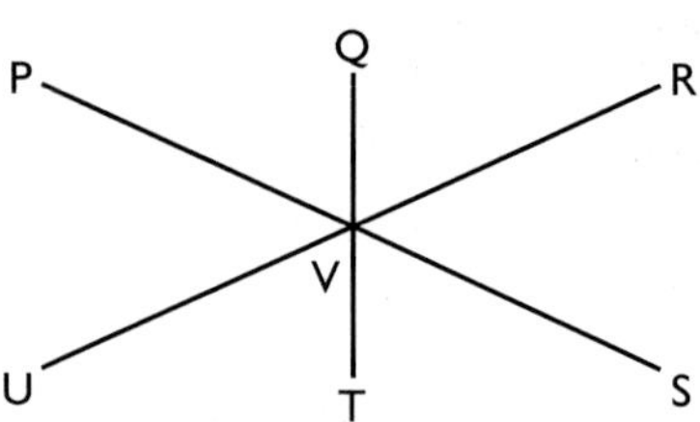

3 The scissors can be simplified as a pair of straight lines.

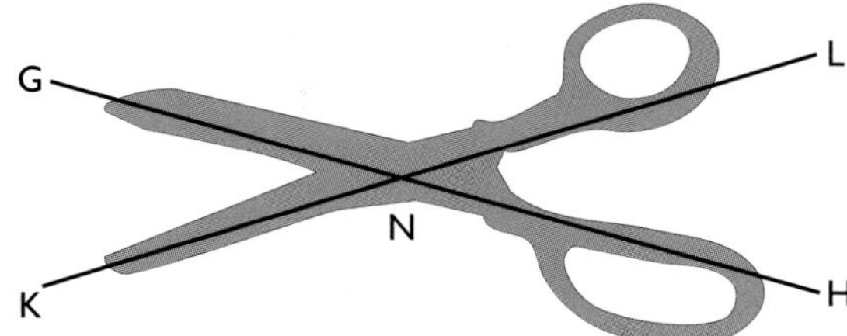

a What is the size of ∠LNH when ∠GNK is
i 34° **ii** 112° **iii** x°?

b What is the size of ∠LNH when ∠GNL is
i 160° **ii** 89° **iii** y°?

c Martin measures ∠GNK as 50°.
He says ∠GNL is three times as big.
Is he correct?

4 In each diagram calculate the size of:
i ∠DGE **ii** ∠DGF **iii** ∠AGF.

a

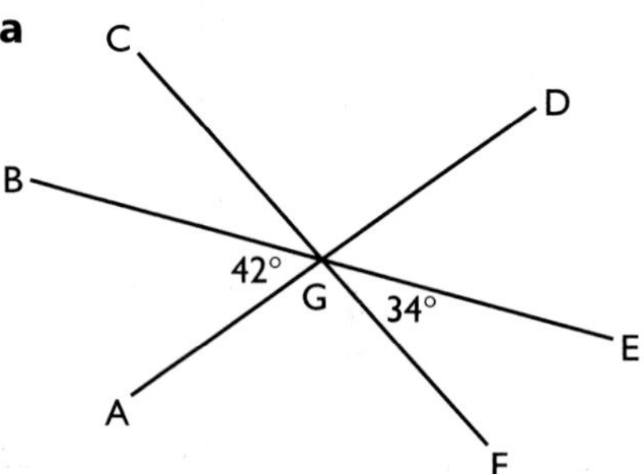

b

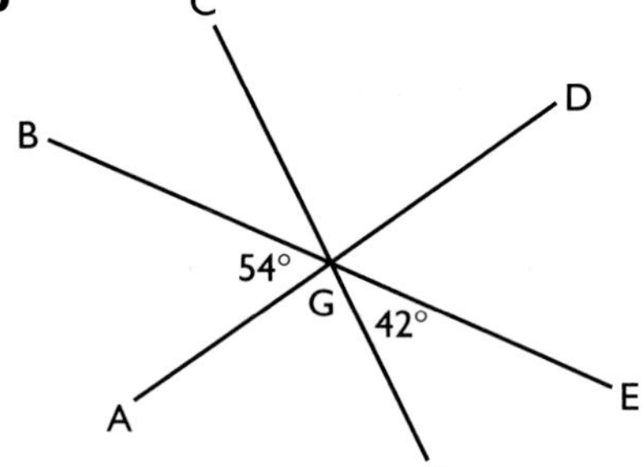

5 SW, TX and UY are straight lines.
Calculate the size of:

a ∠TZV

b ∠SZU

c ∠SZY

d ∠VZX.

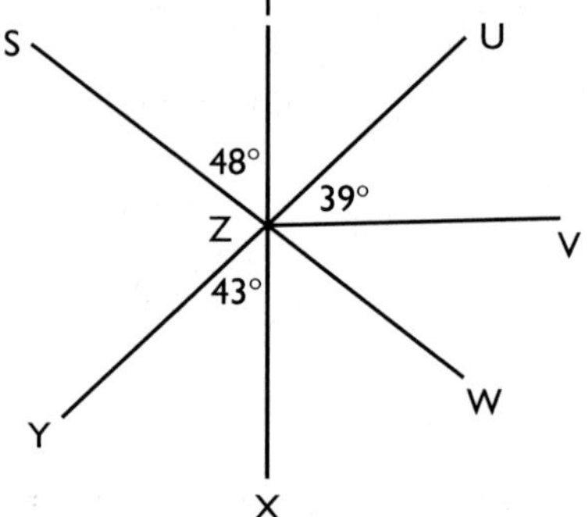

Exercise 3.2

1 Some of the ropes of the rigging of the tall ship are shown.
ACF and BCE are straight lines.
$\angle DCE = 27°$ and $\angle BCF = 150°$.
Calculate the size of:

- **a** $\angle ACD$
- **b** $\angle ACB$
- **c** $\angle DCF$.

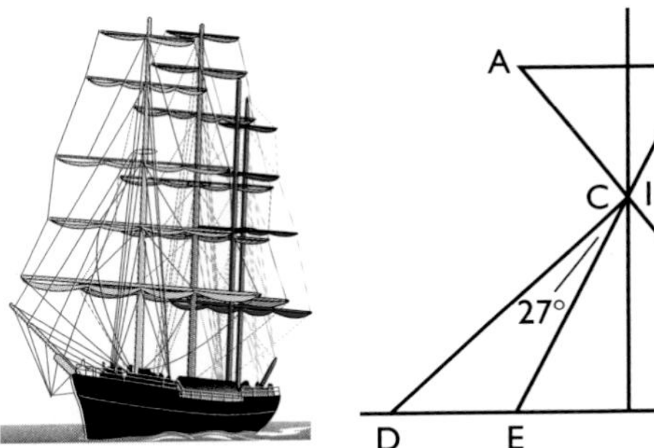

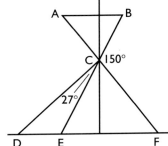

2 Examine each diagram.
i Form an equation in x. **ii** Calculate the value of x and of y.

a

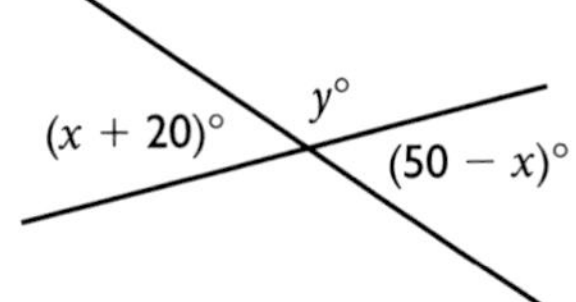

b

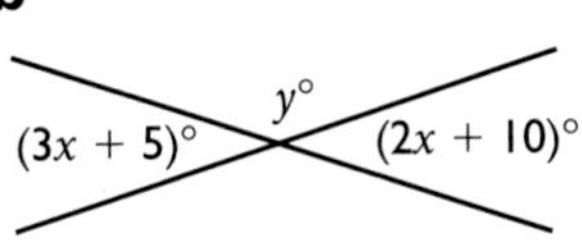

c

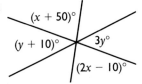

$(x + 50)°$
$(y + 10)°$
$3y°$
$(2x - 10)°$

3 A painter has set up scaffolding up to the roof of the house.
AQS and PQT are straight lines.
$\angle PQR$ is a right angle. $\angle AQP = x°$.

- **a** Express $\angle RQS$ in terms of x.
- **b** If $\angle AQT = 155°$, calculate the size of $\angle RQS$.

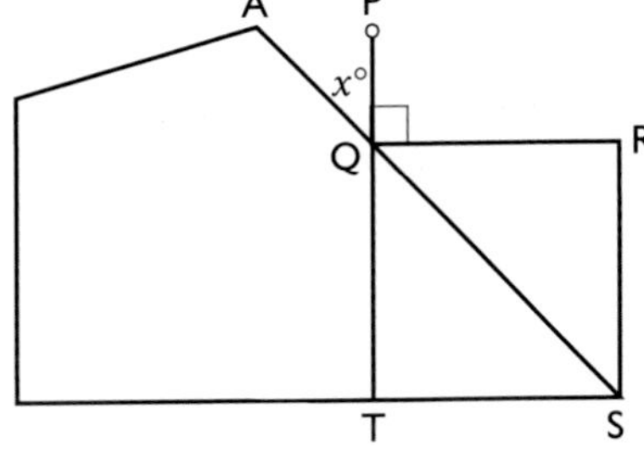

Brainstormer

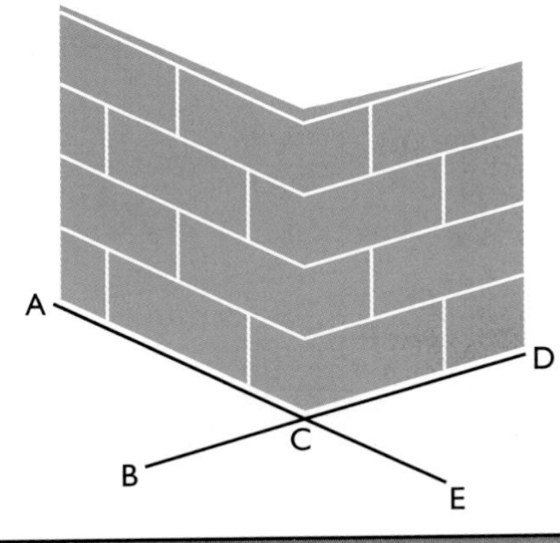

In order to figure out the angle $\angle ACD$ at which the two walls meet, the builder lies two straight canes AE and BD against the walls.
He discovers that $\angle DCE$ is only four-fifths of $\angle BCE$.

What is the size of $\angle ACD$?

E

4 Angles and parallel lines

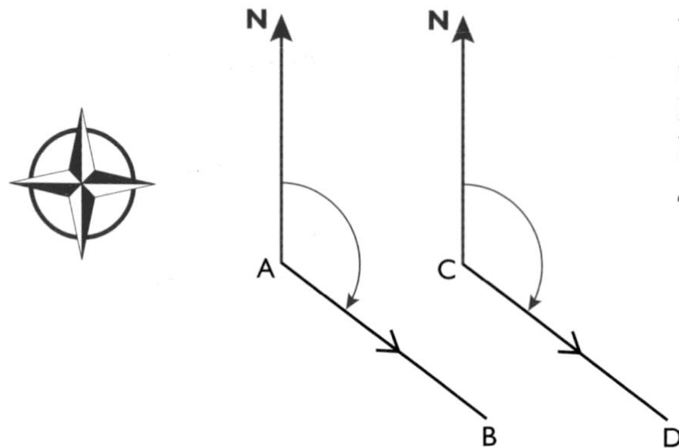

We can say lines are parallel when they run in the same direction. In this example AB and CD are both running south-east.

Thus AB is parallel to CD.

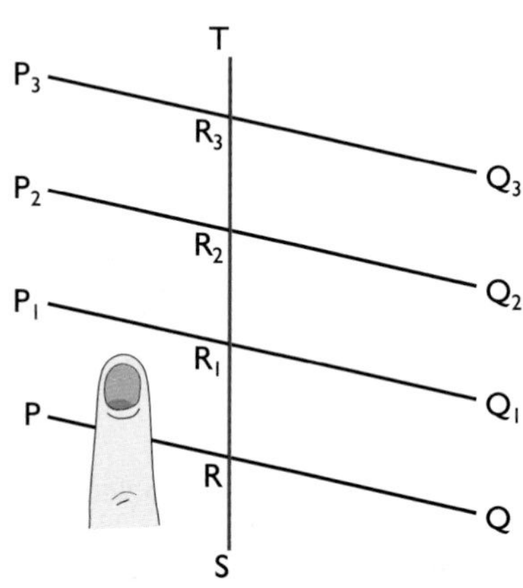

As PRQ is slid along ST without twisting, the angle TRQ keeps its size.

Thus all versions of PRQ are parallel.

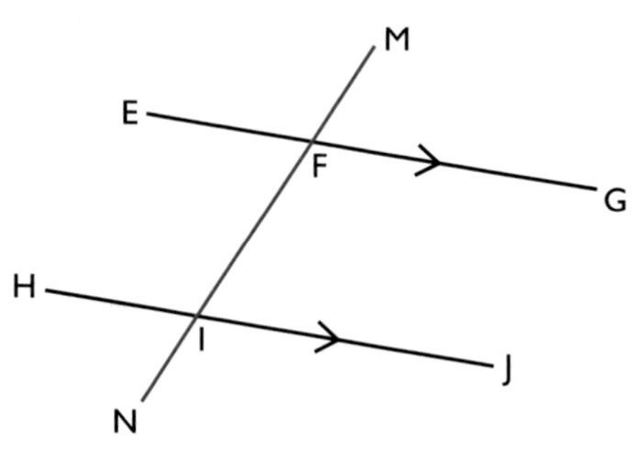

EG and HJ are parallel.

The line MN cuts EG at F and HJ at I.

Such a line is called a transversal.

> When parallel lines are cut by a transversal, the pattern of angles round the points of intersection is identical.

Example Find the size of each angle in the diagram.

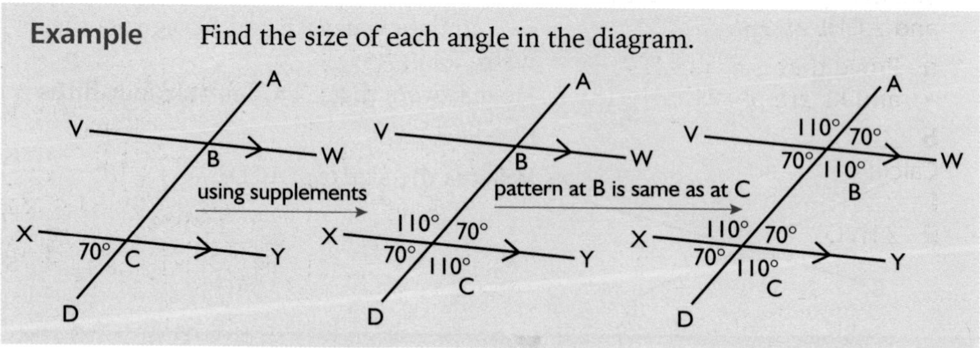

Exercise 4.1

1 Copy each diagram, then fill in the sizes of as many angles as you can.

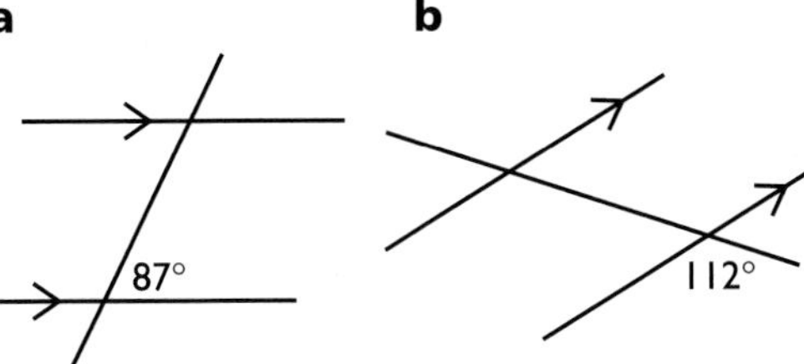

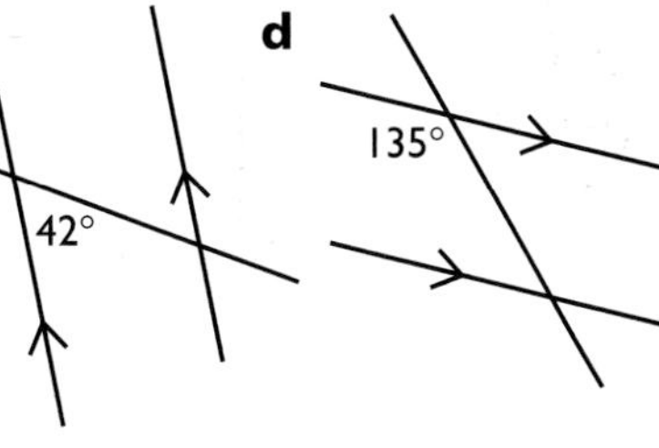

2 ABCD is a rectangle.

a What can be said about the sides AB and CD?

b NK cuts the rectangle at L and M as shown. Calculate the size of:

i ∠MLD **ii** ∠MLC

iii ∠NMA **iv** ∠NMB.

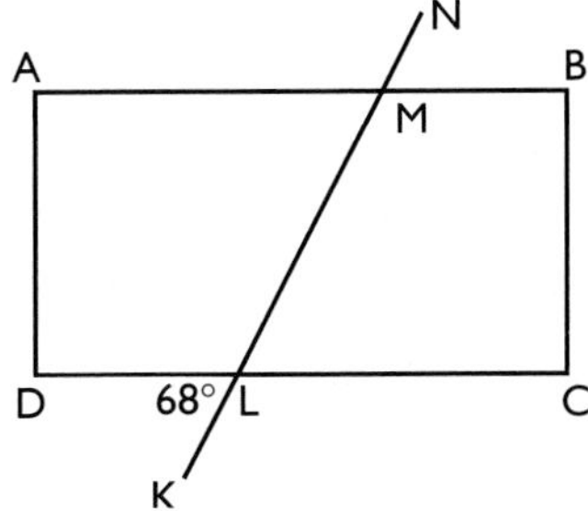

3 The struts AB and CD of an artist's easel are both horizontal.
The easel is symmetrical.
∠CMN = 84°.
Calculate the size of

a $p°$ **b** $q°$

c $r°$ **d** $s°$.

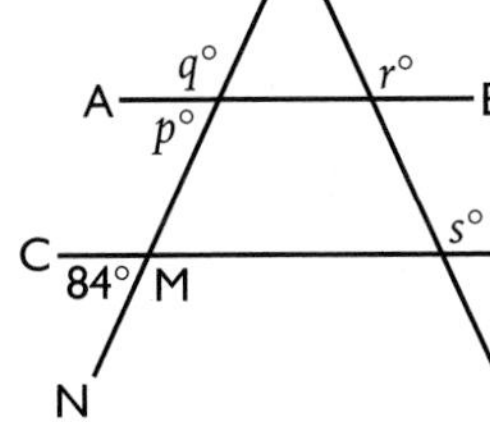

4 Maria took a photo of Tower Bridge.
She measured ∠HGM as 84° and ∠GHL as 96°.

a Prove that the lines NM and KL are parallel.

b ∠PTM = 88°.
Calculate the size of

i ∠TVH

ii ∠HVQ.

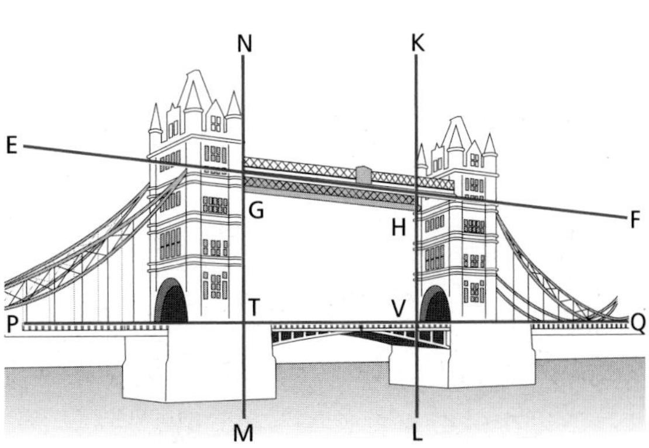

E

5 Three jets fly over a motorway. From above the angles are measured as shown.

a Which two jets are flying on parallel paths?

b The jets also fly over a canal as shown. Calculate the value of x.

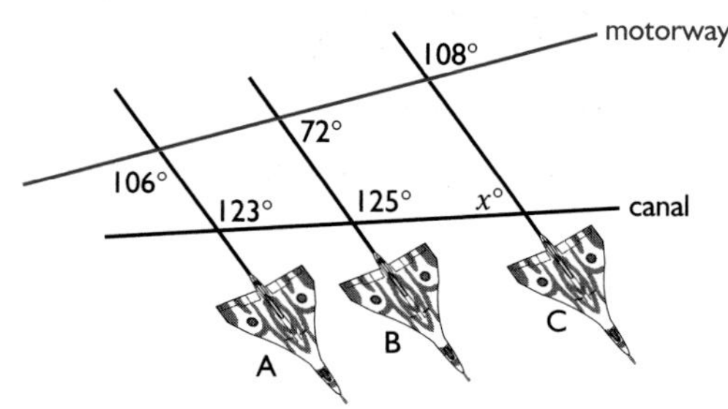

6 The yachts at a regatta have all crossed the winning line. The angle at which each crossed is shown.

a Which two yachts have parallel wakes?

b A motor launch has cut across the wakes. Calculate the size of the angle marked y.

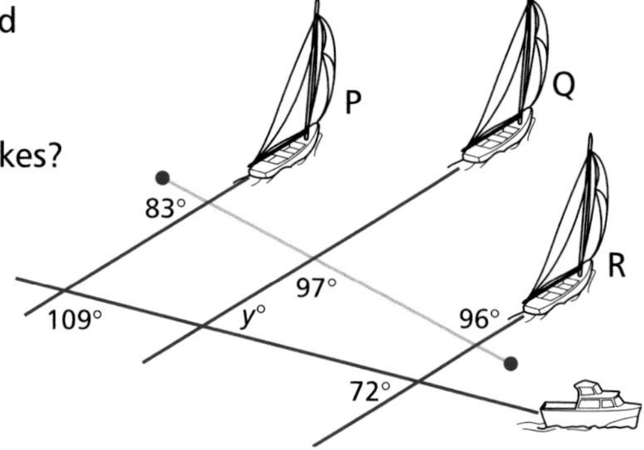

5 Corresponding angles

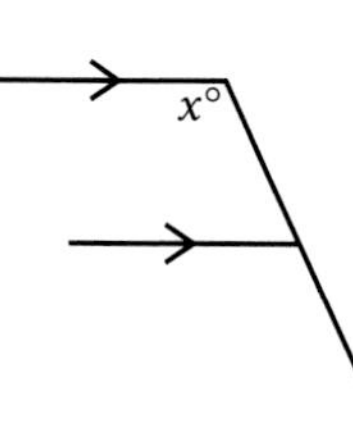

Extend the lines to show parallel lines and a transversal. Mark the angle equal to x at the other intersection.

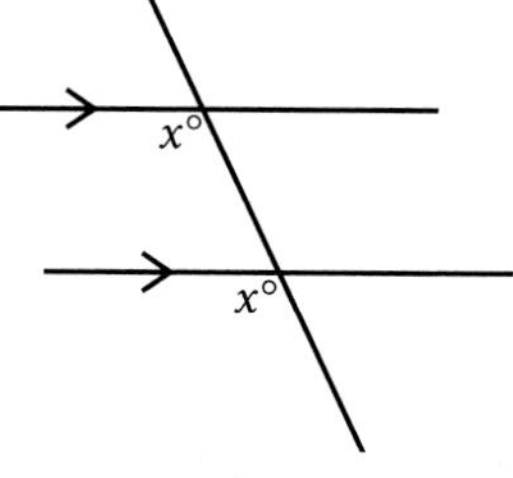

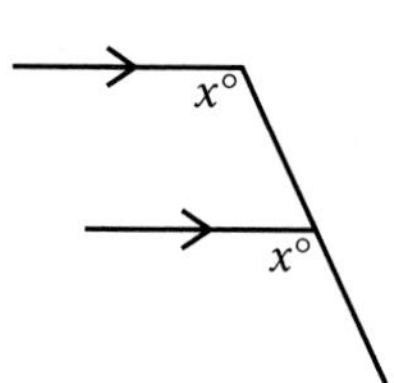

Note that in this case the equal angles are both under a parallel and to the left of the transversal.

Angles arranged like this, both occupying similar positions, are called **corresponding** angles.

> When parallel lines are cut by a transversal, **corresponding** angles are equal.

Examples

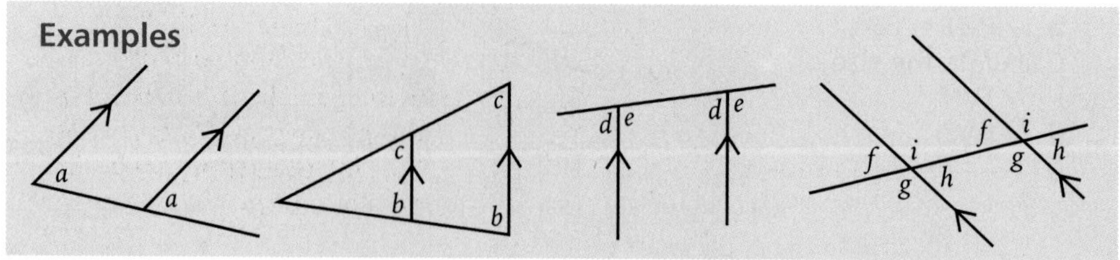

Exercise 5.1

1 Copy each diagram and mark pairs of corresponding angles.

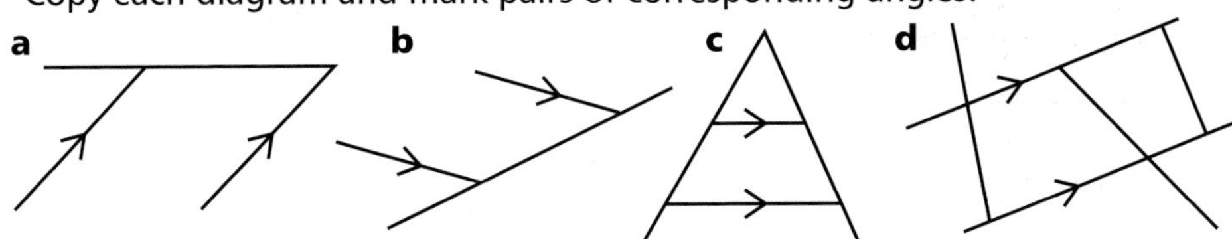

2 Calculate the size of each lettered angle.

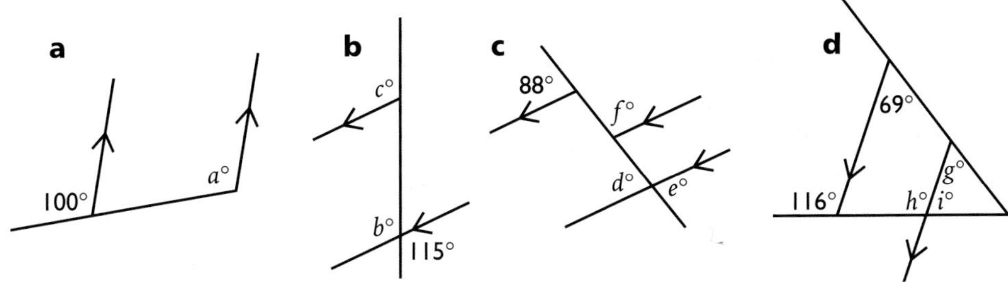

3 Derrick's set of shelves could have been better constructed! Which of the shelves are parallel to the ground?

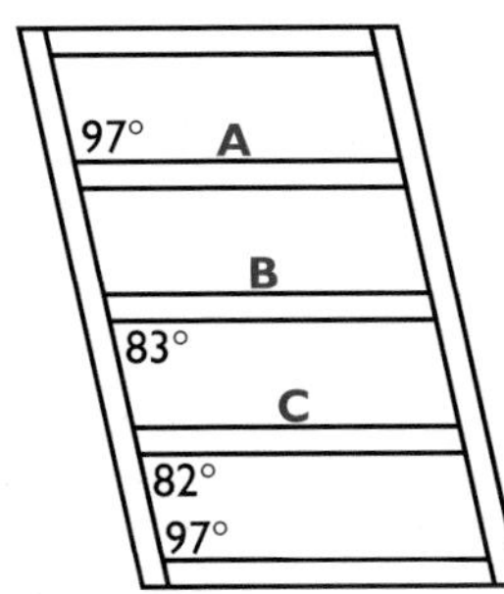

4 In triangle ABC, the line DE is drawn as shown.

a Prove that DE is parallel to BC.

b Calculate the size of ∠ABC.

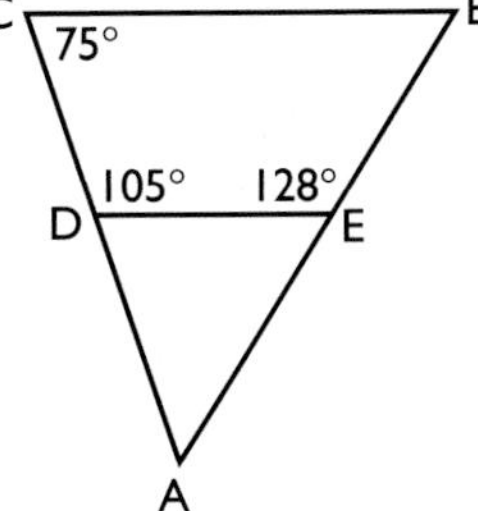

5 EFGH is a parallelogram.

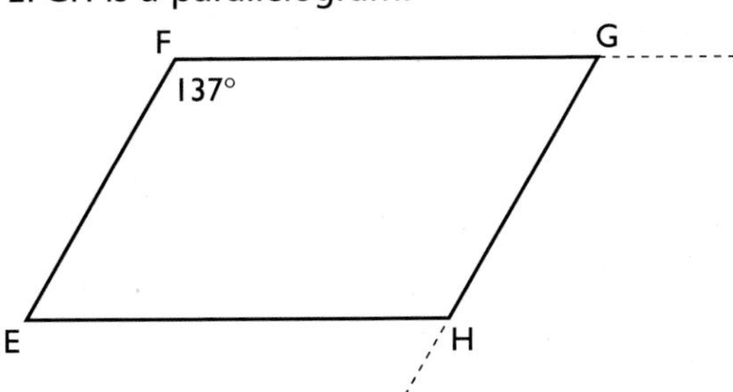

The angle at F is 137°. By considering suitable extensions from the sides of the parallelogram, calculate the size of each angle in the parallelogram.

6

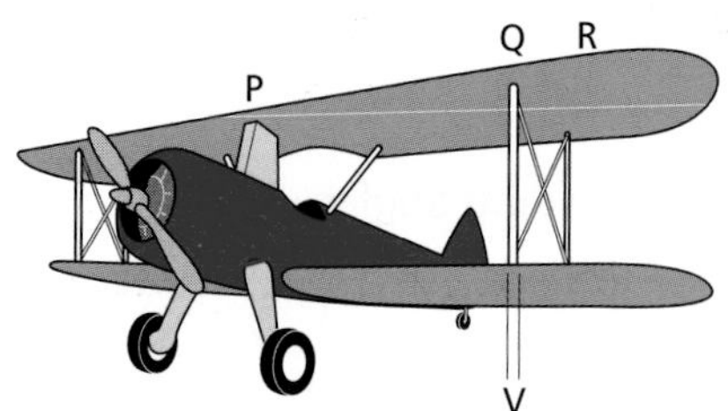

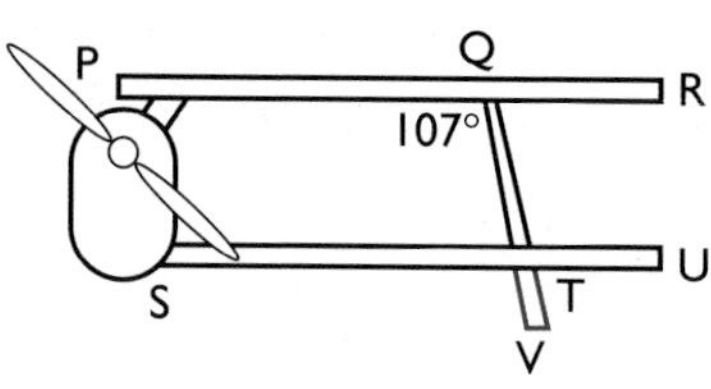

a The wing of the biplane is strengthened by a strut QT which forms an angle of 107° with the upper wing. The wings are parallel.
What is the size of ∠QTS, the angle the strut makes with the lower wing? (Hint: imagine QT continues below the wing to V.)

b From the side, the wings and the struts form two pairs of parallel lines. If ∠TQN = 88°, calculate the size of each angle of the parallelogram.

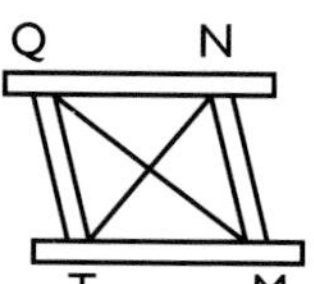

Exercise 5.2

E

1 Find the value of x in each case.

a

$(4x - 35)°$

$(2x + 15)°$

b

$(3x + 26)°$

67°

c

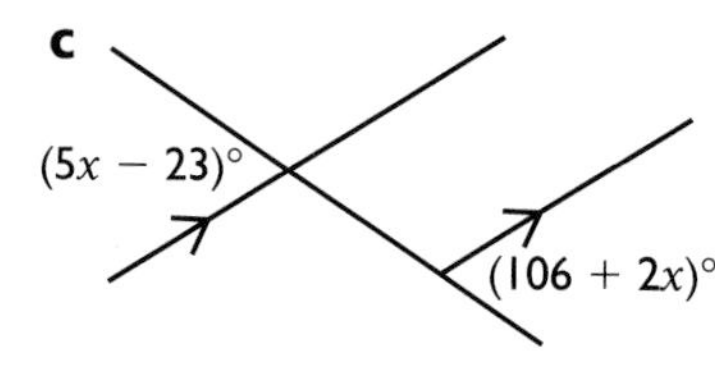

2 In each case, find for what value of x PQ and RS are parallel.

a

R

$(3x + 20)°$

P

$(5x - 4)°$

S

Q

b

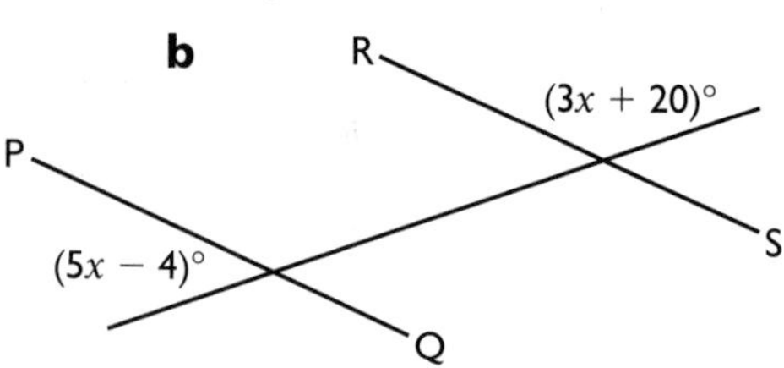

3 The threads of a screw are parallel in the picture, the angle changing depending on the use of the screw.

a Calculate y when x is

i 95°

ii 99°

iii 92°.

b Comment on your answers.

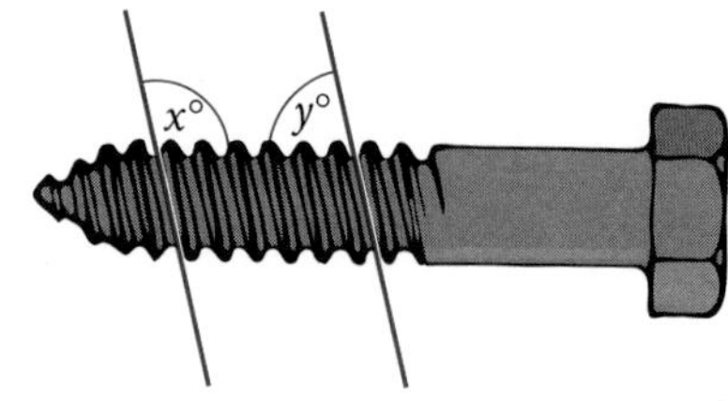

4 Triangle ABC has angles of size $x°$, $y°$ and $z°$.

a Describe the four added lines.

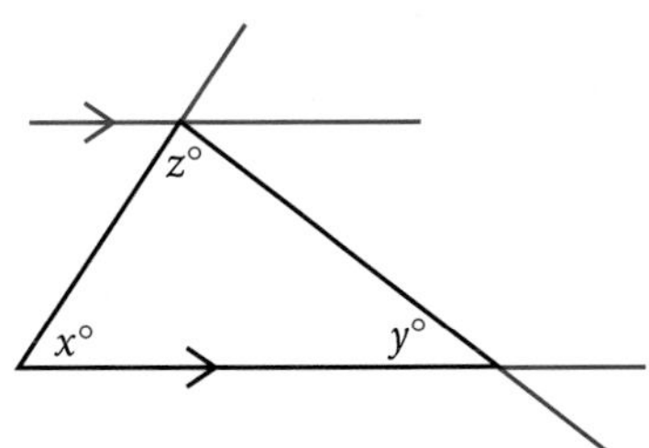

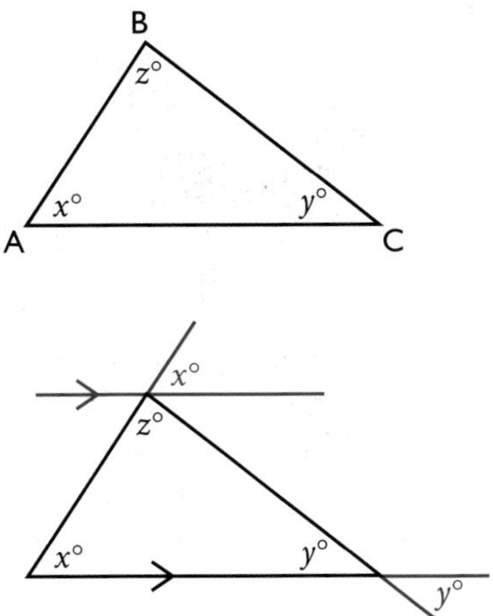

b Give reasons for the additions to the diagram.

c Prove that the sum of the angles of a triangle is 180°.

6 Alternate angles

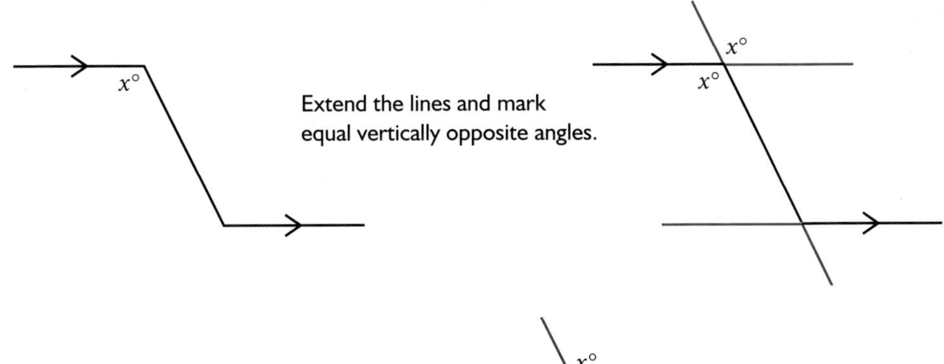

Extend the lines and mark equal vertically opposite angles.

Note the parallel lines and a transversal. Mark the corresponding angles at the other intersection.

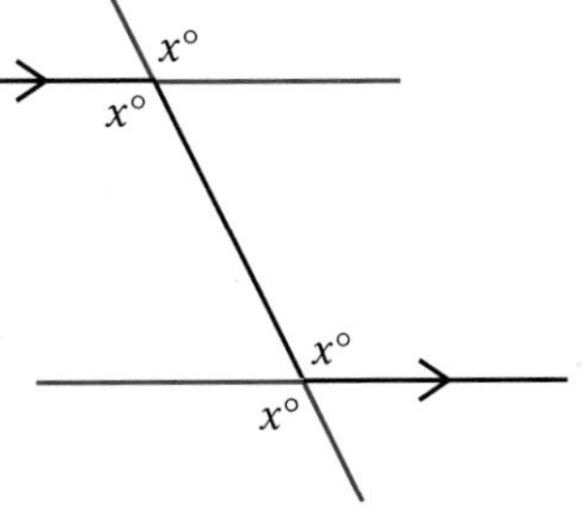

Removing the extra lines leaves this pattern.

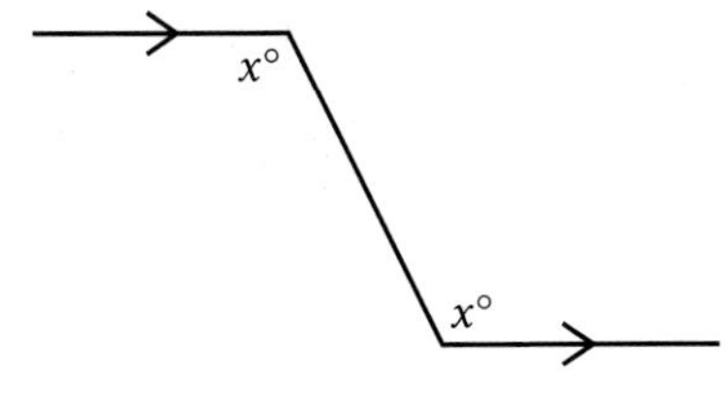

Angles arranged like this are called **alternate** angles.

> When parallel lines are cut by a transversal, **alternate** angles are equal.

E

Examples

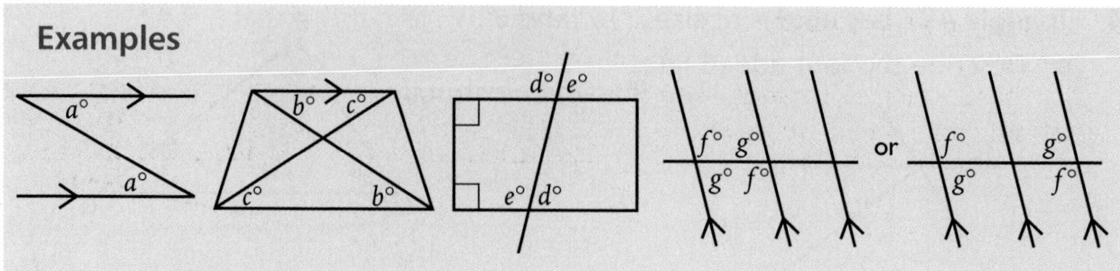

Exercise 6.1

1 Copy each diagram and mark pairs of alternate angles.

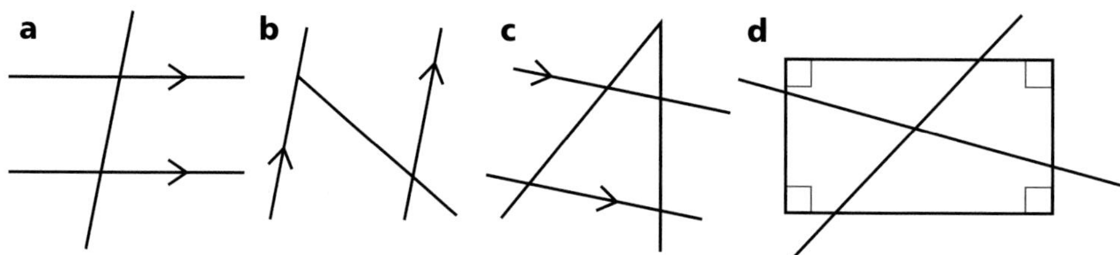

2 Use alternate angles to find the labelled angles.

a

61° a°

119° b°

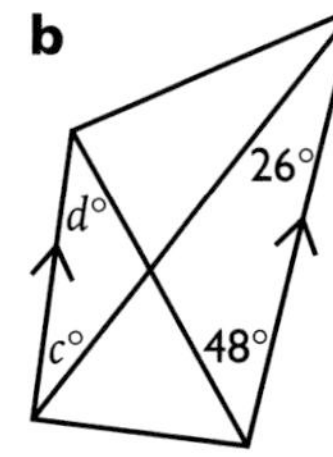

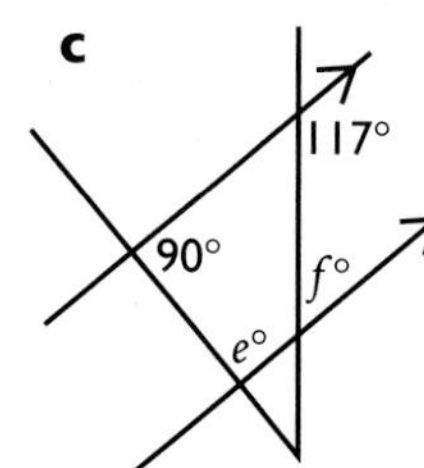

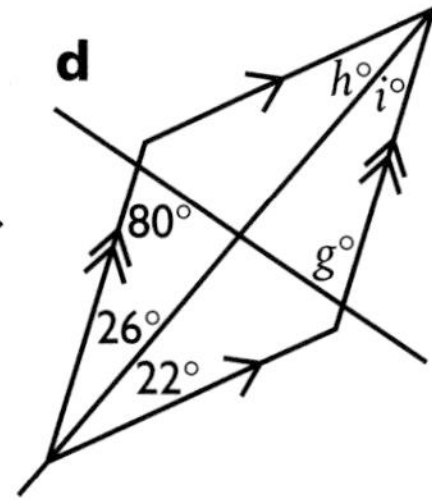

3 During an archaelogical dig, three columns are uncovered.
Some angles are measured in the survey.
Prove that two pillars are parallel.
(Use alternate angles.)

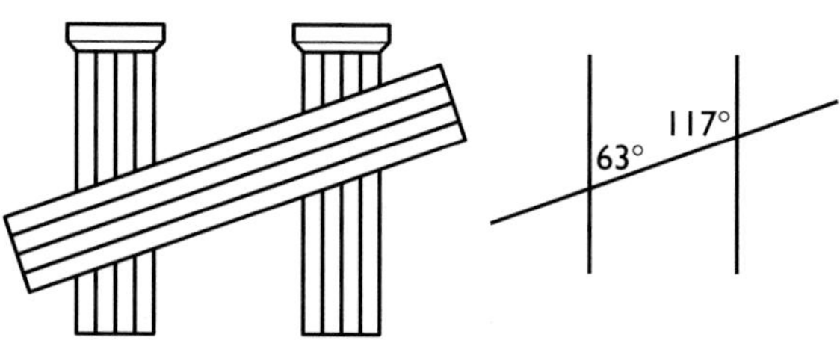

4 In a vending machine, the slot along which the coin runs has parallel sides.
Make a copy of the slot and fill in as many angles as you can.

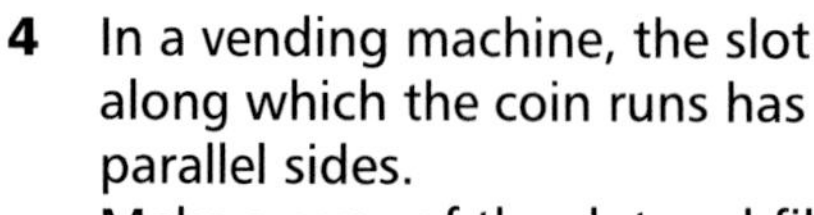

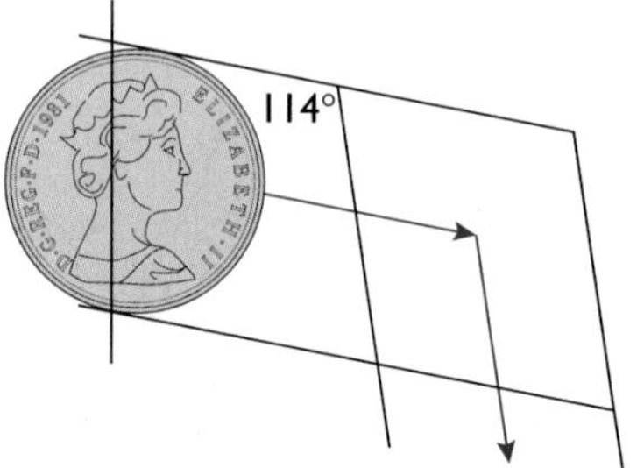

5 A screw goes into a piece of wood at right angles.
Its threads are at an angle of 16° to the surface of the wood.
Calculate the value of a, b and c.

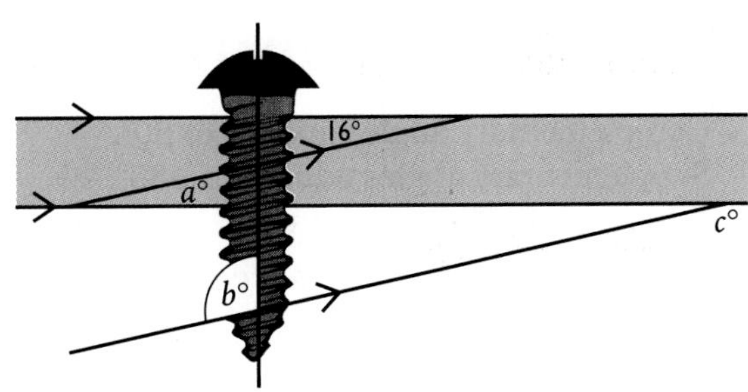

Exercise 6.2

1 The flag is a rectangle.

  a Calculate the value of x.

  b Copy the flag and fill in as many angles as you can.

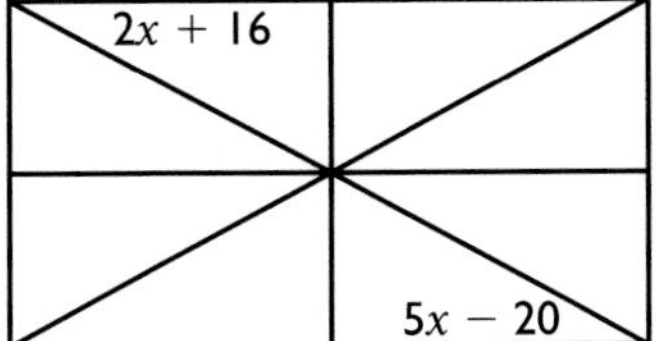

2 ABCD is a rectangle.
EDF is parallel to the diagonal AC.

  a Prove that AD cuts the angle EDG in half.

  b Prove CD bisects ∠GDF.

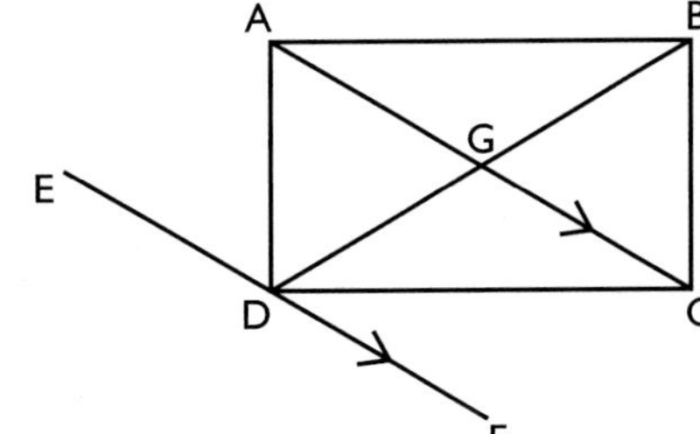

3 ABC is an isosceles triangle.

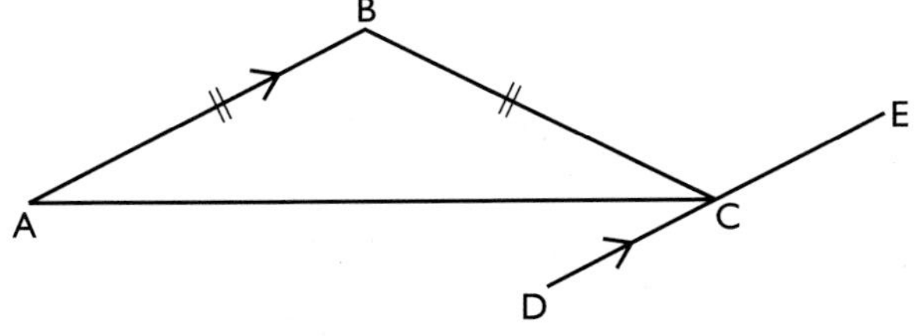

DCE is parallel to AB.
Prove that AC bisects ∠BCD.

4 Draw the triangle ABC.
Draw a line through the vertex, A, parallel to the base.
Use alternate angles to prove that the sum of the angles of a triangle is 180°.

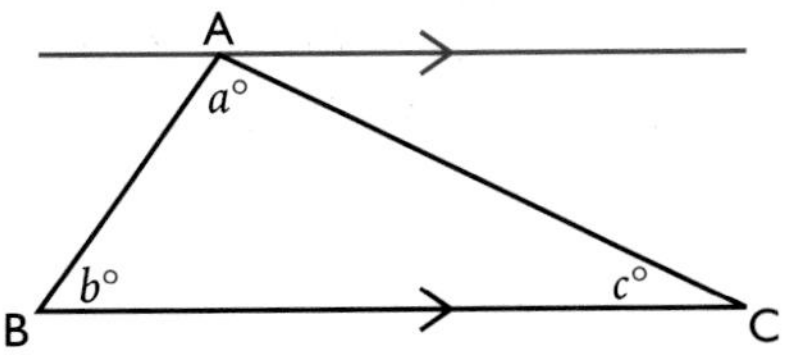

E

7 Mixed examples

Complementary angles add up to 90°.
Supplementary angles add up to 180°.
When parallel lines are cut by a transversal,

- **i** corresponding angles are equal
- **ii** alternate angles are equal.

Using a combination of these facts can lead to other new findings.

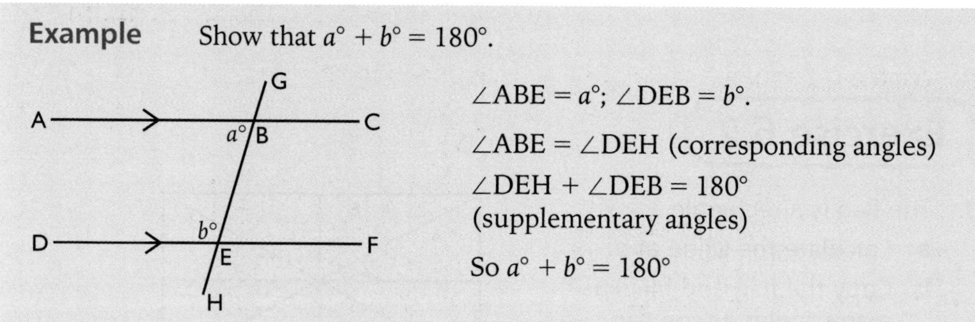

Example Show that $a° + b° = 180°$.

$\angle ABE = a°$; $\angle DEB = b°$.

$\angle ABE = \angle DEH$ (corresponding angles)

$\angle DEH + \angle DEB = 180°$ (supplementary angles)

So $a° + b° = 180°$

Exercise 7.1

1 Use the fact discovered in the example above to calculate the lettered angle in each case.

a $x°$, 127°

b $y°$, 83°

c 135°, $q°$, $r°$, $p°$

2 A railway cutting has a cross-section as shown.

AB, EF and CD are all parallel.
$\angle BCD = 142°$; $\angle CDE = 151°$.
Calculate the size of the reflex angles:

a $\angle ABC$

b $\angle DEF$.

3 The gable-end of a house is as shown. The walls and the chimney stack have vertical sides.

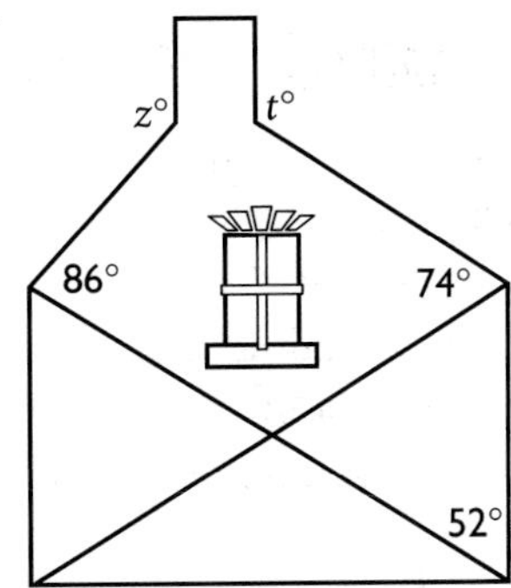

a Calculate the value of:
  i z
  ii t.

b Calculate the size of each angle inside the outline.

4 Asha has designed a chair. Its side view is as shown.

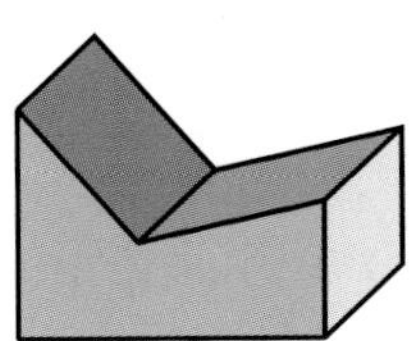

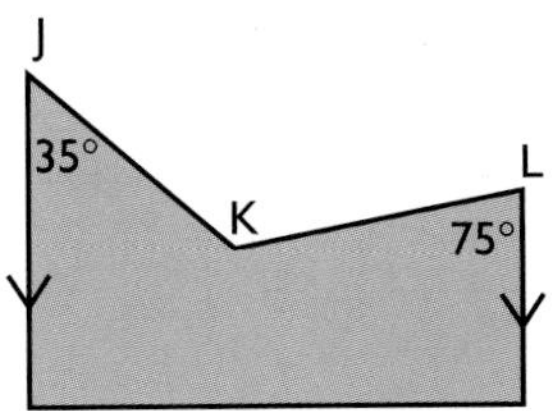

a **i** Make a sketch of this view.
  ii Add a vertical line passing through K.

b Calculate the size of the obtuse angle JKL.

5 Peter (P) takes a sighting of the yacht. It is 26° clockwise from north. Margaret (M) records it as 20° anticlockwise from north. Calculate the size of the angle that the yachtsman measures between Peter and Margaret (∠PYM). (Hint: add a north line through the yacht.)

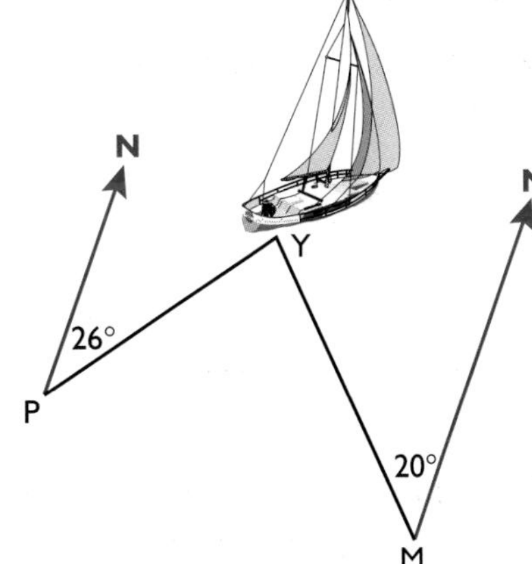

6 By adding a suitable line, calculate the value of x.

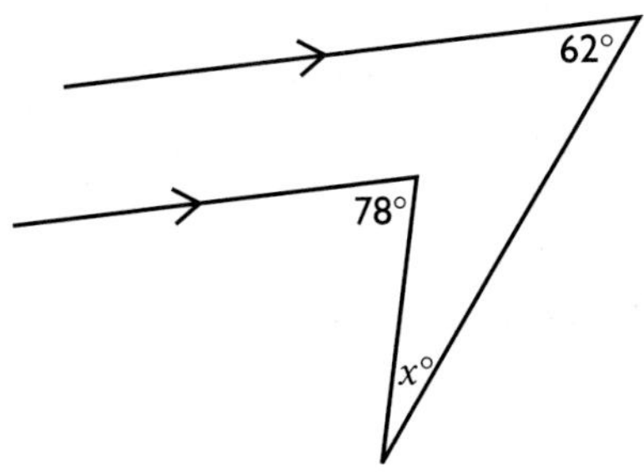

7 A construction company is digging two parallel trenches. Both trenches change direction as shown.

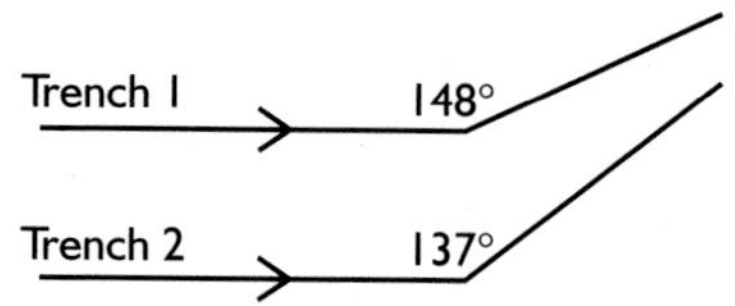

At what angle will the trenches meet?

Investigation

What is the relation between a, b and c in each diagram?

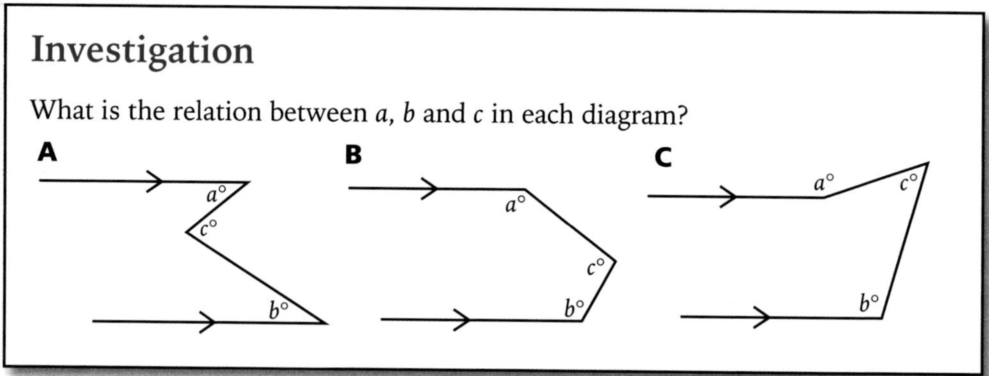

8 Interior and exterior angles

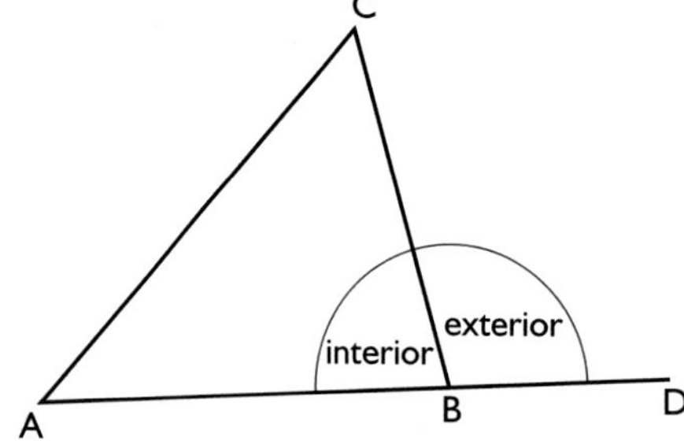

∠ABC is an angle inside the triangle ABC. It is called an **interior** angle. ∠CBD is the supplement of ∠ABC. It is an **exterior** angle of the triangle.

Reminder: A regular polygon is a shape whose sides are all the same length and whose angles are all the same size.

Examples

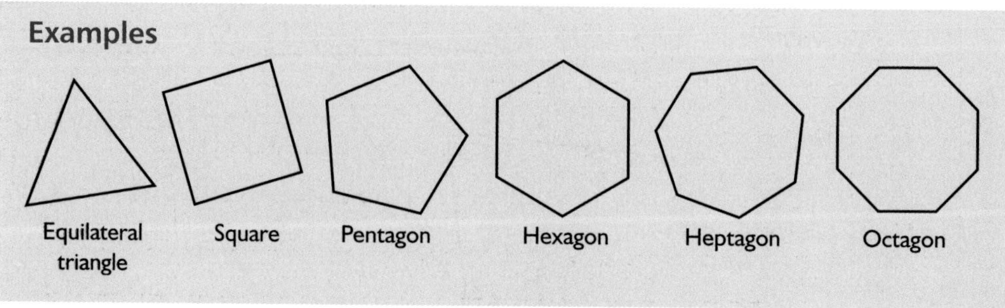

Exercise 8.1

1 The sum of the angles of a triangle is 180°.

a What is the size of one angle in a regular triangle? (Remember all angles are the same size.)

b What is the size of an exterior angle of an equilateral triangle?

c An equilateral triangle has six exterior angles. Make a sketch of an equilateral triangle and its exterior angles.

2 A square can be split into two triangles as shown.

a What is the sum of the interior angles of a square?

b What is the size of one angle in a square?

c What is the size of an exterior angle of a square?

d A square has eight exterior angles. Make a sketch of a square and its exterior angles.

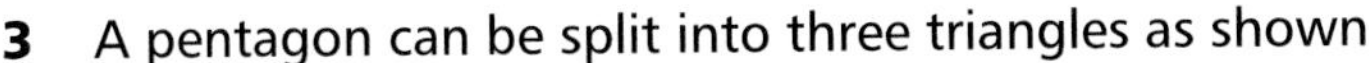

3 A pentagon can be split into three triangles as shown.

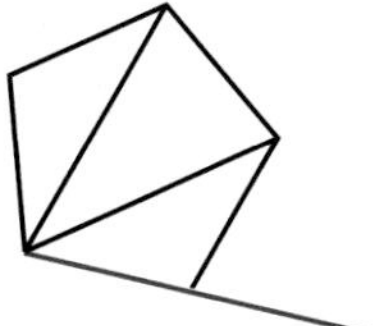

a What is the sum of the interior angles of a pentagon?

b What is the size of one angle in a regular pentagon?

c What is the size of an exterior angle of a regular pentagon?

d A pentagon has ten exterior angles. Make a sketch of a regular pentagon and its exterior angles.

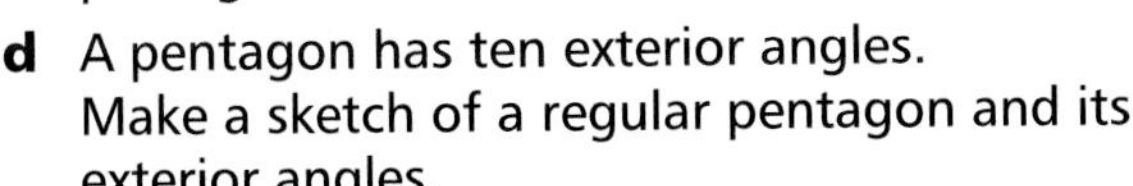

4 Copy and complete the table.

Number of sides	Name of shape	Sum of interiors	Size of 1 interior	Size of 1 exterior	Sum of exteriors
3	triangle	180	$180 \div 3 = 60$	$180 - 60 = 120$	$120 \times 6 = 720$
4	square	$2 \times 180 = 360$	$360 \div 4 = 90$		
5	pentagon	$3 \times 180 = 540$	$540 \div 5 = 108$		
6	hexagon				
8	octagon				
10	decagon				
n	n-gon				

5 A Roamer is a little robot that can draw shapes under the control of a computer.
The following instructions will make it draw a shape:

(FORWARD 10; LEFT 72) REPEAT 5.

Following these instructions, it will move forward 10 units and turn left through 72°. It will repeat these steps 5 times.

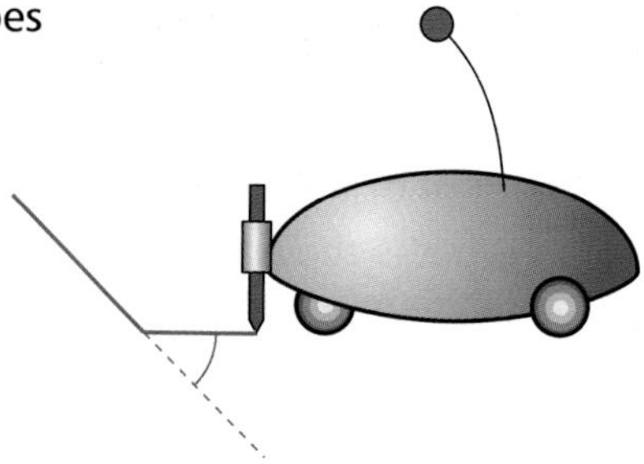

a What shape will it trace out?

b Is 72° an exterior or interior angle of the finished shape?

c What instructions would get the Roamer to draw
i a hexagon **ii** an octagon?

CHECK-UP

1 Calculate the values of the reflex angles:

a ∠ABE

b ∠ABC.

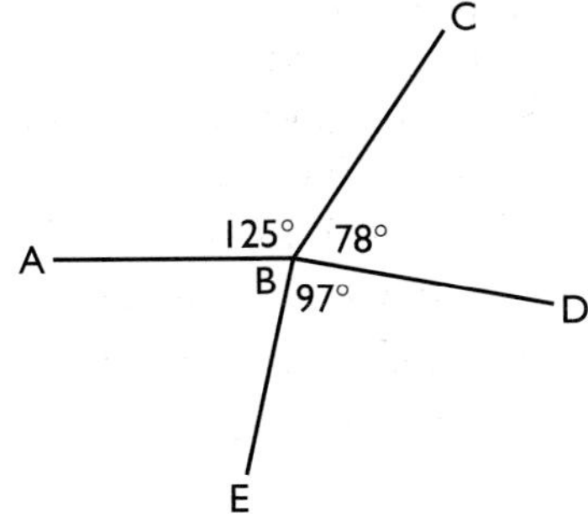

2 Name the relationship between each pair of marked angles.

a

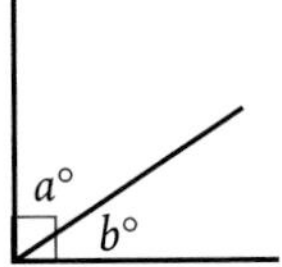

b

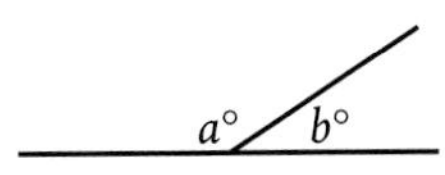

c

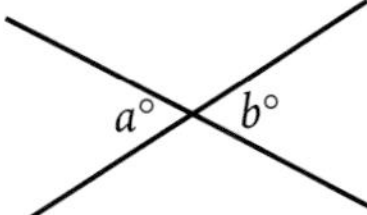

d

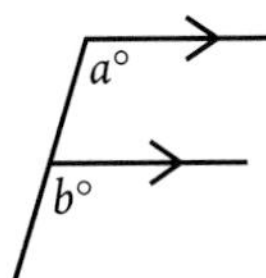

e

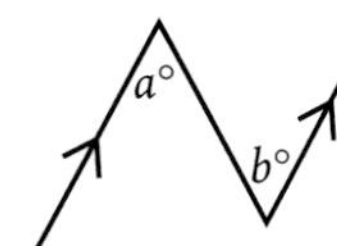

3 Calculate the size of each labelled angle, giving reasons.

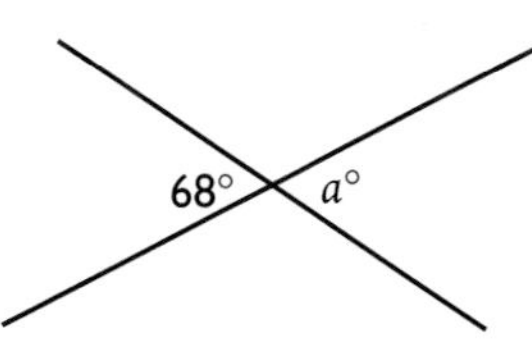

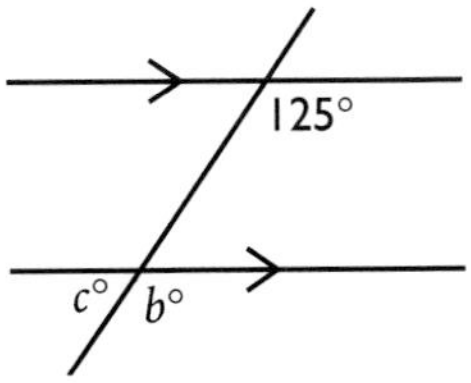

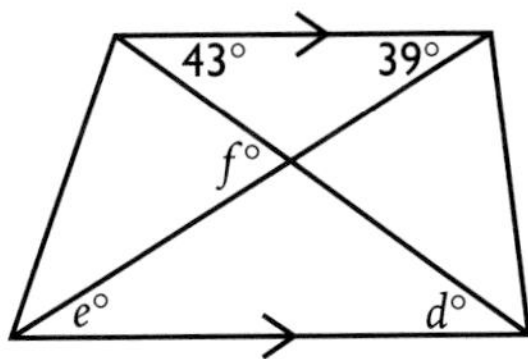

4 Janine is part of the way across the rope on the assault course. Calculate the size of the reflex angle ABC.

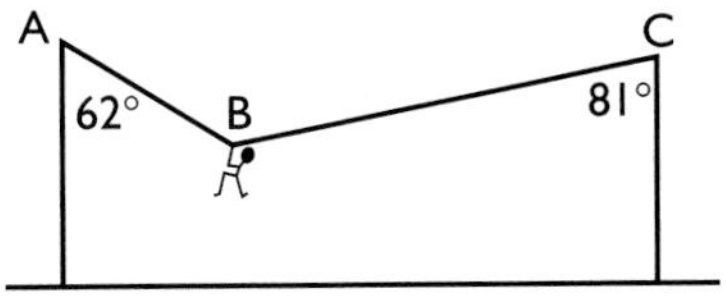

5 **a** Calculate the size of the exterior angle of a regular 12-sided polygon.

b Sketch a heptagon and its exterior angles.

4 Algebraic notation: expressions and formulae

Who used letters for numbers first?

In the Rhind Papyrus the word 'heap' was used to represent an unknown.

Around 350 BC Aristotle used single or double capital Greek letters for numbers, while later around AD 270 Diophantus used a Greek letter with an accent for an unknown number.

In 1202 Leonardo of Pisa (known as Fibonacci) used small Roman letters for unknown quantities.

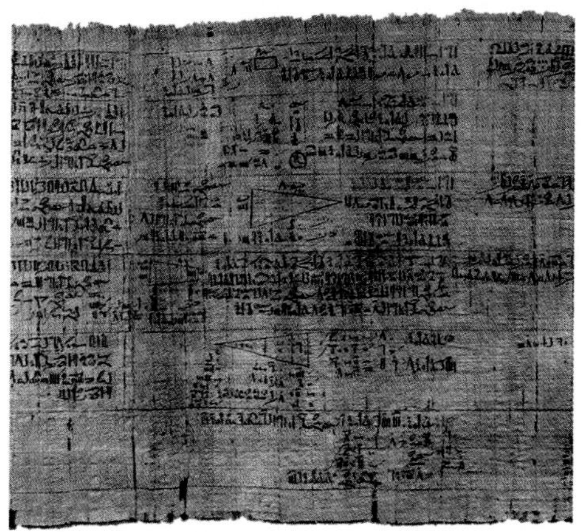

The Rhind Papyrus

1 Looking back

Exercise 1.1

1 Find the value of each letter. Give your answer in the form $x = 2$, etc.

a

Tue	Wed	Thur	Fri
	1	2	x
y	8	9	10
14	z	16	17

b 3, 7, a, 15, 19, …

c 49, 42, 35, m, 21,

d

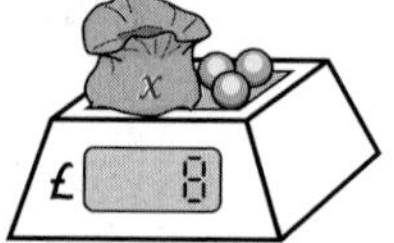

e

2 **a** Peter ate his meal in x minutes.
This was 4 minutes longer than his sister Sue.
His other sister Kerry took 5 minutes to eat hers, 1 minute longer than Sue.
Find x.

b Mario and Luis between them have £35. Mario has £x.
If Luis has £5 more than Mario find x.

3 Write down the missing expressions:

a

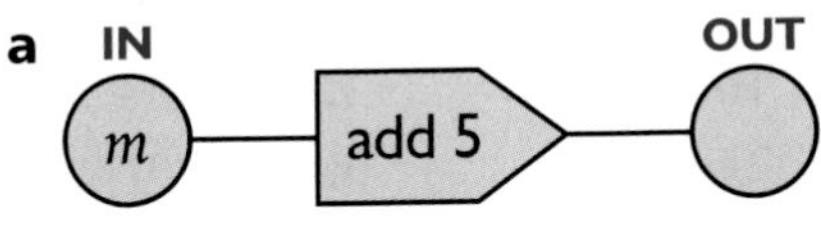

b

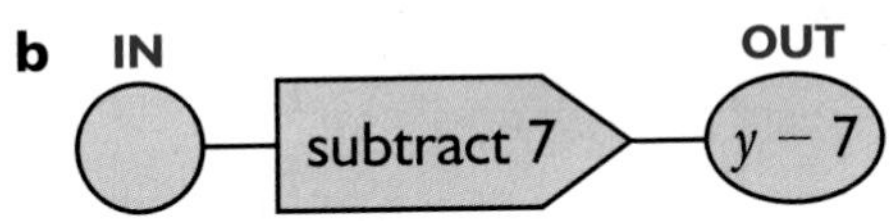

c

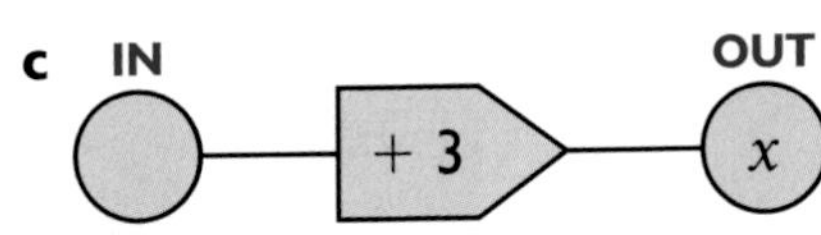

d

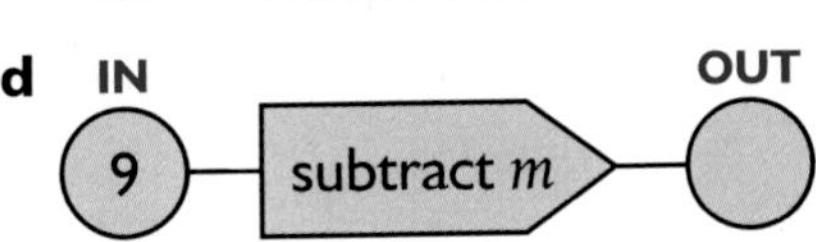

e

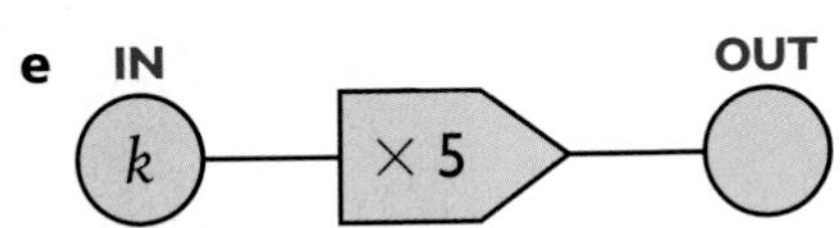

f

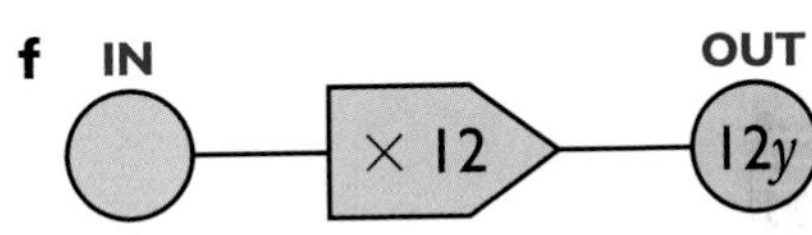

4 Find an expression to answer each question.

a What is the total money here?

b 1 litre was drunk. How much is left?

c A wall had B bricks. 20 were removed. How many are left?

d A rod was 85 cm long.
A d cm length was sawn off.
What length is left?

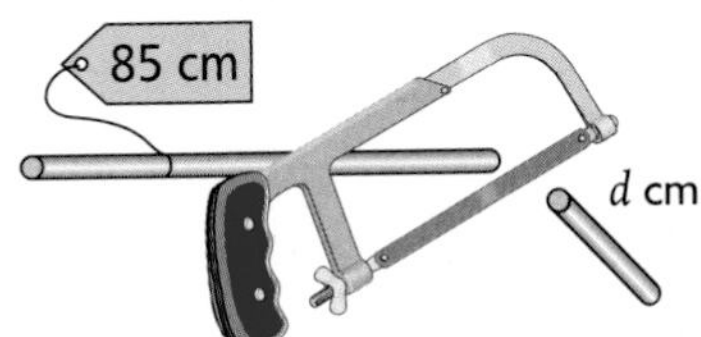

5 Here there are £$(3x + 2)$ in total.

Find an expression for each situation.

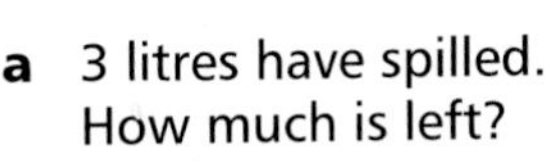

a 3 litres have spilled.
How much is left?

b What does the selection of cakes cost?

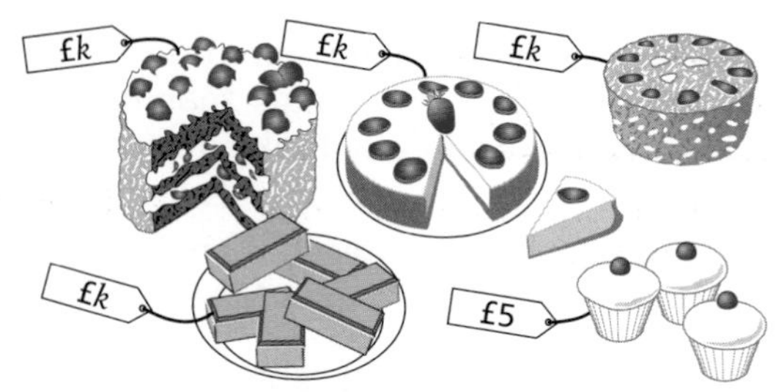

6 If $h = 4$, give the value of:

a $h - 3$ **b** $h + 2$ **c** $10 - h$ **d** $h - 3 + h$
e $3h$ **f** $\frac{1}{4}h$ **g** $2h + 1$ **h** $8h - 9$

7 Find an expression for the number of matches needed to make:

a m triangles **b** x letter Ts **c** k pentagons.

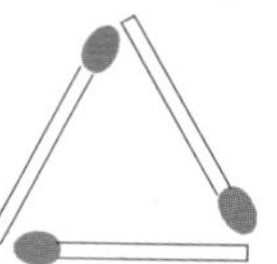

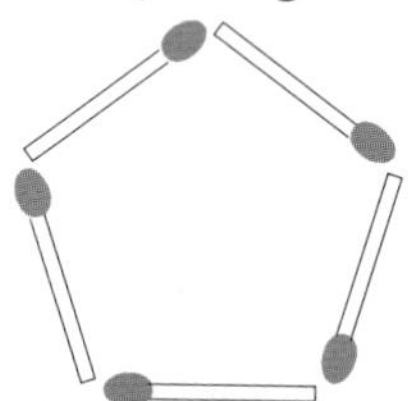

◀◀ E

2 The value of expressions

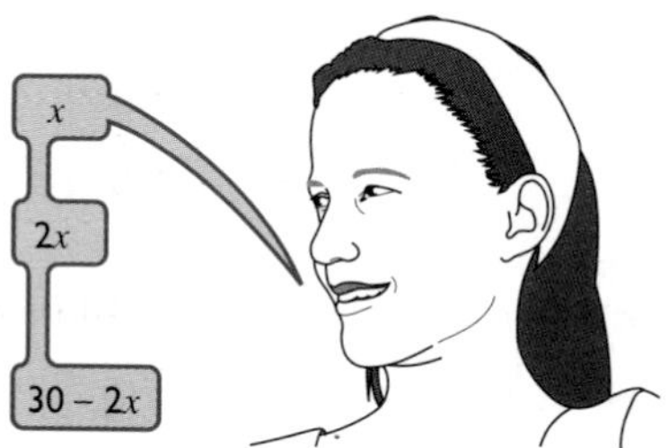

For example, thinking of 7: $x = 7$

$\Rightarrow 2x = 14$

$\Rightarrow 30 - 2x = 16$

We say that, when x is 7, the value of $30 - 2x$ is 16.

Showing the substitution and the calculation we have:
when $x = 7$, $30 - 2x = 30 - 2 \times 7 = 30 - 14 = 16$.

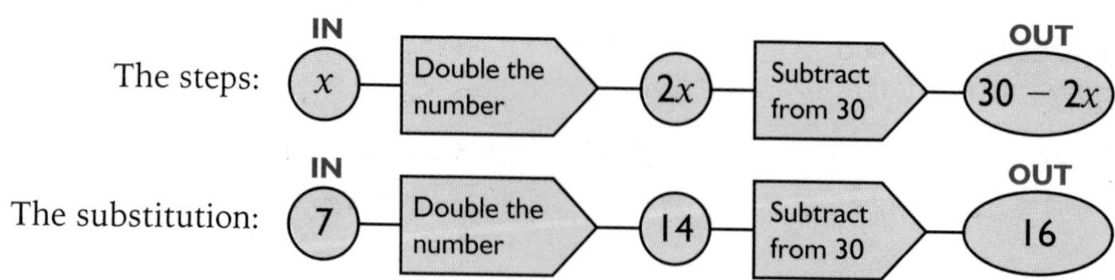

Exercise 2.1

1 Copy and complete each machine to build up an expression and perform a substitution.

a

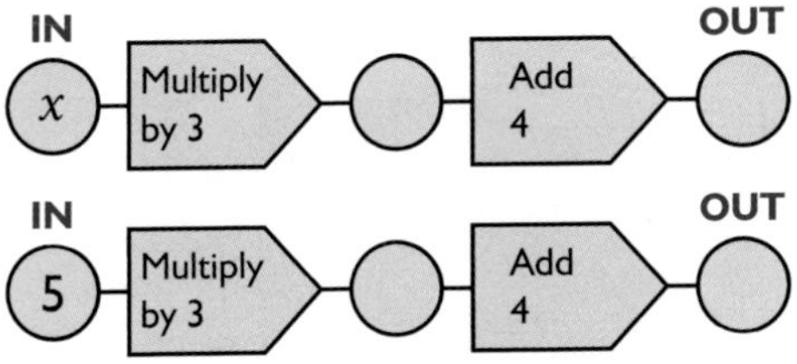

IN x → Multiply by 3 → ○ → Add 4 → ○ OUT

IN 5 → Multiply by 3 → ○ → Add 4 → ○ OUT

b

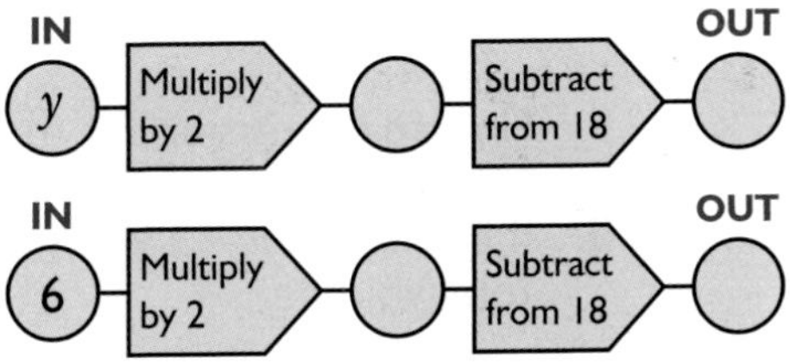

IN y → Multiply by 2 → ○ → Subtract from 18 → ○ OUT

IN 6 → Multiply by 2 → ○ → Subtract from 18 → ○ OUT

c

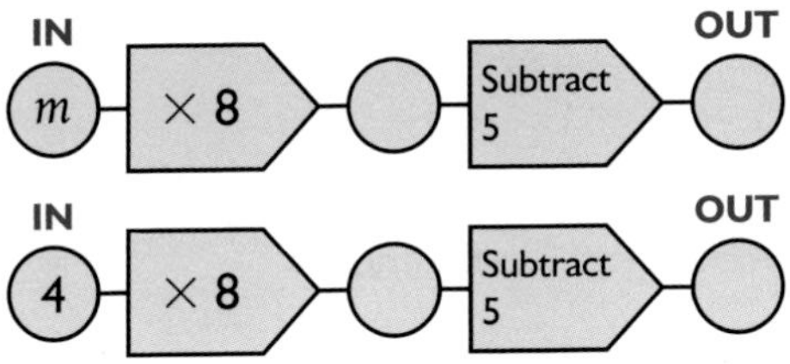

IN m → × 8 → ○ → Subtract 5 → ○ OUT

IN 4 → × 8 → ○ → Subtract 5 → ○ OUT

d

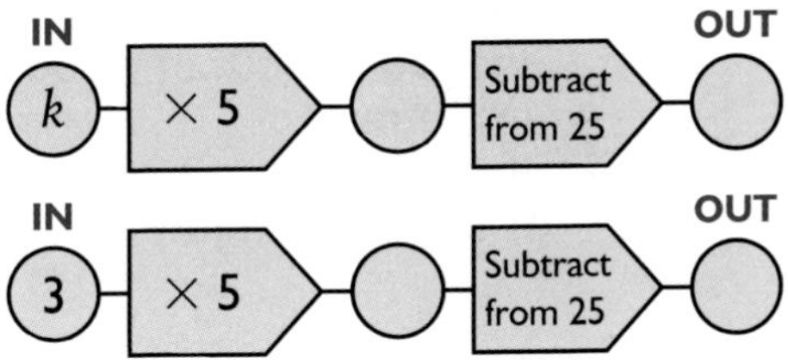

IN k → × 5 → ○ → Subtract from 25 → ○ OUT

IN 3 → × 5 → ○ → Subtract from 25 → ○ OUT

e

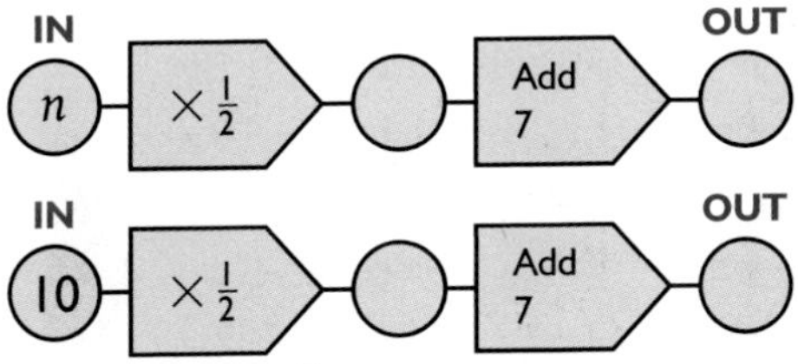

IN n → $\times \frac{1}{2}$ → ○ → Add 7 → ○ OUT

IN 10 → $\times \frac{1}{2}$ → ○ → Add 7 → ○ OUT

f

IN k → × 7 → ○ → Subtract from 40 → ○ OUT

IN 3 → × 7 → ○ → Subtract from 40 → ○ OUT

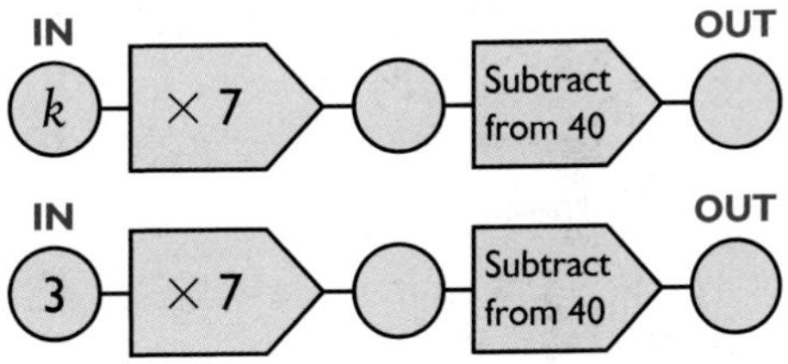

2 Evaluate:

a $4x + 3$ when $x = 1$

b $3y - 2$ when $y = 3$

c $10 - 2m$ when $m = 5$

d $18 - \frac{1}{2}y$ when $y = 16$

e $5 + 3t$ when $t = 4$

f $\frac{1}{2}k - 2$ when $k = 10$

g $10m + 7$ when $m = 0$

h $42 - 4h$ when $h = 4$

i $12 - \frac{1}{3}x$ when $x = 6$

j $13 + 5n$ when $n = 3$

k $\frac{1}{4}y - 1$ when $y = 12$

l $50 - 7e$ when $e = 7$

m $5x + 3 + x$ when $x = 2$

n $7y - 2 + y$ when $y = 3$

o $8 + 2n + 3$ when $n = 5$

p $10 - \frac{1}{2}x + 3$ when $x = 20$

q $\frac{1}{3}x + 1 + \frac{1}{4}x$ when $x = 24$

r $12 - \frac{1}{2}r + \frac{1}{3}r$ when $r = 6$

3 **a** **i** Find an expression for the total cost in £ of these items.

ii If $a = 5$ and $b = 3$ what is the total cost?

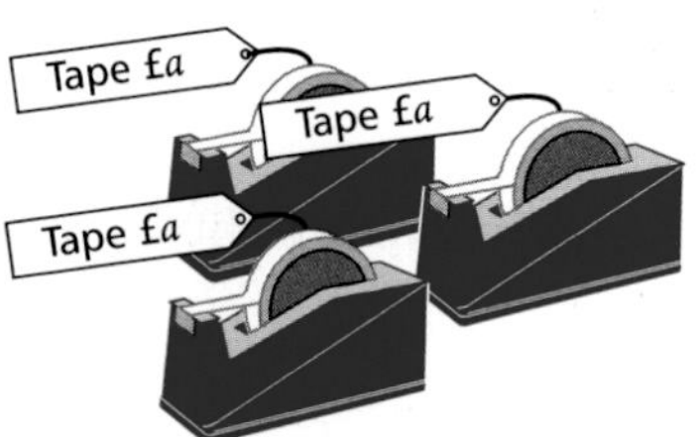

b **i** Find an expression for the total volume in litres.

ii If $m = 8$ and $n = 3$ what is the total volume?

c **i** Find an expression for the total length of wood in metres.

ii If $x = 4$ and $y = 2$ what is the total length?

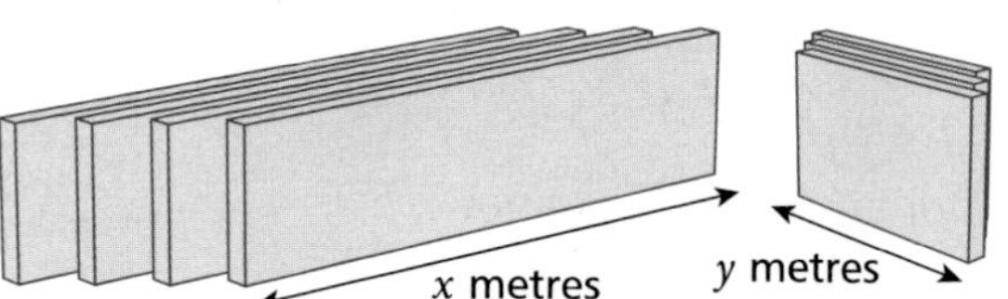

E

4 Find the value of each expression if $m = 3$, $n = 5$, $x = 1$, $y = 7$ and $w = 12$.

a $6n - 1$ **b** $8 - 2m$ **c** $y - x$

d $3n - w$ **e** $4m - n$ **f** $2w - 3y$

g $14 + 8x$ **h** $3w + 5x$ **i** $50 - 7y$

j $m - 2x$ **k** $5n - 24$ **l** $8y - 4w$

m $n - m$ **n** $3m - y + n$ **o** $8x + w - 4n$

p $2w - 3y + 4x$ **q** $13 - w + 3m + x$ **r** $5y - 2w + 2n - 3m$

s $\frac{1}{2}w - 2m + 3y$ **t** $x + \frac{1}{3}m + 2n$ **u** $m - \frac{1}{4}w + \frac{1}{5}n - x$

Challenge

A can holds x litres of oil. A bottle holds y litres.
Ian has $2x + 3y$ litres of oil and Tom has $3x + 2y$ litres.

a They have 25 litres between them.
How much oil is there together in 1 can and 1 bottle?
Explain your working.

b Tom actually has 1 more litre of oil than Ian.
How much oil is in 1 can and in 1 bottle?
Explain your working.

3 Like terms

$3x$ is 3 lots of x.
$4x$ is 4 lots of x.
Together they make 7 lots of x:

$$3x + 4x = 7x.$$

The cost of 3 apples + the cost of 4 apples = the cost of 7 apples

$3x$ and $4x$ are counting the same things.
They are **like** terms and so $3x + 4x$ can be simplified by addition.

$3x$ is 3 lots of x.
$4y$ is 4 lots of y.

They count different things.

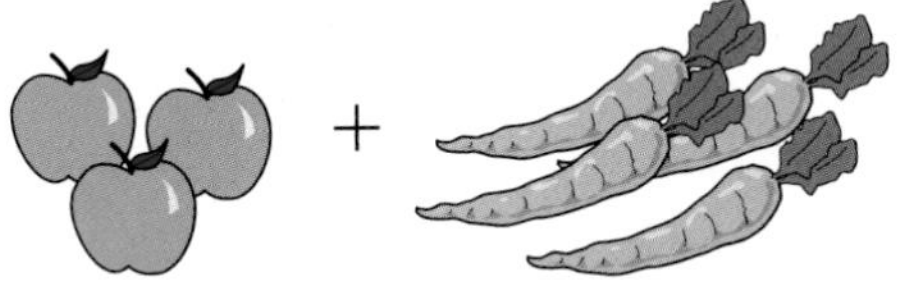

The cost of 3 apples + the cost of 4 carrots = the cost of 3 apples and 4 carrots

$3x$ and $4y$ are **unlike** terms and so $3x + 4y$ cannot be simplified by addition.

Note that $3x + 2$ cannot be simplified as $3x$ and 2 are **unlike** terms.

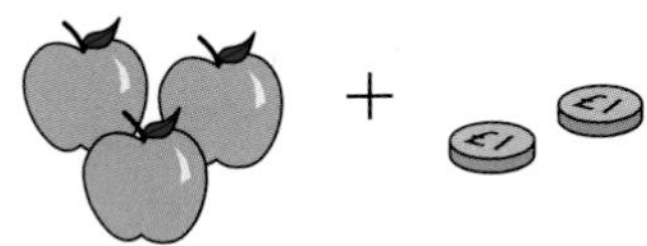

The cost of 3 apples + 2 pounds

Example

Simplify: **a** $x + 2 + x + x$ **b** $a + b + 5 + b + a + b$ **c** $4x + 9y - 2x - 3y$

Answer:

a $3x + 2$ The first, third and fourth terms are all terms in x and can be combined.

b $2a + 3b + 5$ The first and fifth terms (in a) are like; the second, fourth and sixth (in b) are like.

c $2x + 6y$ The first and third terms in the original expression combine to give the first term in the simplified expression.
Note that we are subtracting the third term.

Exercise 3.1

1 For each, identify the required term and say whether it is being added or subtracted in the expression.

a $3x + 4y$ (second term)
b $2a + 3b + 4a$ (third term)
c $4m - n + 2m$ (first term)
d $3d + e + 2e + 3e$ (second term)
e $5k - 3m + k + 4k$ (second term)
f $18c + d + 3d - 4c$ (fourth term)

2 Match each arrow with a destination on the target by considering like terms.

a

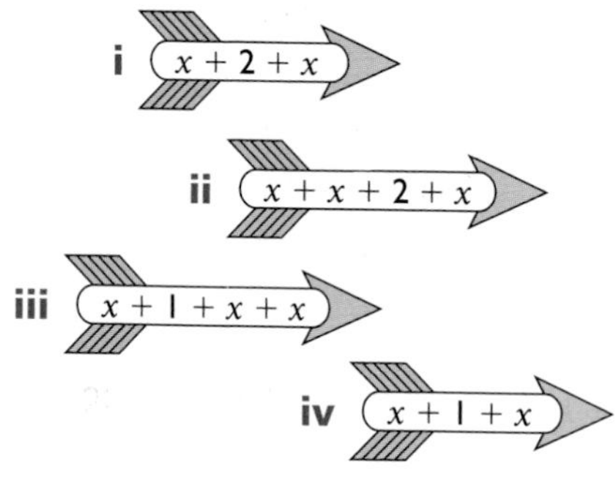

$2x + 1$
$3x + 1$
$2x + 2$
$3x + 2$
D
C
B
A

b

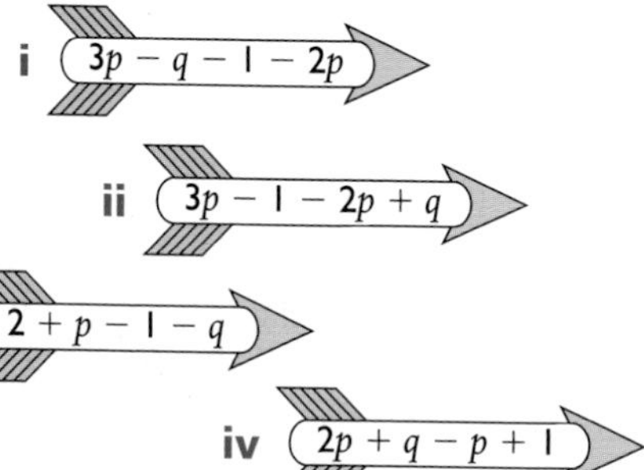

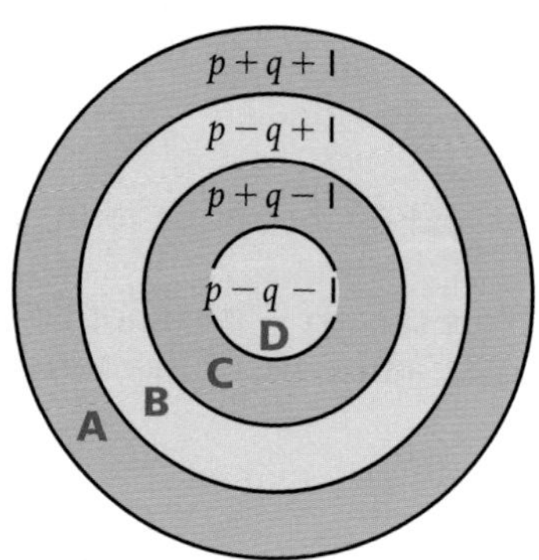

3 There is a shorter way to write each of these expressions by collecting *like* terms. Find it.

a $x + 1 + x + 1 + x$

b $m + 2 + m + 3 + m$

c $y + z + y + y + z + z$

d $a + c + b + c + b + b + a$

e $a + 3 + b + 2 + b + a + a$

f $k - k + k + k - k + k + k$

g $a + b - a - b + a + b + a$

h $h + h + g - h - g + h + g$

4 Simplify each expression.

a $2y - y + 3y$

b $5m + 3m - 4m$

c $2a - a + 3a + 4a$

d $k + 5k + 4k - 10k$

e $3x - 2x + 4x$

f $2n + 5 + n + 3n$

g $5x + 8 - x + 2$

h $4a + 2 - 4a + 3$

i $7 + 2h - 7 + 3h - h$

j $2a + b + 3a - b$

k $5m + 2n - 3m + 3n$

l $4 + 7a + b - 3 + 2a$

m $r + 6 + 2t + 3r - t$

n $5x + 4 + y - 3x + 2y$

o $7 + 3w + y - 2w + 2y + 1$

p $8k + 2m - 3k - m - 5k$

q $2a + 5 + 3b + 2$

r $12m + 12n - m - 2n - 11m$

s $2 + 3c - 2 - 3c + 5d$

t $12k - 12a - 11k + 32$

u $5p - 2q + 3p + 7 - 7p - 6$

5 **i** Simplify each expression.

ii Find its value when the letters are replaced by the given numbers.

a $5x + 7 - 3x + 2y - 5 + 3y$ $(x = 2 \text{ and } y = 3)$

b $12 + 2m + 10n - m - 10 + 3n$ $(m = 5 \text{ and } n = 3)$

c $8k + 13 + 2w - 5k - 13 + 8w$ $(k = 4 \text{ and } w = 6)$

d $12c - d - 10c + 4 + 3c + 5$ $(c = 7 \text{ and } d = 10)$

6 Find expressions for:

a the total length of wood

3x metres
y metres
2x metres
2y metres

b the total of all the four angle sizes

$3y°$
$(2x + 10)°$
$3x°$
$15°$

c the total of all their ages.

Jamie	$(m + 5)$ years
Michelle	$2n$ years
Jason	$3m$ years
Kevin	14 years
Amy	$(m + n)$ years

7 **i** For each of these shapes, find an expression for the perimeter. (All angles are right angles.)

ii Calculate the perimeter for the given letter values. (All measurements are in centimetres.)

a

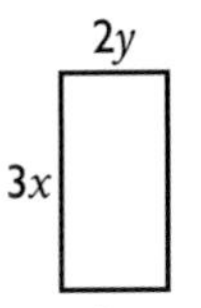

$x = 4, y = 3$

b

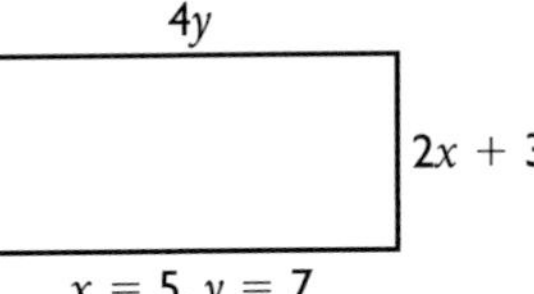

$x = 5, y = 7$

c

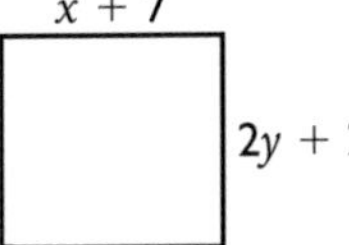

$x = 8, y = 6$

d

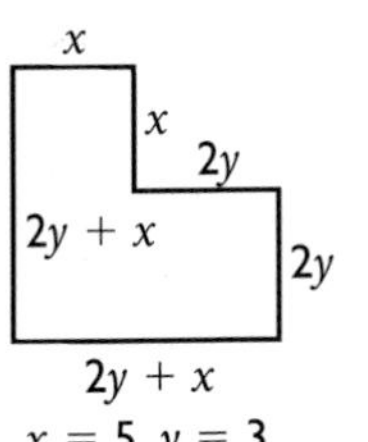

$x = 5, y = 3$

e

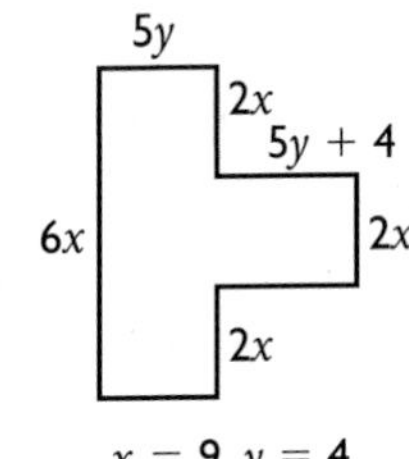

$x = 9, y = 4$

E

Brainstormer

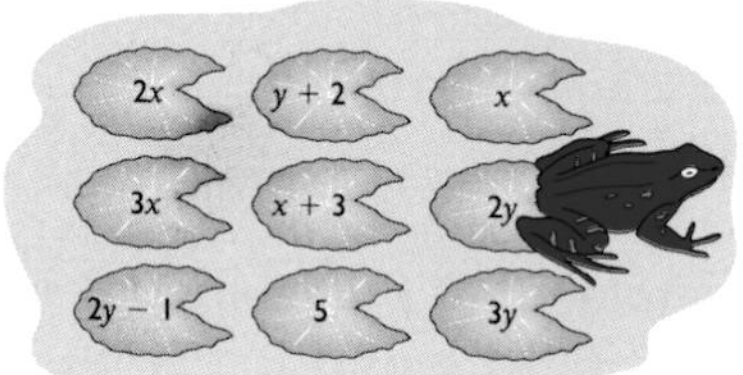

Start on $x + 3$ and 'hop' in the following directions:

north then east then south.
This gives the expression $2x + 3y + 5$.
Can you see why?

This journey can be named $(x + 3)$ N E S.

a Give the resulting expression for each journey:
  i $(3x)$ E S E **ii** (5) E N N W **iii** $(2x)$ S E E S W W

b Give the missing directions:
  i starting at 5 to give $x + y + 10$
  ii starting at $2y$ to give $3y + 3x + 2$
  iii starting at $x + 3$ to give $x + 3y + 13$

c Give the missing starting square:
  i (?) E W E W E W giving $8x + 3y + 6$
  ii (?) S N S N E giving $3x + 3y + 12$
  iii (?) E W S N E W S giving $14x + 4y + 4$

E

4 Which order?

What is the value of $2 + 3 \times 4$?

Joe types    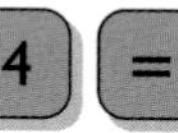 4 = on his arithmetic calculator and gets 20.

Ailsa types the same thing on her scientific calculator and gets 14.
Which calculator is giving the correct answer?

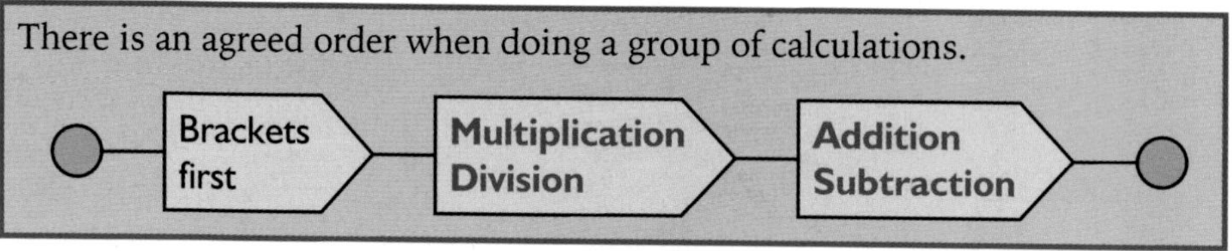

There is an agreed order when doing a group of calculations.
Brackets first
Multiplication Division
Addition Subtraction

Scientific calculators are programmed to follow this order, arithmetic calculators are not.
So Ailsa's calculator is giving the correct answer.

Example 1

$3 + \frac{10}{2}$ ← Do the division first

$= 3 + 5$

$= 8$

Example 2

$(2 + 3) \times 4$ ← Do the brackets first

$= 5 \times 4$

$= 20$

Example 3

$\frac{10}{8-3} = \frac{10}{(8-3)}$ ← Do the brackets first

$= \frac{10}{5}$

$= 2$

Example 4

Find the value of $3a + 2(a + 1)$ when $a = 4$.

Substitute 4 for a:

$3 \times 4 + 2(4 + 1)$
$= 3 \times 4 + 2 \times 5$
$= 12 + 10$
$= 22$

Exercise 4.1

1 Do these calculations:

a $12 + 3 \times 2$ **b** $\frac{10}{5} + 3$ **c** $4 - (2 + 1)$ **d** $\frac{8}{1+3}$

e $(8 - 1) \times 3$ **f** $2 \times 3 + 3 \times 4$ **g** $10 - 3 \times 2 + 1$ **h** $4 \times 2 - 3 \times 2$

i $\frac{2+8}{3-1}$ **j** $6 - \frac{4}{2}$ **k** $8 - (3 - 1)$ **l** $\frac{8}{2} + 3 \times 2$

m $2 \times 3 - 5 \times 1$ **n** $2 + 3 \times (5 - 1)$ **o** $(2 + 3) \times (5 - 1)$ **p** $2(3 - 1)$

q $5 - 3(4 - 3)$ **r** $8 + 5(2 + 1)$

2 If $a = 3$ and $b = 4$ evaluate:

Reminder: ab means $a \times b$

a $20 - ab$ **b** $a(b + 2)$ **c** $5b - 3a$ **d** $\frac{14}{a+b}$

e $\frac{1}{2}b + a$ **f** $ab - 7$ **g** $\frac{b+a}{b-a}$ **h** $a - (b - 3)$

i $\frac{ab}{b-a}$ **j** $3ab$ **k** $2(a + b)$ **l** $ab - a$

Challenge

Copy and complete this cross-number puzzle:

$a = 5, b = 6, c = 2, d = 12$

Across
1 $bc + 1$
3 $a + cd$
4 $2ab + c$
6 $b(d - c)$
7 bc
9 $b(a + c)$
10 bcd

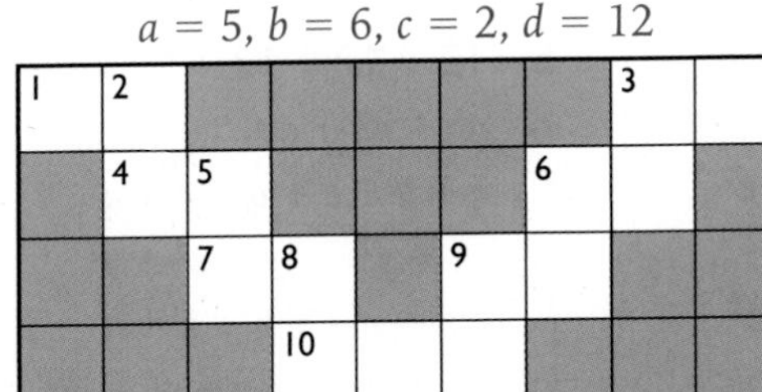

Down
2 $2b(a - c)$
3 $ab - (d - c)$
5 $3(a + c)$
6 $c + ad$
8 $31 - ac$
9 $4d - (b - c)$

E

5 Adding more expressions

Expression	Shorter form	Note
$7 + 7 + 7 + 7$	4×7	four lots of 7
$y + y + y + y + y$	$5y$	five lots of y
$x \times y$	xy	x lots of y
$xy + xy + xy$	$3xy$	three lots of xy
$3 \times 3 \times 3 \times 3$	3^4	four factors of 3
$x \times x \times x$	x^3	three factors of x
$m^2 + m^2 + m^2$	$3m^2$	three lots of m^2
$m^2 + m^2 + m$	$2m^2 + m$	m and m^2 are unlike

Example 1

The diagram shows a stair carpet.

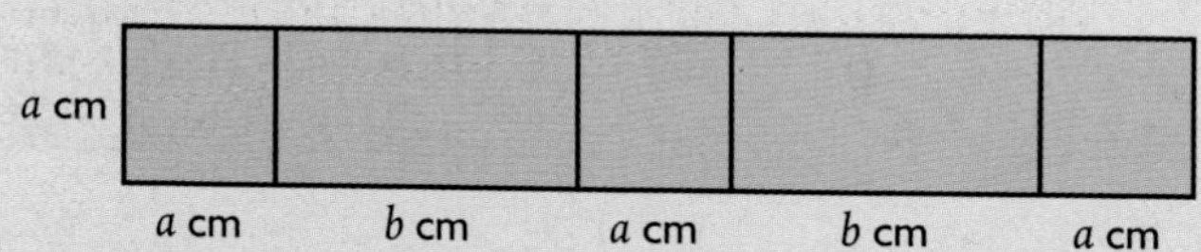

We can use the formula $A = lb$ for the area of a rectangle to get an expression for the area of the carpet.
Area $= (a^2 + ab + a^2 + ab + a^2)$ cm^2
Collecting like terms we get: Area $= (3a^2 + 2ab)$ cm^2
'three lots of a^2 and two lots of ab'

Exercise 5.1

1 Write in shorter form:

a $9 + 9 + 9 + 9 + 9$
b $12 + 12 + 12 + 12 + 12 + 12 + 12$
c $k + k + k + k$
d $ab + ab + ab$
e $x^2 + x^2 + x^2 + x^2 + x^2$
f $q + q + q + q + q + q$
g $y + y + y + m^2 + m^2$
h $xy + y^2 + xy + y^2 + y^2$
i $a^2 + a^2 + b^2 + b^2 + b^2$
j $mn + n + mn + n + n$
k $ab + ac + ac + ac + ab$
l $w^2 + wy + wy + y^2 + w^2$

F

2 Special stamps of different sizes are issued in small sheets. Find an expression for the area of each miniature sheet below, writing your answer in its simplest form.

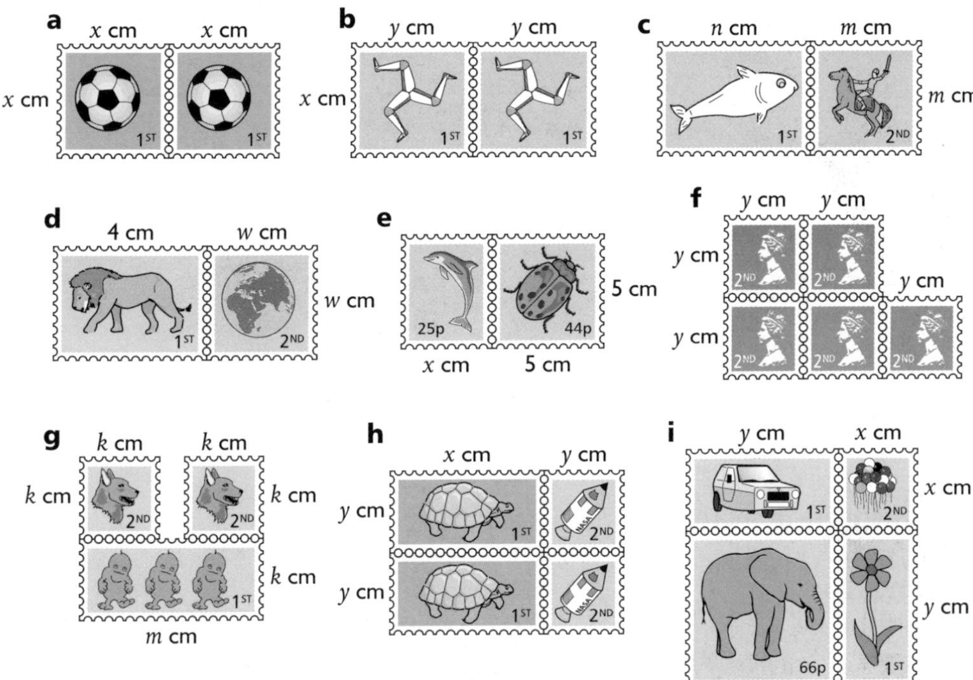

F

3 If $m = 3$, $n = 2$ and $w = 5$, find the values of:

a $2m^2$ (two lots of m^2 so two lots of 3^2)

b	$3n^2$	**c**	$2nw$	**d**	$mn + w^2$
e	$mw - n^2$	**f**	$3n - m$	**g**	$mn - n$
h	$w^2 - m$	**i**	$5mn$	**j**	$4w^2$
k	$m^2 + n^2$	**l**	$w^2 - m^2$	**m**	$nw - nm$
n	$5w - w^2$	**o**	$3w - 5n$	**p**	$4n^2 - m^2$
q	$3w^2 - 3w$	**r**	$6nw + 2n^2$	**s**	$4mn - 2nw$
t	$5m^2 - mnw$				

Example 2 Simplify $2y \times 3y - y \times w \times 2$

$$\begin{aligned} & 2y \times 3y - y \times w \times 2 \\ &= 2 \times y \times 3 \times y - y \times w \times 2 \\ &= 2 \times 3 \times y \times y - 2 \times y \times w \\ &= 6y^2 - 2wy \end{aligned}$$

4

Exercise 5.2

1
a $x \times 2x$ **b** $3y \times 2y$ **c** $5m \times m$
d $w \times w + w \times w$ **e** $3a \times a$ **f** $2a^2 + a \times a$
g $5 + m \times m$ **h** $3 - 2 \times x$ **i** $5 \times k - 2 \times 3$
j $4 \times y \times y - 2 \times y$ **k** $a \times b + a \times b + a + a \times b$ **l** $4y^2 - y \times y \times 3$
m $2k + k \times k - k$ **n** $m^2 \times 3 - 2 \times m^2$ **o** $x^2 \times 5 - 2 \times x \times 2 \times x$

2 Match equal expressions:

a

A $n \times n - 3$
B $3 + n \times n$
C $n \times 3 + n$
D $n \times 3 \times n$
E $3 - n \times n$

i $4n$
ii $3 - n^2$
iii $3n^2$
iv $3 + n^2$
v $n^2 - 3$

b

A $d \times e \times e$
B $e + d \times e$
C $d + e \times e$
D $e \times d + d$
E $e + d + d$

i $ed + d$
ii $2d + e$
iii $de + e$
iv de^2
v $d + e^2$

3 Write these in shorter form:
a $y \times y \times y$ **b** $w \times w \times w \times w \times w$ **c** $3 \times a \times a \times a$
d $t \times 2 \times t \times t$ **e** $k \times k + k$ **f** $k \times k + k \times k$
g $k \times k \times k \times k$ **h** $c^2 \times c$ **i** $d \times d^3$
j $5 \times a^2 \times a$ **k** $2 \times n \times n \times 3 \times n$ **l** $10 \times x \times x \times x$
m $a \times a + a \times a \times a$ **n** $3 \times a \times a \times 2 \times 4 \times a$

4 If $m = 3$ then $m^3 = 3^3 = 3 \times 3 \times 3 = 27$. In a similar way find the values of:
a a^3 when $a = 2$ **b** n^3 when $n = 1$ **c** w^4 when $w = 2$
d x^3 when $x = 9$ **e** y^3 when $y = 5$ **f** $5z$ when $z = 10$
g z^5 when $z = 10$ **h** e^4 when $e = 0$ **i** f^5 when $f = 2$

6 Square values

There are two different ways of finding an expression for each area below. (All measurements are in centimetres.)

Example 1

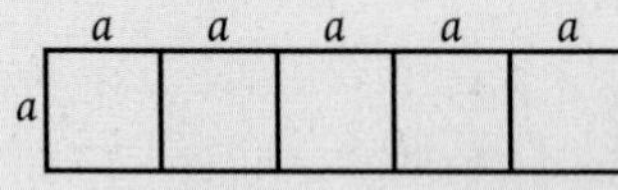

=

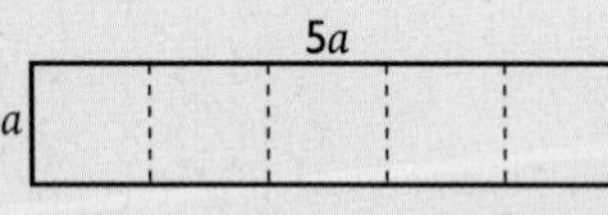

Area = $a^2 + a^2 + a^2 + a^2 + a^2 = \mathbf{5a^2}$ cm^2 Area = $5a \times a = \mathbf{5a^2}$ cm^2

F

Example 2

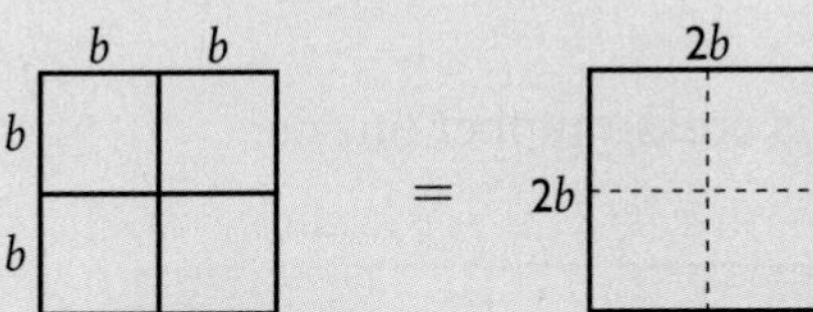

Area = $b^2 + b^2 + b^2 + b^2 = \mathbf{4b^2}$ cm^2 Area = $(2b)^2 = 2b \times 2b = \mathbf{4b^2}$ cm^2

Be careful not to confuse $2x^2$ and $(2x)^2$.
For example when $x = 5$:
$2x^2 = 2 \times 5^2 = 2 \times 25 = 50$ whereas $(2x)^2 = (2 \times 5)^2 = 10^2 = 100$

Exercise 6.1

1 Find, in two different ways (as in the example above), expressions for these areas. All lengths are in centimetres.

a

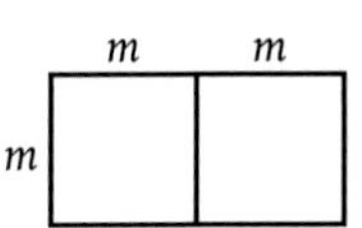

b

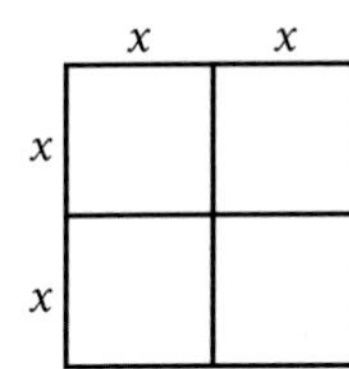

c

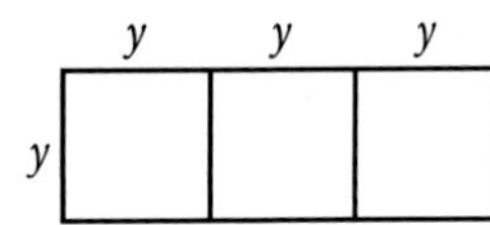

d

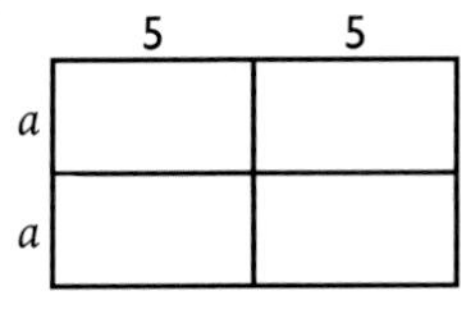

e

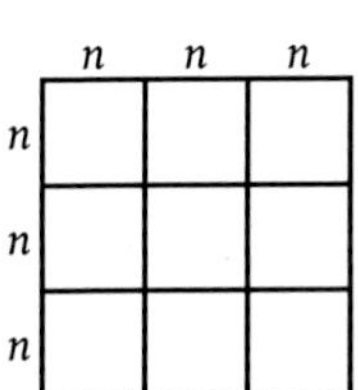

f

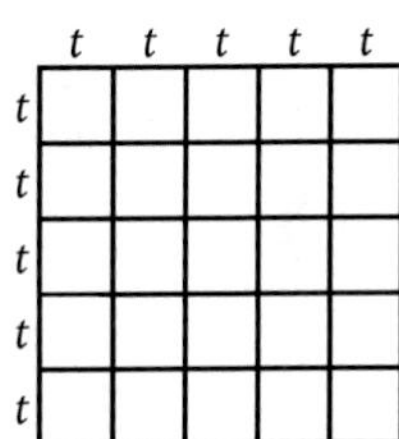

2 Evaluate the following for the given values:

a $2m^2$ when $m = 3$
b $(2m)^2$ when $m = 3$
c $3ab$ when $a = 1$ and $b = 5$
d xy^2 when $x = 2$ and $y = 4$
e x^2y when $x = 2$ and $y = 4$
f $5k^2$ when $k = 2$
g $(5k)^2$ when $k = 2$
h $(ab)^2$ when $a = 4$ and $b = 2$
i $(3a)^2$ when $a = 2$

3 If $a = 3$, $b = 2$, $c = 6$ and $d = 10$, evaluate:

a a^2b **b** $3b^2$ **c** $(ab)^2$ **d** ab^2 **e** $(4a)^2$
f $(a - b)^2$ **g** bd^2 **h** b^2d **i** $(d - b)^2$ **j** $c^2 - a$
k $d^2 - 3b$ **l** $4(c - b)^2$ **m** $4c - b^2$ **n** $4a^2 - b$ **o** $a^2 - b^2$
p $ab^2 + a$ **q** $2c^2 + 3b^2$ **r** $5d^2 - c^2$ **s** $5a^2 - 2b^2$ **t** $(4c)^2 - (5b)^2$

F

Challenge

Copy and complete this cross-number puzzle:

$x = 4$, $y = 3$, $z = 9$ and $w = 25$

Across

1 $(2x)^2$
3 $(zx)^2$
5 $(w - 2z)^2$
6 $z^2 - w$
8 $6y^2 - 1$
9 $4x^2$
10 $(3w + x)^2$
13 $3x^2 + y^2$

		1	2		
	3			4	
5				6	7
8				9	
	10	11	12		
		13			

Down

1 $7y^2 - 1$
2 $(x + y)^2$
3 $(11x)^2$
4 $(9z)^2$
5 $5y^2$
7 $x^2 + 4xy$
11 $(z - x)^2$
12 $3x^2 - 1$

7 Removing brackets

$3a$ means 'three lots of a'

$\dots a + a + a$

Similarly $3(a + 4)$ means 'three lots of $a + 4$'

$\dots a + 4 + a + 4 + a + 4$

Note that this gives 'three lots of a plus three lots of 4'

$\dots a + a + a + 4 + 4 + 4 = 3a + 12$

$$3(a + 4) = 3a + 12$$

Each term within the bracket has been multiplied by the factor outside the bracket.

In general the pattern for removing brackets is:
$a(b + c) = ab + ac$ and $a(b - c) = ab - ac$

Example 1

Expand $7(a + b)$

$$7(a + b) = 7 \times a + 7 \times b$$
$$= 7a + 7b$$

Example 2

Expand $5(y - 3)$

$$5(y - 3) = 5 \times y - 5 \times 3$$
$$= 5y - 15$$

Example 3

Expand $x(x + y)$

$$x(x + y) = x \times x + x \times y$$
$$= x^2 + xy$$

Example 4

Expand $y(3 - y)$

$$y(3 - y) = y \times 3 - y \times y$$
$$= 3y - y^2$$

Exercise 7.1

1 Expand:

a $3(m - 2)$	**b** $5(x + 2)$	**c** $7(2 + y)$	**d** $2(a + b)$	**e** $8(t - 3)$
f $4(1 + x)$	**g** $10(3 + k)$	**h** $3(1 - a)$	**i** $6(t + 4)$	**j** $9(y - z)$
k $7(a - b)$	**l** $5(t + 4)$	**m** $2(n - 10)$	**n** $4(2 - k)$	**o** $8(1 + n)$
p $11(u - w)$	**q** $20(2 - x)$	**r** $9(y + 4)$		

2 Remove the brackets:

a $x(x + 3)$	**b** $y(y - 2)$	**c** $a(4 - a)$	**d** $a(b + a)$	**e** $m(5 - m)$
f $n(m + n)$	**g** $t(4 + t)$	**h** $u(u - 3)$	**i** $w(y - w)$	**j** $x(10 - x)$
k $c(c + 8)$	**l** $x(y + x)$	**m** $r(1 - r)$	**n** $x(1 + x)$	**o** $k(k - 5)$
p $m(a - b)$	**q** $w(x + y)$	**r** $u(4 - u)$	**s** $x(a + b)$	**t** $e(e - 3)$

3 Find an expression for each area in two different ways. (Remember $A = lb$.)

a

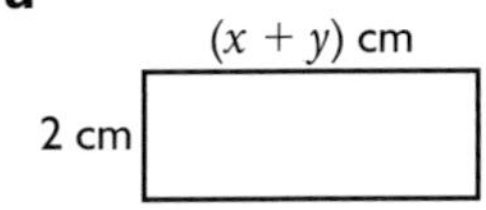

…consider

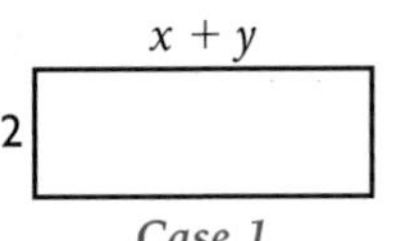

Case 1

and

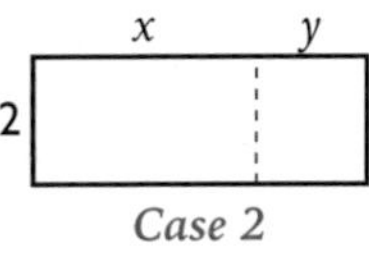

Case 2

b

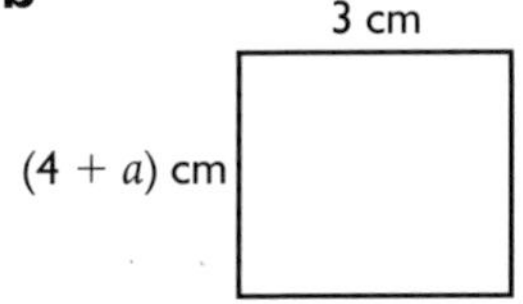

…consider

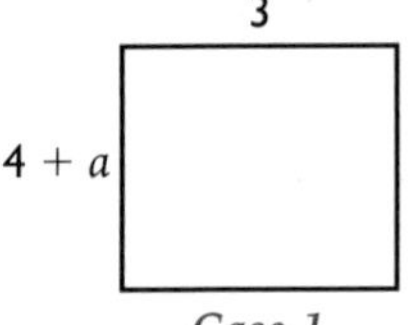

Case 1

and

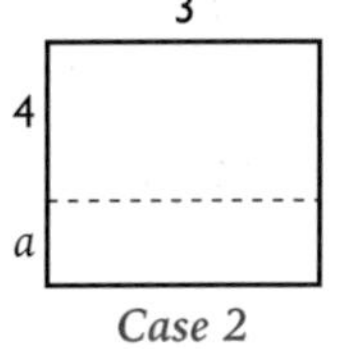

Case 2

c (Sketch the two cases first.)

$(x + 2)$ cm

5 cm

d (Sketch the two cases first.)

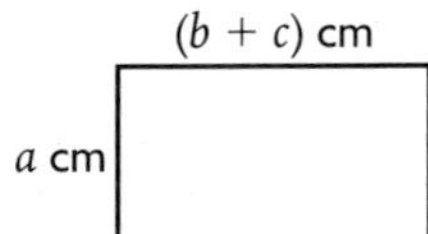

4 **a** Maria pays £x a day for bus fares. She spends £y a day on school lunch. She attends school 5 days a week.
Express the amount she spends per week on bus fares and lunch in two different ways.

b A school day is split by lunch. There are a periods before lunch and p periods after lunch. Each period is 54 minutes long.
Express the length of the school day in terms of a and p in two different ways.

c At the baker's, Peter buys x millionaire shortbreads and $3y$ fruit cakes. Each item is sold at $4z$ pence each. Find two expressions for Peter's bill.

Example 5

Remove the brackets and simplify:

$2(x - 3) - x$

$$\begin{aligned} 2(x - 3) - x &= 2x - 6 - x \\ &= x - 6 \end{aligned}$$

Example 6

Expand and simplify:

$3(y + x) + 2(x + 3)$

$$\begin{aligned} 3(y + x) + 2(x + 3) &= 3y + 3x + 2x + 6 \\ &= 3y + 5x + 6 \end{aligned}$$

Example 7

Expand $3a(2a + 5b) = 3a \times 2a + 3a \times 5b = 6a^2 + 15ab$

Exercise 7.2

1 Remove the brackets and simplify:

a $5(m + 2) + 3m$ **b** $4(n - 2) + n$ **c** $12 + 4(n + 1)$
d $9(x + y) - 9x$ **e** $6(1 + k) + 3k$ **f** $5y + 2(3 + y)$
g $2(3 + a) + 3(2 + a)$ **h** $7(m + n) + 3(m - n)$ **i** $10(x + 4) + 2(x - 20)$
j $8(2 + e) + 5(2 - e)$ **k** $8x + 4(x + 3) - 12x$ **l** $8y + 8(2 - y) - 16$

2 Expand:

a $5(3y - 1)$ **b** $6(2x + 3y)$ **c** $a(4a - 2)$
d $x(4 - 5x)$ **e** $2m(m - 3)$ **f** $5t(4 - 2t)$
g $2a(a - 2b)$ **h** $n(3n - 2m)$ **i** $3w(10 - 2w)$
j $5r(r - s)$ **k** $8w(2x - 3y)$ **l** $3(15a + 7b)$
m $2f(5f - g)$ **n** $7c(10 - 5c)$

3 Find an expression for the area of each postage stamp in two ways, namely
i with brackets **ii** without brackets.
All lengths are in centimetres.

a

b

c

d
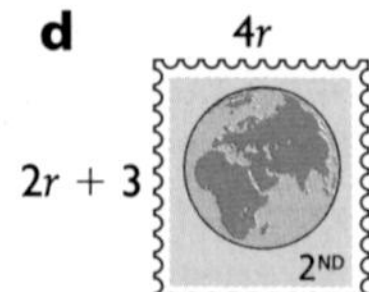

e $x + 2y$, $3y$

f

g

h

Challenge

1 Casey is attempting to write $(2x + 3)(x + 5)$ without brackets.
Remember this means $(2x + 3) \times (x + 5)$.
By considering areas (see opposite) she gets:

$2x^2 + 13x + 15$

Can you explain this by completing the diagram?

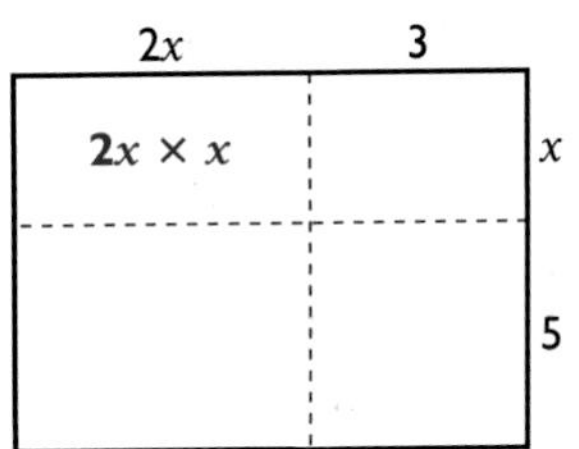

2 In a similar way expand:

a $(2a + b)(3a + b)$ b $(3m + 2n)(m + 5n)$

8 Factorising expressions

$2 \times 3 = 6$ ... 6 is the **product** of 2 and 3.
2 and 3 are **factors** of 6.

Similarly $3x(x + 2) = 3x^2 + 6x$ ... $3x^2 + 6x$ is the **product** of $3x$ and $(x + 2)$.
$3x$ and $(x + 2)$ are **factors** of $3x^2 + 6x$.

In the previous section we learned to expand expressions, for example $3x(x + 2) = 3x^2 + 6x$.
Can we reverse the process and work out that $3x^2 + 6x = 3x(x + 2)$?

We should note that $3x$ is the highest common factor of $3x^2$ and $6x$ since $3x^2 = 3x \times x$ and $6x = 3x \times 2$.

If $3x^2 + 6x = 3x(A + B)$ then on expanding we want $3x^2 = 3x \times A$ and $6x = 3x \times B$.
From this we see that $A = x$ and $B = 2$.

So $3x^2 + 6x = 3x(x + 2)$ ... this process is called **factorising**.

Example 1

Factorise $12y - 16$
Note that $12y = 4 \times 3y$ and $16 = 4 \times 4$
Thus $12y - 16 = 4(3y - 4)$

Example 2

Factorise $8a^2 + 4ab$
Note that $8a^2 = 4a \times 2a$ and $4ab = 4a \times b$
Thus $8a^2 + 4ab = 4a(2a + b)$

Example 3

Factorise $7x - 14x^2$
$7x - 14x^2 = 7x(1 - 2x)$

Example 4

Factorise $10xy - 15x^2y$
$10xy - 15x^2y = 5xy(2 - 3x)$

Always check your answer is correct by mentally expanding the factorised expression.

Exercise 8.1

1 Factorise, then check by mentally removing the brackets:

a $6y - 9$ **b** $x^2 - x$ **c** $2ab + a$ **d** $12 - 6y$
e $5a + 5b$ **f** $9b + 9$ **g** $ay + az$ **h** $12m - 8$
i $ef + e$ **j** $ef - e$ **k** $kl + l^2$ **l** $2n - n^2$
m $5n^2 - 5$ **n** $6n^2 - 3$ **o** $n^2 - 2n$ **p** $3ab + 6b$
q $7b^2 - 14b$ **r** $8x^2 + 4x$ **s** $2ab - 4a$ **t** $8mn + 6n^2$
u $14ef + 21f$ **v** $k^2 - k^2x$ **w** $4a^2b - a^2$ **x** $12pq^2 - 6pq$

2 Match each expression with its factorised form:

a

A $16x^2 - 20x$
B $16x^2 + 14x$
C $8x^2 + 16$
D $8x - 20x^2$
E $16x - 3x^2$
F $3x^2 + 6x$

i $x(16 - 3x)$
ii $8(x^2 + 2)$
iii $3x(x + 2)$
iv $4x(4x - 5)$
v $4x(2 - 5x)$
vi $2x(8x + 7)$

b

A $2ab - 2a^2$
B $2a^2 + ab$
C $b^2 - 2ab$
D $2b^2 + 2ab$
E $2ab - a^2b$
F $a^2b + 2ab$

i $ab(a + 2)$
ii $2b(b + a)$
iii $ab(2 - a)$
iv $2a(b - a)$
v $b(b - 2a)$
vi $a(2a + b)$

F

3 Factorise:

a $10e - 25$ **b** $51x - 17x^2$ **c** $2am - 2bm$
d $9y^2 - 9y$ **e** $a - abc$ **f** $\pi a^2 - \pi b^2$
g $3k^2 - 21ak$ **h** $mn + 2mw$ **i** $6pq - 12pr$
j $ab + abc$ **k** $13xy - 13x$ **l** $6e^2 + 3e$
m $\pi rh + \pi r^2$ **n** $\pi R^2 - \pi r^2$ **o** $\frac{1}{2}ah + \frac{1}{2}bh$
p $a^2b + ab^2$ **q** $2a^2b^2 - 4ab$ **r** $27x^2y - 36xy^2$
s $45m^2 + 54mn^2$ **t** $100k^2 + 120kw$ **u** $aA - bA$
v $4ab^2c - 2ab$ **w** $63m^2n + 81n^2$ **x** $45ef - 90e^2f^2$

4 **a** Calculate $5 \times 17 + 5 \times 83$ without a calculator!
Hint: factorise as $5 \times (17 + 83)$.

b In a similar manner perform the following calculations mentally.

i $8 \times 77 + 8 \times 23$ **ii** $7 \times 2{\cdot}4 + 7 \times 2{\cdot}6$
iii $19 \times 0{\cdot}7 + 19 \times 0{\cdot}3$ **iv** $9 \times 105 - 9 \times 5$
v $14 \times 12{\cdot}4 - 14 \times 2{\cdot}4$ **vi** $27 \times 3{\cdot}9 - 27 \times 2{\cdot}9$

5 A picture frame in a doll's house has dimensions as shown.
Without the aid of a calculator, find:

a the difference between the areas of the inner and outer rectangles

b the shaded area.

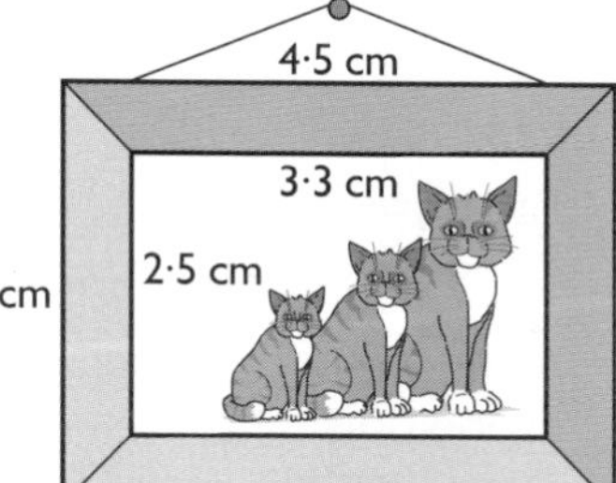

Challenges

A Factorising patterns

Take out the common factor in each expression in these families of expressions:

$a^2 - a$	$a^3 - a$	$a^4 - a$	$a^2b - ab^2$
$a^3 - a^2$	$a^4 - a^2$	$a^5 - a^2$	$a^3b - ab^3$
$a^4 - a^3$	$a^5 - a^3$	$a^6 - a^3$	$a^4b - ab^4$
$a^5 - a^4$	$a^6 - a^4$	$a^7 - a^4$	$a^5b - ab^5$
…	…	…	…

Describe any patterns that you find.

B A boxing match

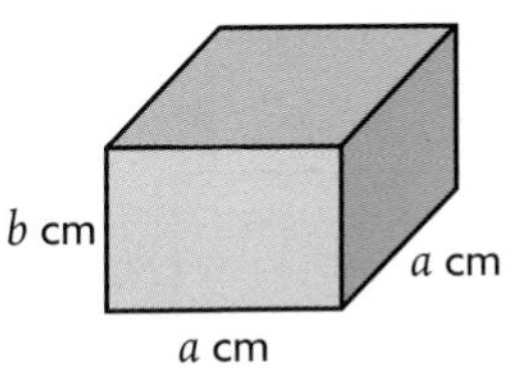

This box has height b cm and square base of side a cm.

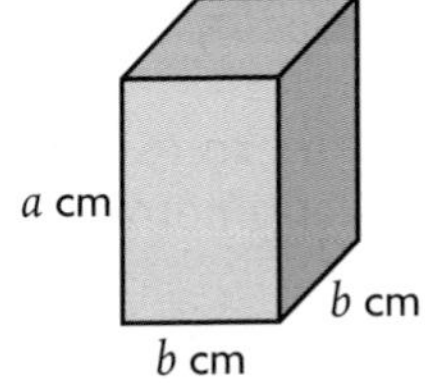

This box has height a cm and square base of side b cm.

a Find an expression in factorised form for the combined volume of the two boxes.

b Use your answer to **a** to give the dimensions of a box that has the combined volume of these two boxes.
(Check your result for some values of a and b.)

CHECK-UP

1 Copy and complete the missing expressions:

a

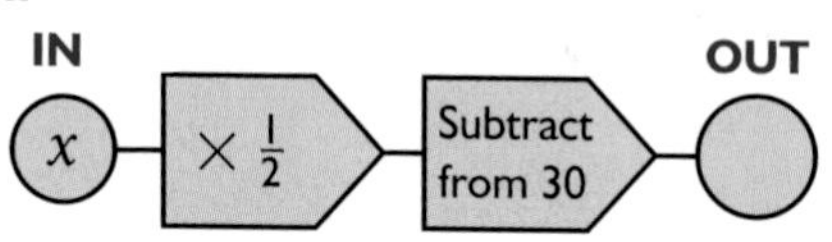

b

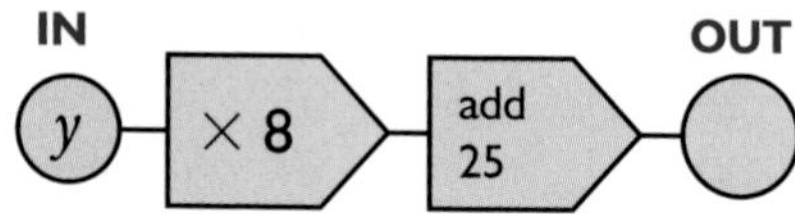

2 Evaluate:

a $2x + 3y + 2$ when $x = 3$ and $y = 5$

b $30 - \frac{1}{2}x$ when $x = 50$

3 Simplify:

a $3a + b - a + 4b$

b $3x + 12 - 2x + y - 10 + 4y$

4 **a** Find and simplify an expression for the perimeter (in centimetres) of this rectangle.

b Find the value of the perimeter if $a = 7$ and $b = 5$.

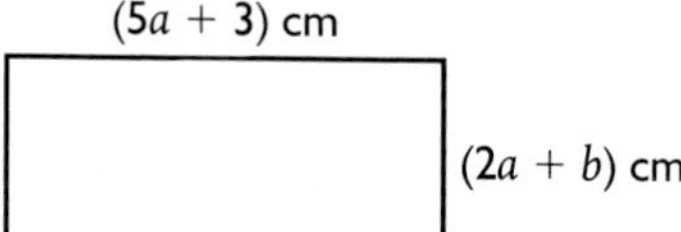

5 If $a = 10$ and $b = 6$ calculate:

a $100 - ab$

b $\dfrac{a + b}{a - b}$

c $a - (a - b)$

d $2ab$

6 Evaluate:

a $m^2 - 2n^2$ when $m = 7$ and $n = 3$

b $4(a - 2)^2$ when $a = 7$

7 Write without brackets:

a $5(k - 2)$ **b** $2a(a - b)$ **c** $6y(2x - y)$

8 Remove the brackets and simplify:

a $2(10 + k) - 2k$

b $3(m + 2n) + 5(m - n) - 8m$

9 Factorise:

a $8y - 12$

b $2x^2 + 6x$

c $a^2b + 3a$

d $7pq - 14p^2q^2$

E F

5 Information handling 1

Data collection has always been seen as an important activity

In Luke 2:1 we read that Caesar Augustus decreed that a census be taken of all the inhabited earth. It was while travelling to this census that Mary and Joseph found themselves in Bethlehem without a place to stay.

William the Conqueror knew of its importance when in December 1085 he ordered the *Domesday Book* to be created.

The Domesday Book

1 Looking back

Exercise 1.1

1 'What size shoe do you take?'
30 answers collected from an S2 class are shown below:

2	4	6	3	4	3
5	7	5	6	2	4
4	3	2	5	5	3
5	5	6	3	7	2
2	5	3	6	4	5

Organise the data using the tally chart given. Check that your total comes to 30.

shoe size	tally	number of pupils
2		
3		
4		
5		
6		
7		
	total	

2 In class 2B, 7 girls and 12 boys said they had a computer at home.
There are 32 pupils in this class, of whom 15 are girls.
Copy and complete the table.

	have a computer at home	don't have a computer at home	totals
girls	7		
boys			
totals			

a How many girls don't have a computer at home?

b What fraction of boys have computers at home?

3 A group of students collected this data:

student	1	2	3	4	5	6	7	8	9	10	11	12
finger span (cm)	18	23	20	18	22	21	23	19	19	20	22	17
shoe size	5	11	5	4	9	8	10	6	5	6	8	4

a Arrange the students in order by shoe size, smallest first.

b Which students have a shoe size smaller than 7?

c Which students have a finger span longer than 20 cm?

4 **a** Construct the frequency table which this bar graph represents.

b How many pupils had more than three pets?

c How many pupils had at least one pet?

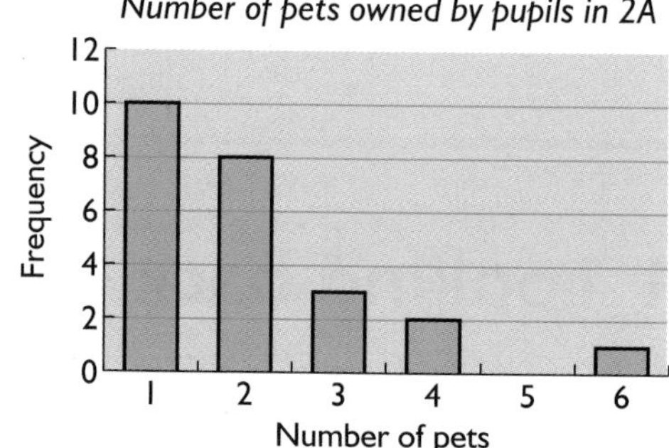

2 Become a data collector

The answers to these and many other questions can be found by collecting data.

How much do second-hand bikes cost?
How often do people eat in 'fast food' outlets?

2 You are designing tables to use for collecting data to find out what kind of magazine is most popular and how many magazines are read each week.

a What responses are there likely to be for

i 'type of magazine'

ii 'number of magazines'?

b What is the difference between the type of data collected at **ai** and **aii**?

3 Kenmair High has four houses: Clova, Isla, Esk and Prosen.
The House Championship board lists the winning houses since 1990.

1990 Clova	1995 Esk	2000 Esk
1991 Isla	1996 Clova and Esk	2001 Clova
1992 Clova	1997 Prosen	2002 Esk
1993 Prosen	1998 Clova and Esk	
1994 Prosen	1999 Esk	

a Complete a table in which the data is organised to show the number of times each house has either won or shared the championship.

b Which house is listed most?

4 National test results in mathematics in S2 were as follows.

Mr Able's class had 24 Es and 6 Fs.
Mrs Bright's class had 15 Es and 14 Fs.
Mr Crook's class had 13 Ds and 4 Cs.
Miss Dunn's class had 1 C, 17 Ds and 6 Es.

a Show this information in a table.

b Which class has the most Fs?

c Which class has no Es?

d How many Es were there altogether?

e How many pupils were there in each class?

f What percentage of these results were Es or Fs?

5 In a maths competition these answers were given for a scale drawing problem.

In team A, Anne 6·1 cm 72°, Barry 6·2 cm 75°, Claire 6 cm 70°, Diane 6 cm 71°.
In team B, Euan 5·8 cm 70°, Freddy 6 cm 66°, Gail 6·2 cm 75°, Hari 6·2 cm 73°.

Any answer between 6 cm and 6·2 cm is correct for the length; between 68° and 70° is correct for the angle.

a Organise the data into two tables, one for each team, which shows which pupils got what correct.

b Which answer was more likely to be correct, the length or the angle?

c Which team got the highest number of correct answers?

E

4 Summarising and comparing data: the mean

The table shows how Jade and Peter faired in their exams.

	English	Maths	French	Science	Art
Jade	90	74	72	89	85
Peter	90	79	69	82	75

Who did better? One way to answer this is to calculate their **mean** scores.

For Jade this is 82%; for Peter 79%.

This one value, an average, can be used as a quick **summary** of results and is useful in comparing Jade's results with Peter's.

Reminder

The **mean** is a type of average. $\text{Mean} = \dfrac{\text{sum of the data values}}{\text{number of data values}}$

Example

The numbers of characters in each word in the sentence 'Jade was pleased her average test mark was 82%' are:

4, 3, 7, 3, 7, 4, 4, 3, 3

Calculate the mean number of characters per word.

$$\text{Mean} = \frac{4+3+7+3+7+4+4+3+3}{9} = \frac{38}{9}$$

The answer, to 1 decimal place, is 4·2 characters.

E

Exercise 4.1

1 Calculate the mean values for the data summarised below.

- **a** Mean height of seedlings when 5 seedlings have a total height of 65 cm.
- **b** Mean price of a book when the total cost of 12 books is £71·88.
- **c** Mean weight of a bag of apples when 8 bags weigh a total of 10·3 kg.
- **d** Mean journey time when the total journey time is 121 minutes for 9 journeys.

2 Calculate the mean value for these samples.

a Takings at stalls at a summer fête: £145, £92, £53, £102, £67, £37, £81.

b Estimates of the number of sweeties in a jar: 402, 650, 240, 555, 199, 450, 330, 606,474, 1000.

c Number of letters in words in a sentence from a children's novel: 3, 5, 3, 6, 5, 8, 7, 7, 4, 3, 2, 3, 6, 1, 8.

d Marks in a test: 31%, 61%, 87%, 39%, 88%, 74%, 65%, 90%, 57%, 82%, 49%, 53%, 56%, 60%, 61%, 57%, 77%, 62%, 60%, 74%, 68%, 59%, 69%, 58%, 76%, 78%, 84%.

3 Patrick is allowed to keep his tips when he works as a waiter.
One evening he collects £26 in tips from waiting at 7 tables.
Jacques, working at the same restaurant, made an average tip of £3·90.
Who had the higher average tip?

4 Leslie regularly plays golf with a friend at a particular course, starting at 6 p.m. The last few times they played they finished their games at 9.15 p.m., 8.50 p.m., 9.10 p.m., 9.30 p.m. and 8.55 p.m.

a Work out how many minutes before or after 9 p.m. each game finished.

b How long did their games take on average?

E

5 Mrs Meek, a midwife, was surprised by the weight of the baby she had just helped deliver.
He weighed in at 5·0 kg. The previous ten babies she had delivered weighed

3·3 kg, 4·1 kg, 3·8 kg, 3·2 kg, 3·5 kg, 4·2 kg, 3·1 kg, 3·9 kg, 4·0 kg and 3·4 kg.

a How many kilograms above the mean of these ten was the new baby?

b What is the mean weight of the eleven babies?

6 Mr and Mrs McKay went on a touring holiday in Europe. When they got home Mr McKay looked at their credit card bills for the various hotels they had stayed in. In Germany their overnight bills were €56, €60, €52, €75, in Italy €50, €68, €72 and in France €46, €52, €80, €63, €45, €48, €70.

a For which country was the overnight accommodation bill lowest and what was this bill?

b Which country was cheaper on average for overnight accommodation? What was this average cost?

Brainstormers

a Kelso Kickarounds have played nine times this season and averaged one goal per game.
How many goals must they score in the next game to bring that average up to two goals per game?

b The mean weight of the team (eleven men) is 13 stone. If you don't count the goalie who weighs 18 stone, what is the mean weight of the rest of the team?

c The mean age of the team is 23 years.
Without the striker this drops to 22 years.
How old is the striker?

Finding the mean without a calculator

Here is a list of ten scores in a maths test: 67, 65, 78, 72, 76, 75, 68, 67, 77, 80.

$$\text{Mean} = \frac{67 + 65 + 78 + 72 + 76 + 75 + 68 + 67 + 77 + 80}{10} = 72{\cdot}5$$

E

Some people may have a problem adding the ten scores without a calculator.

Suppose we considered for each score how far from 70 it is,
e.g. 67 is 3 below 70, (−3).

The list would look like: −3, −5, +8, +2, +6, +5, −2, −3, +7, +10 … a total of 25.

The mean amount a score differs from 70 is $\frac{25}{10} = 2{\cdot}5$.

Thus the mean score is $70 + 2{\cdot}5 = 72{\cdot}5$.

In this example we compared everything to 70;
70 is referred to as the **assumed mean**.

We can choose anything to be the assumed mean, it will not affect the final answer.

Example Find the mean of 112, 118, 121, 124, 129.

scores	112	118	121	124	129	Total
assumed 120	−8	−2	1	4	9	4

Mean difference $= \frac{4}{5} = 0{\cdot}8$

So mean score $= 120 + 0{\cdot}8$
$= 120{\cdot}8$

Exercise 4.2

1 Calculate the mean of the following lists using the suggested assumed mean.

a 26, 28, 29, 29, 31, 33, 35, 35, 37, 37 (assumed mean 30)

b £79, £84, £88, £88, £92 (assumed mean £88)

c £4·90, £4·94, £4·98 £5·06, £5·12, £5·24 (assumed mean £5; work in pennies)

d 1294, 1310, 1324, 1333 (assumed mean 1300)

2 Calculate the mean of the following lists using an assumed mean.

a 49, 49, 50, 52, 52, 54, 56, 57, 57, 59

b €125, €125, €129, €133, €137, €140, €144, €148

c 55 minutes, 58 minutes, 1 hour 2 minutes, 1 hour 5 minutes, 1 hour 12 minutes (work in minutes)

d 12 079, 12 085

3 Whitewaterfoot Golf Course has nine holes. Their yardage is given below. 167, 179, 205, 312, 184, 191, 185, 168, 200.

a Using an assumed mean of 190 yards, calculate the mean yardage of the course.

b What is the difference between the mean yardage for the first four holes and the last four?

E

4 If you are less than 1·60 metres tall you are not allowed on the fairground attraction, Switchback Central. The heights of some customers were measured as: 1·57 m, 1·61 m, 1·68 m, 1·72 m, 1·64 m, 1·58 m, 1·70 m, 1·62 m.

a Calculate the mean height of the group.

b What is the mean height of the people in the group who are allowed on?

5 A CD has ten tracks. The duration of each, in minutes and seconds, is given on the cover as: 4:33, 3:42, 4:27, 4:53, 4:06, 5:04, 3:50, 4:39, 3:59, 4:00.

a Calculate the mean duration of a track on the CD. (Work in seconds.)

b What is the mean duration of the tracks which are shorter than the mean for the CD?

6 The rainfall (in centimetres) at various centres around the country was recorded over four months.

Location	June	July	Aug	September	*Mean*
Paisley	2·1	2·8	1·8	1·9	2·15
Fort William	6·3	5·2	5·4	4·9	5·45
Selkirk	1·3	1·0	1·2	1·1	1·2
Pitlochry	1·0	1·3	1·5	1·0	1·2

a One of the mean values is incorrect. Which one?

b Use the correct mean values to work out the mean of all the readings given.

7 Customers complain about a train journey taking too long. The company decides to try various changes for a week to see if it will make a difference.

The table shows how long the trip takes, in minutes, for the week before the trial and the week after.

	Mon	Tue	Wed	Thu	Fri
Before trial	45	42	47	41	45
After trial	43	43	42	43	42

a Calculate the mean for both sets of times.

b Have the changes made much difference? Consider the percentage improvement in the mean.

E

Brainstormer

The mean can be used to 'smooth out' figures that tend to jump around a lot, so that the trend can be more easily spotted.

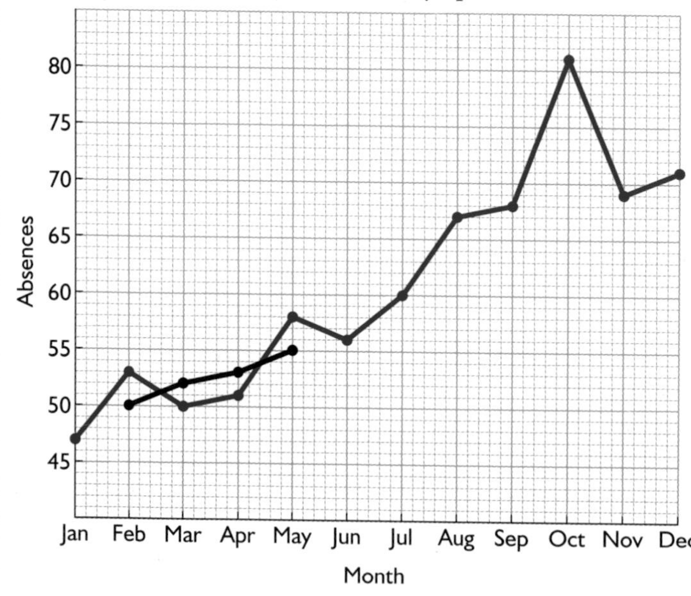

The purple graph shows a school's absentee figures from January to December.

The trend can be made clearer by taking the months three at a time and working out a mean.

Months	Mean
Jan–Mar	50
Feb–Apr	52
Mar–May	53
Apr–Jun	55

a Copy and complete the table of means. The last one will be Oct–Dec.

b Copy and complete the black graph to see the 'smoothing' effect.

5 Finding the mean from a frequency table

When there are lots of data, information is often presented in a frequency table.

This table, for example, shows the number of siblings (brothers and sisters) of pupils in a second year class.

siblings	frequency
0	9
1	13
2	6
3	1
4	0
5	1

Row 1 tells us that 9 pupils had no siblings

Row 3 tells us that 6 pupils had 2 siblings, i.e. $2 \times 6 = 12$ siblings altogether

By adding a third column we can work out the total number of siblings counted

siblings (S)	frequency (f)	$S \times f$
0	9	$0 \times 9 = 0$
1	13	$1 \times 13 = 13$
2	6	$2 \times 6 = 12$
3	1	$3 \times 1 = 3$
4	0	$4 \times 0 = 0$
5	1	$5 \times 1 = 5$
Totals	30	33

30 pupils were asked

33 siblings were counted

So the mean number of siblings per pupil

$$= \frac{\text{sum of data values}}{\text{number of data values}} = \frac{\text{sum of siblings} \times \text{frequency}}{\text{sum of frequency}}$$

$$= \tfrac{33}{30} = 1{\cdot}1$$

Exercise 5.1

1 The frequency table shows the number of newspapers delivered per household on a certain newspaper round.

a Copy and complete the frequency table.

b How many households are there on the round?

c How many newspapers were delivered in total?

d Find the mean number of newspapers delivered per household.

number of newspapers	frequency	number of newspapers × frequency
1	24	$1 \times 24 =$
2	13	
3	3	
totals		

F

2 The frequency table shows the scores of various throws of a dice during a game of Ludo.

a Copy and complete the frequency table.

b How many times was the dice rolled?

c What was the total score for all the rolls?

score	1	2	3	4	5	6	totals
frequency	6	9	5	5	12	3	
score × frequency	1 × 6 =						

d Find the mean score.

3 Calculate the mean values for the data summarised below.

a Mean number of broken eggs in a sample of boxes.

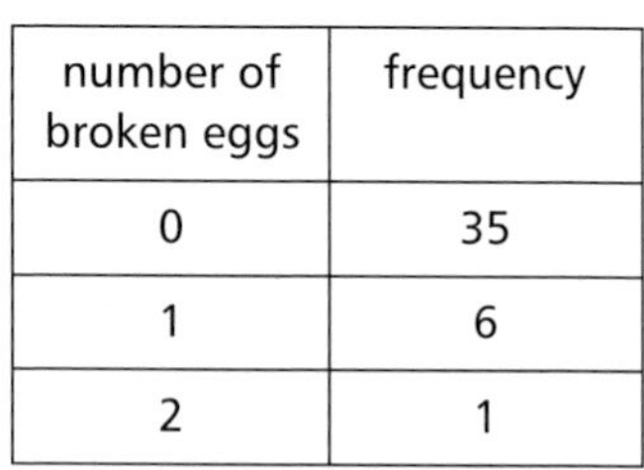

number of broken eggs	frequency
0	35
1	6
2	1

b Mean number of matches in a box.

number of matches	frequency
49	2
50	11
51	8
52	5
53	0
54	1

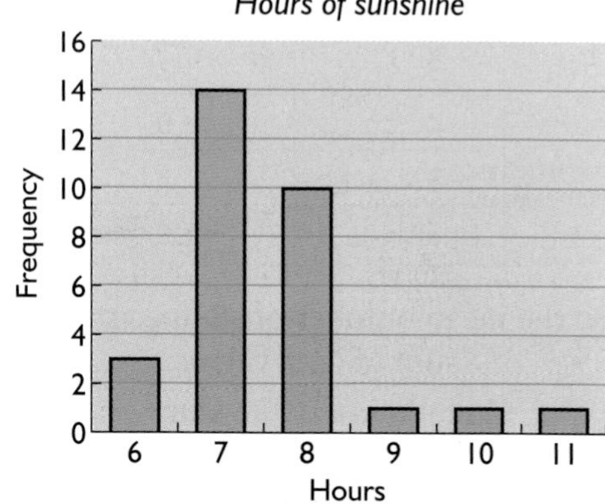

c Mean number of hours of sunshine in June. (Hint: make a frequency table.)

4 The pictograph shows the quantities of wool required to knit various ladies' jumpers in a pattern book.

a 'Number of balls of wool' or 'Number of patterns' – which axis gives the frequency?

b Make a frequency table from the bar chart

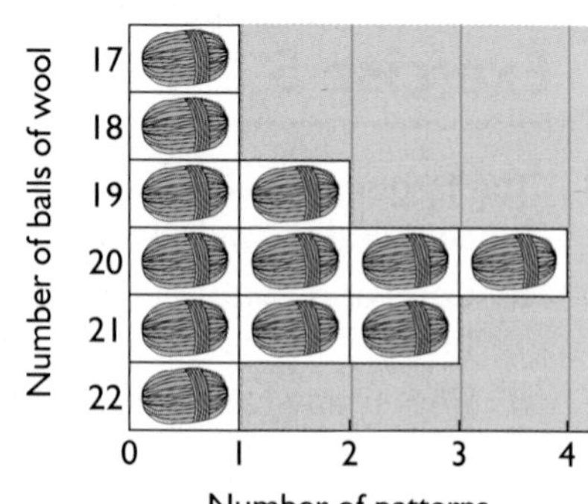

c A novice knitter wants to know roughly how many balls of wool she would need to make a lady's jumper.

i Find the mean number of balls of wool needed to make a lady's jumper from this pattern book.

ii Use your answer to complete the sentence: 'It takes on average just under … balls of wool to knit a lady's jumper.'

F

5 The bar graph shows the number of ice-creams sold per customer one day in summer.

a What is the label on the axis representing *frequency*?

b Make a frequency table from the bar chart.

c Summarise the sales by giving the mean number of ice-creams per customer.

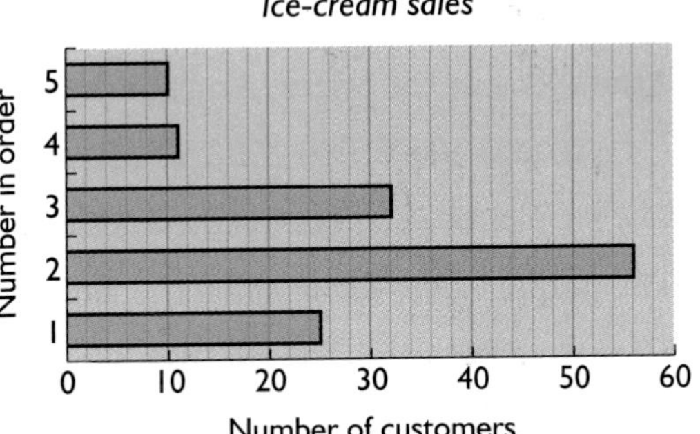

6 The median and the mode

The average is supposed to give you an idea of what is typical for the situation. Consider the following.

A large holiday company offers you a chance to win one of the following prizes when you make a booking:

one prize of £10 000, two prizes of £1000 and ten prizes worth £250 towards a holiday of your choice.

The mean value of these prizes would be

$$\frac{10\,000 + 1000 + 1000 + 250 + 250 + 250 + 250 + 250 + 250 + 250 + 250 + 250 + 250}{13} = \frac{14\,500}{13}$$

$= £1115{\cdot}38$

Is this value typical of the size of a prize?

There are 13 prizes and 10 of these are far less than the mean.

The mode

The most commonly occurring prize value is £250 … we could consider this as a typical prize size.

We call the most commonly occurring value in a list of data the **mode** or **modal value**.

Sometimes we can't quote a single value as the mode, for example when two values are equally frequent.

Example 1 State the mode in the following lists.

a 1, 2, 5, 1, 6, 3, 1, 2, 3, 4

b A, A, B, C, A, C, C, B, D, C, A, B, B, B

c 12 years, 14 years, 14 years, 15 years, 15 years, 15 years, 16 years, 17 years

d 3, 4, 5, 3, 4, 6, 3, 4, 7, 3, 4, 5

Answers:

a 1

b A (note that a mean value could not have been calculated!)

c 15 years

d There is no single most frequent value.

F

5

The median

Again, look at the prizes. Arrange the 13 prizes *in order of size*:

10 000 1000 1000 250 250 250 **250** 250 250 250 250 250 250

The purple value highlights the middle of the list. Note that $13 \div 2 = 6$ remainder 1.

The purple value, £250, splits the list into two smaller lists both holding 6 values.

The value that splits the list into two equal smaller lists is called the **median**.

Note that if the top prize had been £1 000 000 it would not have affected the value of the median, but the mean value would have leapt to £77 269 with now 12 out of 13 values below it.

> When an ordered list contains an even number of values then there will be two values in the middle. The median is defined as the mean of these two values.

F

Example 2 Find the median of the following lists.

a 1, 1, 1, 2, 2, 3, 4, 4, 5, 6, 7

b 12, 13, 13, 14, 15, 16, 17, 18

c 7, 3, 2, 5, 7, 1, 8, 1, 1

d 3, 4, 5, 3, 4, 6, 3, 4, 7, 3, 4, 5

Answers:

a 1, 1, 1, 2, 2, (3), 4, 4, 5, 6, 7 — Median is 3

b 12, 13, 13, (14), (15), 16, 17, 18 — Median is $\frac{14 + 15}{2} = 14{\cdot}5$

c 1, 1, 1, 2, (3), 5, 7, 7, 8 — Median is 3 (having ordered the list)

d 3, 3, 3, 3, 4, (4), (4), 4, 5, 5, 6, 7 — Median is $\frac{4 + 4}{2} = 4$ (having ordered the list)

> The prize list has three averages:
>
> the mean = £1115·38
>
> the mode = £250
>
> the median = £250

Exercise 6.1

1 List these sets in order, smallest first, then find the median.

- **a** 8, 9, 6, 5, 9, 7, 1
- **b** 20, 21, 20, 20, 20, 20, 19, 20
- **c** 50, 30, 100, 50, 90, 200, 100, 50
- **d** 9·3, 9·7, 9·9, 9·5, 8·9, 9·0, 9·7, 8·9, 9·1, 9·2, 9·5, 9·8, 9·7

2 Find the modes for the data sets given in question **1**.

3 The bar chart shows the number of brown eggs in boxes at Fred's Fresh Farm Produce shop.

- **a** Which label refers to the frequency – 'number of boxes' or 'number of brown eggs in a box'?
- **b** What is the modal number of brown eggs in a box?

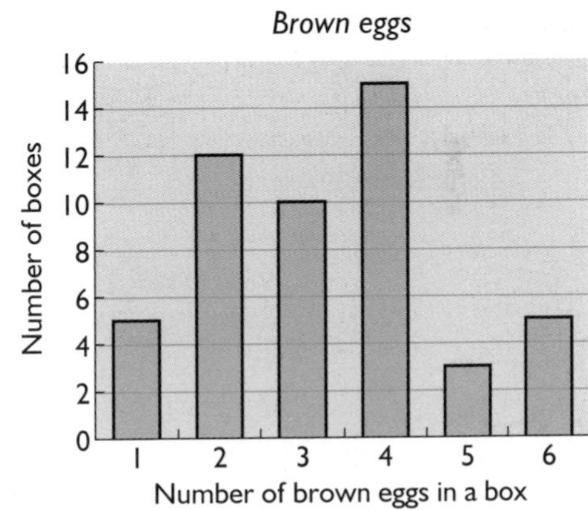

4 The pictograph shows the number of goals scored by a school's U-14 team in each game of a football tournament.

- **a** Which label refers to the frequency?
- **b** What was the modal score for the U-14 team?

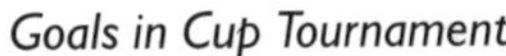

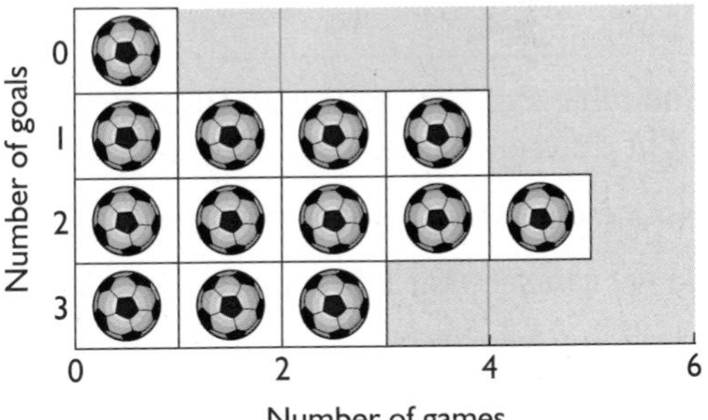

5 The players in a rugby team collect their sports shirts from the coach.
He hands out these sizes:

M, M, L, L, S, L, L, M, L, M, M, L, S, M, L.

- **a** Organise the list in a table like this:
- **b** Which is the modal size?

size	frequency
S	
M	
L	

6 Julie noted the hair colour for girls in her class: brown, brown, blonde, black, red, brown, blonde, black, brown, brown.

- **a** Can the 'total' value of this list be found?
- **b** Can this data be listed in order of size?
- **c** Which average could be used to find a representative for this list – mean, median or mode?

7 A shoe shop owner reviews sales over the weekend of a line of children's trainers. The sizes sold are: 4, 1, 3, 3, 2, 4, 5, 4, 3, 4, 2, 5.

- **a** Write the list in order, smallest first.
- **b** What is the modal size?
- **c** What is the median size?
- **d** Which is more typical of the shoes sold over the weekend – median or mode?

8 These second-hand car sales advertisements appeared in a newspaper one day. Find the median price.

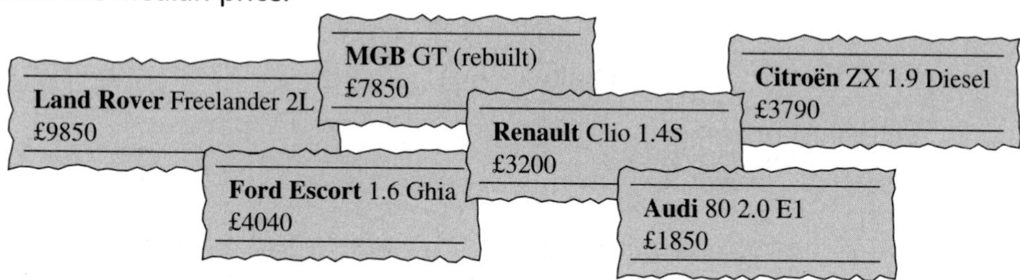

Land Rover Freelander 2L
£9850
MGB GT (rebuilt)
£7850
Citroën ZX 1.9 Diesel
£3790
Renault Clio 1.4S
£3200
Ford Escort 1.6 Ghia
£4040
Audi 80 2.0 E1
£1850

F

7 The range

°F	1	2	3	4	5	6	7	8	mean
Moon	−261	−200	−10	35	97	154	199	140	19·3
Earth	−45	−19	−9	12	32	45	56	82	19·3

The table shows the temperature (°F) as measured at eight different places on **i** the moon and **ii** the earth.

Notice that in both cases the mean temperature is the same.

So we can see that knowing the mean does not give us the whole picture.

The temperature range on the moon is much wider – the data values are more spread out.

To help us measure this spread we have defined a quantity known as the **range**.

> Range = highest data value – lowest data value

Example Which has the biggest range in temperature, the moon or the earth?

For the moon, the range of temperature = 199 – (−261) = 460 degrees

For the earth, the range = 82 – (−45) = 127 degrees

The moon has the bigger range.

Exercise 7.1

1 Mrs Stone looked at her class's marks in their last test. The lowest was 32% but the highest was 95% and the mean was 78%. What is the range of marks?

2 One question in the test had these answers:

45°, 52°, 48°, 50°, 44°, 47°, 50°, 51°, 49°, 46°, 48°, 49°, 45°, 50°, 45°, 48°

a Arrange the answers in order, smallest first.

b Find the range.

3 In Philip's experiment, he grew six plants with a new fertiliser and six without. Those without fertiliser grew to heights between 30 cm and 36 cm; those with, grew to a minimum height of 35 cm and a maximum height of 45 cm.

a Find the range in heights for both sets of plants.

b Which showed more spread in heights?

4 Joe, a cyclist, had practice times for a 7 mile race of 17.28 (17 minutes 28 seconds), 16.56, 17.18 and 17.30 while his team mate, Jim, had practice times of 17.20, 17.29, 17.15 and 17.12.

a Find the range in times for both Joe and Jim.

b Who was the more consistent cyclist?

5 The table shows the scores of Anne and Jo when they played each other at golf.

hole	1	2	3	4	5	6	7	8	9	10	11	12	13	14	15	16	17	18
Anne's score	4	2	6	3	3	4	5	2	3	3	4	5	3	4	3	4	3	2
Jo's score	3	3	4	4	5	4	4	3	4	4	4	4	3	4	4	5	3	3

a Find the range in scores for both Anne and Jo.

b Find their modal scores.

c Who was the more consistent golfer?

d Did the more consistent golfer also have the better (lower) modal score?

e Who won the round (had the lower total)?

F

Challenge

Look in various encyclopedias and books of records to find the information you need to answer the following questions.

a Find the range of annual rainfall in the west coast of Scotland. Is it more or less variable than that in the east coast?

b What is the range in planet size in the solar system? What is the range in satellite size?

Exercise 7.2

1 Mr Khan is a good all rounder at cricket.
In five innings he made the following number of runs: 25, 40, 36, 11, 22.

a Find the mean number of runs Mr Khan made per innings.

b Find the median number of runs Mr Khan made per innings.

c Which average is usually quoted in the game of cricket?

d Find the range for Mr Khan's batting scores.

2 The table gives information on the first six King Class locomotives built in 1927.

Number	Name	Built	Withdrawn	Mileage
6000	King George V	Jun-27	Dec-62	1 910 424
6001	King Edward VII	Jul-27	Sep-62	1 941 044
6002	King William IV	Jul-27	Sep-62	1 891 952
6003	King George IV	Jul-27	Jun-62	1 920 479
6004	King George III	Jul-27	Jun-62	1 917 258
6005	King George II	Jul-27	Nov-62	1 679 275

a Find the mean total mileage for these six locomotives.

b Find the range in the mileages.

c The King George V was in service for 35 years 6 months.
What was King George V's mean mileage per month?

d Find the mean mileage per month for locomotive number 6002.

e Which of these locomotives worked harder on average?

3 In order to qualify for various offers, a supermarket requires its customers to spend an average of £60 per week in the store.
Mr and Mrs Kean looked at their bills over the last 8 weeks.

a Make a list of the amounts spent each week, starting on Saturdays. The list should be in order, largest amount first.

b Find the median amount spent per week.

c Find the range of amounts spent per week.

d Find the mean amount spent per week.

e Do you think that the Keans should qualify for the offers? Explain.

Date	Amount
Sat 1/10	£63·48
Sat 8/10	£67·08
Sat 15/10	£42·56
Sat 22/10	£48·34
Sat 27/10	£28·87
Mon 29/10	£29·65
Sat 3/11	£52·39
Sat 10/11	£74·21
Sat 17/11	£62·68

F

4 The bar chart shows the number of pupils in each year at Seaview High School.

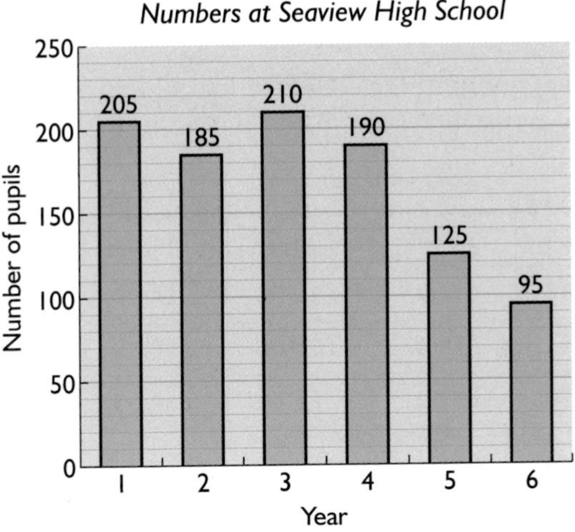

a Find:
  i the mean number of pupils per year
  ii the median number of pupils per year.

b Is there a modal number of pupils per year?

c Find the range of pupil numbers per year.

d Three pupils join S1, one pupil joins S2, two leave S3 and two leave S6. Which of the previous measures (mean, median, mode and range) change? Find any new values.

5 As part of a survey on car use, the local council stopped traffic on certain roads into town for several short periods. Drivers were asked about reasons for their journeys and the number of travellers was noted. Here are some results:

	number of cars starting at	
reason for journey	8.30 a.m.	11.00 a.m.
work	26	3
shopping	7	17
school trip	18	0
pleasure	4	12

	number of cars starting at	
number of travellers	8.30 a.m.	11.00 a.m.
1	23	18
2	20	7
3	8	5
4	3	2
5	1	0

a Find the modal reason for journey for each time period and comment.

b Find the mode and range for the number of travellers for each time period and comment.

F

8 Grouped frequency tables

When the range in a data set is large, the raw data are often organised into groups.

Example Twenty volunteers collected for charity one Saturday afternoon.

When they emptied their tins, the amounts collected were found to be:

£13·42	£20·65	£5·21	£26·03	£11·61
£10·78	£8·52	£12·93	£15·06	£4·97
£13·49	£22·57	£19·42	£16·06	£18·83
£23·24	£29·16	£15·01	£6·89	£14·55

Here the range is approximately £25 and there are only 20 pieces of data.

To summarise the data, it has been grouped in £5 intervals, starting with easy numbers 0, 5, 10, … This makes six groups or classes.

amount	tally	frequency
£0–£4·99	|	1
£5–£9·99	|||	3
£10–£14·99	~~||||~~ |	6
£15–£19·99	~~||||~~	5
£20–£24·99	|||	3
£25–£29·99	||	2
	check total	20

amount	tally	frequency
£0–£9·99	||||	4
£10–£19·99	~~||||~~ ~~||||~~ |	11
£20–£29·99	~~||||~~	5
	check total	20

Notice that if £10 intervals had been chosen the number of intervals would have been rather small.

> Intervals of the same size should be chosen.
> Start with an easy number.
> Aim to give a reasonable number of groups (say 5 to 10).

Adding a tally column can make finding the frequencies easier.

Check that the total frequency in the table is the same as the original number of bits of data.

The class interval with the highest frequency is called the **modal class**.

So the modal class for the first grouping is £10–£14·99.

F

Exercise 8.1

1 Bob is a salesman and needs to keep a weekly record of his mileage for work. His records for the last 6 months are given.

125	306	411	256	277
198	345	264	301	208
366	139	526	185	397
228	284	318	237	329
205	194	236	429	290

mileage	tally	frequency
100–199		
200–299		
	check total	

a Copy and complete the grouped frequency table for this data.
b What is the length of the class interval?
c Which class interval is the modal class?

2 At Parkside Primary School, records are kept of the heights (in centimetres) of all the P7 pupils as they leave for secondary school. This year's records are given in the table.

147	137·5	143	139·5	142	141	130	143·5
136	142	144	139	142	138	149·5	140
135·5	133	135	134·5	142·5	137	145	153·5

a Construct a grouped frequency table for these marks with class intervals of 5 cm, starting with '130 cm to under 135 cm'.
b Find the modal class.
c Find the range from the original data.
Is it possible to find the range from the grouped frequency table?

3 Sara has been working on a project called 'Household Chores'.
Each classmate recorded the number of minutes in total spent on helping around the house in one particular week.
The information is given in the table.

a Find the shortest and longest times spent helping around the house.
b Sara wants to draw a bar chart to illustrate this information.
Which bar size (class interval) would you choose – 30 minutes or 60 minutes?

24	95	75	90	105	48	170
60	118	120	175	75	120	88
90	85	35	140	90	0	102
160	100	90	115	80	130	55

c Make a grouped frequency table which will help her draw the bar chart.
d Draw the bar chart. Don't forget to label the axes and include a title.

4 On a particularly accident-prone section of a motorway, the speeds in miles per hour of all vehicles are regularly monitored. In one session, the speeds of passing vehicles were recorded as follows:

57	70	78	67	74	75	53	71	75	68
66	48	58	78	65	71	68	50	63	72
70	79	69	67	71	75	66	79	92	70
69	64	72	73	51	75	78	70	62	55
52	73	74	65	70	67	59	75	72	62

a What was **i** the slowest **ii** the fastest **iii** the range of the speeds?

b To organise the data in groups, which class interval would be best – 5, 10 or 11?

c Make a grouped frequency table.

d Were the majority keeping to the speed limit of 70 m.p.h.?

Challenge

As part of a promotion, a biscuit company is offering a free puzzle with its multipacks.
There are five free puzzles to collect and each puzzle is randomly enclosed with a pack.
It's just a matter of luck which puzzle you get.

How many multipacks will you have to buy to get the whole set of puzzles?

You don't need actually to 'buy' multipacks to answer this question.
You can do a **simulation** to collect the data.

- Cut out five cards or use five counters, labelled puzzle 1, 2, 3, 4 and 5 and place them in a bag.
- Choose one card or counter and record the puzzle number on it and return it to the bag (a trial).
- Continue until you have chosen each puzzle number at least once.
- Count the number of trials you had to do.
- Repeat the simulation several times.

Combine your results with another person in your class and organise your results in a table.

- What is the range of the data?
- What is the modal value?
- How many simulations have you included in your results?
- Calculate the mean.

Which value can you use to answer the original question?

CHECK-UP

1 Why might the following questions not be suitable for a questionnaire?

a Are you likely to buy a magazine this month?

b Have you ever lied in a questionnaire?

c Do you prefer heads or do you not prefer tails?

2 At the bottle bank, bottles are sorted according to the colour of the glass. A sample of bottles is examined and their colour noted.

a Organise the data into a table which shows how many of each type of bottle there is in the sample.

b What fraction of the bottles were white?

c What colour of glass is more likely to turn up if the sample is anything to go by?

brown	brown	green	white	brown	brown
brown	white	green	green	brown	brown
green	white	white	brown	white	green
brown	brown	white	brown	brown	white

3 The table gives information on scores in a class test.

a Find **i** the highest mark **ii** the lowest mark.

b How many pupils are in the class?

c Find the mean mark.

Mark	Frequency
5	2
6	4
7	4
8	7
9	9

4 The table gives information on a selection of English cathedrals.

Cathedral	Total length (m)	Tower height (m)	Total area (m^2)
Canterbury	157	72	4026
Durham	152	101	9698
Lichfield	141	109	8128
Liverpool	148	65	5669
London	143	66	4148
Winchester	113	79	2578
York	160	46	4974

a Find **i** the greatest length **ii** the shortest length.

b Find the mean total area.

c Find the range in the heights.

d Find the median tower height.

EF

5 Mean, median, mode, range

Which of these:

a requires a total value to be found?

b can be used when the data are categories, e.g. short, standard, long, rather than numbers?

c measures spread rather than average?

d can only be found once the data are ordered in a list or table?

6 Are class sizes too big? At Downtown High School the number of pupils in each maths class is listed by teacher.

Teacher	S1	S2	S3	S4	S5	S6
Mr A	33	22	30	25		
Mrs B	28	33	29	20	26	
Miss C	33	29	24	30		20
Mr D	29	33	30	21	24	
Mr E		33	30	27		12
Mrs F	32	30	29	30	27	
Mr G	23	33	20	30	18	
Mrs H	33	25	23	30	19	

a Copy and complete the frequency table.

Number of pupils	Tally	Number of classes
10 to 14		

b How many different maths classes are there in Downtown High?

c How many maths classes are there with 30 or more pupils?

d What is the modal class interval of class sizes?

e What is the range of class sizes?

f Is it true to say the majority of classes have 30 or more pupils?

F

6 Time, distance and speed

In August 1492, Christopher Columbus left Spain looking for a westward route to the Orient. On 12 October of that year he arrived in Cuba. He averaged **150 miles per day**.

Concorde was designed as the first commercial supersonic aeroplane. Its record time from New York to London is 2 hours 54 minutes 45 seconds.
Its cruising speed is **1336 miles per hour**.

1 Looking back ◀◀

Exercise 1.1

1 Below are listed six activities that Janine did on Tuesday.
The times when she did them are also listed.
Match each activity with the most appropriate time.

Activity	Time
Go to bed	08 10
Listen to music	20 15
Eat breakfast	21 42
Go home after school	16 05
Play badminton	18 30
Go to school	08 39

2 Here is part of a TV guide.

4 35	The Art of Secrecy
5 05	Brookside Omnibus
7 00	Channel 4 News
7 30	Blues Singers of the Year
9 10	The Saturday Evening Film
11 05	Top Ten Female Soap Characters

a Which TV channel is being advertised?

b Which day is the guide for?

c How long does *The Art of Secrecy* last?

d How long does *Blues Singers* last?

e *Top Ten Female Soap Characters* lasts for 1 hour 35 minutes. What time does it finish?

3 Ms Blake puts her car in a multi-storey car park at 11.14 a.m. and arrives back at 4.46 p.m.

a How long has she parked for?

b How much does her parking cost?

City Car Park
Up to
1 hour £2·00
2 hours £3·80
4 hours £7·00
8 hours £12·00

4 Pam checks her alarm clock as she goes to bed.

She presses the alarm set button to check when her alarm will go off in the morning.

How long does she have until the alarm goes off?

5 Calculate how far each person will go in an hour.

a Usman cycled 4 miles in a quarter of an hour.

b Ella walked 2 km in 10 minutes.

c Mike's on a high speed train which travelled 65 km in 20 minutes.

d Mary Foster drove 5 km in 5 minutes.

2 Measuring time

Stopwatches are used to time events.
Most sporting events these days require to be measured to the nearest 100th of a second.
The average person's reaction time is measured in tenths of a second and so the timing of sporting events is generally controlled by mechanical devices or computers.

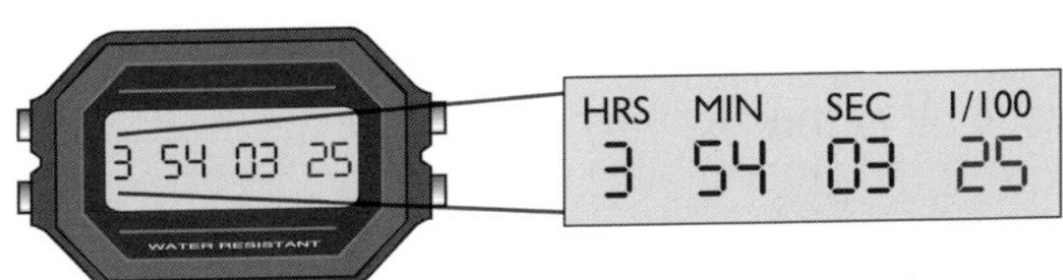

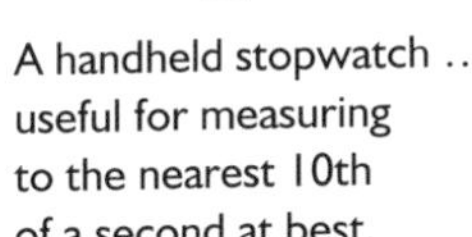

A handheld stopwatch … useful for measuring to the nearest 10th of a second at best.

An electronic timer … capable of measuring to the nearest 100th of a second or better.

This is often written 3h 54′ 03·25″
… 3h 54′ 03·3″ to the nearest 10th of a second
… 3h 54′ 03″ to the nearest second
… 3h 54′ to the nearest minute
… 3h 50′ to the nearest 10 minutes
… 4h to the nearest hour

Exercise 2.1

1 Round the following readings to the nearest

i tenth of a second **ii** second **iii** minute
iv 10 minutes **v** hour.

a

HRS	MIN	SEC	1/100
0	15	53	37

b

HRS	MIN	SEC	1/100
0	24	46	32

c

HRS	MIN	SEC	1/100
9	40	59	99

d

HRS	MIN	SEC	1/100
7	30	50	90

e

HRS	MIN	SEC	1/100
3	59	59	28

f

HRS	MIN	SEC	1/100
8	35	30	25

2 **a** What will **1d** read 10 seconds later?

b What will **1e** read 1 minute later?

c How long will it be before **1e** reads 4 hours exactly?

d How many seconds have elapsed between **1a** and **1b**?

3 A group of people in a fitness class measure their pulse rates.
Using a stopwatch, they count the number of beats over 30 seconds.
They double their answer to calculate the number of *beats per minute* (b.p.m.).

After running on the spot for 2 minutes they check their pulses again. The results are recorded.

For 30 seconds

	Before	After
Iain	34	60
Bill	36	65
Harry	38	71
Phil	32	58

a Calculate the pulse rate, before and after exercise, for each person.

b What happens to a person's pulse rate after exercise?

c The coach says 'The lower the beat, the healthier the person'.
According to the coach who should be the healthiest?

Investigate how your own pulse rate increases after 2 minutes of exercise.

4 In 1999, Maurice Greene (USA) ran the 100 m in 9·79 seconds.

a Estimate his average speed using the graph as a ready reckoner.

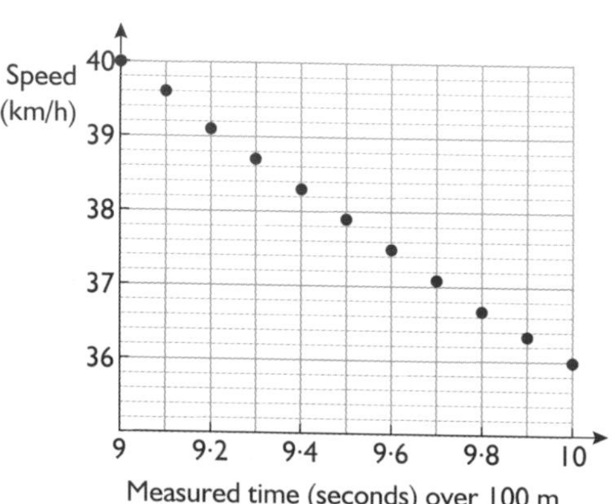

b In 1968, James Ray Hines held the 100 m record at 9·9 seconds.
How much slower was he travelling?

Investigate how fast you can travel over 100 metres using this ready reckoner and a stopwatch.

Speed (km/h): 40, 35, 30, 25, 20

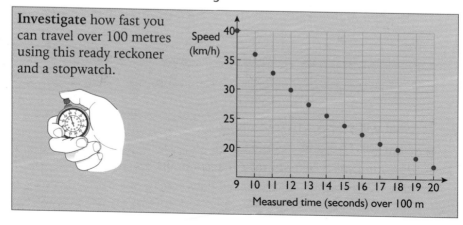

Measured time (seconds) over 100 m: 9, 10, 11, 12, 13, 14, 15, 16, 17, 18, 19, 20

Investigation

In the movie *Gregory's Girl*, one character (the class photographer) estimates seconds by counting '1 elephant, 2 elephants, 3 elephants …'.

a See how good this method is for estimating 1 minute (60 elephants)!

b Experiment with other phrases to see how close you can get.
Compare your results with others in the class and write a short report.

5 *An experiment in time.* You will need a partner and a 30 cm ruler.

Galileo was a mathematician and scientist in the sixteenth century.
His study of the motion of objects produced a formula which allows us to work out just how fast we are at reacting to situations.

- Your partner should sit with his wrist resting on a desk, hand projecting over the edge.
- Hold a ruler, as shown, so that the zero is level with the top of your partner's thumb.
- Release the ruler so that it starts to fall between your partner's thumb and forefinger.
- As soon as he is aware that the ruler is falling, he must react to stop it.
- Note the length of ruler, in millimetres, that has passed between his fingers before he stopped it.
- Use Galileo's formula to work out his reaction time.

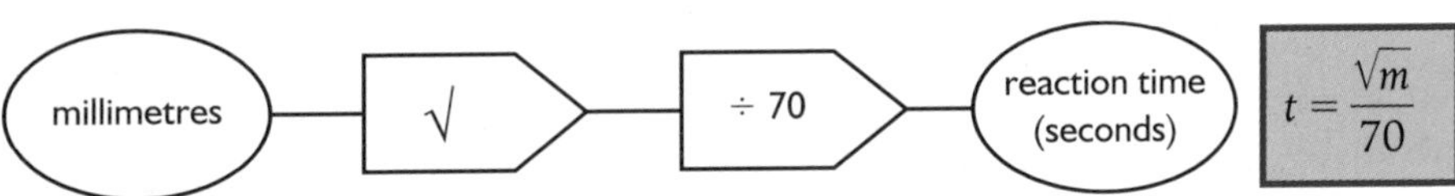

a Work out your own reaction time over several trials.

b What effect does this have on your ability to use a stopwatch to time events to the nearest 100th of a second?

3 Manipulating time

When adding, subtracting, multiplying or dividing times, we must remember that 60 minutes make an hour and 60 seconds make a minute.

Example 1 Add the following times: 12 min 36 s, 24 min 45 s, 32 min 29 s, 10 min 17 s

Step 1

min	s
12	36
24	45
32	29
10	17

127 s

Total the seconds column

Step 2

min	s
12	36
24	45
32	29
10_2	17
	7

= 2 min 7 s

… change to minutes and seconds

Step 3

min	s
12	36
24	45
32	29
10_2	17
	7

80 min

Total the minutes column

Step 4

	min	s
	12	36
	24	45
	32	29
	10_2	17
1 h	20	7

1 h 20 min

… change to hours and minutes

Answer: 1 h 20 min 7 s

Example 2 Subtract 4 h 35 min from 6 h 18 min.

h	min
6	18
4	35

We can't take 35 min from 18 min so we rewrite 6 h 18 min as 5 h 78 min

h	min
5	78
4	35
1	43

Answer: 1 h 43 min

Example 3 Multiply 4 h 35 min by 6.

Step 1

h	min
4	35
	×6
24	210

Multiply each column separately by 6

Step 2

h	min
4	35
	×6
24	**3 h 30 min**

Change minutes to hours and minutes

Step 3

h	min
4	35
	×6
27	30
24	**3 h 30 min**

Combine the hours

Answer: 27 h 30 min

Example 4 Divide 11 h 14 min 24 s by 4.

```
     h   min   s          h   min   s          h   min   s
  4 | 11  14  24       4 | 11  14  24       4 | 11  14  24
                              194                 194  144
                         ----------          --------------
                          2                    2   48   36
```

11 ÷ 4 = 2 remainder 3 hours
= 2 remainder 180 min
180 min + 14 min = 194 min

194 ÷ 4 = 48 remainer 2 min
= 48 remainder 120 s
120 s + 24 s = 144 s

144 ÷ 4 = 36

Answer: 2 h 48 min 6 s

Many calculators now have a button that makes it easy to do calculations with time.
Check your calculator manual for **hexadecimal calculations.**

Exercise 3.1

1 Add each set of times.

- **a** 3 h 24 min and 2 h 45 min
- **b** 5 h 58 min and 1 h 54 min
- **c** 35 min 43 s and 45 min 27 s
- **d** 54 min 26 s and 10 min 50 s
- **e** 2 h 36 min 33 s and 3 h 49 min 42 s
- **f** 4 h 44 min 12 s and 5 h 51 min 56 s
- **g** 2 h 46 min and 47 min 42 s

2 Find the difference between these times.

- **a** 4 h 24 min and 2 h 56 min
- **b** 5 h 17 min and 1 h 50 min
- **c** 17 min 46 s and 12 min 52 s
- **d** 3 h 25 min 17 s and 1 h 25 min 20 s
- **e** 5 h 36 min 42 s and 2 h 40 min 19 s

3 Calculate:

- **a** 2 h 34 min × 3
- **b** 3 h 17 min × 5
- **c** 5 h 40 min × 4
- **d** 1 min 14 s × 10
- **e** 2 min 35 s × 6
- **f** 12 min 15 s × 7
- **g** 5 h 15 min 20 s × 5
- **h** 3 h 25 min 31 s × 4

4 Evaluate:

- **a** 3 h 40 min ÷ 4
- **b** 1 h 36 min ÷ 2
- **c** 6 h 50 min ÷ 5
- **d** 4 h 30 min ÷ 10
- **e** 18 h 33 min ÷ 7
- **f** 24 min 36 s ÷ 6
- **g** 1 h 29 min ÷ 10
- **h** 5 h 21 min ÷ 5
- **I** 7 h 1 min ÷ 3

E

5 A CD has 14 tracks with the following playing times:

4:33 (4 min 33 s), 3:42, 7:27, 4:53, 3:06, 7:04,
3:50, 4:39, 3:22, 5:03, 4:46, 4:26, 3:30 and 11:19.

a What is the total playing time of the first three tracks?

b Calculate the total playing time of the last three tracks.

c What is the difference between the playing times of track 1 and track 14?

d How much longer is track 6 than track 7?

e Calculate the mean playing time of tracks 8 to 11.

6 Janice worked 6 h 25 min each day for 5 days.

a Calculate the total time worked.

b If she had worked 36 hours she would have received a bonus. How much short of that time was she?

7 A biology class were doing an experiment adding iodine to a starch solution. They timed how long it took for the solution to change colour. Here are the results of twelve students.

	minutes	seconds		minutes	seconds		minutes	seconds
Adam	1	6	Ellen	1	3	Iain	0	58
Bill	0	55	Fred	1	7	Jan	1	0
Carol	0	59	Gerry	0	52	Kelly	1	12
Davina	1	10	Hal	0	53	Lianne	0	56

a What is the sum of the times which took over 1 minute?

b What is the difference in time between the fastest and slowest reaction?

c Calculate the mean time for the chemical reaction.

8 Here are some new world records recorded for swimming events in the summer of 2000.

		Time			
Winner	Event	min	s	1/100	Country
Ian Thorpe	200 m freestyle	1	45	69	Australia
Ian Thorpe	200 m freestyle	1	45	51	Australia
Ian Thorpe	400 m freestyle	3	41	33	Australia
Geoff Huegill	50 m butterfly	0	23	60	Australia
Alex Popov	50 m freestyle	0	21	64	Australia
Tom Malchow	200 m butterfly	1	55	18	USA

a i By how much did Ian Thorpe improve his world record for the 200 m freestyle?

ii What is his mean time for this event?

b Which was the best time over a 50 m race?

c How much faster was this race than the other 50 m races?

d How much less than 1 minute is Geoff Huegill's world record?

e How much less than 2 minutes is Tom Malchow's world record?

f Calculate the mean time for the 50 m events.

9 Margaret has a 3-hour video tape. She wishes to record a series of programmes on it. They are all the same length and she has been told that the tape will just hold eight episodes.

a What is the length of one episode?

b There are 18 episodes in all. What total length of time will Margaret need?

c Assuming she fills a tape when she can, what length of time is recorded on the last tape?

d What is the mean time recorded per tape?

10 **a** Malik has worked out that it will take him 3 hours and 25 minutes to prepare the dinner. He starts at 17 minutes to 1. When will the dinner be ready?

b It is recommended that the sweet be taken out the fridge 18 minutes before the meal starts. At what time should it be removed?

c Saida is also preparing a meal.
She knows it will take her 2 hours 35 minutes to prepare.
She wants to start serving at 6 o'clock in the evening.
When should she start her preparations?

11 A water tank holds 1000 litres. At 1.25 p.m. Sam opened a valve to start draining it. By 2.15 p.m. 250 litres had drained away.

a What time did it take to drain 250 litres?

b At what time will the whole tank be drained?

c What assumptions do you make to answer part **b**?

In the previous question we assume that the same amount of water drains out in the same time.
We say that the **rate** at which the water drains is fixed.

Example 5 Oil seeps out of a 1000 ml can so that it is empty in 25 minutes. At what rate per minute is it leaking?

$1000 \div 25 = 40$ ml per minute.

Example 6 Jan has an old fashioned record player. The record she is playing turns at a rate of 45 revolutions per minute.
A song lasts 3 minutes and 24 seconds. How many times will the record turn during the song?

3 min 24 s = $3\frac{24}{60}$ min, so it turn $45 \times 3\frac{24}{60} = 153$ times.

E

Exercise 3.2

1 Express each of the following as a rate.

a A secretary typed up a 5000 word report in 40 minutes (words per minute).

b At a factory a machine can fill 14 400 bags of sugar in one hour (bags per second).

c A record turned 148·5 times as it played a 4 minute 30 second song (revolutions per minute).

d In June 37·5 cm of rain fell over the 30 days (centimetres per day).

2 The following facts were discovered from reading an old book of records. Turn them into suitable rates.

a Ray Craig of Indiana picked 151 bushels of apples in 8 hours.

b The registrar at the US treasury signed 12 500 bonds in a 48-hour period.

c Joseph Raglon layed 3472 bricks in 60 minutes.

d Nicholas Willey clapped his hands 118 440 times in 14 hours and 6 minutes.

e D. Coghlan shovelled 508 kg of coal in 56·6 seconds.

f Bruno Leuthardt, a teacher, over 11 years travelled a total of 4070 miles to work and back, and was late only once.

g Rolf Elfso, a barber, gave 610 haircuts in 80 hours.

h J. Moir of a Belfast shipyard fitted 11 209 rivets in 9 hours.

Perhaps you could find out if any of these records have been broken.

3 From 4.17 p.m. until 6.25 p.m., John managed to address 256 envelopes.

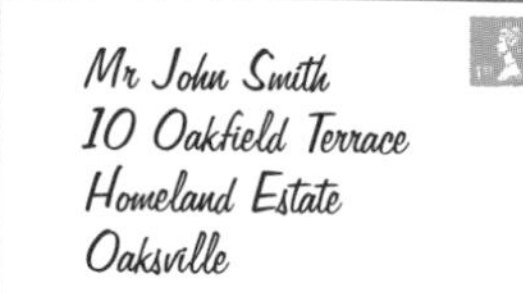

a At what rate (envelopes per minute) is he working?

b At the same rate, by which time will he have completed 300 envelopes?

4 On 1st March a plant first showed above the ground. By the end of 10th March it was 8 cm high.

a At what rate is the plant growing?

b When full grown, the plant is 30 cm tall.

Assuming a fixed rate of growth, on what date will it achieve its full size?

5 Terry and Pat were checking components in a factory. From 9.00 till 10.40 Terry checked 260 components. From 9.15 to 10.40 Pat checked 238.

a Work out, in components per minute, the work rate of

i Terry ii Pat.

b Starting together, both check 500 components each. What is the time difference in their finishing?

c Their supervisor gives them another 999 components to check. Working together, how long will it take the pair of them to complete the check?

4 Speed – a special rate

Speed is the rate at which a distance is covered.

- The slowest mammal is the 3-toed sloth which has a ground speed of about 4 cm per second.
- Man can run at about 9 metres per second.
- A car cannot travel faster than 70 miles per hour on the motorway.

A car may speed up on the straights and slow down on the bends, but if it covers 60 miles in a period of an hour, we would say its **average speed** is 60 miles per hour (m.p.h.).

$$\text{average speed} = \frac{\text{distance covered}}{\text{time taken}}$$

Note that *units must be consistent*. If distance is measured in metres and the time is measured in minutes then the speed is in metres per minute.

Example 1 Drew runs in a marathon and takes four hours exactly to run the 26 miles.
What was his average speed in miles per hour?

$S = \frac{D}{T} = \frac{26}{4} = 6{\cdot}5$ miles per hour (m.p.h.)

Example 2 A cyclist travelled 45 km in 2 hours 15 minutes.
What was her average speed in kilometres per hour?

$S = \frac{D}{T} = \frac{45}{2^h15^m} = \frac{45}{2{\cdot}25}$

$= 20$ kilometres per hour (km/h)

Remember to keep units **consistent**.
15 min $= \frac{15}{60} = 0{\cdot}25$ hour

Exercise 4.1

1 Use the formula $S = \frac{D}{T}$ to calculate the average speed for each example in this table. (Be careful with units.)

	a	b	c	d	e	f	g	h
Distance	95 km	210 miles	171 km	900 miles	75 cm	275 metres	5 km	6 km
Time	5 hours	2 hours	3 hours	2 hours	3 seconds	55 min	10 hours	30 min
Units	km/h	m.p.h.	km/h	m.p.h.	cm/s	m/min	m/h	km/h

2 Find Rob's average walking speed if he takes 2 hours to walk 22 km.

3 Gordon is training for fell-running competitions. His coach times his practice run as 8 miles in 2·5 hours.

a What is his average speed for the run?

b He takes 2 hours for the 4 miles uphill and half an hour for the downhill run.

i What is his uphill speed? **ii** What is his downhill speed?

4 Swifts fly to better feeding grounds in wet Scottish weather.
One group recorded flew 1200 miles to the Baltic coast in exactly one day.
Calculate their average speed in miles per hour.

5 Jenny takes 60 seconds to run 475 metres.
Calculate her average speed in metres per second correct to 2 decimal places.

6 A tennis star's serve travels a distance of 18 metres in 0·31 s.
Calculate the average speed of the serve in:

a metres per second

b kilometres per hour.

F

7 A bus leaves Galashiels at 9.35 a.m.
It arrives in Dalkeith at 10.15 a.m.
The distance between these two towns is 27 miles.

a Calculate the average speed of the bus.

b A car which left 5 minutes after the bus arrived in Dalkeith 3 minutes before it. What was the car's average speed?

Using fractions of an hour

Example 3 In a rally, a car travelled 350 miles in 5 hours 8 minutes. What was the average speed of the rally car?

Answer:

5 hours 8 minutes = $5\frac{8}{60}$ hours = 5·1333 … hours

$$S = \frac{D}{T} = \frac{350}{5\frac{8}{60}} \approx \frac{350}{5 \cdot 1333}$$

= 68 miles per hour (to the nearest mile per hour)

Exercise 4.2

1 George is training for a half marathon race of 13 miles.
His best time so far is 2 hours 10 minutes.
Calculate his average speed over the distance.

2 Carl Lewis, when Olympic champion, ran the 200 metre sprint in 19·8 seconds.
Calculate how fast this is in metres per second correct to 2 decimal places.

3 The fastest of bowlers can reach the batsman in $\frac{1}{2}$ second.
The distance is $\frac{1}{80}$ of a mile. Calculate this speed in miles per hour.

4 Rena travels through country lanes for the first part of her car journey.
She leaves home at 10 past 8 in the morning and looks at her watch as she joins the motorway.
It is a quarter past 9. She has travelled 42 miles.
90 miles later Rena leaves the motorway. Her watch says 25 to 11.

a Calculate the average speed for each part of Rena's journey.

b Calculate the average speed for the whole of Rena's journey.

Investigation

When talking about supersonic speeds, such as with Concorde, we sometimes hear the expression 'Mach numbers' used.
Find out what you can about Mach numbers and what they have to do with speed.
Where did the word 'Mach' come from?

F

5 Back in time

When the speed is known, then the time taken to cover specified distances can be easily calculated.

Example 1

How long does it take to complete a car journey of 180 miles when you travel at an average speed of 45 miles per hour?

Answer:
The car covers 45 miles each hour.
We need to work out how many 45s there are in 180. $180 \div 45 = 4$
The journey will take 4 hours.

$$\text{Time taken} = \frac{\text{distance covered}}{\text{speed}} \qquad T = \frac{D}{S}$$

Example 2 How long does it take for Concorde to reach New York from Heathrow, London, a distance of 2324 miles, travelling at an average speed of 664 miles per hour?

$$T = \frac{D}{S} = \frac{2324}{664} = 3{\cdot}5 \text{ hours} = 3 \text{ hours } 30 \text{ minutes}$$

(0·5 hour = 0·5 × 60 minutes = 30 minutes)

This simple memory aid helps you remember the required formulae

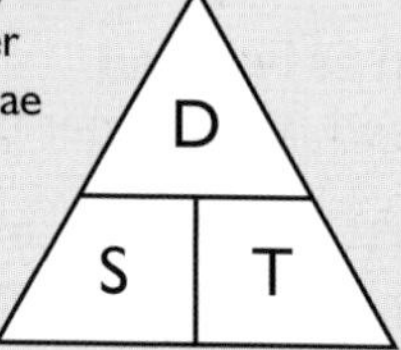

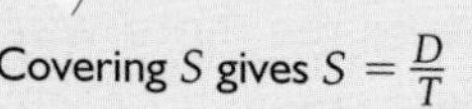

Covering S gives $S = \frac{D}{T}$

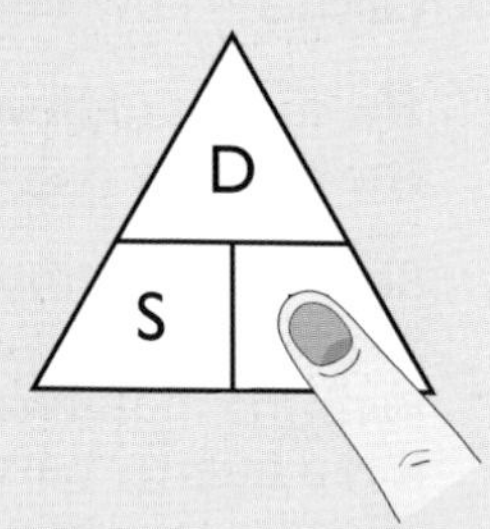

Covering T gives $T = \frac{D}{S}$

F

Exercise 5.1

1 Use the formula $T = \frac{D}{S}$ to calculate the time taken for each of the following:

	a	b	c	d	e	f	g	h
Distance	90 km	210 km	966 km	100 m	37·5 cm	100 m	91 miles	332·8 m
Speed	55 km/h	60 km/h	80·5 km/h	8 m/s	1·5 cm/s	10 km/h	28 m.p.h.	64 m/min

2 A car travels 180 km at an average speed of 60 km per hour.

a How long does it take for the journey?

b If it continues at the same speed for another 30 km, how long would this part of the journey take?

3 Eleanor reckons she can average 50 miles per hour on a journey to visit friends. They live 200 miles away.

a How long does it take for the journey?

b If she leaves home at 10.15 a.m. what time should she arrive at her friends?

4 Kelso to Stirling is 90 miles. Travelling at an average speed of 60 miles per hour:

a how long will the journey take?

b when will you have to leave to arrive at Stirling for 9.30 a.m.?

5 From London to the suburbs of Manchester is 200 miles.
Stan drives at a peak travelling time and averages 40 miles per hour.
Brian does the journey at night when the roads are quieter and averages 50 miles per hour.
How much time does Brian save by travelling at night?

6 Fiona goes to visit her parents at a weekend. They live 75 km away.
She knows she can drive at an average speed of 60 km per hour.

a At this speed, how long will the journey take her?

b If she leaves home at 9.40 a.m., what time will she arrive at her parents?
(Remember $0{\cdot}25$ hour $= 0{\cdot}25 \times 60$ minutes)

7 Nicky is sponsored to do a 10 km walk. In training she has averaged 6 km per hour.
At this speed how long will she take for her walk?

8 Jon has been training to run in the London marathon.
His best average speed is 7·5 miles per hour.
If he can maintain this speed, how long will he take for the 26 mile run?

9 The fastest that any human has travelled is 39 897 km/h.
This was the crew of the Apollo 10 on their return from flying round the moon.

a How long would it take them, in minutes, to cover 1000 km at this speed?
(Answer to 1 d.p.)

b Calculate, in seconds, the time it would take them to cover 100 km.

10 The captain of an aeroplane tells the passengers on a flight to Greece that the cruising speed of the plane is 420 miles per hour. If the distance through the skies is 1540 miles, how long will the flight take at this cruising speed?

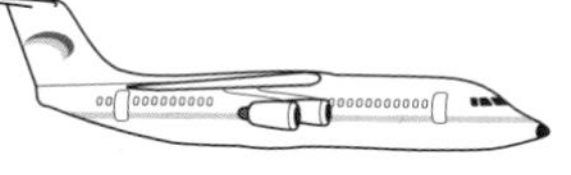

11 Ling runs a 400 metre race at an average speed of 7·5 metres per second.

a At this speed, how long does Ling take to run the race?

b The winner took an average speed of 8 metres per second.
How much sooner did she reach the winning tape in front of Ling?

12 Gill enters for a 'cycle, walk and jog' event.
The 20 mile event is divided up as follows:
cycle for 10 miles, walk for 5 miles, jog for 5 miles.
Gill sets off at nine in the morning.
Her average speed for **i** cycling is 8 miles per hour
ii walking is 3 miles per hour
iii jogging is 4 miles per hour.

a Calculate the time taken for each leg of the race.

b At what time does she finish the event?

F

6 Distance

Example 1 What distance is covered by a car travelling at an average speed of 55 miles per hour for 3 hours?

Answer:
The car covers 55 miles in 1 hour.
So it covers 55 × 3 miles in 3 hours.
It covers a distance of 165 miles.

Distance covered = Speed × Time taken

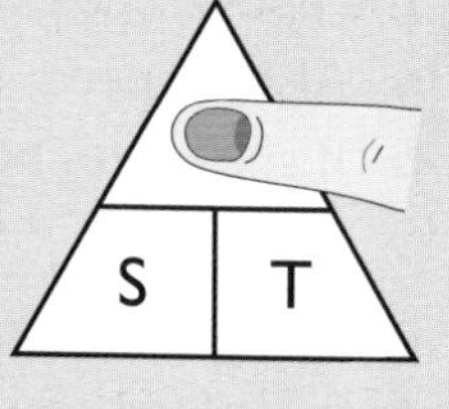

Covering D gives $D = ST$

Example 2
At Waverley station in Edinburgh, the board says
Departure time: 11 00
Arrival time: 15 45 for London.
The train travels at an average speed of 88 mph.
What is the distance from Edinburgh to London?

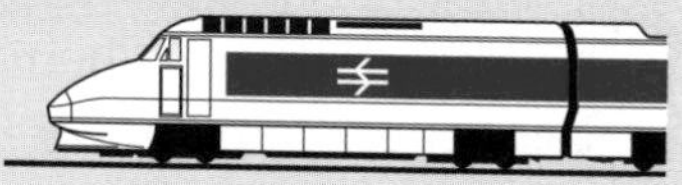

Answer:
Distance = Speed × Time

$D = S \times T$
$= 88 \times 4$ hours 45 minutes
$= 88 \times 4{\cdot}75$ hours **(45 min = 45 ÷ 60 = 0·75 hour)**
$= 418$ miles

Exercise 6.1

1 Use the formula $D = ST$ to calculate the distance in each case.

	a	**b**	**c**	**d**	**e**	**f**	**g**	**h**
Speed	40 km/h	197 km/h	9 m/s	12 m.p.h.	26 cm/s	45 cm/s	7 miles/min	3·5 m/min
Time	6 hours	2 hours	33 s	4·5 hours	17 s	2 min	1 hour	2·5 hours

2 Emma and Chas take a camper van to the 'T in the park' concert.
The journey takes $2\frac{3}{4}$ hours at an average speed of 50 m.p.h.
How far away do Emma and Chas live from the venue for 'T in the Park'?

3 Maya drove her new car at an average speed of 50 miles per hour.
She took 2 hours 15 minutes (2·25 hours) to get to her destination.
How far had she travelled?

4 A cyclist is training for a cycle event. His best speed so far is 22 km per hour.
If he could cycle for $2\frac{1}{2}$ hours at his best speed, what distance could he cover?

5 Helen hired a pony for a day's trekking. She spent 6 hours on the trek, one of which was a picnic break. If she spent the rest of the time in the saddle and the pony averages 5 miles per hour, how far did she trek?

6 A ferry boat sails between the islands of Hydra and Poros at a speed of 20 knots (nautical miles per hour).
The trip took $\frac{3}{4}$ hour.
How far apart are the islands in nautical miles?

7 Geologists monitor the San Andreas Fault which runs through San Francisco.
Measurements tell them that the fault is moving at an average rate of 5 cm per year.

a How many kilometres would it be expected to shift in 1 million years?

b Careful study has shown that in the Jurassic period the fault was only moving at an average speed of 1·2 mm per year.
The Jurassic period lasted 45 million years.
How far did the fault move in this period?

8 A coach travels from Cardiff to Hull at an average speed of 59 miles per hour.
The timetable for the bus journey says it takes 4 hours and 5 minutes.

a Express 4 hours and 5 minutes as hours.

b What is the distance between the two towns to the nearest mile?

9 The Williams set off with their caravan, logging an average speed of 72 km per hour.
What distance had they covered when they stopped for a break 2 hours and 40 minutes later?

10 A racing pigeon was released at Penzance and flew home to Belfast.
Her recorded average speed was 38 miles per hour.
She flew for 17 hours 12 minutes until she reached her loft.

a What fraction of an hour is 12 minutes?

b How far was her flight home?

11 The fastest non-stop run for a train was from Calais to Marseilles in May 2001.
For 3 hours 9 minutes it averaged a speed of 317·5 km per hour.

a How far apart are the two towns?

b If the train set out at 11.45 a.m., how far would you expect it to have gone by 1.30 p.m. at this rate?

F

12 A Sea-king helicopter flies out from its base responding to a May day call from an oil-rig. Here are the details written in the log book.

Leave base:	13 42
Arrive target:	16 16
Average speed:	176 m.p.h.
Distance covered on mission	

If the distance covered includes its return to base, how far did the helicopter fly?

13 Nick is going home for the weekend. He goes by train and gets picked up by car for the last part of the journey home. The train travels at 100 km per hour for the first 15 minutes, then speeds up to 120 km for the remaining 25 minutes. The car trip from the station to home is 27 km.
How long is Nick's journey home altogether?

14 From Almsbury to Besset is a distance of 26 km.
Sandra set out from Almsbury to Crosspatch via Besset at 12.15 p.m. and arrived at 3.40 p.m.
Her average speed was 54·6 km/h.

a What distance did she travel?

b How far is it from Besset to Crosspatch?

Challenge

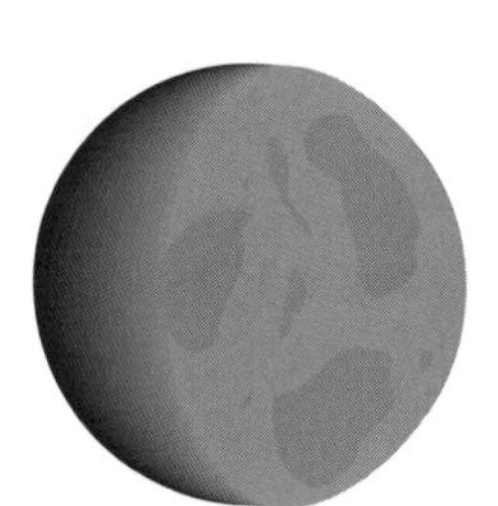

The speed at which light travels is 300 000 km per second. Scientists bounced a laser light off the surface of the moon and noted that it took 2·56 seconds to get there and back.

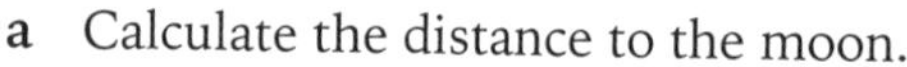

a Calculate the distance to the moon.

b The moon's speed has been calculated as 0·8 km/s.
From full moon to full moon is a period of 29·5 days.
How far, to the nearest kilometre, does the moon travel in this period?

7 All together now

Use the appropriate formula:

D | S | T

$S = \frac{D}{T}$ $T = \frac{D}{S}$ $D = ST$

Exercise 7.1

1 A greyhound can run 60 metres in 6·5 seconds.

a Calculate its average speed in metres per second.

b How far can it go in 4 seconds at this speed?

2 A plane has a cruising speed of 480 km per hour.
It flies at this speed for 3 hours 50 minutes.

a How far has it flown?

b How long will it take to travel a further 76 km at this speed?

3 Sam is travelling from Glasgow to London.
He consults a timetable to find which train is most suitable.

Leave Glasgow	14 42	17 15	18 35
Arrive London	19 26	22 05	23 05

a If the distance by rail is 450 miles. Calculate the speed of each train.

b Sam takes the fastest train. What time does it leave Glasgow?

c Glasgow is 120 miles from Carlisle.
Estimate when the train will be passing through Carlisle.

F

4 The fastest train in the world travels at a speed of 515 km per hour.

a Travelling at this speed, how far does it go in 1 hour 55 minutes?

b Galashiels is 43 km from Dalkeith. How long would it take to go from one to the other at this speed?

5 **a** From Burnt Island, an oil tanker sets out to Ghana.
It travels non-stop to its destination for 2 weeks at an average speed of 14 knots (14 nautical miles per hour).
How far is it from Burnt Island to Ghana by this route?

b The captain logged the distance on another shipping route.
From the mouth of the Mississippi to Mombassa in Kenya, a distance of 10 920 nautical miles, the tanker sailed at an average speed of 13 knots.
How many days was the tanker at sea?

6 A penalty at the 2002 World Cup was recorded at a speed of 71·5 miles per hour.
The penalty spot was 12 yards away from the goal mouth.
How long in seconds did it take the ball to cross the goal line?
Answer to the nearest $\frac{1}{100}$th second.
(**Hint:** 1 mile = 1760 yards)

8 Distance–time graphs

A distance–time graph is a good way to portray journeys.

Example

Mr and Mrs Chambers are flying to Sardinia from Manchester Airport. They set off on their journey from Galashiels at 9 o'clock one morning to drive to Manchester Airport.

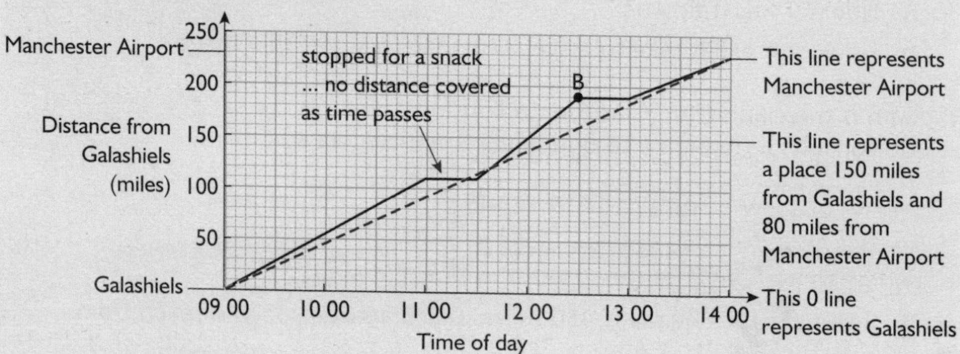

Note that overall they travelled 230 miles in 5 hours ... an average speed of 46 m.p.h.
The dotted line represents a journey made at the average speed.

F

Exercise 8.1

1 Use the graph above to help you answer the following questions.

- **a** How far did they travel in the first hour?
- **b** How far had they travelled when they stopped for a snack?
- **c** What time did they stop to have a snack?
- **d** How many times did they stop on their journey?
- **e** What time did they get to Manchester Airport?
- **f** What was the total distance for the journey?
- **g** Calculate their average speed up until they stopped for the second time (Point B).

2 Stella is taking part in a charity event.
She walks for 5 km, jogs for 5 km and runs for 2 km.
Between each stage she has a break.
She starts at 10 o'clock in the morning.

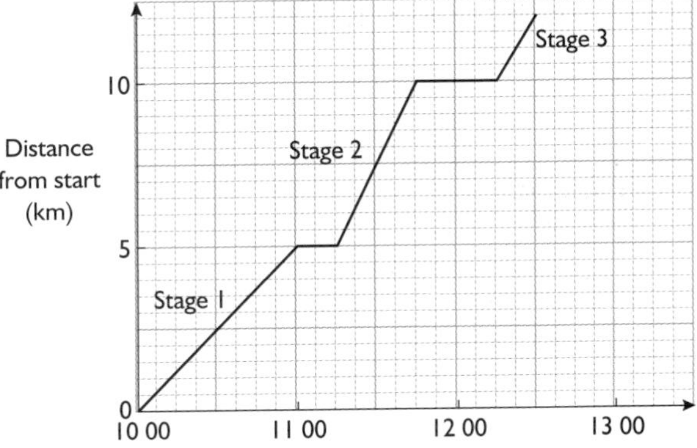

a Which event was stage 1?

b Which event was stage 2?

c How long was the first stop?

d How long did stage 2 take?

e Which event was stage 3?

f What distance was covered in stage 3?

g How far was the total event?

h How long did the whole event take?

i What was her average speed over the whole event?

3 A tour company takes American visitors to Edinburgh to watch the Tattoo at Edinburgh castle.

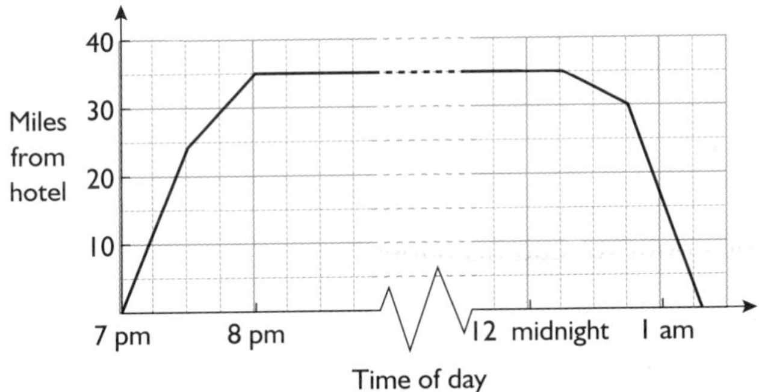

a What time did they set off from the hotel?

b How far did they travel in

i the first half hour **ii** the second half hour

c How far away is Edinburgh from their hotel?

d How long did they stop in Edinburgh?

e How long did the drive to Edinburgh take?

f How long did the drive back take?

g What time did they arrive back at the hotel?

h How long was the round trip?

i Comment on the average speed to Edinburgh and from Edinburgh.

9 Making distance–time graphs

- Time is always measured along the horizontal axis.
- Distance from start is always shown along the vertical axis.
- Scales should be in units that are easy to read.

Exercise 9.1

1 Lin and Sue are going to visit friends who live 60 miles away.
- They set off at 10 a.m. and complete the first 40 miles in an hour.
- They stop and have a cup of coffee for half an hour.
- They complete their journey in another half an hour.

Draw a graph of their journey using suitable scales.

2 Brad cycles from school to his home 4 km away.
- He sets off at 3.50 p.m. and in 20 minutes has cycled 3 km.
- He stops for 5 minutes at a shop to buy a packet of crisps.
- Then continues his journey and arrives home at 4.20 p.m.

Draw a graph of his journey.

F

3 Mike works for a delivery company. He has a delivery to make 90 km away.
- He leaves the depot at 11 o'clock in the morning.
- He travels the first 60 km in an hour.
- He stops for $\frac{1}{4}$ hour to read his paper.
- He continues his journey at the same speed until he arrives at his destination.
- He takes half an hour to complete his tasks.
- He drives back home without stopping.
  He arrives back at the depot at 2.15 p.m.

a Draw a graph of his journey using suitable scales.

b What was Mike's average speed for his homeward journey?

4 Frank and Tommy are on an army cadet training weekend.
One morning they have a 40 km cycle run to complete.
Frank sets off at 7 a.m. He travels 25 km in $1\frac{1}{2}$ hours, then he stops for half an hour to have a rest.
He travels the rest of the distance in $\frac{1}{4}$ of an hour.
Tommy sleeps in and sets off at 8 a.m. and arrives at the destination 2 hours later without stopping.

a Draw their journeys on the same graph, using appropriate scales.

b What was Tommy's average speed in kilometres per hour?

c How much later than Frank did Tommy arrive?

CHECK-UP

1 A chemistry class are doing an experiment where a red dye turns yellow due to a chemical process.
They use a stopwatch to check the time it takes to complete the process.
The experiment is repeated five times as shown:

Trial	1	2	3	4	5
Time	3 min 11 s	2 min 58 s	3 min 05 s	3 min 15 s	2 min 51 s

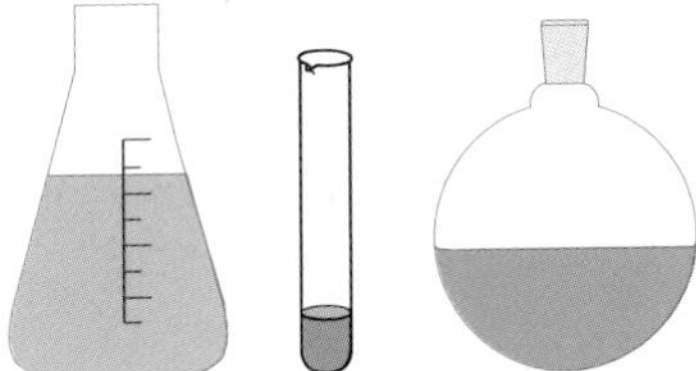

a Write down
  i the longest time taken
  ii the shortest time taken.

b Calculate the mean reaction time.

2 Calculate:

a 4 h 27 min + 3 h 42 min

b 3 h 25 min − 1 h 30 min

c 2 h 20 min × 5

d 3 h 36 min ÷ 6

3 Peter worked 6 h 30 min for 3 days and 5 h 20 min for 2 days.

a How long did he work in total?

b If he had worked 35 hours he would have been given a bonus.
How much longer would that have taken him?

4 Laurie drove along the motorway for $1\frac{1}{2}$ hours at an average speed of 92 km per hour.
How far did he travel?

5 Rachel reckons she can average 80 km per hour on a trip to visit friends.
They live 152 km away.
How long will it take for the journey?

6 Frank is in training for a boxing match.
His trainer sends him jogging every morning and records his speeds.
One day he ran 9 miles in 1 hour 15 minutes.
What was his average speed for the run?

E F

7 Jack and Jenny have tickets for a rock concert.
They set off from home at 7 p.m. on Jack's motorbike.
The graph shows their journey.

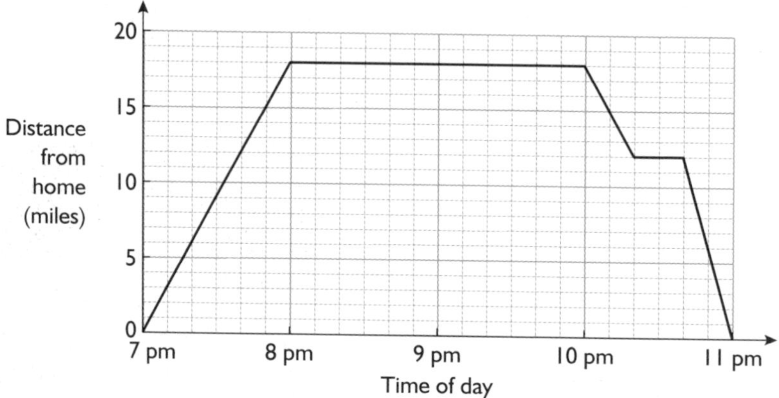

a At what time do they get to the concert?

b How far away is the concert from their home?

c How long do they stay at the concert?

d Calculate their average speed on their journey home.

8 Ali is training for a charity cycle event. His club has worked out a route for him. He is told to log his journey.

- He leaves the club at 10 a.m. and cycles 30 km in the first hour.
- He stops for half an hour.
- He then continues at a steady speed of 28 km per hour for the next $1\frac{1}{2}$ hours.

a Draw a graph of his journey using suitable scales.

b What was his average speed for the total distance?

7 Scales and coordinates

Over the centuries man has tried to describe position and journeys by drawing maps. The maps of early explorers bear little resemblance to the satellite maps we are used to today.

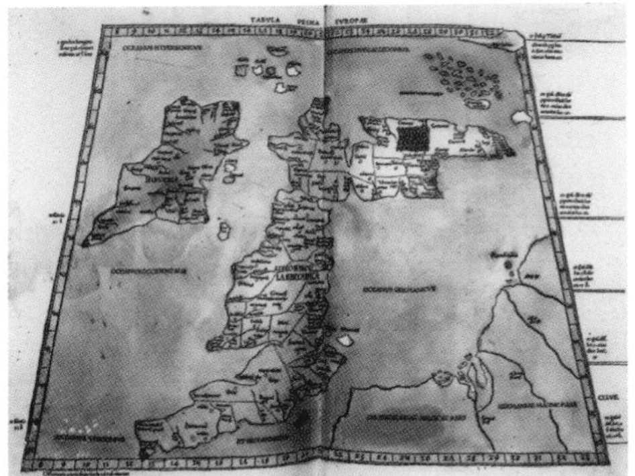

A map of Britain based on Ptolemy, 2AD

A satellite image of Britain from AD 2000

1 Looking back ◀◀

Exercise 1.1

1 Measure these angles as accurately as you can.

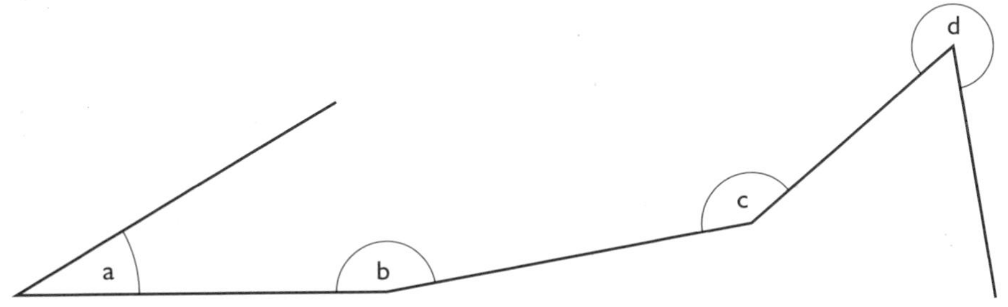

2 **a** Write down the coordinates of each point on the grid.

b Which point lies on the x axis?

c Which two points have a y coordinate of 4?

d Which point has its x coordinate equal to its y coordinate?

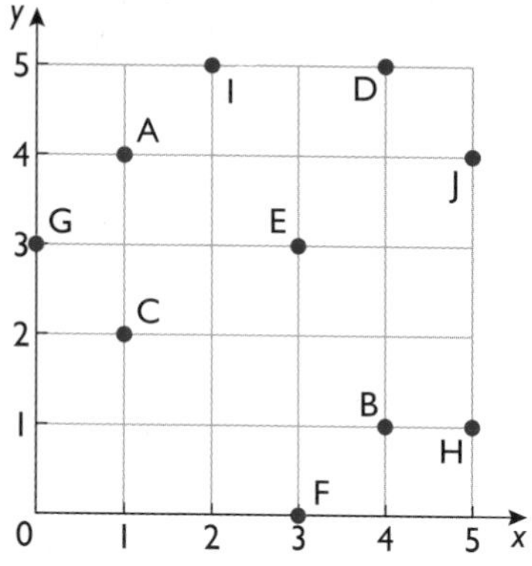

3 Draw a coordinate grid on squared paper.
Plot these points, remembering to label each one:
K (3, 5), L (1, 1), M (4, 3), N (5, 0),
O (0, 0), P (2, 1), Q (0, 2), R (5, 2).

4

apple	pear	plum
cherry	damson	crab apple
gooseberry	blackcurrant	raspberry

N

An orchard is laid out neatly in rows.

a What is north of the cherry tree?

b What is south-east of the damson?

c Two trees are north-east of the gooseberry bush.
What are they?

E

2 Scale drawings

Architects, engineers, builders and designers need accurate drawings of what they want to build or make. They need to *scale down* the sizes to fit the paper or screen they are using.

Here is a plan of a garden.
The sizes have been reduced to a scale where
1 cm represents 10 metres.

Garden of No. 16 High St

N

flowers

grass

path

vegetables

0 10 20 30 km

This means for every 10 metres of actual garden, 1 cm is drawn.
The actual garden is 60 metres long and 22 metres wide.

Scaling it down:

10 m is represented by 1 cm

$\Rightarrow$ 60 m is represented by $(60 \div 10)$ cm $= 6$ cm

Similarly 22 m is represented by 2·2 cm.

On the plan the vegetable patch is 5·3 cm long and 1·2 cm wide.
This means that the actual garden is $5{\cdot}3 \times 10 = 53$ metres long
and $1{\cdot}2 \times 10 = 12$ metres wide.

Exercise 2.1

1 **a** Measure the height of the tree in centimetres.

b What is the height of the real tree?

Scale: 1 cm *represents* 1 metre.

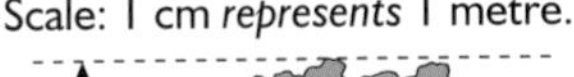

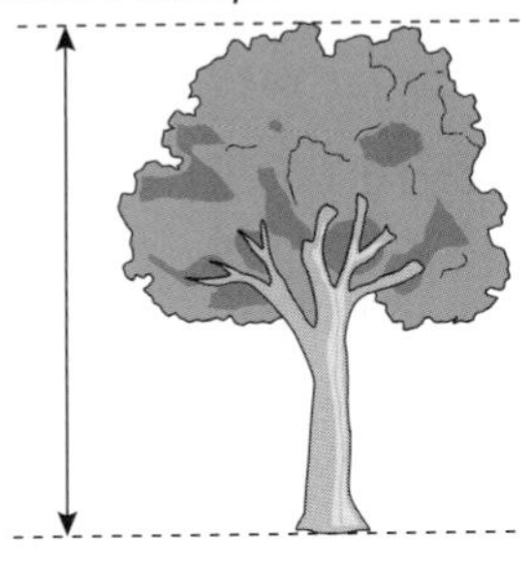

2 **a** Measure the height of the building in centimetres.

b How tall is the actual building?

Scale: 1 cm *represents* 2 metres.

3 This is a scale drawing of an advertising board.

a Write down the dimensions of the actual board.

b How tall is the bottle in the advert?
Scale: 1 cm represents 2 metres.

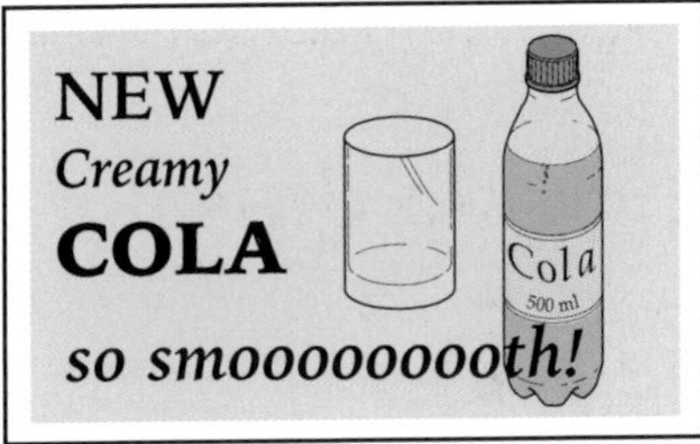

4 This is a scale drawing of a car approaching a garage. It has been drawn to a scale of 1 cm to 1 m.

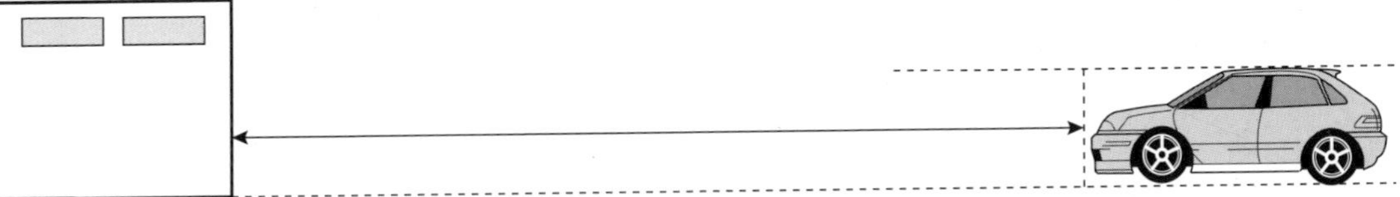

a How high is the garage?

b How tall is the car?

c How much clearance is there between the top of the car and the roof of the garage?

d How far is the car from the front of the garage?

5 The map shows the farms around Loch Leerie.
The scale of the map is 1 cm to 2 km.

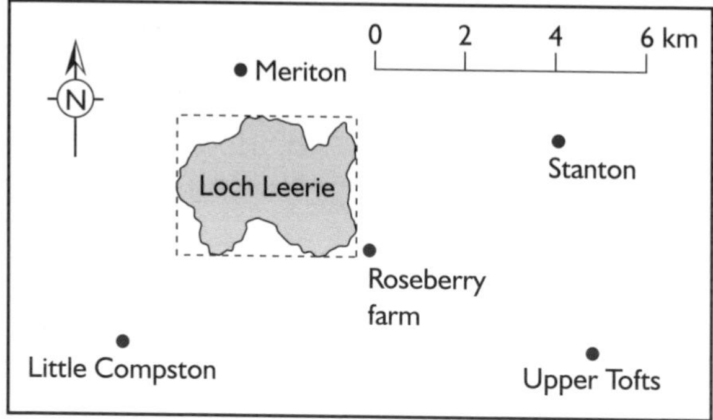

a **i** Measure the length and breadth of Loch Leerie at its widest.
ii Write down its actual dimensions.

b **i** Measure the distance between Roseberry farm and Little Compston on the map.
ii What is the actual distance between them?

c This distance has been placed on the distance chart.
Copy and complete the chart.

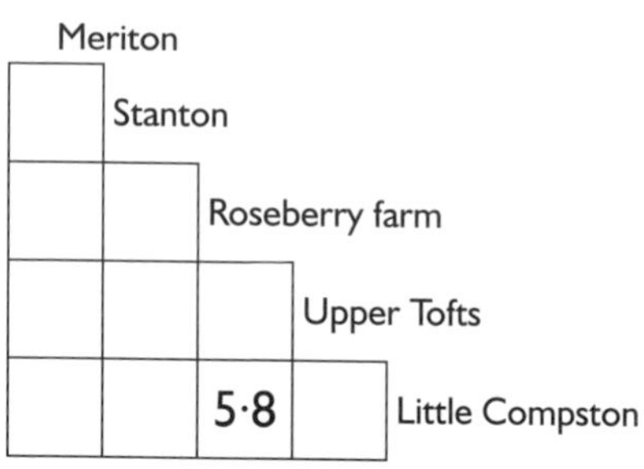

6 This is a plan of Bert's garden.

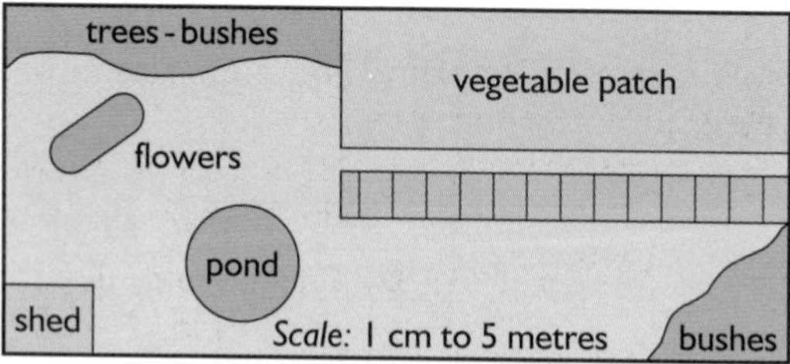

a What are the dimensions of the actual vegetable patch?

b Write down the diameter of the pond.

c Bert needs to place a new fence round his garden.
It costs £4 per metre.
How much will it cost him to replace his fence?

7 An orienteering course is laid out as shown in the diagram. The scale of the map is 1 cm to 200 metres.

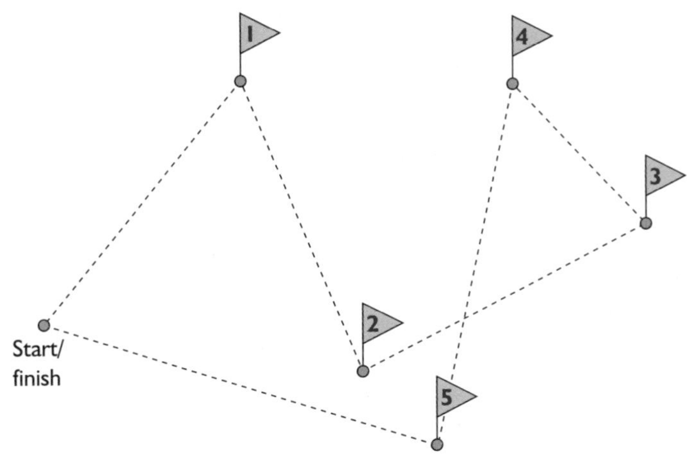

a Copy and complete the table.

	Distance on map	Distance on ground
Start to 1	cm	m
1 to 2		
2 to 3		
3 to 4		
4 to 5		
5 to Finish		

b What is the total length of the course?

c Write this distance in kilometres.

8 Here is a map of the region round Ben Law.

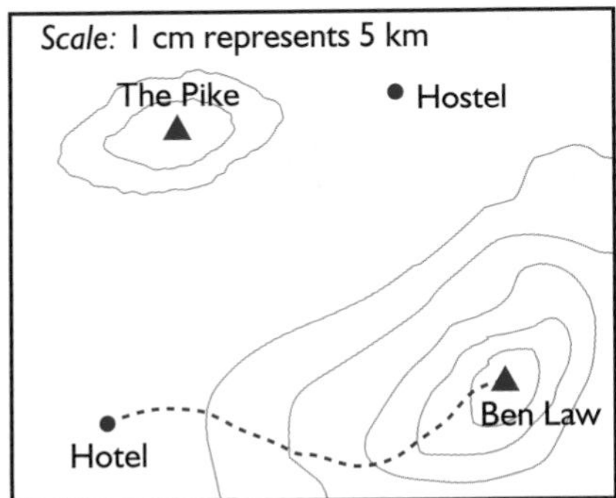

a How far is it between the hostel and the hotel?

b Cairns mark the top of each mountain.
How far is it from the top of The Pike to Ben Law?

c The dotted line shows the path that runs from the hotel to the top of Ben Law.
Estimate the length of the path.

E

3 Making scale drawings

The larger the plan, the more accurate the measurements we take from it will be. So we try to make the most use of the paper available.

Example A builder has a plot of land he wishes to develop. He visits the site and makes a rough sketch, marking on it the actual measurements he needs.

N
400 m
100 m
250 m
100 m
150 m
High St Plot

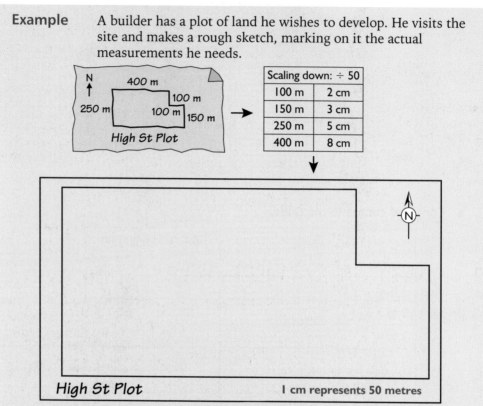

Scaling down: ÷ 50	
100 m	2 cm
150 m	3 cm
250 m	5 cm
400 m	8 cm

N

High St Plot **1 cm represents 50 metres**

Choosing the best scale he can, he makes an accurate scale drawing.
He can now use his drawing to try out different building layouts without having to return to the site.

Exercise 3.1

Make accurate drawings of these sketches using the scales given.
You will need a sharp pencil, a ruler, and an angle measurer to make right angles, and a set of compasses.

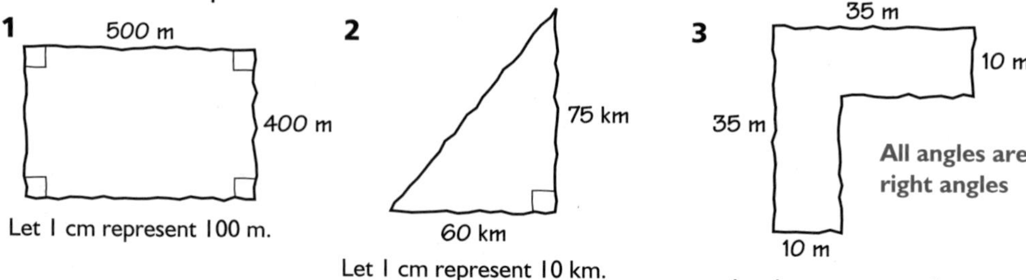

Let 1 cm represent 100 m.

Let 1 cm represent 10 km.

Let 1 cm represent 5 m.

4

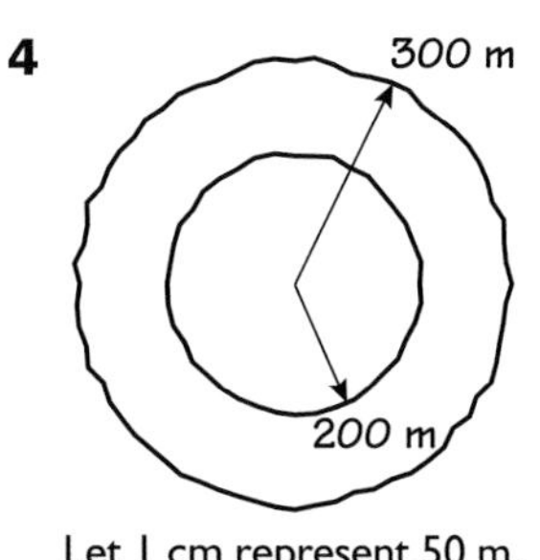

Let 1 cm represent 50 m.

5

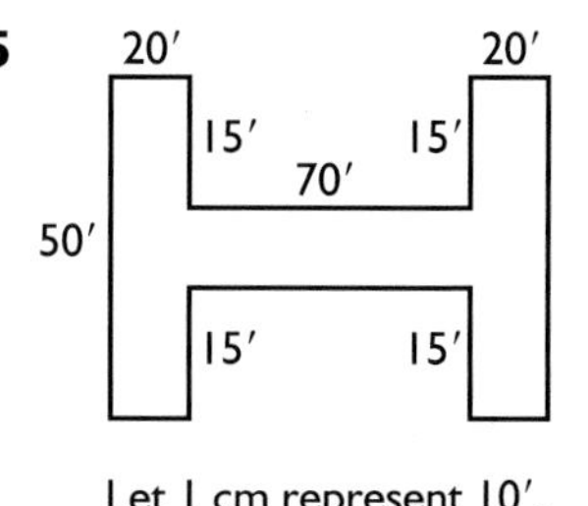

Let 1 cm represent 10′.

6

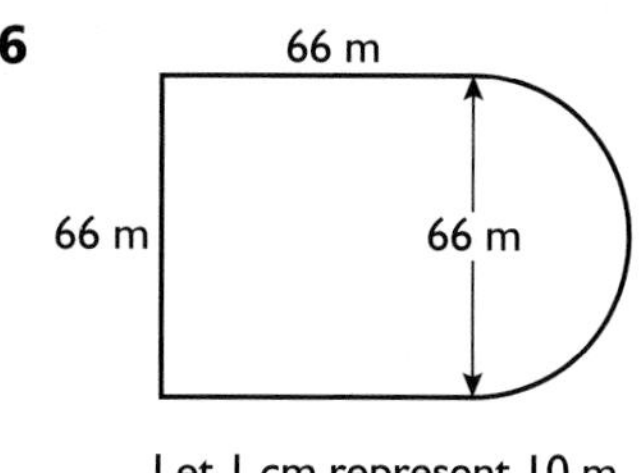

Let 1 cm represent 10 m.

Sometimes there is a need to scale up objects!

7

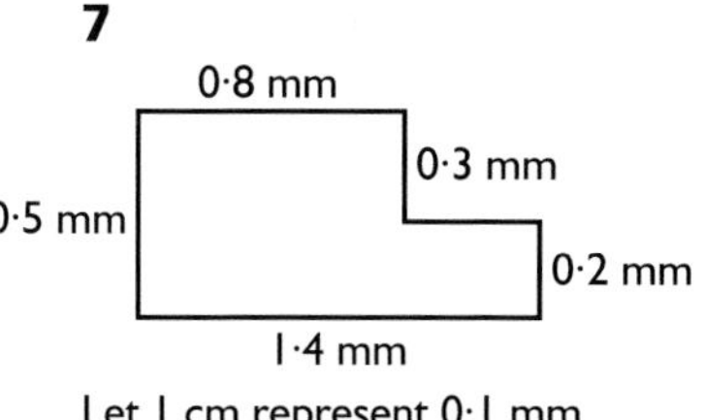

Let 1 cm represent 0·1 mm.

8

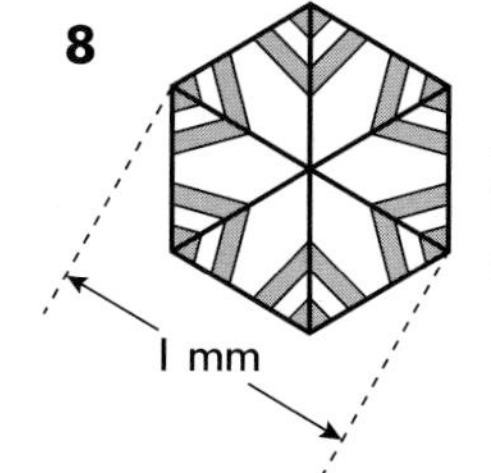

A snowflake is hexagonal and 1 mm across.

Let 1 cm represent 0·25 mm.

4 Directions and journeys

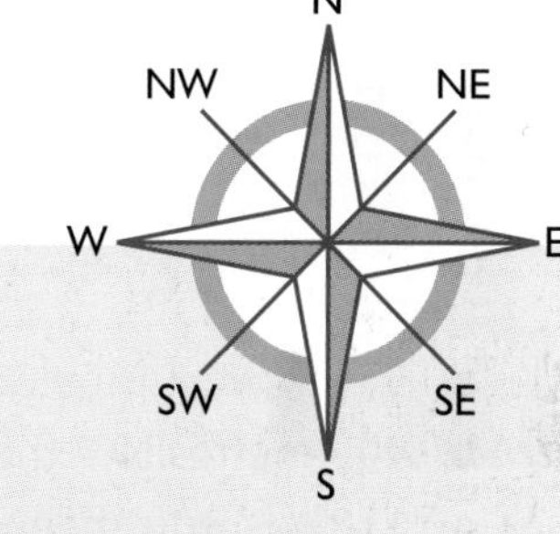

Plans of journeys can be drawn by using compass directions and scales.

Example From home, Julie cycles 20 km east, then 15 km south-east.

a Make a drawing of the journey, using a scale of 1 cm to 5 km.

b Work out from the drawing how far she is from home.

Answer:

First draw a sketch.

N
90°
180° − 45° = 135°
20 km
45°
15 km
? km

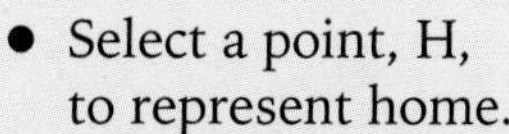

- Select a point, H, to represent home.
- Draw a line 4 cm east to represent 20 km.
- Measure an angle of 135° as shown.
- Make the line 3 cm long to represent 15 km and find F, the end of the journey.
- Measure HF: 6·5 cm
- Scale it up to find her distance from home:
  actual distance = 6·5 × 5 = 32·5 km

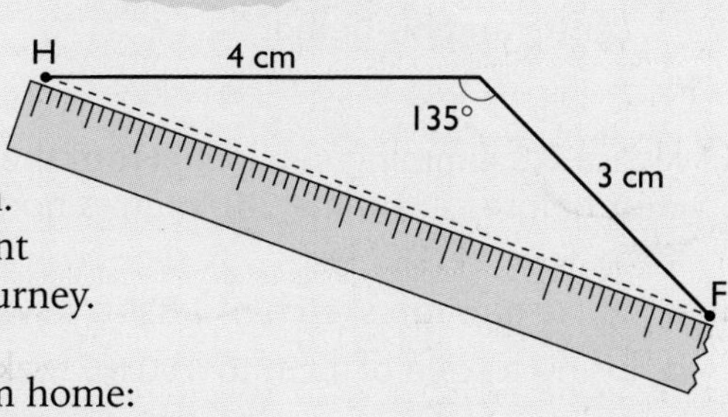

Exercise 4.1

1 A ship leaves port and sails 70 km east, then 50 km north.

   a Make an accurate scale drawing of the journey. Remember to put in a north line.

   b i Measure the distance on your drawing between the ship and the port.

   ii Work out how far the ship has to travel to return to port.

2 Maya leaves home and drives south-east for 6 miles, then drives south for 4 miles.

   a Calculate the size of the angle between north and south-east.

   b Use a scale of 1 cm to 1 mile to make an accurate scale drawing of Maya's journey.

   c Use your drawing to work out the direct distance between Maya and her home.

3 For each of these journeys make an accurate scale drawing and from it work out the direct distance to the starting point. Remember to draw a sketch first.

   a 55 km west then 68 km north

   b 400 metres NW then 650 m west

   c 110 m south then 74 m NE

4 Craig set off from home on a run to the sports centre. He ran 88 m in a north-westerly direction, 1400 m east then 1100 m south to reach the sports centre.

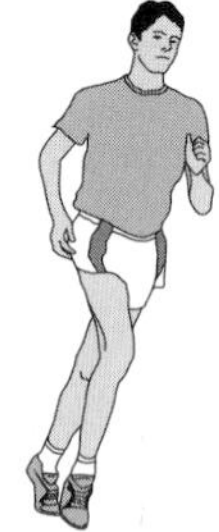

   a Using a scale of 1 cm to represent 200 metres, make a scale drawing of Craig's run.

   b What is the direct distance between the sports centre and his home?

5 Jessica is swimming in a loch. From the jetty Jessica swims 450 metres south-west before swimming 740 metres north. She then swims straight back to the jetty.

   a Make a rough sketch of Jessica's swim.

   b Using a scale of 1 cm to 100 m, make an accurate scale drawing.

   c Use your drawing to work out how far she swam altogether.

5 Three-figure bearings

Using the mariner's compass allows us to describe eight main directions.
We can add more by defining directions halfway between these eight, e.g. between *north* and *north-east* we have *north-north-east*.
However, the names become long and slightly confusing.

A method has been developed which, for all practical purposes, allows us to describe any direction easily.

Using a compass we can always find north.

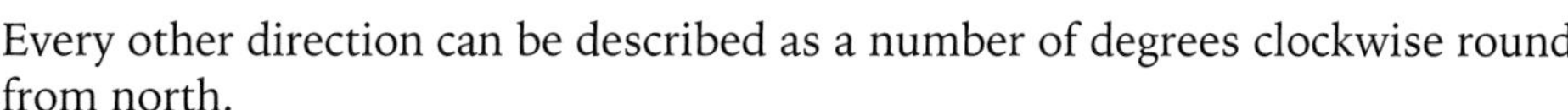

Every other direction can be described as a number of degrees clockwise round from north.

Generally the angle is quoted using three digits, and such angles are called **3-figure bearings**.

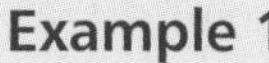

Example 1 A plane flies from A to B.
On what bearing is it flying?

Measure angle NAB. It is 115°.
So the direction would be described as a **bearing of 115°**.

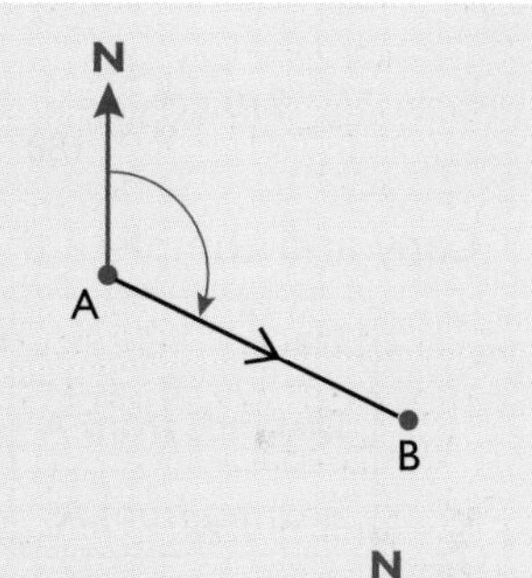

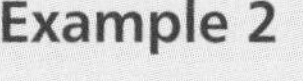

Example 2 The plane returns from B to A.
On what bearing is it flying now?

Measure angle NBA clockwise.
It is 295°.
So the direction would be described as a **bearing of 295°**.

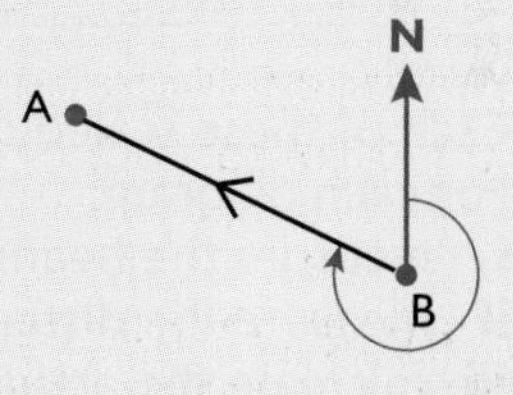

- On one map all arrows indicating north are parallel.
- When an angle is less than 100° we add a leading zero to give it three figures, e.g. 079°.

Exercise 5.1

1 Express each of the following compass points as a 3-figure bearing.

a E	**b** S	**c** W	**d** N
e NE	**f** SW	**g** NW	**h** SE

2 The *SS Arctic Explorer* is caught in the ice. Four survey teams set out from it in different directions.

Use an angle measurer to find the 3-figure bearing of each.

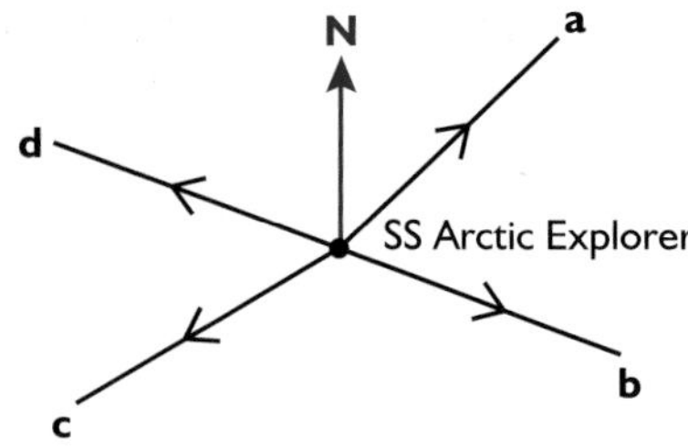

3

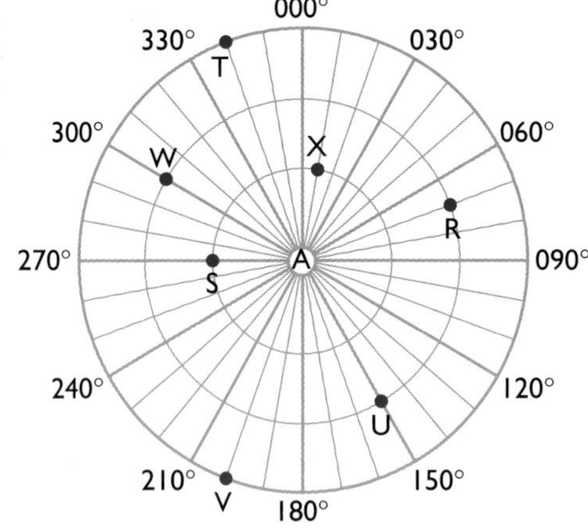

A radar station is situated at Airport A.
It shows the positions of planes on a screen.
The airport itself is in the centre of the diagram.
The rings represents distances of 50 km, 100 km and 150 km.
Plane R is 100 km from the airport, on a bearing of 070°.

Copy and complete the table:

Plane	R	S	T	U	V	W	X
Distance from A	100 km						
Bearing from A	070°						

4 Each of these scaled diagram shows the relative position of two towns. For each diagram:

i measure the bearing of the town (S) from the town (P)
ii measure the distance on the diagram from one town to the other
iii calculate the actual distance between the towns.

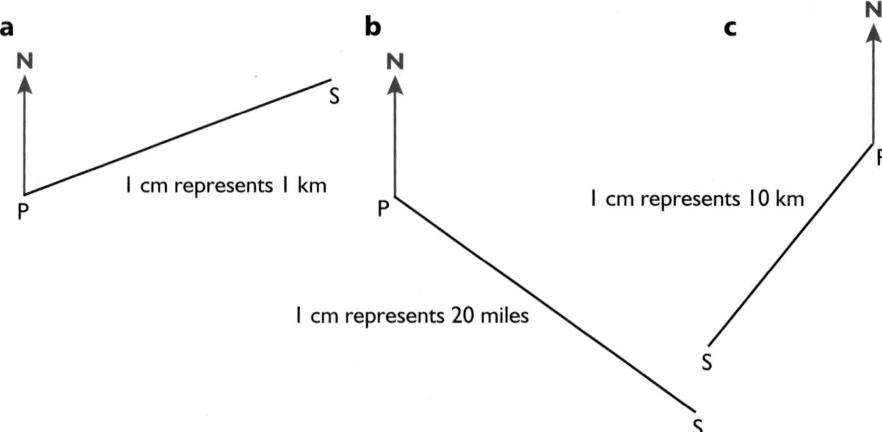

5 This scaled diagram shows the course for a cross-country bike race.
The cyclists go from A to B to C to A.

Copy and complete the table:

	Bearing	Distance
Leg 1		
Leg 2		
Leg 3		

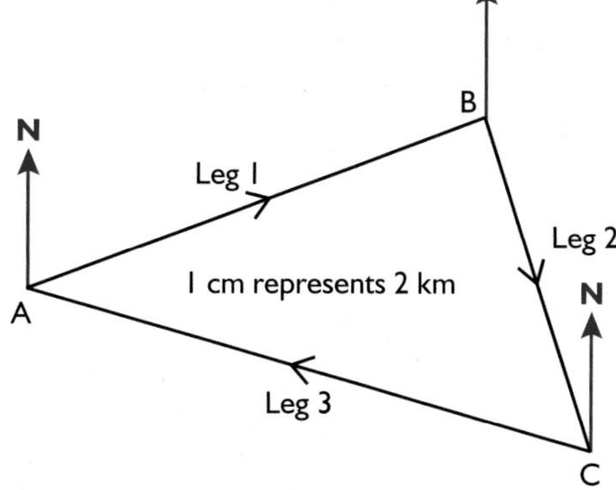

6 P, Q and R are marker buoys for sailing trials.
A boat sails from P round Q and R then back to P.

a For each part of the course:
  i calculate the actual distance it represents
  ii measure the bearing the boat has to take.

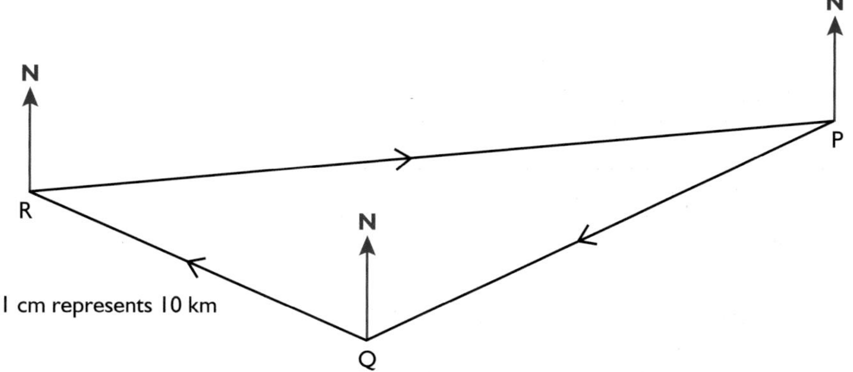

b In the second part of the trials, the boat has to go round the course in the other direction.
Measure the bearing of:
i R from P **ii** Q from R **iii** P from Q.

Investigation

The bearing from A to B is $x°$
The bearing from B to A is $y°$.
By trying several examples,
find the connection between x and y.

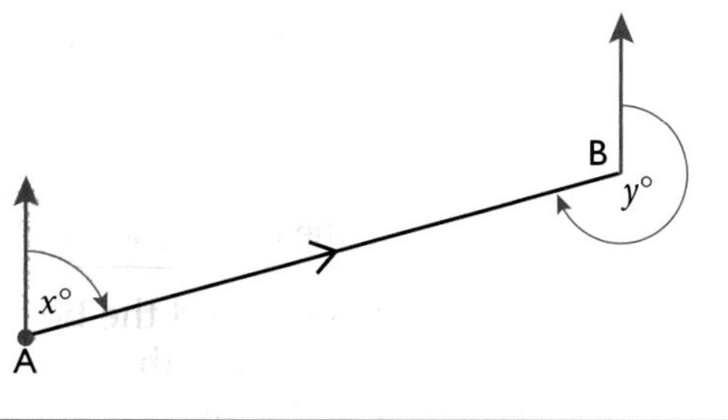

E

There and back again

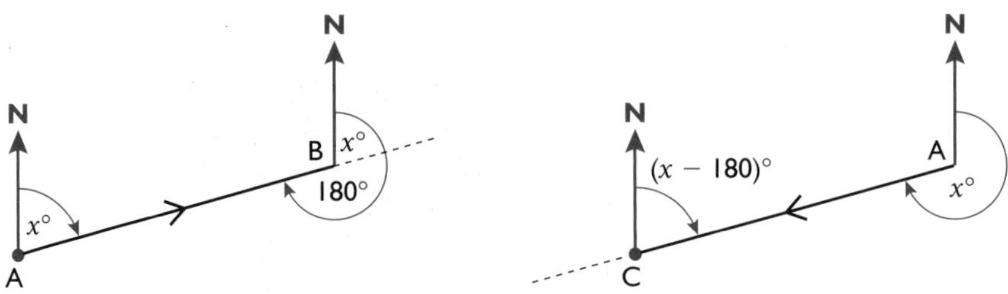

When a bearing is less than 180°, add 180° to get the return bearing.

When a bearing is greater than 180°, subtract 180° to get the return bearing.

The return bearing is also referred to as the **back-bearing**.

Exercise 5.2

1 A ship sails from Learmonth and visits three islands before returning directly to port.

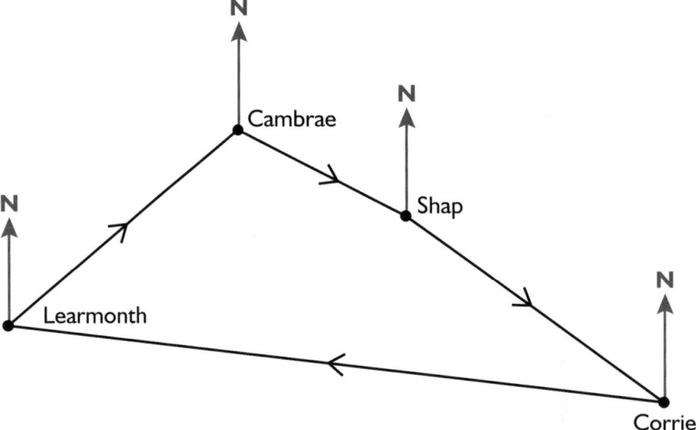

On the map of the journey shown here, 1 cm represents 10 km.

a Copy and complete the table.

	Distance (km)	Bearing
Learmonth to Cambrae		
Cambrae to Shap		
Shap to Corrie		
Corrie to Learmonth		

b Without measuring, find the bearing of

i Cambrae to Learmonth

ii Learmonth to Corrie.

2 A quad-bike course goes from Start to markers 1, 2, 3 and 4, then back to the start.

For each part of the course work out:

a the bearing the drivers take

b the actual distance driven.

Scale: 1 cm represents 200 m

c Calculate the bearing of
i 2 from 3 **ii** 4 from the start.

3 A small plane flies from island to island delivering mail. It does a round trip from Hannay, visiting Woodley, Greater Brossay and Lesser Brossay.

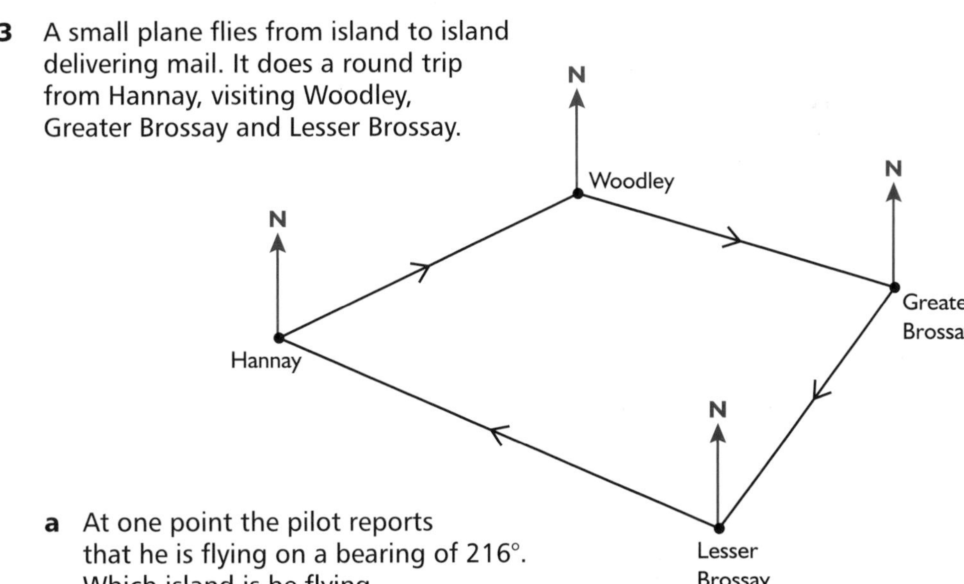

a At one point the pilot reports that he is flying on a bearing of 216°. Which island is he flying
i away from **ii** towards?

b Measure the bearing that the plane takes for each part of the journey.

c The distance between the two Brossay islands is 8 km. How far does the plane fly altogether?

d Calculate the bearing of Hannay from Woodley.

6 Drawing maps

If we make accurate drawings using information we have, we can then find more information by measurement.

Example A car travels for 11 km on a bearing of 290°.
How far **a** north **b** west is it from its start?

Answer: Make a scale drawing (1 cm represents 2 km)

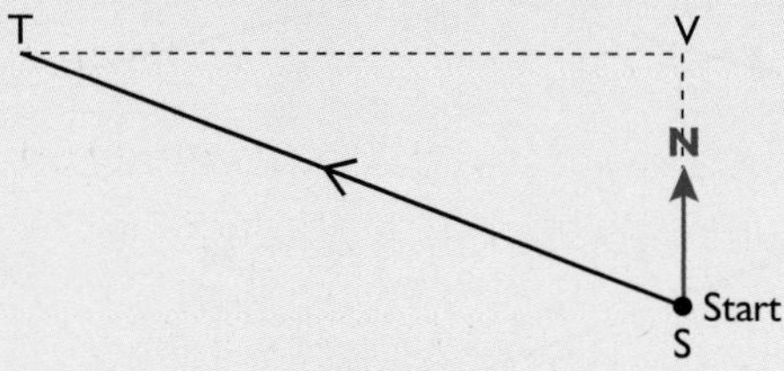

a By measuring we find SV = 1·9 cm,
so distance required = 2 × 1·9 = 3·8 km

b TV = 5·1 cm, so distance = 2 × 5·1 = 10·2 km

Exercise 6.1

1 Make an accurate scale drawing of each sketch to represent each journey, from P, using the scales given.
Then find out how far east or west the end point is from the start.

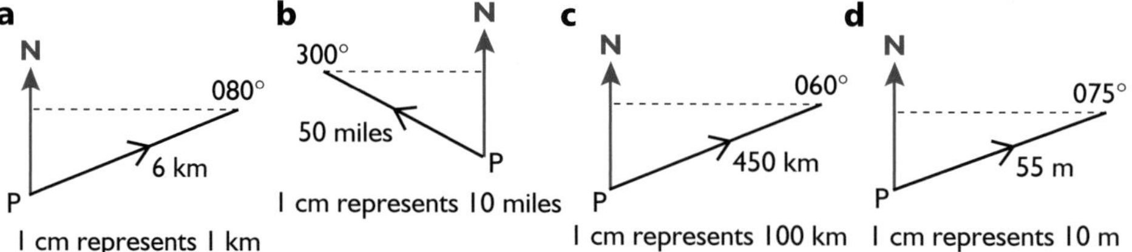

2 A car leaves its garage (G) and is driven 750 metres on a bearing of 070° to the shopping centre (C).

a Using a scale of 1 cm to 100 m, make an accurate drawing of the journey.

b How far east of the garage is the shopping centre?

3 Anthony sets off from home (H) and jogs 12 km on a bearing of 230°.

a Make an accurate drawing of Anthony's run, using a scale of 1 cm to 2 km.

b How far south of his home is he?

4 A truck leaves a factory (F) and is driven 53 km on a bearing of 320° to a depot (D).

a Make an accurate scale drawing of this journey, using a scale of 1 cm to 10 km.

b Find out how far north of the factory the depot is.

5 A ship sails from port (P) on a bearing of 060° for 50 km to R, then changes course, sailing on a bearing of 150° for 40 km to S.

a Make a scale drawing of the ship's journey. (Use 1 cm to represent 10 km.)

b Use your drawing to find the distance (PS) the ship is from the port.

c Measure the bearing the ship should take to return to port.

6 At the Tall Ships Regatta, two ships sail out of Port Henry (P).

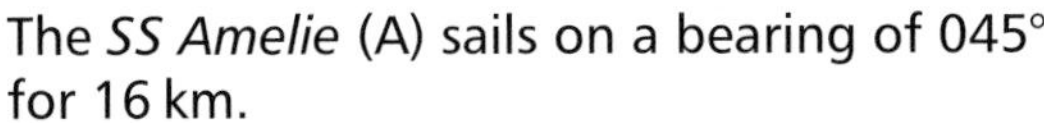

The *SS Amelie* (A) sails on a bearing of 045° for 16 km.
The *Beagle* (B) sails 9 km on a bearing of 200°.

a Make a scale drawing showing both ships' journeys. (Use a scale of 1 cm to 2 km.)

b Use your scale drawing to find out how far apart the ships are.

c What is the bearing of the *Beagle* from the *Amelie*?

7 Appleton is 67 km from Jackson on a bearing of 165°.
Greenlees is 73 km from Jackson on a bearing of 240°.
By means of a scale drawing, calculate:

a how far Greenlees is from Appleton

b the bearing of Appleton from Greenlees.

8 Pete and Billy leave school and walk home.
Pete walks 1600 metres on a bearing of 075°.
Billy walks 900 metres on a bearing of 200°.
Using a scale drawing, work out:

a how far apart Pete and Billy live

b what bearing Pete would have to take to get to Billy's house.

9 Rio sets off from work and cycles 7 km on a bearing of 105°, then cycles 5 km on a bearing of 085° to arrive home.

a What is the direct distance from Rio's work to his home?

b From Rio's home what is the bearing of his work?

7 Scales written as ratios

So far we have expressed scale in the form '1 cm represents 100 m', etc.
On maps and plans, the scale is often written as a ratio, e.g. 1 : 100.
This means that

one unit on the map represents *one hundred units on the ground.*

It could mean 1 cm to 100 cm, or 1 inch to 100 inches, or 1 metre to 100 metres. This way of writing the scale does not dictate what units the reader of the map must use.
The ratio is referred to as a **representative fraction.**

Example 1 Express the scale '1 cm represents 100 km' as a representative fraction.

$$\begin{aligned} & 1\text{ cm} : 100\text{ km} \\ &= 1\text{ cm} : 100 \times 1000\text{ m} \\ &= 1\text{ cm} : 100\,000 \times 100\text{ cm} \\ &= 1 : 10\,000\,000 \end{aligned}$$

Note that we drop the use of units when they are the same on both sides of the ratio.

Example 2 On a map, the distance between two towns is 7·8 cm.
The scale of the map is given as 1 : 100 000.
How far apart are the two towns on the ground?

$$\begin{aligned} & 7{\cdot}8\text{ cm represents } 1000\,000 \times 7{\cdot}8\text{ cm} \\ &= 7\,800\,000\text{ cm} \\ &= 78\,000\text{ m} \\ &= 78\text{ km} \end{aligned}$$

E

Exercise 7.1

1 Calculate the missing entries in the table.

Length on map	3 cm	5 cm			44 mm	1·5 cm	4·6 cm	59 mm	
Length on ground	12 km	30 km	100 km	15 m					20 km
Scale			1 cm rep. 20 km	1 mm rep. 3 m					
Representative fraction					1 : 20	1 : 100	1 : 50	1 : 10	1 : 500 000

2 A map has a scale of 1 : 10 000. The distance between two houses on the map measures 7 cm.
Work out the real distance between them in metres.

3

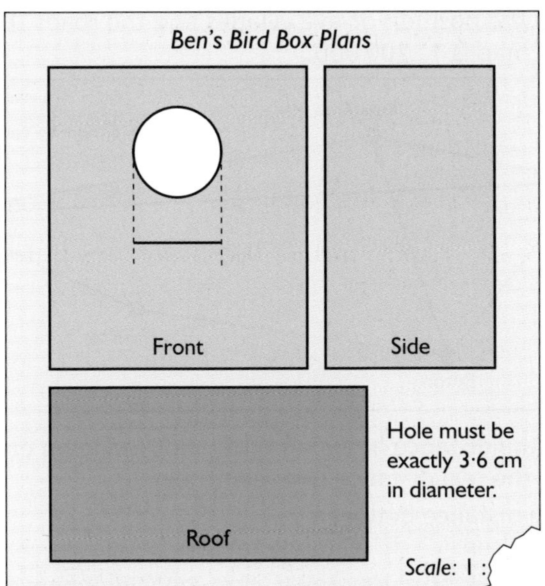

This drawing is part of the plan for a bird house. Unfortunately the scale is missing.

a Measure the size of the hole in the plan.

b Its actual size should be 3·6 cm.
Calculate the scale of the plan, giving it as a representative fraction.

c Work out the actual dimensions of the
   i front
   ii side
   iii roof.

4 This map shows where a gardener intends planting trees in an orchard.

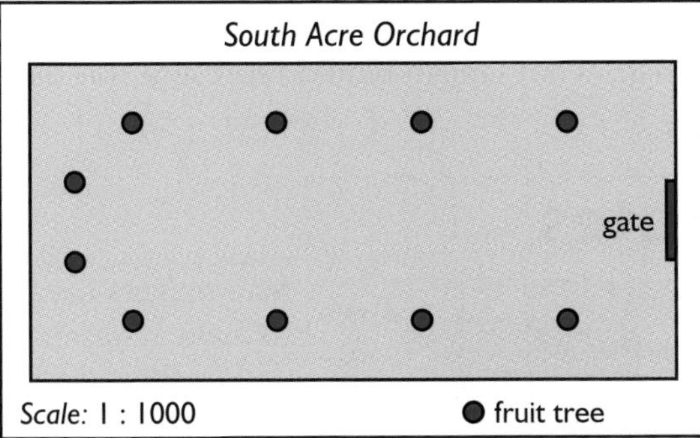

a Work out the actual dimensions of the orchard in metres.

b How far apart, in metres, are the two trees nearest the gate?

c Fruit trees should never be planted closer than 5 metres from each other. Does this gardener stick to the rule?

5 This map shows the position of five villages and the roads that join them.
The scale of the map is 1 : 200 000.

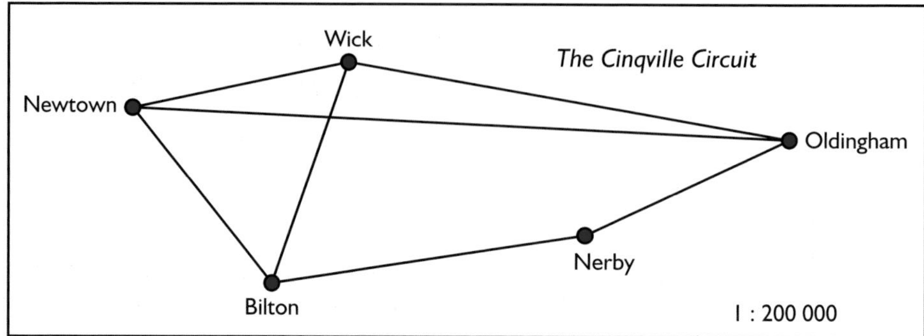

a **i** Measure the distance between Wick and Newtown on the map.
ii Calculate the real distance between them.

b Work out the distance between
i Wick and Bilton **ii** Oldingham and Newtown

c Mary plans to walk from Newtown, through Oldingham and Bilton to Wick.
She estimates that she will be walking at 10 km/h.
If she sets out at 9 a.m., estimate her arrival at Wick.

6 Faisal measures his local football pitch. It is a rectangle 110 metres by 60 metres.
With the aid of a scale drawing (1 : 1000), work out the distance between diagonally opposite corners of the pitch in metres.

7 A map used a scale of 1 : 500 000. On the map the distance between Grantsmill and Hilldon is 6 cm, between Hilldon and Mead is 4·5 cm and between Mead and Grantsmill is 7·3 cm.
Cycling at an average speed of 48 km/h, how long, to the nearest minute, will it take to complete a circuit of all three towns?

8 Violethill and Moles are 7·5 cm apart on a map. They are actually 1·5 km apart.

a Express the scale of the map as a representative fraction.

b The distance between Tain and Dunmuir is 4 km.
On the same map, what length would represent this distance?

FE

8 Coordinates

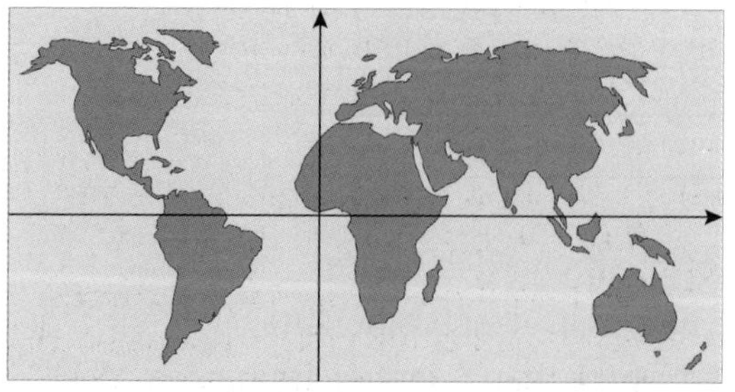

Map makers use a coordinate system to make it easier to refer to positions within their maps.

The axes used for the world map are shown.

What names are given to the axes?

What is the part above the '*x* axis' called?

Let's look at a simplified version of this which we use in mathematics.

Reminders

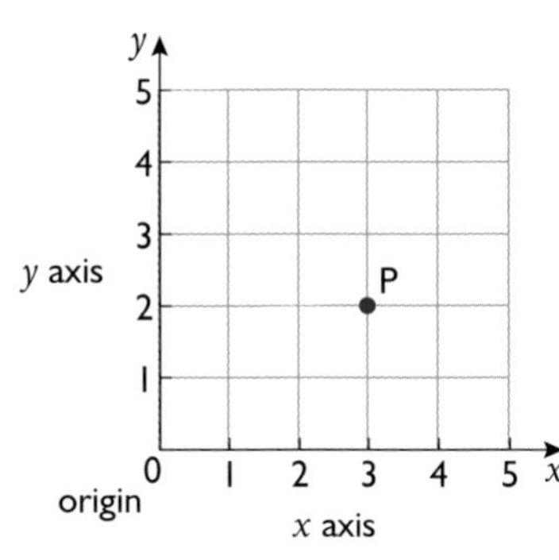

P is the point (3, 2).

From the origin, go 3 along and 2 up.

3 is the x coordinate of P.
2 is the y coordinate of P.

O (0, 0) is the origin.

Any point on the x axis has a y coordinate of 0.
Any point on the y axis has an x coordinate of 0.

Using negative numbers, we can extend the axes to the left and down as shown below.

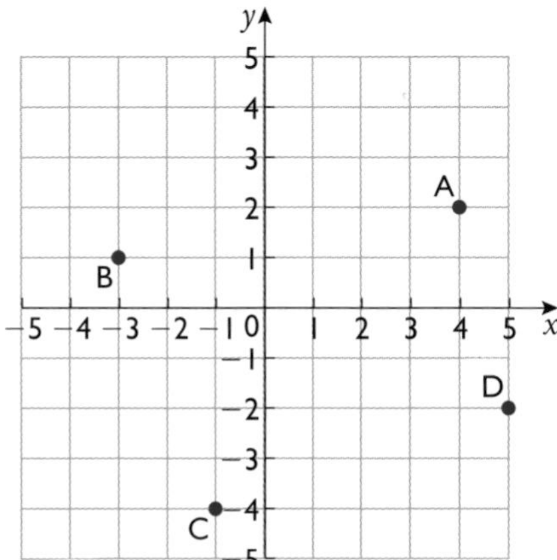

Note that the axes now break the plane up into four sections.
These are called **quadrants**.

The point A(4, 2) is in the first quadrant.
B(−3, 1) is in the second quadrant.
C(−1, −4) is in the third quadrant.
D(5, −2) is in the fourth quadrant.

Exercise 8.1

1

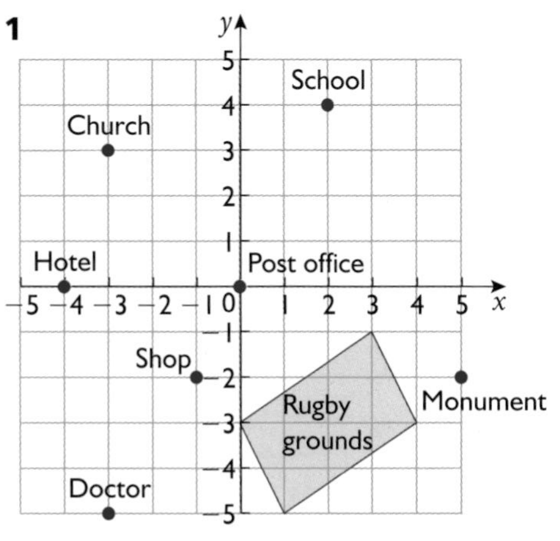

This coordinate grid shows the layout of a village.

a Copy and complete this list.
Monument (5, …), School (…, 4), Shop (…, …), Post office (…, …), Church (…, …), Doctor's surgery (…, …), Hotel (…, …).

b Write down the coordinates of the four corners of the rugby grounds.

c The telephone box is exactly halfway between the post office and the hotel. Write down the coordinates of the telephone box.

2 **a** Name the point at
i (−1, 1)
ii (5, −2).

b Write down the coordinates of
i W
ii Q
iii S.

c Which point has
i an x coordinate of 0?
ii a y coordinate of −5?
iii equal x and y coordinates?

d Name two points with the same
i x coordinate
ii y coordinate.

e Which three points can be joined by a straight line?

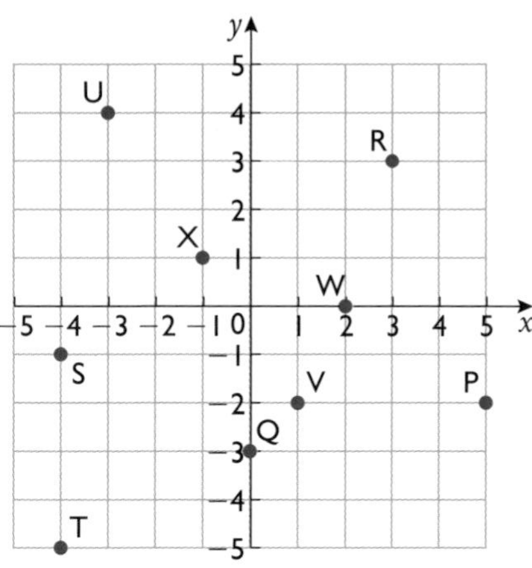

3

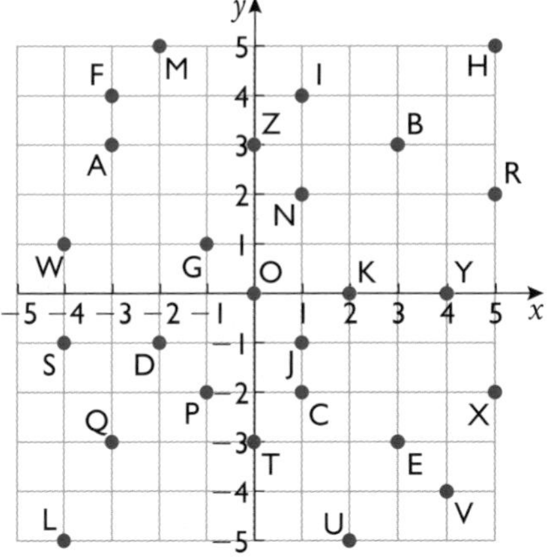

Coordinate codes!

a Work out the secret message by finding the letters on the grid:
(−2, −1) (0, 0) (1, 4) (1, 2) (−1, 1);
(−2, 5) (−3, 3) (0, −3) (5, 5)
(−4, −1); (1, 4) (−4, −1); (−1, 1)
(5, 2) (3, −3) (−3, 3) (0, −3); (−3, 4)
(2, −5) (1, 2).

b Using the coordinates, write this message in code:
HOLIDAYS ARE EVEN BETTER

c Write a message to a friend using the code.
Get them to work out the message.

4 Many games can be simulated on a computer by using coordinates.
In a darts simulation, the darts of four players fell at the following points:

Adam:	A(1, −4)	B(2, 2)	C(−4, 1)
Debi:	D(−5, −4)	E(−3, −3)	F(1, 0)
George:	G(0, 5)	H(1, −3)	I(−2, 4)
Jemima:	J(−5, 0)	K(0, −1)	L(5, 4)

a A is worth 10 points.
Find the value of each of the other 'darts'.

b Which player scored the most with their three darts?

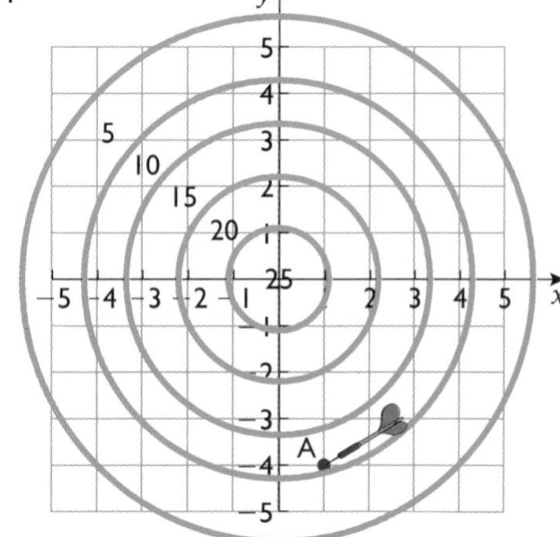

5 Coordinates can also help you make geometric drawings.
Draw a coordinate grid with both axes numbered from −10 to 10.

i Plot each set of points, joining them as indicated.

ii Each set makes a mathematical shape. Write its name inside the shape.

a A(7, 10) → B(5, 8) → C(7, 4) → D(9, 8) → A

b P(−2, 5) → Q(0, 3) → R(3, 6) → S(1, 8) → P

c K(2, −2) → L(4, 2) → M(8, 2) → N(10, −2) → K

d E(2, −5) → F(1, −8) → G(−5, −8) → H(−4, −5) → E

e W(−7, 4) → X(−9, −1) → Y(−7, −6) → Z(−5, −1) → W

f T(9, −6) → U(4, −4) → V(6, −9) → T

6 *Do you know what it is yet?*
Draw a set of axes each numbered from −10 to 10.
Plot each set of points in order, joining them as you go.

a Join (−5, 8) to (−5, 10) Stop

b Start (−1, −2), (0, −3), (0, −6), (−2, −6), (−2, −3), (−1, −2) Stop

c Start (2, −8), (2, −5), (3, −4), (4, −5), (4, −8) Stop

d Start (6, −3), (7, −2), (8, −3), (8, −6), (6, −6), (6, −3) Stop

e Start (−4, 3), (−6, 3), (−6, 6), (−4, 6), (−4, −5) Stop

f Join (−6, 9) to (−4, 9) Stop

g Start (10, −1), (−3, −1), (−3, 2), (8, 2), (10, −1), (10, −8), (−3, −8)
(−3, 6), (−5, 8), (−7, 6), (−7, −8), (−3, −8) Stop

Challenge

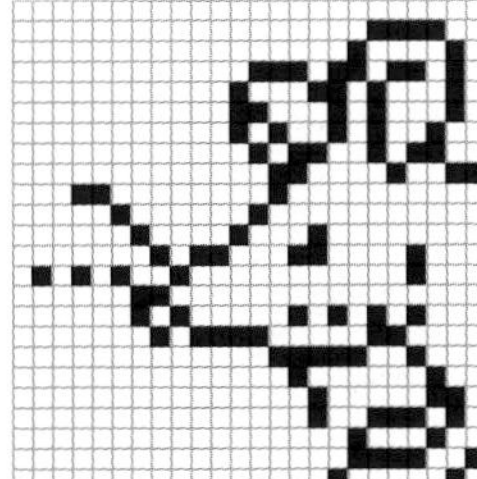

Write instructions to communicate a drawing of your own to a friend.

Digitising pictures can also be done using coordinates.

Squares are either black or white. If you give the coordinates of the lower left-hand corner of all the black squares then you can communicate the picture as a series of points.

Try one of your own.

9 Distance on a grid

When the scale of the grid is known, then distances can be counted, measured or estimated by treating it as a scaled drawing.

Example This grid shows the position of four oil-rigs in the North Sea. Each unit on the grid represents 10 km.

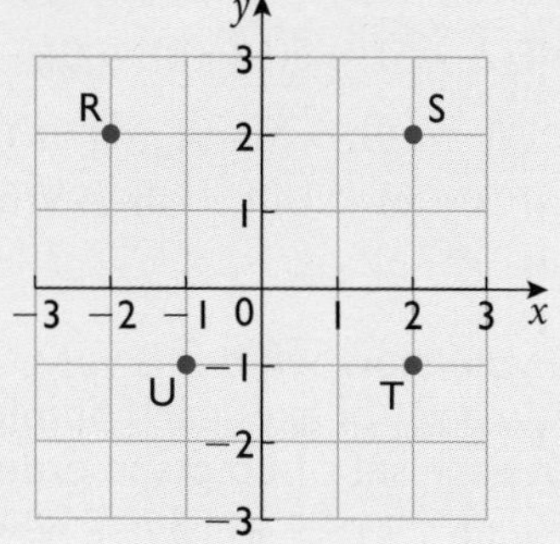

From Oilrig R to Oilrig S there are 4 units, so the actual distance is $4 \times 10 = 40$ km.

It is $3 \times 10 = 30$ km from Oilrig S to T.

Note:
Since R and U do not lie on the same gridline some other method for calculating their distance must be found.

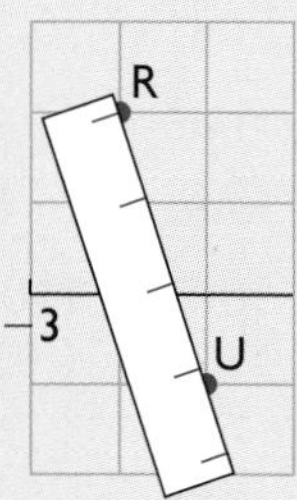

We could transfer the units on the grid onto a piece of paper and use it as a ruler to estimate the distance.
We see that RU ≈ 3·2 cm, giving an estimate of 32 km.

Exercise 9.1

1 This grid shows the positions of some wind turbines on a hillside.

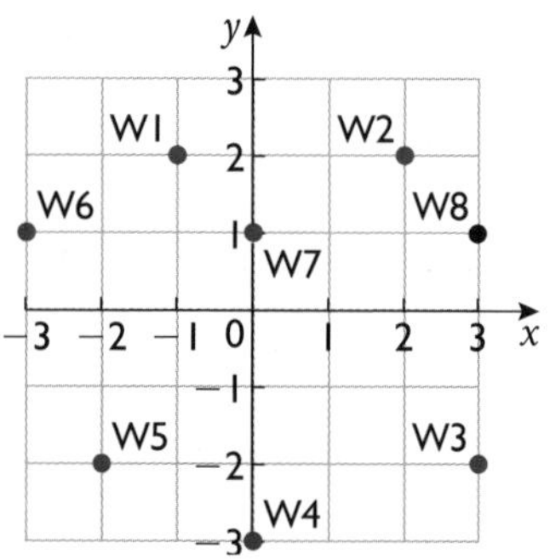

a Which turbine is at
- **i** (−1, 2)
- **ii** (3, −2)?

b Calculate the actual distance between
- **i** W1 and W2
- **ii** W6 and W8
- **iii** W4 and W7
- **iv** W3 and W5

if each unit represents 20 m.

2 Two Paint Ball teams are taking part in a game.
The crosses on the grid show the position of each person.
The scale on the grid is 1 unit to 5 metres.

a Which person is at

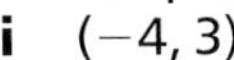

i (−4, 3)
ii (2, −2)
iii (−2, −2)?

b How far is it between participants
i P1 and Q4
ii P4 and P5
iii Q3 and P3?

c Q3 fired a paint ball in a southerly direction. Which participant did he hit?

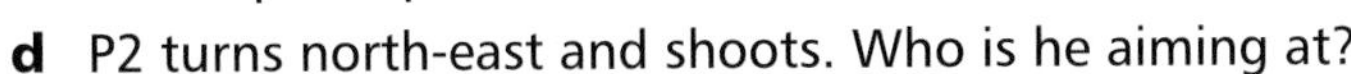

d P2 turns north-east and shoots. Who is he aiming at?

e P5 turns north-west, hoping to hit Q4, and fires. Explain what might happen.

f Q1 advances south 30 metres and west 5 metres. Which participant will she make contact with?

3 Boats at a regatta are positioned at:

R(4, −4), S(0, 3), T(−1, 2), U(−1, −4),
V(3, 0), W(4, 2), X(−3, 0), Y(−2, −2) and Z(5, −2).

a Make a coordinate grid and plot the points.

b Each unit on the grid represents 500 metres.
Work out the distance, in kilometres, between the following boats:
i V and X **ii** R and U **iii** T and U **iv** Y and Z.

c Estimate the distance between
i S and V **ii** X and Z.

10 Sets of points

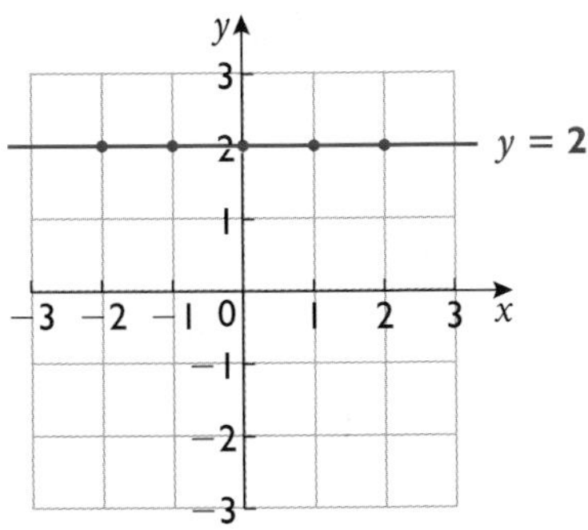

A selection of wind turbines all lie in a straight line.

Their coordinates are
(−2, 2), (−1, 2), (0, 2), (1, 2) and (2, 2).

Note that in each case their *y* coordinate was 2. Every point with a *y* coordinate of 2 lies on this line … and no other points!

For this reason the line is referred to as **the line** $y = 2$.

Similarly, this set of turbines lie on the line $x = -1$.

$y = 2$ and $x = -1$ are referred to as the **equations of the lines**.

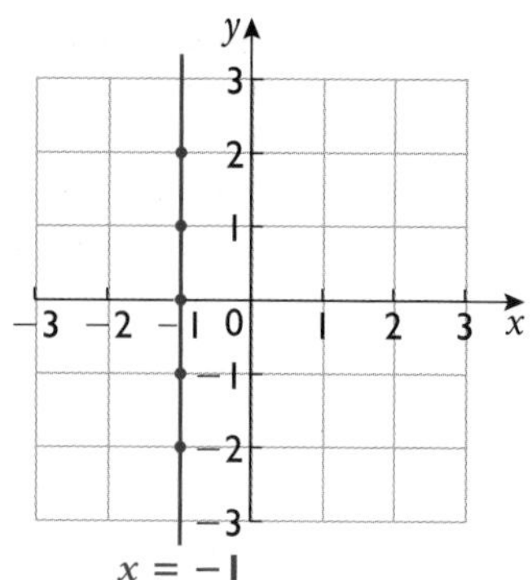

Exercise 10.1

1 a i State the coordinates of the three points marked on the line AB.
ii Write down the equation of the line AB.
b i State the coordinates of the three points marked on the line CD.
ii Write down the equation of the line CD.
c Copy and complete the sentence: The point (..., ...) lies on both the line $x = \ldots$ and the line $y = \ldots$.

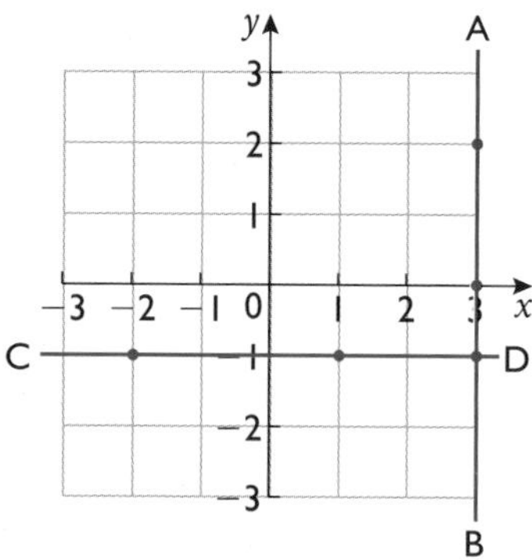

2

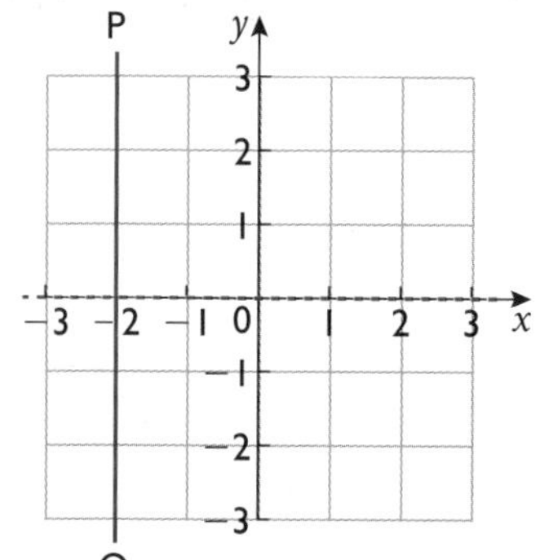

a i Write down the coordinates of three points on the line PQ.
ii Write down the equation of the line PQ.
b i List three points on the x axis.
ii Write down the equation of the x axis.
c Write down the equation of the y axis.

3 a Write down the equation of each labelled line.
b What point lies on the intersection of the lines
i $x = 1$ and $y = 1$
ii $x = 3$ and $y = 1$
iii $x = -3$ and $y = 1$?

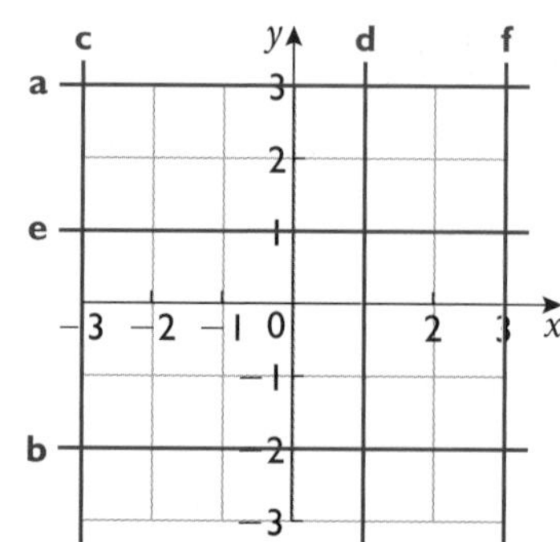

4 **a** **i** Follow these instructions to draw the line $x = 4$.
- List three points with an x coordinate of 4.
- Plot the points and draw a line through them.
- Label the line $x = 4$.

ii On the same diagram draw the lines $x = 1$ and $x = -4$.

b Draw the lines **i** $y = -4$ **ii** $y = -2$ **iii** $y = 5$.

c Complete the following sentences.

i A line with equation $x = a$, where a is a number, is parallel to the … axis.

ii A line with equation $y = b$, where b is a number, is ……… axis.

5 The sides of a rectangle lie along the lines $x = 4$, $y = 3$, $x = -2$ and $y = -3$.

a Draw the rectangle on a coordinate grid.

b List the coordinates of the vertices of the rectangle.

c Where do its diagonals intersect?

d What is the area of the rectangle?

6 Not all lines are parallel to the axes.

a List five points on the line PQ.

b State a simple relation between the points you have listed.

c For obvious reasons this line is called $y = x$.
Which of the following points lie on this line?
i (0, 0) **ii** (10, 10) **iii** (99, 100)
iv (70, −70) **v** (−56, −56)

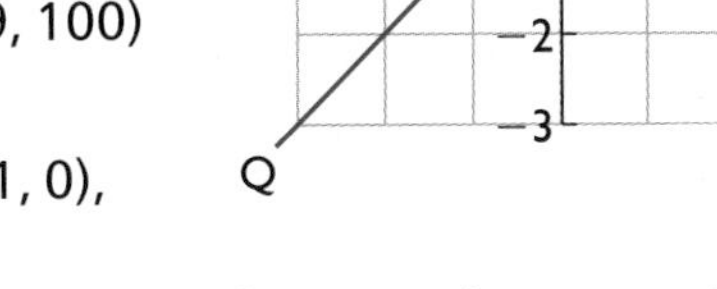

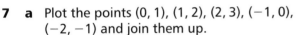

7 **a** Plot the points (0, 1), (1, 2), (2, 3), (−1, 0), (−2, −1) and join them up.

b They all lie on the line with equation **$y = x + 1$ because the y coordinate is always 1 more than the x coordinate.**
Which of the following points lie on this line?
i (17, 18) **ii** (23, 22) **iii** (−19, −20) **iv** (−28, −27)

8 **a** Plot the points (0, 0), (1, 2), (2, 4), (3, 6), (−1, −2), (−2, −4) and join them up.

b The line is called $y = 2x$. Why?

c Which of the following points lie on this line?
i (18, 9) **ii** (44, 88) **iii** (−20, −10) **iv** (−50, −100)

Challenge

Use a graphic calculator or a computer package to find out more about the names (or equations) of straight lines.

1 Can you draw: a $y = x + 2$ b $y = x + 3$ c $y = x - 1$?
Use the graphic calculator to see if you are correct.

2 Examine $y = x$ and $y = 2x$. Where would you find:
a $y = 3x$ b $y = -4x$ c $y = 0{\cdot}5x$?
Check to see if you are right.

F

CHECK-UP

1 This is a map of Reef Isle.

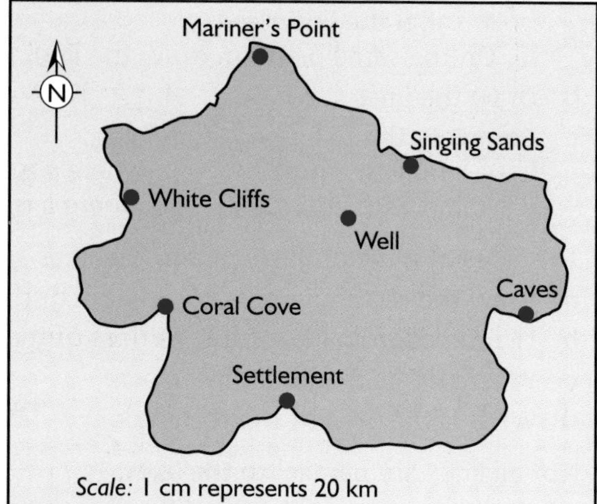

a Calculate the distance between
- **i** Mariner's Point and the Settlement
- **ii** Singing Sands and Coral Cove
- **iii** White Cliffs and the Well.

b What lies
- **i** due east of Coral Cove
- **ii** south-east of White Cliffs?

c If you walked due south from Mariner's Point, how far would you walk before you reached the coast?

2 Make a scaled drawing of each of these shapes using the given scales.

a

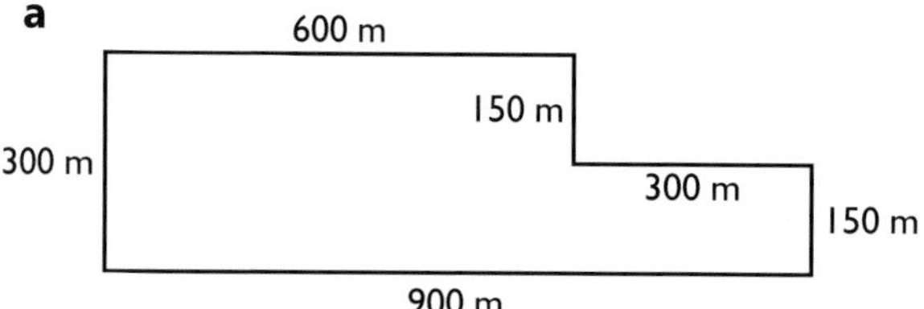

***Scale:* 1 cm to 100 m.**

b

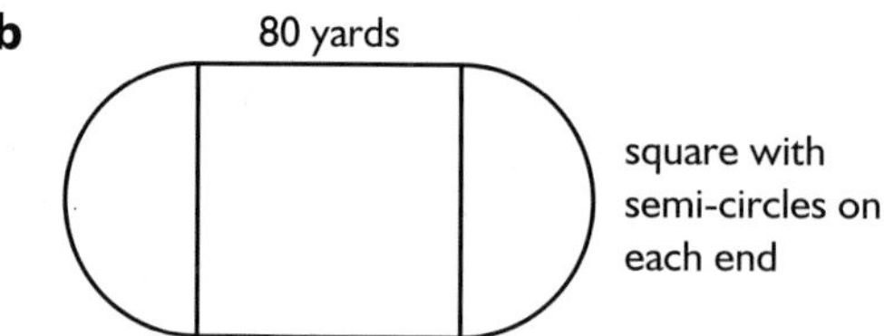

***Scale:* 1 cm to 10 yards.**

3 On a plan the front of a drawer is 5·5 cm long. The scale of the map is 1 : 10. How long is the actual drawer?

4 Work out the bearing of Q from P.

a

N
Q
73°
P

b

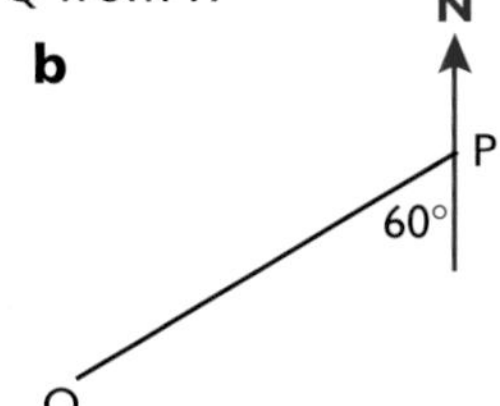

c

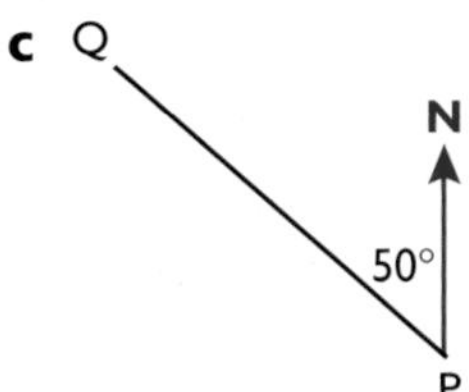

5 For each of the following journeys

i make a scaled drawing

ii use the drawing to work out the direct distance back to the start.

a From home, James travelled 500 m east then 280 m north. (Let 1 cm represent 100 m.)

b From the port, a yacht sailed 42 km on a bearing of 050°, then 35 km on a bearing of 140°. (Let 1 cm represent 10 km.)

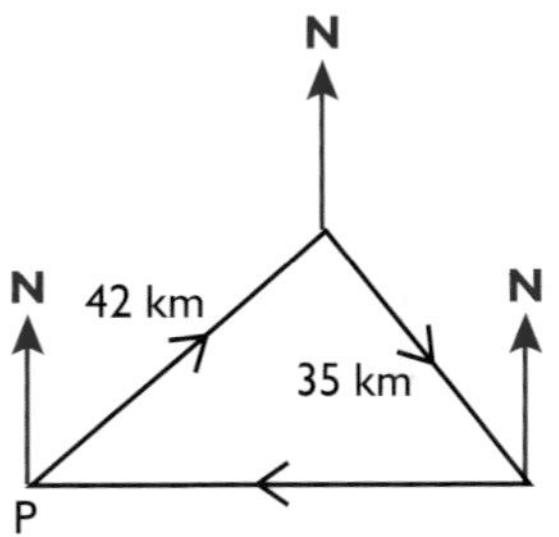

6 Two ships sail out of Aberdeen.
The *Moray Princess* sails for 14 km on a bearing of 110°.
The *Titania* sails for 19 km on a bearing of 165°.

a Make a scale drawing of the ships' journeys, using a scale of 1 cm to 2 km.

b How far apart are the two ships?

7 Write down the coordinates of each of the points A to G.

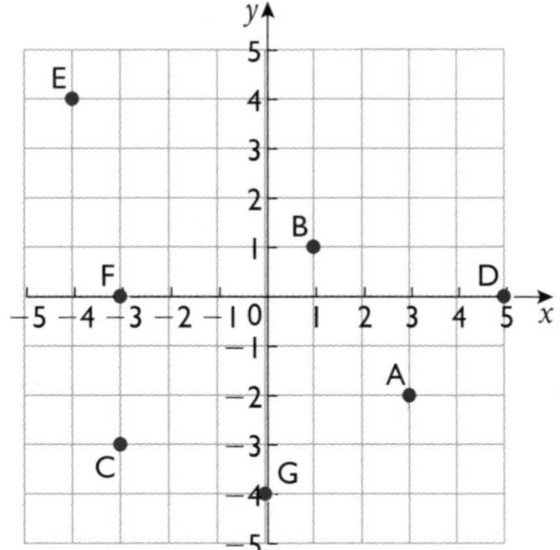

8 a Plot the following points:
P(−4, 1), Q(0, 5), R(2, 1) and S(−2, −3).

b Join up the points to make quadrilateral PQRS.

c What shape is PQRS?

d Draw the diagonals and write down the coordinates of the point of their intersection.

E

9 On coordinate grids, draw the lines with equations:

a $x = 3$ **b** $y = 4$ **c** $x = -4$ **d** $y = -1$.

10 Give the equation of each labelled straight line.

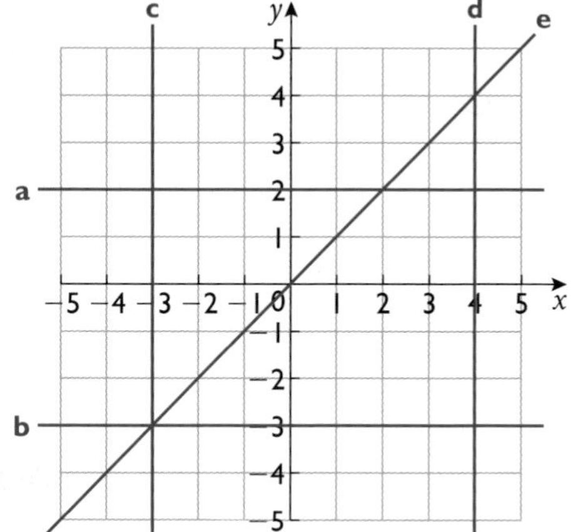

F

8 Solving equations and inequations

Mathematicians have made great efforts over the centuries to solve different types of equations.

Around 300 BC, Euclid (born in Greece) was using geometry (diagrams) to solve equations of a special type.

By AD 1400, Al'Kashi (born in Iran) was solving equations by a trial and improvement method called **iteration**.

In 1535, Nicola Fontana Tartaglia (born in Italy) won a public maths contest by discovering a new method of solving equations.

In 1799, Ruffini (also born in Italy) published a book called *General Theory of Equations* in which he claimed some special equations could not be solved.

And in 1937, Isograph Bell Laboratories built a machine to solve equations.

1 Looking back

Exercise 1.1

1 Solve each equation. Give the solutions like this: $y = 6$.

a $u + 4 = 8$ **b** $t - 3 = 7$ **c** $5y = 40$

2 For each picture

i write an equation and solve it

ii say what the solution means.

a

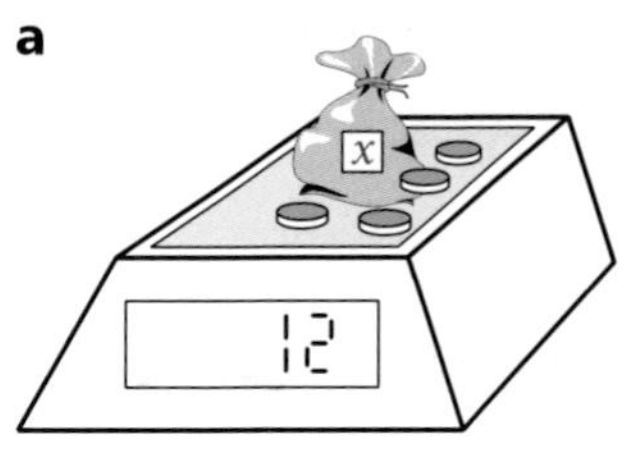

b

3 litres poured out, 7 litres left

c

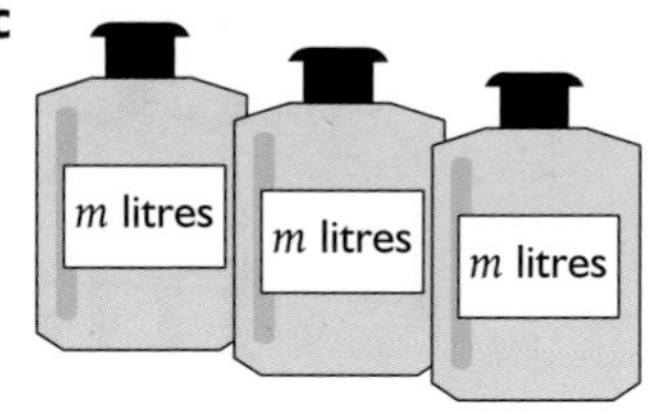

15 litres in total

3 Solve each equation:

a $2x + 1 = 9$ **b** $4y - 3 = 5$ **c** $8k + 10 = 10$

4 Make an equation for each machine and solve it to find the IN number.

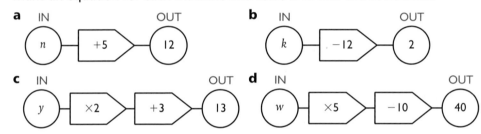

a IN n → $+5$ → 12 OUT

b

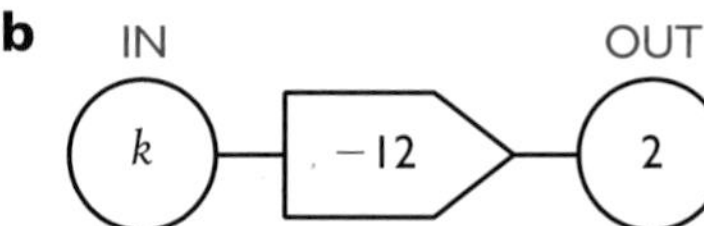

c IN y → $\times 2$ → $+3$ → 13 OUT

d

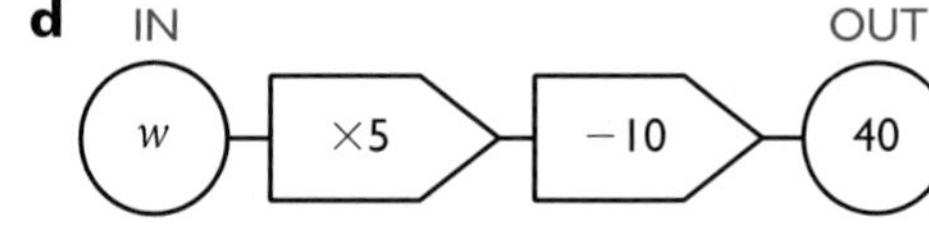

E

5 Five CDs and £8 worth of batteries cost Ian £43 altogether.

a Let the cost of one CD be £x. Make an equation in x.

b Solve the equation to find the cost of one CD.

2 Checking solutions

Example Is $m = 2$ a solution of the equation $15 - 2m = m + 6$?

Answer:

When $m = 2$ then $15 - 2m = 15 - 2 \times 2 = 15 - 4 = 11$

and $m + 6 = 2 + 6 = 8$

So, when $m = 2$, $15 - 2m \neq m + 6$

and $m = 2$ is therefore not a solution to the equation.

Is $m = 3$ a solution?

$15 - 2m = 15 - 2 \times 3 = 15 - 6 = 9$

and $m + 6 = 3 + 6 = 9$

So, when $m = 3$, $15 - 2m = m + 6$

and $m = 3$ *is* a solution.

Exercise 2.1

1 In each case check whether the given value is a solution of the equation.

a $x = 4;\ 3x = x + 8$

b $x = 5;\ 4x - 12 = x$

c $x = 6;\ x + 4 = 2x - 1$

d $x = 10;\ x - 7 = 2x - 17$

e $x = 1;\ 5x - 1 = x + 7$

f $x = 4;\ 10 - x = 14 - 2x$

g $x = 2;\ 3 + 2x = 18 - 3x$

h $x = 7;\ 49 - 2x = 4x + 7$

2 One of the given values is a solution of the equation. Find it. Show your working!

a $14 - x = x + 2$; pick from {3, 4, 5, 6}

b $5x = x + 12$; pick from {2, 3, 4, 5}

c $3x + 4 = 12 - x$; pick from {0, 1, 2, 3}

d $5x = 35 - 2x$; pick from {2, 3, 4, 5, 6}

e $8x - 1 = 2x + 23$; pick from {2, 3, 4, 5, 6}

f $50 - 3x = 43 - 2x$; pick from {4, 5, 6, 7, 8}

Challenge

Martin and Irene have each found a solution to the equation among the given values.

Their solutions are different.

Each is convinced their solution works.
Can you help them?

$$x^2 + 3 = 4x$$

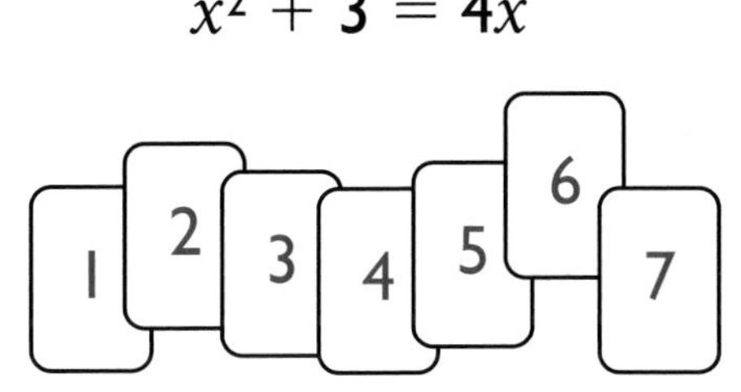

E

3 A cover-up

Example 1 Solve $4x - 5 = 15$

It is possible to cover up $4x$ (since x appears nowhere else in the equation)

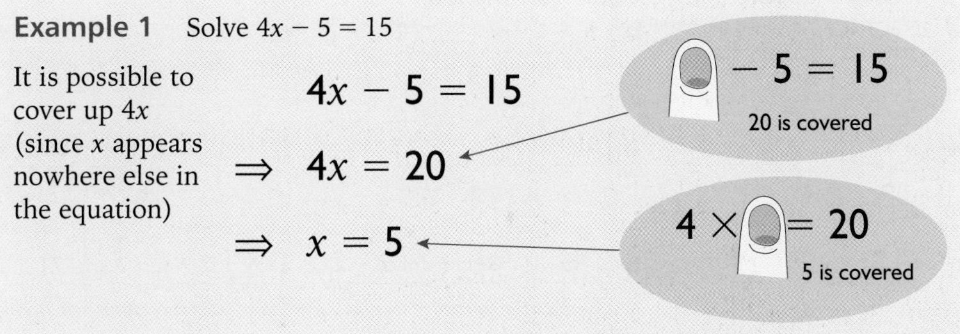

What happens when you try to solve $2x + 5 = 7x$ by covering up?

? $2x + 5 = 7x \longrightarrow$ [finger] $+ 5 =$ [finger]

Example 2 Solve $10 - \frac{1}{3}x = 4$

$$10 - \tfrac{1}{3}x = 4$$
$$\Rightarrow \quad \tfrac{1}{3}x = 6$$
$$\Rightarrow \quad x = 18$$

$10 -$ [finger] $= 4$
6 is covered

$\frac{1}{3}$ of [finger] $= 6$
18 is covered

Exercise 3.1

1 Solve each equation.

a $3x + 2 = 14$ **b** $10 - 2m = 0$ **c** $14 + 3n = 20$ **d** $7y - 3 = 11$
e $18 = 2t + 8$ **f** $7 = 22 - 3a$ **g** $47 = 2 + 9w$ **h** $7 = 5k - 3$
i $25 - 4x = 5$ **j** $3 + 10y = 33$ **k** $8c - 5 = 35$ **l** $2 = 17 - 5x$

2 Solve these equations. Be careful with the fractions.

a $8 - \frac{1}{2}x = 3$ **b** $6 = 8 - \frac{1}{5}y$ **c** $3 + \frac{1}{4}y = 5$ **d** $\frac{1}{3}w + 2 = 4$
e $5 = \frac{1}{4}k + 2$ **f** $\frac{1}{6}x - 1 = 1$ **g** $7 = 12 - \frac{1}{3}m$ **h** $11 - \frac{1}{7}e = 9$
i $7 = 3 + \frac{1}{2}n$ **j** $6 = \frac{1}{3}a - 4$ **k** $2 = 5 - \frac{1}{6}f$ **l** $4 + \frac{1}{2}x = 9$
m $14 = \frac{1}{4}x + 7$ **n** $\frac{1}{9}y + 1 = 3$ **o** $\frac{1}{3}z - 2 = 25$ **p** $9 - \frac{1}{10}a = 2$
q $1 = 8 - \frac{1}{5}x$ **r** $2 = 1 + \frac{1}{3}y$

3 More equations to solve … some have fractions and some don't.

a $5 + 2x = 11$ **b** $5 + \frac{1}{2}x = 11$ **c** $13 - 3y = 4$ **d** $13 = 18 - \frac{1}{3}m$
e $4 = \frac{1}{4}w - 2$ **f** $18 = 4a - 2$ **g** $3 + 7x = 52$ **h** $8 - \frac{1}{7}x = 1$
i $\frac{1}{4}e - 3 = 0$ **j** $3c - 3 = 12$ **k** $4 = \frac{1}{3}n + 2$ **l** $3n + 2 = 14$
m $2 = \frac{1}{2}f - 4$

4 These scales are balanced. Make an equation for each and solve it. Check that your solution balances the scales.

a 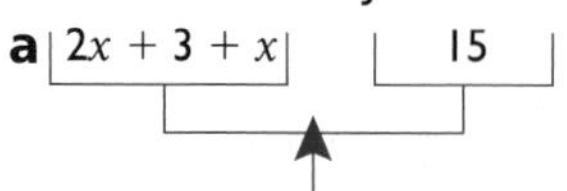

b 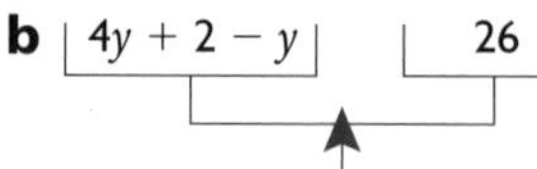

c 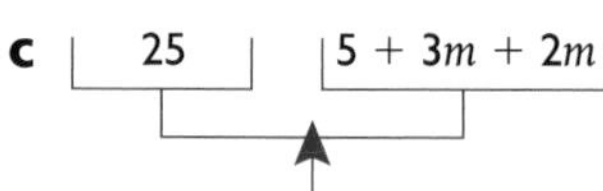

d 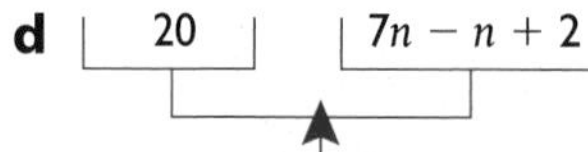

e 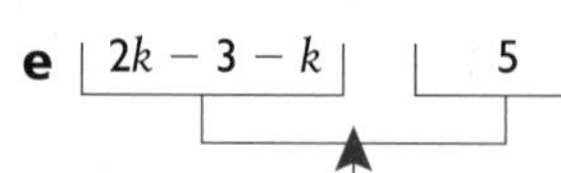

f 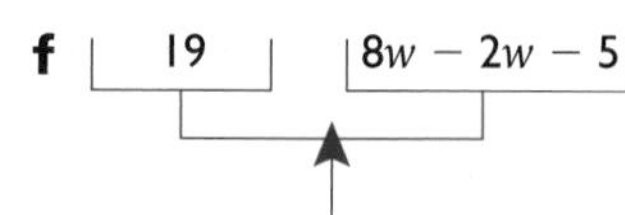

g $14 + 3a + 2$ | 31

h 40 | $4x + 3 + x + 2$

i 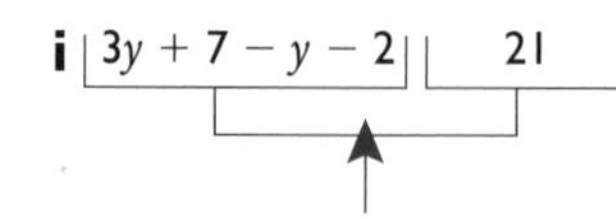

5 Mystery numbers

Form an equation and solve it to find the mystery number in each case.

Example

I think of a number	... x
I halve it	$\frac{1}{2}x$
I subtract the answer from 10	... $10 - \frac{1}{2}x$
I get 6	... $10 - \frac{1}{2}x = 6$

a I think of a number.
I multiply it by 5.
I subtract 8.
I get 37.

b I think of a number.
I halve it.
I add 9.
I get 15.

c I think of a number.
I third it.
I subtract the answer from 15.
I get 8.

d I think of a number.
I multiply it by 9.
I subtract the answer from 60.
I get 6.

e I think of a number.
I quarter it.
I then subtract 7.
I get 3.

f I think of a number.
I find a fifth of it.
I then add 6.
I get 11.

g I think of a number then
divide it by 10.
I take the result away from 10
and get an answer of 3.

Challenge

A This carpet is one third as wide as it is long. If it takes 40 m of tape to seal the edges, what are its dimensions?
(Hint: let the width be x metres and then form an equation.)

B This carpet is 3 metres longer than it is broad. It takes 34 metres of tape to seal its edges.
What are its dimensions?

E

4 The failed cover-up … keeping your balance

An equation like $3x = x + 4$ cannot be solved by the cover-up method:

$3x = x + 4 \longrightarrow$ [thumb] $=$ [thumb] $+ 4$

In this case you have to alter the equation so that x appears on only one side. However, the equation must always be kept balanced, so **do the same action to both sides.**

Remove x from both sides

$3x = x + 4$

$\Rightarrow \quad 3x - x = x + 4 - x$

$\Rightarrow \quad 2x = 4$

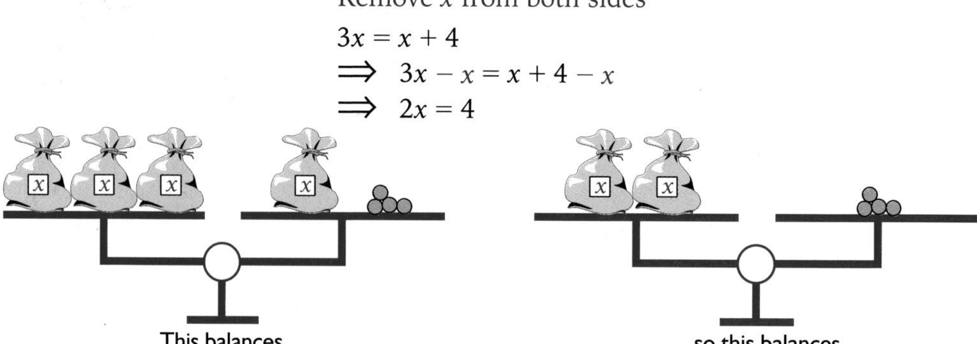

E

Divide both sides by 2

$\Rightarrow \quad 2x \div 2 = 4 \div 2$

$\Rightarrow \quad x = 2$

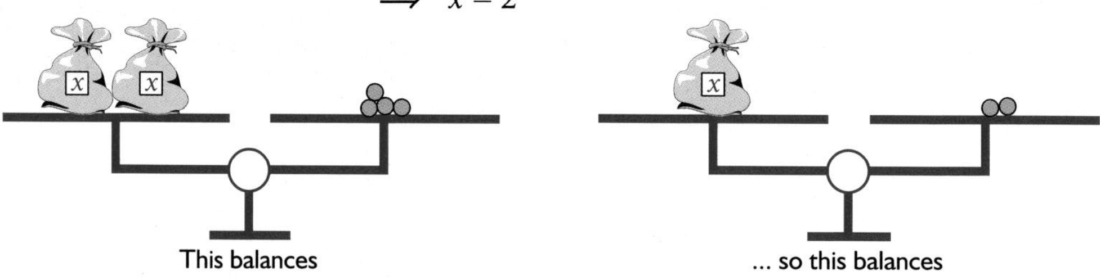

Check: Put $x = 2$ in the original equation. $3x = 3 \times 2 = 6$; $x + 4 = 2 + 4 = 6$

These are equal.

Example 1

$10x = 2x + 16$

$\Rightarrow \quad 10x - 2x = 2x + 16 - 2x$

$\Rightarrow \quad 8x = 16$

$\Rightarrow \quad 8x \div 8 = 16 \div 8$

$\Rightarrow \quad x = 2$

Check: $10 \times 2 = 2 \times 2 + 16 = 20$ ✓

Example 2

$3x + 12 = 7x$

$\Rightarrow \quad 3x + 12 - 3x = 7x - 3x$

$\Rightarrow \quad 12 = 4x$

$\Rightarrow \quad 12 \div 4 = 4x \div 4$

$\Rightarrow \quad 3 = x$

$\Rightarrow \quad x = 3$

Check: $3 \times 3 + 12 = 7 \times 3 = 21$ ✓

Exercise 4.1

1 Copy these equations and solve them by using the indicated action on both sides. Check your solution in the original equation.

a $2x = x + 5\ (-x)$	**b** $4x + 3 = 5x\ (-4x)$	**c** $5x + 6 = 7x\ (-5x)$
d $5y = 3y + 10\ (-3y)$	**e** $3 + m = 2m\ (-m)$	**f** $7n = 8 + 6n\ (-6n)$
g $7k = 4k + 6\ (-4k)$	**h** $10y = 16 + 6y\ (-6y)$	**i** $t + 15 = 6t\ (-t)$
j $18 + x = 3x\ (-x)$	**k** $8c = 4c + 20\ (-4c)$	**l** $5w = 2 + 3w\ (-3w)$
m $8r = 3r + 25\ (-3r)$	**n** $2m + 21 = 5m\ (-2m)$	**o** $9 + 4a = 7a\ (-4a)$
p $n + 36 = 5n\ (-n)$	**q** $9f = 24 + 6f\ (-6f)$	**r** $30 + 2m = 7m\ (-2m)$
s $11k = 35 + 6k\ (-6k)$	**t** $32 + x = 5x\ (-x)$	**u** $12y + 10 = 14y\ (-12y)$

2 Solve these equations and check your solution in the original equation.

a $7m = 6m + 5$	**b** $2y + 6 = 4y$	**c** $1 + x = 2x$	**d** $5x = 8 + x$
e $5k = 3k + 12$	**f** $15 + 2y = 5y$	**g** $7a + 4 = 8a$	**h** $8e = 10 + 3e$
i $2f = 3 + f$	**j** $10c = 7c + 18$	**k** $14 + x = 3x$	**l** $w + 28 = 5w$
m $9n = 4n + 35$	**n** $2y + 21 = 5y$	**o** $20 + 5h = 9h$	

3 Each situation shows equal lengths. For each pair

i make an equation

ii solve it

iii find the lengths required.

a pencils (lengths in centimetres)

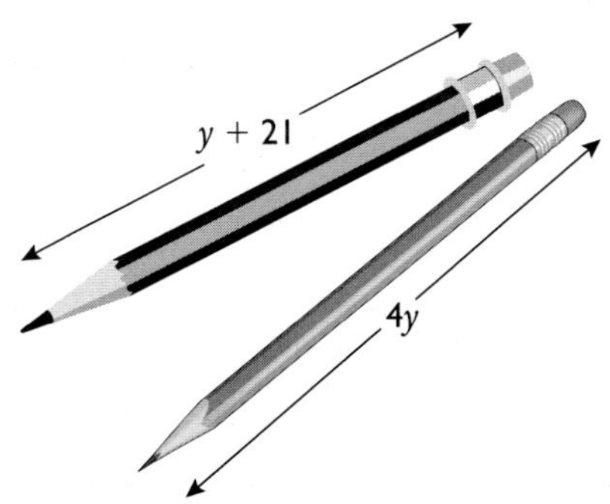

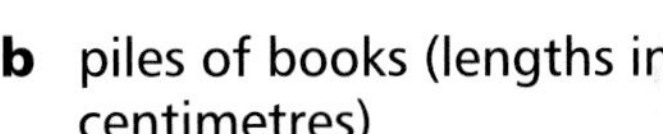

b piles of books (lengths in centimetres)

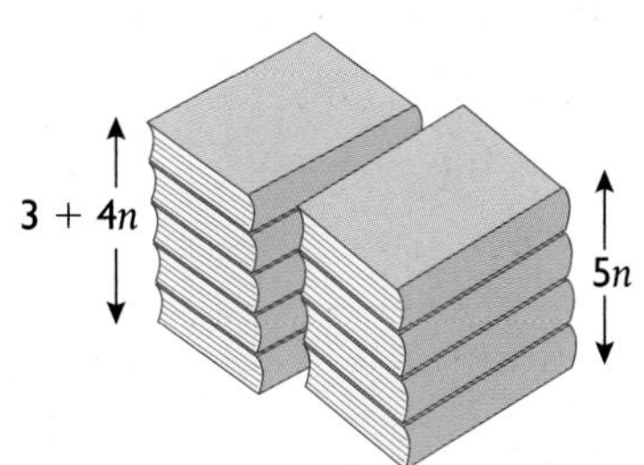

c rows of chalets (lengths in metres)

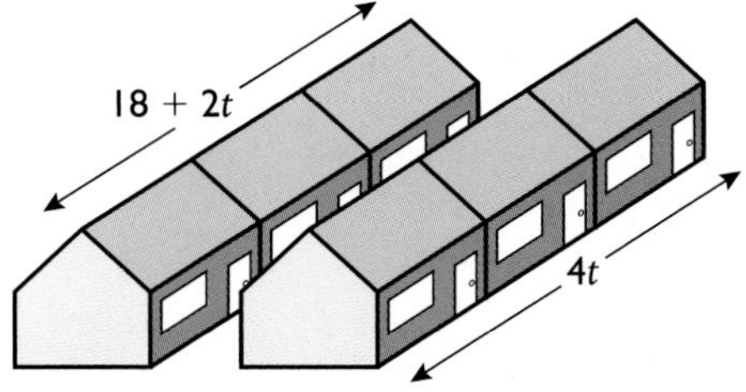

d ranks of taxis (lengths in metres)

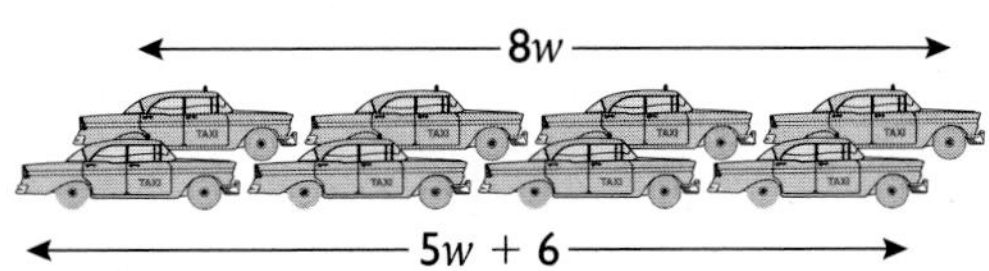

4 Solve:

a $y = 9 - 2y$ $(+2y)$
b $m = 8 - m$ $(+m)$
c $16 - x = 3x$ $(+x)$
d $15 - 4x = x$ $(+4x)$
e $k = 6 - k$
f $12 - 2w = 2w$
g $5a = 18 - a$
h $n = 15 - 2n$
i $21 - 2c = 5c$
j $24 - 2y = y$
k $2f = 16 - 2f$
l $36 - 3h = 3h$
m $3q = 20 - 2q$
n $x = 6 - 5x$

5 Remember that vertically opposite angles are equal.
For each situation form an equation and find the size of each angle.

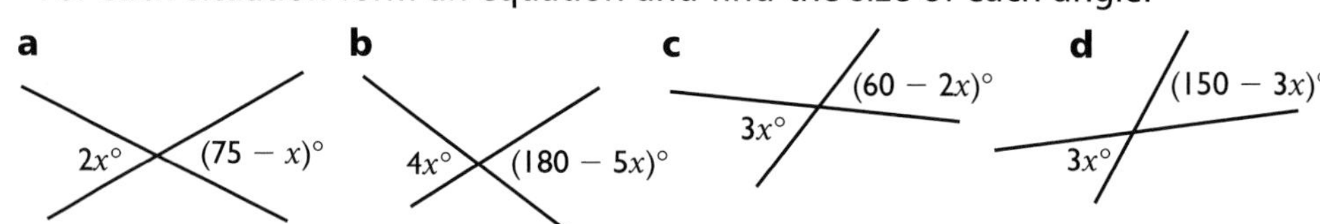

Challenge

Copy and complete this cross-number puzzle.

Across

2 $2x = 696 - x$
4 $33 + 3x = 6x$
5 $x = 244 - 3x$
7 $5x = 82 + 3x$
8 $9x = x + 96$
9 $7x = 250 - 3x$
11 $186 - 5x = x$
12 $3x + 115 = 4x$

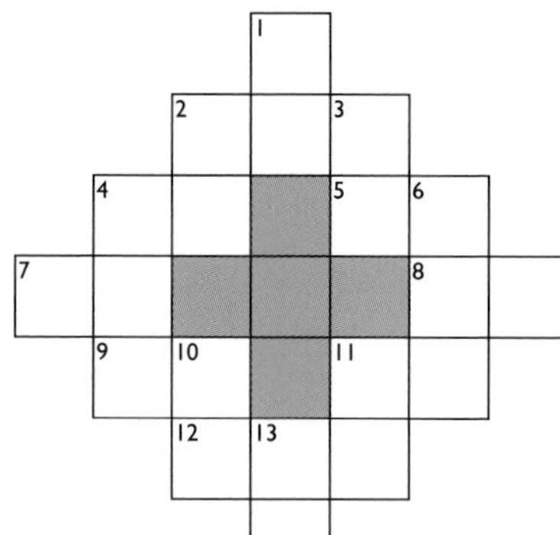

Down

1 $3x = x + 26$
2 $4x + 84 = 8x$
3 $130 - x = 4x$
4 $336 - 2x = x$
6 $3x + 555 = 8x$
10 $306 - 3x = 3x$
11 $10x = 105 + 7x$
13 $2x = 76 - 2x$

Example 3 Solve $3 + 3x - 3 = 2x - x + 2$

Simplifying: $3x = x + 2$
Balancing: $3x - x = x + 2 - x$
$\Rightarrow 2x = 2$
$\Rightarrow x = 1$

Exercise 4.2

1 Solve these equations. If one or both sides can be simplified then do that first.

a $4y - y = 8 - y + 4$

b $a + 5 + 5a - 5 = 2a - a + 15$

c $k + 1 + 2k + 3 = k + 10 - k$

d $8x + 2 - 4x - 2 = 5x + 21 - 4x$

e $m + 5m - 4m = 10 - m + 14$

2 Opposite angles of a parallelogram are equal.
Find the size of the labelled angles in each parallelogram.

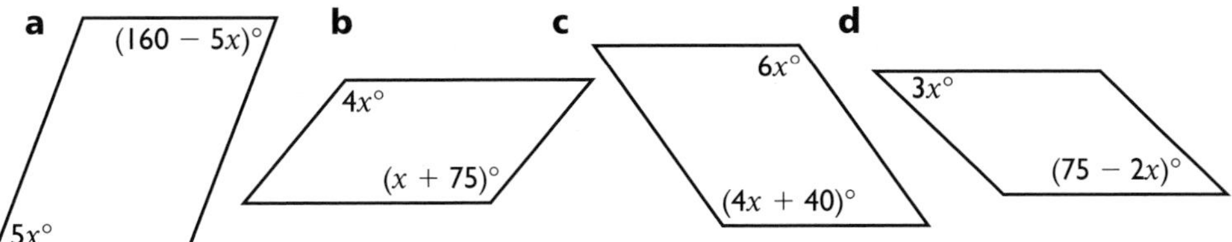

3 For each of these situations, make an equation and solve it.
Use your solution to solve the problem.

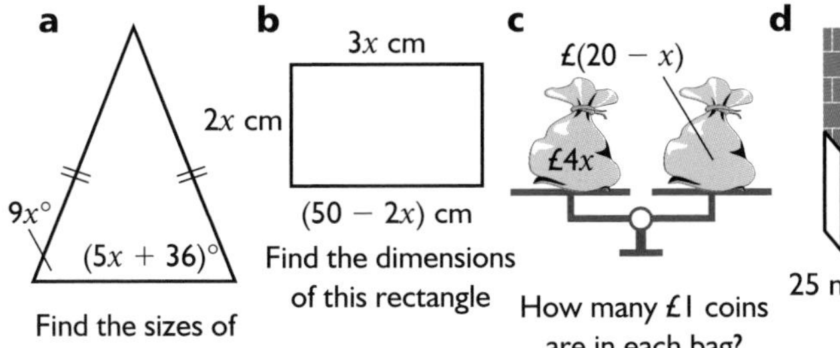

Challenge

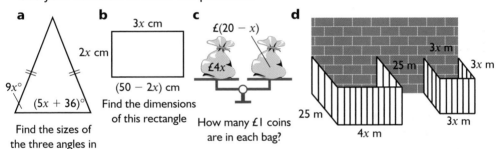

Each frame requires exactly the same length of wood.
Find the dimensions of each frame.

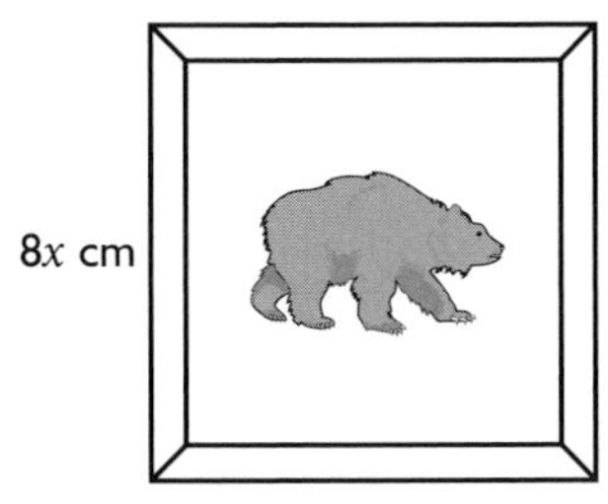

This is a square frame

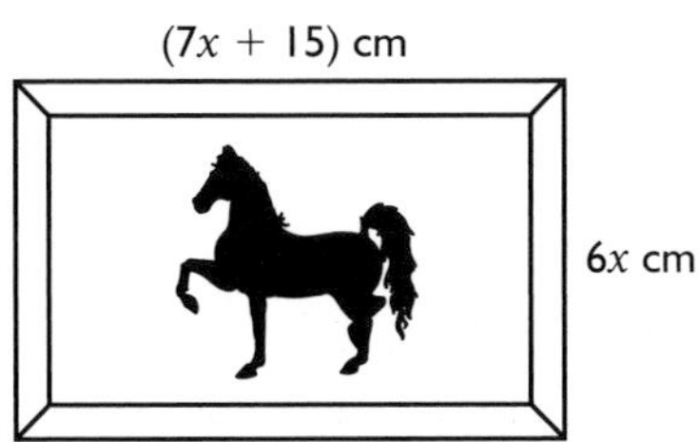

This is a rectangular frame

E

5 Inequations

If it's less than 3 then it must be 0 or 1 or 2 … $x < 3 \Rightarrow x = 0, 1, 2$

If it's less than or equal to 3 then it must be 0 or 1 or 2 or 3 … $x \leqslant 3 \Rightarrow x = 0, 1, 2, 3$

If it's greater than 3, it could be 4 or 5 or 6 or … … $x > 3 \Rightarrow x = 4, 5, 6, 7, \ldots$

If it's greater than or equal to 3, it could be 3 or 4 or 5 or … … $x \geqslant 3 \Rightarrow x = 3, 4, 5, 6, 7, \ldots$

These are **inequality** signs.

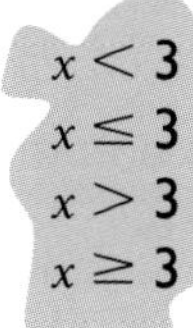

These are inequalities or **inequations**.

Inequations can describe situations.

Inequations have solutions.

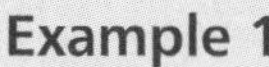

Example 1

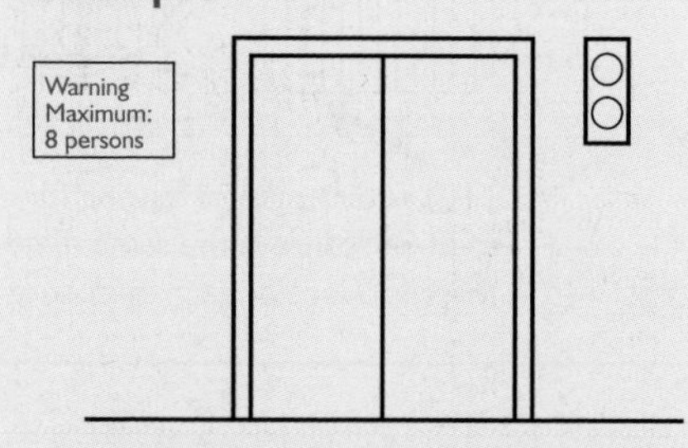

If there are n people in the lift safely then $n \leqslant 8$.

Example 2

Solve $x + 2 > 5$ choosing solutions from $\{1, 2, 3, 4, 5, 6, 7\}$.

$1 + 2 = 3$
$2 + 2 = 4$
$3 + 2 = 5$
not greater than 5 ✗

$4 + 2 = 6$
$5 + 2 = 7$
$6 + 2 = 8$
$7 + 2 = 9$
greater than 5 ✓

So the solutions are $x = 4, 5, 6,$ or 7.

Exercise 5.1

1 Place $<$, $\leqslant$, $>$ or $\geqslant$ between the two given numbers to make a true statement. All questions have two possible answers.

a 1 … 3	**b** 5 … 4	**c** 5 … 5	**d** $\frac{1}{2}$ … 1
e 2·6 … 3	**f** 9 … $8\frac{1}{2}$	**g** 10 … 100	**h** 13 … 12
i 0 … 0	**j** 0 … 5	**k** −3 … 0	**l** −3 … −2

2 Use the given inequality sign to order the pair of numbers (e.g. with 2, 3 and $>$ we get $3 > 2$).

a 8, 4 using $<$ **b** 3, 2 using $>$ **c** 0, 6 using $\geqslant$ **d** 14, 3 using $\leqslant$
e 1, 7 using $<$ **f** 2, 3 using $>$ **g** 7, 3 using $\leqslant$

3 Write an inequation that describes each situation.

a

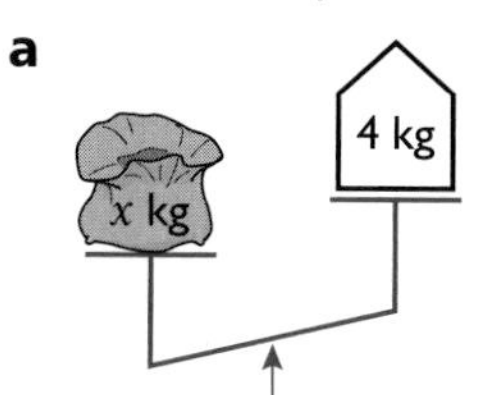

b

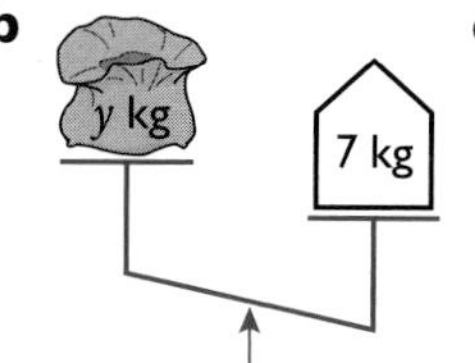

c

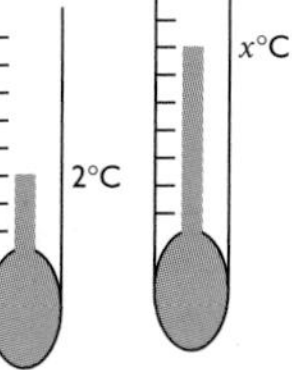

d

e

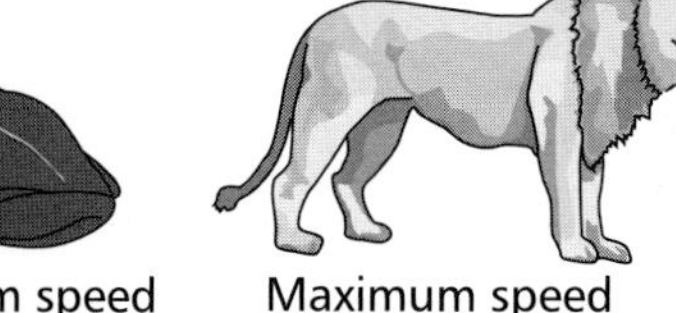

Maximum speed x mph

Maximum speed 60 mph

f

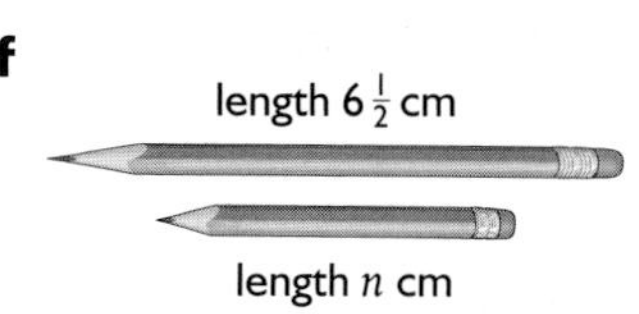

4 Solve these inequations, choosing solutions only from the listed numbers:

a $x \leqslant 3$ from {1, 2, 3, 4, 5} **b** $m \geqslant 2$ from {0, 1, 2, 3, 4}
c $y > 6$ from {4, 5, 6, 7} **d** $a < 5$ from {2, 3, 4, 5}
e $e < 9$ from {8, 9, 10, 11} **f** $k \leqslant 1$ from {1, 2, 3, 4, 5}
g $w \geqslant 5$ from {2, 3, 4, 5, 6, 7} **h** $x > 3$ from {0, 1, 2, 3}

5

I must have at least 300 points to qualify.
I will qualify since I've got n points.
Inequation: $n \geqslant 300$.

Treat each of the following situations in a similar way and write an inequation that describes it.

a 'Your maximum speed is 30 mph.' 'That's OK since I'm travelling at x mph.'

b 'If you take less than 2 hours you'll be in time,' 'I'll take h hours so I'll be in time.'

c 'Tickets cost £3.' 'Good, I've got £m so I can buy one.'

d 'Has the temperature of the oven reached 200 °C yet?' 'Yes it's at T °C which is more than that.'

e 'You need more than 5 litres of paint.' 'I've only got y litres. That's not enough.'

f 'I'm gaining weight. I was 60 kg, I'm now w kg.'

g 'What was the passmark?' '60%.' 'I've passed! I got n%.'

E

6 **i** Describe each of these using an inequation.
ii Solve it using the allowed weights listed below each diagram. Give your solution like this: $x = 2, 3$

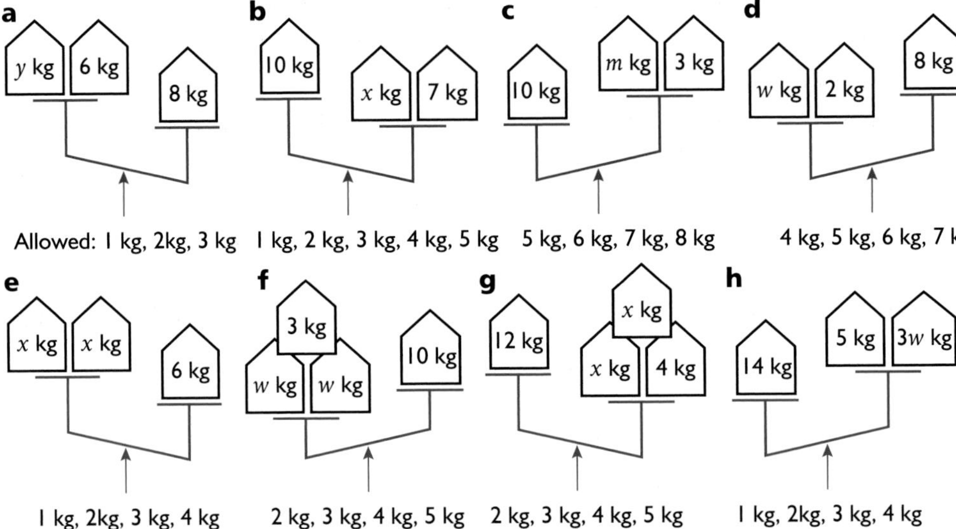

Challenges

A i This costs £x. You'll get change from £3.

ii This costs £y. You'll get change from £5.

iii £5 is not enough if you want to buy both.

a Write inequations to describe these statements.

b Find whole number values to satisfy the three inequations.

B
- m and n are two whole numbers.
- $m + n < 10$
- $m > n + 2$
- $n > 2$

Find the only pair of numbers that fit this description.

Exercise 5.2

1 Solve these inequations, choosing values from the given list:

a $3m \geqslant 9$ {2, 3, 4, 5}
b $2x < 9$ {3, 4, 5, 6, 7}
c $12 > 4n$ {1, 2, 3, 4, 5}
d $y + 4 \leqslant 6$ {1, 2, 3, 4}
e $18 - w > 15$ {1, 2, 3, 4, 5}
f $8 \leqslant x + 3$ {2, 3, 4, 5, 6}
g $14 \leqslant 5k$ {1, 2, 3, 4, 5}
h $y - 5 \geqslant 1$ {3, 4, 5, 6}
i $14 < 20 - x$ {1, 2, 3, 4, 5}
j $5w \leqslant 10$ {2, 3, 4, 5}
k $10 \leqslant 16 + y$ {1, 2, 3, 4}
l $5x < 2$ {1, 2, 3, 4}

2 Match the inequations and solutions. All values are chosen from 1 to 10 only.

A	$2x + 1 \leqslant 9$	**i**	$x = 1, 2,$ or 3
B	$10 - x > 6$	**ii**	$x = 7, 8, 9$ or 10
C	$4 > 16 - 2x$	**iii**	$x = 9$ or 10
D	$25 < 3x + 1$	**iv**	$x = 1$ or 2
E	$4x - 3 \leqslant 5$	**v**	$x = 8, 9$ or 10
F	$30 - 3x < 9$	**vi**	$x = 1, 2, 3$ or 4

3 For each situation
i set up an inequation
ii solve it using the extra information.

a **i** The lift takes no more than a 2000 kg load safely.
A load of three identical crates and a 500 kg box is safe. (Hint: let the weight of one crate be x kg.)
ii Crates weigh 450 kg, 550 kg or 650 kg.

b **i** It is possible to fill seven identical cans from the 50 litres left in the tank. More than 30 litres must always remain in the tank for emergency use. (Hint: let one can contain x litres.)
ii Cans come in 2·5 litre, 3 litre or 3·5 litre sizes.

c **i** The store room is 400 cm high, floor to ceiling.
Eight identical crates are stacked on top of each other followed by two packets each 30 cm high, again on top of each other. There is still space at the top. (Hint: let each crate be x cm high.)
ii Crates come in various heights: 42 cm, 45 cm and 48 cm.

4 Solve these inequations, choosing whole number values from 5 to 10 only:

a $3x + 3 > 30$
b $2x - 6 \leqslant 10$
c $35 \leqslant 4x + 3$
d $40 > 5x - 5$
e $30 - 3x > 6$
f $8 \leqslant 38 - 5x$
g $5x \geqslant 4x + 6$
h $4x < 3x + 8$
i $3x - 18 \geqslant x$
j $2x - 5 > 16 - x$
k $x + 6 \geqslant 36 - 2x$
l $3 + 2x \geqslant 3x - 4$
m $9 + 3x \leqslant 4x + 2$
n $3x < 35 - 2x$
o $9x + 7 \leqslant 3x + 61$
p $38 - x \leqslant 48 - 3x$
q $30 - x > 36 - 2x$
r $19 - \frac{1}{2}x < 22 - x$

E

6 Solving more equations

Example 1

Solve $4m - 1 = 2m + 5$

$4m - 1 = 2m + 5$
$\Rightarrow 4m - 1 + 1 = 2m + 5 + 1$
$\Rightarrow 4m = 2m + 6$
$\Rightarrow 4m - 2m = 2m + 6 - 2m$
$\Rightarrow 2m = 6$
$\Rightarrow 2m \div 2 = 6 \div 2$
$\Rightarrow m = 3$

Check: $4 \times 3 - 1 = 2 \times 3 + 5 = 11$ ✓

Example 2

Solve $8 + 3x = 7x - 12$

$8 + 3x = 7x - 12$
$\Rightarrow 8 + 3x + 12 = 7x - 12 + 12$
$\Rightarrow 20 + 3x = 7x$
$\Rightarrow 20 + 3x - 3x = 7x - 3x$
$\Rightarrow 20 = 4x$
$\Rightarrow 20 \div 4 = 4x \div 4$
$\Rightarrow 5 = x$
$\Rightarrow x = 5$

Check: $8 + 3 \times 5 = 7 \times 5 - 12 = 23$ ✓

Intermediate steps can often be omitted.

Example 3 Solve $40 - 2x = 3x + 5$

$40 - 2x = 3x + 5$
$\Rightarrow 35 - 2x = 3x$ (by subtracting 5)
$\Rightarrow 35 = 5x$ (by adding $2x$)
$\Rightarrow 7 = x$ (by dividing by 5)
$\Rightarrow x = 7$

Check: $40 - 2 \times 7 = 3 \times 7 + 5 = 26$ ✓

F

Exercise 6.1

1 For each equation, carry out the given action and then solve the resulting simpler equation. Check your solutions.

a $5y - 2 = 2y + 4$ $(+2)$
b $10 + 2n = 8n - 8$ $(+8)$
c $28 - x = 2x + 4$ (-4)
d $6m + 5 = 25 + m$ (-5)
e $7t - 1 = 11t - 9$ $(+9)$
f $9w + 2 = 35 - 2w$ (-2)

2 Solve each equation in two different ways suggested by the given actions. Your final solutions should be the same! Remember to check them.

a **i** $5x + 2 = x + 22$ (-2) **ii** $5x + 2 = x + 22$ $(-x)$
b **i** $20 - y = 5y - 4$ $(+4)$ **ii** $20 - y = 5y - 4$ $(+y)$
c **i** $9c - 8 = 2c + 41$ $(+8)$ **ii** $9c - 8 = 2c + 41$ $(-2c)$
d **i** $18 - 7w = 2 + w$ (-2) **ii** $18 - 7w = 2 + w$ $(+7w)$

3 Solve these equations and check your solutions.

a $4e + 1 = e + 7$ **b** $5w - 3 = 2w + 6$ **c** $8x - 12 = 2x - 6$

d $24 - 5y = 2y + 3$ **e** $21 + m = 1 + 5m$ **f** $13 - 2a = 3 + 8a$

g $5x - 2 = 22 - x$ **h** $2n + 13 = 5 + 4n$ **i** $29 - 5k = 9k + 1$

j $4 + 8c = 3c + 39$ **k** $23 - 5x = x - 7$ **l** $10 - 8y = 1 + y$

m $16 - 2a = 5a - 40$ **n** $14x + 2 = 26 + 11x$ **o** $46 + 7t = 12t + 6$

4 Each diagram shows a pair of fields.

i Find an expression for the perimeter of each field.

ii Each of the two fields requires the same length of fencing.
Set up an equation and solve it to find the length of fencing required.

iii Give the dimensions of each field. (All measurements are in metres.)

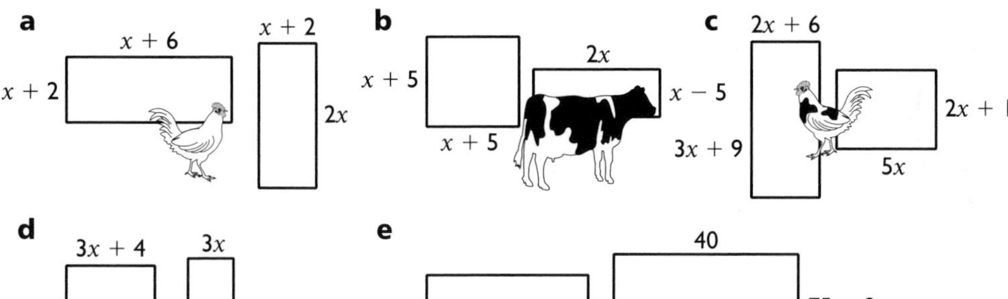

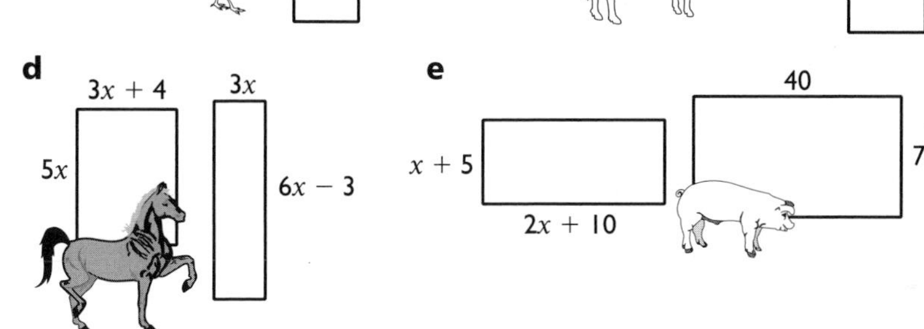

5 Solve this cross-number puzzle.

Across

1 $4x - 20 = x + 49$

3 $9 + 8x = 2x + 81$

5 $x - 31 = 6x - 406$

8 $8x - 17 = 337 + 5x$

10 $9 - 5x = 93 - 9x$

11 $340 - 2x = 5x - 227$

13 $137 - x = 50 + 2x$

15 $17 - 3x = 514 - 10x$

17 $223 + 3x = 5x - 1$

18 $28 + 5x = 646 - x$

1	2	3	4	5	6
7	8	9		10	
11	12	13	14	15	16
17			18		

Down

2 $x + 52 = 176 - 3x$

4 $10x - 52 = 200 + x$

6 $60 + 3x = 4x + 9$

7 $60 - 2x = 6 + x$

9 $2x + 90 = 700 - 3x$

10 $300 - 8x = 3x + 3$

12 $5 + x = 27 - x$

14 $45 + 13x = 500 + 8x$

16 $100 + 2x = 10x - 4$

7 Negative numbers and expressions

Example If $x = -2$ and $y = -3$ then find the values of:

a $x - y$ b $5xy$ c $\frac{x^2}{y}$ d $5(x + y)$ e $4x - 6y$ f $\frac{10 + 2x}{2y}$

Answers:

a $x - y = -2 - (-3)$
$= -2 + 3$
$= 1$

b $5xy = 5 \times (-2) \times (-3)$
$= 5 \times 6$
$= 30$

c $\frac{x^2}{y} = \frac{(-2)^2}{-3}$
$= \frac{4}{-3}$
$= -1\frac{1}{3}$

d $5(x + y) = 5 \times (-2 + (-3))$
$= 5 \times (-5)$
$= -25$

e $4x - 6y = 4 \times (-2) - 6 \times (-3)$
$= -8 - (-18)$
$= -8 + 18$
$= 10$

f $\frac{10 + 2x}{2y} = \frac{10 + 2 \times (-2)}{2 \times (-3)}$
$= \frac{10 + (-4)}{-6}$
$= \frac{6}{-6}$
$= -1$

F

Exercise 7.1

1 If $a = -3$ and $b = -5$, find the value of:

a $a - b$ **b** $3a$ **c** b^2 **d** $b - a$ **e** ab **f** $a + b$

2 If $m = -1$ and $n = -2$, find the value of:

a $2m + 3$ **b** $\frac{n}{m}$ **c** $m + 2n$ **d** $5 - mn$
e m^2 **f** $2n^2$ **g** $2 - n^2$ **h** $(m - n)^2$
i mn^2 **j** m^2n **k** $(mn)^2$ **l** $m - n^2$
m $m^2 - n$ **n** $\frac{m}{n}$ **o** $\frac{m + n}{m}$ **p** $\frac{m + n}{m - n}$
q $m(n + 2)$ **r** $-3(n - 1)$ **s** $-4(m - n)$ **t** $m(2n - 3m)$

3 Evaluate each expression using the given values:

a $10 - x;\ x = -7$ **b** $3(y - 2);\ y = -5$
c $-2(3 + m);\ m = -1$ **d** $3a - 2b;\ a = -2,\ b = -3$
e $xy - x;\ x = -2,\ y = 3$ **f** $5n^2;\ n = -4$

g $(3-k)^2;\ k=-2$

h $10-pq;\ p=-2,\ q=-3$

i $\dfrac{4-y}{4+y};\ y=-2$

j $ab^2-a^2b;\ a=2,\ b=-1$

k $-(x-y);\ x=-5,\ y=-2$

l $\dfrac{10-m^2}{m^2-10};\ m=-3$

Challenge

In order, the expressions: $a-b$, dc, $a-(b+c)$, $\dfrac{b}{d}$, $ad-c$, ac, a^2+c, bc, $(c+d)^2$ and $c(a+c)$ have values 1 to 10.
The values -1, -2, -3 and -4 are to be assigned to the letters a, b, c and d in some order. Find the correct order.

8 Negative numbers and equations

Example 1

Solve $-3+x=-5$

$-3+x=-5$
$\Rightarrow\ -3+x+3=-5+3$
$\Rightarrow\ x=-2$

Example 2

Solve $-2x=6-x$

$-2x=6-x$
$\Rightarrow\ -2x+x=6-x+x$
$\Rightarrow\ -x=6$
$\Rightarrow\ x=-6$

Example 3 Solve $5-2x=-7$

$5-2x=-7$
$\Rightarrow\ 5-2x-5=-7-5$
$\Rightarrow\ -2x=-12$
$\Rightarrow\ -2x\div(-2)=-12\div(-2)$
$\Rightarrow\ x=6$

Exercise 8.1

1 Solve each equation.

a $-2+y=-1$ **b** $-3+x=-7$ **c** $4-w=6$

d $7-t=-2$ **e** $-2m=6$ **f** $6+2n=0$

g $12+x=3$ **h** $a-2=-1$ **i** $3n=-9$

j $3x+12=0$ **k** $18-4y=2$ **l** $-7-2y=1$

m $3=7+2n$ **n** $7w-1=-15$ **o** $-y+8=-2$

2 Match equations and solutions:

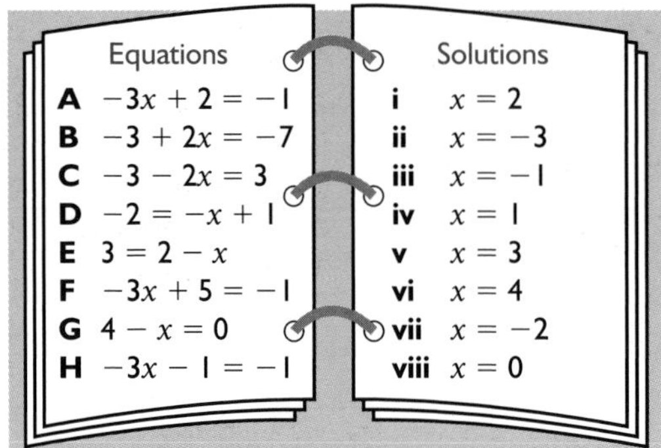

Equations
A $-3x + 2 = -1$
B $-3 + 2x = -7$
C $-3 - 2x = 3$
D $-2 = -x + 1$
E $3 = 2 - x$
F $-3x + 5 = -1$
G $4 - x = 0$
H $-3x - 1 = -1$
Solutions
i $x = 2$
ii $x = -3$
iii $x = -1$
iv $x = 1$
v $x = 3$
vi $x = 4$
vii $x = -2$
viii $x = 0$

3 Solve these equations:

a $5w + 7 = 3w + 3$ **b** $x - 1 = 3x + 5$ **c** $3 - 2y = 4 - y$
d $4t - 3 = 1 + 6t$ **e** $-7a - 5 = 1 - 4a$ **f** $10x - 1 = -2x - 25$
g $1 - m = 6 + 4m$ **h** $-7 - 3n = 10n + 6$ **i** $3k - 5 = -10 - 2k$
j $-1 - 8y = y - 10$ **k** $-w - 8 = -2 + 5w$ **l** $-3 - 8t = 12 - 3t$

9 Brackets and equations

Example 1

Solve $2(x + 4) = 12$

$2(x + 4) = 12$ ... remove the brackets
$\Rightarrow 2x + 8 = 12$
$\Rightarrow 2x + 8 - 8 = 12 - 8$
$\Rightarrow 2x = 4$
$\Rightarrow x = 2$

Example 2

Solve $5x = 3(8 - x)$

$5x = 3(8 - x)$ ... remove the brackets
$\Rightarrow 5x = 24 - 3x$
$\Rightarrow 5x + 3x = 24 - 3x + 3x$
$\Rightarrow 8x = 24$
$\Rightarrow x = 3$

Exercise 9.1

1 Solve these equations, first removing the brackets:

a $3(x - 2) = 6$ **b** $25 = 5(x + 4)$ **c** $4(y + 3) = 28$
d $8 = 2(a - 1)$ **e** $42 = 6(w + 3)$ **f** $8(k - 3) = 40$
g $50 = 10(x - 3)$ **h** $7(m + 2) = 63$ **i** $72 = 9(n + 2)$
j $2(c - 7) = 20$ **k** $5(x + 9) = 50$ **l** $2(t + 7) = 22$

2 Solve:

a $2(3 - x) = 4x$ **b** $3x = 5(x - 2)$ **c** $2(x + 1) = x + 3$
d $4(5 - x) = x$ **e** $5x = 3(x + 2)$ **f** $x - 2 = 7(x - 2)$
g $6(x + 1) = 20 - x$ **h** $9(1 - x) = 3 - 6x$ **i** $11(x - 1) = 8x - 2$
j $17x = 8(x + 9)$ **k** $3(12 - x) = 2x + 1$ **l** $7(2 - x) = 6 - 3x$

3 Complete this cross-number puzzle.

Across

1 $6(x - 7) = 3x$
3 $6(x + 2) = 396 - 2x$
4 $2(x - 17) = 50 - x$
6 $4x = 3(x + 15)$
8 $104 - x = 2(x - 29)$
9 $8x = 16(x - 36)$

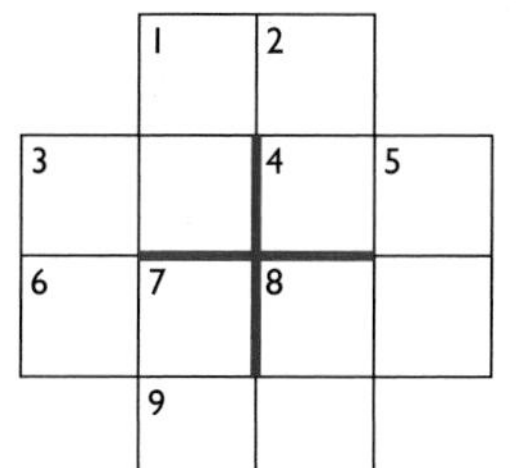

Down

1 $5x = 6(x - 3)$
2 $3x - 46 = 2(x - 2)$
3 $60 - x = 2(x - 36)$
5 $2(x - 8) = 3x - 100$
7 $3(x - 56) = 60 - x$
8 $3(x + 8) = 5x - 80$

4 Solve these equations:

a $3(2x - 1) = 5(x - 3)$
b $2(12 - 3x) = 3(x + 2)$
c $2(1 - 4x) = 3(x + 8)$
d $2(3x + 11) = 4(1 - 3x)$
e $2(3x - 5) = 8(7 - 2x)$
f $2(6x - 1) = 5(3x - 1)$
g $2(6 - x) = 4(2x + 13)$
h $2(x + 11) = 6(x + 9)$
i $2(10 - 2x) = 3(3x - 2)$
j $4(26 - 2x) = 5(3x - 16)$
k $4(6 - 2x) = 8(x + 9)$
l $6(4 - 2x) = 3(x + 58)$
m $2(3 - 7x) = 5(3 - x)$
n $7(2x + 14) = 2(4 - 2x)$
o $3(9x + 1) = 5(7x - 1)$

10 A negative multiplier

Example 1

Remove the brackets in the expression $-3(2x - 5)$

$$\begin{aligned}-3(2x - 5) &= -3 \times 2x - (-3) \times 5\\ &= -6x - (-15)\\ &= -6x + 15\end{aligned}$$

Example 2

Simplify $-(2a - 6)$

$$\begin{aligned}-(2a - 6) &= -1(2a - 6)\\ &= -1 \times 2a - (-1) \times 6\\ &= -2a + 6\end{aligned}$$

Example 3 Simplify $5 - (2a - 6)$

$$\begin{aligned}5 - (2a - 6) &= 5 - 1(2a - 6)\\ &= 5 - 2a + 6 \text{ ... see Example 2}\\ &= 11 - 2a\end{aligned}$$

Example 4 Solve $10 - 3(2x + 6) = 4$

$10 - 3(2x + 6) = 4$

$\Rightarrow 10 - 6x - 18 = 4 \quad -3(2x + 6) = -3 \times 2x + (-3) \times 6$

$\Rightarrow -8 - 6x = 4$

$\Rightarrow -6x = 12$

$\Rightarrow \dfrac{-6x}{-6} = \dfrac{12}{-6}$

$\Rightarrow x = -2$

F

Exercise 10.1

1 Remove the brackets:

a $-5(x-3)$ **b** $-2(8+y)$ **c** $-3(a-2b)$ **d** $-(m+n)$
e $-10(2t-3)$ **f** $-(2x-3y)$ **g** $5-2(x-2y)$ **h** $x-3(5y+2)$
i $2w-3(x+1)$ **j** $7(e-2f)+3$ **k** $5m-(n-2)$ **l** $18-2(a+3b)$

2 Simplify:

a $3-(x+2)$ **b** $-3(y-1)-3$ **c** $2x-(x+y)$
d $5-3(m-1)$ **e** $t-(8-3t)$ **f** $-2a-3(b+2a)$
g $9-7(w+2)$ **h** $8w-2(w-3)$ **i** $5n-(n+1)$
j $-1-5(k-2)$ **k** $10-(10-e)$ **l** $-(11+a)+a$
m $-4(2-f)+2f$ **n** $2a-7(a-b)$ **o** $-(x+y)-2(x-y)$

3 Solve these equations. Remove the brackets and simplify first.

a $8-2(x-1)=4$ **b** $5x-(3+x)=1$
c $-3(x+1)=2x+7$ **d** $-2(x+3)=8(x-7)$
e $2x-3(3x+1)=18$ **f** $6-5(2-3x)=14x$
g $7-2(3x+1)=10-x$ **h** $-3(2-2x)=10(x-3)$
i $12-5(8-2x)=-3x-80$ **j** $8-3(x-2)=15-5(x+1)$

F

11 Fractions and equations

Remember $\frac{A}{4} \times 4 = A \div 4 \times 4 = A$

Example 1

Solve $\frac{3x}{4} = 6$

$\frac{3x}{4} = 6$

$\Rightarrow \frac{3x}{4} \times 4 = 6 \times 4$

$\Rightarrow 3x = 24$

$\Rightarrow x = 8$

Example 2

Solve $\frac{2}{3} = \frac{3x}{5}$

$\frac{2}{3} = \frac{3x}{5}$

$\Rightarrow \frac{2}{3} \times 3 \times 5 = \frac{3x}{5} \times 3 \times 5$

$\Rightarrow 2 \times 5 = 3x \times 3$

$\Rightarrow 10 = 9x$

$\Rightarrow \frac{10}{9} = \frac{9x}{9}$

$\Rightarrow \frac{10}{9} = x$

$\Rightarrow x = \frac{10}{9}$

Example 3 Solve $\frac{2x-3}{5} = -1$

$$\frac{2x-3}{5} = -1$$
$$\Rightarrow \frac{2x-3}{5} \times 5 = -1 \times 5$$
$$\Rightarrow 2x - 3 = -5$$
$$\Rightarrow 2x = -2$$
$$\Rightarrow x = -1$$

Exercise 11.1

1 Solve these equations by first getting rid of the fractions.

a $\frac{x}{7} = 8$ **b** $\frac{y}{2} = 1$ **c** $\frac{3x}{4} = 6$ **d** $8 = \frac{2x}{3}$

e $9 = \frac{3x}{4}$ **f** $\frac{5w}{6} = 10$ **g** $\frac{7m}{9} = 21$ **h** $4 = \frac{2n}{11}$

i $\frac{2a}{3} = -4$ **j** $-12 = \frac{4n}{7}$ **k** $\frac{x+2}{3} = 2$ **l** $\frac{y-5}{2} = 3$

2 Solve:

a $\frac{5k}{2} = \frac{1}{3}$ **b** $\frac{2}{3} = \frac{4y}{5}$ **c** $\frac{8x}{7} = \frac{5}{6}$ **d** $\frac{1}{9} = \frac{3w}{4}$

3 Solve each of these equations:

a $\frac{2x+1}{3} = 5$ **b** $1 = \frac{3x-1}{5}$ **c** $\frac{2x+5}{3} = -1$

d $\frac{8-x}{3} = 3$ **e** $\frac{5-3x}{5} = -2$ **f** $\frac{9+3x}{4} = -3$

F

12 Inequations revisited

If $A > B$ then
- $A + 4 > B + 4$
- $A - 4 > B - 4$
- $A \times 4 > B \times 4$
- $A \div 4 > B \div 4$

However
- $A \times (-4) < B \times (-4)$
- $A \div (-4) < B \div (-4)$

Notice how the relationship between *A* and *B* changes when you multiply or divide by a negative quantity.

Using these ideas, inequations can be *balanced* in a similar manner to equations.

Example 1 Solve this inequation: $-x < -6$

$$-x < -6$$
$$\Rightarrow -x \times (-1) > -6 \times (-1)$$
$$\Rightarrow x > 6$$

Example 2 Solve $8 \geqslant -2x$

$8 \geqslant -2x$
$\Rightarrow \quad 8 \div (-2) \leqslant -2x \div (-2)$
$\Rightarrow \quad -4 \leqslant x$
$\Rightarrow \quad x \geqslant -4$

Example 3 Solve $2x - 3 < 7$

$2x - 3 < 7$
$\Rightarrow \quad 2x - 3 + 3 < 7 + 3$
$\Rightarrow \quad 2x < 10$
$\Rightarrow \quad 2x \div 2 < 10 \div 2$
$\Rightarrow \quad x < 5$

Exercise 12.1

1 Rewrite each inequation in the form '$x >$ …' or $x \geqslant$ …' or '$x <$ …' or '$x \leqslant$ …'.

a $8 < x$ **b** $2 \geqslant x$ **c** $5 > x$ **d** $4 \leqslant x$
e $-x > -2$ **f** $-x \leqslant 5$ **g** $-x < -7$ **h** $-x \geqslant 2$
i $3 \leqslant -x$ **j** $-2 > -x$ **k** $4 \geqslant -x$ **l** $-7 < -x$

2 Solve these inequations:

a $-2x > 4$ **b** $9 \leqslant -3x$ **c** $14 < 7x$ **d** $5x \geqslant -15$
e $28 \geqslant -7x$ **f** $56 < -8x$ **g** $-6x \leqslant -30$ **h** $-2 > -2x$

3 Solve:

a $x - 3 \geqslant 7$ **b** $8 - x < 17$ **c** $9 > 10 - x$
d $4 - x < 8$ **e** $x + 8 \geqslant 2$ **f** $3 \leqslant x + 7$

4 Solve:

a $3x + 2 < x - 3$ **b** $x - 4 \geqslant 2x + 1$ **c** $8 - 3x \leqslant 10 - x$

5 For each picture **i** form an inequation (the first one is done) **ii** solve it.

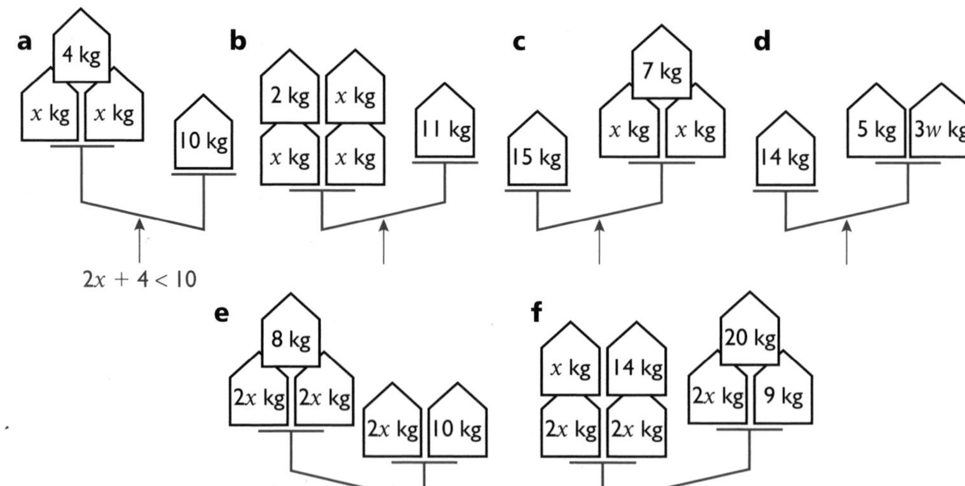

CHECK-UP

1 Solve these equations:

a $2x - 4 = 14$ **b** $\frac{1}{3}n + 2 = 5$ **c** $13 - 5m = 3$

d $25 = 2x + 1 + x + 3$ **e** $16 = 20 - \frac{1}{4}y$

2 **a** Form an equation.

b Solve the equation.

c Say what the mystery number is.

I think of a number.
I halve it.
I subtract the answer from 11.
I get 2.

3 Solve these equations:

a $16 + y = 3y$ **b** $x = 12 - 3x$ **c** $14 - 4k = 3k$

4 These two angles are equal. Find their size.

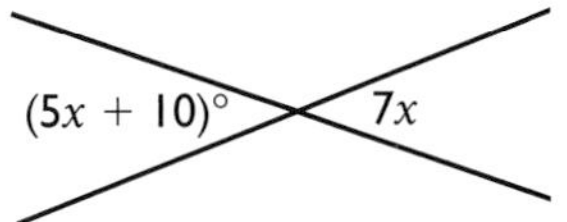

5 Use the information in the diagram to find the dimensions of the rectangle.

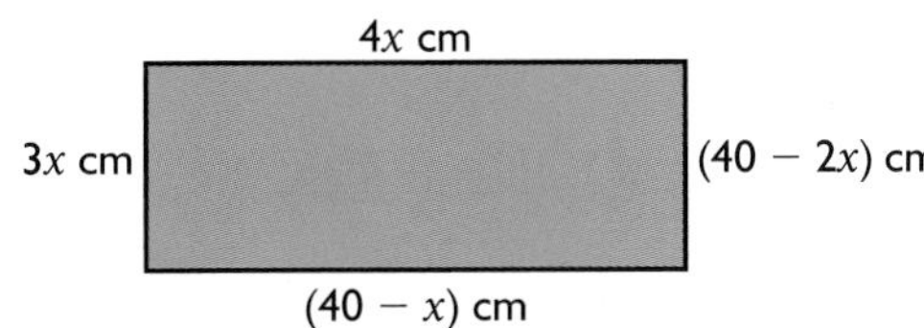

6 Solve these inequations, choosing solutions from 1, 2, 3, 4 or 5 only.

a $3x > 9$ **b** $18 - x \leqslant 15$ **c** $5x - 2 \leqslant 2x + 7$

7 Solve these equations:

a $6x - 1 = x + 9$ **b** $7 - 2y = 1 + y$ **c** $11 - 8m = 2 + m$

8 These two fields require the same length of fencing.

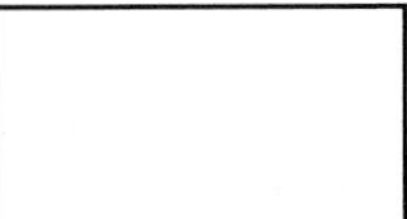

12 m

$4x$ m

a Find an expression for the perimeter of each field.

b Set up an equation and solve it.

c Find the length of fencing each field requires.

d Give the dimensions of each field.

9 $p = -3$, $q = -4$ and $r = 5$. Find the value of:

a $2pq$ **b** $3p - 4q$ **c** qr^2 **d** $r(p + q)$ **e** $\frac{r - q}{p}$

E
F

10 Solve these equations:

a $2(x - 3) = 8$ **b** $7 - (8 + 2x) = -7$ **c** $6y + 7 = 4y + 3$

d $2(5x - 1) = -3(3 - x)$ **e** $\frac{x + 2}{3} = \frac{x - 1}{2}$

11 Solve these inequations:

a $-5x > 15$ **b** $-18 \leqslant -3x$ **c** $10 - 3x \geqslant 12 - x$

9 Calculating distance

Measuring lengths and finding distances which are inaccessible to direct measurement have been major activities in the history of mathematics and science.

3000 years ago the Egyptians were measuring and building pyramids to an accuracy which is still considered astonishing today.

In the third century BC, the Greek mathematician Eratosthenes calculated the circumference of the earth, while another Greek, Aristarchus, was able to work out the distance to the sun and moon by considering the relative positions of the earth, moon and sun at the time of a half-moon.

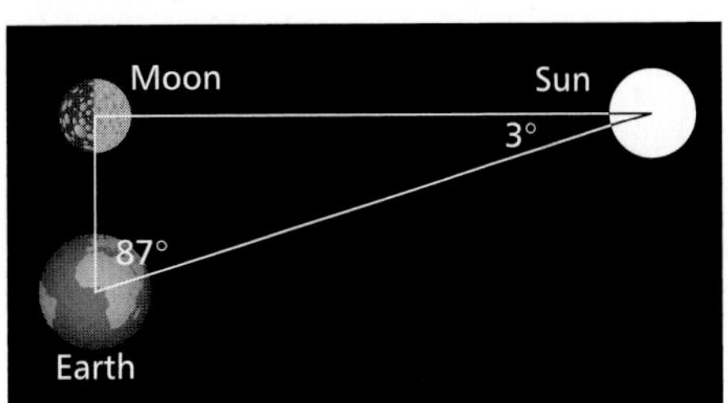

1 Looking back ◀◀

Exercise 1.1

1 How many centimetres are in:
a 3 m **b** 7 m 4 cm **c** 11·54 m
d 90 mm **e** 147 mm **f** 8 mm?

2 Work out how many metres are in:
a 450 cm **b** 83 cm **c** 17 km **d** 9·2 km.

3 Round to the nearest whole number:
a 14·235 **b** 785·76 **c** 19·93.

4 Round to one decimal place:
a 5·55 **b** 23·456 **c** 7·073 **d** 86·023 **e** 0·418.

5 Round to three significant figures:
a 36 844 **b** 39·5831 **c** 2·938 46 **d** 0·857 240 1 **e** 10·037 8.

6 State the value of each labelled number.

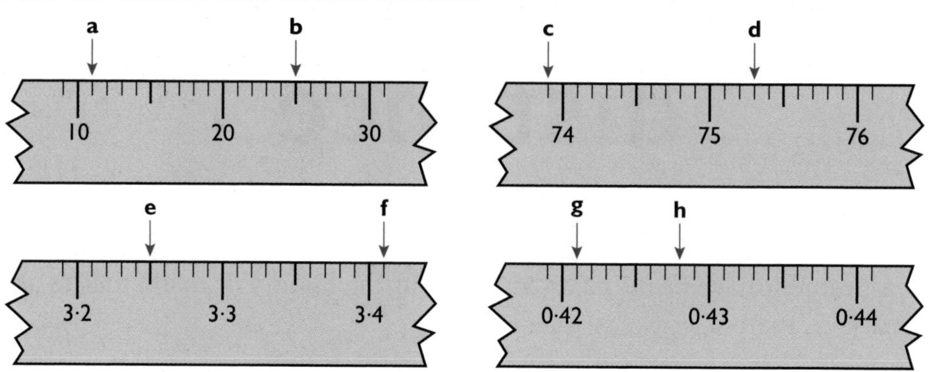

7 Without using a calculator, work out:

a 5^2 **b** 9^2 **c** 30^2 **d** $0·7^2$

8 Use the x^2 button on your calculator to work out:

a 23^2 **b** $4·6^2$ **c** $1·04^2$ **d** $0·37^2$

◀◀ E

9 Calculate:

a $8^2 + 5^2$ **b** $6·6^2 + 4·1^2$

10 Work out, without a calculator:

a $\sqrt{16}$ **b** $\sqrt{81}$ **c** $\sqrt{400}$ **d** $\sqrt{0·64}$

11 Use a calculator to help you work out, correct to 1 decimal place:

a $\sqrt{1369}$ **b** $\sqrt{30·25}$ **c** $\sqrt{237}$
d $\sqrt{0·2209}$ **e** $\sqrt{1·81}$ **f** $\sqrt{5^2 + 12^2}$

2 Working with length

Remember: 10 000 000 metres is the distance from the Pole to the Equator.

10 millimetres = 1 centimetre
100 centimetres = 1 metre
1000 millimetres = 1 metre
1000 metres = 1 kilometre

When working with lengths, units should be consistent.

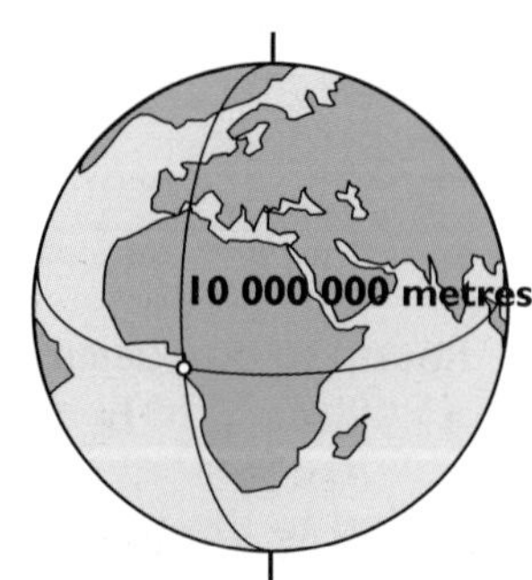

Example 1 Add 35 cm, 99 cm, 2·75 m, 1 m and 3 m 4 cm.

Converting all lengths to metres: 0·35 m + 0·99 m + 2·75 m + 1·00 m + 3·04 m
Total = 8·13 m

Example 2 An engineer has to examine 3 km of road in a day.
He has examined 1094 metres so far.
How much more does he have to examine?

Working in metres: 3000 m − 1094 m = 1906 m
or working in kilometres: 3 km − 1·094 km = 1·906 km

Whatever units you choose, make sure you state them in the answer.

Exercise 2.1

1 Work out the following, being mindful of the units.

- **a** 3·45 m + 1·05 m + 2 m 35 cm + 76 cm
- **b** 2 m + 34 cm + 1·9 m + 1 m 9 cm
- **c** 2·121 km + 5 km 29 m + 126 m
- **d** 6 km + 89 m + 2·7 km + 3 km 7 m
- **e** 6·54 m − 1 m 6 cm
- **f** 3 m − 9 cm
- **g** 7 km − 82 m
- **h** 3·87 km − 942 m

2
- **a** Express the quotient of 2·76 m ÷ 3 in centimetres.
- **b** Express the result of 34·8 km ÷ 4 in metres.
- **c** Calculate 78 cm × 23 and express your answer in metres.
- **d** Calculate 326 m × 45 and express your answer in kilometres.

3 Put the following lists of lengths in order, smallest first.

- **a** 1 m 25 cm, 1·06 m, 1·5 m, 1 m 5 cm, 124 cm
- **b** 3·78 km, 3 km 78 m, 378 m
- **c** 8·712 km, 8 km 71 m, 8714 m, 817 m

4 In the long jump finals, Colin jumped 7·66 metres on his first jump and 7·79 metres on his second.

- **a** By how many centimetres was his second jump better than his first?
- **b** His third attempt was 7·62 metres.
  What was the mean of the three jumps?

E

5 The table shows the distances jumped by four competitors in the triple jump.

a How far in total did each competitor jump?

b Arrange them in order, winner first.

metres	Hop	Skip	Jump	Total
Allan	5·76	5·21	4·88	
Bostan	4·99	5·66	5·07	
Charles	5·80	5·00	4·87	
Daniel	4·87	4·65	5·11	

6 The *Titanic* was 268·16 metres long.
The *Queen Elizabeth* was 315·48 metres.

a How much longer was the *Queen Elizabeth*?

b Express this difference as a fraction of the length of the *Queen Elizabeth*.

7 The table gives the depths of the five deepest caves in the world.

Country	Austria	Iran	Mexico	Poland	Switzerland
Depth	913 m	751 m	859 m	783 m	827 m

a Put the list in order, deepest first.

b **i** Calculate the mean depth.

ii State the value of the median depth.

E

8 A roll contains 15 metres of ribbon.
Charity workers are making twists of ribbon to sell to raise funds.
Each twist of ribbon uses 11 cm.

a How many can they make from the roll of ribbon?

b How many centimetres of ribbon are left?

c The ribbons are sold for 20p each.
How much money will they make if they sell them all?

9 A fence has five strands of wire on it.
475 metres of roadside needs to be fenced.
How many kilometres of wire are needed?

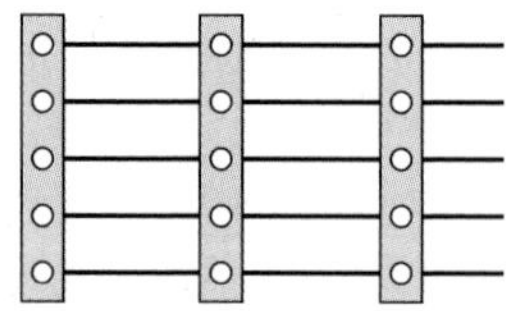

10 A building plot has straight edges and all angles are right angles, as shown in the diagram.

a Calculate the perimeter of the building plot.

b How many metres less than a kilometre is this?

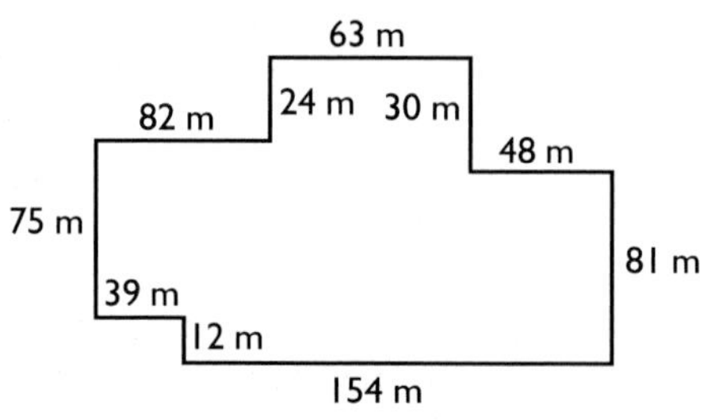

11 a When a metal bar was heated its length increased by 0·0025 m.
By how many millimetres did it increase?

b A metal rail is heated until its length increases by 0·1%.
What is its new length if it originally was
i 23 metres **ii** 3 metres?

c In very cold weather a metal rail contracts by 0·1%.
What is its new length if it originally was
i 23 metres **ii** 3 metres?

12 Fiona kept a log of her height over several years.
At the start of the record she was 1·2 metres tall.
The table shows her height increases in each year.

Year 1	Year 2	Year 3	Year 4
3·5 cm	0·02 m	55 mm	4·3 cm

a How tall was Fiona at the end of the fourth year?

b What was her average increase in height per year?

We tend to use the most convenient units of measurement.
Sometimes the kilometre is not big enough.
Sometimes the millimetre is not small enough.

E

Exercise 2.2

1 a How many centimetres are in 0·0045 km?

b Write 76 mm as a decimal part of a kilometre.

2 The Franz Joseph Glacier in New Zealand is moving down the mountain.
It is estimated that the ice flow in the interior of the glacier is moving at 1·5 metres per day.

a How many kilometres will it have moved in 100 years?
(Answer to 1 decimal place.)

b How far does the glacier move in a second?

3 We often give our height in feet, which is an old imperial unit.
To change feet to metres we multiply by 0·305.

a Jamie is a basketball player and is seven and a half feet tall.
Calculate his height in metres, to 2 decimal places.

b Loch Morar in Scotland has a maximum depth of 1017 feet.
Lake Superior in Canada has a maximum depth of 405 metres.
Which is deeper, and by how much?

4 250 sheets of light card make a pile 3·2 cm thick.
Calculate the thickness of one sheet of card in millimetres (correct to 2 decimal places).

5 Astronomers, when discussing the solar system, do not use kilometres. The most convenient unit is called the **astronomical unit**. It is the distance between the sun and the earth.

1 astronomical unit (a.u.) = 149 600 000 km

Planet	Mercury	Venus	Earth	Mars	Jupiter
Distance to sun (a.u.)	0·39	0·72	1·00	1·52	5·20

a How many kilometres is

i Venus **ii** Jupiter from the sun?

b The diagram shows the distance between Mercury and Mars:

i at their closest **ii** at their furthest apart.

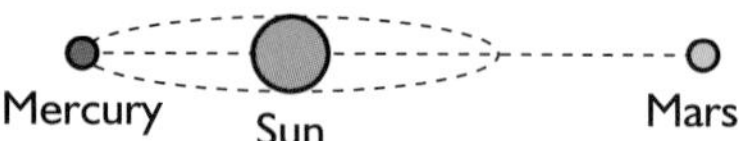

Calculate both distances in astronomical units.

E

6 When studying the distance to the stars, a more convenient unit is the **light year**.
A light year is the **distance** light will travel in space over a period of 1 year.

1 light year = 9 460 500 000 000 km

a How many astronomical units are in a light year?

b The first three stars whose distances were measured are:

- 61 Cygni (by Bessel in 1838) … 11·2 light years
- Proxima Centauri (by Thomas Henderson of Scotland) … 4·3 light years
- Vega (by von Struve) … 26 light years.

i Express the distance to 61 Cygni in astronomical units.

ii The distance to Proxima Centauri is 9000 times as far as it is from the sun to Pluto.
How far from the sun is Pluto in kilometres?

7 When physicists measure microwaves and study the atom, then the most convenient unit is the **angstrom**, named after Anders Ångström, a Swedish physicist of the nineteenth century.

1 angstrom = 0·000 000 01 cm

a Express 1 angstrom in metres.

b The wavelength of yellow sodium light is 0·000 059 cm
Express this in angstroms.

3 Estimating length

We estimate the length of an object by comparing it with a length we already know.

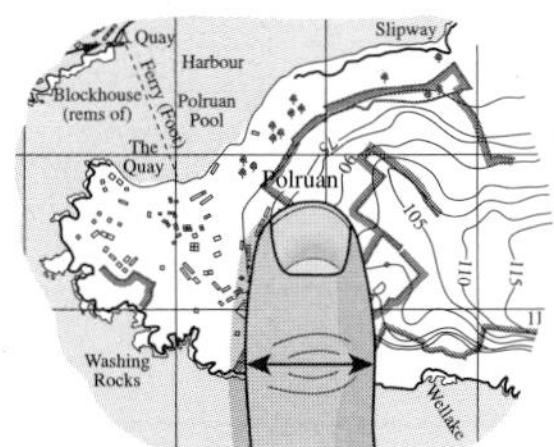

Many hillwalkers use their thumb to judge distances on maps. A thumb is about 2·5 cm wide.

A good pace is about 1 metre.

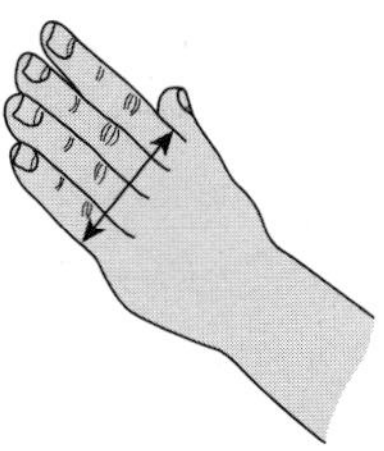

A hand is about 10 cm.

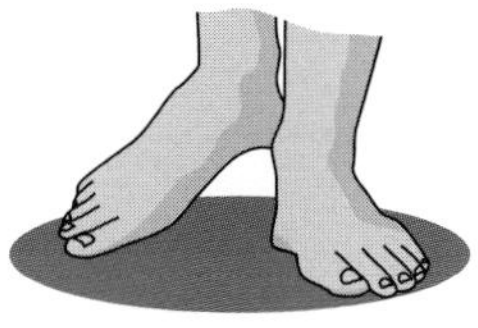

If your shoe size is $6\frac{1}{2}$, your foot is about 25 cm long.

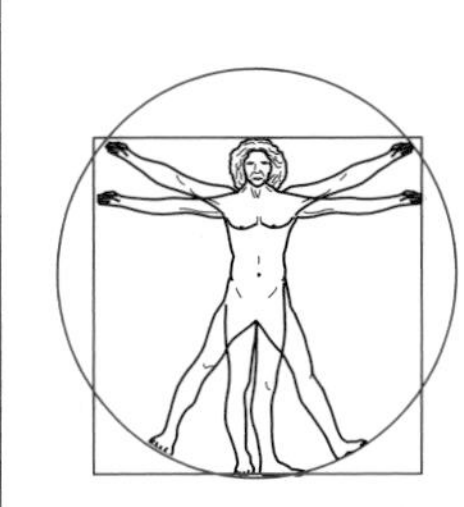

How many of these are true for you?

Waist to ground … 1 metre
Nose to fingertip … 1 metre
Elbow to fingertip … 50 cm
Height … between 1·5 m and 2 m
Thumb to pinkie (stretched) 20 cm

Exercise 3.1

1 We have to be careful when estimating size. Sometimes illusion plays a big part. For each pair

i estimate the size of the objects
ii decide which is bigger
iii measure each to the nearest millimetre. Were you correct?

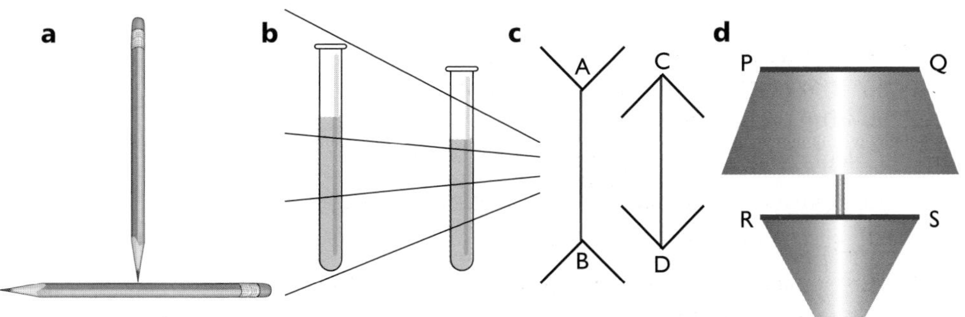

2 A thumb is roughly 25 mm wide. Estimate the length of …

a

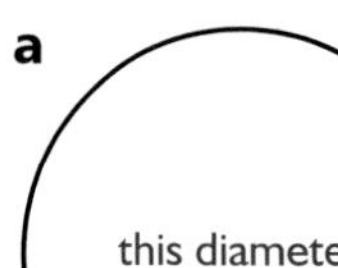

b

the diagonal

c

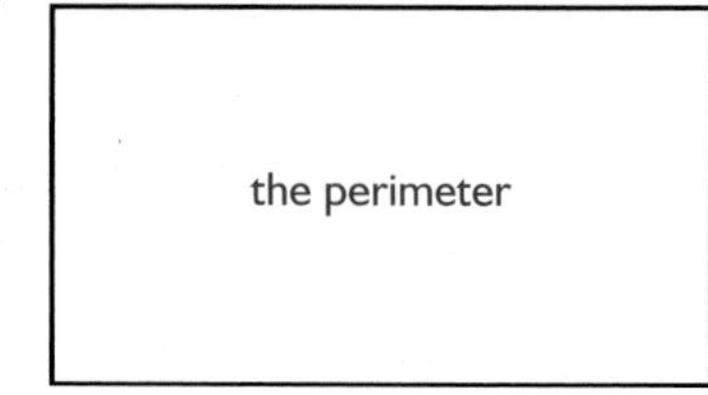

3 Estimate, in centimetres, the length of:

a PQ

b RS

c the 150 metre contour.

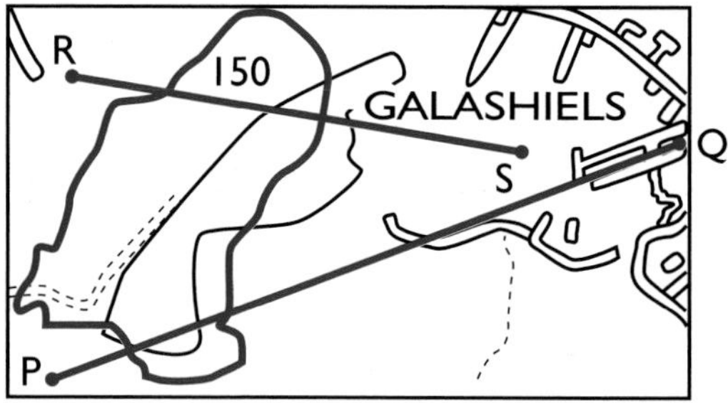

4 **a** Near the top of a page in your jotter mark a point A.

b Without the aid of a ruler, try to place the following points on the page. Their distance from A is given.

i B 6 cm **ii** C 13·5 cm

iii D 25 mm **iv** E 20 cm

v F 19 mm

c Use a ruler to find the number of millimetres you are out in each case. Ignore whether it is over or under.

d Calculate your mean error.

e Repeat the exercise with these points:

i G 5 cm **ii** H 12·5 cm

iii I 26 mm **iv** J 18 cm

v K 21 mm

f Has your mean decreased? Should it have?

5 **a** Estimate, in metres:

i the height of your desk

ii the length of the classroom

iii the height of the door

iv the width of the blackboard.

b Calculate your mean error.

c Compare this with the results of question **4**.

Relatively speaking ...

When one size in a picture is known, other sizes can be guessed at.

Suppose you know that Pat is 1·62 metres tall.

a The bin looks about $\frac{2}{3}$ the size of Pat.
You can estimate that the bin is $\frac{2}{3} \times 1{\cdot}62 = 1{\cdot}08$ metres
It would be reasonable to say the bin is about 1 metre high.

b Using a piece of paper it is easy to compare the width of the top of the bin with Pat's height.
It looks about $\frac{1}{3}$ of Pat.
The bin is about 0·5 metre wide at the top.

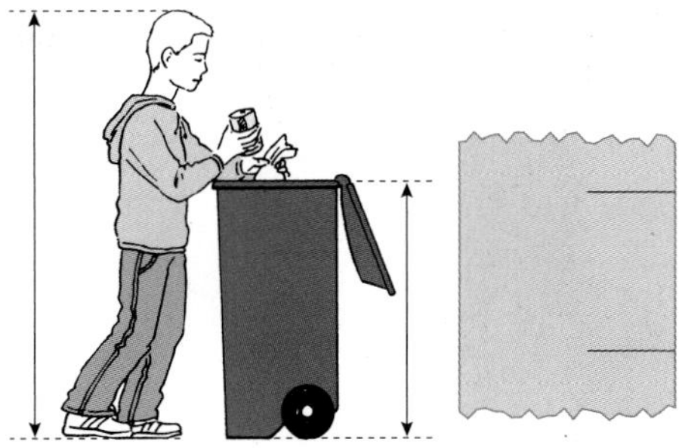

Mark the bin's width on a piece of paper

Exercise 3.2

1 If the car is 2·4 m long, estimate:

a the height of the car
b the length of the truck
c the height of the truck
d the diameter of the wheel of **i** the car **ii** the truck
e the length of the car's side windows.

2 Meg is 1·75 metres tall.

a Estimate:
  i the height of the door
  ii the width of the door.

b **i** Use a ruler to measure the height of Meg and of the door in the picture.
  ii Calculate what fraction of the door's height is Meg's height.
  iii Compare this with your estimate. Remember that Meg is 1·75 m tall.

E

3 Peter is a tree surgeon. He is 1·5 m tall.
Use this information to make an informed guess at the height of each tree.

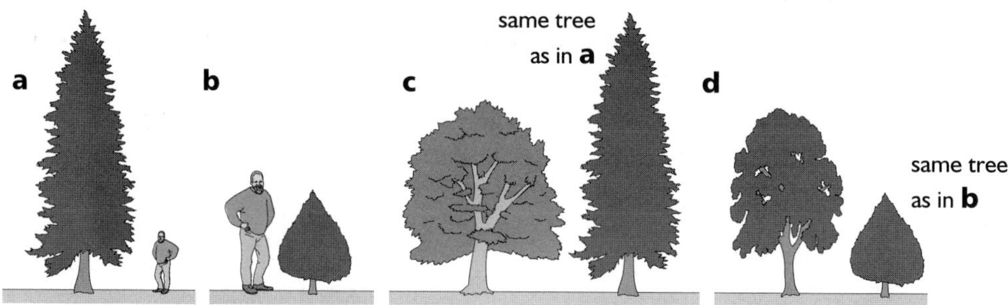

4 The garage door is 2·5 m tall.

a Estimate, in metres:
- **i** the height of the front door
- **ii** the height of the house
- **iii** the width of the garage
- **iv** the width of the whole building.

b The drawing is actually a plan with a scale 1 : 250.
Measure each of the above and hence calculate the actual sizes.

c How good were your estimates?
Was there any difference between the errors in estimated heights and estimated widths?

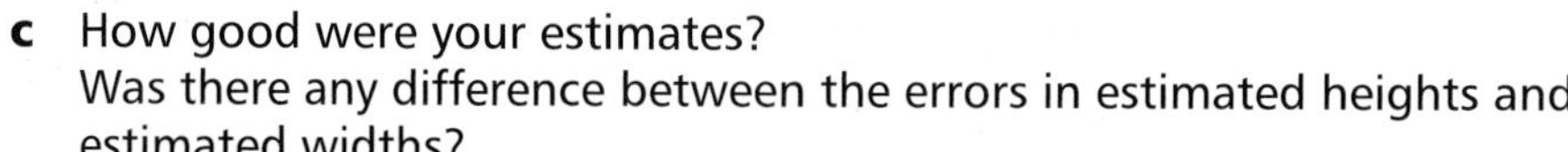

4 Reading between the lines …

The ruler is marked off in 10 cm lengths.
The pen measures more than 10 cm but less than 20 cm.

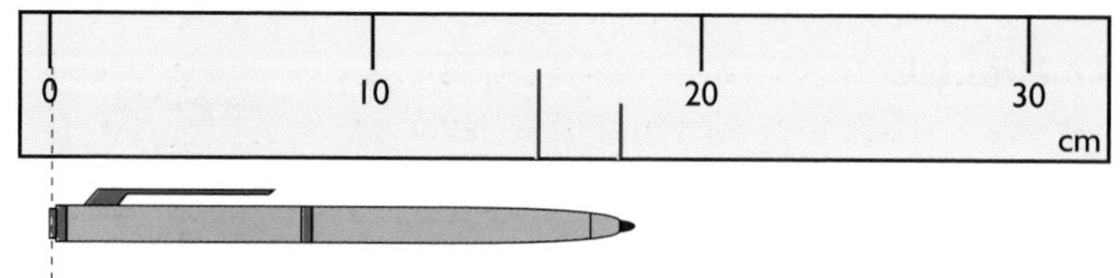

It is fairly easy to judge halfway between 10 and 20 … 15 cm is marked in **purple**.
Then in turn, halfway between 15 and 20 can be visualised. … 17·5 cm is marked.
It is reasonable to guess with some confidence that the pen is about 18 cm long.
It is definitely closer to 18 cm than it is to either 17 cm or 19 cm.

Exercise 4.1

1 Estimate the lengths or heights of each of these objects as accurately as you can by imagining *midway* marks.

a

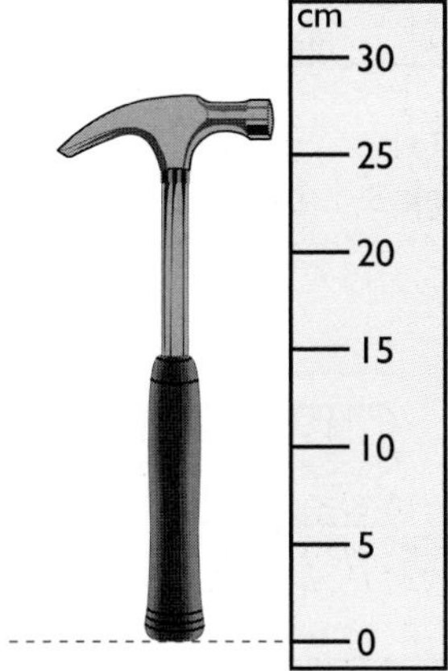

b

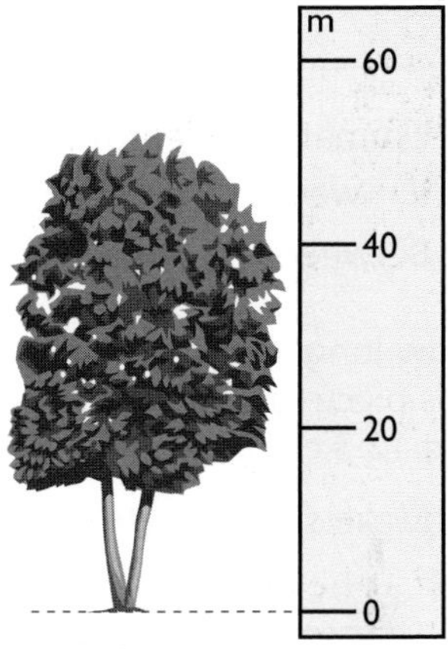

c

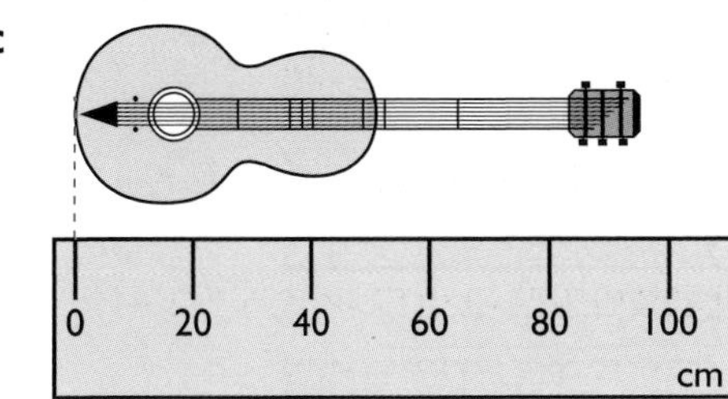

d

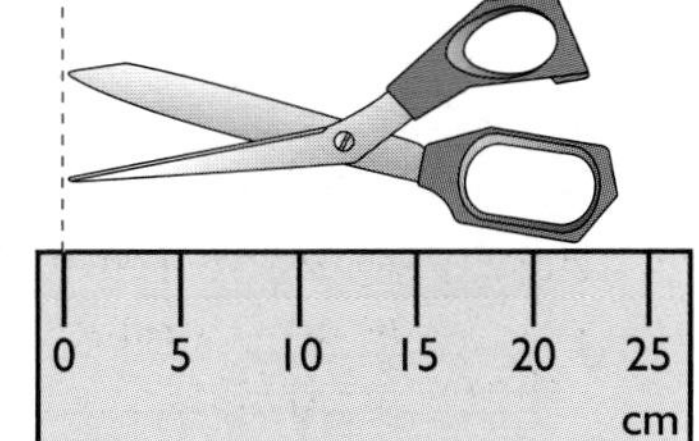

e

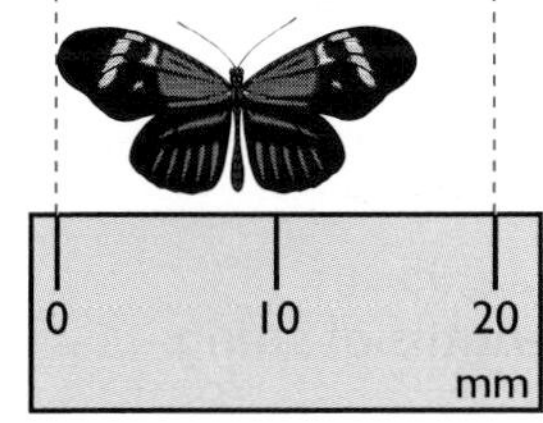

2 Some members of a class mark their heights on a chart. From the chart we can see that Ali's height is between 1·6 metres and 1·7 metres and is closer to 1·7 metres. To the nearest tenth of a metre Ali's height is 1·7 m.

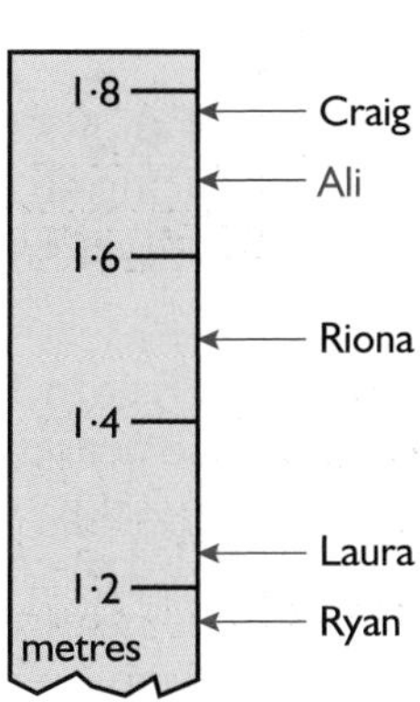

a Make similar statements about the other four students.

b Use these results to state the difference in height between Laura and Ryan. Comment.

c Estimate each student's height to the nearest 5 cm.

E

3 The length of a ground worm is recorded every week.

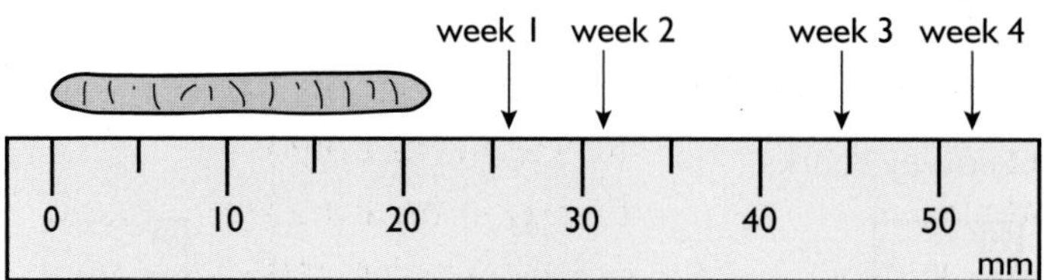

a Estimate the length of the worm at the end of

i week 1 **ii** week 2 **iii** week 3 **iv** week 4.

b Between which two weeks did it grow most?

4 'How long is a piece of string?'
This piece of string is between 12·2 cm and 12·3 cm and is closer to 12·3 cm.

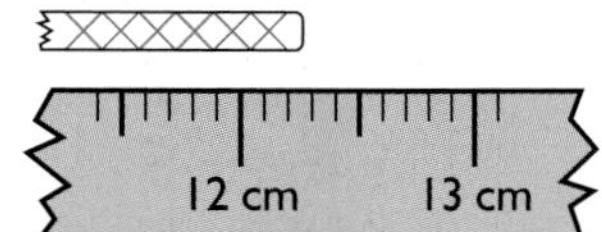

a Make similar statements about these pieces.

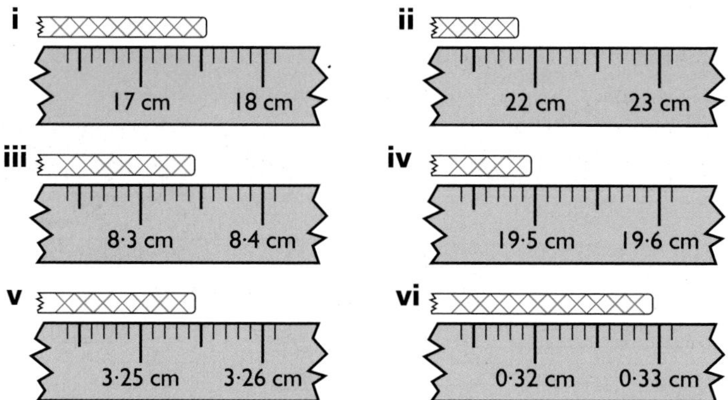

b When we said that the piece of string was 12·3 cm long, we meant 12·3 was the closest mark.
In truth, its length was between 12·25 cm and 12·35 cm.
Make similar statements about the following lengths of string:

i 12·8 cm **ii** 8·4 cm **iii** 9·5 cm.

Question **4** shows that no matter how accurately we measure, we are still at some level producing an *estimate*. Whenever we quote the length of an object, we accept that the number was a choice between two 'marks'.

For example:

3·6 cm (correct to 1 d.p.) ... lies between 3·55 cm and 3·65 cm
4 cm (to the nearest centimetre) ... lies between 3·5 cm and 4·5 cm
2·54 cm (to 2 d.p.) ... lies between 2·535 cm and 2·545 cm
5·6 cm (to 1 d.p) could actually be as large as 5·65 cm ... a possible error of 0·05 cm.
5 cm (to the nearest centimetre) could actually be as large as 5·5 cm ... a possible error of 0·5 cm.

Exercise 4.2

1 Between what two marks do the following measurements lie?

a 5·7 cm (to 1 d.p.)
b 0·9 cm (to 1 d.p.)
c 12·1 cm (to 1 d.p.)
d 4·5 cm (to 1 d.p.)
e 6 cm (to nearest cm)
f 18 cm (to nearest cm)
g 1 cm (to nearest cm)
h 76 cm (to nearest cm)

2 For each measurement
i state the biggest it could actually be
ii the size of the possible error.

a 2·3 cm (to 1 d.p.)
b 4·7 cm (to 1 d.p.)
c 7·0 cm (to 1 d.p.)
d 6.5 cm (to 1 d.p.)
e 7 cm (to nearest cm)
f 12 cm (to nearest cm)
g 10 cm (to nearest cm)

3 Two planks of wood are measured to the nearest centimetre.
Plank A is 26 cm and plank B is 32 cm long.

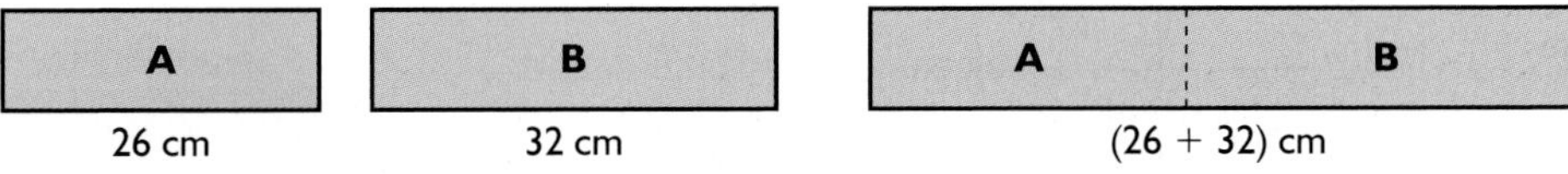

a What is the biggest **i** plank A
ii plank B might actually be?

b What is the biggest possible error in each case?

c The two planks are joined.
i What is the total length expected to be?
ii If the biggest possible error is made in both cases, what will the total length actually be?
iii What is the error (the difference between what is expected and what it actually is)?

d Two measurements are added. How do you work out the error in the sum?

4 Two pencils are measured to the nearest centimetre.
The larger one is 17 cm long.

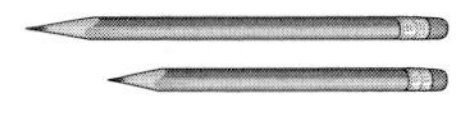

a How small might this pencil actually be?

b It is decided to trim this pencil by 3 cm to make it the same size as the other.
3 cm is measured from the tip correct to the nearest centimetre.
What is the biggest this measurement might actually be?

c One would expect the resulting pencil length to be 17 − 3 = 14 cm.
By using the results from **a** and **b** calculate how small the resulting pencil might turn out.

d Two measurements are subtracted. How do you work out the error in the difference?

5 The length and breadth of a rectangle are measured to the nearest centimetre. It is a 12 cm by 9 cm rectangle.

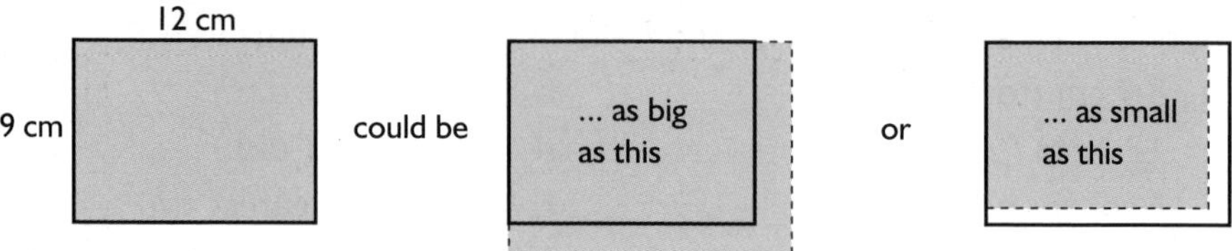
12 cm
9 cm
could be
... as big
as this
or
... as small
as this

a What is **i** the largest
ii the smallest the length might actually be?

b What is **i** the largest
ii the smallest the breadth might actually be?

c Its area is expected to be $12 \times 9 = 108\ \text{cm}^2$.
Calculate **i** how big
ii how small this area might actually be.

5 Calculating lengths

Around 2500 years ago a Greek mathematician called Pythagoras discovered that if a triangle was right-angled then the three sides formed a special relationship.

A recent postage stamp of Greece illustrates this relationship.

ΠΥΘΑΓΟΡΕΙΟΝ
ΘΕΩΡΗΜΑ
ΕΛΛΑΣ-ΔΡΧ.3 50

Notice that the areas of the squares drawn on the two smaller sides add up to the same area as the square drawn on the biggest side. (Count the small squares.)

The biggest side is given the name **hypotenuse**, which comes from the ancient Greek meaning 'stretched under'.

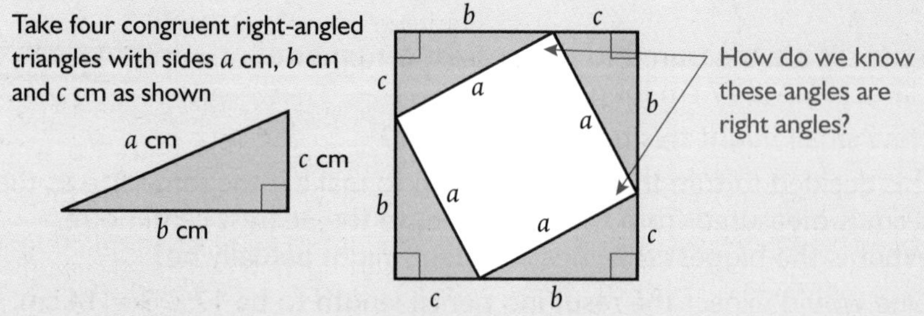
Take four congruent right-angled triangles with sides *a* cm, *b* cm and *c* cm as shown
a cm
c cm
b cm
b
c
c
a
a
b
b
a
a
c
c
b
How do we know these angles are right angles?

Arranged like this they form a large square of side $(b + c)$ cm.
The area of the square is equal to the area of the four triangles plus a^2, that is the area of the white square.

Arranged like this they also form a large square of side $(b + c)$ cm.
The area of the square is equal to the area of the four triangles plus b^2 plus c^2, the area of the two white squares.

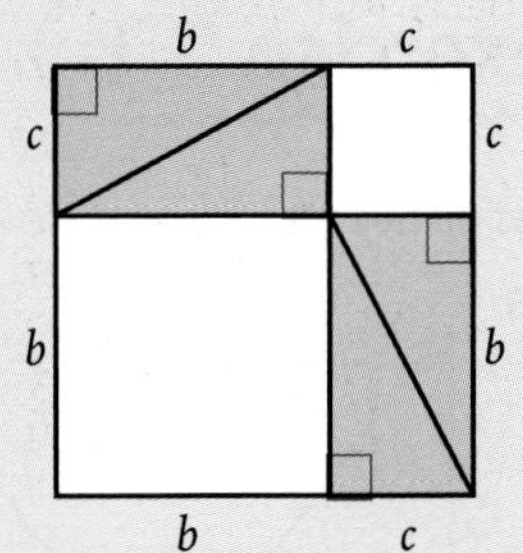

Since both arrangements produce the same large square we have

four triangles + a^2 = four triangles + $b^2 + c^2$
$\Rightarrow a^2 = b^2 + c^2$

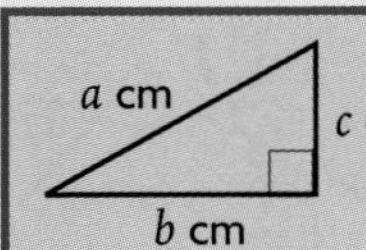

Given this right-angled triangle then $a^2 = b^2 + c^2$

In any right-angled triangle the square on the hypotenuse is equal to the sum of the squares on the other two sides.

Example 1 The triangle is right-angled.
The hypotenuse is p cm long.

$\Rightarrow p^2 = m^2 + n^2$

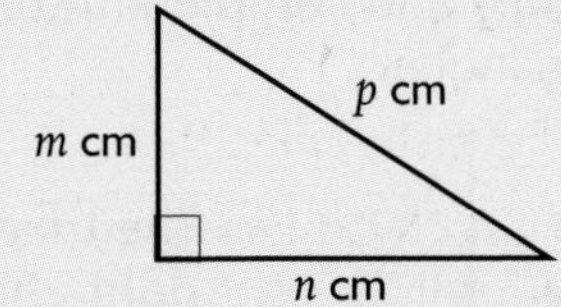

Example 2 The triangle is right-angled.
The hypotenuse is RE.

$\Rightarrow \text{RE}^2 = \text{GE}^2 + \text{RG}^2$

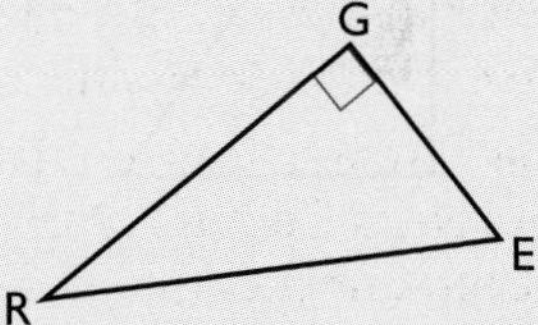

Example 3 The triangle is *not* right-angled.
Pythagoras's theorem does not apply.

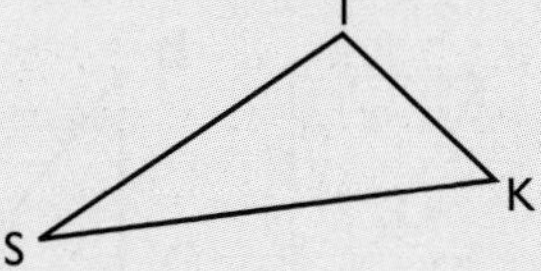

Example 4 The area of the square = $m \times m = m^2$

$\Rightarrow m^2 = 49$
$\Rightarrow m = \sqrt{49}$
$\Rightarrow m = 7$

The side of the square is 7 cm long.

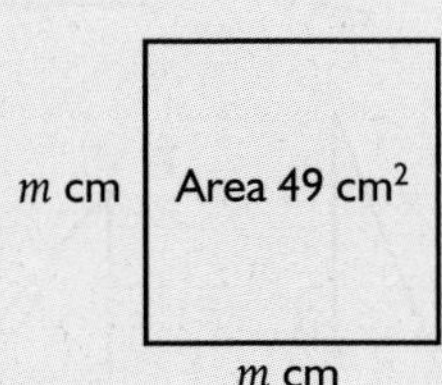

Exercise 5.1

1 Identify the hypotenuse of each triangle where possible.

a **b**

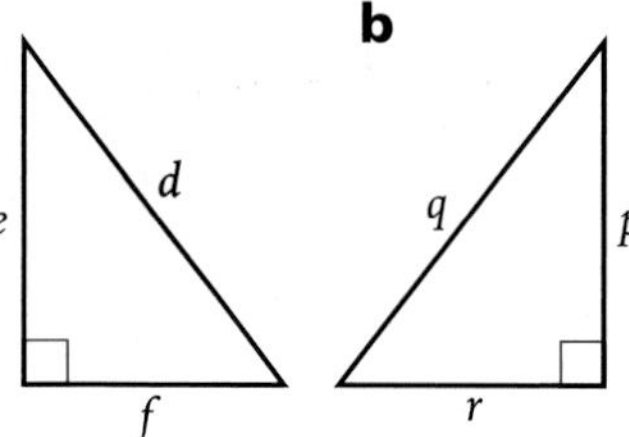

c **d**

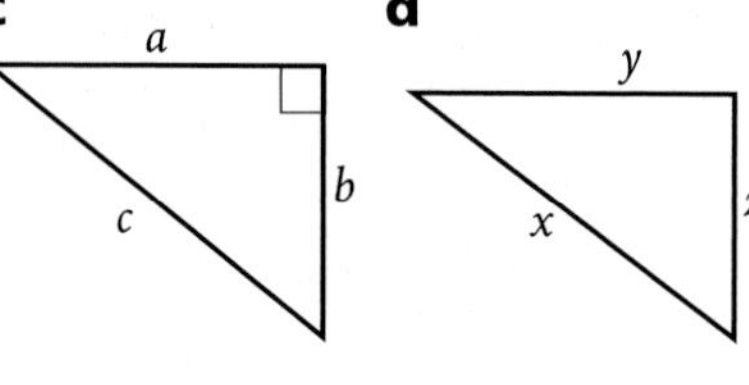

e

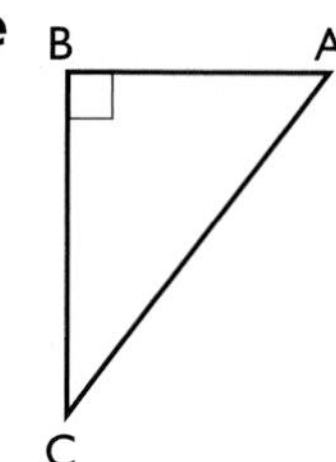

f **g**

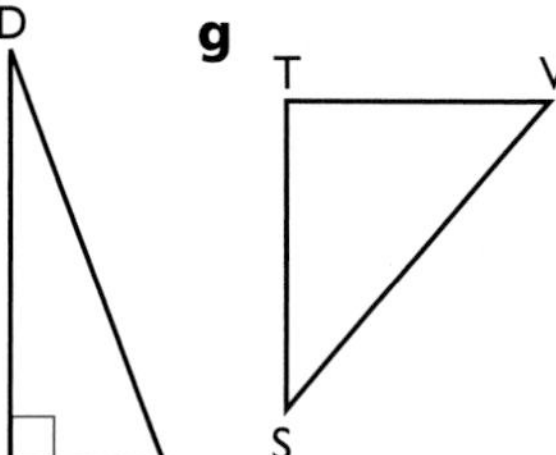

h **i**

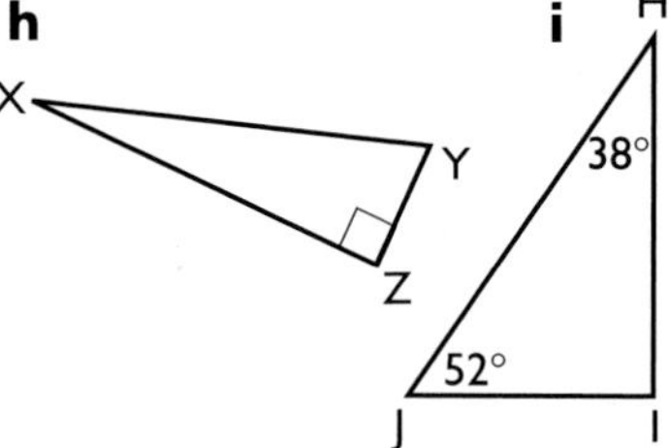

j

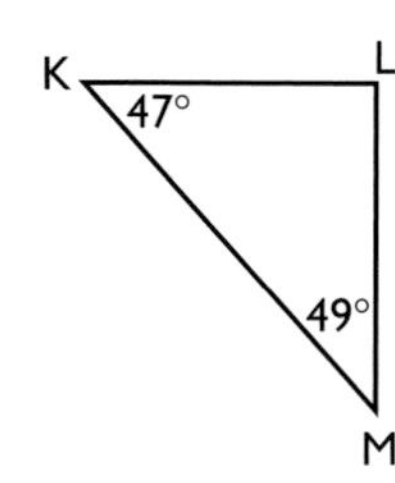

2 Copy and complete the statement of the theorem of Pythagoras for each triangle.

a

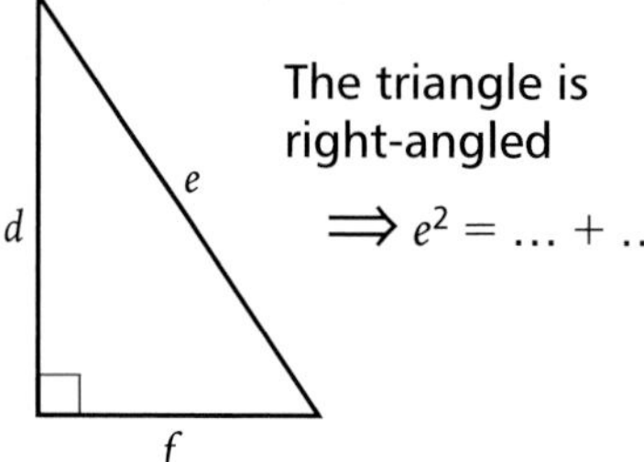

b

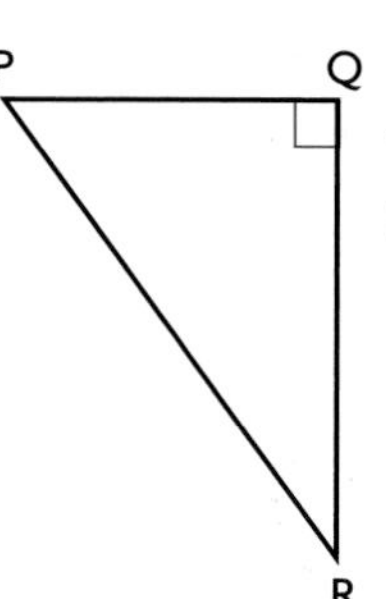

The triangle is right-angled

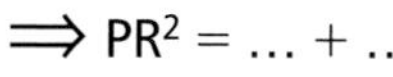

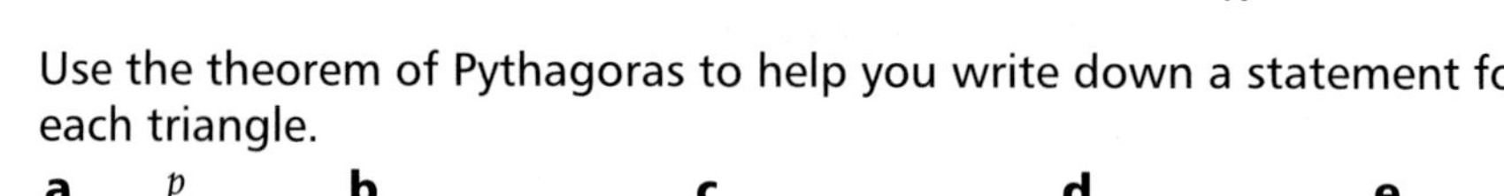

3 Use the theorem of Pythagoras to help you write down a statement for each triangle.

a

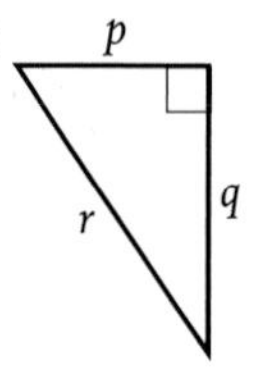

b

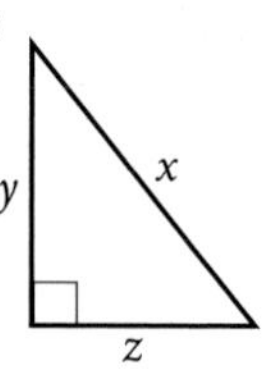

c

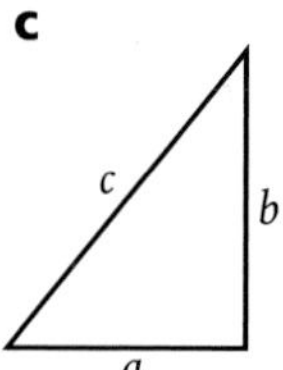

d

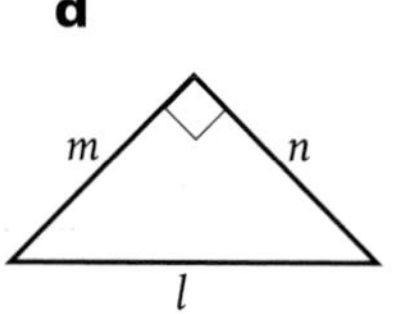

e

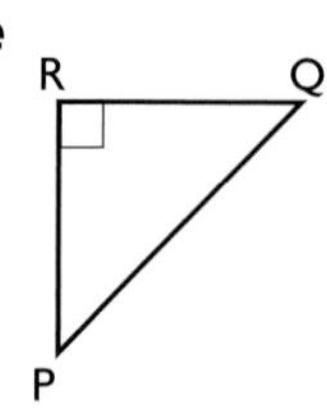

f

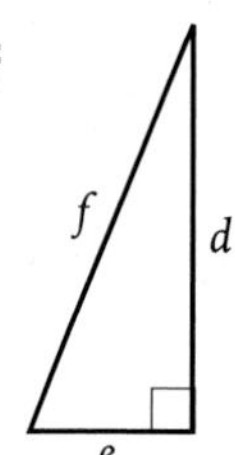

f

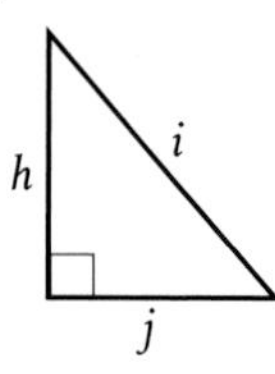

h

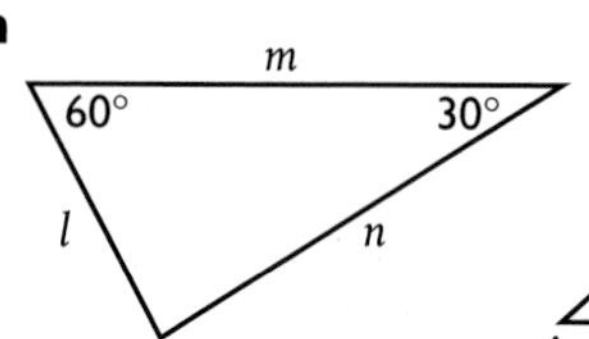

i

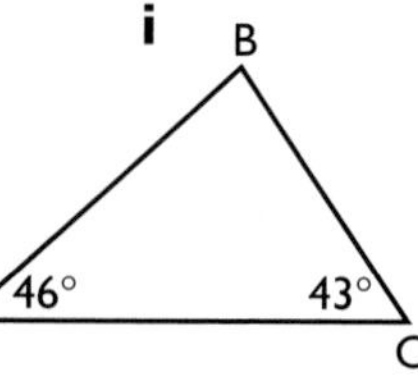

6 Calculating the length of the hypotenuse

Example 1 Calculate the length of AB.

The triangle is right-angled

$\Rightarrow$ $p^2 = 5^2 + 12^2$

$\Rightarrow$ $p^2 = 25 + 144$

$\Rightarrow$ $p^2 = 169$

$\Rightarrow$ $p = \sqrt{169}$

$\Rightarrow$ $p = 13$

The hypotenuse is 13 cm long.

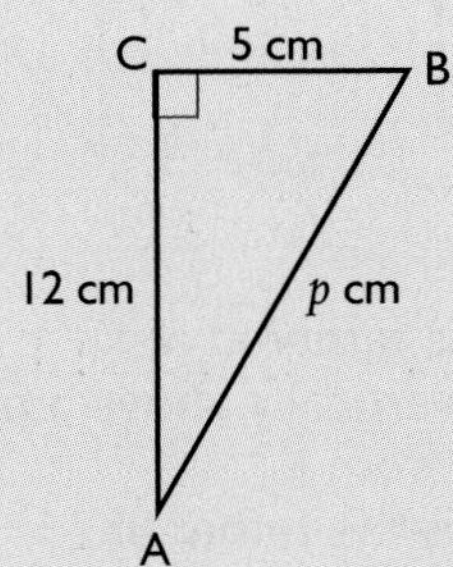

Example 2 Calculate the length of SU.

The triangle is right-angled

$\Rightarrow$ $SU^2 = 6{\cdot}4^2 + 4{\cdot}8^2$

$\Rightarrow$ $SU^2 = 40{\cdot}96 + 23{\cdot}04$

$\Rightarrow$ $SU^2 = 64$

$\Rightarrow$ $SU = \sqrt{64}$

$\Rightarrow$ $SU = 8$

SU is 8 cm long.

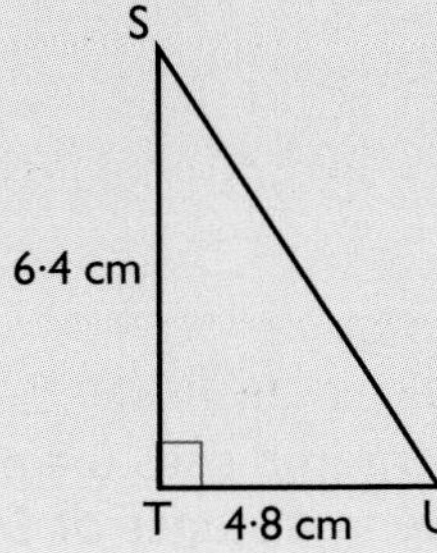

F

Exercise 6.1

1 For each triangle, calculate the length of the hypotenuse.

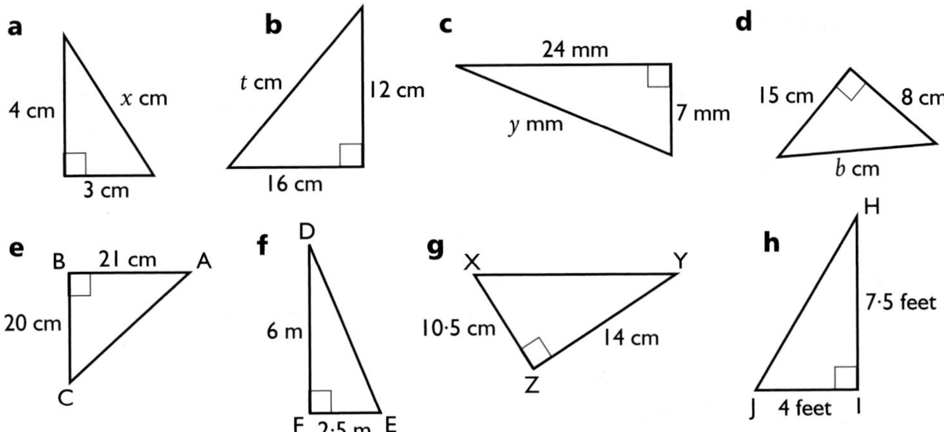

2 Calculate the length of the hypotenuse correct to 1 decimal place.

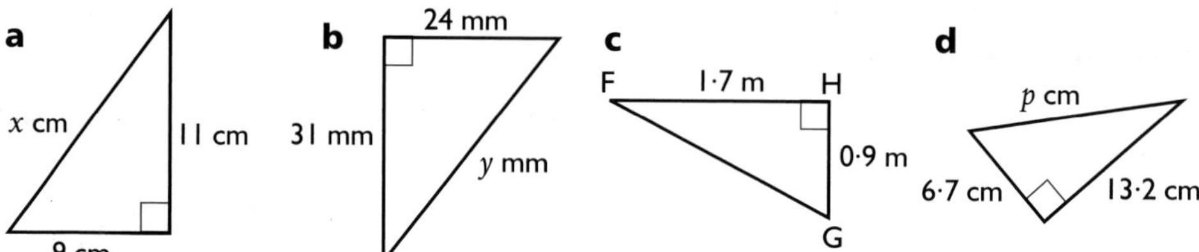

3 A balloon is tethered at K.
It is 3·5 m vertically above a point M.
M is 2·9 m from K.
How long is the tether BK?

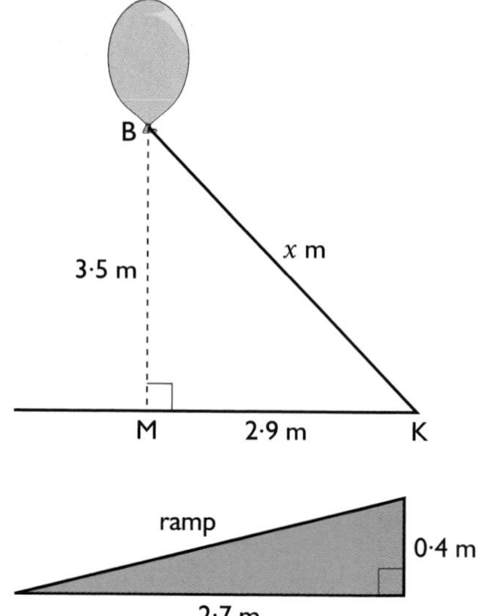

4 A wheelchair ramp rises 0·4 m vertically over a distance of 2·7 m.
How long is the ramp?

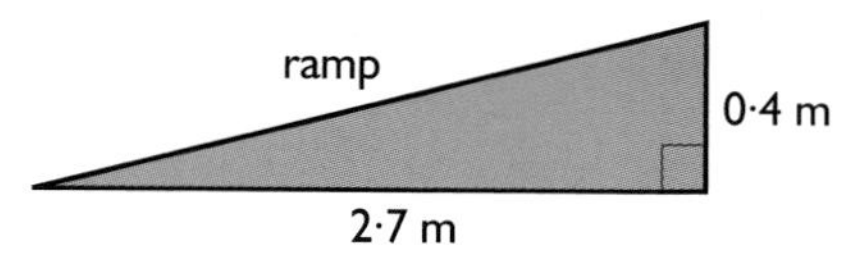

F

7 Calculating a shorter side

Example Calculate the size of AB.

The triangle is right-angled.
The hypotenuse is 46 cm long.

$\Rightarrow \quad 46^2 = y^2 + 35^2$
$\Rightarrow \quad y^2 = 46^2 - 35^2$
$\Rightarrow \quad y^2 = 2116 - 1225$
$\Rightarrow \quad y^2 = 891$
$\Rightarrow \quad y = \sqrt{891}$
$\Rightarrow \quad y = 29{\cdot}8$ correct to 1 d.p.

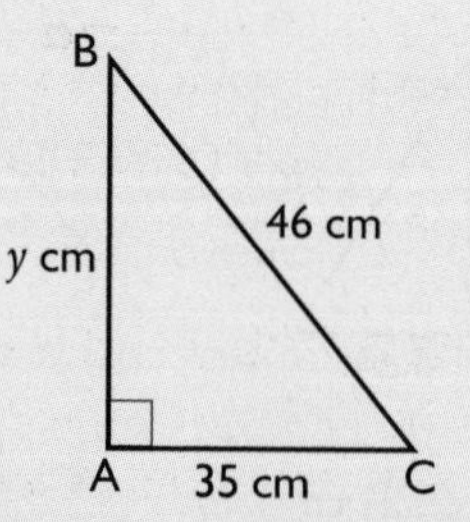

Note: the hypotenuse is the largest side in a triangle. Always check your answers make sense, for example your answer here should be less than the length of the hypotenuse.

Exercise 7.1

1 Calculate the length of the unknown side in each triangle (to 1 decimal place, where necessary).

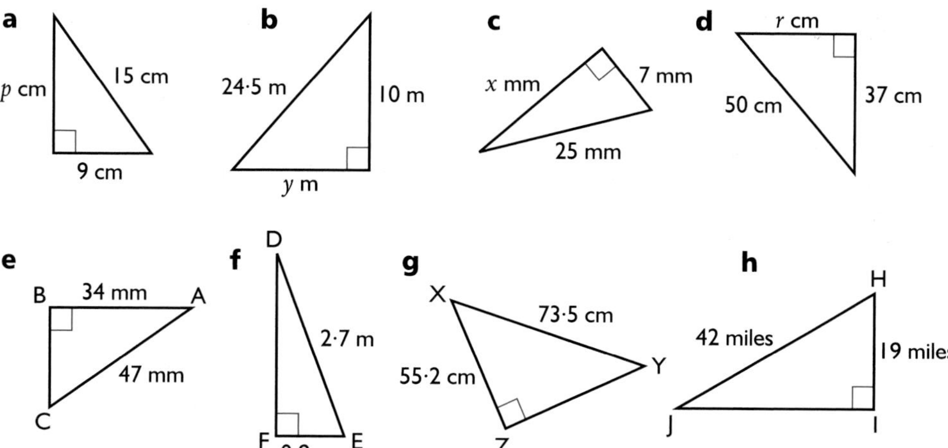

2 A 4 m ladder is propped up against a wall. The foot of the ladder is 1·4 m from the base of the wall. How far up the wall does the ladder reach?

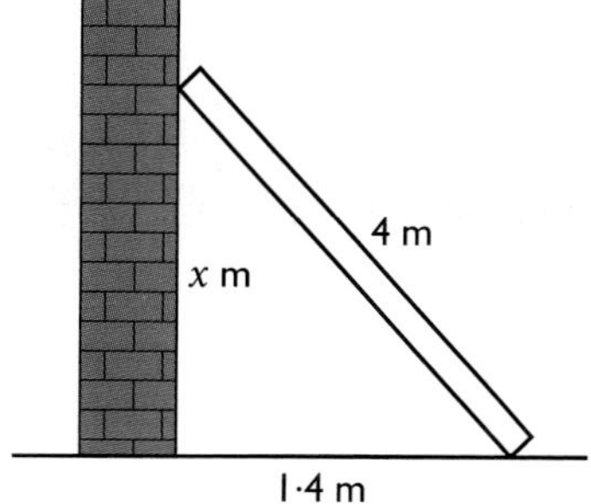

3 A playground slide looks like a triangle from the side. The ladder is 7·3 m long. The chute is 10·4 m long. How long is it from the foot of the chute to the foot of the ladder?

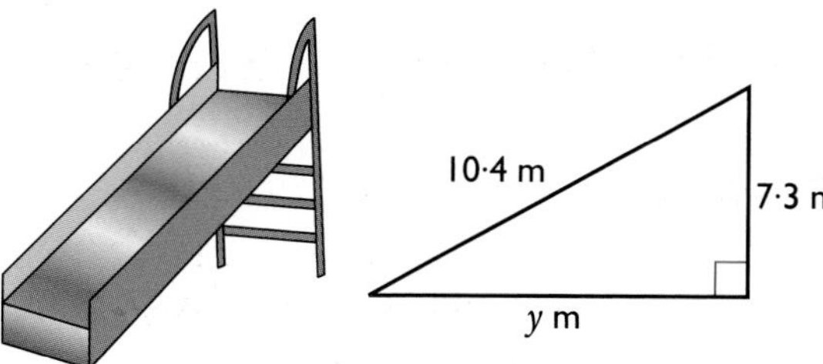

4 The Christmas tree in the town square is kept upright by two guy ropes. AB is 5·4 m long and is tethered 1·9 m from the base of the tree.

a How high is the tree?

b Jamie says the other guy rope is 6 m long and tethered 2 m from the base of the tree. Is this possible?

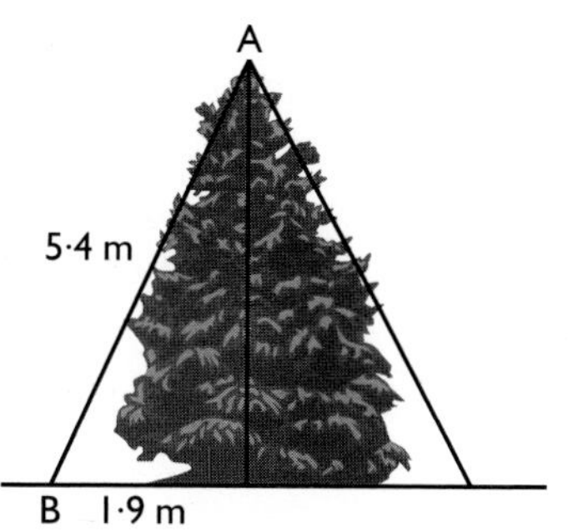

F

8 First find your right-angled triangle …

Many geometric shapes contain right-angled triangles.

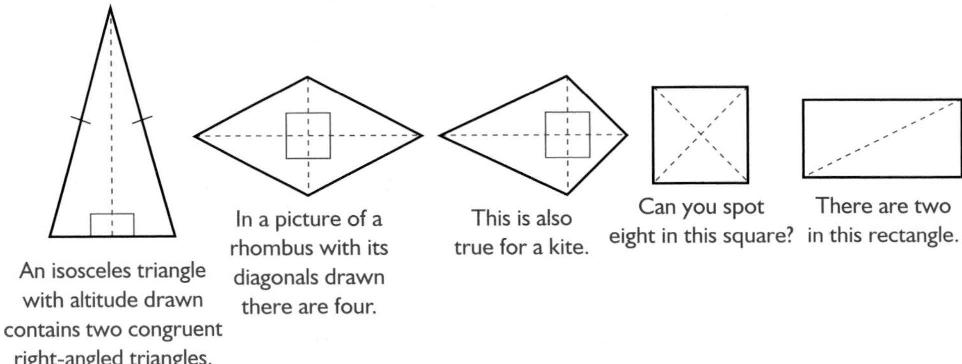
An isosceles triangle with altitude drawn contains two congruent right-angled triangles.
In a picture of a rhombus with its diagonals drawn there are four.
This is also true for a kite.
Can you spot eight in this square?
There are two in this rectangle.

Exercise 8.1

Work to 1 decimal place where appropriate.

1 **a** Find the altitude of the isosceles triangle ABC by considering the triangle ABD.

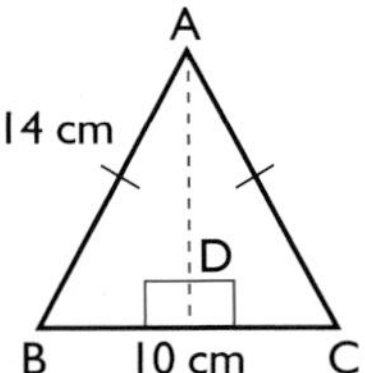
A
14 cm
D
B
10 cm
C

b Similarly calculate the altitude of each of these isosceles triangles.

i

40 cm
36 cm

ii

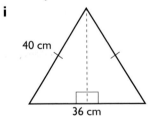

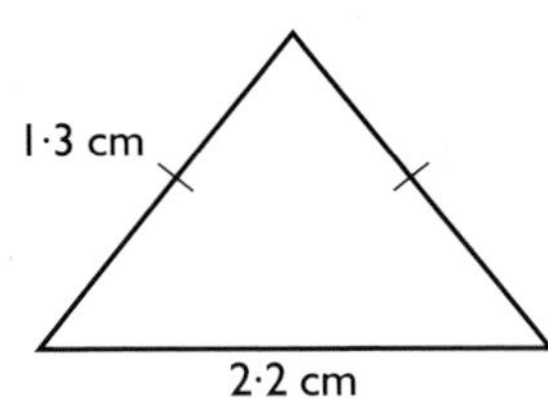
1·3 cm
2·2 cm

c Calculate the length of the equal sides in these isosceles triangles.

i

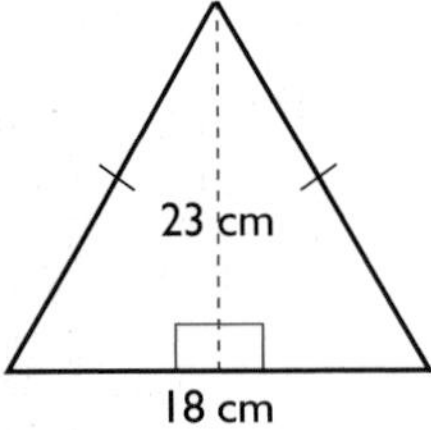
23 cm
18 cm

ii

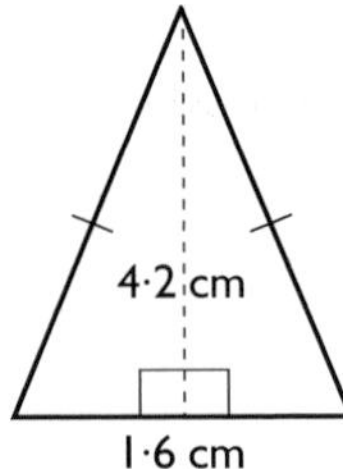
4·2 cm
1·6 cm

d Calculate the length of the base of each of these isosceles triangles.

i

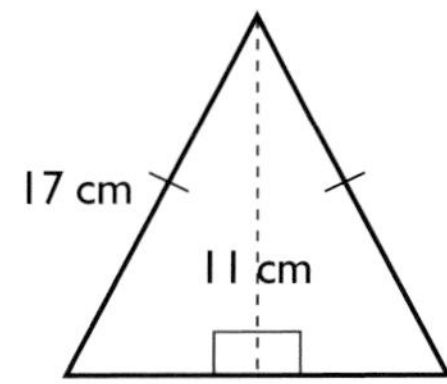

ii

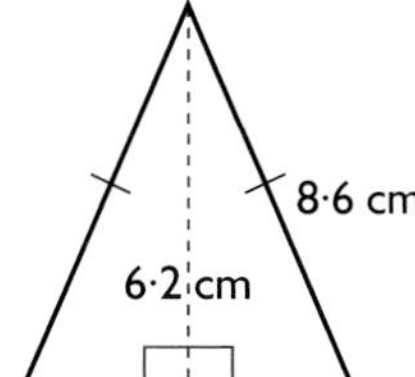

2 Find the labelled lengths in each rhombus or kite. Unless otherwise indicated, the figures given represent diagonal lengths.

a

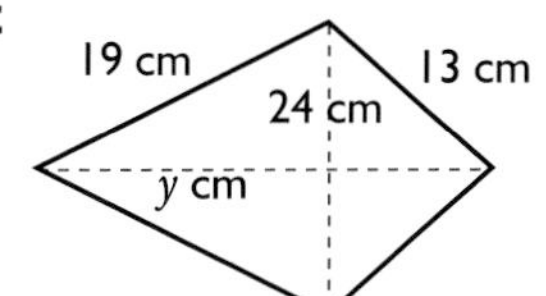

b

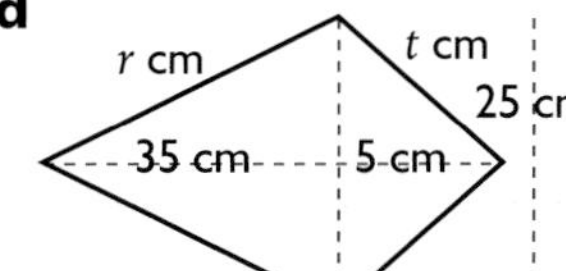

c

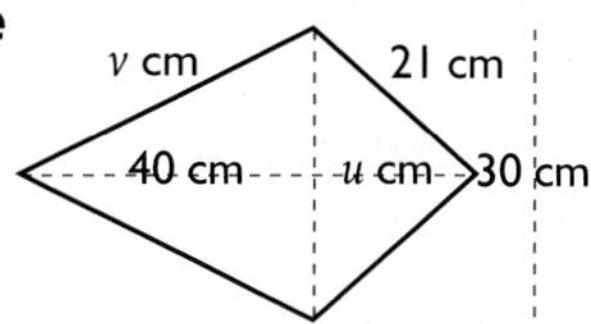

d

e

(Hint: consider the diagonal in two parts.)

3 Calculate the value of x in each diagram.

a

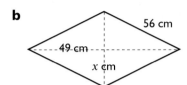

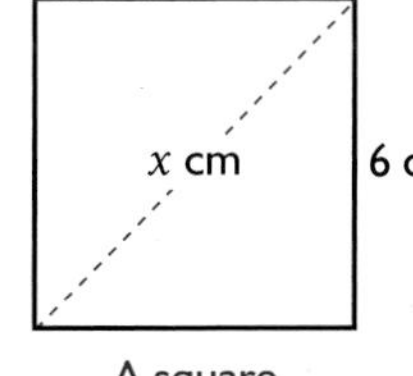

A square

b

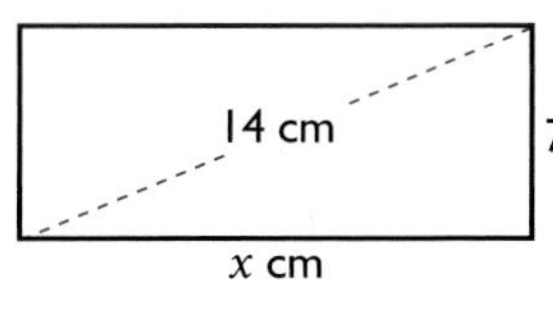

A rectangle

c

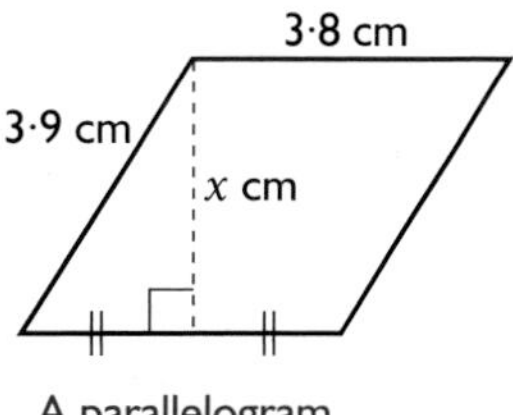

A parallelogram

4 A lean-to shed is 1·4 m high at the front and 1·8 m at the back.
It is 1·3 m wide.

a Calculate the length of the slope of the roof.

b Calculate the length of each diagonal of the side of the shed.

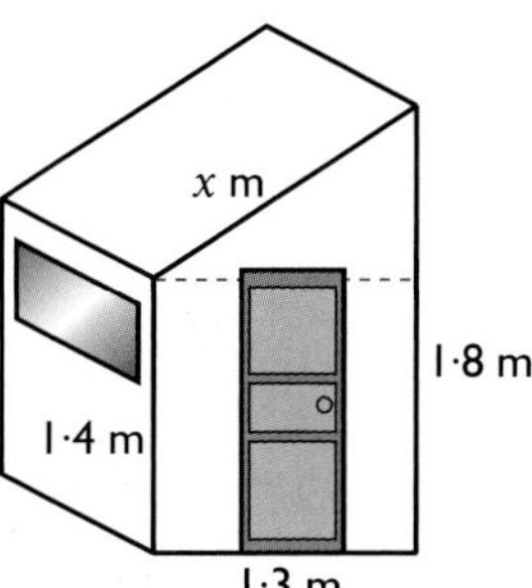

F

5 A swimming pool has dimensions as shown.

a Sketch the trapezium which represents the side of the pool and identify a right-angled triangle by the addition of one line.

b Calculate the length of the sloping floor.

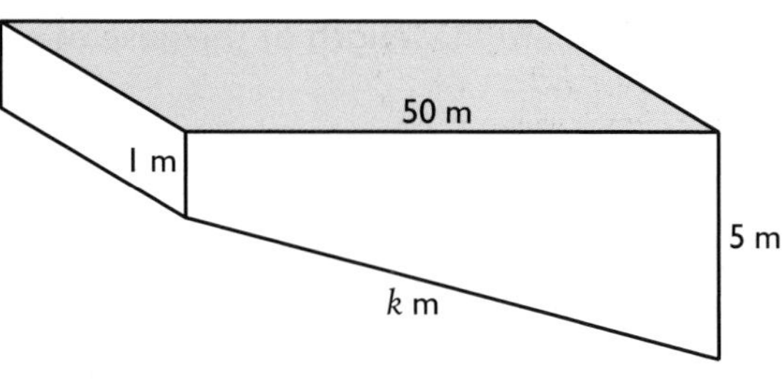

9 Distances on a grid

In Chapter 7 we saw that the distance between points on a grid can be easily obtained as long as the two points lie on the same *horizontal* or *vertical* line. Where this is not the case then the theorem of Pythagoras can be employed.

Example 1

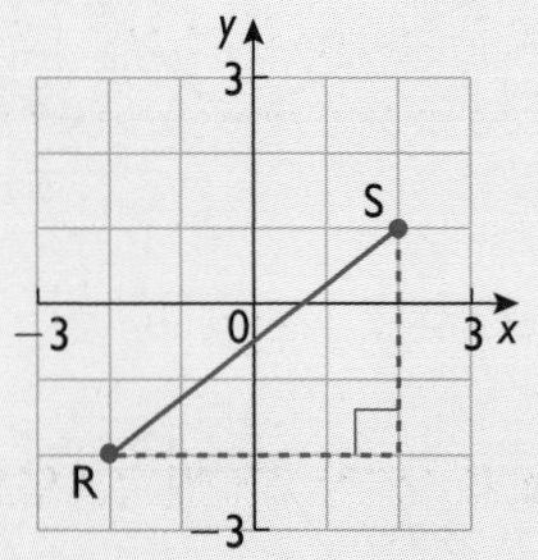

What is the distance between R(−2, −2) and S(2, 1)?

A sketch of the situation helps.
On the sketch draw a right-angled triangle with the required distance as the hypotenuse.

Of the other two sides, one will be parallel to the x axis and the other parallel to the y axis.

Their lengths can be found by counting squares.
The triangle is right-angled

$\Rightarrow$ $RS^2 = 4^2 + 3^2$
$\Rightarrow$ $RS^2 = 16 + 9$
$\Rightarrow$ $RS^2 = 25$
$\Rightarrow$ $RS = \sqrt{25}$
$\Rightarrow$ RS = 5 units long

Example 2

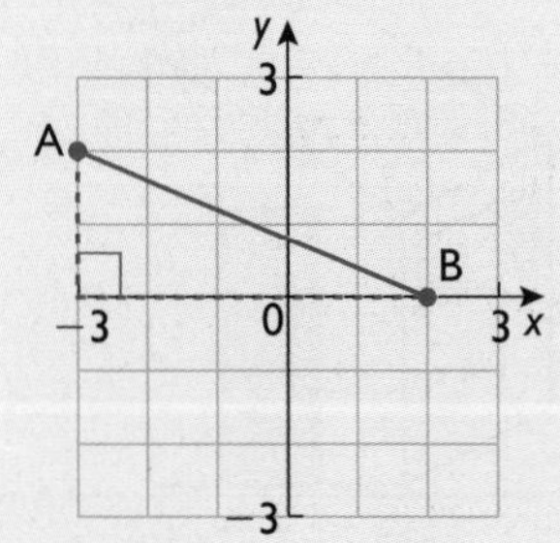

Calculate, correct to 1 decimal place, the distance between A(−3, 2) and B(2, 0).

A right-angled triangle is formed

$\Rightarrow$ $AB^2 = 2^2 + 5^2$
$\Rightarrow$ $AB^2 = 4 + 25$
$\Rightarrow$ $AB^2 = 29$
$\Rightarrow$ $AB = \sqrt{29}$
$\Rightarrow$ AB = 5·4 units long (1 d.p.)

Exercise 9.1

Calculate correct to 1 decimal place where appropriate.

1 Calculate the distance between:

a C(3, −4) and D(3, 1) **b** E(−3, −2) and F(5, −2)

c G(0, −1) and H(0, 5) **d** I(−2, 0) and J(3, 0)

2 **a** Use the diagram to help you calculate the distance:

i AB **ii** UV

ii AU **iv** BV.

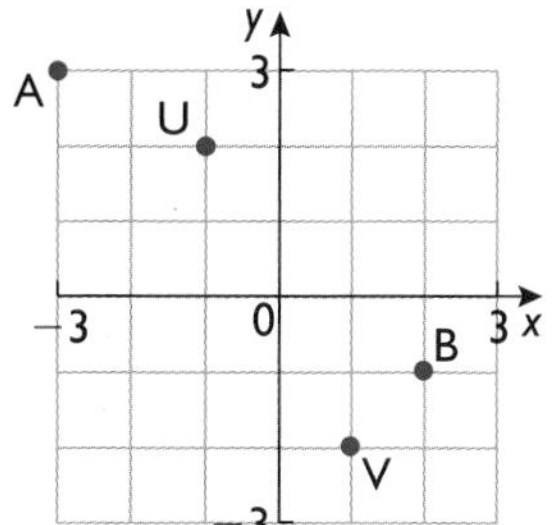

b Helen suggested that the triangle UVB was isosceles.
Perform some calculations to show her wrong.

3 Plot the pairs of points and use the theorem of Pythagoras to work out the distance between them.

a A(4, 1), B(1, 5) **b** C(2, 2), D(−1, 3) **c** E(0, 4), F(−3, −5)

d G(1, −3), H(−3, 1) **e** K(−4, 0), L(5, −5) **f** M(3, 3), N(−1, −1)

Challenge

Can you work out the sides which form the right angle without drawing the points on a grid? Explain!

4 The map shows the position of three towns.
Each unit on the map represents 5 km.

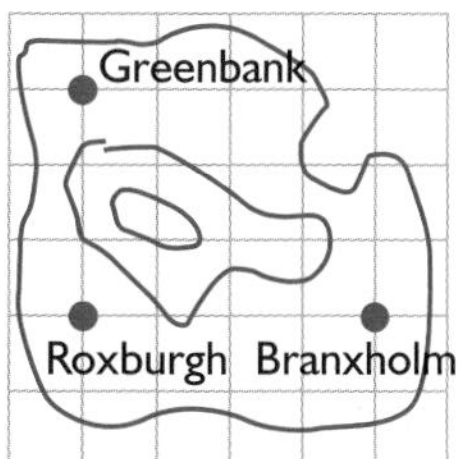

a Check that the distance between Roxburgh and Branxholm is 20 km.

b Work out the distance between Roxburgh and Greenbank.

c Calculate the distance between Branxholm and Greenbank.

5 S(−1, 1), T(−1, −4), U(3, −1) and V(2, 2) are points on a coordinate grid.
Show that STUV is a kite by calculating the lengths of the sides.

6 ABCD is a rectangle, with A(−4, 0), B(−3, −3), C(3, −1) and D(2, 2).

a Calculate

i the length

ii the breadth of the rectangle.

b Work out the length of the diagonal of the rectangle.

7 How much further is it from Langbrae to Harehill than from Langbrae to Jacksonville? (Give your answer to the nearest kilometre.)

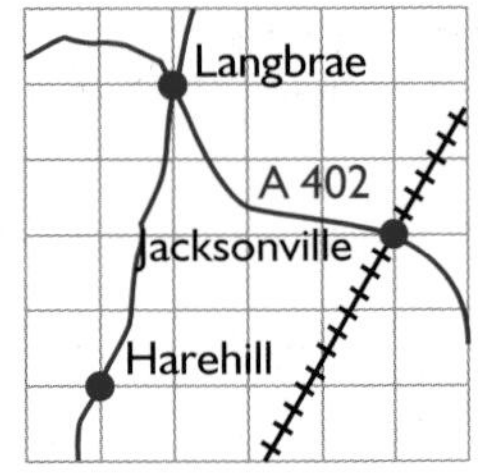

Scale: 1 unit represents 10 km

8 **a** Plot the points P(3, 3), Q(−1, 2) and R(−2, −2).
b Show that triangle PQR is isosceles.
c How much longer, to 1 decimal place, is the base than the equal sides?

Investigation

Archeologists have found many Babylonian clay tablets.

The one shown, called Plimpton 322, when translated proved to be a table of values of sides of right-angled triangles with whole number sides, e.g. 3 4 5 ($3^2 + 4^2 = 5^2$) or 5 12 13 ($5^2 + 12^2 = 13^2$)

The Babylonians had knowledge of the theorem at least 1000 years before Pythagoras lived.

See if you can find some more sets of such number triples.

F

CHECK-UP

1 Estimate the lengths indicated in these pictures.

a

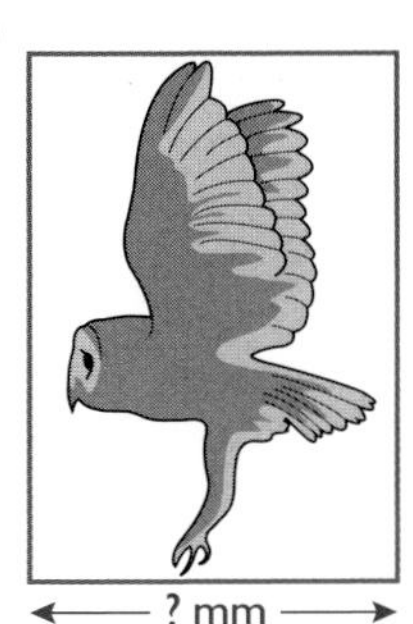

b

? cm

2 Estimate the length of each object.

a

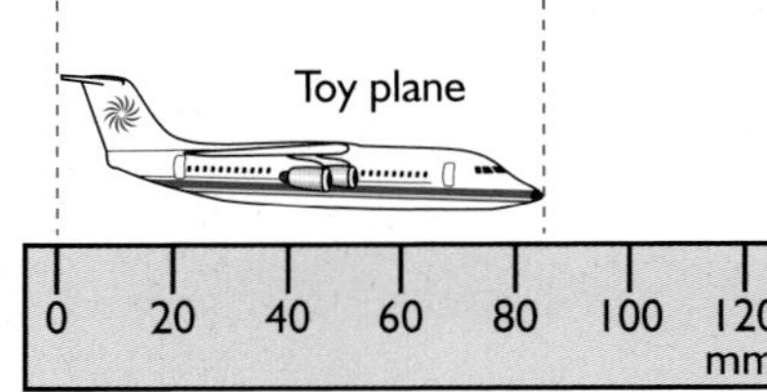

b

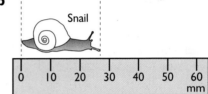

Snail

0 10 20 30 40 50 60 mm

3 To make a piece of wood fit in the space for a shelf, the joiner cut 0·0035 m off the end.
Express this distance in

a centimetres **b** millimetres.

4 When describing a book, Janine said, 'To the nearest centimetre it is 21 centimetres long'.

a What is the longest the book might actually be?

b What is the biggest possible error to be made when measuring to the nearest centimetre?

5 Calculate the length of the side marked x, correct to 1 decimal place.

a

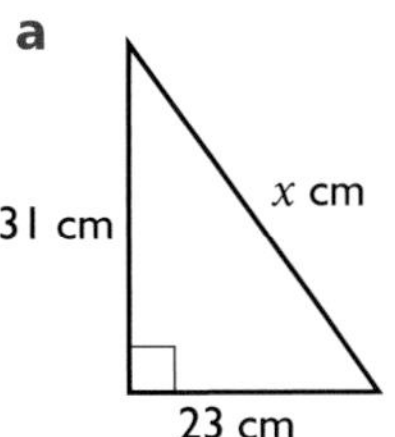

b

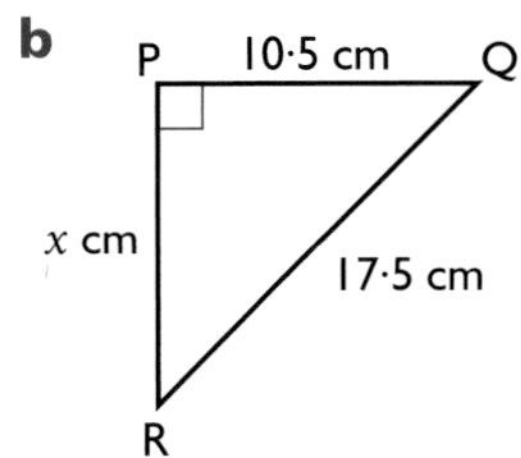

E F

6 DEFG is a rhombus with diagonals DF 14 cm and EG 9 cm. Calculate the length of the sides of the rhombus.

7 Calculate the distance between the following pairs of points.

a S(1, 3) and T(1, −4)

b L(−4, 3) and M(2, −5)

8 The map shows the position of two towns. Calculate the distance between Dryden and Fallin.

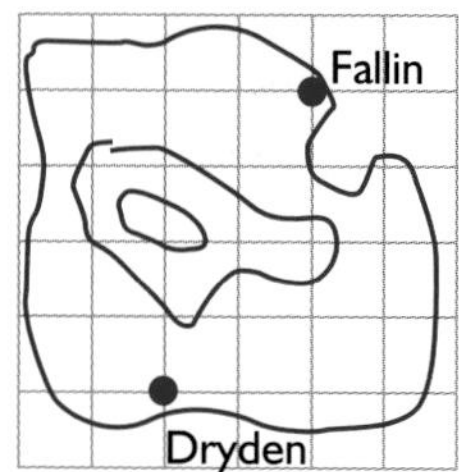

Scale: 1 unit represents 20 km

F

10 Transformation

In the early twentieth century Professor D'Arcy Thompson of St Andrews University tried to explain the relation between species by considering mathematical changes or **transformations**.

The diagrams illustrate his attempts to show the relation between human and chimpanzee skulls.

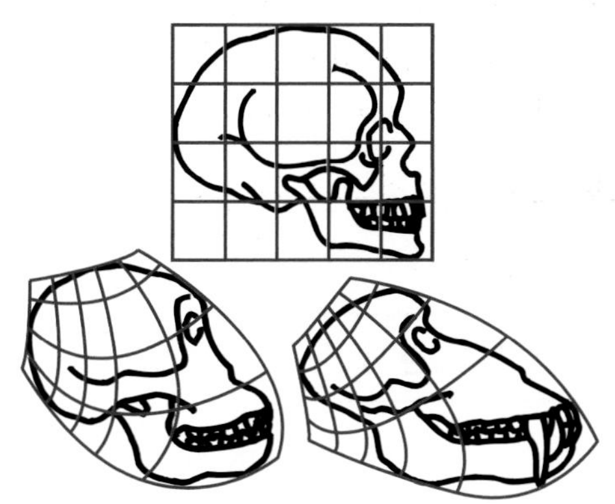

1 Looking back

Reminder
A **transformation** is a change, like **reflection**.

If a shape looks the same after such a change the shape is said to possess **symmetry**.

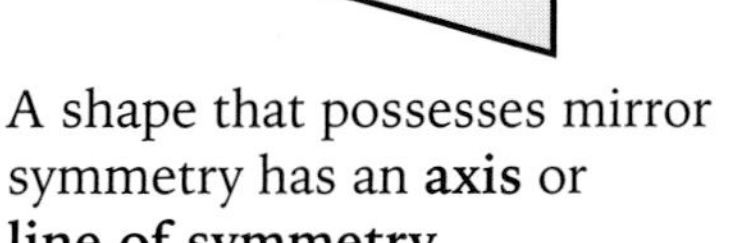

Reflection

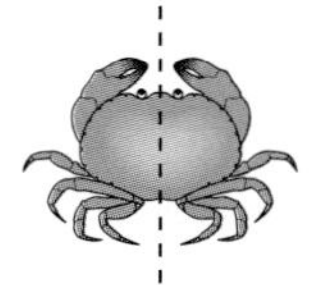

A shape that possesses mirror symmetry has an **axis** or **line of symmetry**.

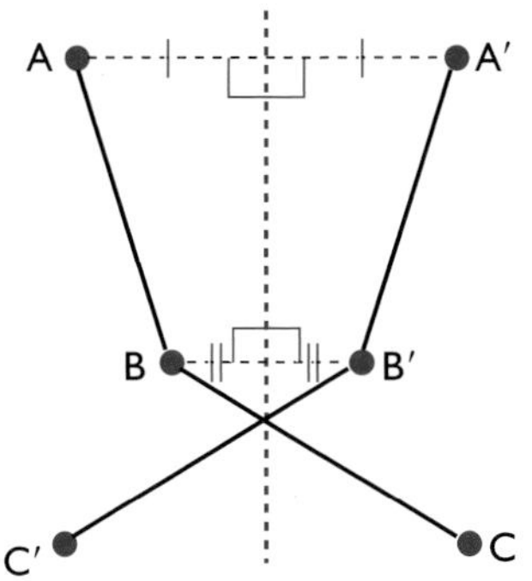

- The point A has an image A′ under reflection in the axis.
- This image is the same perpendicular distance away from, but on the other side of, the axis.
- The image of the line joining A to B is the line joining A′ to B′.
- A line and its image will intersect on the axis of symmetry.
- A shape and its image under reflection will form a picture which has **mirror** or **reflective symmetry**.

Tiling

A shape is said to tile if congruent copies can be used to fill space without either overlapping or leaving gaps.

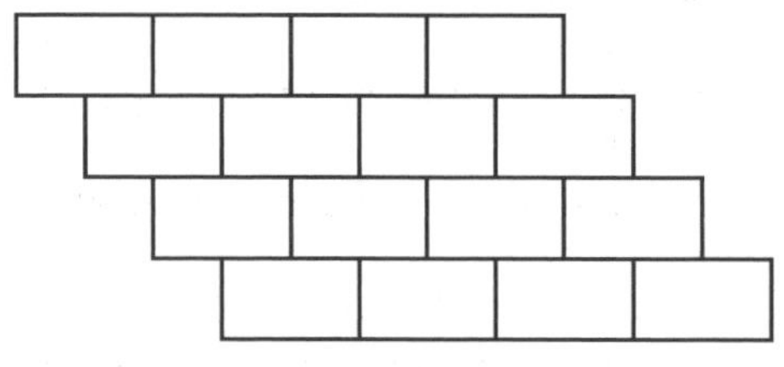

Rectangles

Elephants based on the rectangle

Exercise 1.1

1 Copy each diagram and shade in enough squares to give the shape reflective symmetry about the axis shown.

a

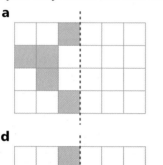

b

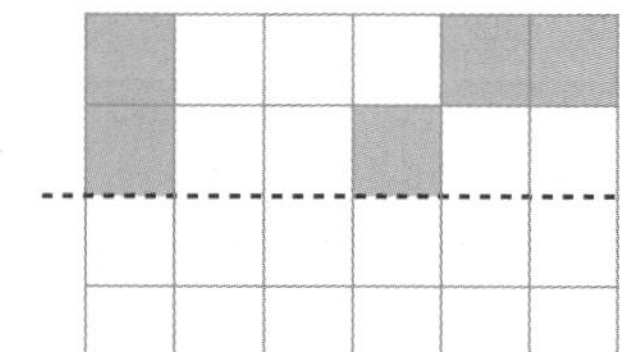

c

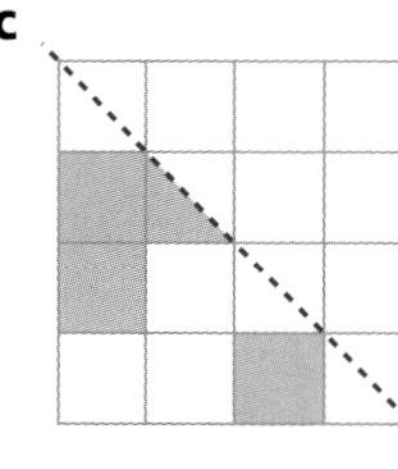

d

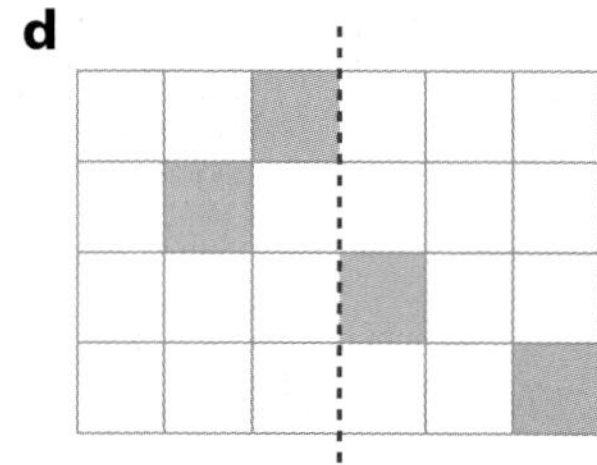

e

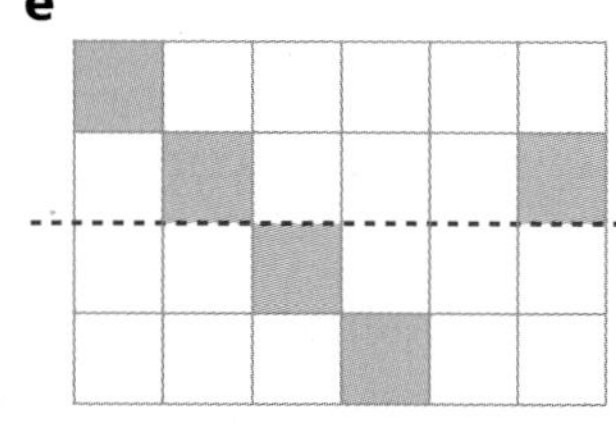

f

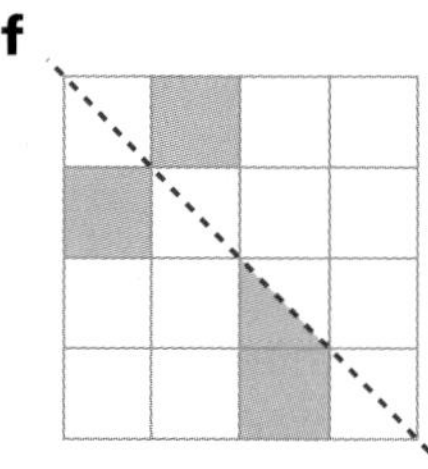

2 a Sketch the geometric shapes and indicate each axis of symmetry by a broken line.

i Rectangle (two)

ii

Square (four)

iii

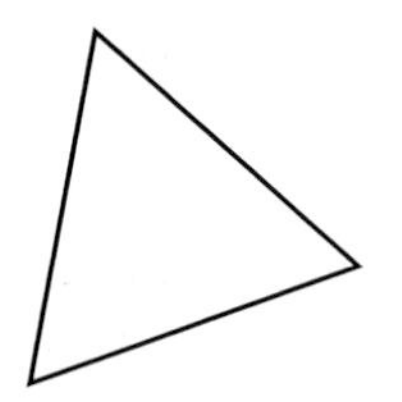

Equilateral triangle (three)

iv

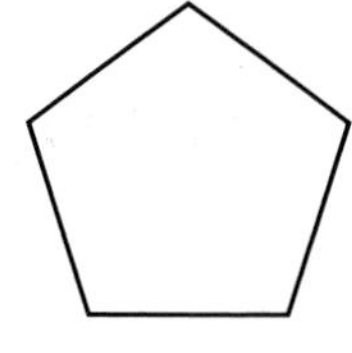

Pentagon (five)

b This hexagon has six axes of symmetry.
Can you sketch a hexagon that has only

i one axis
ii two axes
iii three axes?

3

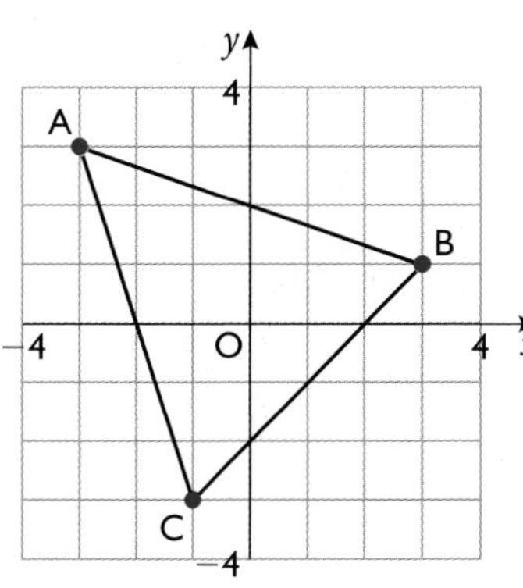

a Copy the diagram onto squared paper.

b **i** State the coordinates of A′, B′ and C′, the images of A, B and C under reflection in the x axis.

ii Plot these points and draw the image of triangle ABC.

iii State the point of intersection of BC with B′C′.

iv Where do AC and A′C′ intersect?

v What do the points found in parts **iii** and **iv** have in common?

4 Triangle PQR has vertices P(4, 0), Q(−4, 2) and R(−4, −4).

a State the coordinates of P′, Q′ and R′, the images of P, Q, and R under reflection in the y axis.

b What can be said about P and P′ and also about Q and Q′?

c What kind of shape is PQRR′?

5 STR is a triangle with vertices as shown. MN is a line passing through (2, 0) parallel to the y axis.

a State the coordinates of

i S, T and R

ii S′T′ and R′, the images of S, T and R under reflection in MN.

b Which point has the same coordinates as its image?

c Where do TS and T′S′ intersect?

d What can be said about ∠TSR and ∠T′S′R′?

e What can be said about the y coordinate of a point and its image under this reflection?

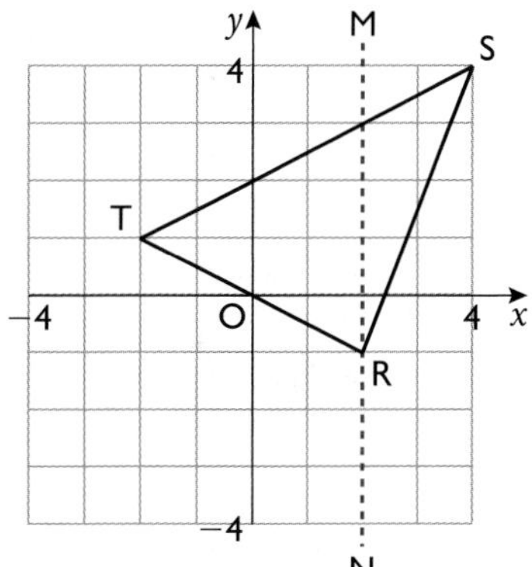

Challenge

A plane of symmetry

Look for pictures showing reflection and reflective symmetry.
Look for art that uses, or misuses, reflection.

You can find lots in magazines or by surfing the net.

Make a class poster to remind you of where reflection crops up in everyday life.

'Vanity'

2 Rotation

Example 1

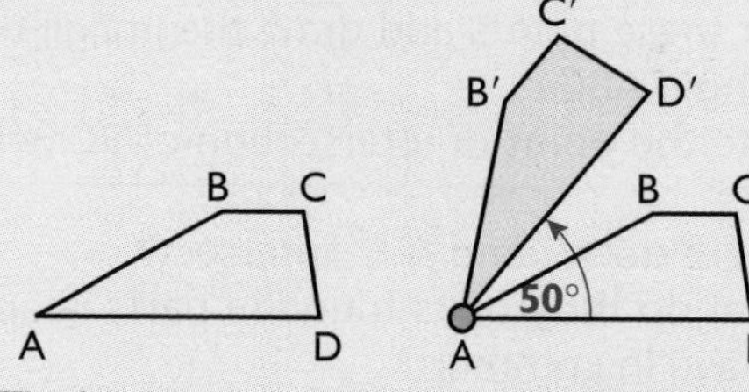

Imagine the shape ABCD pinned at A and turned through 50° anticlockwise.

ABCD would end up at AB′C′D′.

AB′C′D is the image of ABCD under rotation of 50° anticlockwise about A.

The fixed point is called the **centre of rotation.**

Example 2

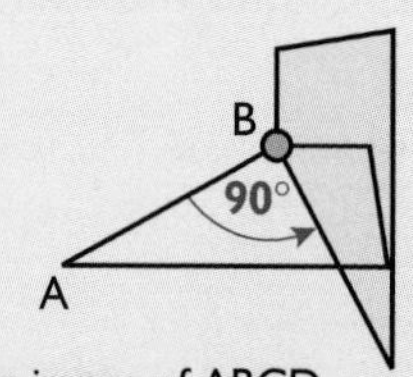

The image of ABCD under rotation of 90° anticlockwise about B

Example 3

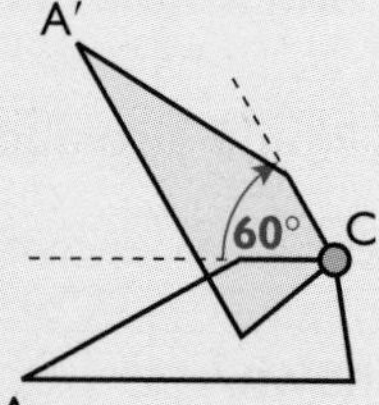

The image of ABCD under rotation of 60° clockwise about C

Example 4

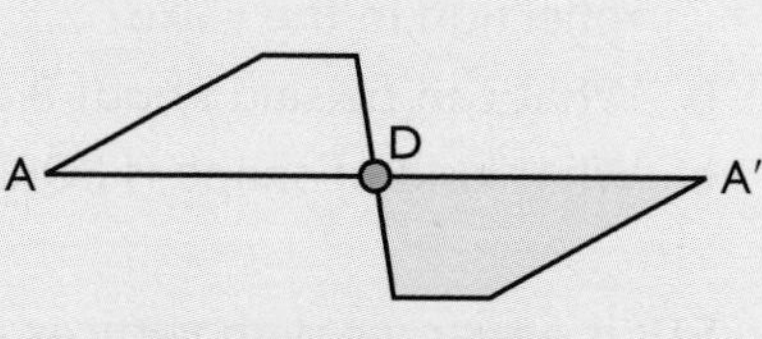

The image of ABCD under rotation of 180° about D

Example 5

Using tracing paper, we can let any point be the centre of rotation. Suppose we wish to rotate the shape 30° anticlockwise around a point P.

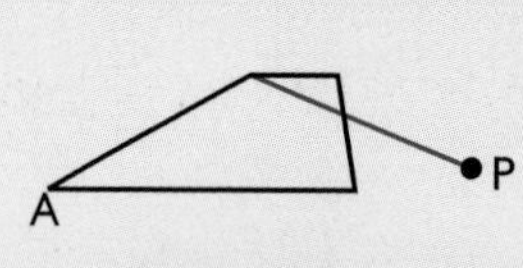

Step 1 Draw a line through P to any point on the shape.

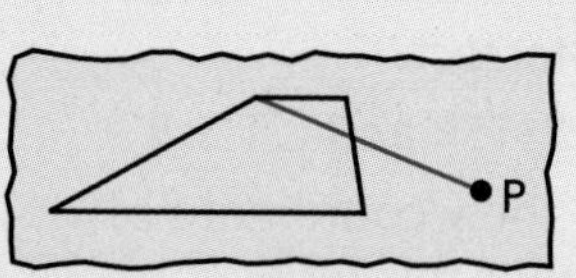

Step 2 Trace the shape, the point and the line.

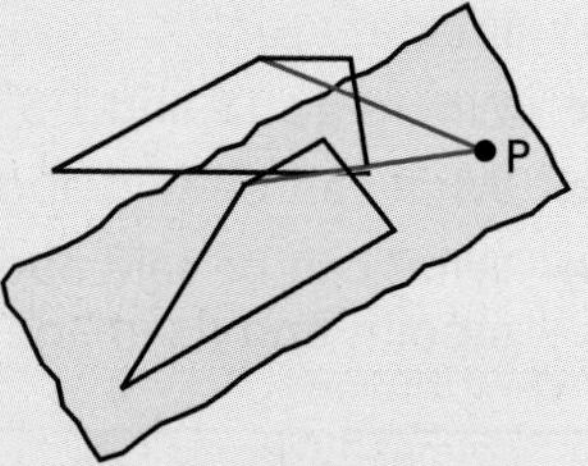

Step 3 Position the tracing with the points P in the same spot and the image of the line 30° around.

Example 6

The angle of rotation can be measured by drawing a line through any two points on the shape and also drawing the image of the line.

The angle at which they intersect is the desired angle.

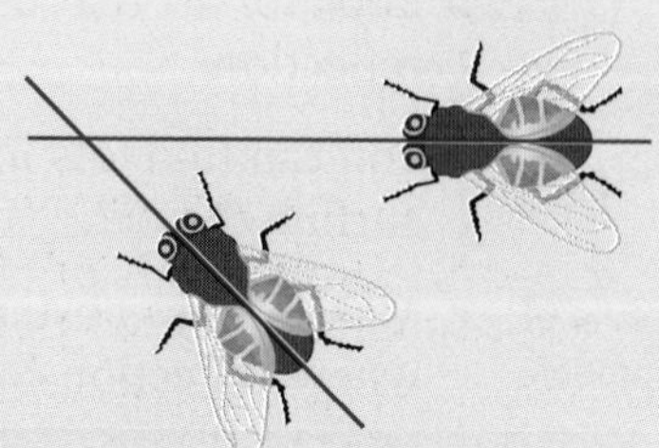

Exercise 2.1

1 Draw each shape accurately and then its image under the given rotation.

a

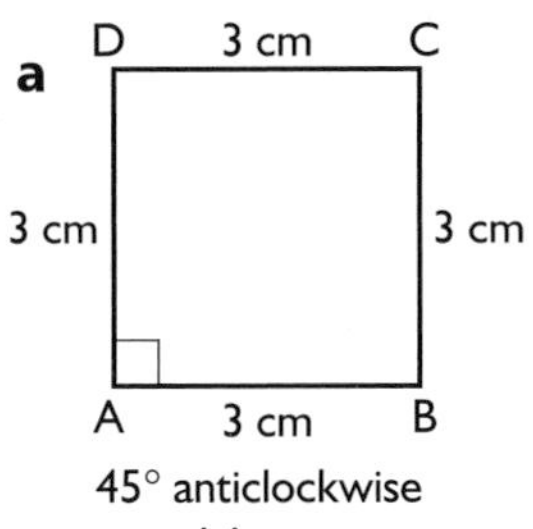

45° anticlockwise round A.

b

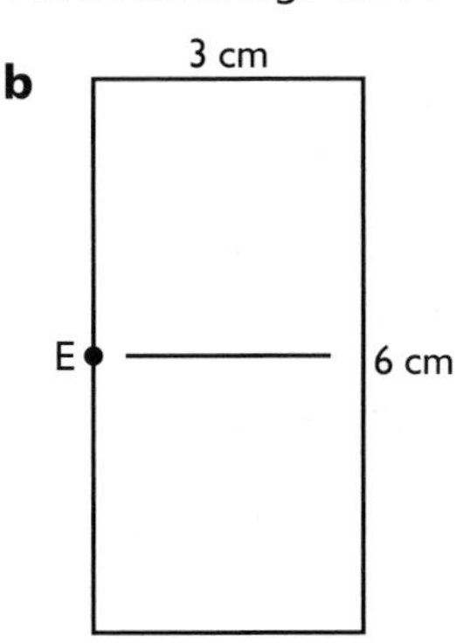

90° clockwise round E.

c

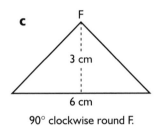

F

3 cm

6 cm

90° clockwise round F.

d

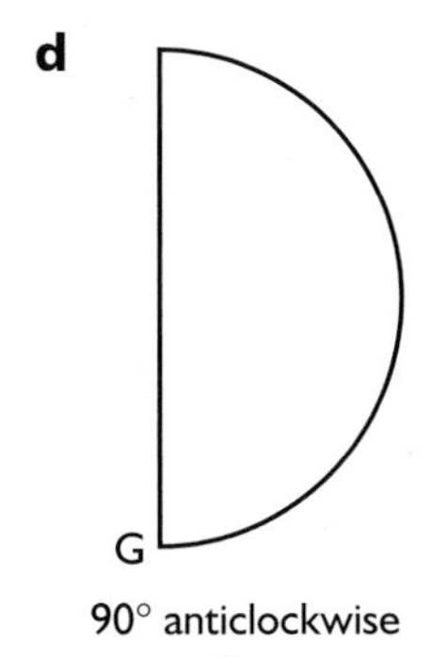

90° anticlockwise round G.

2 An executive toy has a little aeroplane (A) counterbalanced by a weight (B), spinning round a point P.

a What kind of triangle is AA′P?

b What is the length of

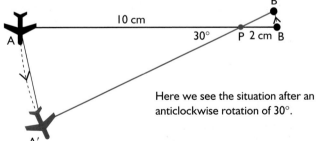

i A′P

ii B′P?

c What is the size of angle

i PAA′

ii B′PB

iii PB′B?

A 10 cm 30° P 2 cm B B′ A′

Here we see the situation after an anticlockwise rotation of 30°.

d To get to A′, A follows the dotted path.

i Describe the dotted path, AA′, in geometric terms.

ii Describe the dotted path, BB′, in a similar fashion.

e What kind of triangle would AA′P be if the size of the rotation had been

i 60° **ii** 90°?

3 A star is made from four equilateral triangles and a square.

a Draw the image under a clockwise rotation about C of
i 45°
ii 90°
iii 135°
iv 180°.

b Comment on the outcomes of **ii** and **iv**.

c What other size of rotation will produce this effect?

4 The picture shows a triangle ABC being rotated 50° anticlockwise round a point P. Note that each point travels in a circle.

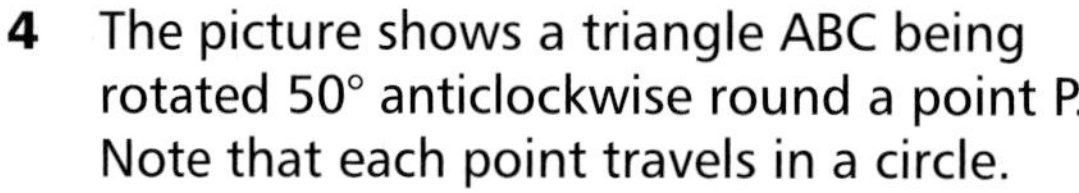

a Use a protractor and a set of compasses to help you rotate this square through 65° anticlockwise round T.

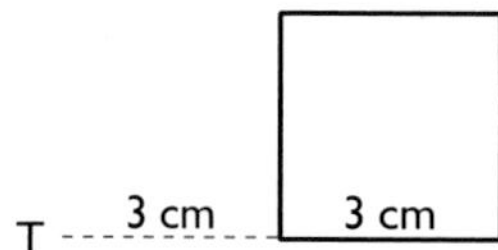

(Hint: you don't need to draw the whole circle each time.)

b Rotate this triangle 80° clockwise round K.

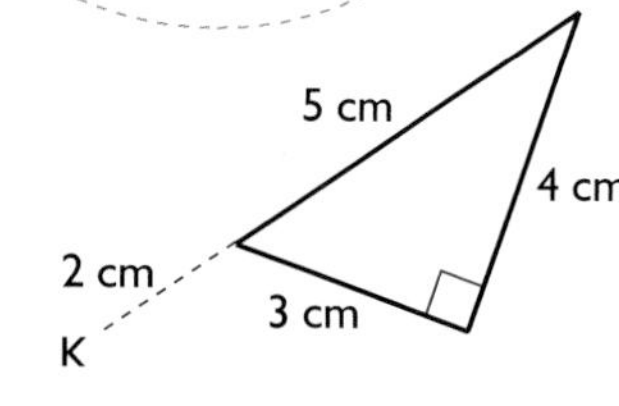

Use tracing paper to check your working.

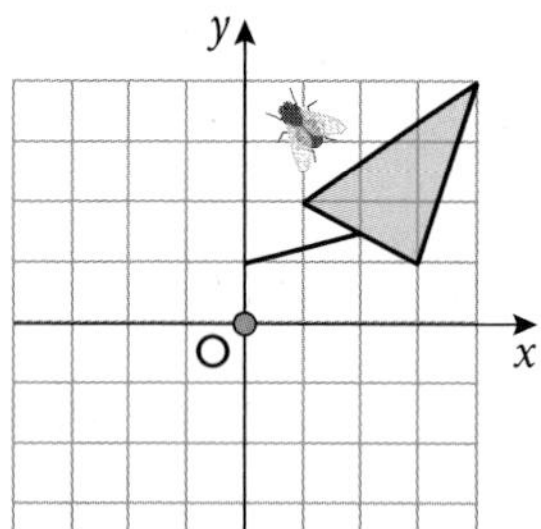

Here is a shape in the first quadrant.

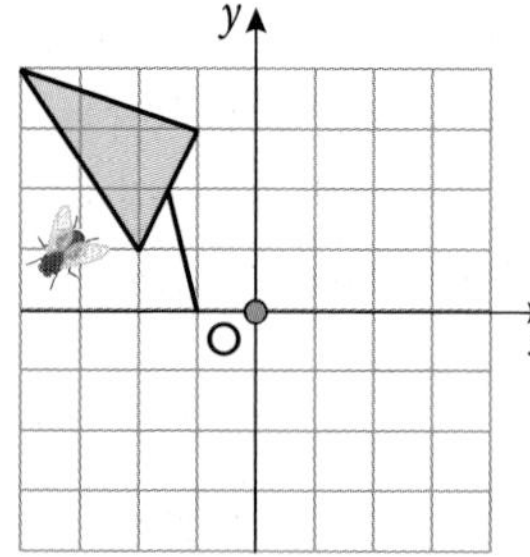

Here it is after a 90° anticlockwise rotation about O.

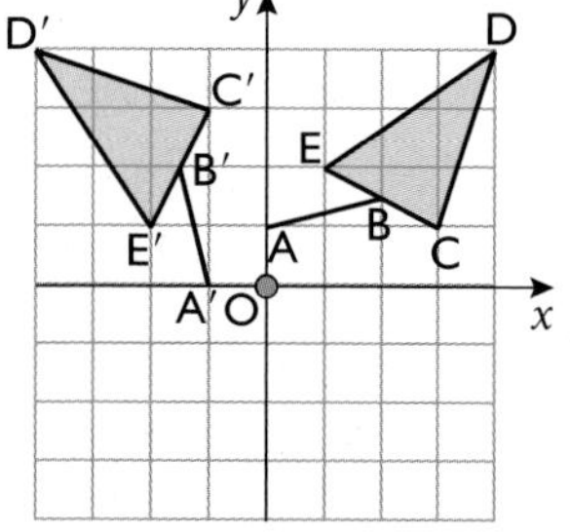

The object and its image … note, for example, that C(3, 1) has an image C′(−1, 3) and that ∠COC′ = 90°

Exercise 2.2

1 a Use the above diagram to copy and complete the table.

Point	A(0, 1)	B	C	D	E
Image	A′(−1, 0)				

b What would be the image of M(10, 12) under this rotation?

2 The triangle PQR has been placed on a grid as shown.

a Copy the drawing and add its image under a 90° anticlockwise rotation about O.

b Copy and complete the table.

Point	Image
P(−3, 2)	P′
Q	
R	

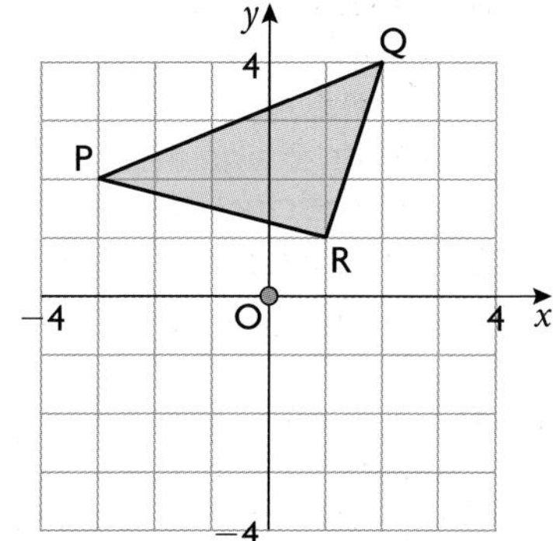

c Copy and complete each sentence:

i If the point K(4, 7) is rotated through 90° anticlockwise, its image is K′(,).

ii If the point L(−4, 7) is rotated through 90° anticlockwise, its image is L′(,).

iii If the point M(−4, −1) is rotated through 90° anticlockwise, its image is M′(,).

iv If the point N(5, −2) is rotated through 90° anticlockwise, its image is N′(,).

v If the point P(a, b) is rotated through 90° anticlockwise, its image is P′(,).

E

3 A point T(7, 2) is rotated 90° anticlockwise about O and then a further 90° anticlockwise about O.

a What are the coordinates of its image, T′, after the first rotation?

b What are the coordinates of its image, T″, after the second rotation?

c What was the total rotation which moved T to T″?

d This type of rotation is referred to as a half-turn rotation. Why?

4

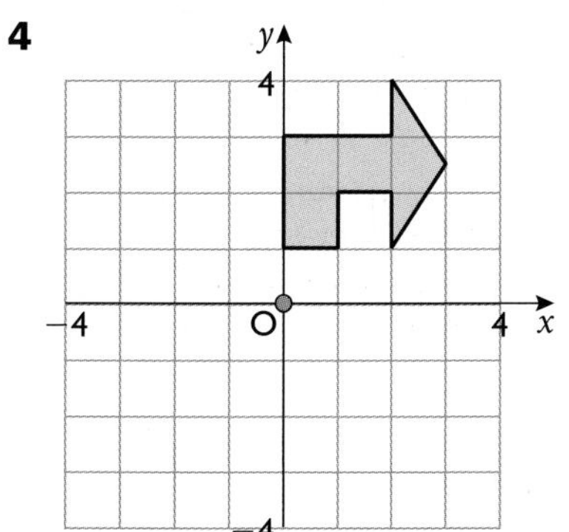

a Copy the diagram and show the image of the shape after

i a 90° anticlockwise rotation (quarter turn) about O

ii a 180° anticlockwise rotation (half turn) about O.

b Make a table of the points and their images under a half-turn rotation about O.

c Copy and complete these statements:

i Under a half turn about O the point F(4, 3) has the image F′(,).

ii Under a half turn about O the point I(−1, 2) has the image I′(,).

iii Under a half turn about O the point P(a, b) has the image P′(,).

5 A line passes through the points $(-2, 1)$ and $(-4, -3)$.

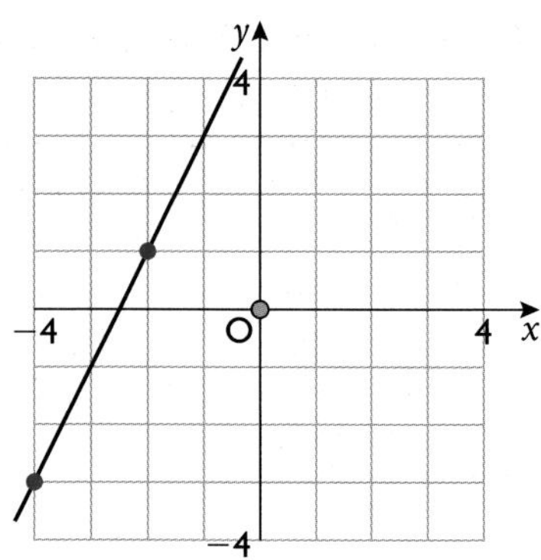

a On the same diagram draw
   i the line
   ii its image after a quarter turn anticlockwise about O
   iii its image after a quarter turn clockwise about O
   iv its image after a half turn about O.

b A quadrilateral is formed by these four lines.
   i What kind of quadrilateral is it?
   ii What are the coordinates of its vertices?
   iii Where do its diagonals intersect?

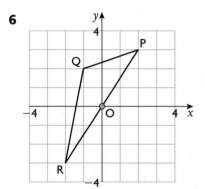

6 In triangle PQR, O is the midpoint of PR.

a State the image, after a half turn about O, of
   i P **ii** Q **iii** R.

b Draw the triangle and its image on the same diagram.

c What can be said about the line
   i PQ and its image
   ii QR and its image?

d What shape is formed by PQRQ′?

e Complete the following statement:
Under half-turn rotation a line and its image are equal in length and …

7 Using isometric paper, 60° rotations can be explored.

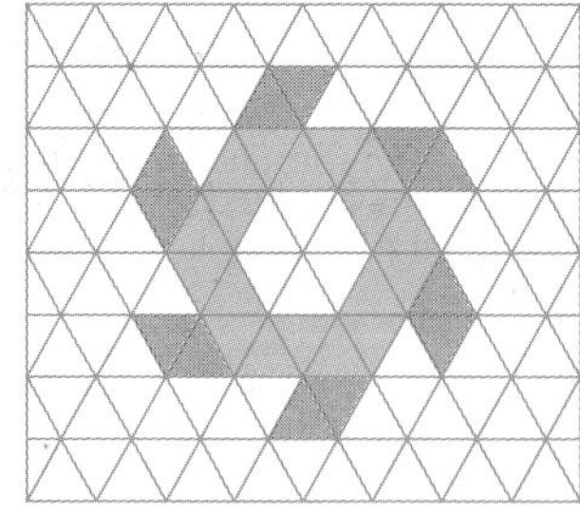

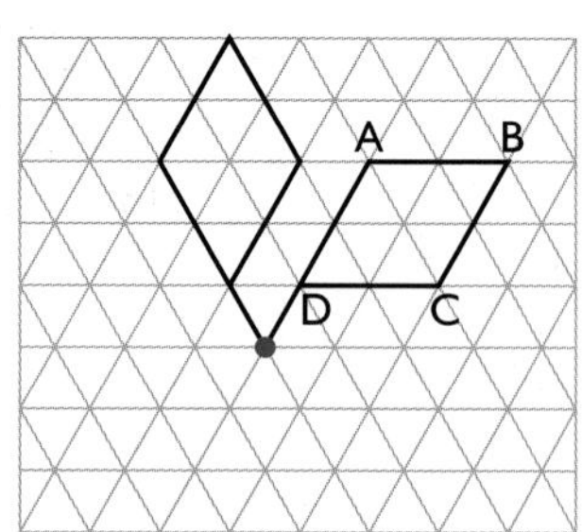

a On isometric paper draw ABCD and its image after a 60° rotation anticlockwise.

b **i** Rotate the image a further 60°
   ii … and then another.

c Rotate the original object through 60° clockwise.

d How many such rotations does it take to complete a half turn?

8 The stars in the sky rotate round the Pole Star once a day.
This diagram shows the constellation 'The Small Bear', the tip of whose tail is the Pole Star, A. Its other stars have been labelled by brightness.

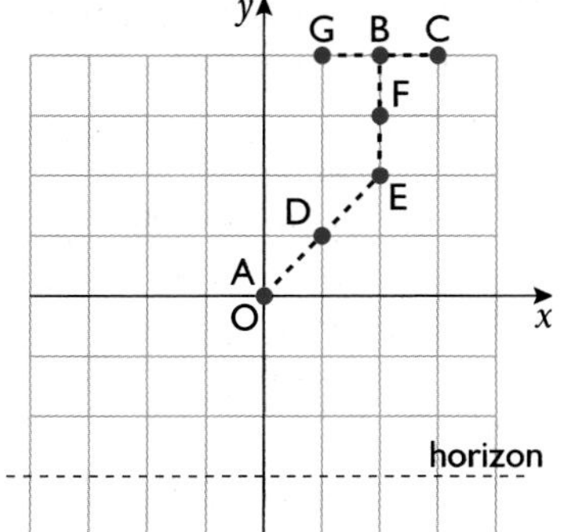

a Plot the images of the stars in the Small Bear after 6 hours (90° anticlockwise around A).

b **i** Plot the images after 12 hours.
ii If the broken line represents the horizon, which of the stars will have set below it at this time?

9 A rectangle has coordinates A(1, 1), B(5, 1), C(5, 11) and D(1, 11).

a On squared paper draw ABCD.

b State the coordinates of E, the point where the diagonals of ABCD intersect.

c ABCD is rotated through 90° anticlockwise around E.
What are the coordinates of the vertices of the resulting image?

10 A pentagon has coordinates P(3, 1), Q(4, 2), R(4, 4), S(2, 4) and T(1, 3).

a On squared paper draw the pentagon.

b It is rotated through 90° anticlockwise around K(1, 1).
What are the coordinates of the vertices of the image of PQRST?

c Find the image of the pentagon after a half turn about (2, 2).

11 Find the angle of rotation in each case.

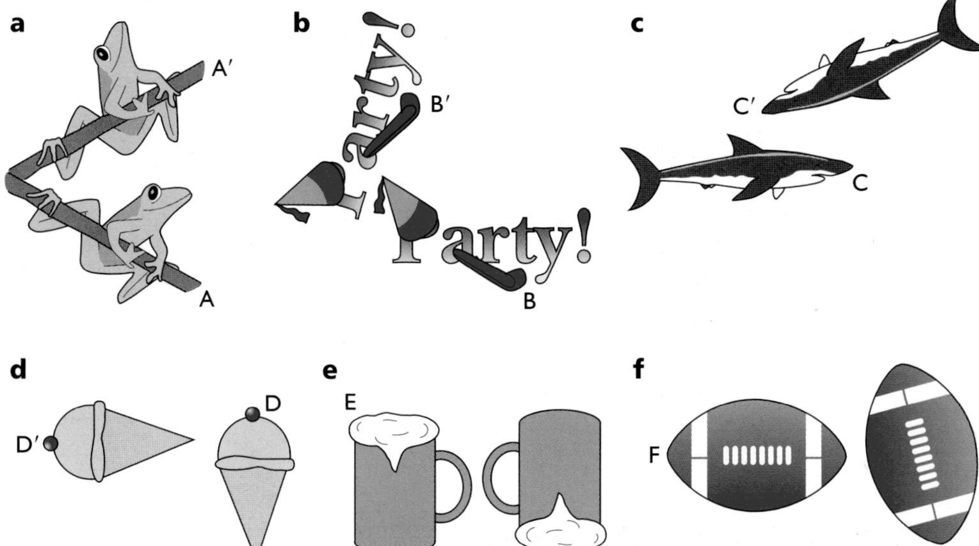

3 Finding the centre of rotation

When rotation about a point occurs, each point traces out a circular path to its image.

The centre of each circle is the centre of rotation.

So if we were to draw all the circular paths we would get a pattern of concentric circles.

The photograph shows the pattern traced out by the stars as they rotate around the Pole Star.

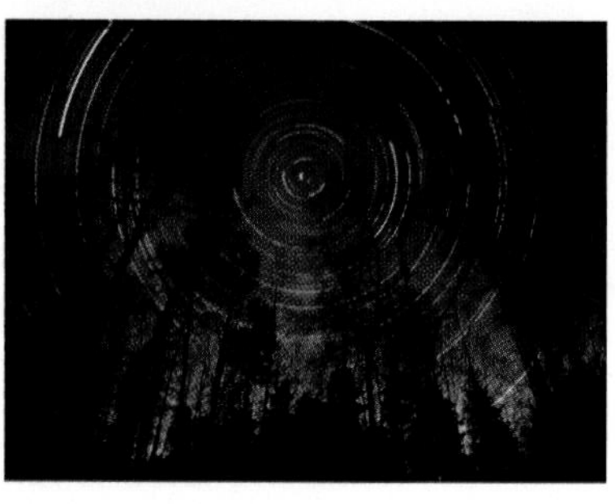

To find the centre of rotation, follow these steps:

- Join any point to its image by a straight line, say AA′.
- Draw the line which is perpendicular to AA′ and cuts it in half. (This is known as the perpendicular bisector of AA′.)
- Join another point to its image by a straight line, say BB′.
- Draw the perpendicular bisector of BB′.

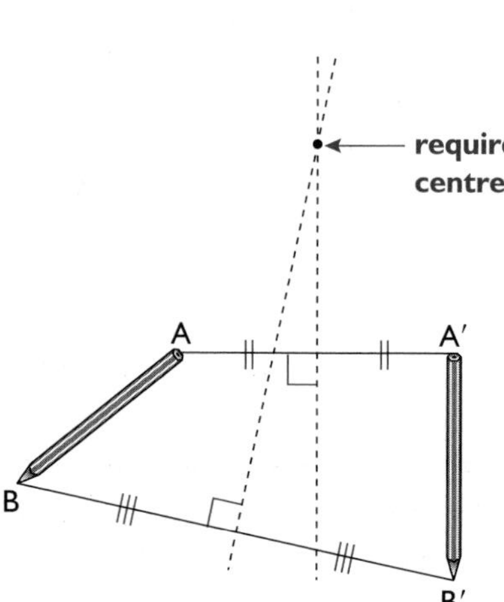

Where these two bisectors intersect is the centre of rotation.

You should be able to check this using a set of compasses.
A and A′ should lie on the same circle, centre C.
B and B′ should lie on the same circle, centre C.

Also, any point and its image will be the same distance from the centre, C.

Exercise 3.1

1 **i** Trace each line and its image into your jotter, then find the centre of rotation for each pair.
ii State the angle of rotation in each case.
iii Check your accuracy using a set of compasses.

a
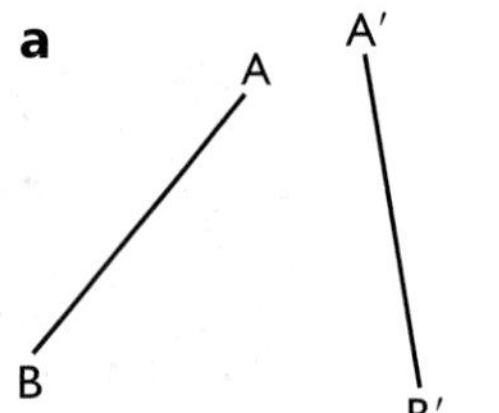

b
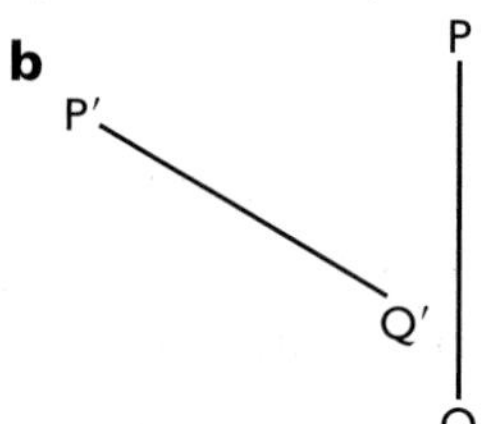

c
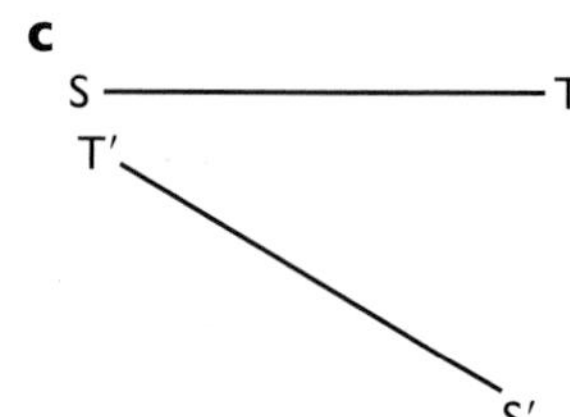

2 The constellation of The Plough rotates around the Pole Star.

a Trace the constellation and its image into your jotter

b Find the location of the Pole Star.

c The stars labelled A and B are often referred to as The Pointers. Why do you think that is?

3
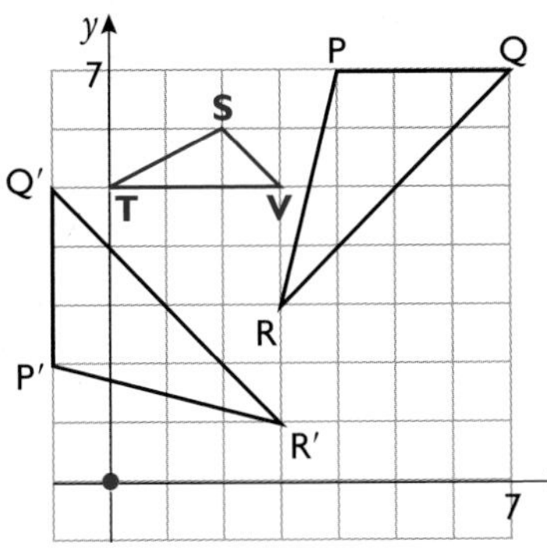

P′Q′R′ is the image of PQR under an anticlockwise rotation of 90°.

a What are the coordinates of the centre of rotation?

b What are the coordinates of the vertices of the image of the triangle STV under the same transformation?

4 WVFT is rotated through 180°. Its image is W′V′F′T′.

a State the coordinates of F′ and T′.

b What are the coordinates of the centre of rotation?

c EGH has undergone the same rotation. It is a triangle with vertices E(0, 7), G(7, 2) and H(1, −1). Find the image of each vertex.

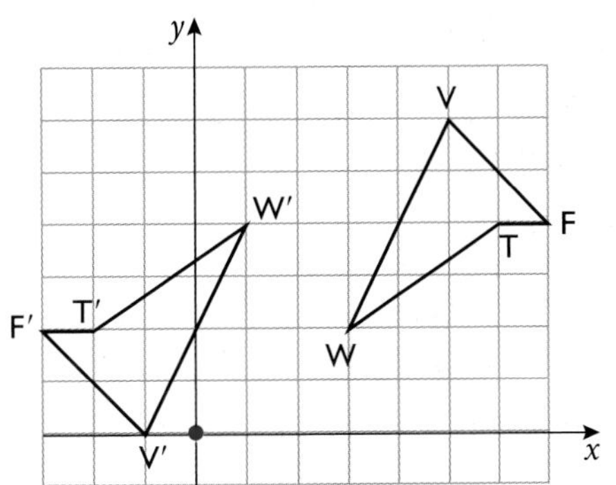

4 Rotational symmetry

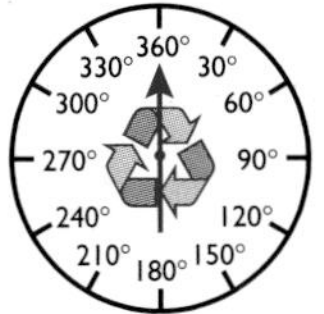

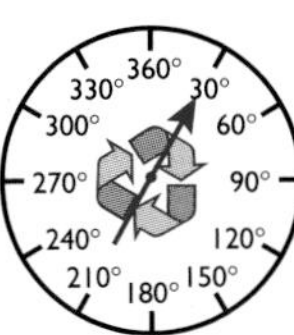

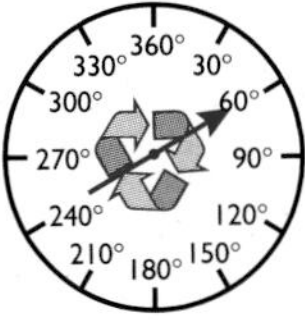

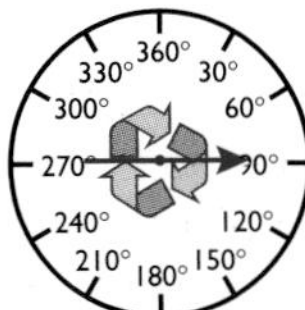

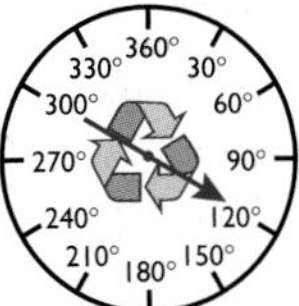

Examine the logo for 'recycling'.

As it rotates clockwise we can see the transformation.

However, when we rotate it through 120°, it looks the same as it started. It has **rotational symmetry**.

In one revolution it looks the same *three* times.

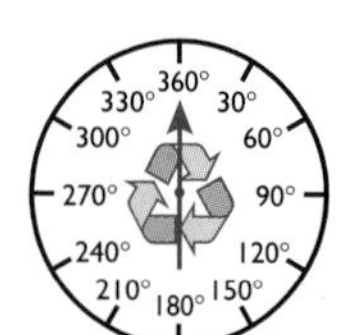

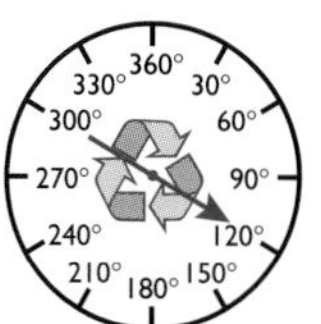

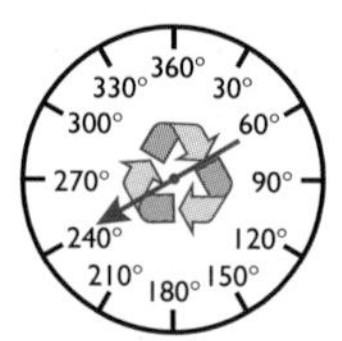

We say that the logo possesses **rotational symmetry of order 3.**

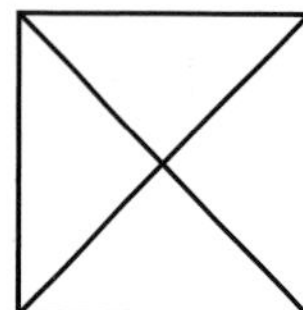

The square possesses quarter-turn symmetry … rotational symmetry of order 4.

The parallelogram possesses half-turn symmetry … rotational symmetry of order 2.

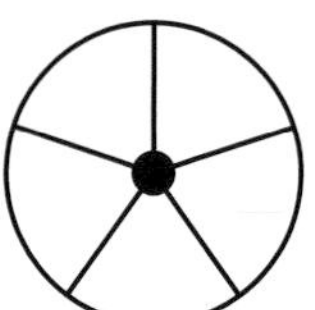

This shape has rotational symmetry of order 5.

Exercise 4.1

1 Identify the order of rotational symmetry for each object.

a

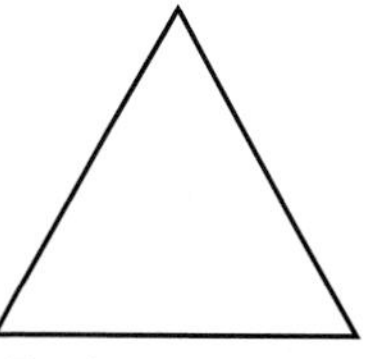

Equilateral triangle

b

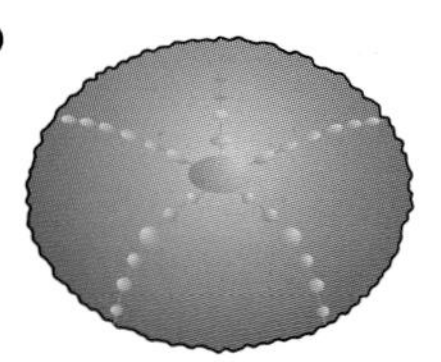

Sea urchin

c

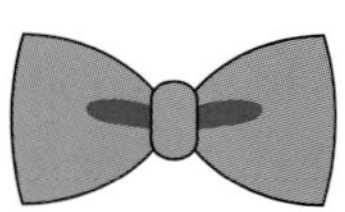

Bow tie

d

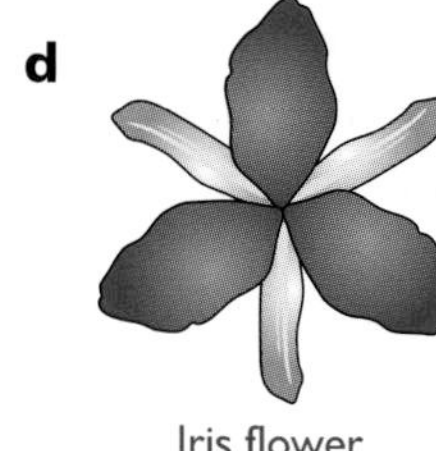

Iris flower

e

Starfish

f

Snowflake

2 This equilateral triangle undergoes a rotation.

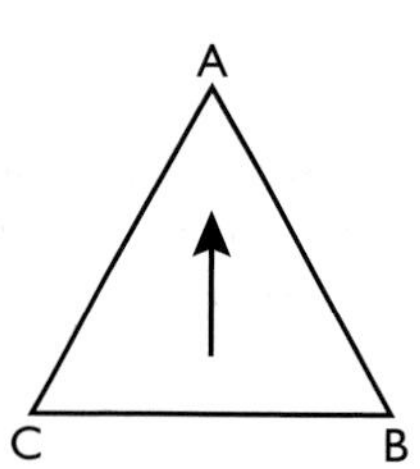

The image of A is C, of C is B and of B is A.

a What is the size of the rotation?

b **i** Draw the triangle.

ii Draw the perpendicular bisector of AA′ (i.e. AC).

iii Draw the perpendicular bisector of CC′ (i.e. CB).

iv Label the centre of rotation (the point of intersection) P.

The point P is known as the **centre of symmetry**.

3 **i** Copy each diagram accurately into your jotter.
ii Use the method described above to find the centre of symmetry of each shape.

a
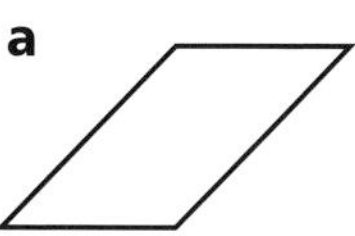

b
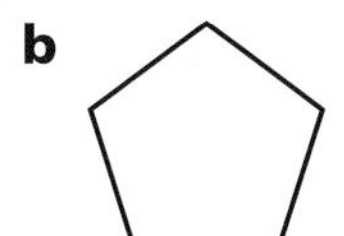

c
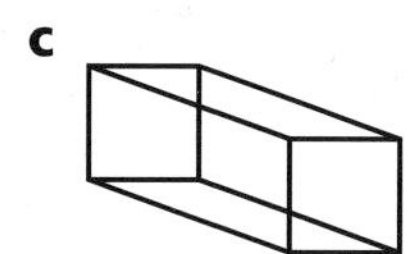

d
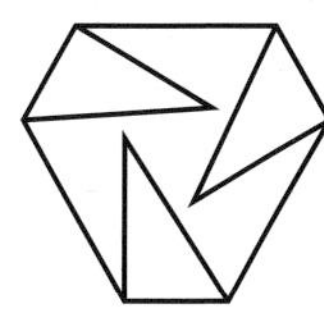

4 Use the fact that each shape possesses rotational symmetry to calculate the labelled angles.

a
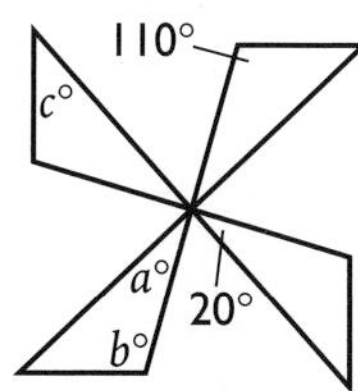

b
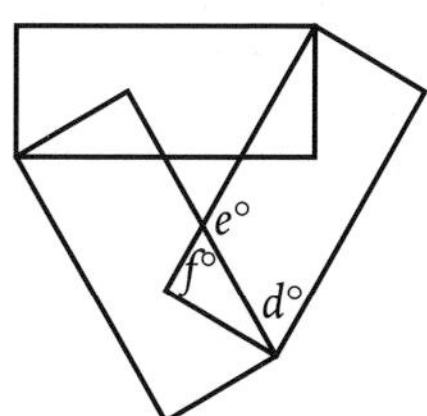

c
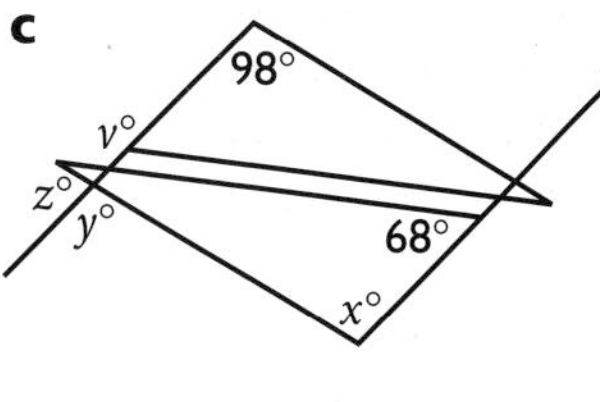

5 ABCD possesses rotational symmetry.

a What is the order of the symmetry?

b Find the coordinates of the centre of symmetry.

c The triangle with vertices E(3, 3), F(2, 6) and G(5, 7) undergoes a half turn about this centre.
What are the coordinates of the images of E, F and G?

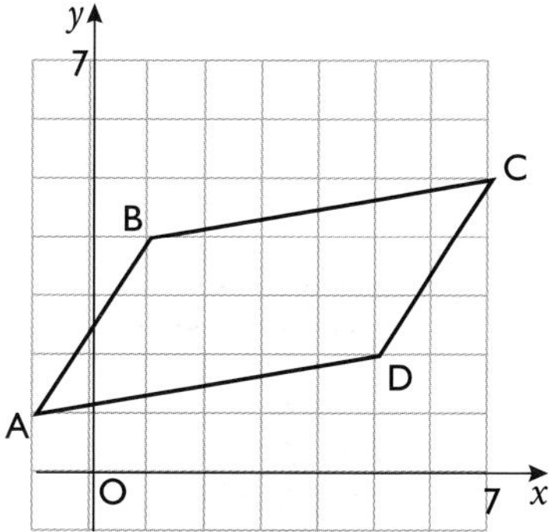

6 We can take any shape and create a picture with rotational symmetry of any order.

- To make symmetry of order 3, first calculate $360 \div 3 = 120°$.
- Draw three guidelines 120° apart as shown.
- Prepare a template of the element you wish to rotate.
- Draw it three times, once on each guideline.

120°
120°
120°

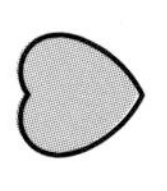
template

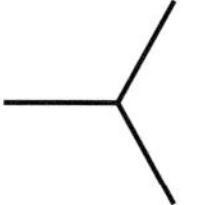
guidelines

Clover leaves have rotational symmetry of order 3.

a The flower celandine has rotational symmetry of order 4.
i At what angle should the guidelines be set?
ii Use the petal template to help you draw a celandine flowerhead.

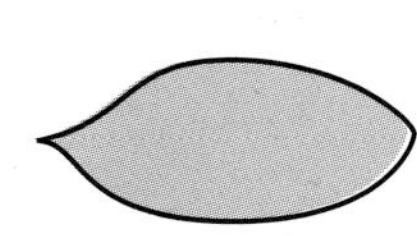

b The buttercup has a flowerhead with rotational symmetry of order 5.

i At what angle should the guidelines be set?

ii Use the petal template to help you draw a buttercup. (The petals will overlap.)

c The wood anemone has a flowerhead with rotational symmetry of order 6. Draw the flower head of the wood anemone.

Investigation

Find out what you can about symmetry in plant life. Consider both reflective and rotational symmetry.

Rotational

Reflective (one axis)

E

7 **a** A design has rotational symmetry of order 3. The diagram shows where the centre is and one part of the design. Copy and complete the design on isometric paper.

b Another design has rotational symmetry of order 6. Copy and complete this second design on isometric paper.

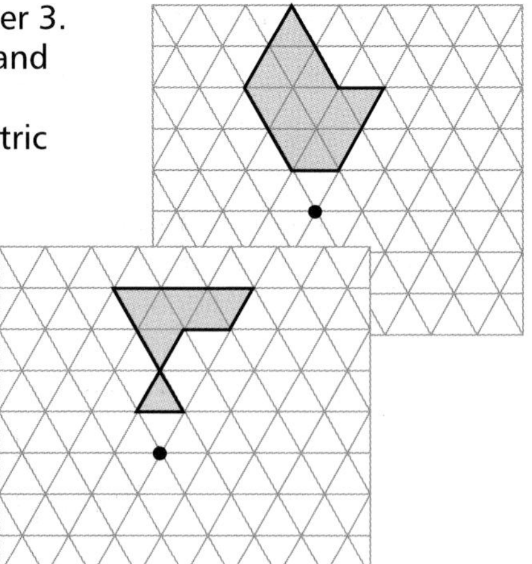

c Use isometric paper to explore the patterns that can be made using 3-fold and 6-fold symmetry.

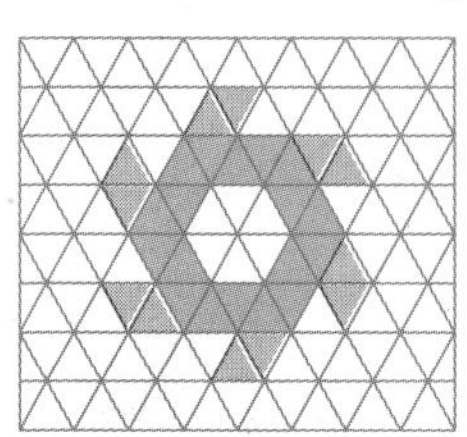

5 Translation

When an object is moved, without rotation, then we say it has undergone a **translation**.

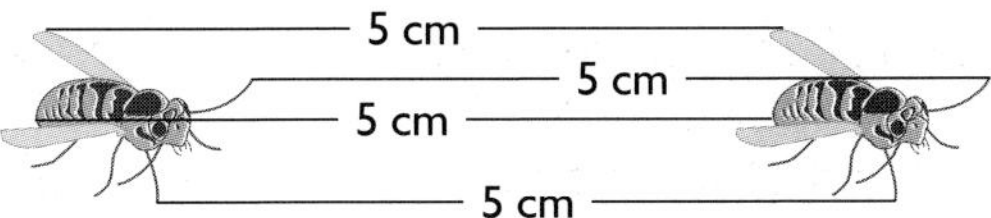

Note that each point of the wasp (the wing tip, the sting, the foot) has moved 5 cm to the right.

The wasp has undergone a translation of 5 cm to the right.

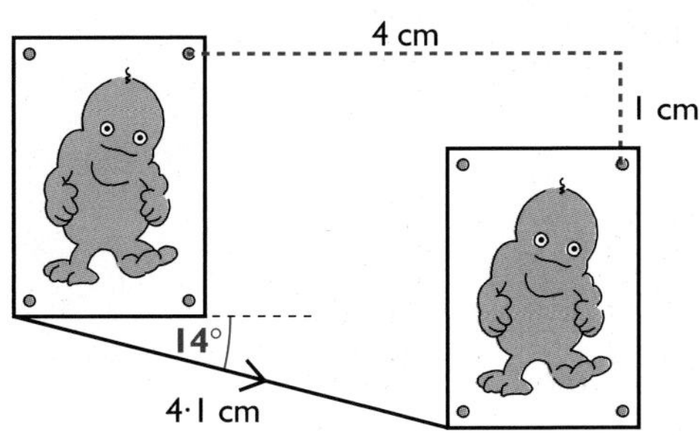

This picture has undergone a translation of 4 cm to the right and 1 cm down.

All points on the picture are displaced *exactly the same*.

The translation could also be described as a path which is 14° down from the horizontal for a distance of 4·1 cm.

E

Exercise 5.1

1 Each pair of pictures, except one, illustrates a translation. Describe that translation in each case.

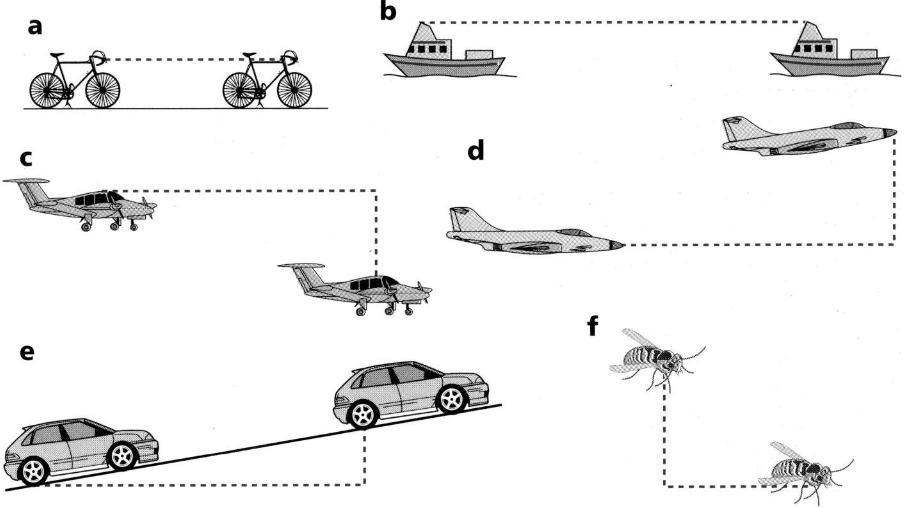

2 A rectangle is 3 cm long and 1 cm high.
It undergoes a translation of 2 cm to the right.

3 cm
1 cm

a Draw the rectangle.

b Draw its image under the translation.

c **i** Shade in the area of overlap between the rectangle and its image.
ii What shape is the overlap?

3 A regular hexagon is arranged as shown.
It undergoes a translation of 2 cm to the right.

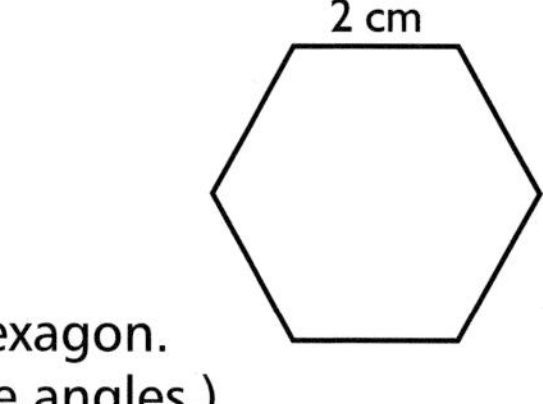

a Make a sketch of the hexagon and its image.

b What is the shape of the overlap created?

c Describe each of the following translations of the hexagon.
(It may help to draw some diagonals … to find some angles.)

(i) **(ii)** **(iii)**

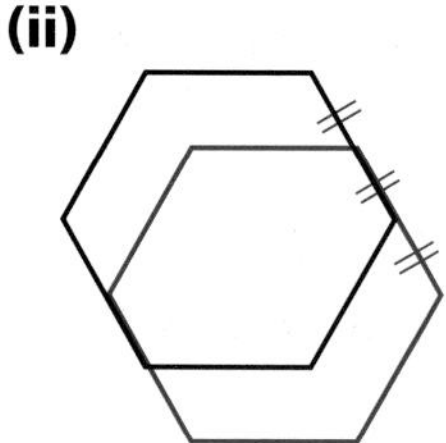

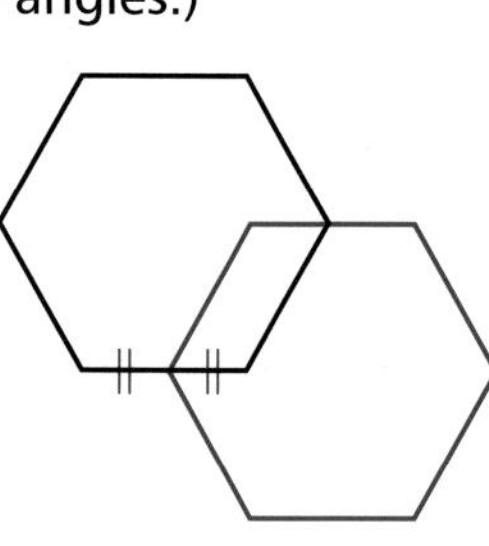

4

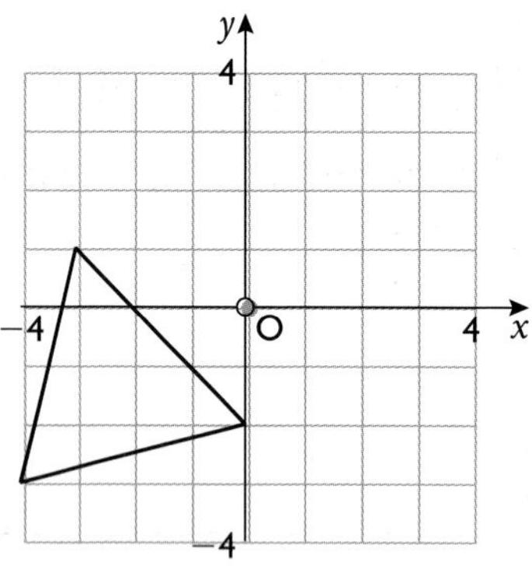

A triangle has vertices A(−4, −3), B(−3, 1) and C(0, −2).

a The triangle undergoes a translation of *4 units to the right and 1 up*.
i Draw the triangle and its image under this translation.
ii Write down the coordinates of A′, B′ and C′, the vertices of the image.

b If A′B′C′ also undergoes this transformation, write down the coordinates of the vertices of its image.

c A second translation takes each triangle *1 unit to the right and 4 up*.
Draw these images on the same diagram.

5 **a** Sketch the parallelogram ABCD.

b Under a certain translation the image of A is B.
i Draw the image of the parallelogram under this translation.
ii Explain why $a + b = 180$.

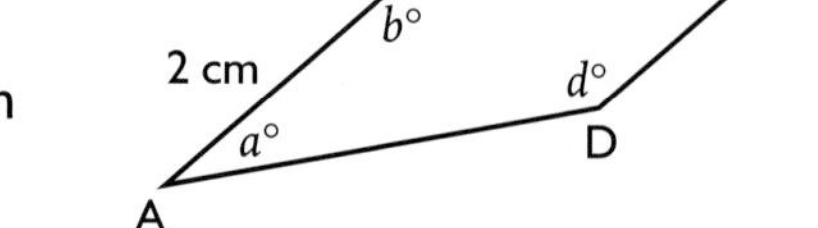

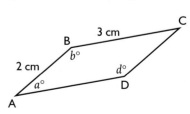

c Under another translation the image of A is D.
i Draw the image of the parallelogram under this translation.
ii Explain why $b = d$.

6 The translation which moves A to K is often written as $\begin{pmatrix} 5 \\ -1 \end{pmatrix}$ … *5 to the right and 1 down.*

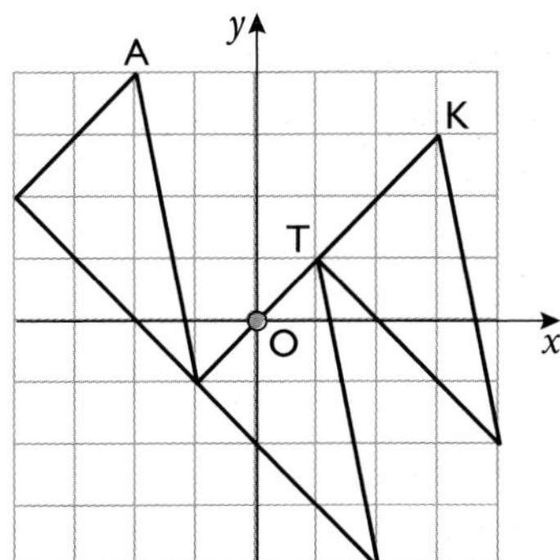

a Write down the following translations in a similar manner:
i K to A **ii** A to T **iii** T to A **iv** T to K.

b If going from P to Q is the translation $\begin{pmatrix} -3 \\ 4 \end{pmatrix}$, write down the translation which takes you from Q to P.

c Going from K to T, then from T to A is a roundabout way of going from K to A.

i Comment on the following:

$$\begin{pmatrix} -2 \\ -2 \end{pmatrix} + \begin{pmatrix} -3 \\ 3 \end{pmatrix} = \begin{pmatrix} -5 \\ 1 \end{pmatrix}$$

ii Make a similar *addition* to describe the fact that going from T to A, then from A to K is a roundabout way of going from T to K.

iii Make a similar addition to cover the fact that going from T to A, then from A to T is a roundabout way of staying at T.

d Describe the translation in which A is its own image.

E

6 Translational symmetry

Here is a regular pattern created by translating a single motif 2 cm to the left.

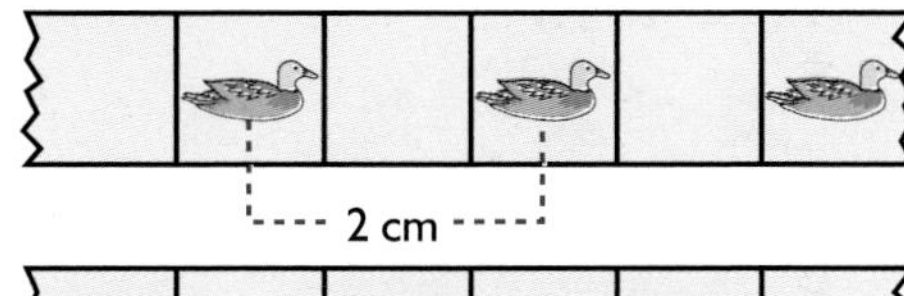

If the pattern were to be moved 1 cm to the right you would spot the difference …

… but if it were to be moved 4 cm to the right it would appear unchanged.

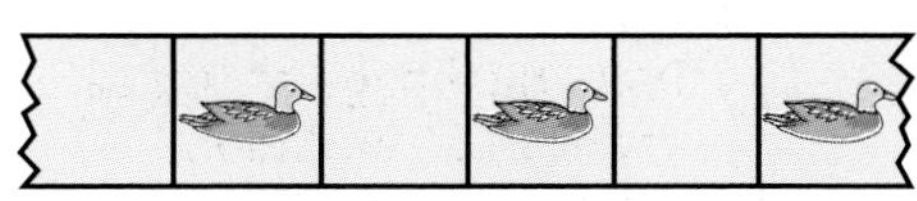

This type of symmetry is called **translational symmetry**.
The size of the smallest translation needed to produce this symmetry is called the **period** or the **repeat** of the symmetry.

Example 1

An array of radio telescopes exhibits translational symmetry.

Example 2

The colonnades of many buildings exhibit translational symmetry.

Example 3

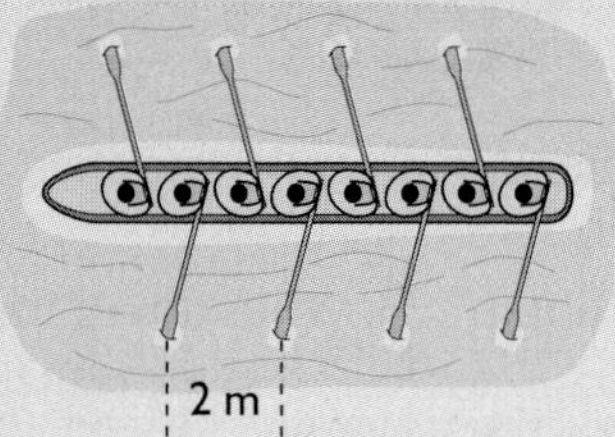

Looking from above and taking rowers in pairs produces translational symmetry with a repeat of about 2 metres to the right.

Example 4 This tiling exhibits many translational symmetries

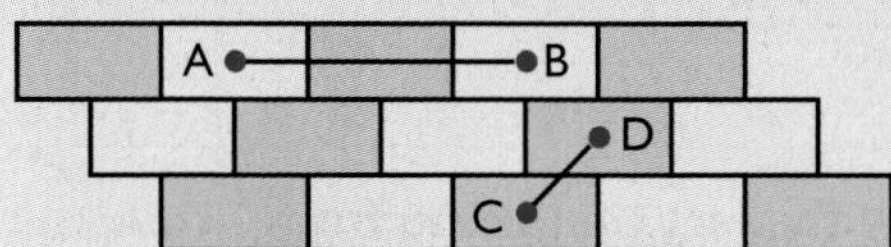

- the translation which takes A to B ... a *repeat* of 2 cm to the right.
- the translation which takes C to D ... a *repeat* of 1 cm to the right and 1 up.

E

Exercise 6.1

1 Measure the period of each case of translational symmetry to the nearest millimetre.

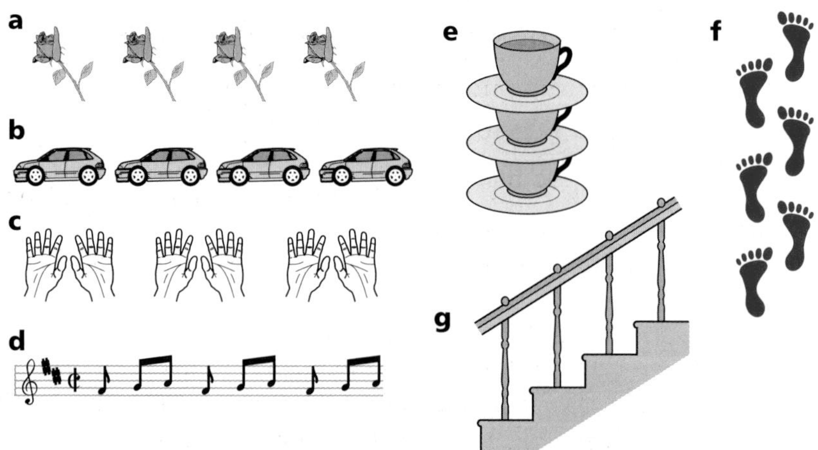

2 The threads of each screw exhibit translational symmetry. Measure the length indicated, then perform an appropriate division to calculate the period in each case.

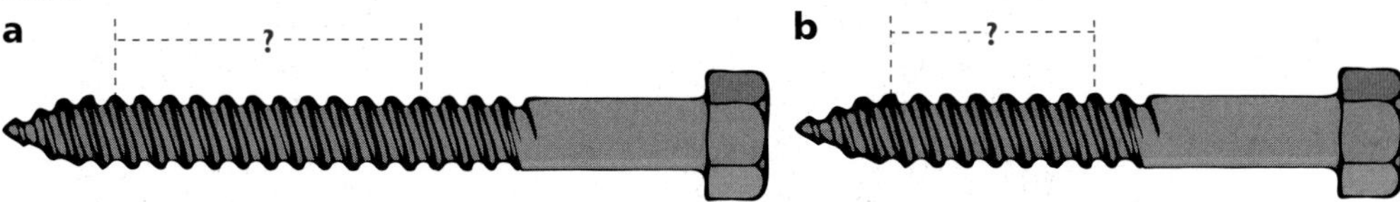

3 Make the measurements indicated to help you calculate the period if translational symmetry is to be seen in the picture of the oarsmen. Note there is a horizontal and vertical shift.

4 The bodies of cars on an assembly line exhibit translational symmetry. They can be represented on a coordinate grid as shown.

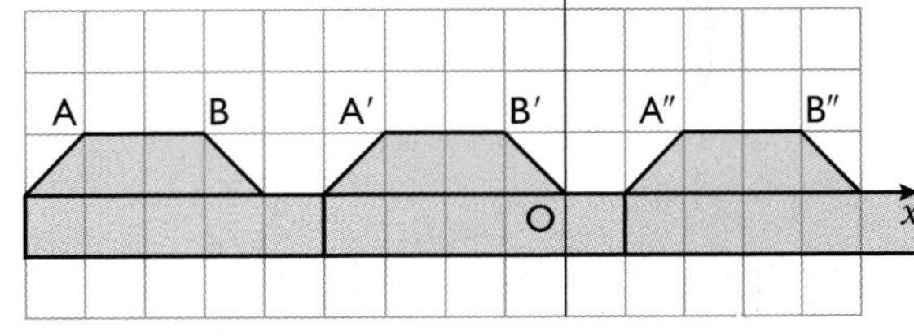

a Describe the translation by giving the distance and direction of the repeat.

b The image of A(−8, 1) under this translation is A′(−3, 1).

i What are the coordinates of the image of A in the third car (A′′)?

ii Calculate the coordinates of the image of A in the fourth car.

iii What are the coordinates of the image of A in the tenth car?

c Calculate the coordinates of the image of B on the fifteenth car.

5 The row of windmills at the wind farm have translational symmetry.

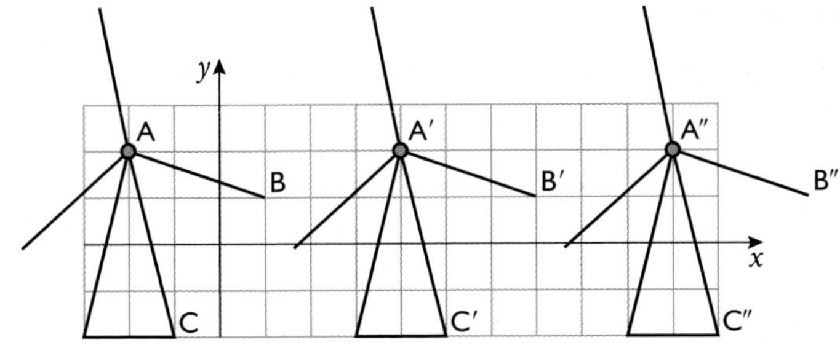

a State the coordinates of **i** A **ii** A′, the image of A in the second mill **iii** the image of A in the tenth mill.

b What is true about the y coordinate of a point which is the image of A in this situation?

c **i** Calculate the image of B in the tenth mill.

ii What is always true about the y coordinate of the images of B?

d Meg says that (29, −1) is an image of C under this scheme. Is that true?

e The point (41, −2) is an image of C. In which mill is it to be found?

E

6 A boulevard of trees running uphill has translational symmetry.
When placed on a suitable coordinate grid, P and its images are P(−3, −2), P′(0, −1), P″(3, 0), …

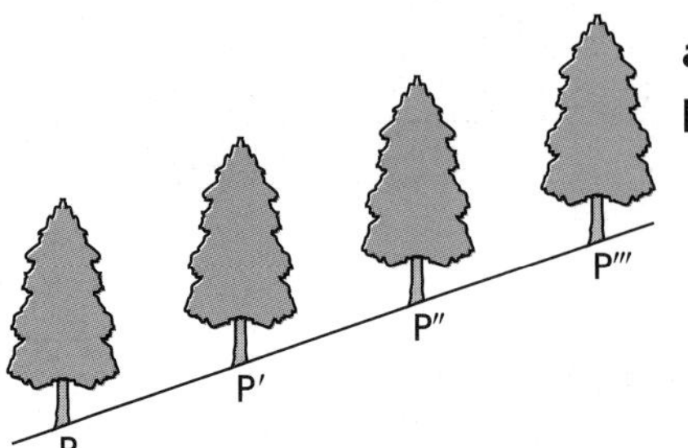

a Describe the *repeat* of the symmetry.

b **i** Calculate the coordinates of the image of P on the tenth tree.

ii A formula for finding the x coordinate of the image of P is $x = 3t - 6$ where t is the tree number.
Check this with the first four trees.

c Find a similar formula for the y coordinate of the image of P.

Investigation

Explore the translational symmetries to be found in tilings.

Try a search for images on the internet using the keywords:

tiling, regular tiling, Escher.

7 Enlargement and reduction

An object can be enlarged or reduced by multiplying each length within it by a suitable factor.

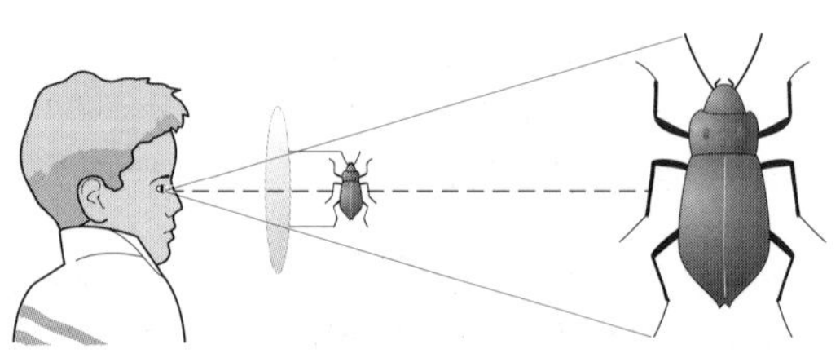

The boy here is looking at a beetle which has been enlarged by a factor of 4 by the lens.
Note that the length of each leg, feeler, wing case in the image is 4 times as long as in the original.

Example 1 **a**

Example 2 **b**

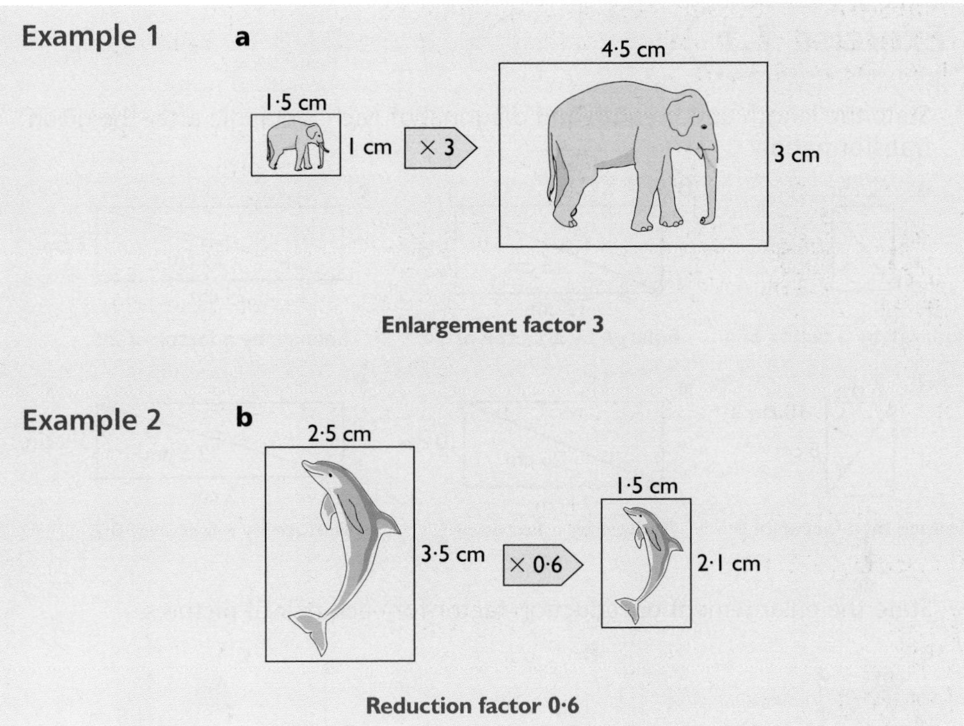

Multiply by a factor between 0 and 1 to reduce the shape.
Multiply by a factor bigger than 1 to enlarge the shape.

Example 3 What is the factor of reduction in this pair of pictures?

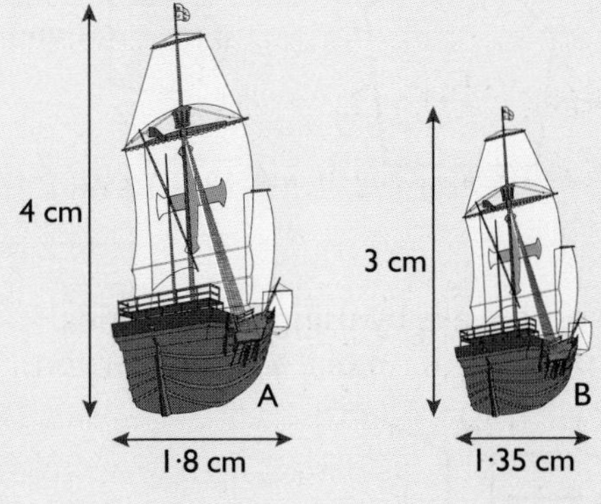

Height of A = 4 cm;
height of B = 3 cm

Reduction factor

$$= \frac{\text{height of image (B)}}{\text{height of object (A)}} = \frac{3}{4} = 0{\cdot}75$$

Width of A = 1·8 cm;
width of B = 1·35 cm

Reduction factor

$$= \frac{\text{width of image (B)}}{\text{width of object (A)}} = \frac{1{\cdot}35}{1{\cdot}8} = 0{\cdot}75$$

F

10

F

Exercise 7.1

1 State the length and breadth and diagonal of each rectangle after the given transformation.

a 1·2 cm, 1·6 cm, 2 cm
Enlarge by a factor of 4

b 13 cm, 5 cm, 12 cm
Enlarge by a factor of 3

c 25 cm, 7 cm, 24 cm
Enlarge by a factor of 2·5

d 6 cm, 10 cm, 8 cm
Reduce by a factor of 0·5

e 26 cm, 10 cm, 24 cm
Reduce by a factor of $\frac{1}{4}$

f 12·5 cm, 3·5 cm, 12 cm
Reduce by a factor of 0·2

2 State the enlargement or reduction factor for each pair of pictures.

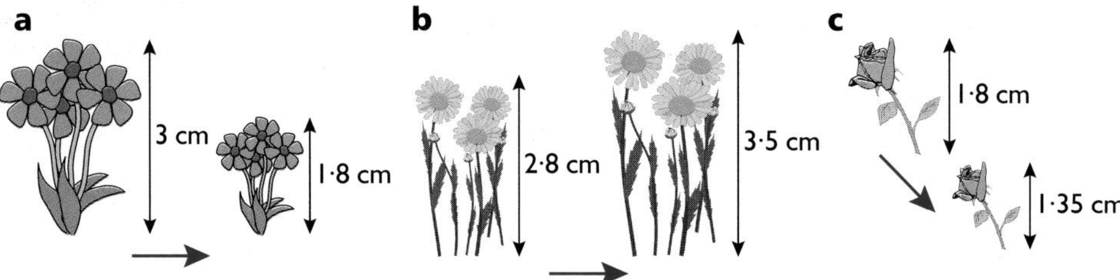

3 For each shape **i** calculate the enlargement or reduction factor
ii calculate the missing lengths.

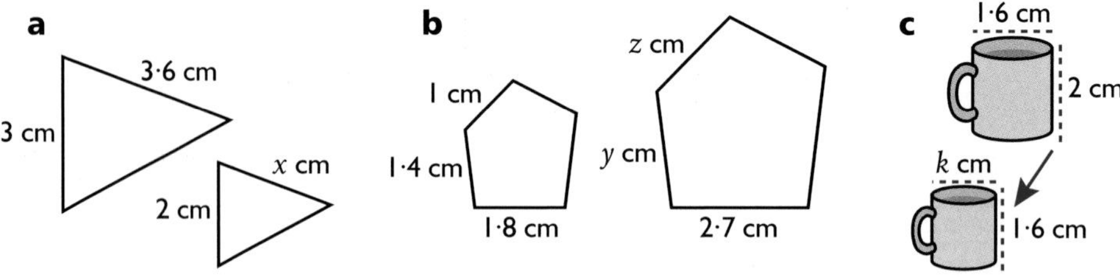

4 The ancient Egyptians enlarged drawings onto walls by using square grids.
Use square paper to **i** copy each picture **ii** make a scaled version.

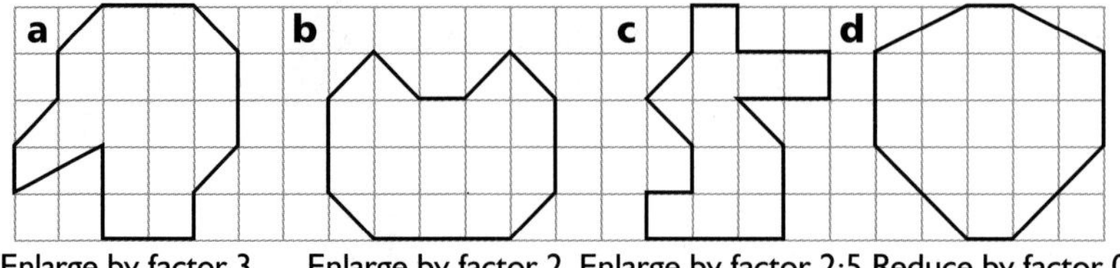

Enlarge by factor 3 Enlarge by factor 2 Enlarge by factor 2·5 Reduce by factor 0·5

5 A rectangle has vertices A(1, 0), B(5, 0), C(5, 4) and D(1, 4).

a Plot the points and draw ABCD.

b Draw the shape whose vertices A′B′C′D′ have coordinates double those of ABCD.

c What can be said about the length of AB and of A′B′?

d Without measuring it, what can be said about the length of the diagonal A′C′?

6 A pentagon has vertices E(4, 2), F(0, 4), G(−4, 2), H(−2, −2) and I(2, −2).

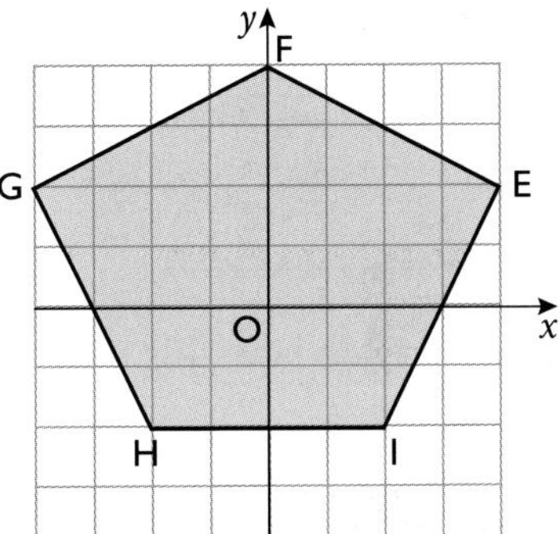

a Find a new set of points E′ to I′ whose coordinates are twice the size of E to I respectively.

b Use these new points to help you draw a pentagon twice as large.

c In a similar fashion find the vertices of a pentagon which is only half as big.

d **i** Draw a line through E and E′, through F and F′, through G and G′. Where do they intersect?

ii Check that HH′ and II′ also converge on this point.

7 Artists make use of this sort of enlargement to make perspective drawings.

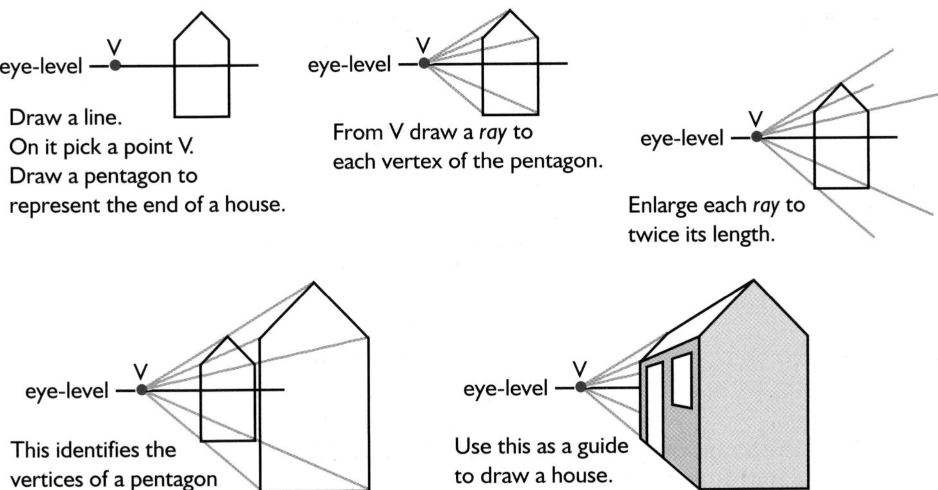

eye-level
V
Draw a line.
On it pick a point V.
Draw a pentagon to
represent the end of a house.
eye-level
V
From V draw a *ray* to
each vertex of the pentagon.
eye-level
V
Enlarge each *ray* to
twice its length.
eye-level
V
This identifies the
vertices of a pentagon
twice as big.
eye-level
V
Use this as a guide
to draw a house.

Explore with different shapes and different scale factors.

8 A triangle has vertices P(−2, 2), Q(−3, 1) and R(−2, −1). V is the point (−4, 1)
Using a technique similar to that described in question **7**, VP is drawn, then extended three times as far to P′. VP′ = 3 × VP.

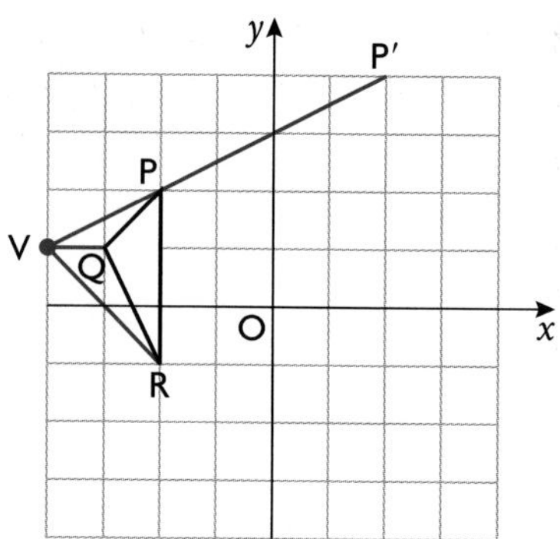

a State the coordinates of P′.

b In a similar way find Q′ and R′ and state their coordinates.

c Draw the image of the triangle PQR, namely P′Q′R′, which is 3 times as big.

V is often referred to as the **centre of enlargement**.

d Using this centre, draw the image of the square with vertices A(−3, 2), B(−1, 2), C(−1, 0) and D(−3, 0) which is twice as large.

Investigation

Investigate how this technique could be used to reduce objects.

CHECK-UP

1 Draw this shape and its image after a half turn about P.

P

2 a Copy this diagram onto squared paper.

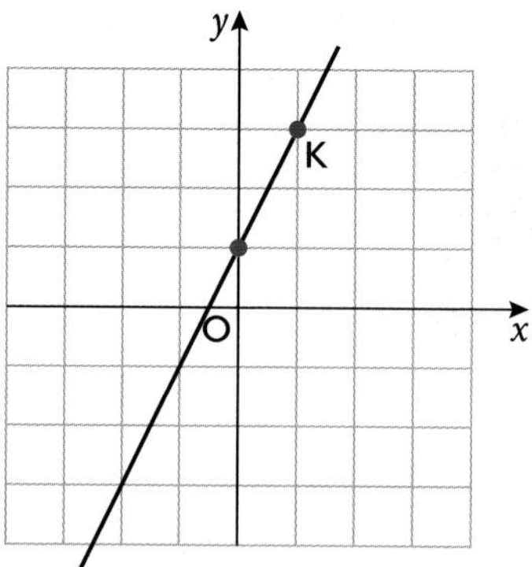

b On the same diagram, draw the image of the line after

i a half turn about the origin

ii a quarter turn clockwise about the origin

iii a 90° turn anticlockwise about the origin.

c State the image of K after each transformation.

3 With the aid of tracing paper and a protractor, describe the size of the rotation required if Fish B is the image of Fish A.

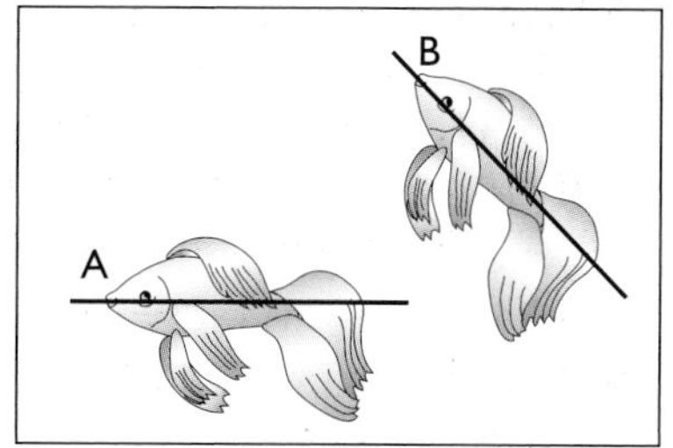

4 State

i the order of symmetry of each shape

ii the smallest angle needed to rotate the shape onto itself.

a

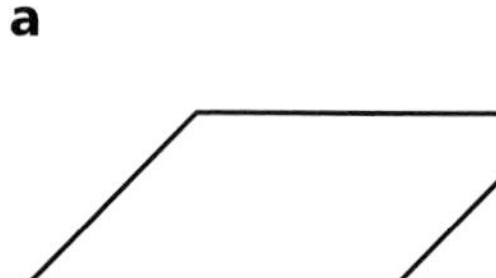

Parallelogram

b

Star

c

Snowflake

5 A quadrilateral has half-turn symmetry.
Its vertices are P(3, 2), Q(−1, 4), R and S.
Its centre of symmetry is the origin.
Calculate the coordinates of

a R and

b S.

6 Describe the translation that slides A onto B in each case.

a

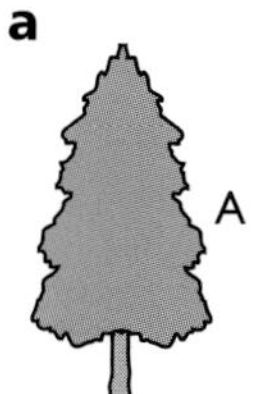

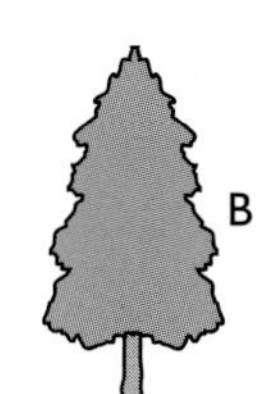

b

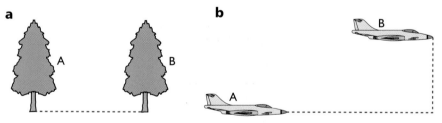

7 The line AB undergoes a translation $\begin{pmatrix} 3 \\ -1 \end{pmatrix}$, i.e. 3 to right and 1 down.

a If A has coordinates (4, 3) what are the coordinates of its image under the translation?

b If the *image* of B has coordinates (−2, −4), what are the coordinates of B?

8 A row of houses exhibits translational symmetry,

a What is the repeat of the symmetry?

b The first house's roof peaks at A$(-2, 3)$.
State the coordinates of its image A′.

c Calculate the coordinates of the image of A on the

i third

ii fourth

iii tenth house.

d Which of the following is a formula for the x coordinate of the image of A on the hth house?

i $x = 4h$ **ii** $x = 4h - 2$ **iii** $x = 4h - 6$ **iv** $x = 4h - 8$

e Find a formula for the x coordinates of the image of B on the hth house.

9 Make a copy of each of the following pictures and another version scaled by the factor given.

a

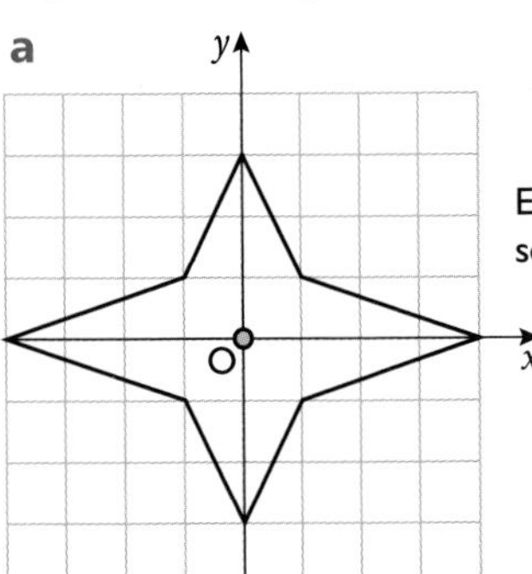

Enlarged, scale factor 3

b

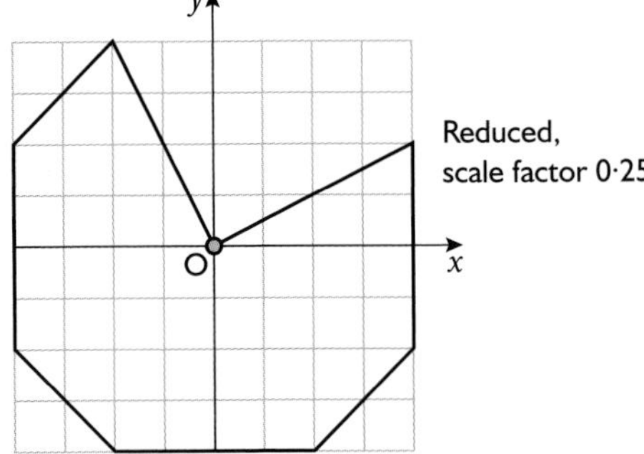

Reduced, scale factor 0·25

10 Consider views of this bridge from different places.
By making a quick sketch indicate a view which exhibits:

a reflective symmetry

b rotational symmetry

c translational symmetry

d enlargement/reduction transformation.

11 Area

Early mathematics originated in parts of the world to the east of Greece. Its main uses were in practical arithmetic including measurement of areas.

The Babylonians as long ago as about 2000 BC used formulae for the area of a rectangle to solve problems in the division of farming land.

Babylon was situated in modern Iraq and when the River Euphrates burst its banks, the areas of land that were flooded had to be calculated.

1 Looking back

Exercise 1.1

1 For each rectangle, write down:

i the number of squares in each row

ii the number of rows

iii its area (assume each small square represents 1 cm^2).

a 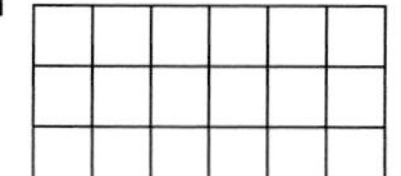

b 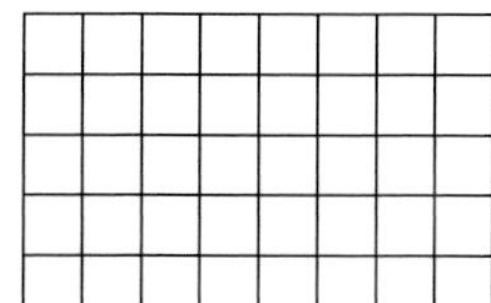

c 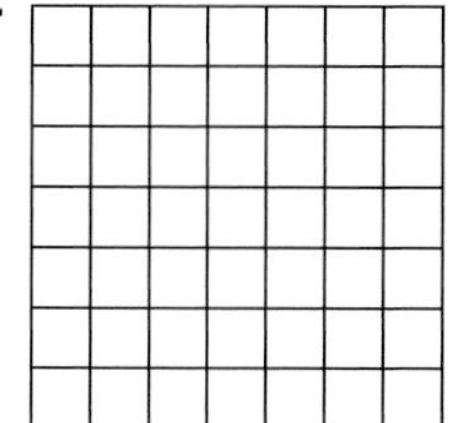

d 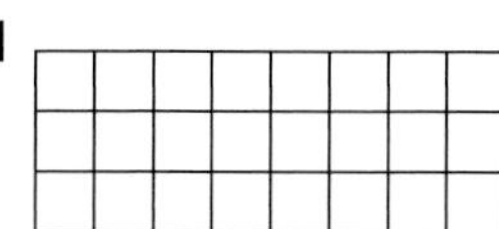

2 The diagram represents a tiled path through a rectangular lawn.
Assume the path is made of square tiles each with area 1 m^2.

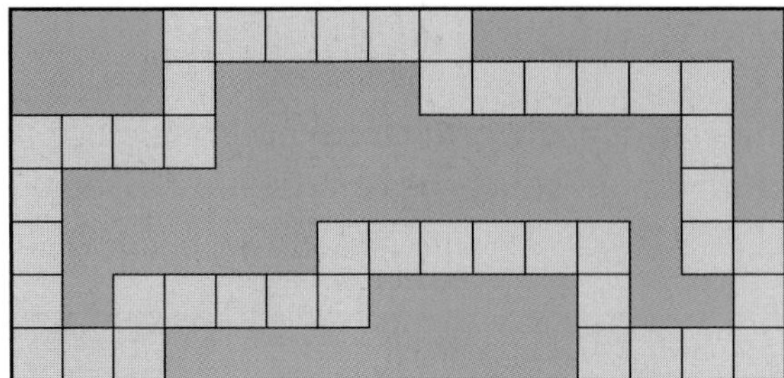

Calculate:

a the area of the path **b** the total area of the rectangular lawn.

3 Calculate the area of:

a rectangle ABCD

b right-angled triangle ACD.
Assume each square on the grid has an area of 1 cm^2.

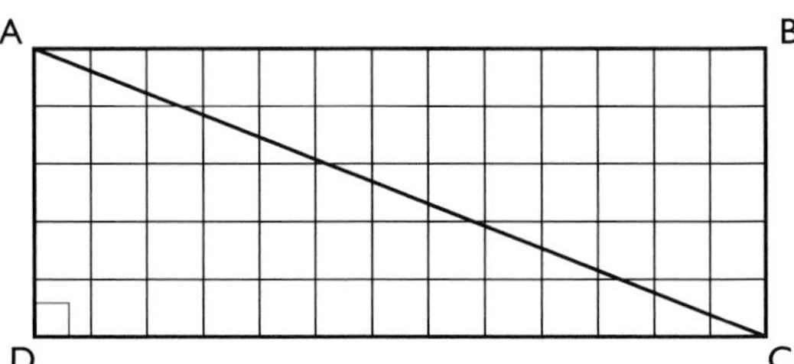

4 What is the area of each of these right-angled triangles?
Assume each square represents 1 cm^2.

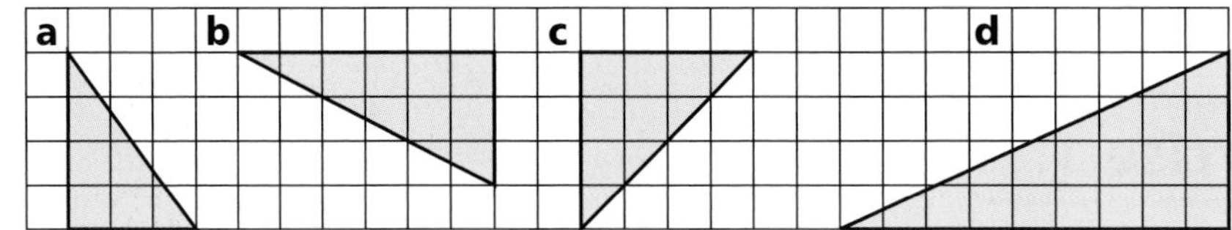

5 **a** Plot the points P(1, 2), Q(8, 6) and R(8, 2) on a coordinate diagram and join them to form △PQR.

b What is the area of △PQR in square units?

Reminder

1 cm

1 cm 1 square centimetre (1 cm^2)

1 mm
1 mm 1 square millimetre (1 mm^2)

$$1 \text{ cm} = 10 \text{ mm}$$
$$\Rightarrow 1 \text{ cm}^2 = 100 \text{ mm}^2$$

6 **a** Convert these areas to square millimetres:
i 2 cm^2 **ii** 8 cm^2 **iii** 85 cm^2 **iv** 0·25 cm^2.

b Convert these areas to square centimetres:
i 1200 mm^2 **ii** 750 mm^2 **iii** 6875 mm^2.

7 The stamp is placed on a 1 cm squared grid.

a Estimate its area in cm^2.

b Give a more accurate estimate of the stamp's area in mm^2.

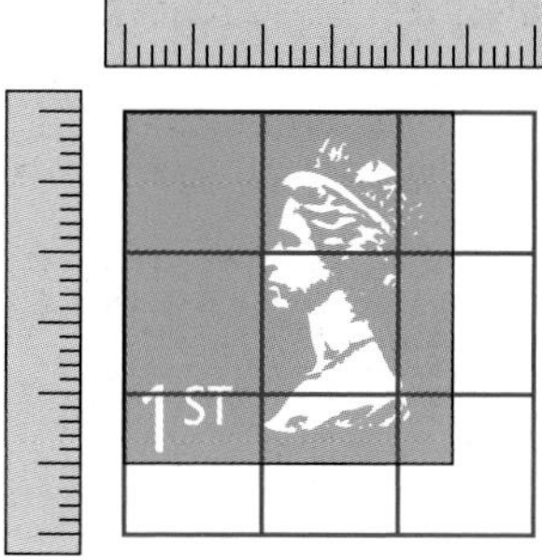

8 **a** Estimate, in cm^2, the area of:

i the cover of your textbook

ii the cover of your jotter

iii the sole of your foot.

b Give better estimates using a 1 cm squared grid.

9

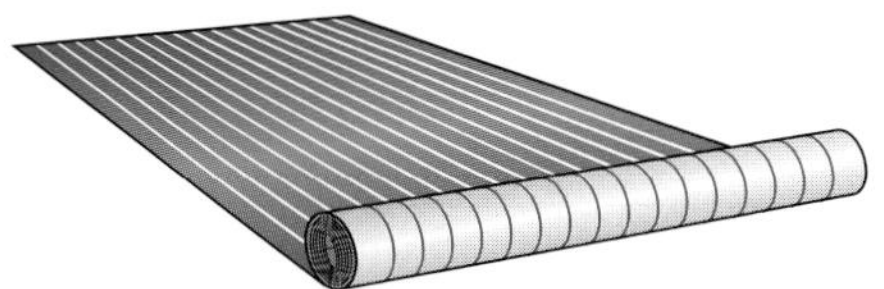

Best value carpet £29 a square metre or £24·25 a square yard

The Queen's Balmoral Estate 9700 hectares (ha) or 24 000 acres

24 square inches or 155 cm^2

LOCH LOMOND
70 square kilometres or 27 square miles

Use the above information to decide which is bigger:

a 1 square metre or 1 square yard

b 1 hectare or 1 acre

c 1 square kilometre or 1 square mile

d 1 square centimetre or 1 square inch

A useful guide:

$6 \text{ m}^2 \approx 5 \text{ yards}^2$

$2 \text{ hectares} \approx 5 \text{ acres}$

$5 \text{ km}^2 \approx 2 \text{ square miles}$

$13 \text{ cm}^2 \approx 2 \text{ square inches}$

(1 hectare is roughly the size of a football pitch)

2 The area of a rectangle: a formula

Example 1

What is the area of a rectangle which is 3 cm by 5 cm?

3 cm

5 cm

On placing a 1 cm square grid over the rectangle we see there are three rows of five 1 cm squares.

The area of the rectangle is $3 \times 5 = 15\ \text{cm}^2$.

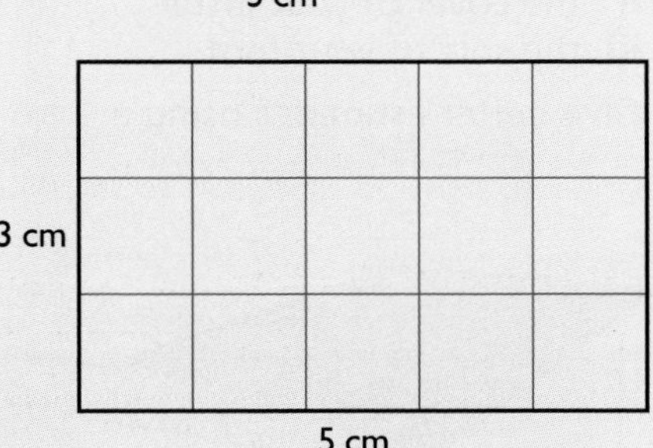

In general, we can find the area, A, of any rectangle by multiplying its length, l, and breadth, b.

$$\textit{Area} = \textit{length} \times \textit{breadth}$$

For a rectangle: $A = lb$ For a square: $A = l^2$

Units must be consistent.

Example 2

Find the area of a rectangle with length 12 cm and breadth 8·5 cm.
(Note: both measurements are in centimetres so the units are consistent.)

$A = lb$
$\Rightarrow A = 12 \times 8{\cdot}5\ \text{cm}^2$
$\Rightarrow A = 102\ \text{cm}^2$

Note: we read the answer as '102 square centimetres' and not as '102 centimetres squared', which means something completely different!

Exercise 2.1

1 Use the formula $A = lb$ to calculate the area of each of these rectangles.

a

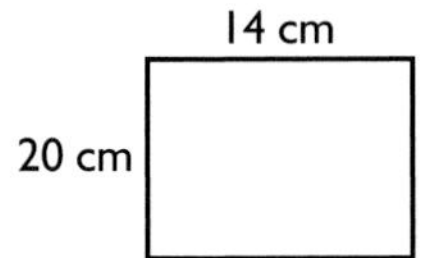

b

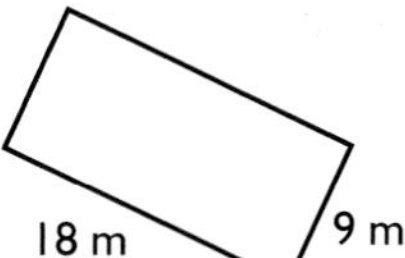

c

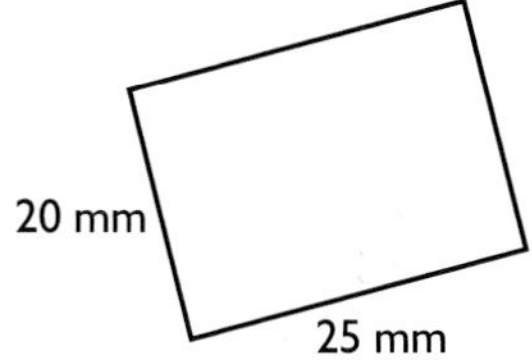

d

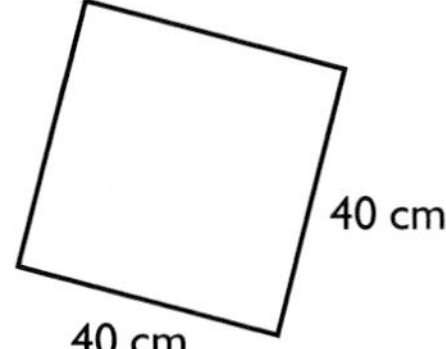

2 Use the formula $A = l^2$ to calculate the area of each square.

a

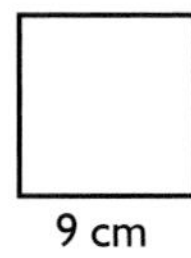

b

c

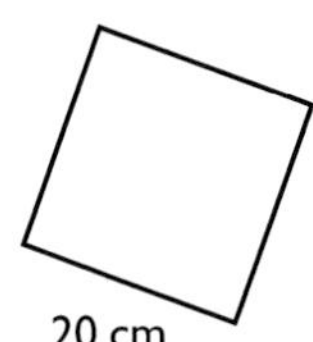

3 Calculate the area of each rectangle and square.

a

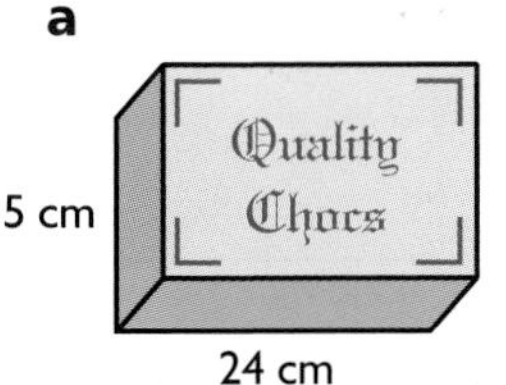

b

c

d

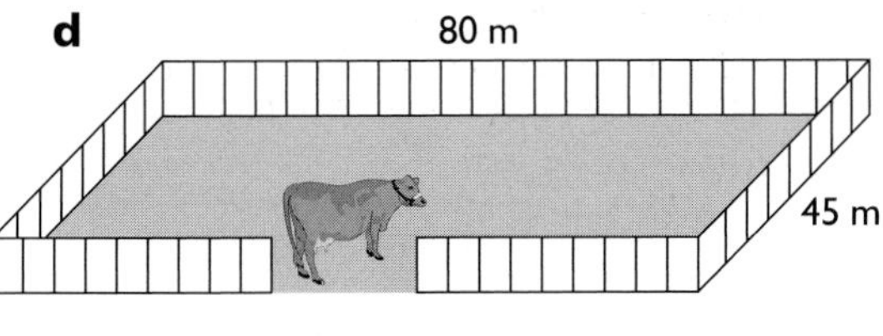

10·6 m

e 5 m

g 90 cm

f 5·3 m

10 m

4 There is a uniform border of 8 cm surrounding the picture.
Calculate the area of the picture.

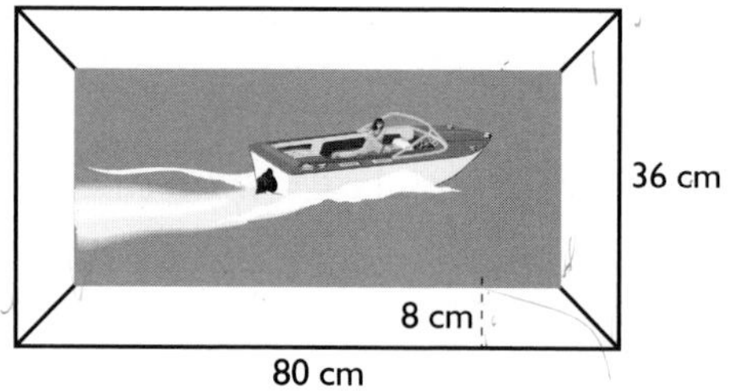

5 The plan of a rectangular children's playground is shown.
Rectangular areas for swings, a roundabout, a chute and a climbing frame are set in the grass playground.

a Calculate the area of the playground.

b Calculate the area set aside for:

i the swings
ii the roundabout
iii the climbing frame
iv the chute

c What area is grassed?

swings
chute
12 m
7·5 m
15 m
15 m
35 m
climbing frame
6 m
6 m
11 m
roundabout
24 m
42 m

6 Monkton High School is shown in the plan opposite.
It sits in rectangular grounds and is made up of a number of rectangular buildings.

a Calculate the area of:

i the PE block
ii the Technical block
iii the main block
iv the three buildings.

b What area of the school grounds is not built on?

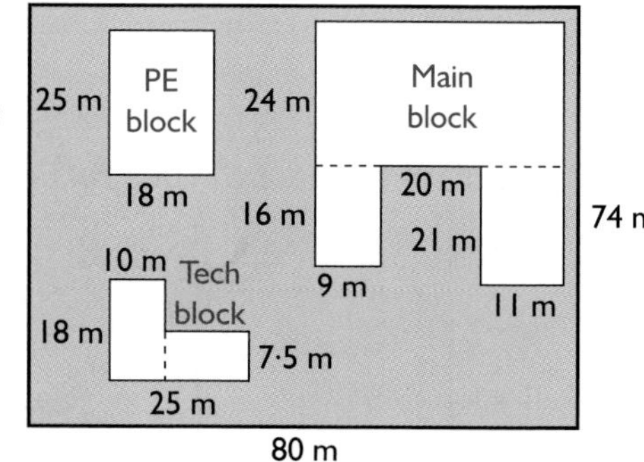

7 A kitchen wall 4·6 m by 2·7 m can be completely tiled with rectangular tiles 20 cm by 15 cm without any of the tiles needing to be cut.
How many of the tiles are needed?

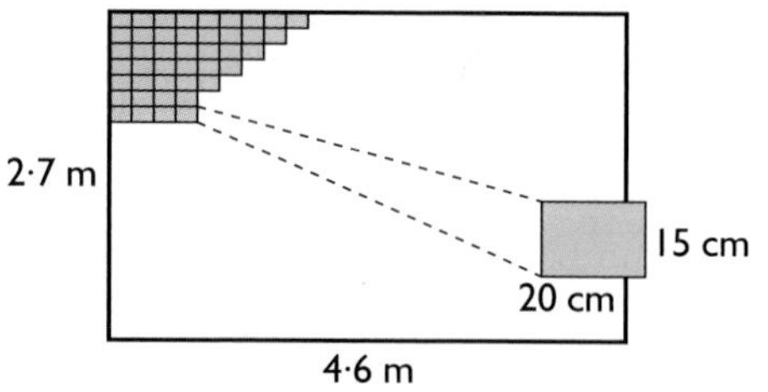

8 **a** Estimate the length and breadth of your classroom floor (if it is rectangular) in metres.
Hence write down an estimate in m^2 for the area of the classroom floor.

b Repeat **a** for **i** the blackboard **ii** the classroom door **iii** the assembly hall floor.

c Check your area estimates with those calculated from actual measurements.

d Copy and complete a table like the one below. Include some other rectangular areas.

Item	Length (m) (Estimate)	Breadth (m) (Estimate)	Area (m^2)	Length (m) (Measurement)	Breadth (m) (Measurement)	Area (m^2)
floor						
blackboard						
door						
assembly hall floor						

3 Getting into shape

The areas of some awkward shapes can be worked out using the formula for the area of a rectangle.

Example 1

Calculate the area of this shape.
All angles are right angles.

All measurements are in centimetres.

Break the shape into rectangles.

Area = A + B + C
$= 16 \times 12 + 20 \times 10 + 9 \times 7$
$= 192 + 200 + 63$
$= 455\ \text{cm}^2$

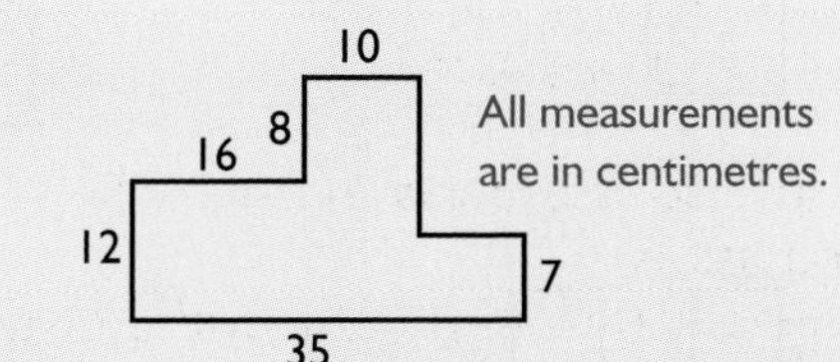

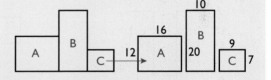

Example 2

Calculate the area of this shape.
All angles are right angles.

All measurements are in metres.

A different strategy to the one above is to draw a surrounding rectangle.

Area = outer rectangle − B − C − D
$= 17 \times 12 - 6 \times 3 - 4 \times 3 - 4 \times 5$
$= 204 - 18 - 12 - 20$
$= 154\ \text{m}^2$

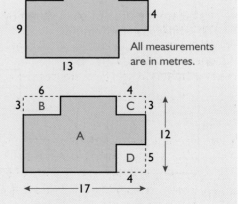

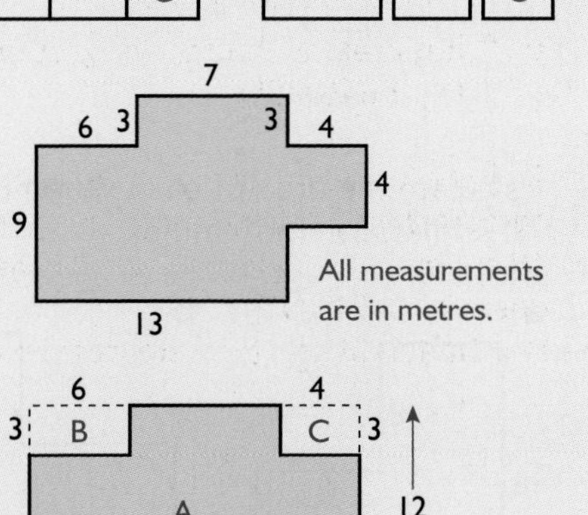

Exercise 3.1

1 Divide the shape in Example 1 above into rectangles in a different way and calculate its area.
Check that the answer you get for the area is the same as the answer above.

2 Divide the shape in Example 2 into rectangles.
Find its area using this method and check that it comes to 154 m^2.

3 Calculate the areas of these *symmetrical* shapes by first dividing them into rectangles.
All angles are right angles.

a

6
5
4
4
8

centimetres

b

10
50
10
15

millimetres

c

25
25
60
25
60
25

metres

d

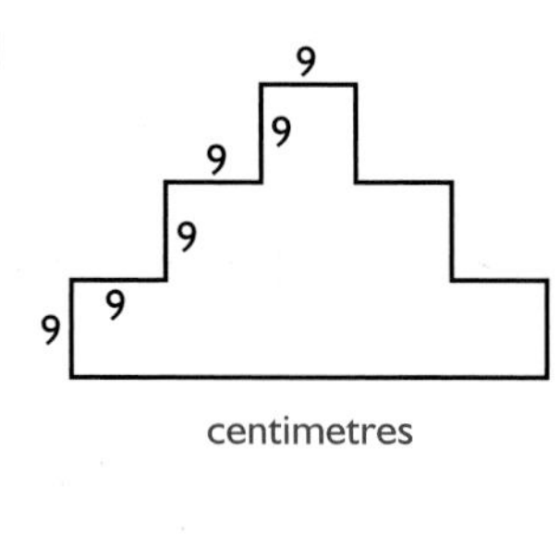

4 Calculate the area of each shape by first completing the rectangle.
All angles are right angles.

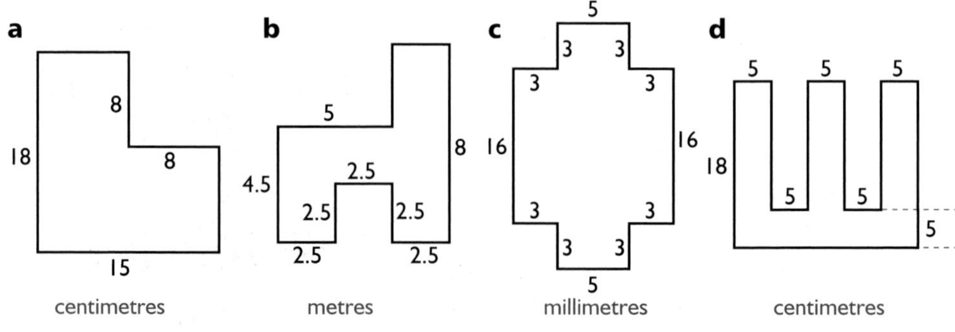

Right-angled triangles

Example 3

Calculate the area of the right-angled triangle ABC.

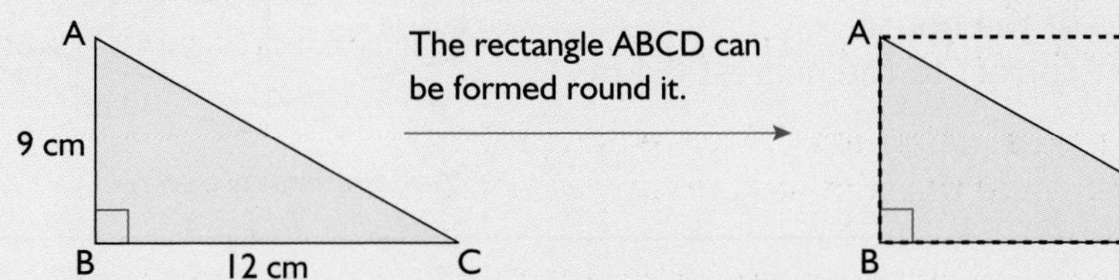

The area of $\triangle$ABC = $\frac{1}{2}\times$ the area of rectangle ABCD

$\Rightarrow$ the area of $\triangle$ABC = $\frac{1}{2}\times 9\times 12 = \frac{1}{2}\times 108\text{ cm}^2 = 54\text{ cm}^2$

Exercise 3.2

1 Calculate the area of each of these right-angled triangles.

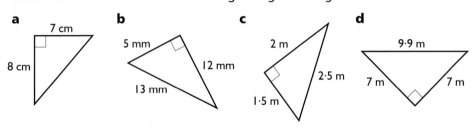

a 7 cm, 8 cm

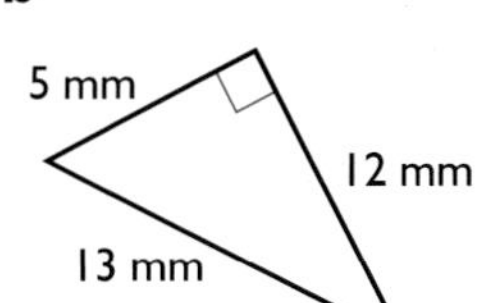

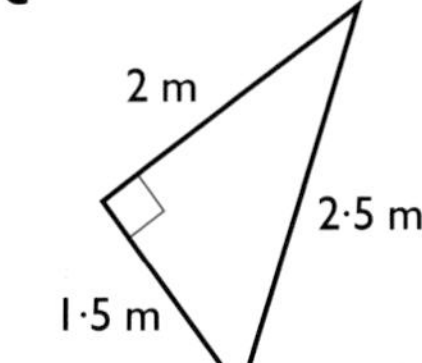

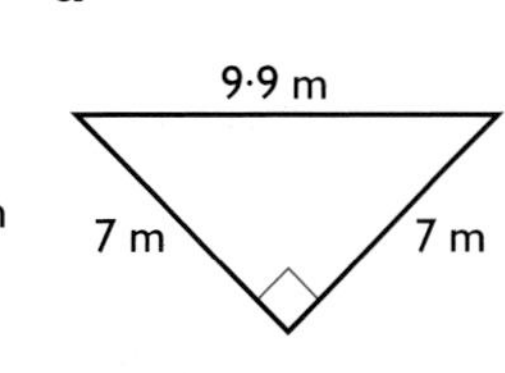

2 Calculate the area of each of these shapes by considering rectangles and right-angled triangles.

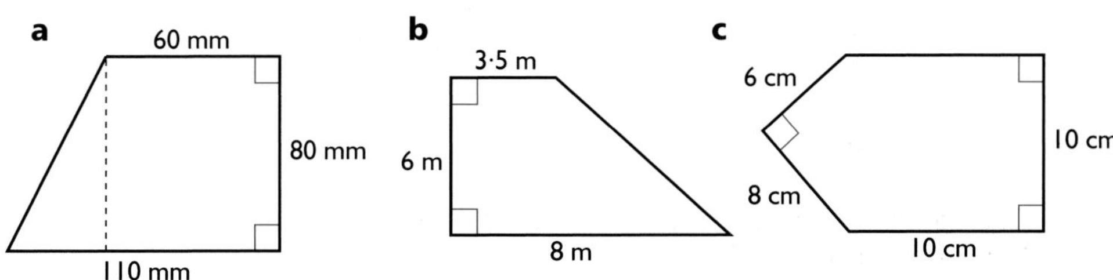

3 The picture represents a life-size wall painting.
Calculate the area of:

a the whole painting

b each sail

c the hull

d the area not representing part of the ship (ignore the area of the mast).

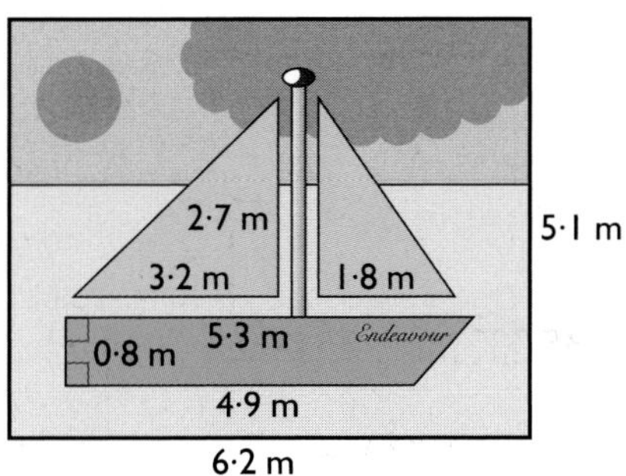

4 **a** Calculate the area of:
i the front of the house
ii a side of the house
iii the roof (front and back).

b Calculate the total area of the six surfaces of the house.
(Answer correct to the nearest 0·1 m^2.)

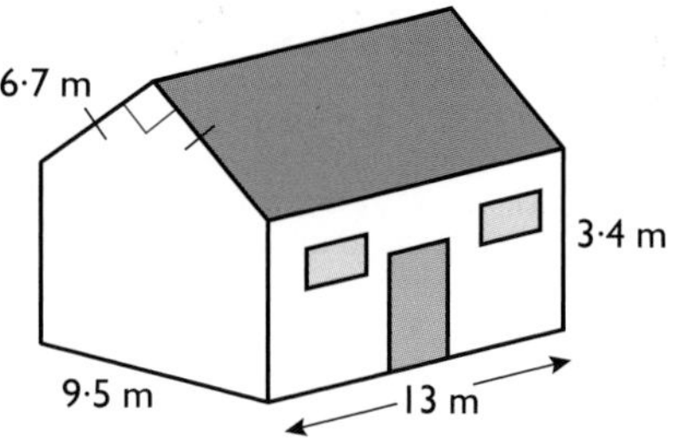

Measurements are correct to 1 d.p.

Brainstormer

The squares have sides of length 1 cm, 3 cm, 5 cm and 7 cm.

a Calculate the black area.
b Calculate the purple area.

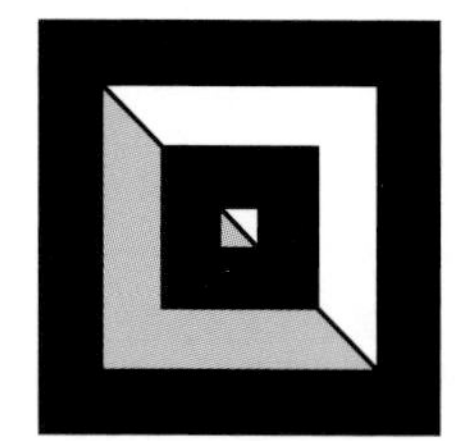

E

4 Large areas

Large areas are measured in **hectares (ha)**.

1 hectare = 100 m × 100 m
⇒ 1 hectare = 10 000 m^2

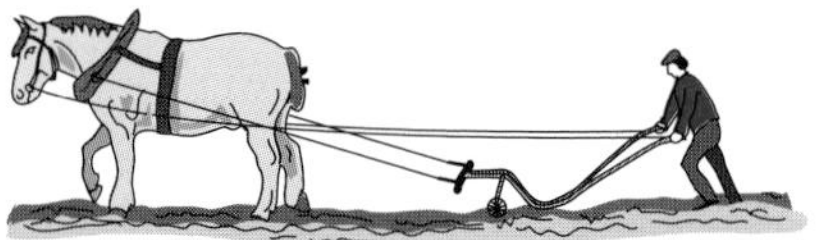

An acre was the amount a man could plough in a day. A hectare ≈ 2·5 acres.

Very large areas are measured in **square kilometres (km^2)**.

1 km^2 = 1000 m × 1000 m
⇒ 1 km^2 = 1 000 000 m^2

The area of Scotland is approximately 79 000 km^2.

Example 1

Change 35 000 m^2 to hectares.
35 000 m^2 = 35 000 ÷ 10 000 hectares
= 3·5 hectares or 3·5 ha

Example 2

Change 0·8 km^2 to m^2.
0·8 km^2 = 0·8 × 1 000 000 m^2
= 800 000 m^2

Exercise 4.1

1 Change to hectares:

a 20 000 m^2 b 80 000 m^2 c 65 000 m^2

d 300 000 m^2 e 7 000 000 m^2

2 Change to m^2:

a 11 hectares b 25 hectares c 0·5 hectare

d 8·2 hectares e 4·25 hectares

3 Change to m^2:

a 4 km^2 b 60 km^2 c 45 km^2

d 5·8 km^2 e 0·5 km^2

4 The area of Scotland is 80 000 km^2 correct to 1 significant figure.
Use the map opposite to estimate the area of:

a England b Wales

c Northern Ireland d Eire.

5 Each square on the grid represents an area of 1 km^3.

a Estimate the area of each island.

b Oil has been discovered in the triangle formed by the ports of Yolk, Salty and Olive.
Calculate the area of this triangle.

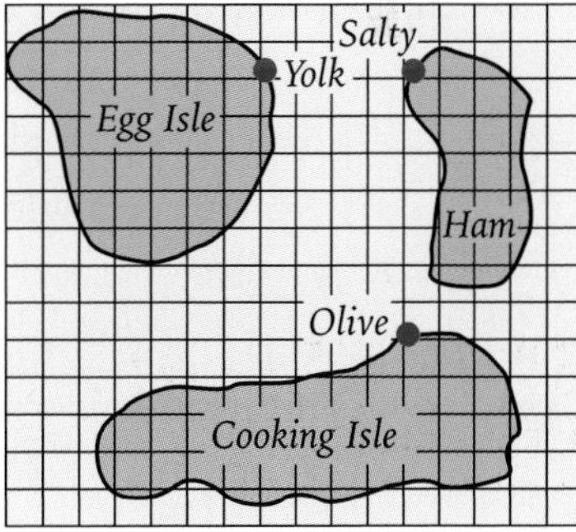

6 a Work out the number of hectares in 1 km^2.

b Change these measurements to km^2:

i 650 ha ii 1250 ha

iii 825 ha iv 85 000 ha.

c Change these measurements to hectares:

i 7 km^2 ii 21 km^2

iii 14·5 km^2 iv 0·65 km^2.

E

5 The area of a triangle

Case 1 The foot of the altitude (perpendicular height) falls inside the triangle

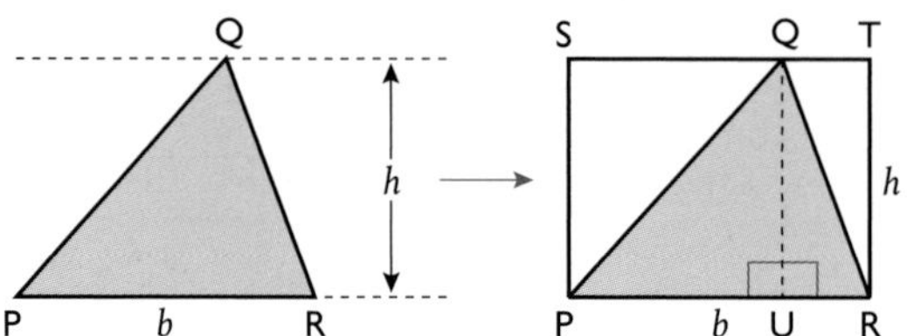

Area of $\triangle$PQR = A

A = Area of $\triangle$PQU + Area of $\triangle$RQU

= $\frac{1}{2}$ of rectangle PSQU + $\frac{1}{2}$ of rectangle RTQU

= $\frac{1}{2}$ of rectangle PSTR

$\Rightarrow$ $A = \frac{1}{2}bh$

Case 2 The foot of the altitude falls outside the triangle

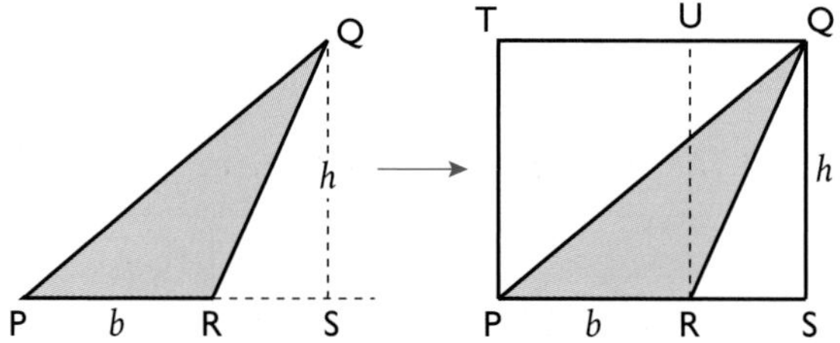

Area of $\triangle$PQR = A

A = Area of $\triangle$PQS − Area of $\triangle$RQS

= $\frac{1}{2}$ of rectangle PTQS − $\frac{1}{2}$ of rectangle RUQS

= ($\frac{1}{2}$ of rectangle PTUR + $\frac{1}{2}$ of rectangle RUQS) − $\frac{1}{2}$ of rectangle RUQS

= $\frac{1}{2}$ of rectangle PTUR

$\Rightarrow$ $A = \frac{1}{2}bh$

Case 3 The altitude is a side of the triangle

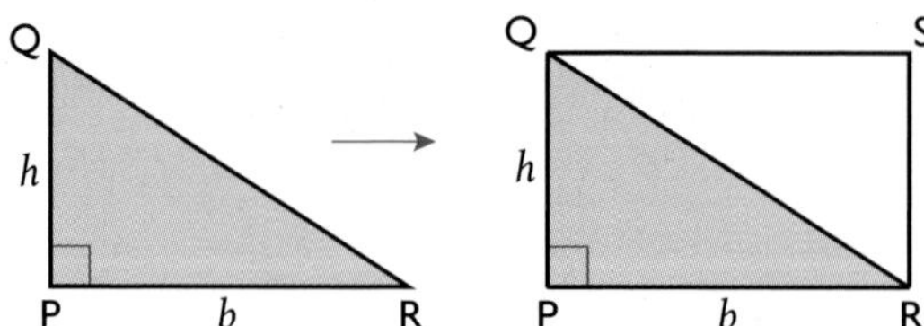

$\triangle$PQR is a right-angled triangle

Area of $\triangle$PQR = A

A = $\frac{1}{2}$ of rectangle PQSR

$\Rightarrow$ $A = \frac{1}{2}bh$

> So, for *any* triangle ABC,
> $A = \frac{1}{2}bh$

F

Example 1

Calculate the area of △PQR.

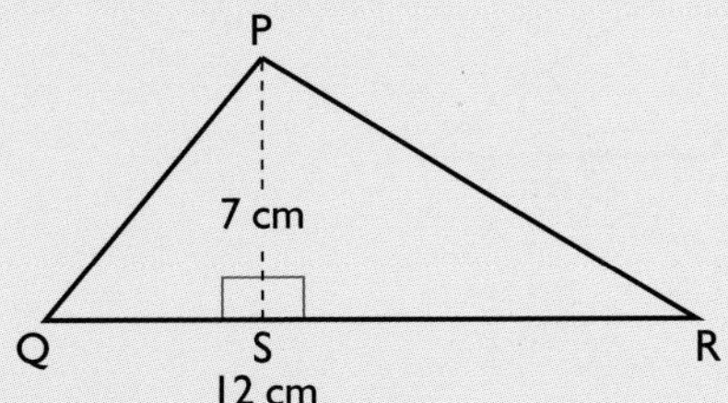

base b = QR = 12 cm
height h = PS = 7 cm

$A = \frac{1}{2}bh$

$\Rightarrow A = \frac{1}{2} \times 12 \times 7$

$\Rightarrow A = 42 \text{ cm}^2$

Example 2

Calculate the area of △KLM.

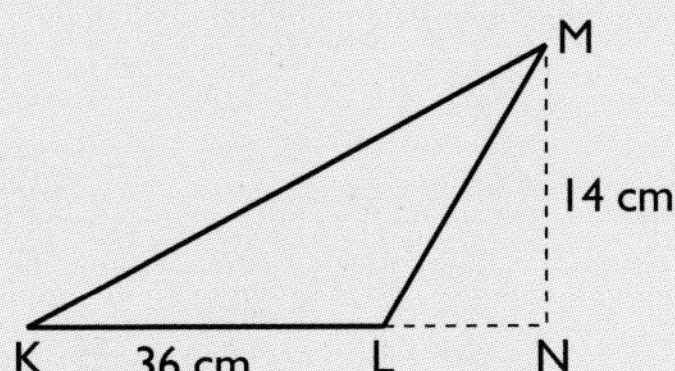

KL is the base b in this example.
MN is the height h.

$A = \frac{1}{2}bh$

$\Rightarrow A = \frac{1}{2} \times 36 \times 14$

$\Rightarrow A = 36 \times 7 = 252 \text{ cm}^2$

Exercise 5.1

1 Use the formula $A = \frac{1}{2}bh$ to find the area of each of these triangles.

a

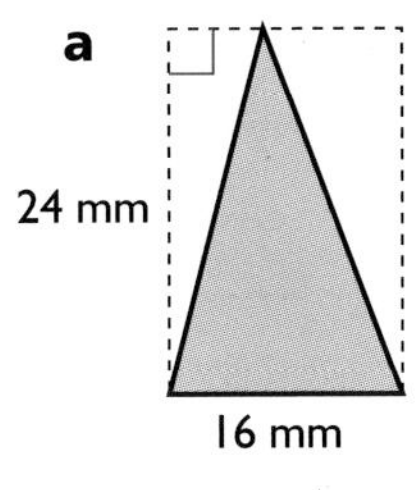

b

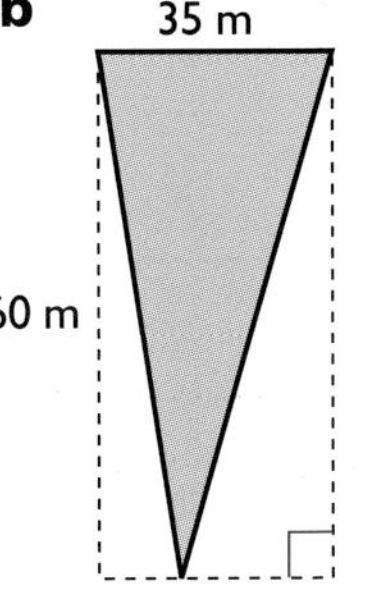

c

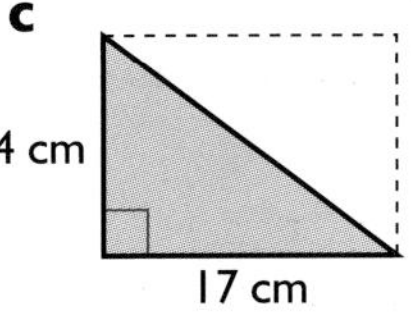

d

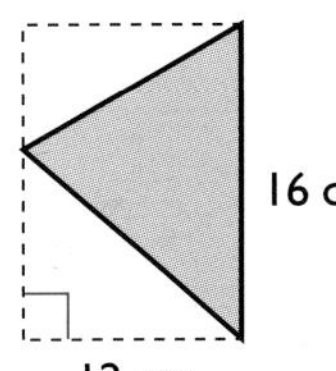

e

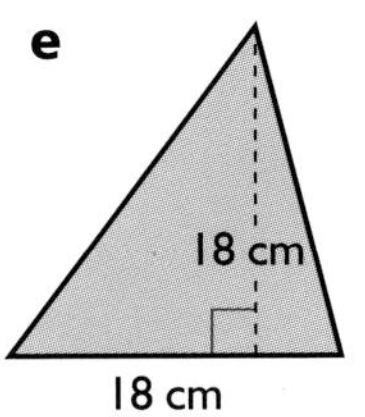

f

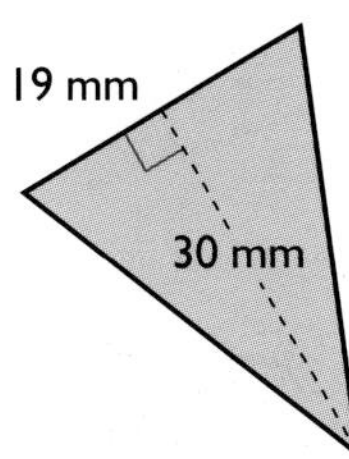

g

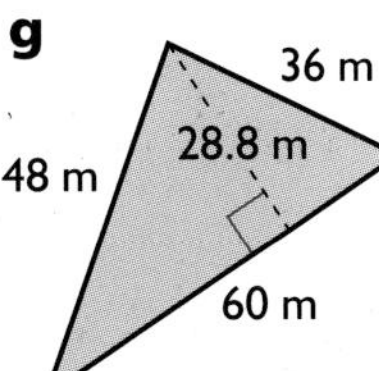

h

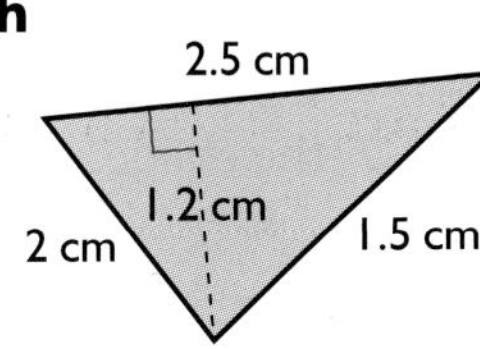

2 Find the area of the three triangles enclosed in this rectangle.

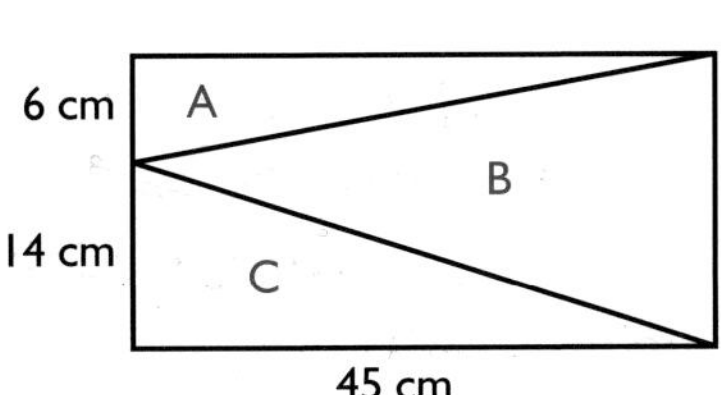

3 Calculate the areas of these four triangles.

a

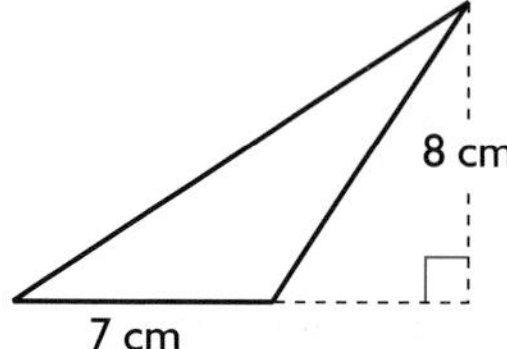

b

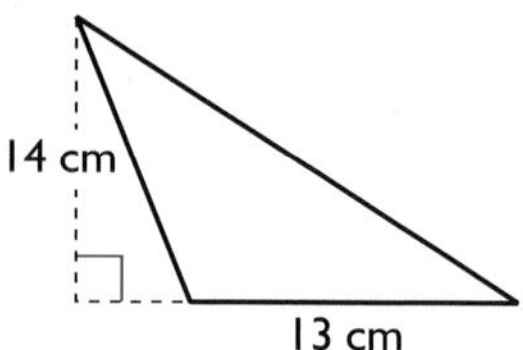

c

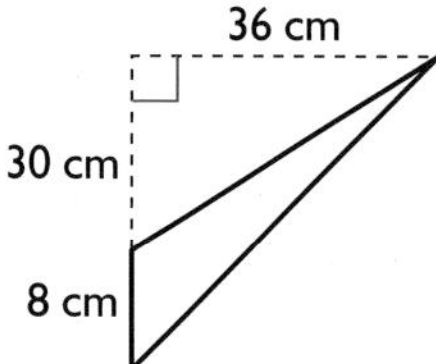

d

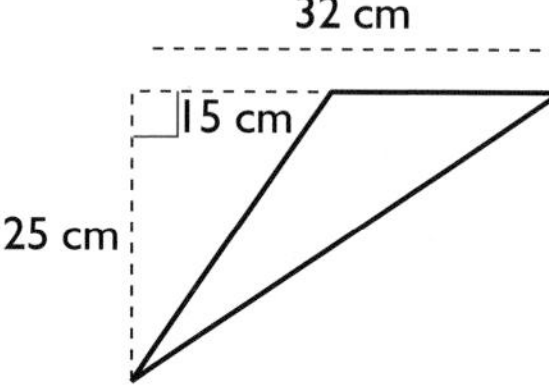

4 Calculate the area of the side of each house.

a

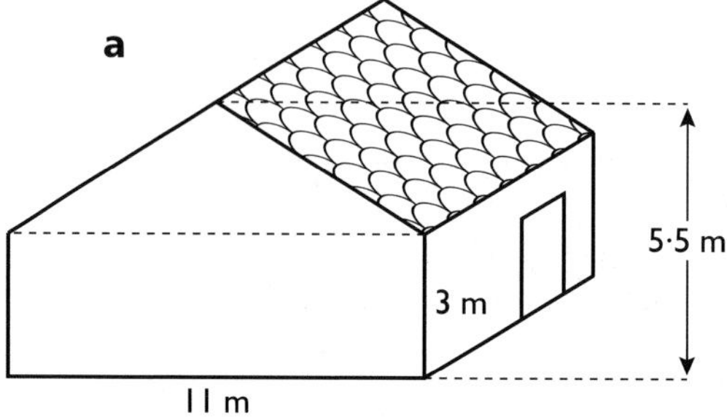

b

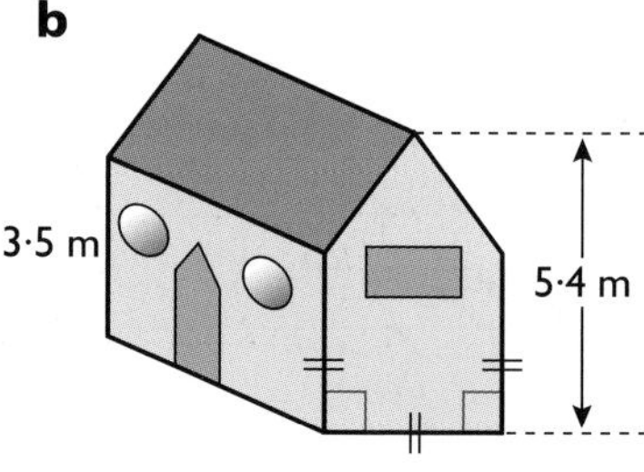

F

Challenge

A Rectangle ABCD of length 12 cm and breadth 8 cm can be drawn round this shape. Calculate the area of the shape.

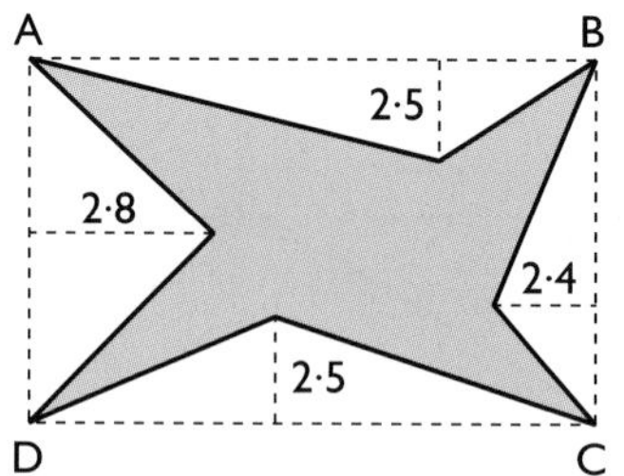

Sizes are in centimetres.

B By considering finding the area of this triangle in two ways, calculate the length of AE.

AB = 16 cm
DC = 10 cm
BC = 12 cm

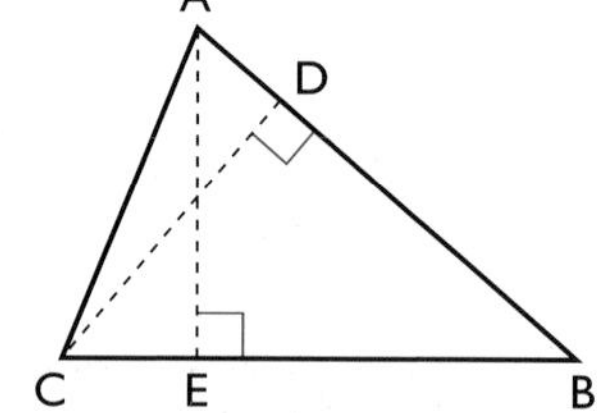

6 Area of the kite, rhombus and parallelogram

1 Kite and rhombus

Both the kite and rhombus are made up of four right-angled triangles. Each right-angled triangle is half the area of its surrounding rectangle.

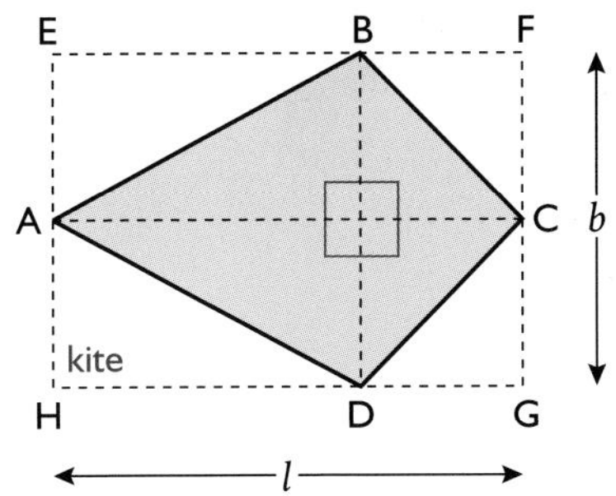

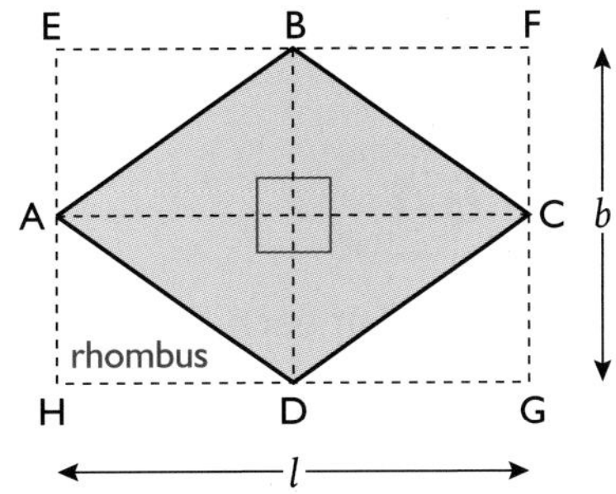

So, in both cases, the area of ABCD is half the area of rectangle EFGH.
So area of ABCD $= \frac{1}{2}lb$.

> For both the **kite** and the **rhombus**:
> the area of ABCD $= \frac{1}{2}$ the product of the diagonals AC and BD

Example 1 Find the area of kite PQRS.

Area of kite $= \frac{1}{2} \times \text{PR} \times \text{QS}$
$= \frac{1}{2} \times 14 \times 8$
$= 56\ \text{cm}^2$

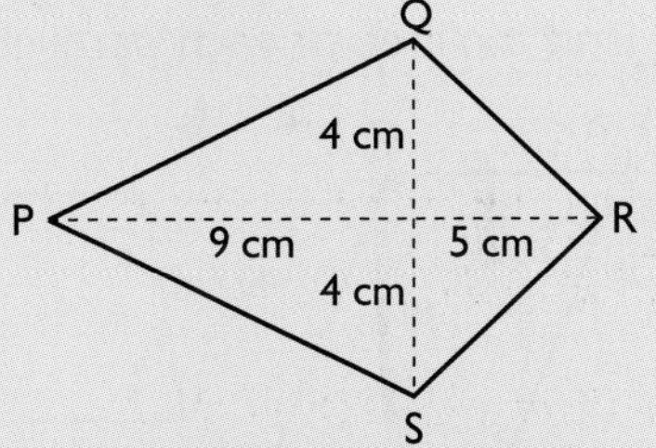

The area could, of course, also be found by adding the areas of the four right-angled triangles.

2 Parallelogram

Parallelogram PQRS can be changed to rectangle SRTU by translating △PUS to position QTR.

Thus UT = PQ = b

$\Rightarrow$ area of parallelogram PQRS = area of rectangle SRTU

$\Rightarrow$ area of parallelogram PQRS = bh

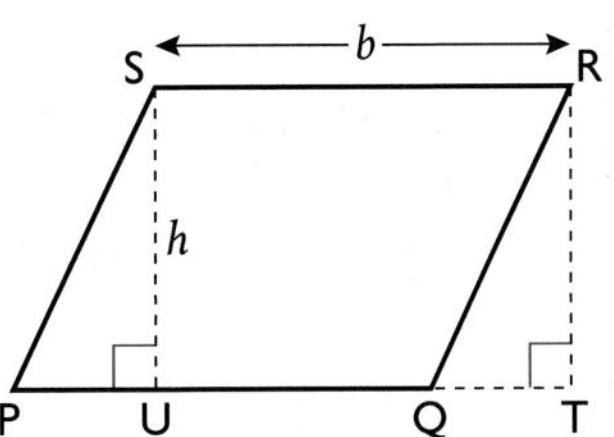

> Area of parallelogram = length of a side × the perpendicular distance to the opposite side

Example 2

Find the area of parallelogram ABCD.

$$\text{Area} = 9 \times 11$$
$$= 99\ \text{cm}^2$$

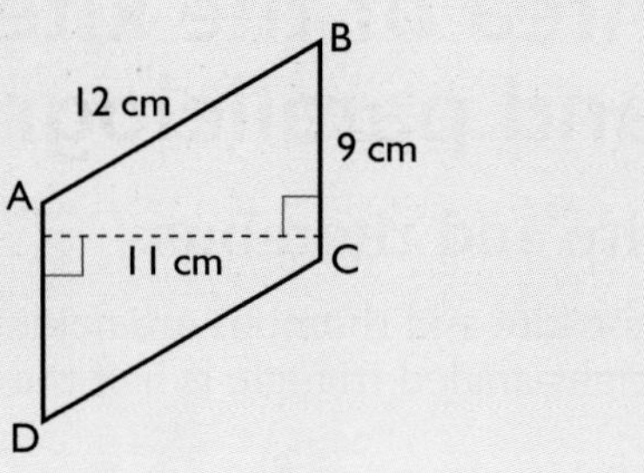

Exercise 6.1

1 Calculate the area of each rhombus or kite.

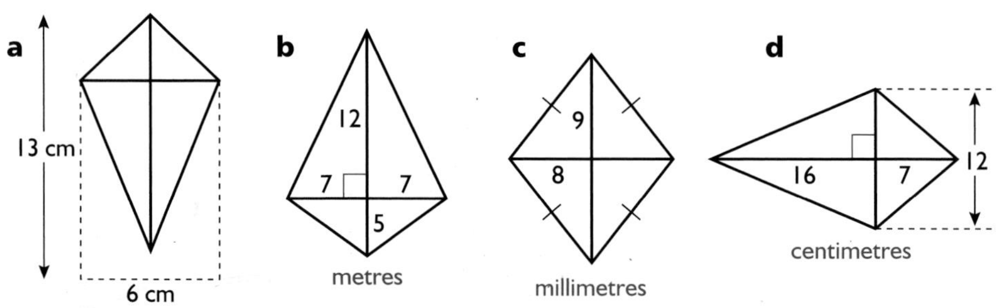

2 Find the area of each parallelogram.

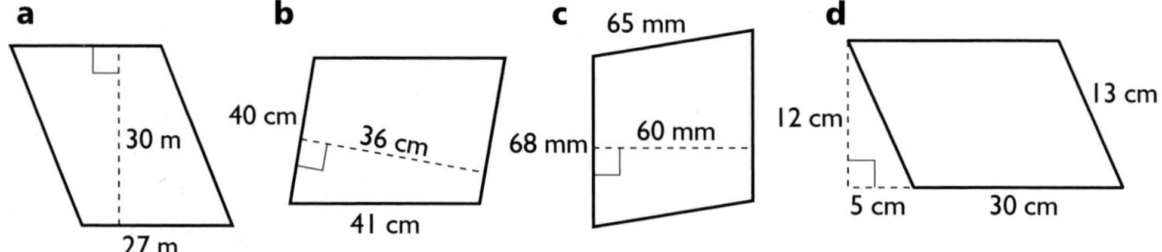

3 Find the area of kite BCDE and the area of rhombus KLMN in three ways:

a Use the *diagonals* formula.

b Add the areas of the four right-angled triangles.

c Find the area of the surrounding rectangle and subtract the areas of four triangles.

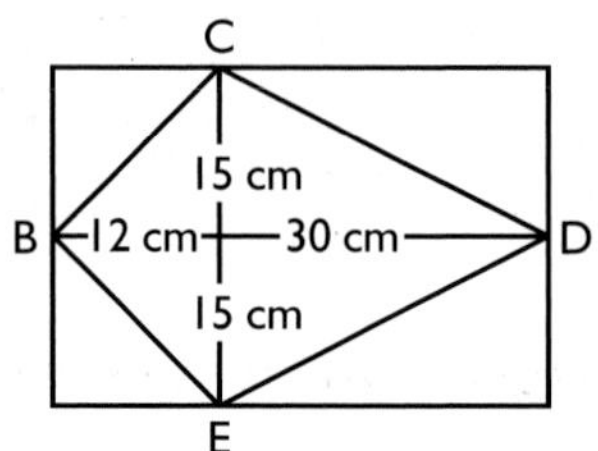

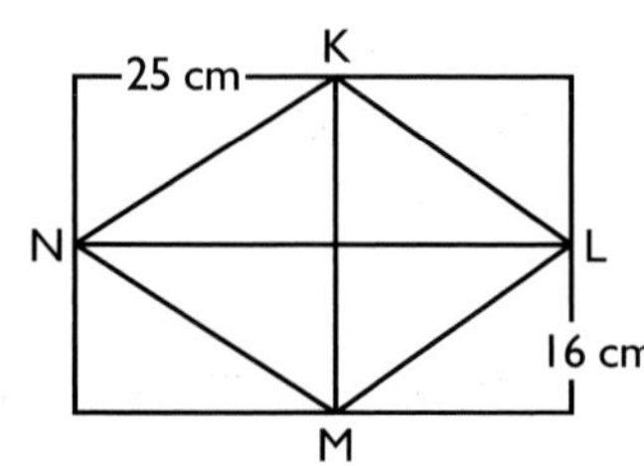

4 **a** Calculate the area of V-kite STUV by finding:

i the areas of rectangles (ASCV, BTCS) and right-angled triangles (SAV, VUC, SBT and TUC)

ii the areas of triangles SVU and STU.

b The diagonals of the V-kite are SU and TV. Show that the area of the V-kite can be found by halving the product of its diagonals.

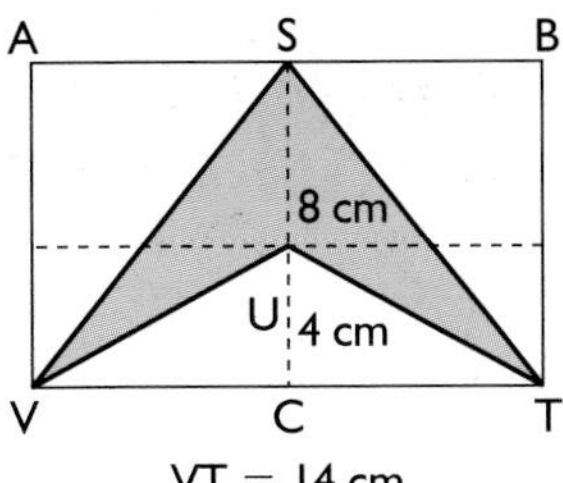

5 Find the area of each V-kite.

a

6
16
8
centimetres

b

9
58
32
metres

c

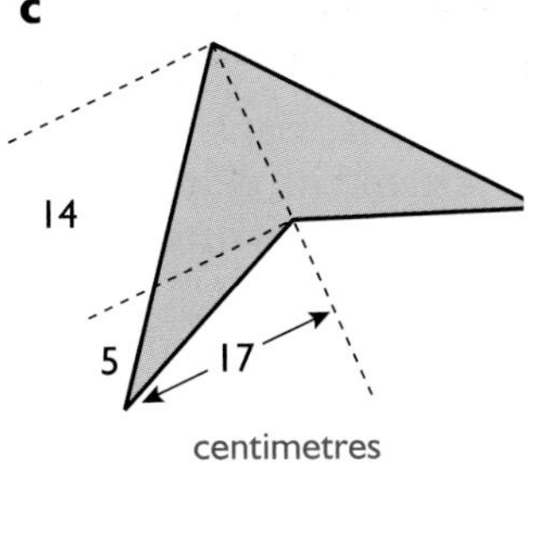

6 The diagram represents the plan of a kitchen floor made up of two parallelograms and a kite. Calculate the area of the floor.

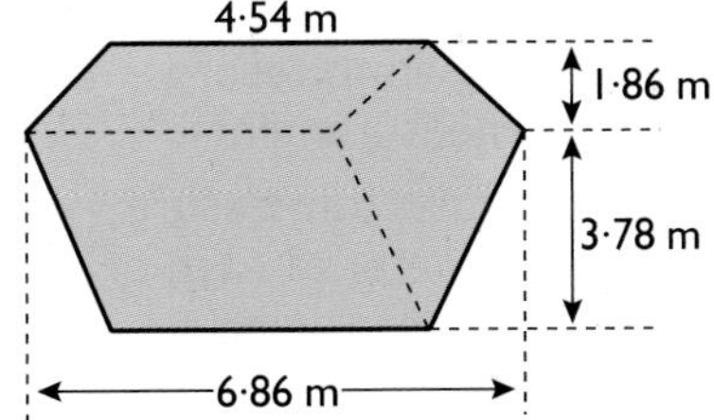

Challenge

ABCD is a trapezium.
Find its area.
(Consider the trapezium with one diagonal drawn forming two triangles.)

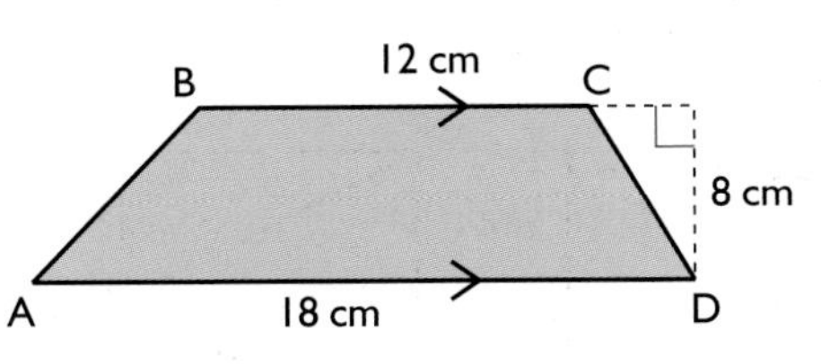

7 The circle: radius, diameter and circumference

Definitions

- All points on a circle are the same distance from the centre, O.
- Any straight line from the centre to the edge of the circle is called a **radius**.
- A line drawn from one point on a circle to another and passing through the centre is called a **diameter**.
- The distance round a circle is called its **circumference**, the perimeter of the circle.

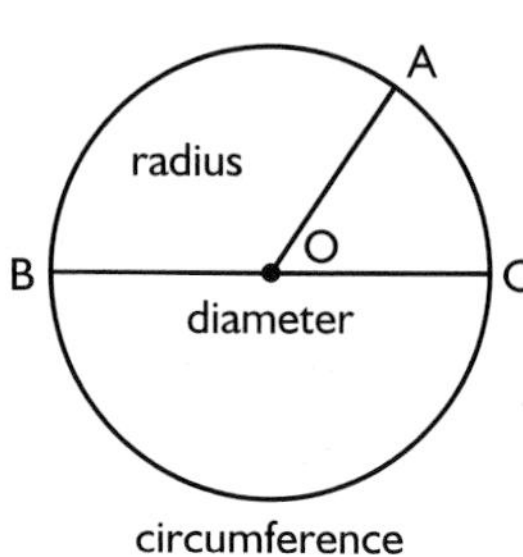

Mathematicians have known for thousands of years that the circumference of a circle and its diameter are related.
The earliest written record of the relation occurs in the Rhind Papyrus, an ancient Egyptian scroll.
It was found that the **circumference is approximately three times the diameter.**

Exercise 7.1

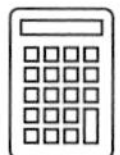

F

1 **a** Collect some circular objects to measure. Make a table like the one shown to record your measurements.

Object	Diameter (D)	Circumference (C)	$C \div D$

b Use a ruler to measure the diameter of each of your circular objects.

c Use thread and a ruler to measure the circumference.

d Divide each circumference (C) by its diameter (D).
Do your findings agree with the findings of the ancient Egyptians?

2 Use the formula $C \approx 3D$ to estimate the circumference of each of these circular objects.

a

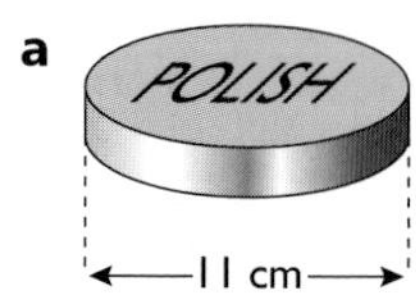

b

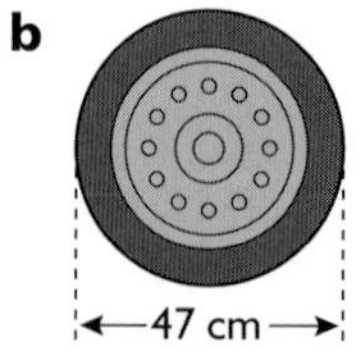

3 A more accurate formula for estimating the circumference of a circle is

$$C \approx 3{\cdot}14D$$

Calculate the circumference of each circle below using this formula.

a diameter = 26 mm

b diameter of roundabout = 20 m

c

diameter of sundial = 1·5 m

d both inner and outer circle

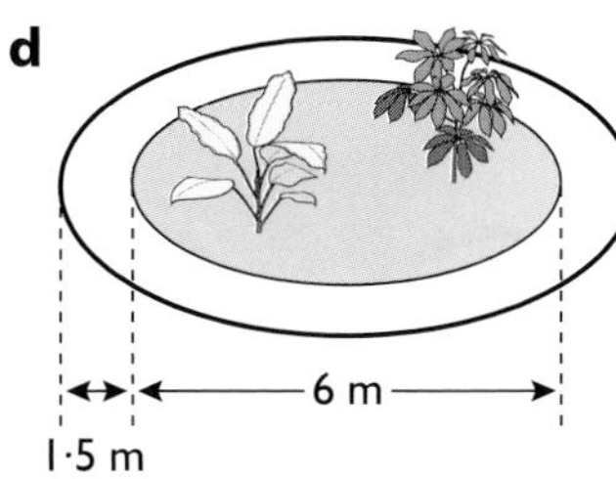

6 m

1·5 m

e

radius 4·5 cm

f both inner and outer circle

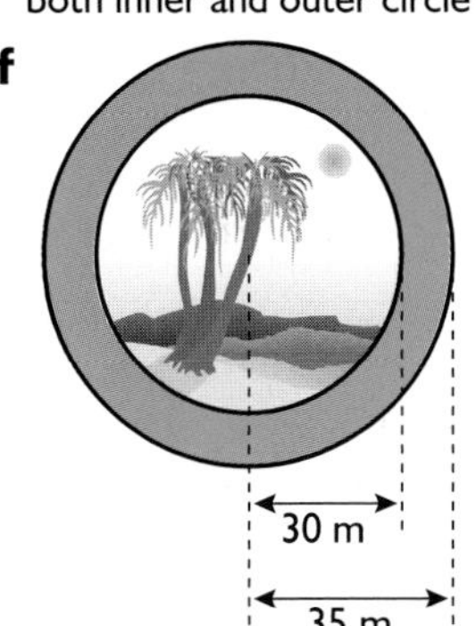

30 m

35 m

F

The most accurate estimate for the circumference of a circle is found by using the π button on a calculator, $\boxed{\pi}$

The formula becomes $C = \pi D$.

(π is a Greek letter and is pronounced 'pie' and spelled 'pi'. It is the first letter of the Greek word for *perimetros*, meaning 'to measure around'.)

The value of π to 7 decimal places is 3·141 592 7.

Example Use the formula $C = \pi D$ to calculate the circumference of a circle with diameter 12·5 cm.

$$\begin{aligned} C &= \pi D \\ &= \pi \times 12{\cdot}5 \text{ cm} \\ &= 39{\cdot}269\,908 \text{ cm} \\ &= 39{\cdot}3 \text{ cm to 3 significant figures} \end{aligned}$$

4 Use the formula $C = \pi D$ to calculate the circumference of a circle with:

a diameter **i** 5 cm **ii** 12 mm **iii** 8·5 m

b radius **i** 8 cm **ii** 5·5 m **iii** 65 mm

Give all your answers rounded to 3 significant figures.

5 A lampshade has its top and bottom edges trimmed with braid.
Use the formula $C = \pi D$ to work out the total length of trim required.
Give your answer correct to 3 significant figures.

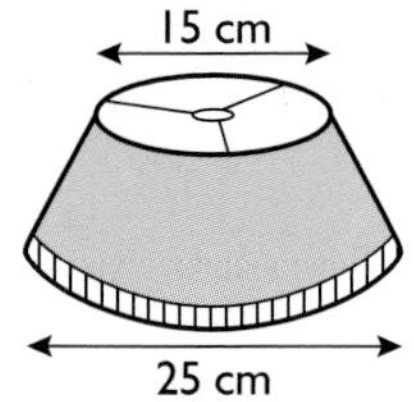

6 All the pieces of a tea set are being gold-plated round the rims.
Calculate the length of gold plating needed for

a the plate (diameter 19 cm)

b the saucer (diameter 15 cm)

c the cup (diameter 8·8 cm).

Give all your answers correct to 1 decimal place.

7 The radius of the wheel of the bike is 0·6 m.
How far does the bicycle travel in 40 complete turns of the wheel?
Give your answer to the nearest metre.

F

8 The area of a circle

A circle, radius r, has a large number of 'spokes' drawn. These spokes divide the circle into a large number of sectors.

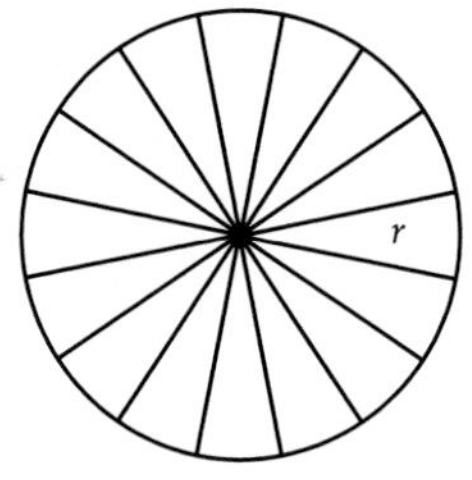

The sectors can be cut out and placed together to form a shape that approximates very closely to a parallelogram. Note that the greater the number of sectors, the closer the shape formed is to a parallelogram.

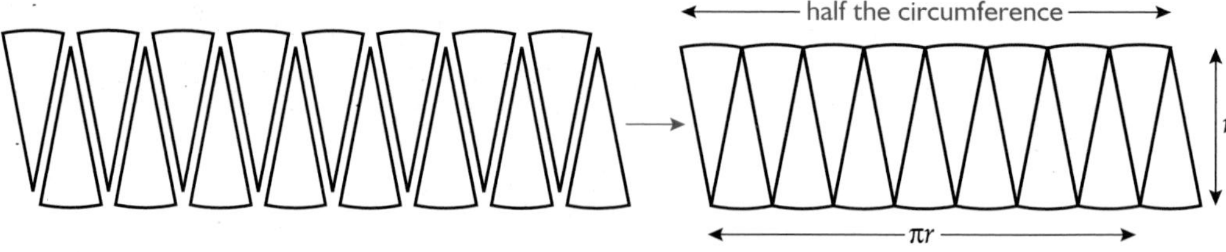

The length of the parallelogram is πr, half the circumference of the circle.
The breadth of the parallelogram is r, the radius of the circle.

The area of the parallelogram is therefore $\pi r \times r = \pi r^2$.

This gives us the formula for the area of the circle: $A = \pi r^2$

where r is the radius of the circle.

Example Calculate the area of a circle of diameter 16 cm.

$$D = 16 \Rightarrow r = 8$$
$$A = \pi r^2$$
$$\Rightarrow A = \pi \times 8 \times 8$$
$$= 201 \text{ cm}^2 \text{ to 3 significant figures}$$

Exercise 8.1

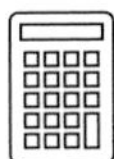

Give all your answers to 3 significant figures.

1 Use the formula $A = \pi r^2$ to find the area of a circle with:

a radius 6 cm **b** radius 10 cm
c radius 25 mm **d** radius 1·5 m
e diameter 14 cm **f** diameter 32 mm
g diameter 23 cm **h** diameter 3·9 m.

2 Calculate:

i the circumference **ii** the area of each coin.
The diameter of each is given.

a

24 mm

b

18 mm

c

20 mm

d

25 mm

3 Calculate the area of each shape:

a

2·8 mm

b

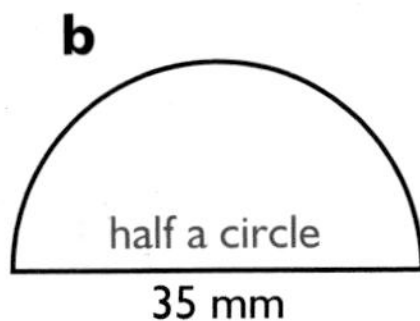

c

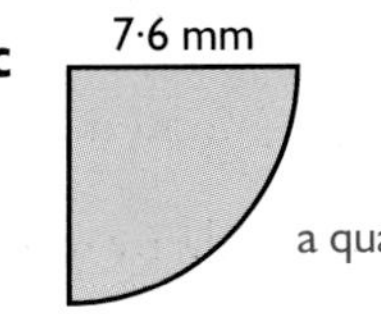

a quarter circle

4 Calculate the area of:

a the £2 coin

b **i** the silver

ii the gold, on one side of the coin.

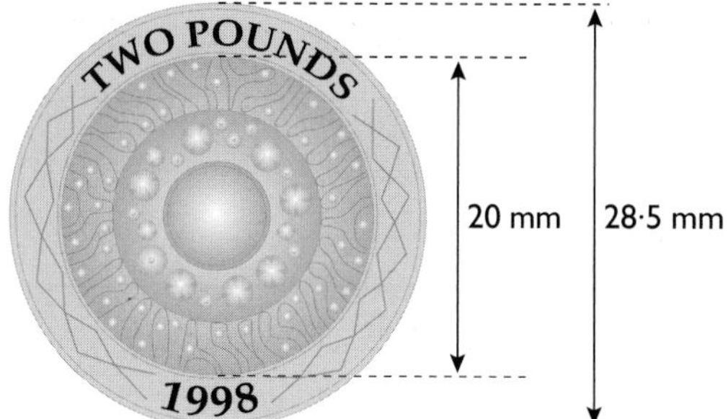

5 The shot-put circle in athletics is 2 m 13 cm in diameter.
Calculate the area of the circle.

6 A goat in a field is tied by a rope to a post so that the furthest she can be from the post is 15 metres.
Find the area of grass the goat has to graze on.

7 A rectangular swimming pool has three circular fountains in it as shown in the diagram.
Calculate the surface area of the water in the swimming pool. Give your answer in square metres.

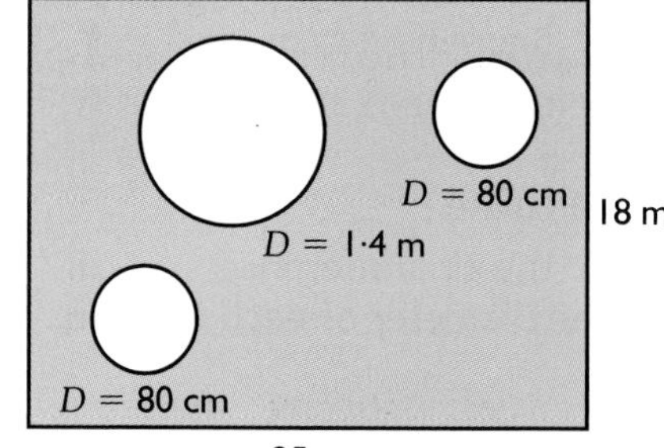

CHECK-UP

1 Use the formula $A = lb$ to calculate the area of

a the stamp

b the notice board.

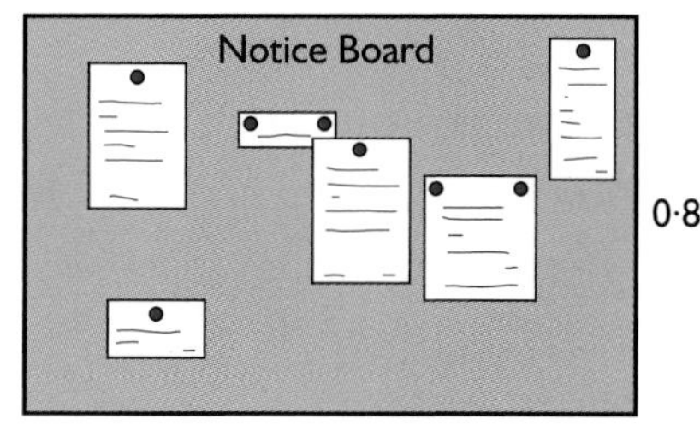

2 A uniform path 1 metre wide surrounds the rectangular flower bed. Calculate the area of:

a the flower bed

b the path.

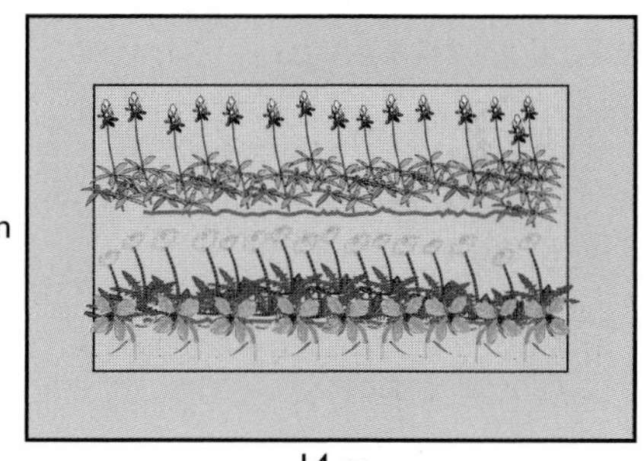

3 Calculate the area of each shape.

a

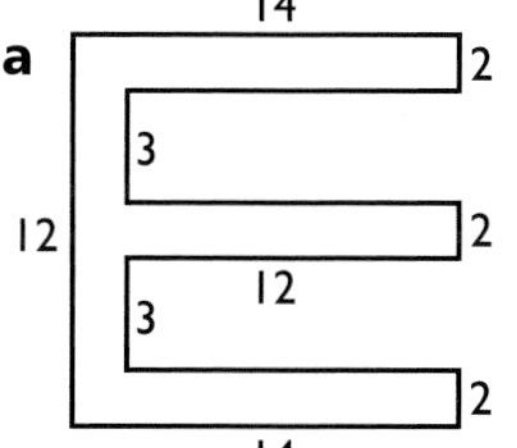

b

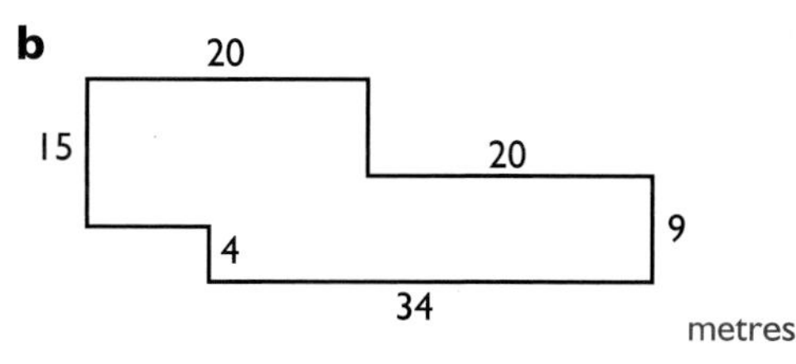

4 Change:

a 85 000 m^2 to hectares **b** 3·75 hectares to m^2 **c** 1·5 km^2 to m^2.

5 Calculate the areas of triangles ABC and PSR.

a

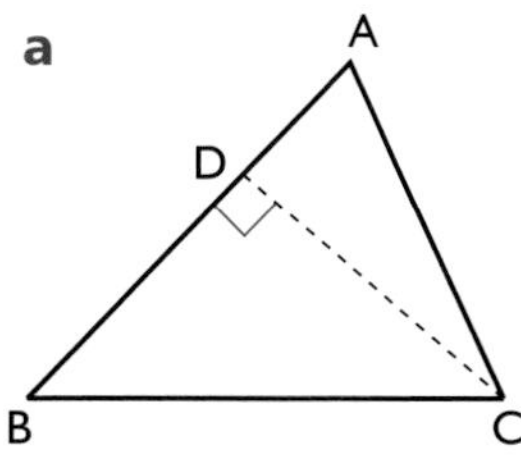

AB = 8 cm, BC = 9 cm, CD = 7 cm

b

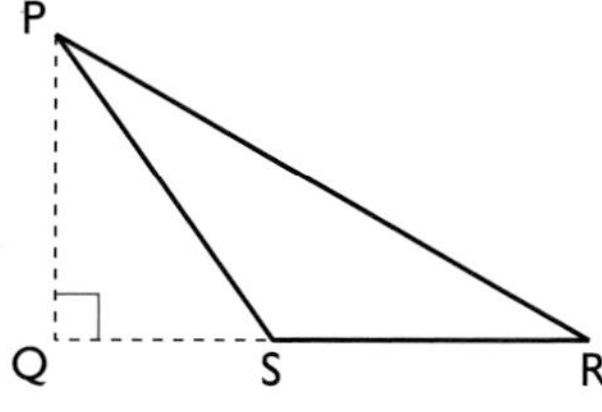

PS = 10 cm, SR = 9 cm, PQ = 8 cm, QS = 6 cm

EF

6 Calculate the shaded area.

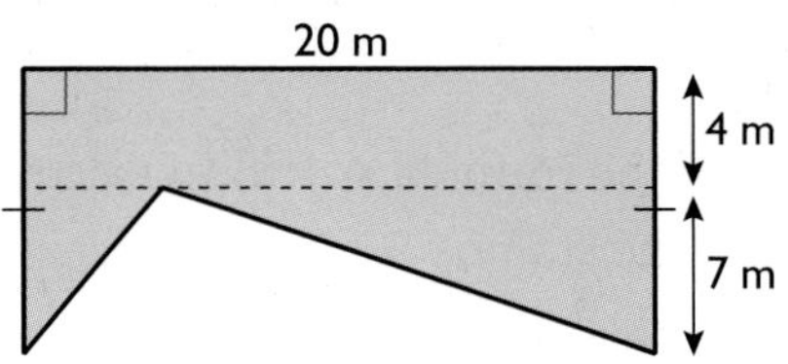

7 Calculate the area of:

a the kite

b the diamond-shaped brooch (rhombus)

c the field, which is a parallelogram.

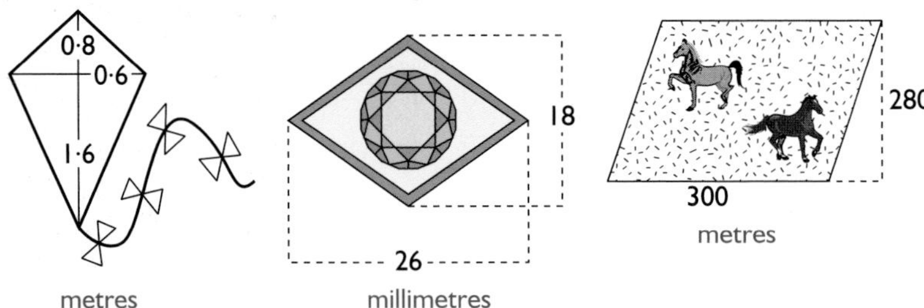

8 Calculate the area of the V-kite.

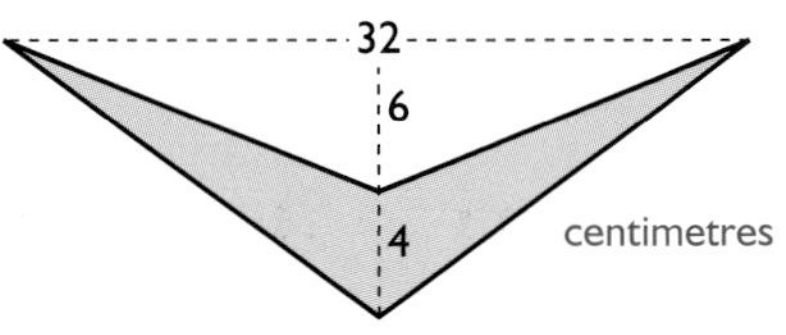

9 Calculate:

a the circumference

b the area of the circular Chinese fan. (Give your answers to 3 significant figures.)

10 Calculate the area of the washer, to the nearest mm^2.

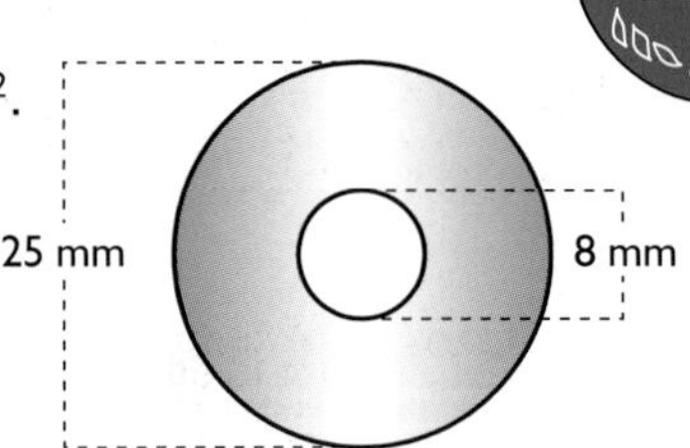

11 In a children's playground, a circular roundabout is set in a rectangular area made of rubber.

a Calculate the area of the roundabout.

b Calculate the area of the rubber.

c Calculate the distance travelled by point A on the outside edge of the roundabout in 50 revolutions.

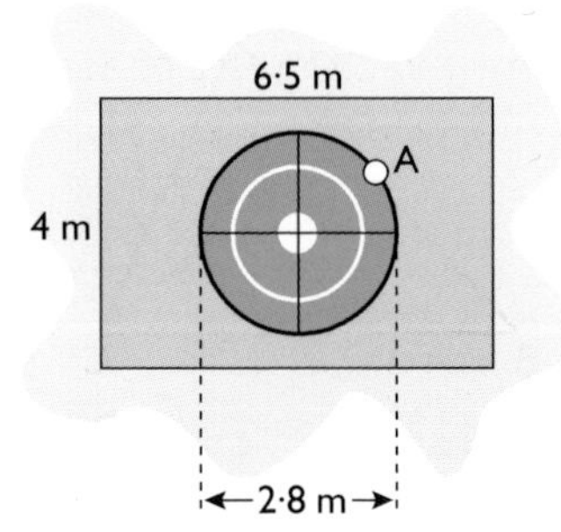

15 cm

F

12 Sequences

The earliest record of a sequence of numbers with a rule that adds a fixed amount to one term to get the next term occurs in the Rhind Papyrus. This papyrus is really the oldest maths book in existence and was written around 1650 BC but possibly copied from much older papyri.

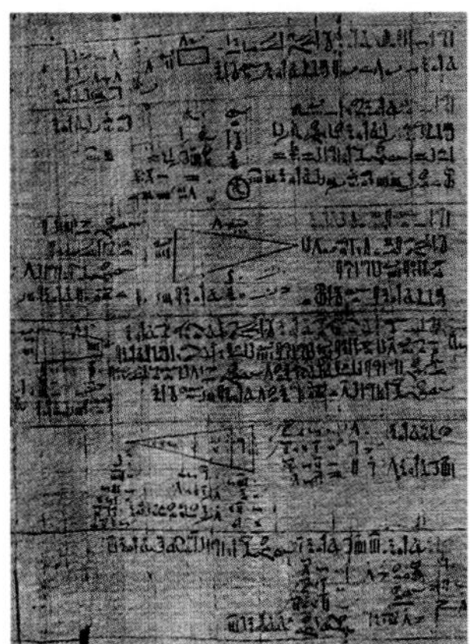

1 Looking back

Exercise 1.1

1 Find the next three terms in each sequence.
Write a sentence describing the rule you used.

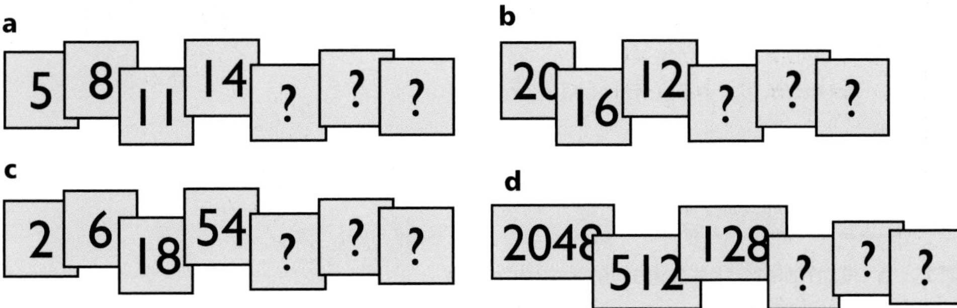

2 Copy and complete these tables:

a t becomes $t - 4$

t	5	6	7	8	9
$t - 4$					

b y becomes $5y$

y	5	6	7	8	9
$5y$					

3

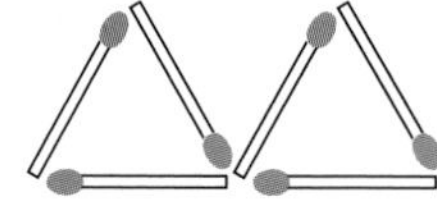

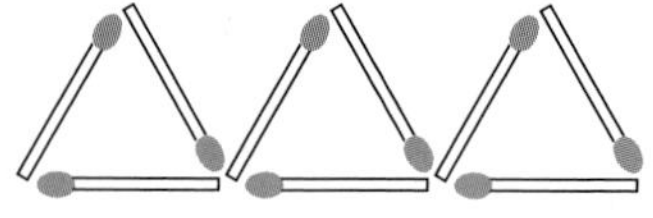

Pattern 1 Pattern 2 Pattern 3

This pattern continues in this way…

Copy and complete the table.

Pattern number	1	2	3	4	5		18		n
Number of matches									

2 The shape of numbers

The followers of Pythagoras studied numbers as arrays of dots. From these they discovered many properties.

Example 1

Consecutive whole numbers
1, 2, 3, 4, …

Example 2

Consecutive even numbers
2, 4, 6, 8, …

Example 3

Consecutive odd numbers
1, 3, 5, 7, …

Other patterns can be generated from these.

Exercise 2.1

1 **a** Complete the following additions:

i 0 + 1 **ii** 0 + 1 + 2

iii 0 + 1 + 2 + 3 **iv** 0 + 1 + 2 + 3 + 4

b Continue this pattern of additions for another five times.

c Copy and complete this sequence of diagrams for another three diagrams.

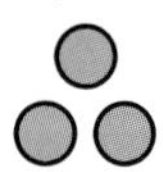

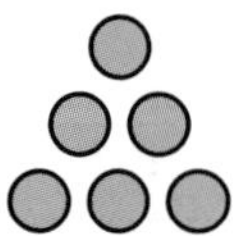

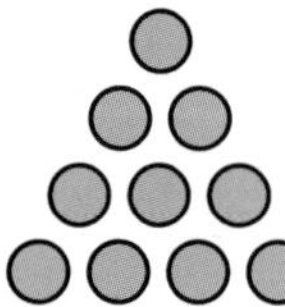

d The Pythagoreans called the sum of the whole numbers up to n the nth triangular number.
i Why do you think that was?
ii What is the seventh triangular number?
iii List the first ten triangular numbers.

e **i** Take a pair of consecutive whole numbers, e.g. 5 and 6.
ii Form a right-angled triangle using these numbers as the base and altitude.
iii Calculate its area.
iv Repeat steps **i–iii**.
v What do you notice about your answers?
vi What is the 100th triangular number?

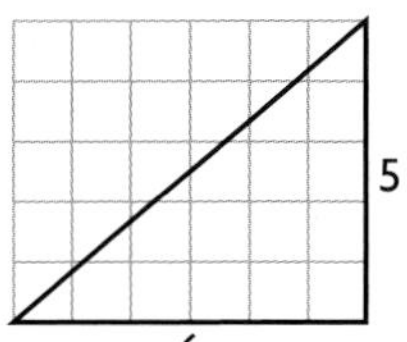

$A = \frac{1}{2} \times 5 \times 6 = 15$

This is the fifth triangular number.

2 If you made a set of dominoes using only the numbers 0 (blank), 1, 2 and 3, you would end up with a set like this:

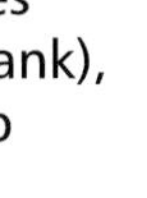

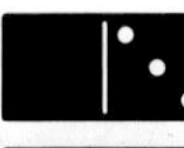

a How many dominoes are in the set whose biggest domino is the double 3 (i.e. the set shown).
b How many dominoes would be in a double 4 set?
c The set which is usually sold in shops is called a double 6 set. How many dominoes are in a set of this size?
d For tournaments people often play with a double 9 set. How many are in this set?
e How many dominoes would there be in a double 20 set?

E

3 **a** Complete the following additions:
i 1 **ii** 1 + 3 **iii** 1 + 3 + 5 **iv** 1 + 3 + 5 + 7
b Continue this pattern of additions for another five times.
c Copy and complete this sequence of diagrams for another three diagrams.

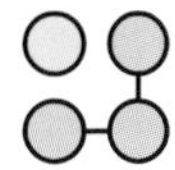
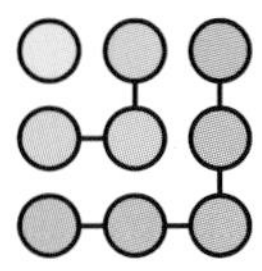
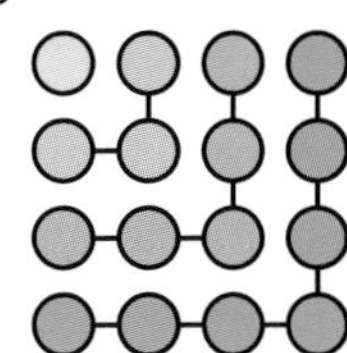

d The Pythagoreans called the sum of the first n odd numbers the nth square number.
i Why do you think that was?
ii What is the tenth square number?
iii List the first ten square numbers.

e **i** Calculate the areas of squares of side 6, 7 and 8 units.
ii What do you notice about your answer?
iii What is the 100th square number?

4 Think of a number. Add 2.
Multiply by the number you first though of and add 1.

a What is special about your answer?

b If I end up with 100 when doing this, what number did I start with?

5 **a** Complete the following additions:
i 2 **ii** $2 + 4$ **iii** $2 + 4 + 6$ **iv** $2 + 4 + 6 + 8$

b Continue this pattern of additions for another five times.

c Copy and complete this sequence of diagrams for another three diagrams.

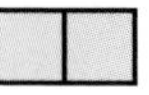
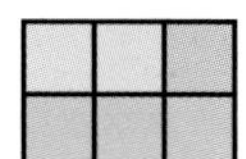

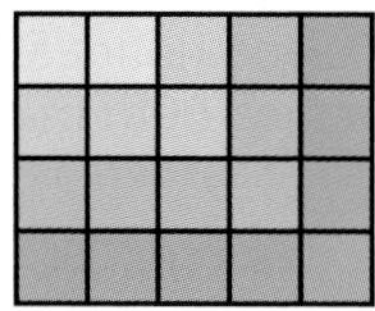

d The Pythagoreans called the sum of the first n even numbers the nth oblong number.
i What is the tenth oblong number?
ii List the first ten oblong numbers.

e **i** Calculate the area of each rectangle above.
ii What do you notice about the numbers in your working?
iii What is the 100th oblong number?

E

Exercise 2.2

1 Use the 'recipes' to calculate:

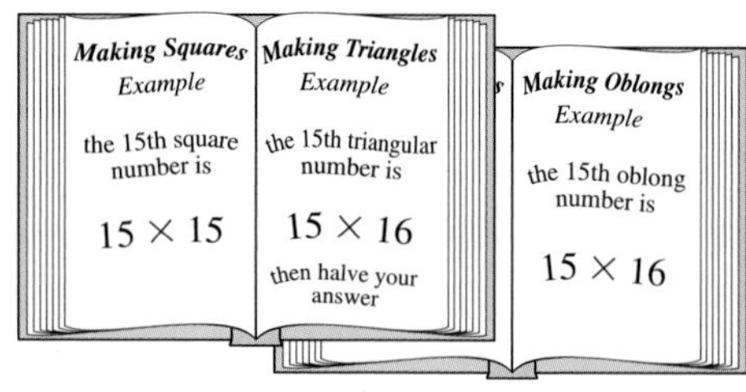
Making Squares
Example
the 15th square number is
15 × 15
Making Triangles
Example
the 15th triangular number is
15 × 16
then halve your answer
Making Oblongs
Example
the 15th oblong number is
15 × 16

a **i** the ninth square number
ii the ninth triangular number
iii the eighth triangular number.

b **i** the seventh square number
ii the seventh triangular number
iii the sixth triangular number.

c What's the relationship between **i**, **ii** and **iii** in each case?

d Examine the diagram below and then complete the sentence 'the third and fourth triangular numbers combine to make …'.

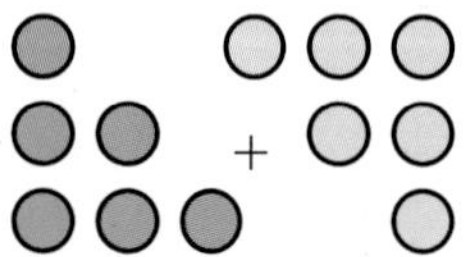
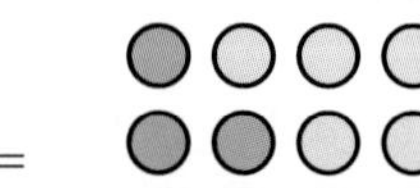
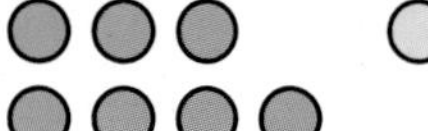
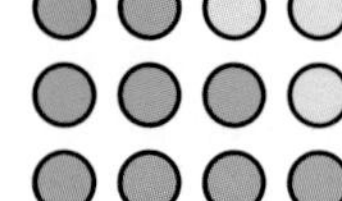

e Make a general statement relating the triangular numbers to the squares.

2 Use the recipes to calculate:

a **i** the ninth oblong number **ii** the ninth triangular number

b **i** the seventh oblong number **ii** the seventh triangular number

c What do you notice about your answers?

d Examine the diagram below and then complete the sentence 'The fourth triangular number is … the fourth oblong'.

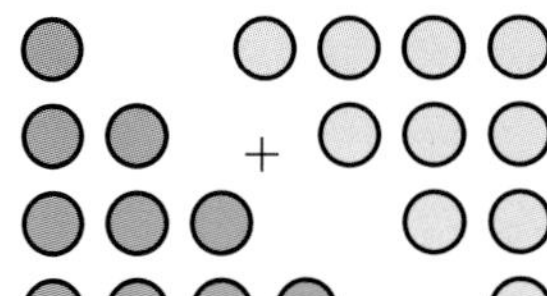

e Make a general statement relating the triangular numbers to the oblongs.

3 Find the simple connection between the squares and the oblongs.

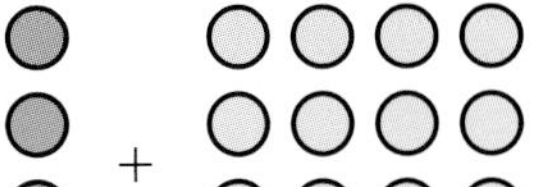

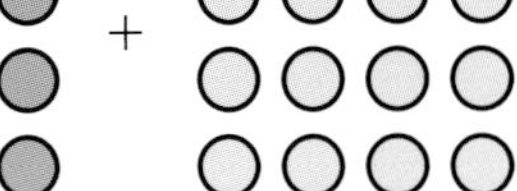

Investigation

Search the internet for 'Figurative numbers' or 'Polygonal numbers' and write a short report on your findings.

Challenge

Each clue is the sum of two numbers. The first is triangular, the second square, e.g. T(3) + S(2) means the 3rd triangular plus the 2nd square number.
So T(3) + S(2) = 6 + 4 = 10

Across

1 T(7) + S(23)
4 T(33) + S(11)
6 T(100) + S(72)
7 T(22) + S(23)
9 T(33) + S(20)
11 T(15) + S(18)
14 T(22) + S(20)
16 T(242) + S(160)
17 T(29) + S(4)
18 T(3) + S(13)

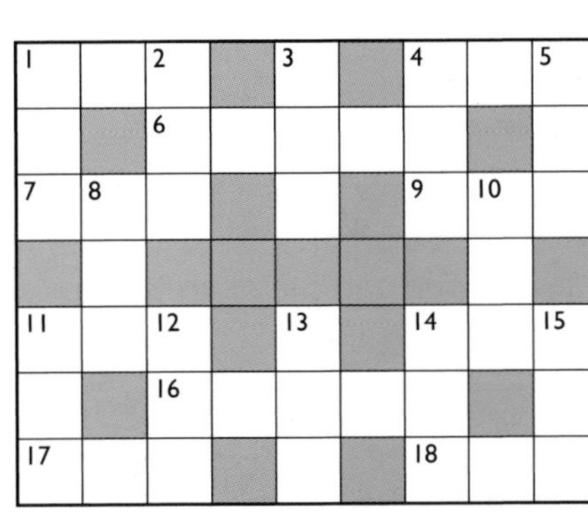

Down

1 T(16) + S(21)
2 T(26) + S(19)
3 T(14) + S(4)
4 T(25) + S(18)
5 T(15) + S(9)
8 T(40) + S(2)
10 T(33) + S(8)
11 T(4) + S(22)
12 T(26) + S(10)
13 T(8) + S(8)
14 T(19) + S(21)
15 T(8) + S(17)

E

3 Generating sequences

The sequence of natural numbers is 1, 2, 3, 4, 5, 6 … n, …
We can devise rules that convert this sequence to some other.

Example 1 Write down the sequence whose nth term is $3n$, where $n = 1, 2, 3, 4, 5, 6 \ldots$

$3n = 3 \times 1, 3 \times 2, 3 \times 3, 3 \times 4, 3 \times 5, 3 \times 6 \ldots$
$= 3, 6, 9, 12, 15, 18, \ldots$ the 3 times table.

Example 2 Write down the sequence whose nth term is $3n - 1$, where $n = 1, 2, 3, 4, 5, 6, \ldots$

$3n - 1 = 3 \times 1 - 1, 3 \times 2 - 1, 3 \times 3 - 1, 3 \times 4 - 1, \ldots$
$= 2, 5, 8, 11, \ldots$ the 3 times table less 1.

Exercise 3.1

1 The formula nth term $= 4n + 1$ is used to generate a sequence.

a List the first five terms of the sequence.

b Calculate:
i the 10th term **ii** the 25th term.

c How are the terms of the sequence related to the multiples of 4?

2 The nth term of a sequence is given by $5n - 2$.

a List the first four terms of the sequence.

b Calculate:
i the 12th term **ii** the 30th term.

c Compare the terms of the sequence with the multiples of 5.
What do you notice?

3 Copy and complete:

a

n	1	2	3	4	5		15
$7n - 3$							

Compare with the multiples of 7.
Comment on the size of the gap between terms.

b

n	1	2	3	4	5		23
$2n + 5$							

Compare with the multiples of 2.
Comment on the size of the gap between terms.

c

n	1	2	3	4	5		17
$6n - 5$							

Compare with the multiples of 6 and comment.

d

n	1	2	3	4	5		30
$10n - 3$							

Compare with the multiples of 10 and comment.

4 Match each nth term expression with a sequence:

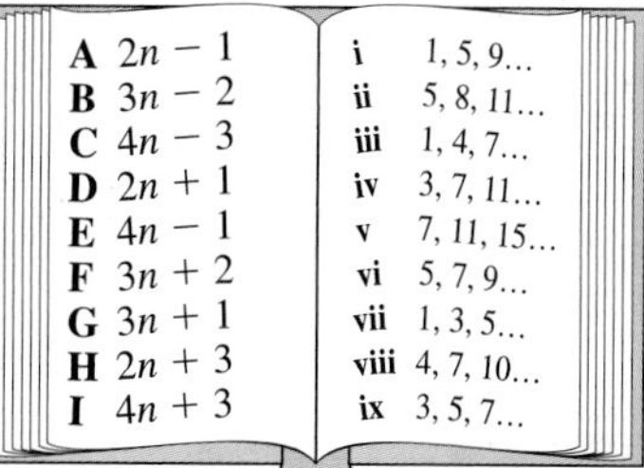

A 2n − 1
B 3n − 2
C 4n − 3
D 2n + 1
E 4n − 1
F 3n + 2
G 3n + 1
H 2n + 3
I 4n + 3
i 1, 5, 9...
ii 5, 8, 11...
iii 1, 4, 7...
iv 3, 7, 11...
v 7, 11, 15...
vi 5, 7, 9...
vii 1, 3, 5...
viii 4, 7, 10...
ix 3, 5, 7...

Challenge

a Jack was attempting to work out the nth term expression for this sequence:
2, 9, 16, 23, …
Look back over the nth term formulae in this exercise.
Give him some hints as to how he can find the nth term.

b Test your method on these two sequences:
i 2, 7, 12, 17, … **ii** 7, 10, 13, 16, …

E

4 Finding the *n*th term

In certain sequences it is easy to find an expression for the nth term.
Consider the sequence 4, 9, 14, 19, …
The terms go up in fives, so let's compare the sequence with the multiples of 5:

	1st term	2nd term	3rd term	4th term	…	nth term
Think of the multiples of 5	5	10	15	20		$5n$
Compare with the sequence	4	9	14	19		?
We need to make this adjustment	−1	−1	−1	−1		−1

Each term in the sequence is 1 less than a multiple of 5.
Hence, the nth term $= 5n - 1$.
We can now generate other members of the sequence.

Example 1 For 5th term use $n = 5$: $5n - 1 = 5 \times 5 - 1 = 25 - 1 = 24$

Example 2 For 32nd term use $n = 32$: $5n - 1 = 5 \times 32 - 1 = 160 - 1 = 159$

Exercise 4.1

1 For each sequence:

i find an expression for the nth term by copying and completing the table

ii check that the expression generates the sequence by using $n = 1, 2, 3$ and 4.

a 6, 8, 10, 12, …

term number	1	2	3	4	…	n
multiples of 2	2	4	6	8	…	$2n$
sequence	6	8	10	12	…	?
adjustment	+4	+4	+4	+4	…	+4

b 6, 11, 16, 21, …

term number	1	2	3	4	…	n
multiples of 5	5	10	?	?	…	?
sequence	6	11	16	21	…	?
adjustment	+1	+1	+1	+1	…	+1

c 2, 6, 10, 14, …

term number	1	2	3	4	…	n
multiples of ?	?	?	?	?	…	?
sequence	2	6	10	14	…	?
adjustment	?	?	?	?	…	?

d 6, 13, 20, 27, …

term number	1	2	3	4	…	n
multiples of ?	?	?	?	?	…	?
sequence	6	13	20	27	…	?
adjustment	?	?	?	?	…	?

e 11, 20, 29, 38, …

term number	1	2	3	4	…	n
multiples of ?	?	?	?	?	…	?
sequence	11	20	29	38	…	?
adjustment	?	?	?	?	…	?

f 8, 11, 14, 17, …

E

2 Find an expression for the nth term of each of these sequences.
You should make up a table comparing the sequence with suitable multiples.
Remember to check that the expression generates the sequence.

a 9, 11, 13, 15, … **b** 1, 6, 11, 16, … **c** 9, 12, 15, 18, …
d 5, 11, 17, 23, … **e** 1, 11, 21, 31, … **f** 8, 15, 22, 29, …
g 2, 8, 14, 20, … **h** 5, 13, 21, 29, … **i** 12, 17, 22, 27, …

3 For each sequence
i find an expression for the nth term
ii use this expression to find the requested term.

a 8, 10, 12, 14, … the 25th term **b** 4, 10, 16, 22, … the 30th term
c 4, 13, 22, 31, … the 35th term **d** 9, 13, 17, 21, … the 41st term
e 7, 12, 17, 22, … the 50th term **f** 0, 3, 6, 9, … the 23rd term
g 11, 17, 23, 29, … the 37th term **h** 5, 12, 19, 26, … the 100th term
i 11, 21, 31, 41, … the 1000th term

Challenge

Sequence A: 11, 15, 19, 23, …
Sequence B: 11, 19, 27, 35, …
Sequence C: 11, 24, 37, 50, …

Tracey wasn't sure to which sequence each of the numbers 1007, 1011 and 1012 belonged.

All she knew was that each belonged to a different sequence.

Can you sort them for her?

E

Example

a Find the nth term expression for 52, 49, 46, 43, …
b Calculate the 14th term.

Answer:

a The terms go down in threes. So we consider the -3 times table.

term number	1	2	3	4	…	n
multiples of -3	-3	-6	-9	-12	…	$-3n$
sequence	52	49	46	43	…	?
adjustment	$+55$	$+55$	$+55$	$+55$	…	$+55$

You need to add 55 to each multiple to generate the sequence, giving an nth term $= -3n + 55$ which is normally written $55 - 3n$.

b The 14th term $= 55 - 3 \times 14 = 13$.

Exercise 4.2

1 Find the nth term expression for each sequence:

a 38, 36, 34, 32, … **b** 32, 29, 26, 23, … **c** 80, 73, 66, 59, …

d 41, 36, 31, 26, … **e** 46, 42, 38, 34, … **f** 91, 82, 73, 64, …

g 80, 74, 68, 62, … **h** 69, 61, 53, 45, … **i** 37, 36, 35, 34, …

2 For each sequence:

i find the nth term

ii calculate the requested term.

a 54, 51, 48, 45, … the 17th term

b 114, 108, 102, 96, … the 18th term

c 200, 198, 196, 194, … the 82nd term

d 300, 296, 292, 288, … the 29th term

e 422, 417, 412, 407, … the 59th term

f 1000, 989, 978, 967, … the 59th term

E

3 The first row in a cinema has 15 seats.
The second row has 17 seats.
The third row has 19 seats.
It continues in this fashion to the back of the cinema.

a Find an expression for the number of seats in the nth row.

b How many seats are in the 14th row?

4 Jafar is taking a taxi ride.
Each mile he reads the meter and makes a note of the cost.

Miles gone	1	2	3	4		n
Cost so far (£)	3	7	11	15		?

a Treating the costs as a sequence, find an expression for the cost after n miles.

b What will the cost be after 15 miles?

5 Margaret built up the following table by examining two thermometers.

Degrees Celsius	1	2	3	4		n
Degrees Fahrenheit	33·8	35·6	37·4	39·2		?

a Treating the Fahrenheit temperatures as a sequence, find an expression for the Fahrenheit temperature at n degrees Celsius.

b What will be the Fahrenheit reading when n is 100 °C?

6 Simone adds weights to the end of a spring and measures the length of the spring.

Weight (kg)	1	2	3	4		n
Length (mm)	60	67	74	81		?

a Find an expression for the length of the spring when n kg have been added to it.

b What is the length of the spring when 8 kg has been added to the spring?

5 Which term?

Example 1 For the sequence 7, 15, 23, 31, ..., which term is 159?

The sequence goes up in eights. So we see the nth term = $8n - 1$.
The nth term = 159 (given)

$\Rightarrow$ $8n - 1 = 159$
$\Rightarrow$ $8n = 160$
$\Rightarrow$ $n = 20$
$\Rightarrow$ 159 is the 20th term in the sequence.

Exercise 5.1

1 For each sequence, a term is highlighted.
Find which term in the sequence it is.

a 10, 13, 16, 19, ..., **52**, ...
b 3, 9, 15, 21, ..., **135**, ...
c 13, 22, 31, 40, ..., **157**, ...
d 3, 11, 19, 27, ..., **243**, ...
e 11, 13, 15, 17, ..., **139**, ...
f 7, 17, 27, 37, ..., **277**, ...
g 14, 27, 40, 53, ..., **521**, ...
h 1, 8, 15, 22, ..., **694**, ...

2 Match each term to a sequence and say which term of the sequence it is.

a

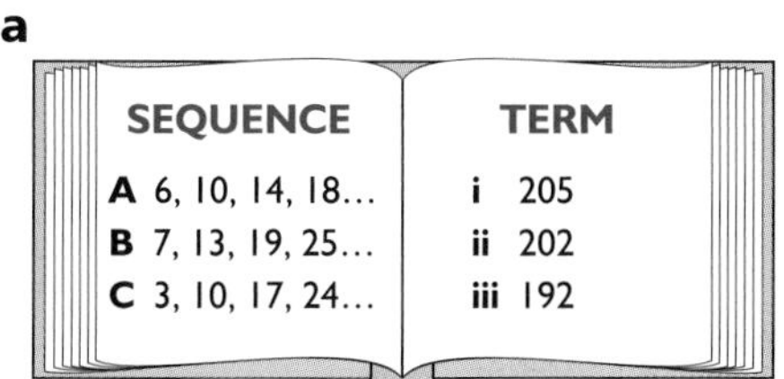

b

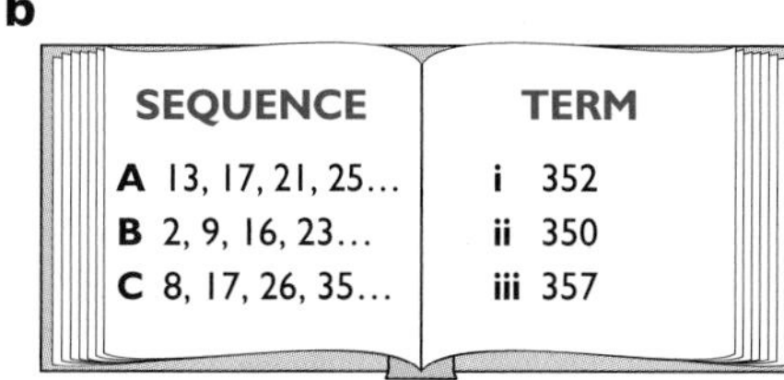

c

SEQUENCE	TERM
A 9, 19, 29, 39...	**i** 297
B 12, 21, 30, 39...	**ii** 299
C 9, 17, 25, 33...	**iii** 291

Brainstormer

Jacob is puzzling over these five sequences. He is convinced that there is more than one way of matching the five terms to the five sequences.

His friend Emma is convinced that there *is* only one possible way.

Who is correct?

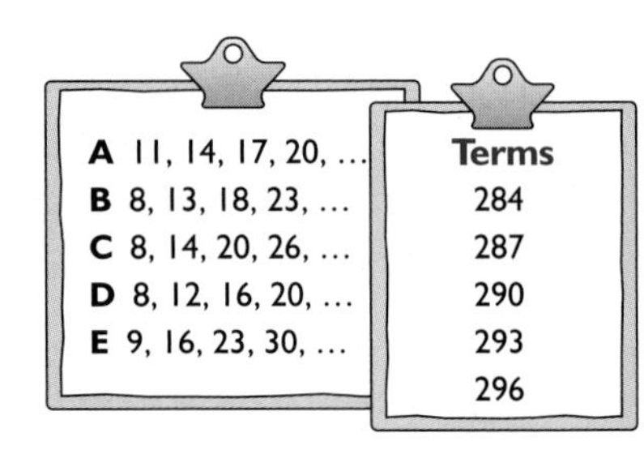

A 11, 14, 17, 20, ...
B 8, 13, 18, 23, ...
C 8, 14, 20, 26, ...
D 8, 12, 16, 20, ...
E 9, 16, 23, 30, ...
Terms
284
287
290
293
296

Example 2

Is 7034 a term of the sequence 2, 9, 16, 23, 30, ... ?

By inspection we see that the nth term $= 7n - 5$.
If 7034 is a term then $7n - 5 = 7034$

$\Rightarrow \quad 7n = 7039$
$\Rightarrow \quad n = 7039 \div 7 = 1005{\cdot}57$ (to 2 d.p.)

But n has to be a whole number.
Thus 7034 is not a term of the given sequence.

Two sequences are said to have a *term in common* when the *same* number occupies the *same* position in both sequences.

Example 3

The sequences 2, 9, 16, 23, 30, ... and 23, 27, 31, 35, ... have a term in common. What is it?

By inspection, the nth terms are $7n - 5$ and $4n + 19$.
For the common term $7n - 5 = 4n + 19$

$\Rightarrow \quad 3n = 24$
$\Rightarrow \quad n = 8$

When $n = 8$, the term $= 7 \times 8 - 5 = 51$ (or $4 \times 8 + 19 = 51$)
Thus, for both sequences, the 8th term is 51.

Exercise 5.2

1 Prove 1234 is not a term of the sequence 1, 12, 23, 34, ...

2 Show that 77 is not in the sequence 7, 13, 19, 25, ...

3 99 is not in the sequence 13, 20, 27, 34, ...

a Prove this is true.

b Between which two terms of the sequence does it lie?

4 Terence is paying off a loan in instalments. The amount owed, week after week, forms a pattern:

£700, £677, £654, £631, …

a Is £0 part of this sequence?

b He pays off the loan when what is owed is less than one instalment. How big is the last payment?

5 For each pair of sequences find the term which is common, giving
i its position in the sequence and
ii its value.

a 0, 5, 10, 15, … and 44, 45, 46, …

b 2, 5, 8, 11, … and 22, 24, 26, 28, …

c 3, 9, 15, … and 21, 24, 27, …

6 Show that the sequences 7, 12, 17, 22, … and 28, 31, 34, 37, … don't share a common term.

7 Toni and Seth each have a pack of 52 cards.
They both take turns at placing the cards in piles.
Toni places six down and thereafter deals them in fours.
Her pile grows according to the sequence 6, 10, 14, …
Seth lays down 17 and thereafter deals them in threes.

a Is there a time when they both have the same amount of cards in their piles?

b How many cards does each person have in their hands at this point?

6 Problem solving

Example

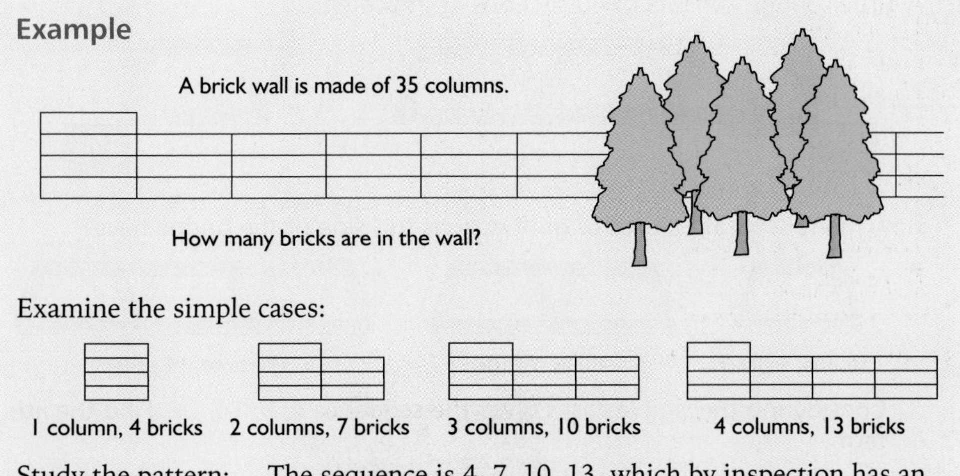

A brick wall is made of 35 columns.
How many bricks are in the wall?
Examine the simple cases:
1 column, 4 bricks
2 columns, 7 bricks
3 columns, 10 bricks
4 columns, 13 bricks

Study the pattern: The sequence is 4, 7, 10, 13, which by inspection has an nth term $= 3n + 1$.

Describe the rule: A wall with n columns has $3n + 1$ bricks.

Check the rule: We know it works for $n = 1, 2, 3, 4$, since we used these to form the rule.
The rule predicts that five columns will have $3 \times 5 + 1 = 16$ bricks.

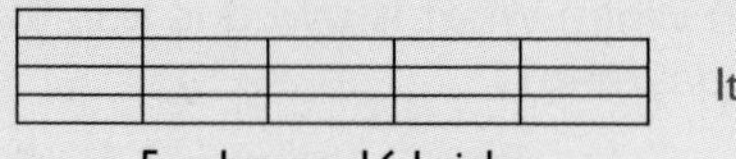

5 columns, 16 bricks

It seems OK!

Solve the problem: For a wall with 35 columns, $n = 35$

$\Rightarrow$ $3n + 1 = 3 \times 35 + 1 = 106$

$\Rightarrow$ 106 bricks make up the wall.

Exercise 6.1

1 A toy train has an engine and 18 trucks.
How many wheels does the assembly have?

a

1 truck, 8 wheels

2 trucks, 12 wheels

3 trucks, 16 wheels

8, 12, 16, … What is the nth term of this sequence?

b How many wheels does a train with n trucks have?

c So how many wheels does an 18-truck train have? (Hint: use $n = 18$)

2 A girder bridge consists of 40 sections as indicated:

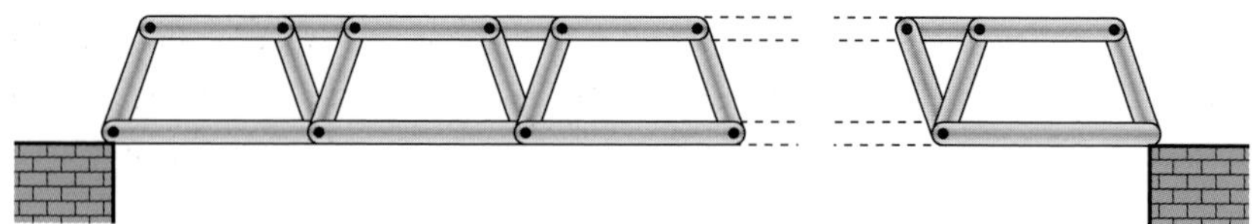

How many separate pieces of girders does this side of the bridge have?

a

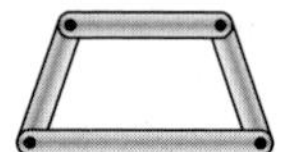

1 section, 4 girders

2 sections, 9 girders

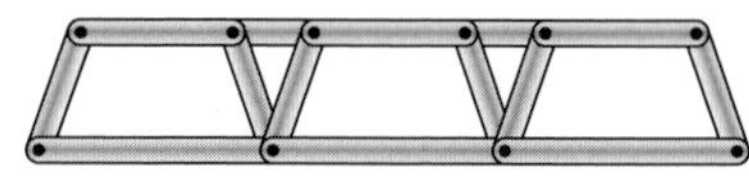

3 sections, 14 girders

Considering the simple cases gives the sequence 4, 9, 14, … . Find the nth term.

b How many girders are used to make the side of a bridge with n sections?

c So how many girders are there in the side of a 40-section bridge? (Hint: use $n = 40$)

3 A metalworker is making a decorative frieze for the outside of a building. It consists of 55 large and a number of small rings welded together as shown. The purple spots indicate welds.

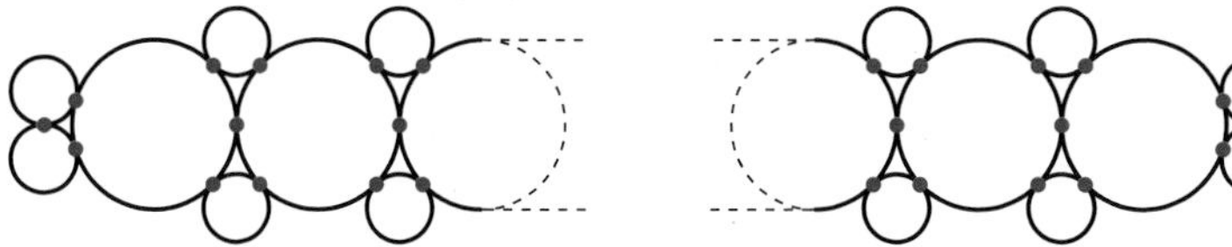

How many welds must the metalworker make to construct the frieze?

a

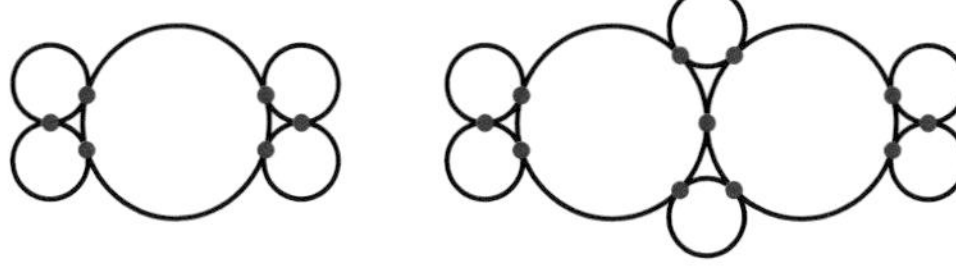

1 large ring, 6 welds   2 large rings, 11 welds

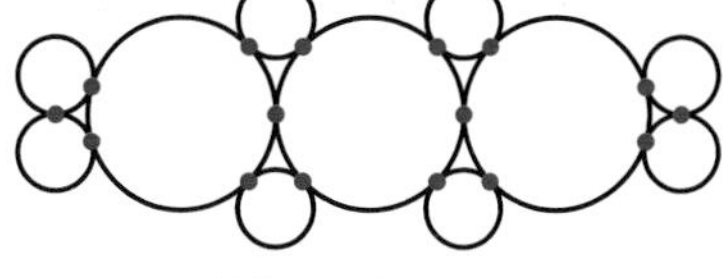

3 large rings, …

i Write down the sequence generated by counting the number of welds up to the 4th term.

ii Write down an expression for the nth term of this sequence: the number of welds needed to construct a frieze with n large rings.

b How many welds will the metalworker need to make the frieze with 55 large rings?

c How many small rings will he need?

4 A wooden fence is made by stapling wooden sections together.

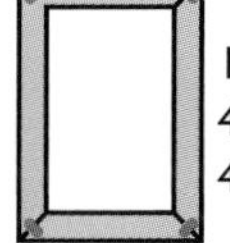

1 section
4 pieces of wood
4 staples

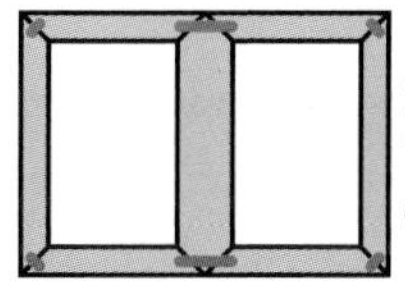

2 sections
7 pieces of wood
6 staples

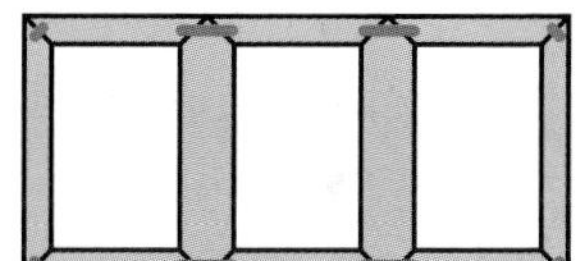

a Find the nth term of the sequence generated by counting pieces of wood.

b How many pieces of wood are needed to make a frame that has 43 sections?

c How many staples are needed to make a frame that has 43 sections?

5 A garden trellice is built up as shown.
Notice that as the trellice gets taller we can use longer pieces of wood.

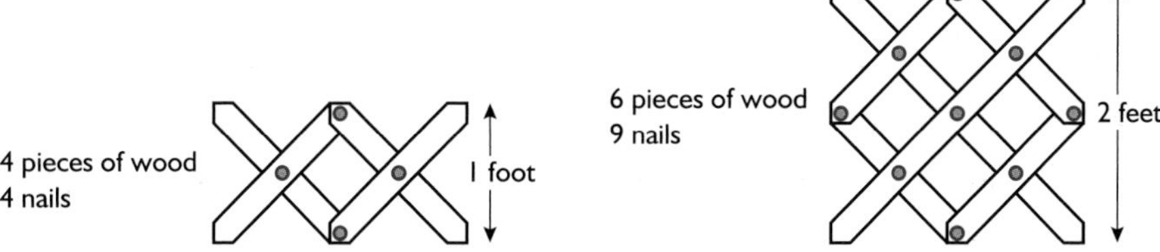

If the trellice is 22 feet tall, calculate the number of:

a pieces of wood needed   **b** nails needed.

Example

A train has 52 wheels.
How many trucks does it have?
We see that a train with n trucks has $4n + 4$ wheels.

52 wheels … how many trucks?

$\Rightarrow \quad 4n + 4 = 52$
$\Rightarrow \quad 4n = 48$
$\Rightarrow \quad n = 12$

The train has 12 trucks.

Exercise 6.2

1

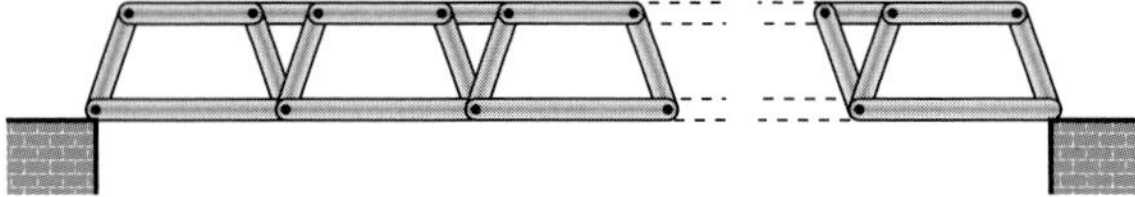

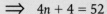

a A girder bridge of this design needs 159 girders to make a side.
How many sections does it have?

b The engineers are building another bridge of the same design.
They have 170 girders on site.
If they use as many girders as possible to make the side, how many are left over?

2

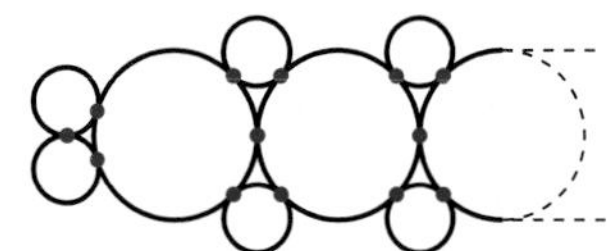

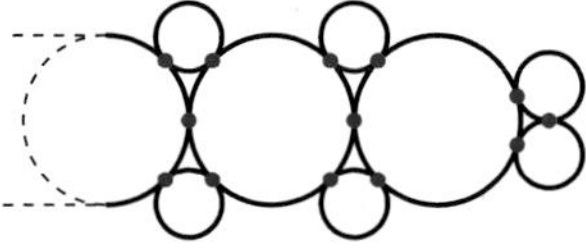

a A decorative frieze, of the same design as the one in the previous exercise, requires 211 welds.
How many **i** large rings **ii** small rings does it have?

b A worker said he made a frieze like this and needed to make 300 welds.
Is this possible?

3

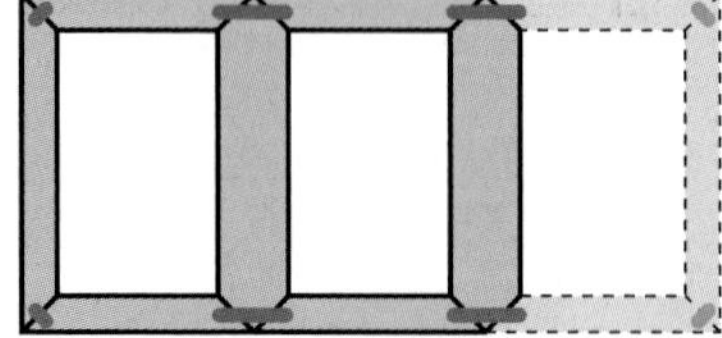

a 94 pieces of wood were used to build a fence similar to the one in question **4** of Exercise 6.1.
How many sections does it have?

b If 61 staples were used, does the fence have a complete number of sections? Explain your answer.

E

4 **a** A trellice is made from 52 pieces of wood. How high is it, if it is only as wide as shown?

b How high is a similar trellice that requires 104 nails to construct?

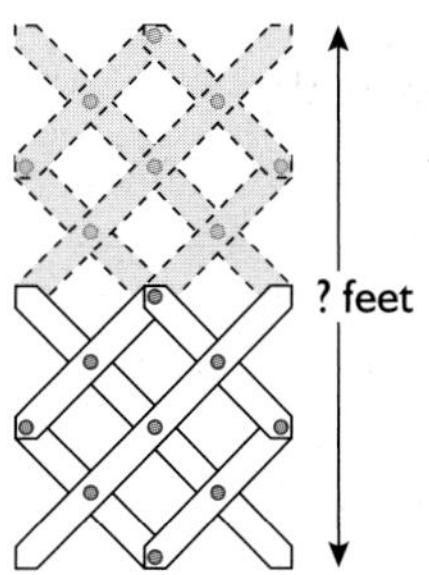

Challenge

Sequence A 3, 11, 19, 27, …
Sequence B 57, 62, 67, 72, …
Sequence C 93, 96, 99, 102, …

Catriona declared that these three sequences have a term in common. Which term? (Hint: find *n*th terms and set them equal.)

7 Finding formulae

Example 1

A construction kit uses joints and rods to make a series of related models.

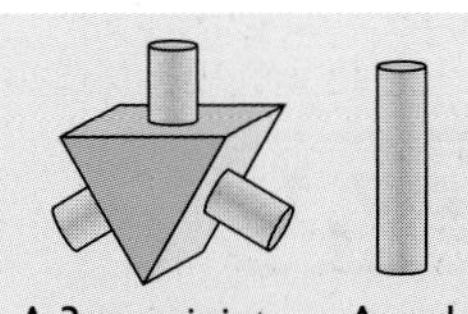

Model 1

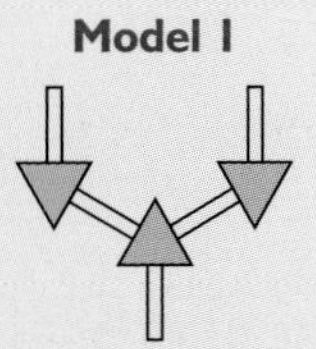

3 joints, 5 rods

Model 2

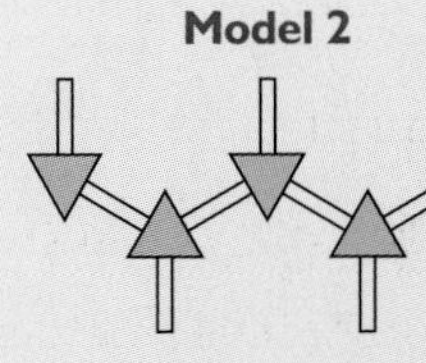

5 joints, 9 rods

Model 3

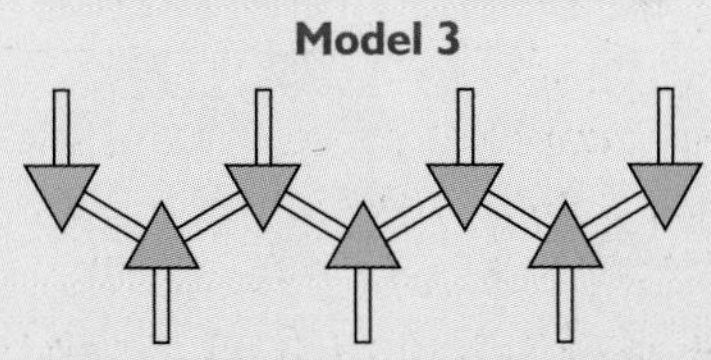

Find formulae for the number of joints (J) and the number of rods (R) in terms of model number (n).
Look for sequences and find expressions for the nth terms.

Model number (n)	1	2	3		n
Number of joints (J)	3	5	7		$2n + 1$
Number of rods (R)	5	9	13		$4n + 1$

By inspection, the required formulae are $J = 2n + 1$ and $R = 4n + 1$.
These formulae may now be used to solve further problems.

Example 2

How many joints and rods do you need to build model 38?

Use $n = 38$ in the formulae:

$J = 2n + 1 = 2 \times 38 + 1 = 76 + 1 = 77$
$R = 4n + 1 = 4 \times 38 + 1 = 152 + 1 = 153$

So 77 joints and 153 rods are required to build model 38.

Example 3

What is the largest model I can make if I have 105 joints and 201 rods?

$J = 105$
$\Rightarrow \quad 2n + 1 = 105$
$\Rightarrow \quad 2n = 104$
$\Rightarrow \quad n = 52$

$R = 201$
$\Rightarrow \quad 4n + 1 = 201$
$\Rightarrow \quad 4n = 200$
$\Rightarrow \quad n = 50$

You can make model 50 (using all 201 rods).
There are not enough rods to make a larger model (even though there are enough joints to make model 52).

F

Exercise 7.1

1 Here is another series of models made with the construction set.

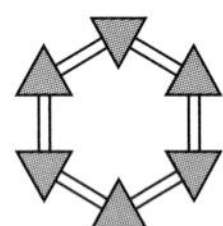 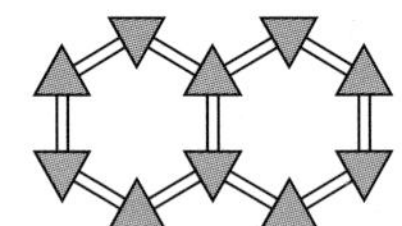 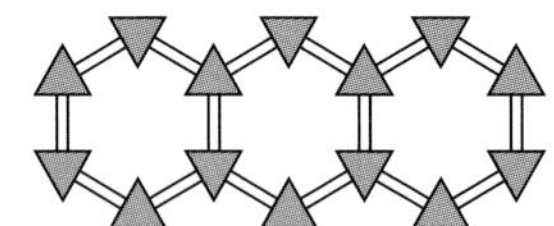

a Copy and complete the table.

Model number (n)	1	2	3		n
Number of joints (J)					
Number of rods (R)					

b Write down formulae for J and R in terms of n.

c How many joints and rods are needed to make model 43?

d One of the models requires 94 joints.
Which model is this and how many rods does the model need?

e What is the largest model you can make with 138 joints and 166 rods?

2 A third series of models look like this:

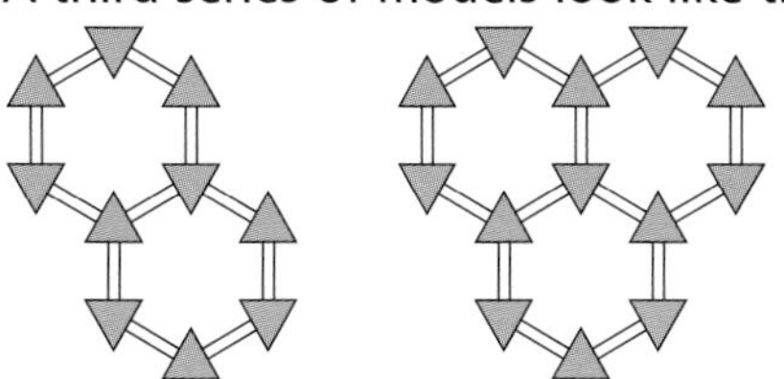

a Find formulae for **i** J **ii** R in terms of n.

b You built model 27 of this series.
How many **i** joints **ii** rods would you need?

c Peter has 163 rods. How many joints does he need to construct the largest model possible with these rods?

3 The Patio Designs Company sells mosaics for patios.
Here is an example of a 2 m by 2 m patio.
It requires 4 slabs, 12 framing pieces, 9 corner squares and 8 border pieces.

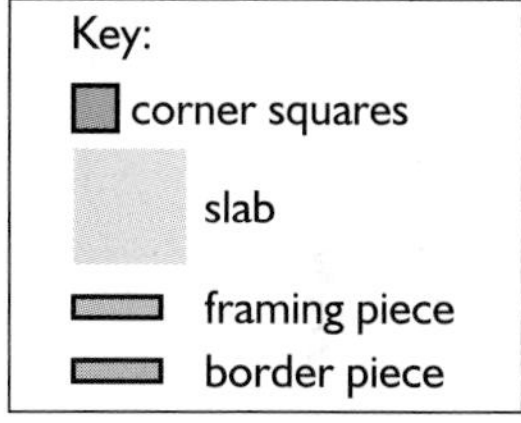

Here is a sequence of designs:

Design 1

1 m × 2 m

Design 2

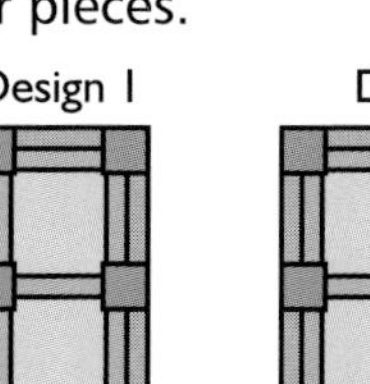

2 m × 2 m

Design 3

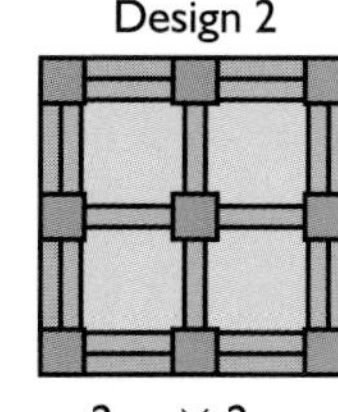

3 m × 2 m

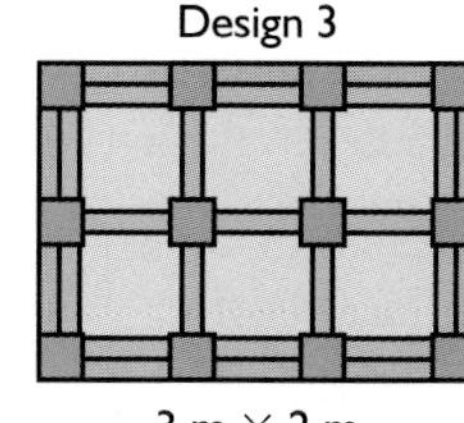

a Copy and complete the table for this sequence of designs.

Design number (n)	1	2	3	4		n
Number of slabs (S)						
Number of frames (F)						
Number of corners (C)						
Number of borders (B)						

b Write down formulae for
i S **ii** F **iii** C **iv** B in terms of n.

c Use your formulae to find the cost of a 13 m × 2 m patio of this design.
Costs are: slabs £4; frame piece £2; corner connector £3; and border piece £6.

Challenge

Mr and Mrs Thomson have £1000 to spend on a 3 metre wide patio.
They are not sure if they can afford an 18 metre or a 19 metre long patio.
Develop formulae for S, F, C and B in terms of n for 3 metre wide patios to help you advise them.

F

8 Problem solving and equations

Example

The first bottle contains twice as much as the second bottle.
The third bottle contains 1 more litre than the second bottle.
In total the three bottles hold 13 litres.
How much is in each bottle?

A picture sometimes helps

Use a letter to stand for one of the unknowns.
Let the second bottle hold x litres.
So the first bottle holds $2x$ litres
and the third bottle contains $x + 1$ litres.

Form an equation.
The total is $x + 2x + x + 1 = 4x + 1$
$\Rightarrow \quad 4x + 1 = 13$

Solve the equation.
$4x + 1 = 13$
$\Rightarrow \quad 4x = 12$
$\Rightarrow \quad x = 3$

Use the solution.
First bottle: $2x = 2 \times 3 = 6$ litres
Second bottle: $x = 3$ litres
Third bottle: $x + 1 = 3 + 1 = 4$ litres

Check your solution. Total $= 6 + 3 + 4 = 13$ litres, as required.

F

Exercise 8.1

1 In a triangle, the largest angle is six times the size of the smallest angle. The other angle is 20° larger than the smallest.

a Let the smallest angle be $x°$.
Write down the sizes of the other two angles in terms of x.

b The angles in a triangle add up to 180°.
Use this fact to write an equation and solve it to find the value of x.

c Find the sizes of the three angles.

2 In triangle ABC, angle A is 10° more than angle B and angle C is three times the size of angle B.
Find the sizes of the three angles. (Hint: let angle B be $x°$)

3 John's brother Dan is twice his age.
His other brother George is three years younger than him.

- **a** Let John's age be x years. Write Dan's age and George's age in terms of x.
- **b** If their ages total 53 years, write an equation and solve it to find x.
- **c** What ages are John, Dan and George?

4 Robbie's mum is three times his age and his dad is 30 years older than him.
Find their ages if they total 110 years. (Hint: let Robbie's age be x years.)

5 The pages in a notebook are 2 cm longer than they are broad.

- **a** If the breadth is x cm write down the length.
- **b** The perimeter of a page is 36 cm. Write an equation and solve it to find x.
- **c** What are the dimensions of a page?

6 The angles of a quadrilateral add up to 360°.
In order of size there is a 10° difference between each of the four angles in this quadrilateral.
Find their sizes. (Hint: let the smallest angle be $x°$.)

7 Use algebra to solve these problems.

- **a** Three sisters have ages that are, in order, 2 years apart.
  Find their ages if they total 42 years.
- **b** In triangle PQR, angle P is 20° less than angle Q and angle R is twice the size of angle Q.
  Find the sizes of the three angles.
- **c** A drum contains five times more liquid than a bottle.
  The bottle contains 2 more litres than a flask.
  In total the three containers hold 19 litres.
  How much liquid is in each?
- **d** Runner A took twice as long as runner C to run a race.
  Runner B finished only 1 minute behind runner C.
  If their total time was 29 minutes, how long did each take?
- **e** Northfield required twice as many seedlings planted as Southfield.
  Westfield required 40 more seedlings than Southfield.
  In total 680 seedlings were planted.
  How many were planted in each field?

Brainstormer

A Ewan's mum is three times his age.
Four years ago she was four times his age. How old are they?
(Hint: present age $= x \Longrightarrow$ age 4 years ago $= x - 4$.)

B Sally's dad is two years older than her mum. Her mum at present is three times Sally's age. When Sally was born, her parent's ages totalled 42 years.
How old are they all now?
(Hint: present age $= x \Longrightarrow$ age at birth $= x - x = 0$.)

F

9 Problem solving with graphs

A car is travelling at a steady average speed on a motorway.
The amount of petrol, L litres, left in the tank after t hours is given by the formula:
$L = 60 - 8t; \ 0 \leqslant t \leqslant 7{\cdot}5$
Using this formula, values for L may be calculated:

t	0	1	2	3	4	5	6	7
L	60	52	44	36	28	20	12	4

The pairs of values (0, 60), (1, 52), … lie in a straight line when plotted on a graph. The resulting graph can be used to help solve problems about the petrol remaining in the car.

For example:

- From the graph it is clear that after about $7\frac{1}{2}$ hours of driving the car will run out of petrol (point A on the graph).
- Following trail B indicates that after $2\frac{1}{2}$ hours there are approximately 40 litres left.
- Following trail C indicates that half the petrol is used up after around 3 hours 45 minutes.

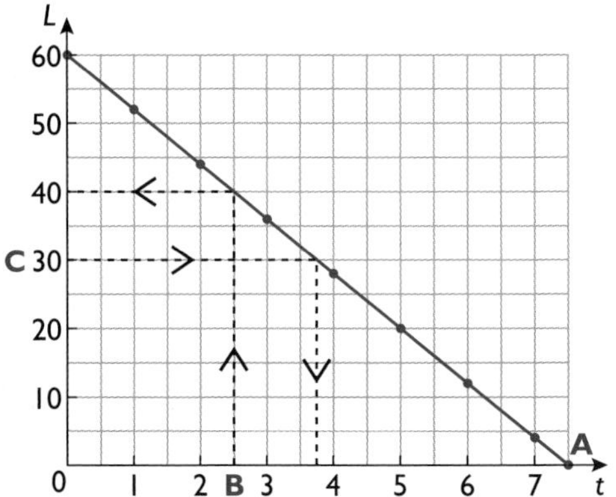

F

Exercise 9.1

1 A catering company uses the formula:

$F = \frac{1}{5}P + 3 \ (0 < P \leqslant 50)$

to calculate the number of French baguettes, F, required for a buffet party of P people.

a Copy and complete the table:

P	10	20	30	40	50
F					

b Use suitable scales to draw a graph for this formula with $0 \leqslant P \leqslant 50$ and $0 \leqslant F \leqslant 13$.

c From the graph estimate the number of baguettes required for a party of 43 people.

d Eight baguettes would be enough for a party of how many people?

2 The recommended number of lights, L, required for a Christmas tree of height h feet is given by the formula:

$L = 20(h - 2)$ for $3 \leqslant h \leqslant 12$.

a Copy and complete the table:

h	3	6	9	12
L				

b Draw a graph for this formula with $3 \leqslant h \leqslant 12$ and $20 \leqslant L \leqslant 200$.

c Estimate the number of lights required for a $5\frac{1}{2}$ ft tree.

d Lights come in sets of 60. What is the maximum height of tree for which two sets could be recommended?

3 A 30-year-old male of medium build with height H cm should ideally have a weight, W kg, given by the formula: $W = \frac{1}{2}(H - 40)$ with $150 \leqslant H \leqslant 200$.

a Copy and complete the table:

H	150	160	170	180	190	200
W						

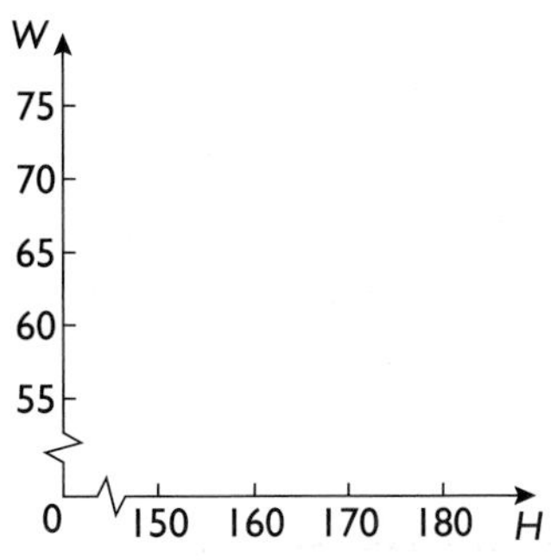

b Draw a graph using the indicated scales.

c Matt has a height of 1·65 m. If he is of medium build what is his ideal weight?

d Joe, who is also of medium build, weighs himself at 64·5 kg. If he is 1·79 m tall, is he overweight or underweight according to the graph?

4 A frozen turkey thawing at room temperature will take t hours to thaw. This can be calculated using the formula: $t = \frac{1}{2}(7w + 26)$ for $0 < w \leqslant 10$ where w kg is the weight of the frozen turkey.

a Copy and complete the table:

w	2	4	6	8	10
t					

b Choose suitable scales and draw a graph for this formula with $0 \leqslant w \leqslant 10$.

c Estimate from your graph the thawing time for a 2·6 kg turkey at room temperature.

d Rahil is planning turkey curry for dinner. It is now 12 noon and the turkey has to be thawed, at room temperature, for 6 p.m. next day. What is the maximum weight of frozen turkey he can thaw in the time available?

CHECK-UP

1 Complete this number snake using the clues.

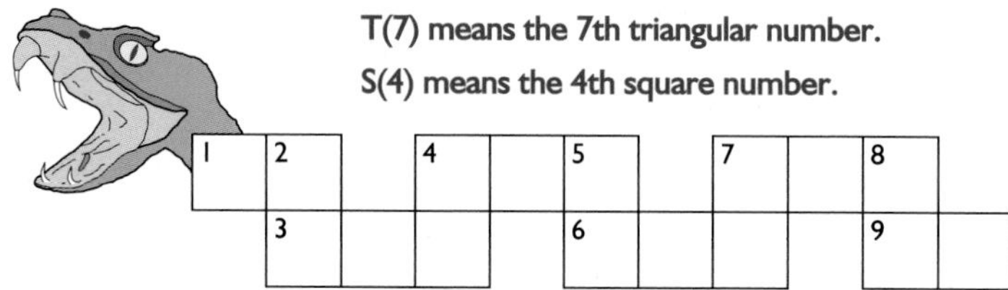
T(7) means the 7th triangular number.
S(4) means the 4th square number.
1
2
4
5
7
8
3
6
9

Across
1 T(7)
3 S(4) + S(11)
4 S(23)
6 T(7) + S(11)
7 The sum of T(20) and T(21)
9 The difference between S(8) and T(4)

Down
2 S(9)
4 T(6) + T(8)
5 The difference between S(10) and S(3)
7 S(7)
8 T(5)

2 The nth term of a sequence is given by $8n - 5$. Find:

a the tenth term

b the difference between the fourth and fifth terms.

3 Find an expression for the nth term of these sequences:

a 11, 20, 29, 38, … **b** 17, 37, 57, 77, … **c** 61, 57, 53, 49, …

4 Which term is highlighted in each sequence?

a 9, 11, 13, 15, …, **207**, …

b 1, 9, 17, 25, …, **393**, …

5 Here is a sequence of girder bridges:

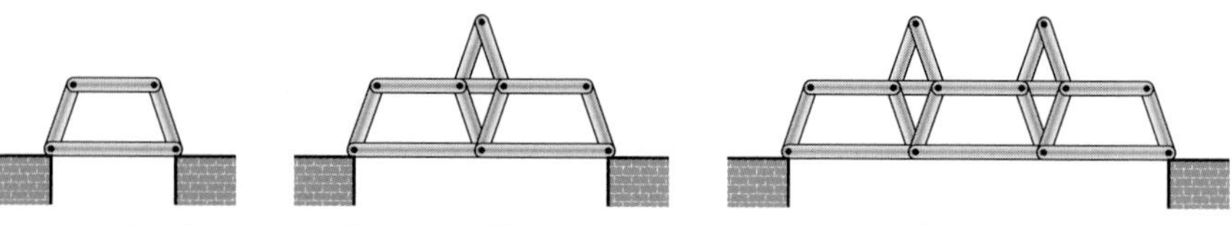

1 section, 4 girders 2 sections, 11 girders 3 sections, 18 girders

a Find an expression for the number of girders required for an n section bridge.

b How many girders are required for a 13 section bridge?

c A bridge of this design required 158 girders. How many sections does it have?

E

6

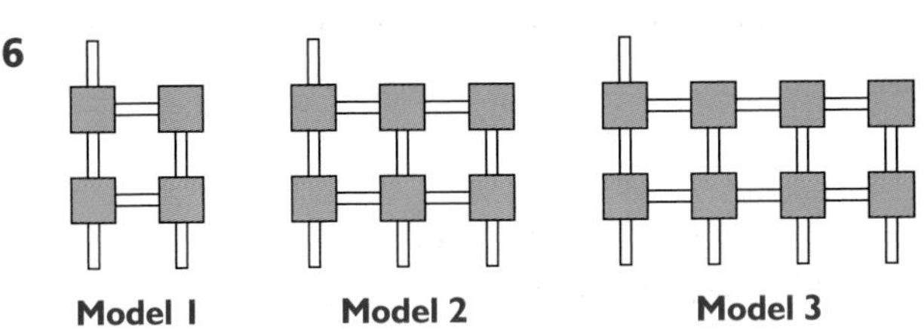

a Copy and complete the table for the above sequence of models.

Model number (n)	1	2	3		n
Number of joints (J)					
Number of rods (R)					

b Write down formulae for J and R in terms of n.

c How many joints and rods do you need to build model 39?

d I have 64 joints and 126 rods.
What is the largest model in this sequence that I can build?

7 In triangle RST, angle R is four times the size of angle T.
Angle S is 54° smaller than angle R.
Find the sizes of the three angles.

8 The length of time, D days, that certain foods can be safely frozen at various temperatures, T °C, is given by the formula:

$D = -6(T + 4)$ for $-20 \leqslant T \leqslant -5$

a Copy and complete the table.

T	-20	-15	-10	-5
D				

b Draw a graph using the indicated scales.

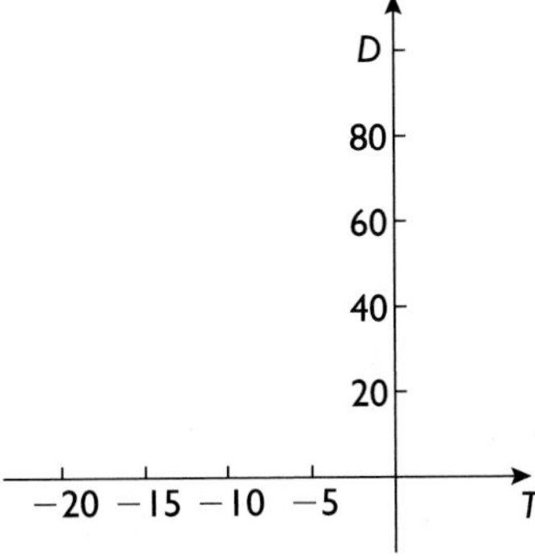

c Estimate, from your graph, how long you can safely store food at a temperature of -12 °C.

d What is the maximum temperature you can freeze food for 2 months?
Write a few sentences about how you arrived at your answer.

F

13 The triangle

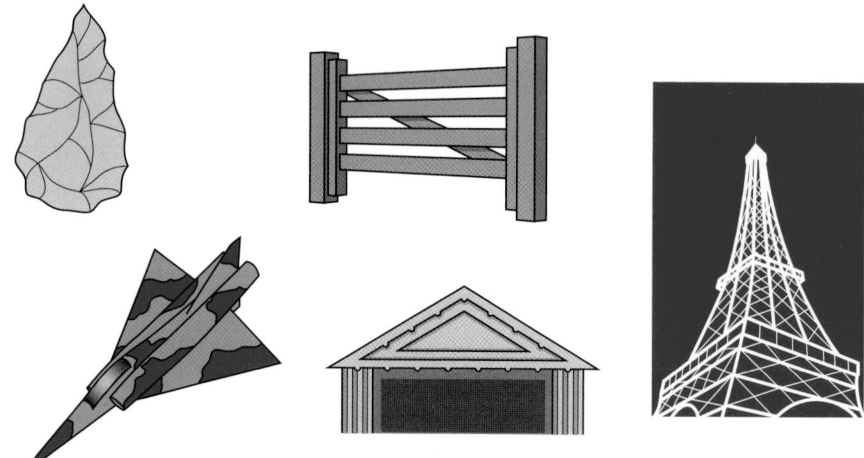

Triangles have been used and studied for thousands of years.

One of their uses is to strengthen structures.

1 Looking back

Reminder

Sorting triangles

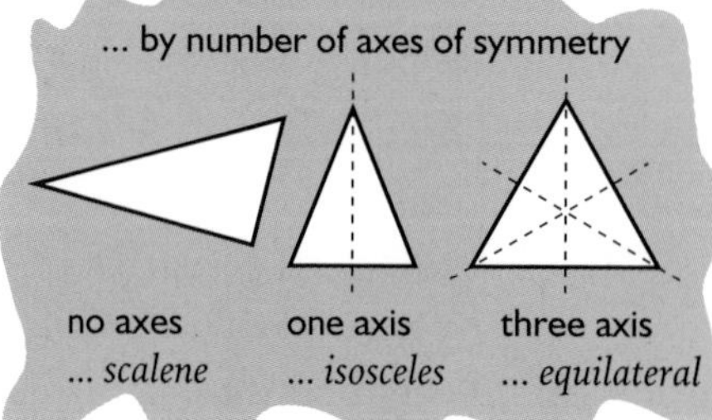

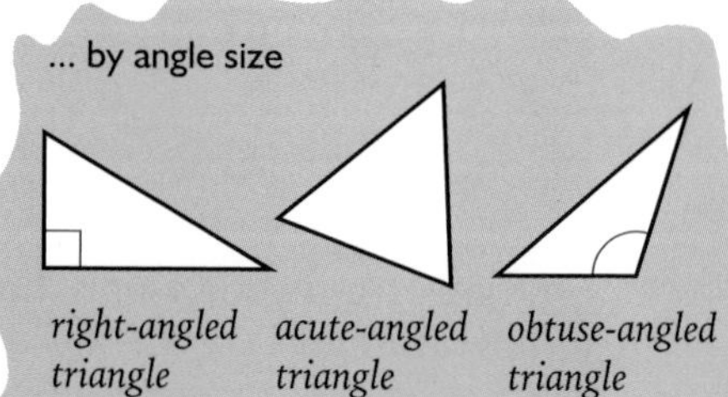

Exercise 1.1

1 ∠ACB is a right angle. Name:

a the other right angle

b the acute angles

c the obtuse angles.

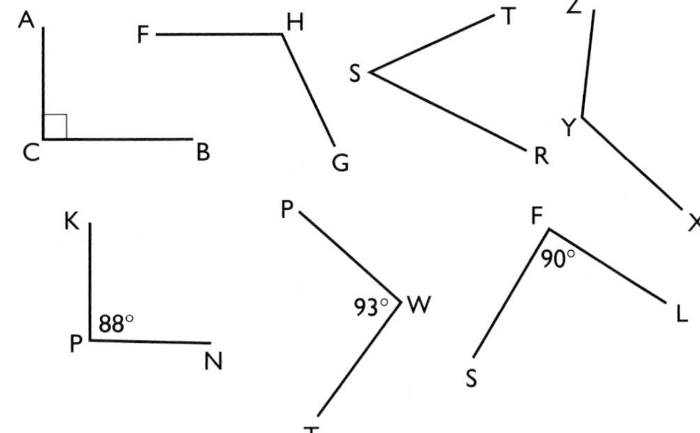

2 △RST is a right-angled triangle. Name:

a the other right-angled triangle

b the acute-angled triangles

c the obtuse-angled triangles.

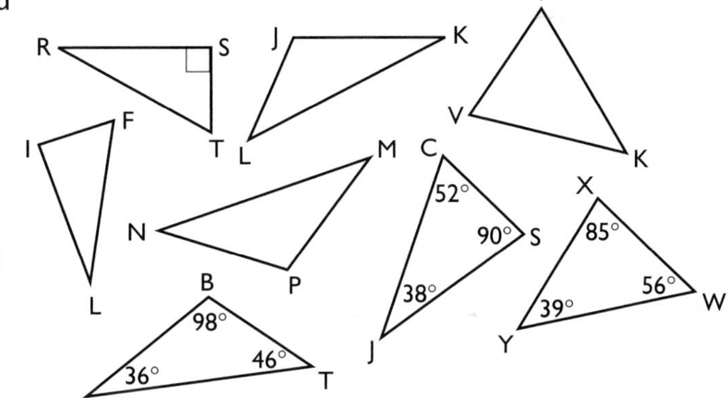

3 Name:

a the isosceles triangles

b the equilateral triangles in this collection.

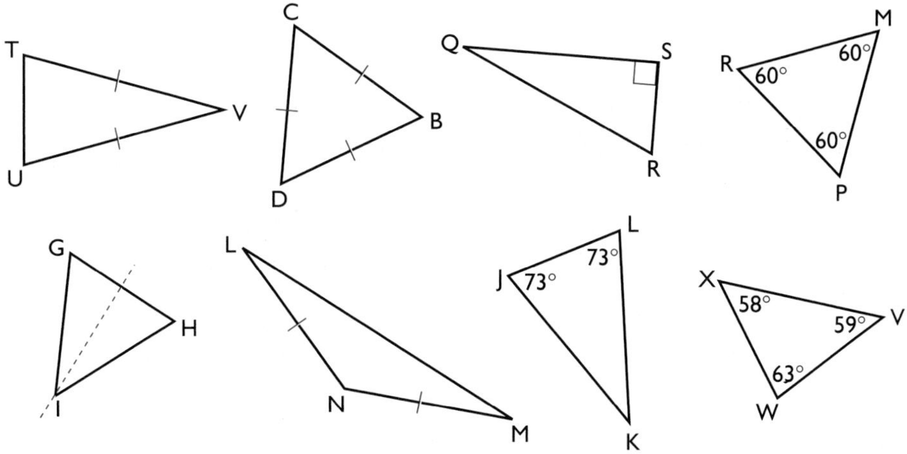

4 **a** On a coordinate diagram, plot the points T(7, 8), U(0, 5) and V(4, 1), and join them up.

b What kind of triangle is △TUV?
How do you know?

c Draw the axis of symmetry of △TUV as a dotted line.

d Find the coordinates of two possible positions for W such that △TUW is isosceles with TU = TW. (Don't choose V as one of your positions for W.)

5 **Remember**: vertically opposite angles are equal.
Which pairs of angles in these diagrams are equal because they are vertically opposite?

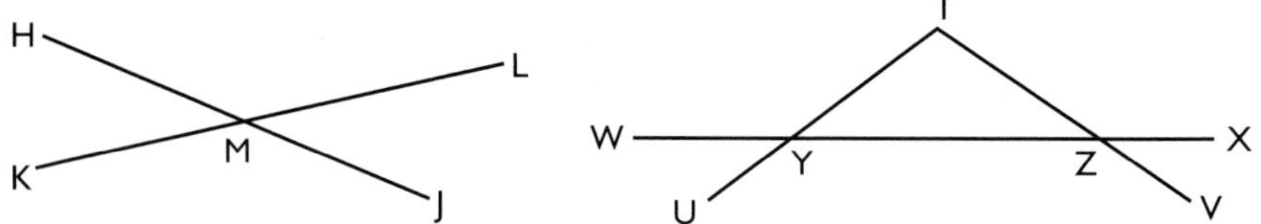

6 The diagram represents part of a roofing structure.

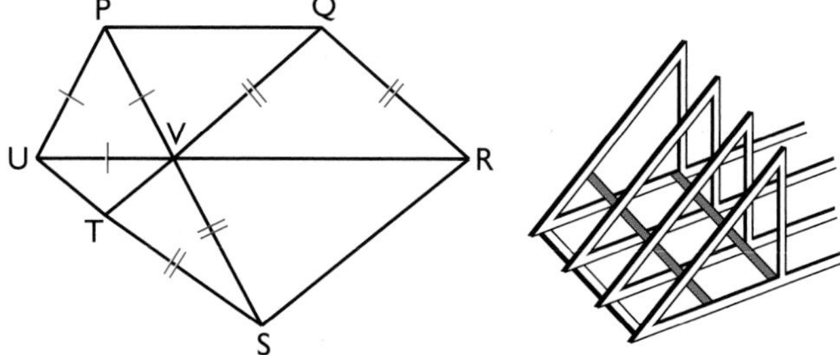

PS, QT and UR are straight lines.

a Name all the isosceles and equilateral triangles you can find in the diagram.

b Name six pairs of vertically opposite angles.

2 The sum of the angles of a triangle

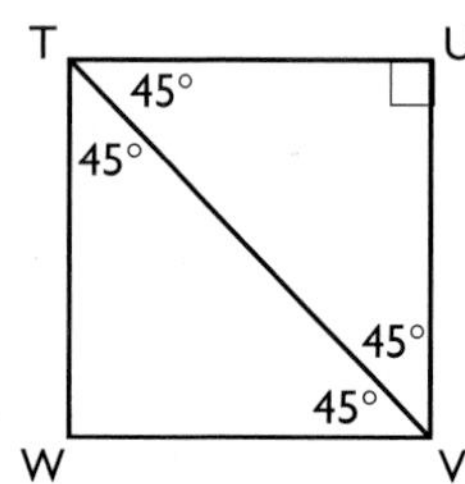

A square is halved by its diagonal. We see that the sum of the angles of the triangle TUV is 180°.

Each angle of an equilateral triangle is 60°. So the sum of the angles of an equilateral triangle is 180°.

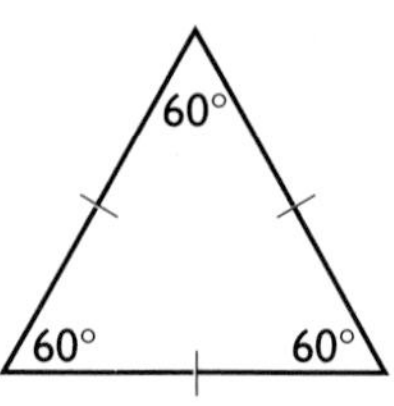

What about other kinds of triangles?

Class activities

Activity 1

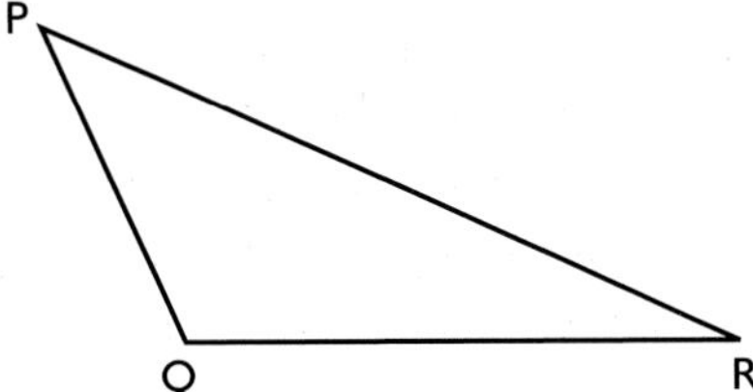

a Measure the sizes of the three angles of triangle PQR.

b Calculate the sum of the three angles.

Activity 2

a Draw your own:
  - **i** obtuse-angled triangle
  - **ii** acute-angled triangle
  - **iii** isosceles triangle.

b For each triangle:
  - **i** measure its angles **ii** calculate the sum of its angles.

c
  - **i** Mark three points anywhere on a page of your jotter.
  - **ii** Join them to form a triangle.
  - **iii** Find the sum of its angles.
  - **iv** Compare your findings with others.

Your findings should confirm the fact that the angles of any triangle add up to 180°.

Proof

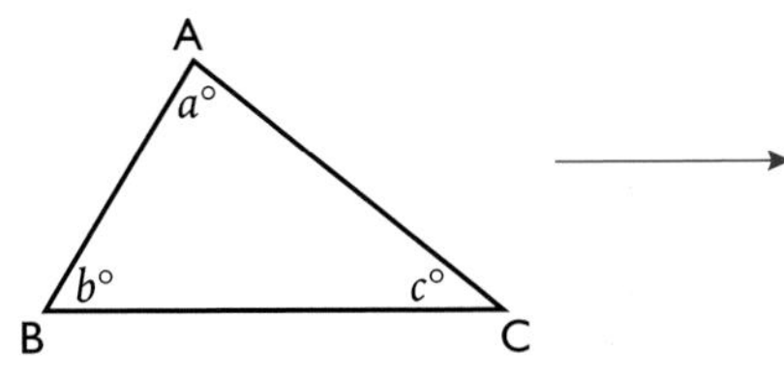

Draw any triangle ABC with angles of size $a°$, $b°$, $c°$ as shown.

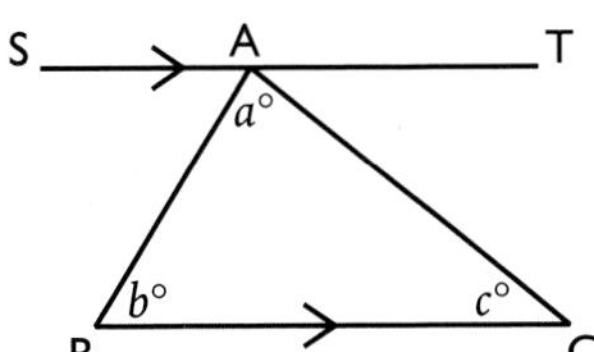

Draw a line ST through A parallel to BC.

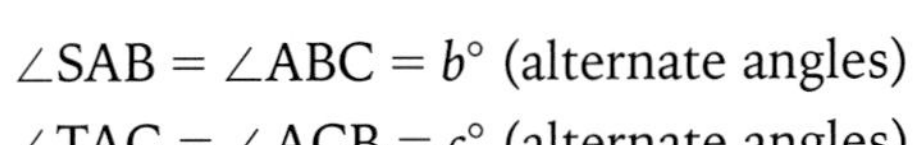

$\angle SAB = \angle ABC = b°$ (alternate angles)

$\angle TAC = \angle ACB = c°$ (alternate angles)

$\angle SAB + \angle BAC + \angle CAT = 180°$ (ST is a straight line)

$\Rightarrow \quad b° + a° + c° = 180°$

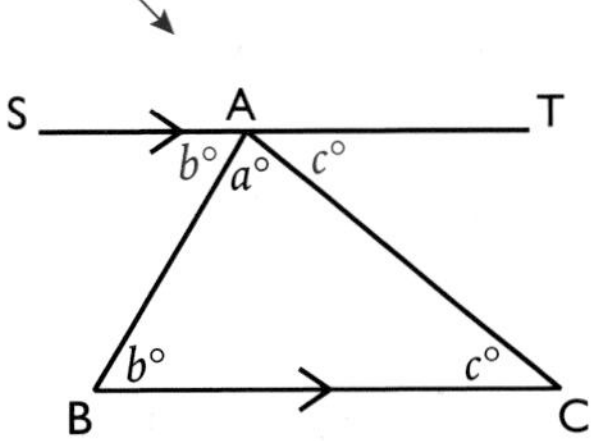

The three angles of any triangle add up to 180°.

Example 1 Calculate the size of ∠LKM.

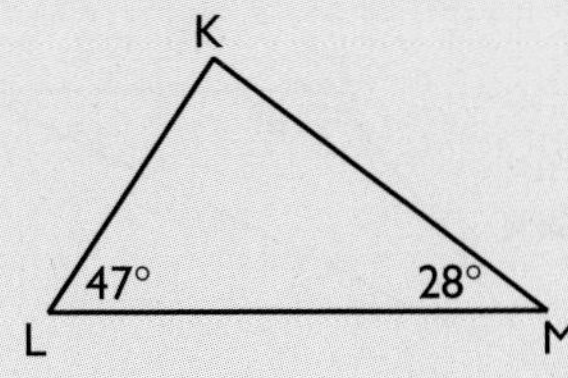

$\angle LKM = 180° - (47° + 28°)$ (third angle in a triangle)

$= 180° - 75°$

$= 105°$

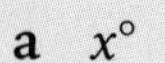

Example 2 Calculate the value of: **a** $x°$ **b** $y°$.

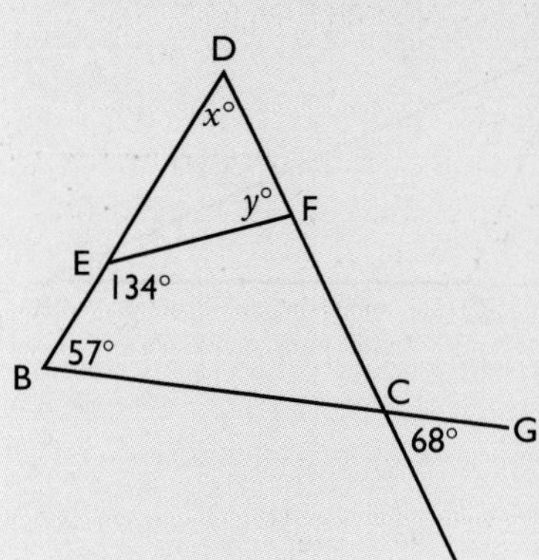

a $\angle DCB = \angle GCH = 68°$ (vertically opposite angles)

$\Rightarrow x° = 180° - (57° + 68°)$ (third angle in triangle BCD)

$= 180° - 125°$

$\Rightarrow x° = 55°$

b $\angle DEF = 180° - \angle BEF$ (DEB is a straight line)

$= 180° - 134° = 46°$

$\Rightarrow y° = 180° - (46° + 55°)$ (third angle in triangle DEF)

$= 180° - 101°$

$\Rightarrow y° = 79°$

Remember to show your reasoning where possible.

Exercise 2.1

1 Calculate the size of the third angle in each of these triangles:

a

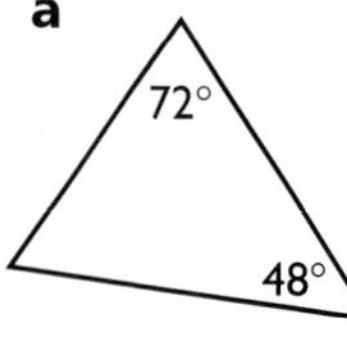

b

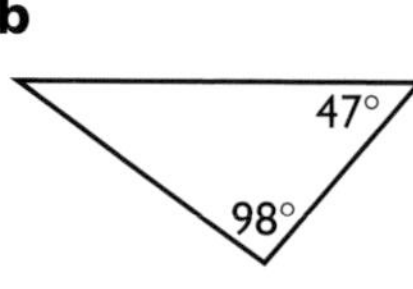

c

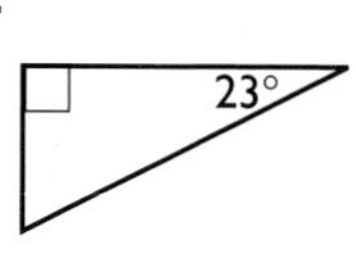

d

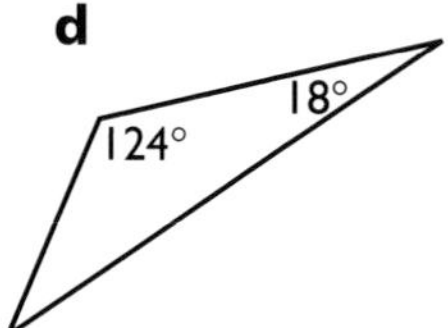

2 Find the size of each unmarked angle in the triangular shapes:

a 123° 28°

b

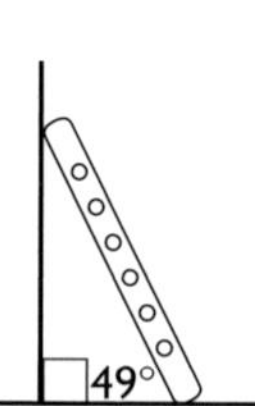

c

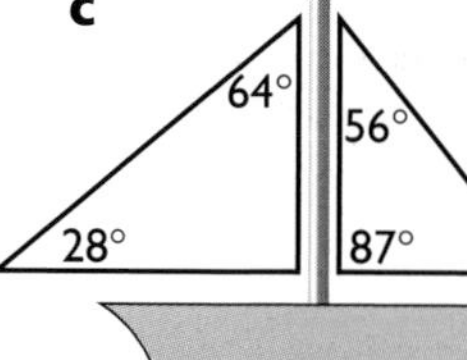

d

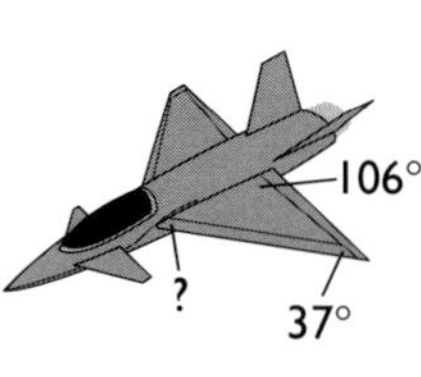

3 These triangles are isosceles. Calculate the size of each unmarked angle.

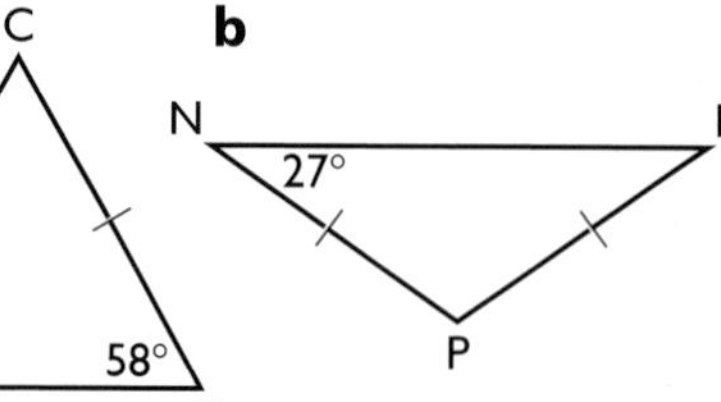

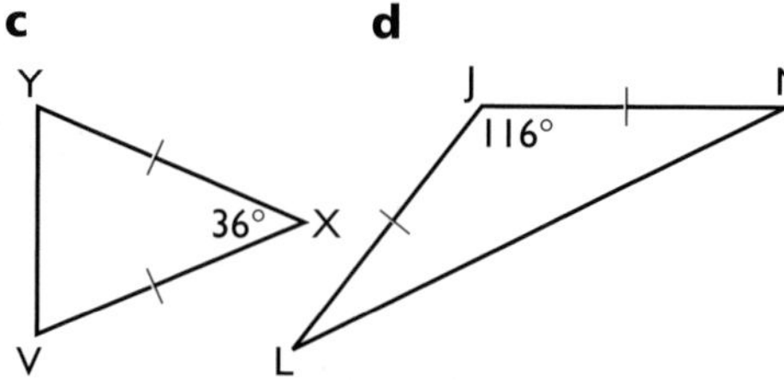

4 For each triangle: **i** calculate the size of each unmarked angle
ii decide whether the triangle is isosceles or not.

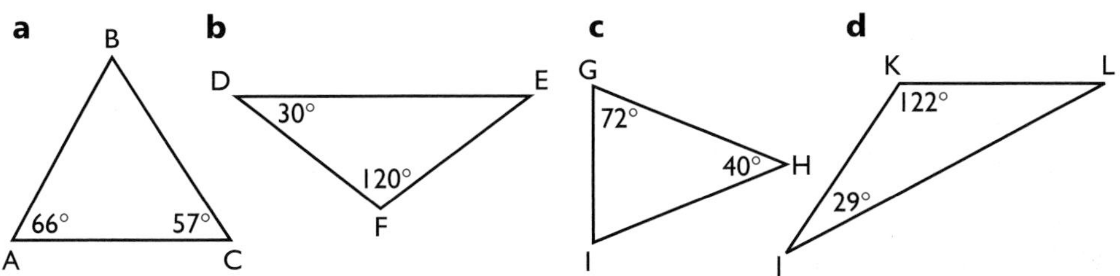

5 Copy each rectangle and fill in the size of each unmarked angle.

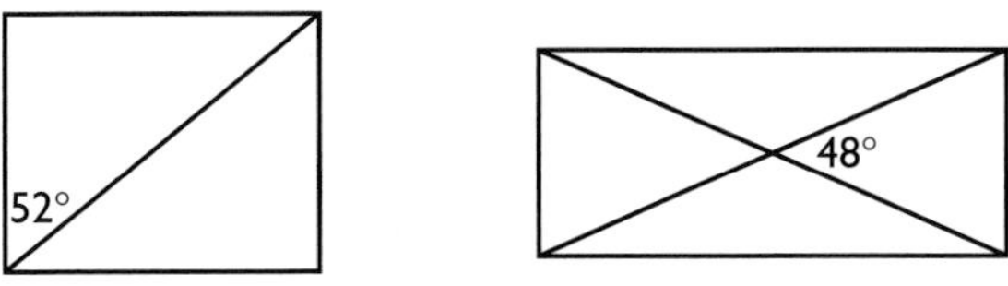

6 Find the size of each lettered angle.

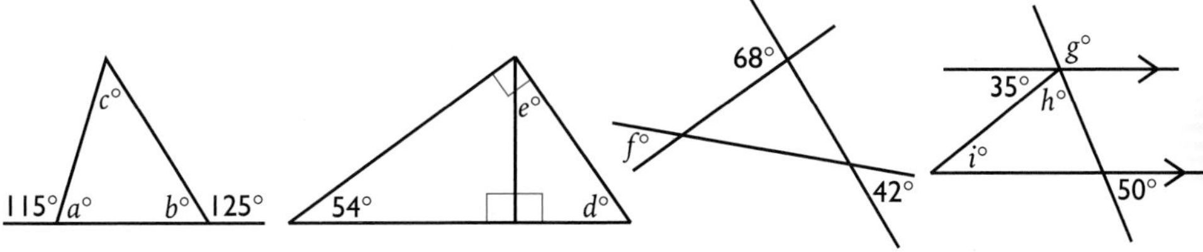

7 Copy the diagrams and find the size of each angle.

a

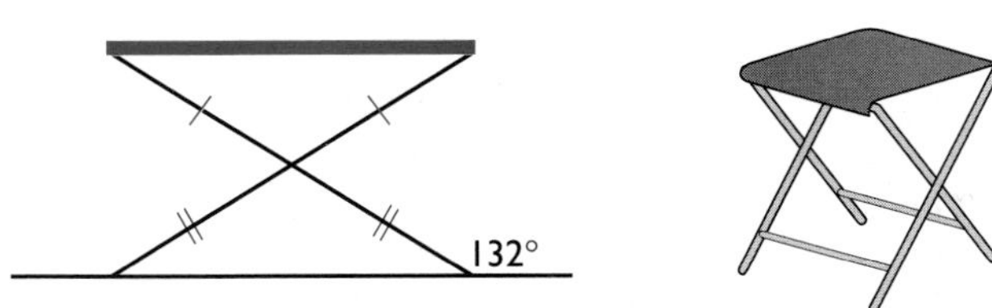

b

Exercise 2.2

1 **a** Show that △ABC is a right-angled triangle.

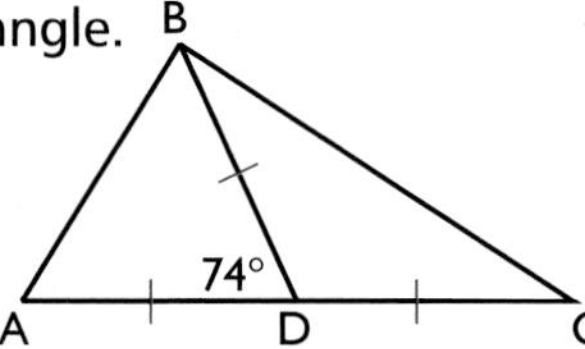

b Show that △PQR is a right-angled triangle when $x =$

i 60

ii 40

iii 100.

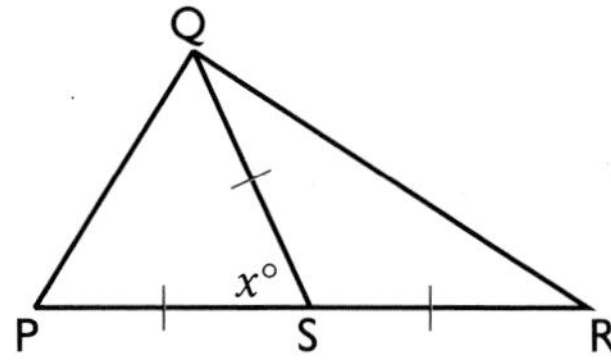

c Can you prove that the triangle is right-angled for all x° between 0° and 180°?

2 **a** What does $x° + 2x° + 3x°$ equal in △KLM?

b Hence find the value of x.

c What are the sizes of the angles of △KLM?

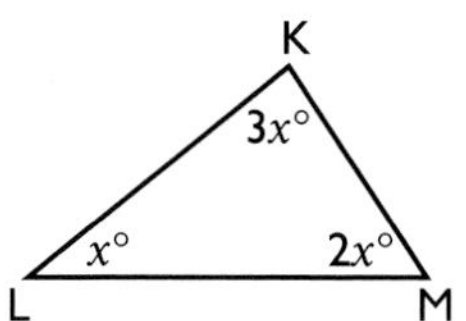

3 **i** For each of the triangles below form an equation in a.

ii Solve each equation and hence find the sizes of the angles of the triangles.

a

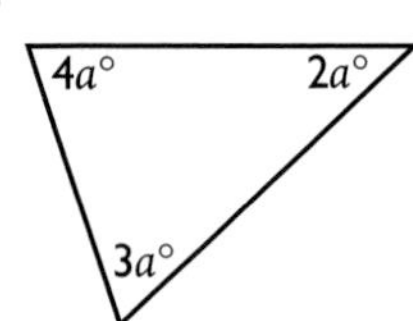

b

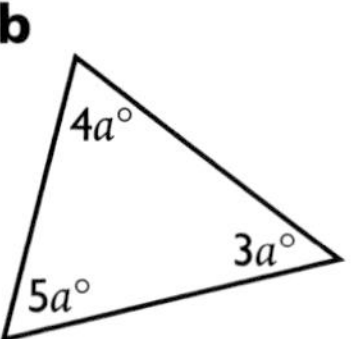

c

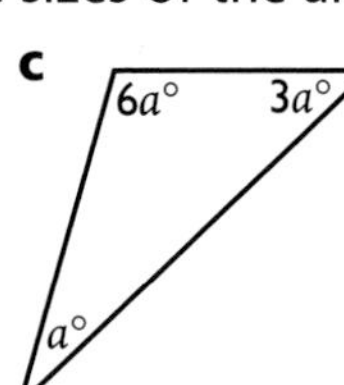

d

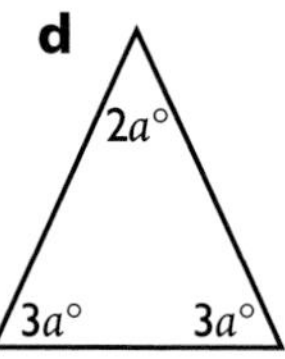

4 **a** Find the value of x and hence find the sizes of the angles of △DEF.

b Can you find another way of calculating the value of x?

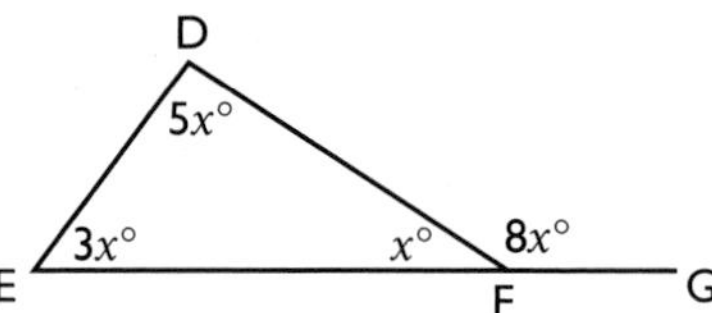

5 For each triangle: **i** form an equation in x **ii** solve it
iii calculate the angles of the triangle.

a

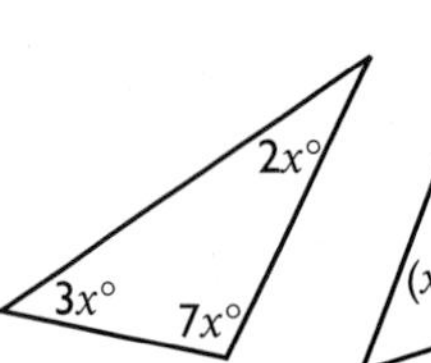

b

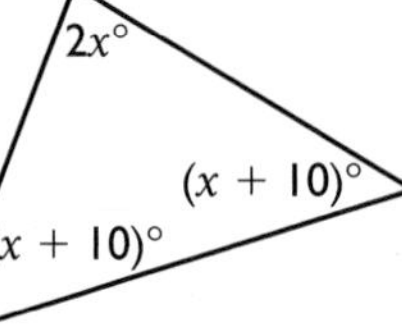

c

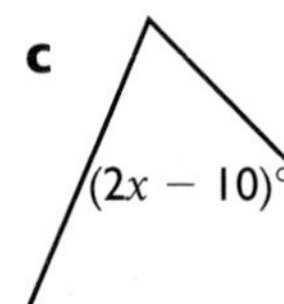

d

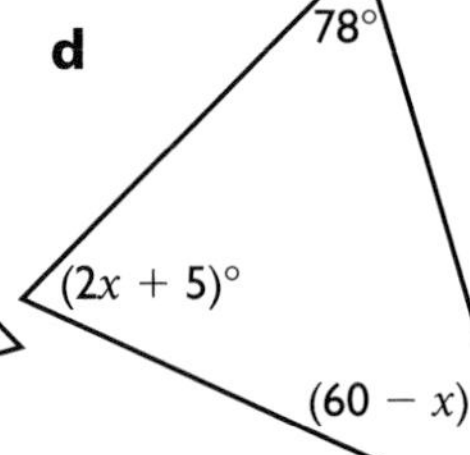

Investigation

Draw any two lines PQ and RS.
Draw a third line TU,
cutting across them.
Find the sum $a + b$ by measurement.
Draw another line, VW, cutting the first two, and find the sum $c + d$.

Why is $a + b = c + d$?

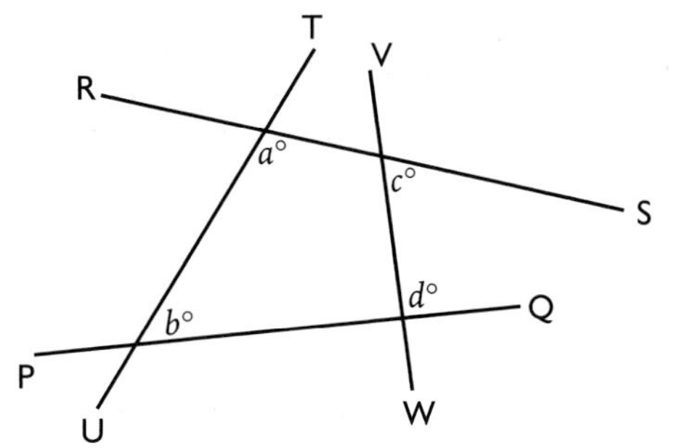

Brainstormer

A

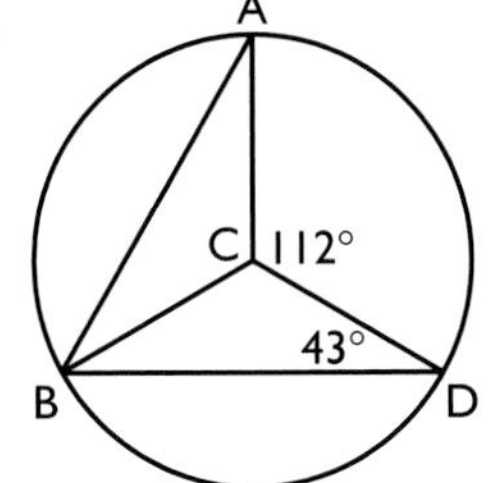

C is the centre of the circle.
Calculate the sizes of the angles of $\triangle ABC$.
(Hint: mark equal lengths.)

B

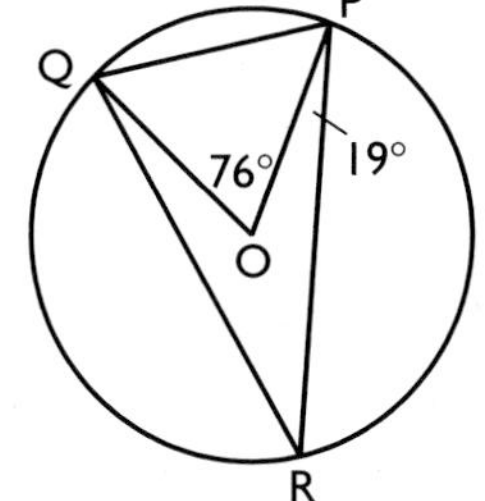

O is the centre of the circle.
Calculate the size of $\angle PRQ$.

(Hint: draw another radius.)

3 Drawing triangles

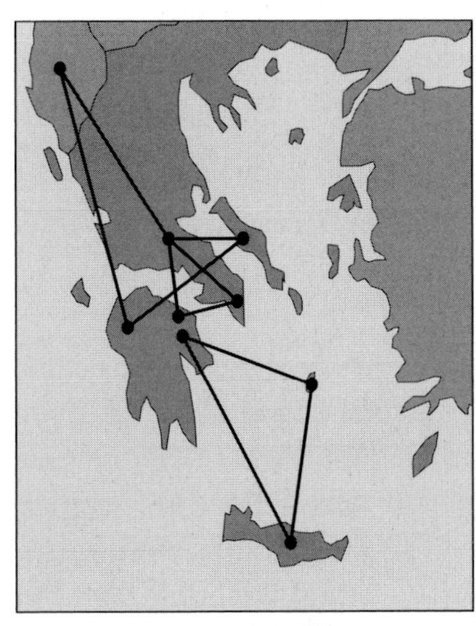

To be able to draw triangles accurately is an important skill.
We can use the drawings to solve real-life problems.

Map makers use a process called **triangulation** to construct their maps accurately.

What is the least amount of information we need before we can draw a triangle?

Note: Because we know the three angles of a triangle sum to 180°, we can calculate the size of the third angle when we are given the size of two.

E

Given the size of two/three angles (AAA)

As these three triangles illustrate, just knowing the angles is not enough information for us to draw a triangle as many different sized triangles fit this description.

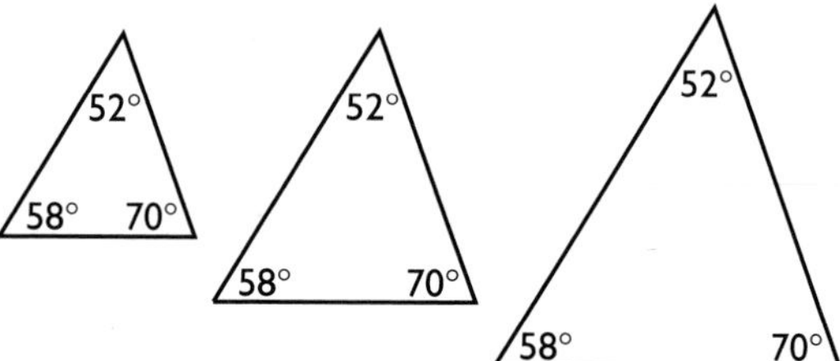

Given the length of one side and the size of two angles (ASA)

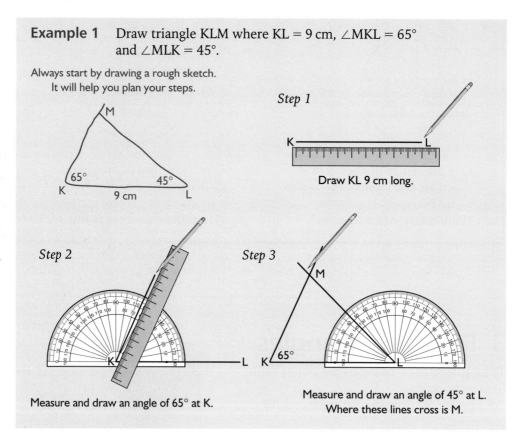

Example 1 Draw triangle KLM where KL = 9 cm, ∠MKL = 65° and ∠MLK = 45°.

Always start by drawing a rough sketch. It will help you plan your steps.

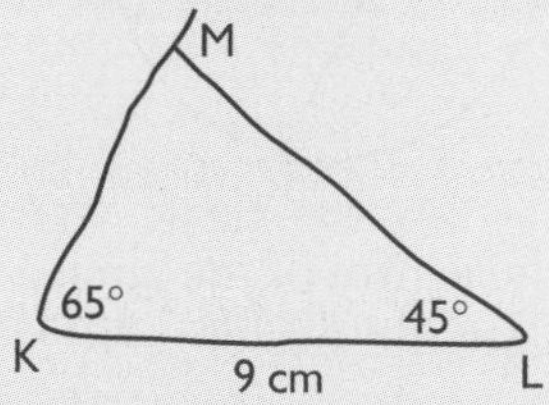

M
65°
45°
K
9 cm
L

Step 1

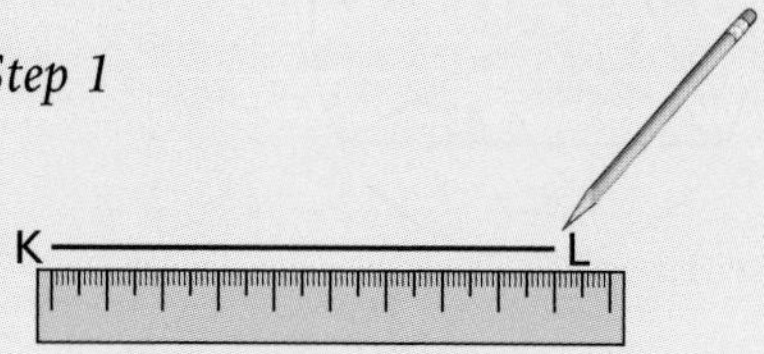

Draw KL 9 cm long.

Step 2

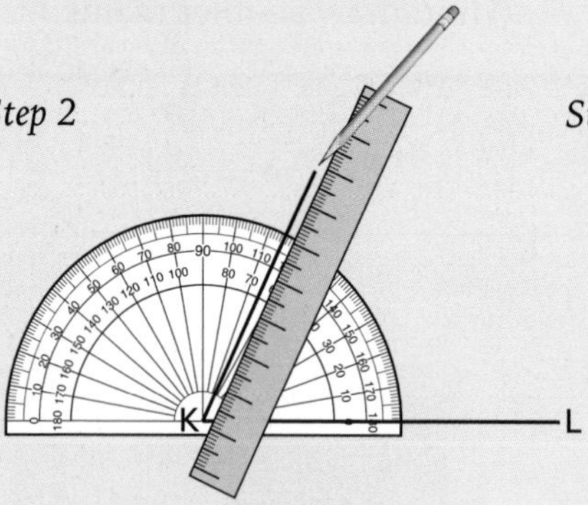

Measure and draw an angle of 65° at K.

Step 3

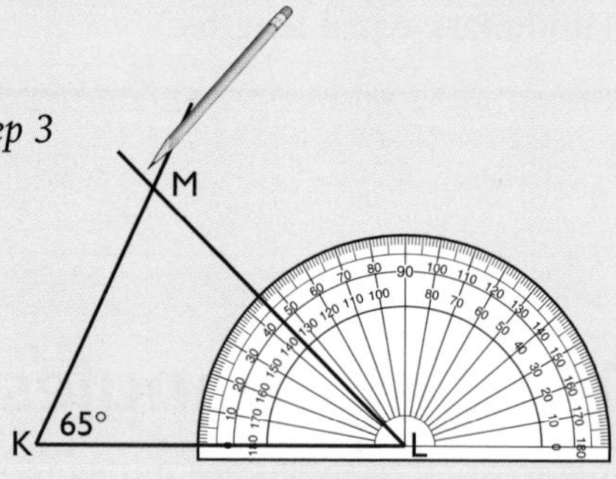

Measure and draw an angle of 45° at L. Where these lines cross is M.

Exercise 3.1

1 **a** Follow the three steps above to draw triangle KLM.

b Measure the third angle, KML, and check your accuracy by calculation, using the angle sum of a triangle.

2 Draw the following triangles as accurately as you can. Always start by drawing a rough sketch.
Measure the third angle of each triangle, then check your accuracy by calculation.

- **a** Triangle ABC, with AB = 10 cm, ∠CAB = 52° and ∠CBA = 78°.
- **b** Triangle CEG, with CE = 8 cm, ∠GEC = 100° and ∠GCE = 46°.
- **c** Triangle LMN, with LN = 9·5 cm, ∠MNL = 95° and ∠MLN = 54°.

3 Draw these triangles as accurately as you can.
In each case measure the length of the shortest side of the triangle.

- **a** Triangle STU, with ST = 9 cm, ∠SUT = 86° and ∠UTS = 48°.
(Hint: first of all calculate the size of ∠UST.)
- **b** Triangle XYZ, with YZ = 5·4 cm, ∠XZY = 54° and ∠YXZ = 62°.

4 Make an accurate drawing of these two rectangles. Measure the lengths of the diagonals, giving your answers correct to the nearest millimetre.

a

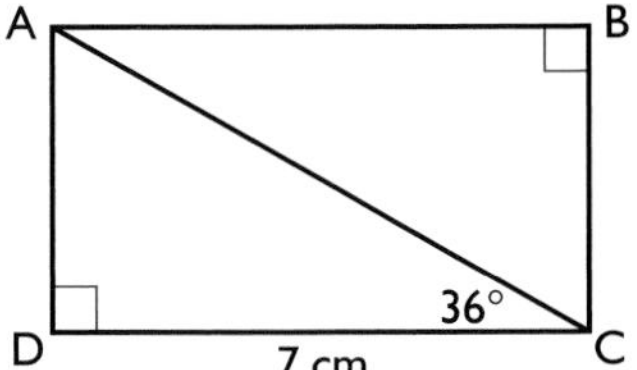

b

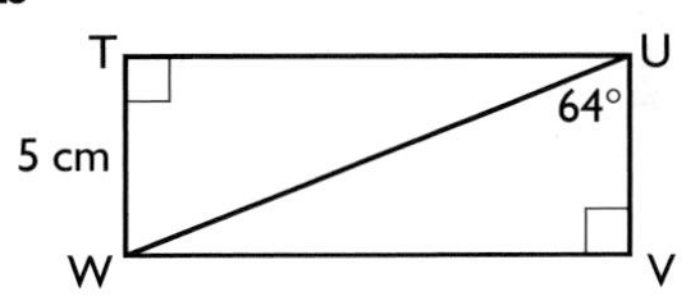

Given two sides and the angle between them (SAS)

Example 2 Draw triangle EFG with EF = 8 cm, FG = 7 cm and ∠EFG = 57°.

First draw a rough sketch.

G
7 cm
57°
E
8 cm
F

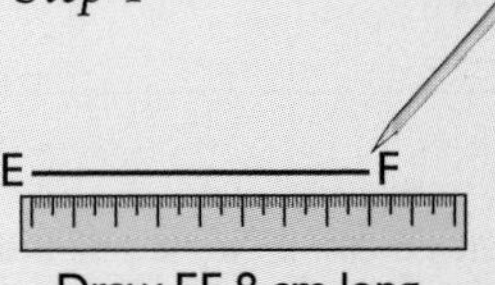

Draw EF 8 cm long.

Step 2

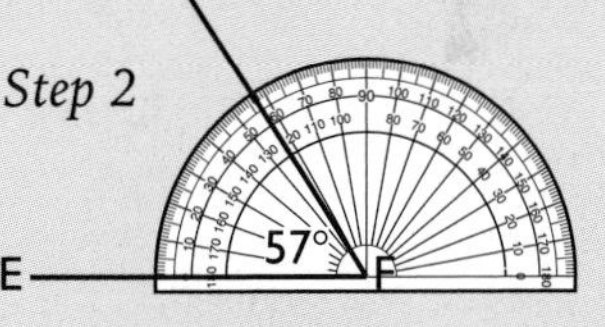

Draw an angle of 57° at F.

Step 3

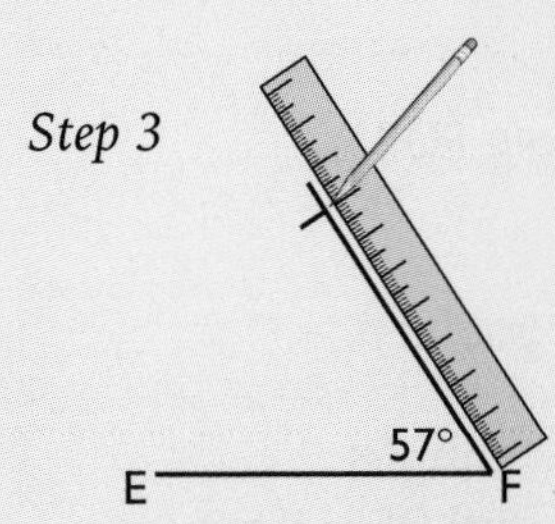

Mark G, 7 cm from F.

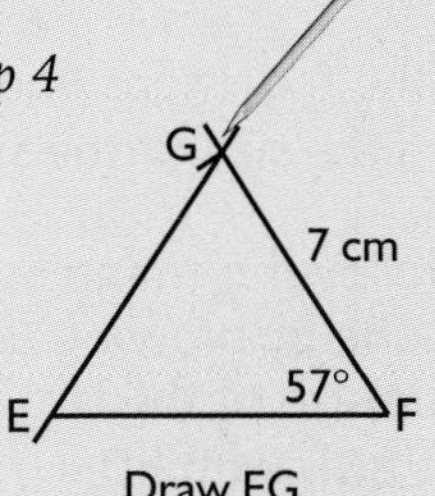

Draw EG.

5 **a** Follow the four steps above to draw △EFG.
b Measure the length of the third side, EG.

6 Draw these triangles as accurately as you can. Start each one by drawing a rough sketch. Measure the length of the third side of each triangle.

a Triangle HIJ, with HI = 7 cm, IJ = 9 cm and ∠HIJ = 46°.

b Triangle QRS, with QR = 8·5 cm, RS = 6·4 cm and ∠QRS = 110°.

c Triangle VWX, with XW = 5·8 cm, VX = 7·8 cm and ∠VXW = 84°.

7 Make an accurate drawing of these two isosceles triangles. In each case, measure the length of the third side.

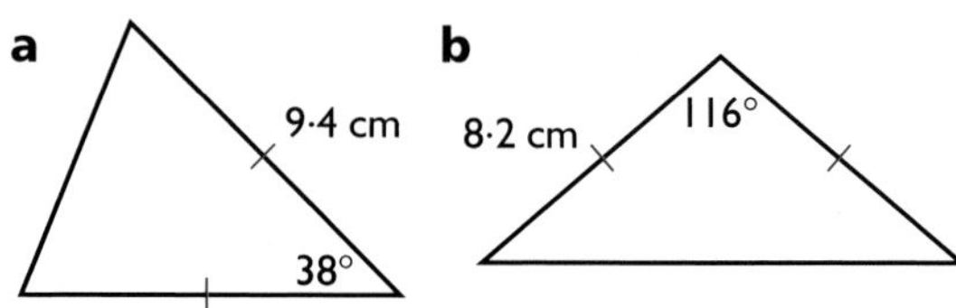

Given three sides (SSS)

Example 3 Draw triangle PQR with PQ = 6 cm, QR = 9 cm and PR = 10 cm.

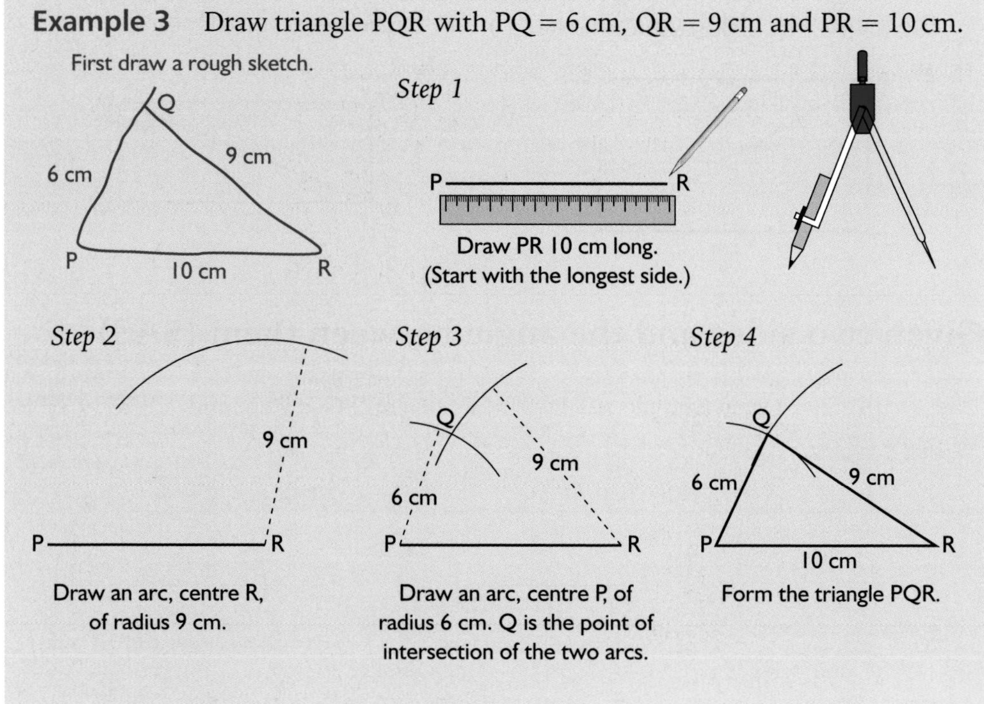

8 **a** Follow the four steps above to draw triangle PQR.

b Measure the size of the smallest angle.

9 Draw the following triangles as accurately as you can. Start each one by drawing a rough sketch. Measure the size of the largest angle of each triangle.

a Triangle BDF, with BD = 7 cm, BF = 8·5 cm and DF = 8 cm.

b Triangle JKL, with KL = 8·4 cm, JL = 9·5 cm and JK = 10·6 cm.

c Triangle VWX, with VX = 5·8 cm, WX = 8·8 cm and VW = 11·6 cm.

10 Draw a triangle whose sides are all 8 cm. Measure the sizes of the angles.

E

Exercise 3.2

1

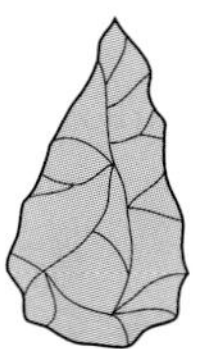

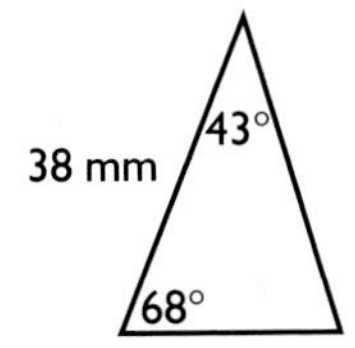

Archaeologists examining a flint arrowhead took various measurements. Some of these are shown in the diagram. By making a suitable drawing, find the sizes of the other two sides of the triangle representing the arrowhead.

2 Make an accurate drawing to help you find the perimeter of this postage stamp.

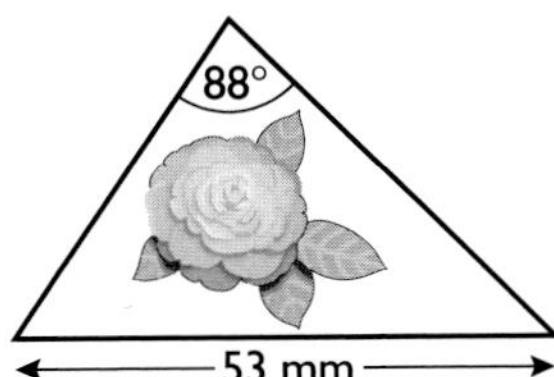

3 Triangles can be dangerous! Make an accurate drawing of the triangle representing the shark's tooth to help you find all the angles.

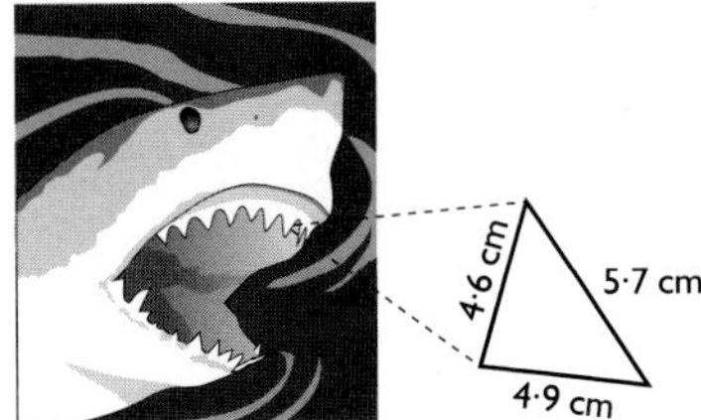

4

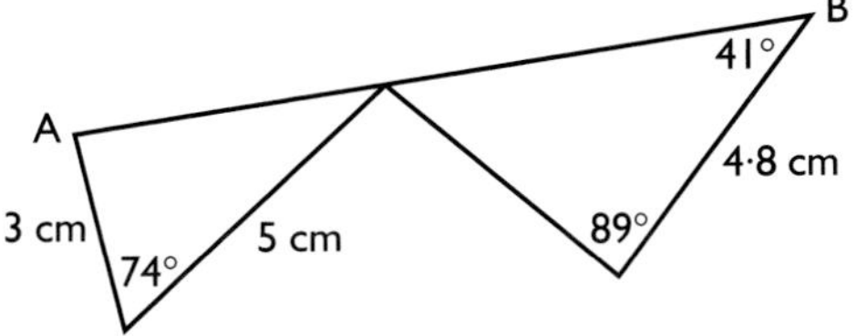

The picture shows a train crossing a bridge in the Yukon. Various measurements have been taken from an enlargement of the picture. Use the information to find the length of the bridge, AB, in the enlargement.

5 Michel was asked to draw a triangle with sides 3 cm, 5 cm and 9 cm.

a Try this yourself. Comment.

b Which of the following sets cannot be the three sides of a triangle?

i 3 cm, 6 cm, 5 cm **ii** 7 cm, 5 cm, 1 cm

iii 4 cm, 8 cm, 3 cm **iv** 7 cm, 7 cm, 5 cm

c Make up a rule that must be true about three lengths before they can be used as the sides of a triangle.

6 Sam drew this rough sketch.

a Draw the 6 cm line.

b Draw the 35° angle.

c Use a set of compasses to draw an arc of radius 3 cm. Comment.

4 Measuring heights and distances

For thousands of years accurate drawings of triangles have been used to solve problems. Scale drawings of triangles allow us to measure lengths and angles which otherwise would be difficult or impossible to measure.

Example

A castle is 580 m due east of a tower. A bridge is 750 m from the tower on a bearing of 142°. How far is the bridge from the castle?

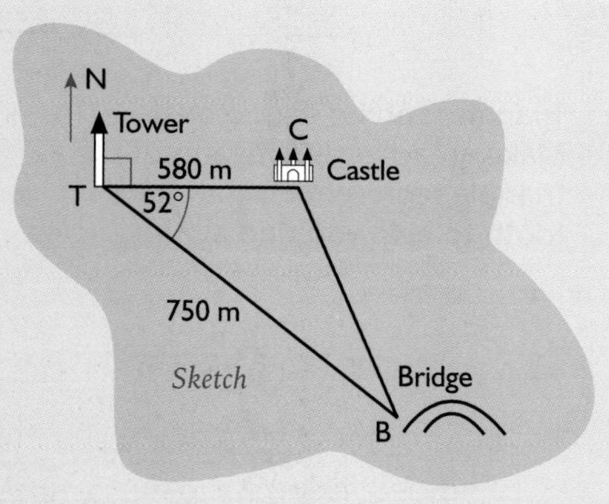

Step 1

Decide on a suitable scale.
If we let **1 cm represent 100 m**, then the line representing 750 m will be 7·5 cm long and the line representing 580 m will be 5·8 cm long.

Step 2

Draw the triangle TCB to this scale.
∠CTB will be 52°.

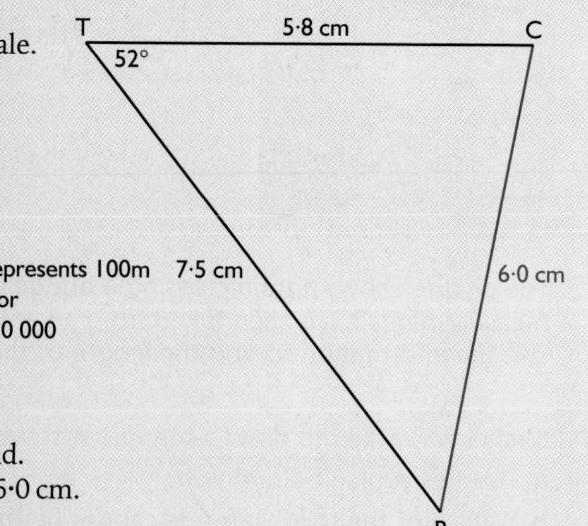

Step 3

CB is the distance we want to find.
Measure CB and you'll find it is 6·0 cm.

Step 4

Scale it up: 6·0 × 100 m = 600 metres.
The bridge is 600 m from the castle.

E

Exercise 4.1

1 **a** Using a scale of 1 cm to represent 4 m, make a scale drawing of $\triangle TSF$. (You will need a ruler and a protractor.)

b From your scale drawing find the height of the tree.

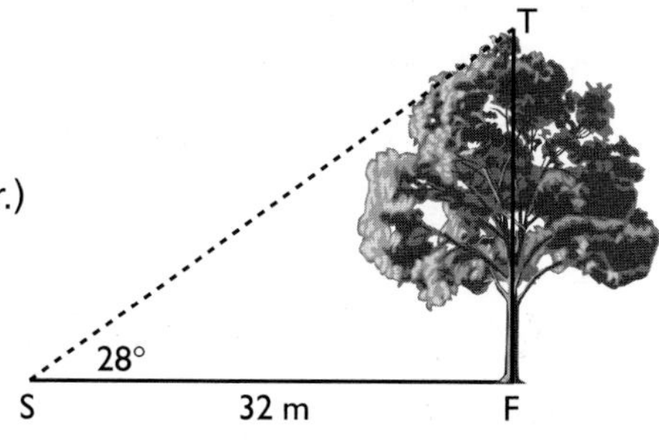

2 Two buildings are 60 metres apart. The angle of elevation from the top of the smaller building to the top of the taller building is 33° (see sketch).

a Choose a suitable scale and make a scale drawing of triangle TAS.

b From your scale drawing find the difference in height of the two buildings.

3 The boat at B is 520 m due north of the harbour at H. The lighthouse at L is 840 m from the harbour on a bearing of 068° from the harbour.

a Using a scale of 1 : 10 000, make a scale drawing of the triangle.

b From your scale drawing find the distance from the boat to the lighthouse.

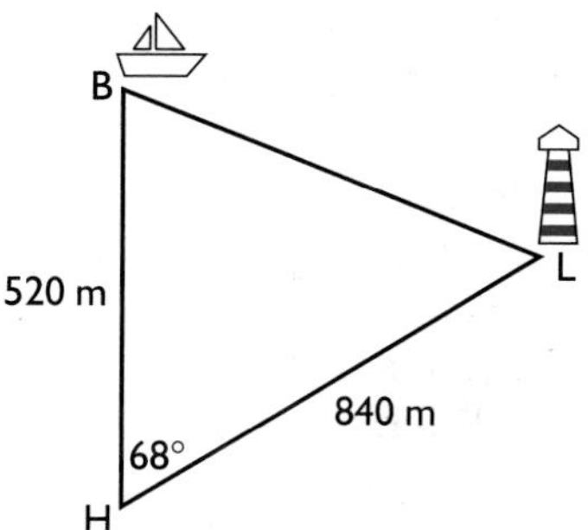

4 **a** Choose a suitable scale and make a scale drawing of $\triangle ABC$.

b From your scale drawing find the height of the roof (i.e. the length of the dotted line).

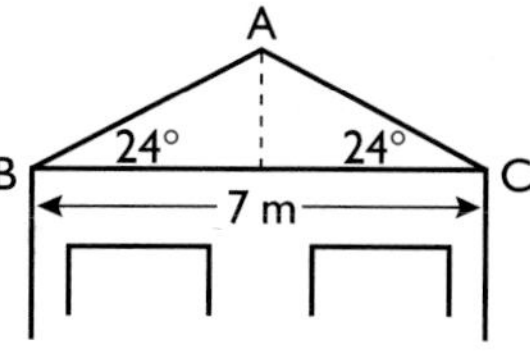

5 The well is due south of the farmhouse.

a Using 1 cm to represent 200 m, make a scale drawing of $\triangle FWC$.

b From your scale drawing find the bearing of the camp from

i the well

ii the farmhouse.

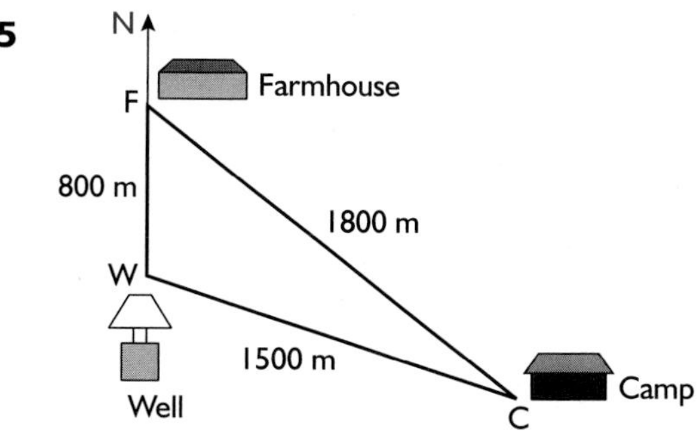

E

6 A section of the side of a bridge is shown in the diagram.

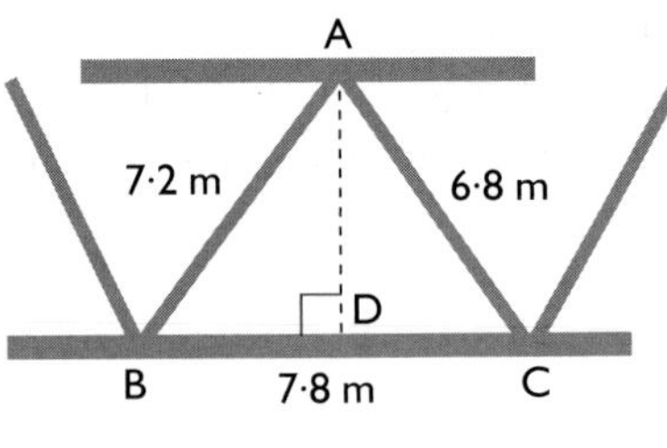

- **a** Choose a suitable scale and make a scale drawing of $\triangle ABC$.
- **b** From your scale drawing measure the angles of the triangle.
- **c** Find the height of the bridge, AD.

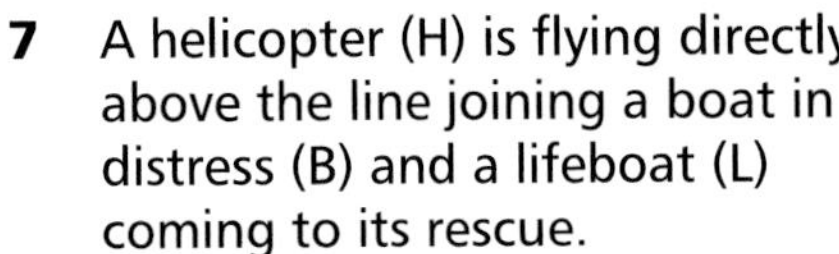

7 A helicopter (H) is flying directly above the line joining a boat in distress (B) and a lifeboat (L) coming to its rescue.

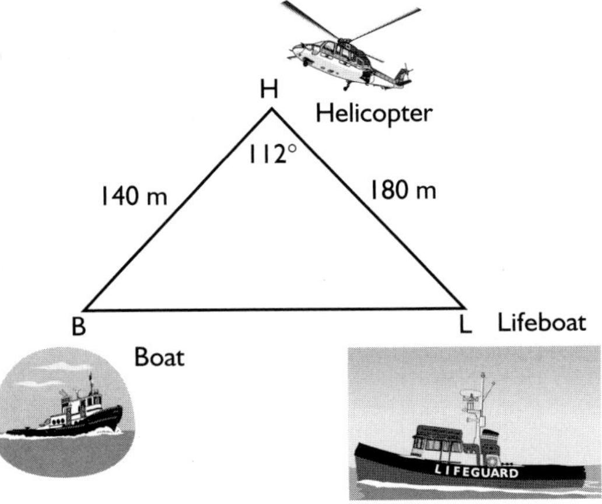

- **a** Using a scale of 1 : 2000 make a scale drawing of $\triangle HBL$.
- **b** From your scale drawing find how far the lifeboat is from the boat in distress.
- **c** What is the height of the helicopter?

E

Exercise 4.2

1 A hang-glider takes off from the side of a hill at T.
His friend is 300 m downhill at F.
His flight path is at an angle of 39° to the slope of the hill and it takes him directly over his friend after flying 190 metres.

- **a** How high above his friend is he as he passes over him?
- **b** How far is he from his friend after another 100 m of flight in the same direction?

190 m T
H 39°
h
300 m
F

2 A helicopter searching for a man overboard flies 20 metres above the sea.
A yachtsman measures the angle of elevation of the helicopter.
At H_1 this angle is 42°. At H_2 it is 15°.

- **a** How far has the helicopter gone between these two points?
- **b** The helicopter creates a disturbance in the sea at D_1 and D_2. How far are these points from the yacht?

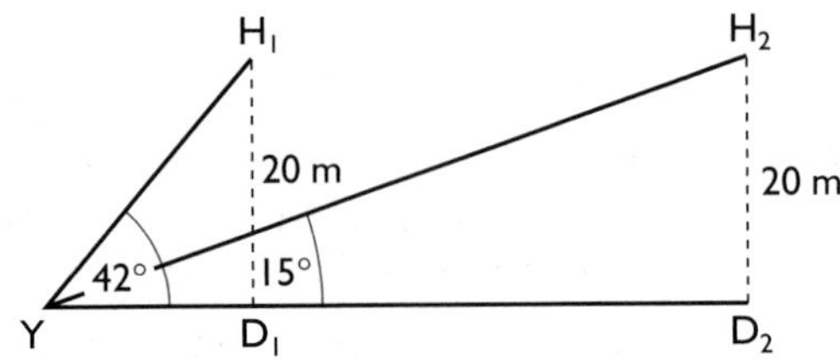

3 Helene wants to find out how tall the Eiffel tower is.
From point A she measures the angle of elevation to the top as 37°.
From point B, 170 m closer to the tower, the angle of elevation is 52°.

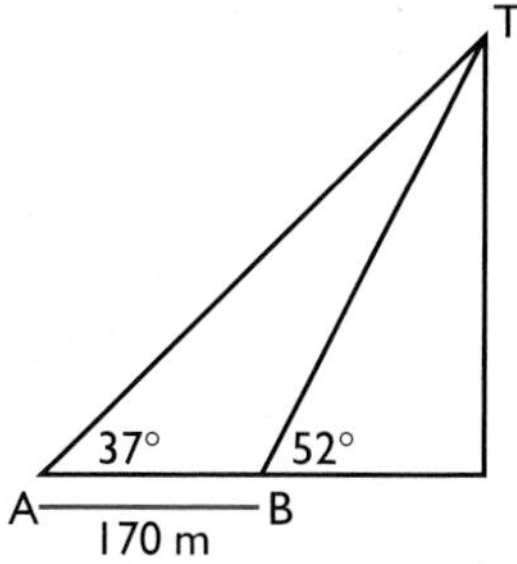

a How high is the Eiffel tower according to Helene's measurements?

b The Eiffel tower is 320 m tall.
How does Helene's figure compare?

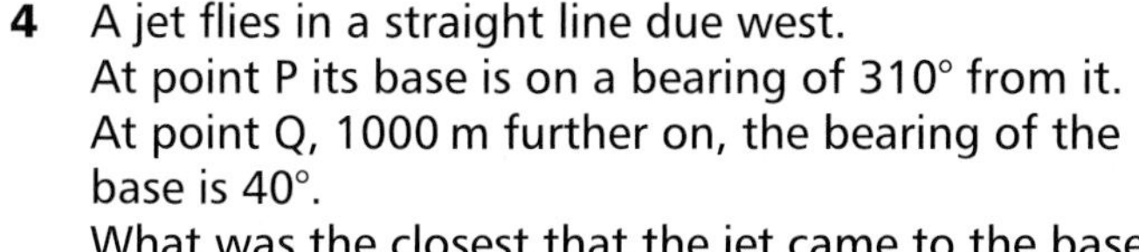

4 A jet flies in a straight line due west.
At point P its base is on a bearing of 310° from it.
At point Q, 1000 m further on, the bearing of the base is 40°.
What was the closest that the jet came to the base?

Brainstormer

The receiver on a radio telescope sits on the vertex of a tetrahedron structure made out of girders. Each of the six girders is 15 metres long.

How high above the triangle ABC is the receiver R?

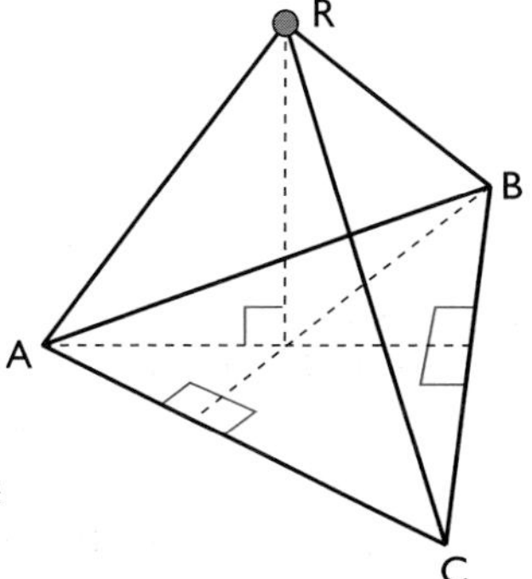

5 Drawing more triangles

We are able to draw a triangle if we are given any one of these sets of data:

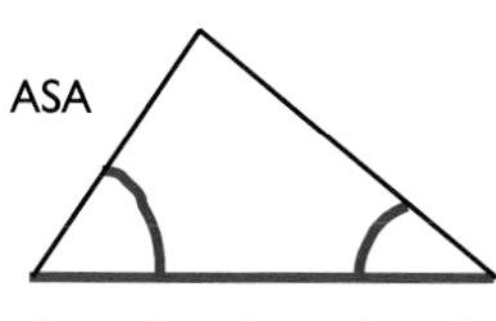

Given 2 angles and a side

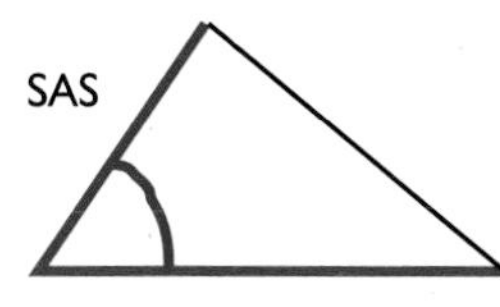

Given 2 sides and the angle between them

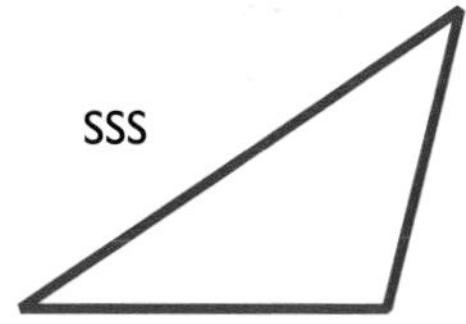

Given 3 sides

Are there any other sets of data that will enable us to draw a specified triangle?

Given two sides and an angle – not the angle between the two sides (ASS)

Example 3 Draw triangle RST with RS = 9 cm, ST = 8 cm and ∠TRS = 47°.

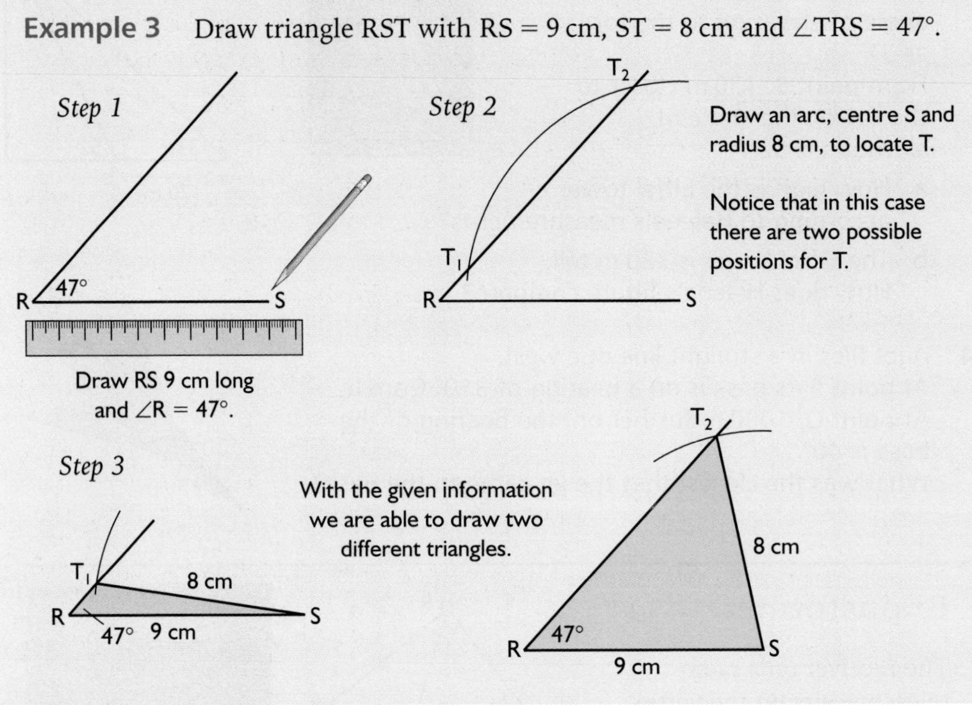

We will not always be able to draw two triangles.
Given two sides and an angle (not the angle between the two sides), we are sometimes able to draw two triangles, as in the example above, or one triangle (when RS ≤ ST or ∠STR = 90°) or indeed none, as shown in the diagrams below.

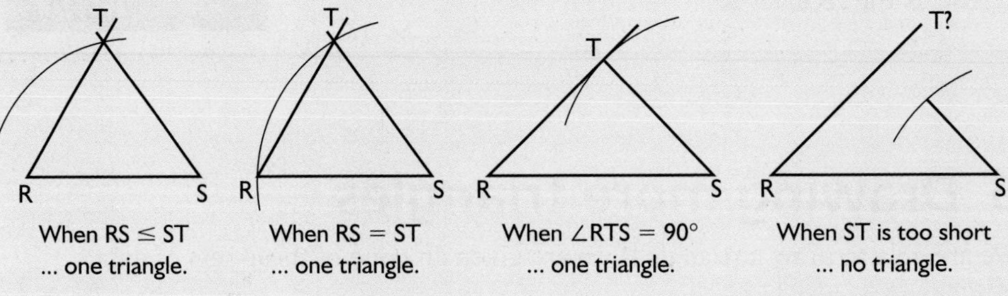

Exercise 5.1

1 **a** Carry out the steps in the example above to draw, as accurately as you can, the two possible triangles RST.

b What are the two possible lengths of RT?

c What are the sizes of the angles in the two triangles?

2 Attempt to draw the following triangles.
In each case say whether there are two possible triangles, one possible triangle or if it is impossible to draw the triangle.
Where it is possible to draw the triangle, find the length(s) of the third side.

- **a** Triangle VWX, with VW = 10·2 cm, WX = 7·4 cm and ∠XVW = 38°.
- **b** Triangle DEF, with DE = 8·7 cm, EF = 8·2 cm and ∠FDE = 68°.
- **c** Triangle LMN, with LM = 9·6 cm, MN = 9·6 cm and ∠NLM = 72°.
- **d** Triangle GHI, with GH = 10·4 cm, GI = 9·2 cm and ∠GHI = 66°.
- **e** Triangle CDE, with CD = 9·6 cm, CE = 7·8 cm and ∠CDE = 42°.

3 The cave is 850 metres due east of the bridge.
It is known that treasure is buried north-east of the bridge and at a distance of 700 metres from the cave.
Make a scale drawing of the map and use it to find the possible distances of the treasure from the bridge.

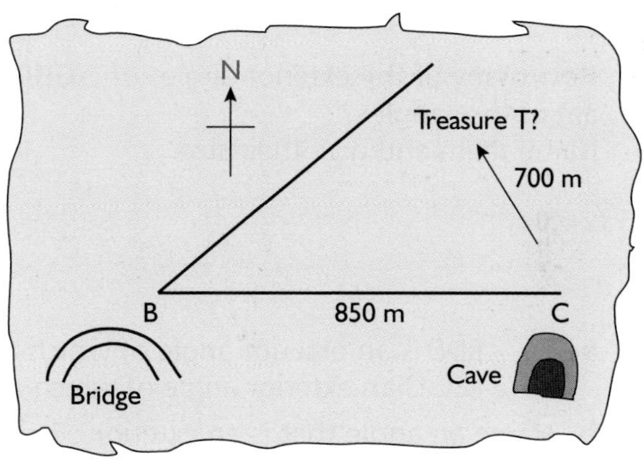

6 The exterior angles of a triangle

In triangle ABC, BA has been extended to D.
The supplement of ∠BAC is ∠CAD.

∠BAC is an **interior** angle of the triangle.
∠CAD is an **exterior** angle of the triangle.

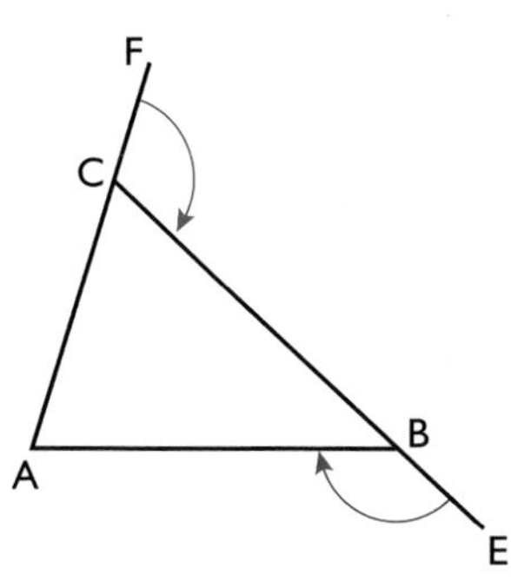

Similarly, ∠ABE is an exterior angle of triangle ABC.
So is ∠BCF.

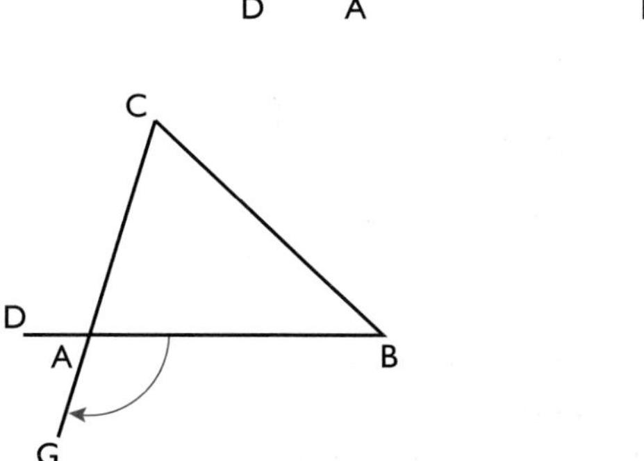

∠BAG is an exterior angle, but ∠DAG is not.

Exercise 6.1

1 **a** Copy the diagram. Mark on it all the exterior angles of △JKL.
(You should find six altogether.)

b Some of the exterior angles are equal. Which ones?
How do you know they are equal?

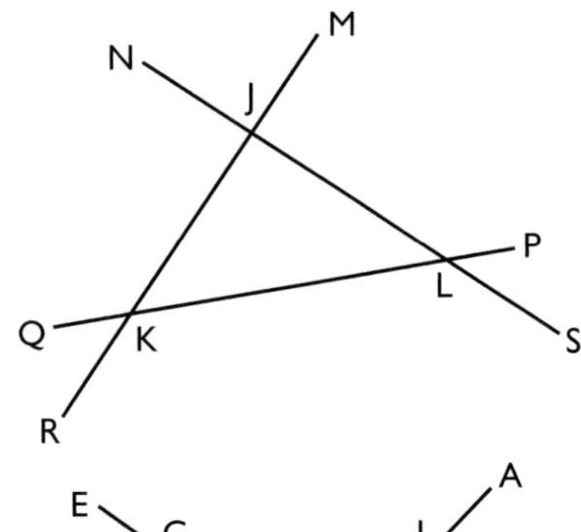

2 How many of the exterior angles of △GHI are obtuse angles?
Name them and give their size.

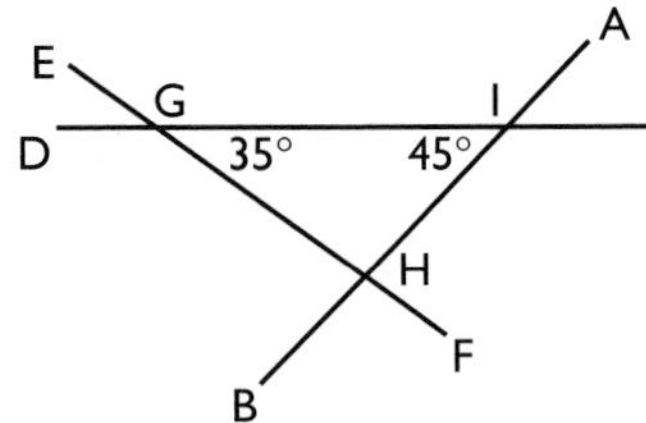

3 **a** **i** ∠BDE is an exterior angle of which triangles?
ii ∠FEC is an exterior angle of which triangles?

b Name an angle that is an exterior angle of both triangles KON and LON.

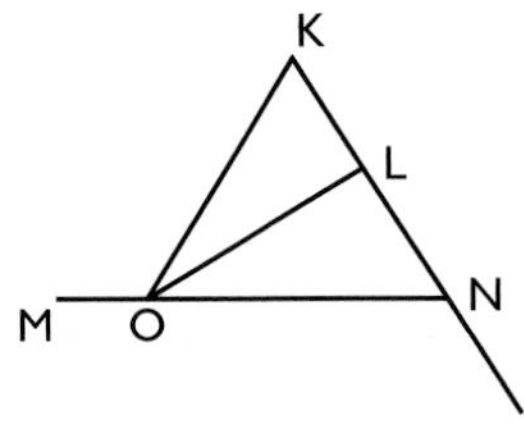

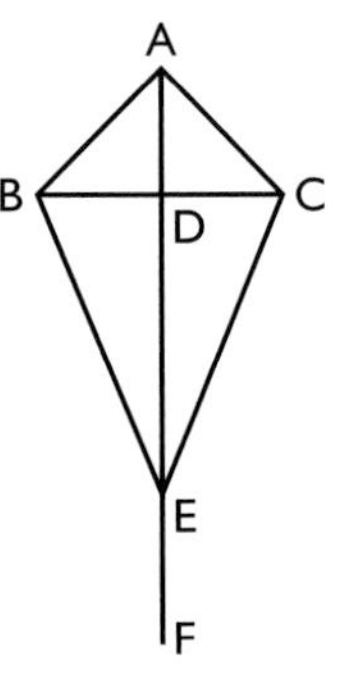

4 Calculate the lettered angle in each diagram and comment.

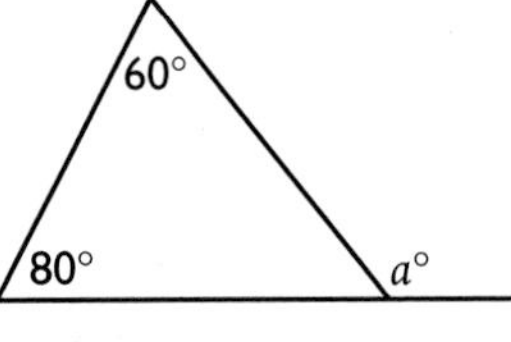

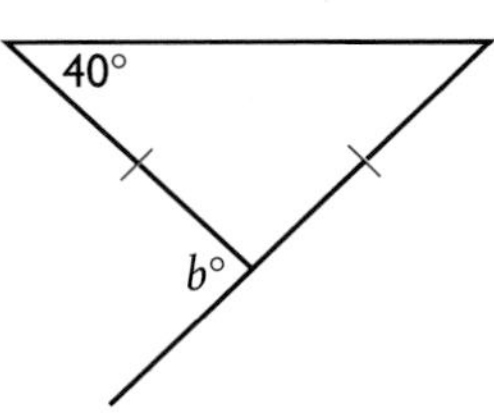

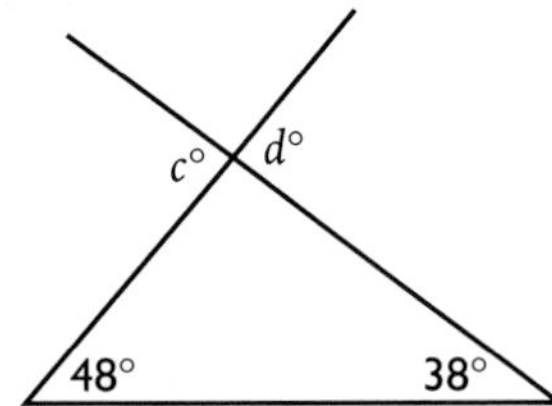

5 **a** Find an expression for the size of ∠ACB in terms of a and b.

b Find an expression for the size of ∠ACD in terms of a and b.

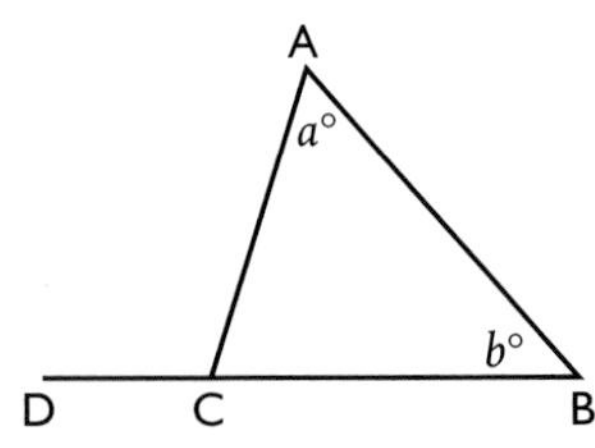

An exterior angle of a triangle is equal to the sum of the two interior opposite angles.

6 **a** Express $\angle$PRS in terms of p and q.

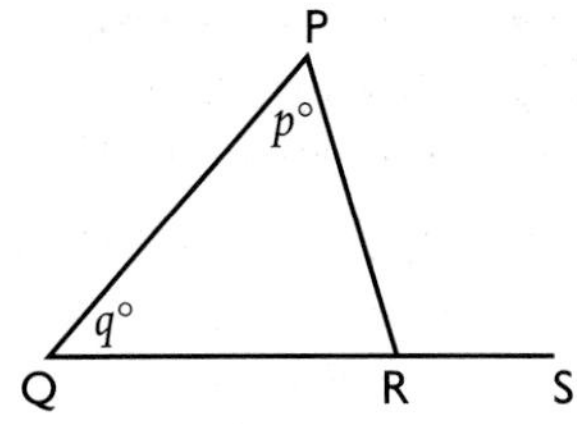

b Find two expressions for the size of $\angle$WXY.

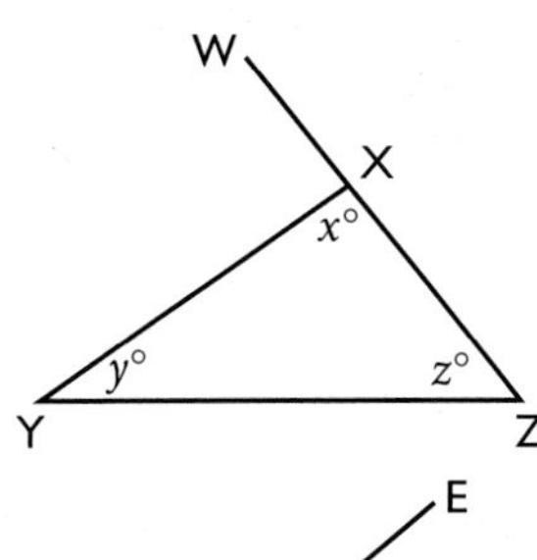

c Find an expression for the size of $\angle$EFG.

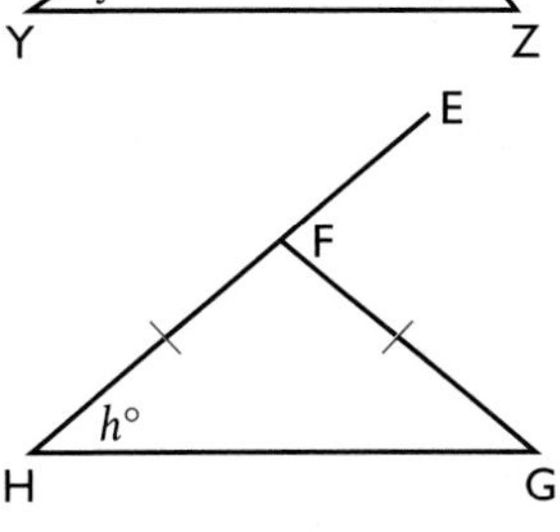

7 Express $\angle$TUV in terms of x.

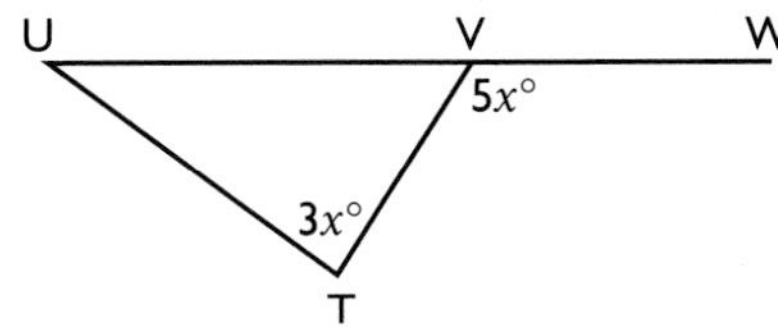

CHECK-UP

1 Calculate the sizes of the lettered angles in these triangles.

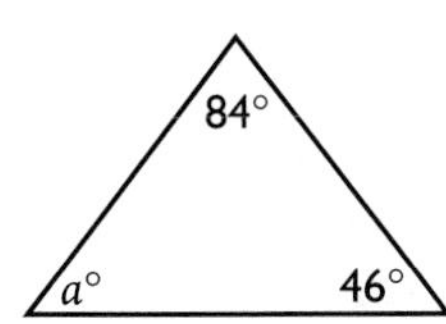

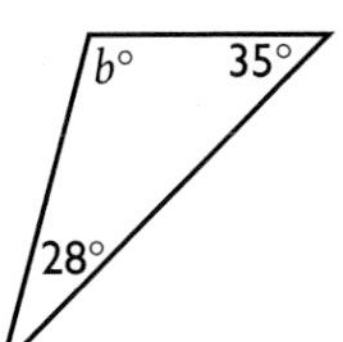

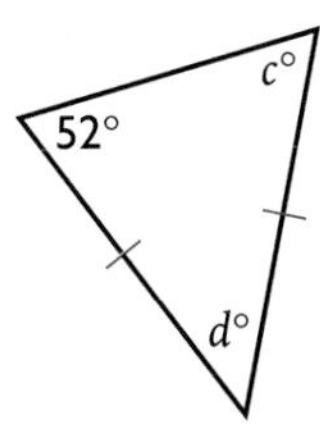

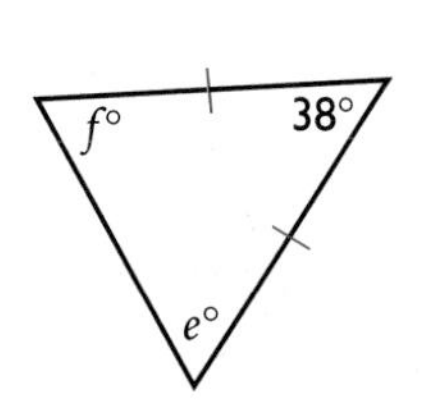

2 Calculate the sizes of all the unmarked angles in the diagrams.

a

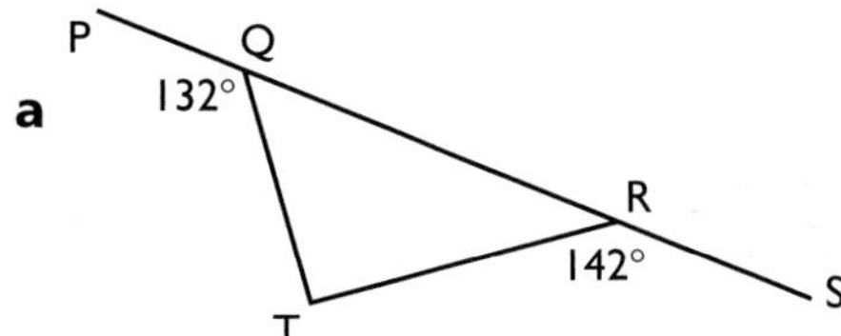

b

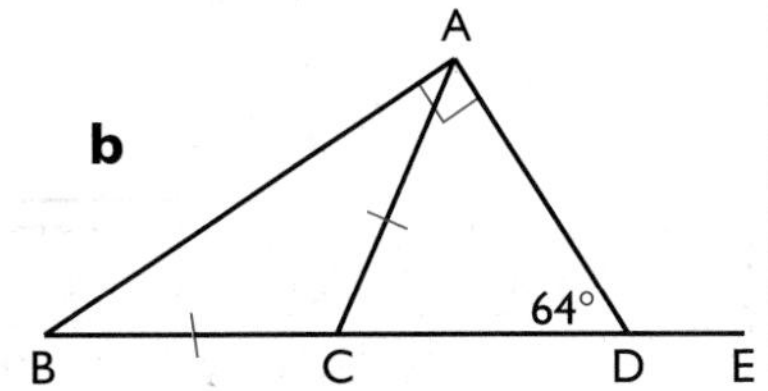

3 **a** **i** Form an equation for each triangle.
ii Solve the equations and hence find the sizes of the angles of the sails.

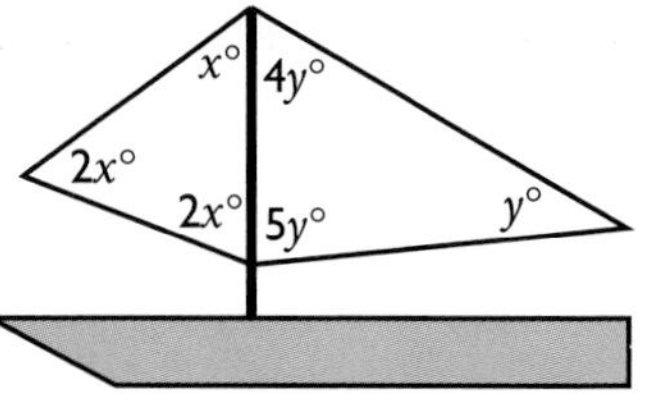

b Copy the rectangular flag and fill in the sizes of all the angles.

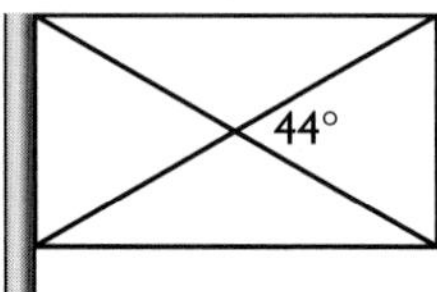

4 **a** Draw △WXY with WX = 10·2 cm, WY = 8·7 cm and ∠XWY = 95°.
b Measure the length of the third side, XY.

5 **a** Draw △FGH with FH = 7·8 cm, GH = 9·6 cm and FG = 8·5 cm.
b Name and measure the size of the largest angle of △FGH.

6 **a** Draw △KLM with ∠KLM = 82°, ∠LKM = 54° and LM = 9·2 cm.
b What is the length of the longest side of △KLM?

7 Gull Island is 70 km south-east of Puffin Island.
Seal Island is 62 km north-east of Gull Island.

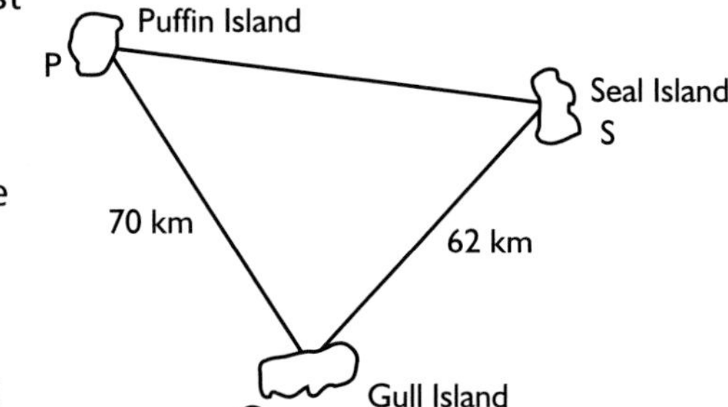

a What angle of the triangle formed by the three islands can you calculate?
b Choose a suitable scale and make a scale drawing of the triangle.
c From your scale drawing find the distance between Puffin Island and Seal Island.

8 **a** Draw △ABC with AB = 10 cm, BC = 8 cm and ∠CAB = 53°.
b Measure the possible lengths of the third side, AC.

9 **a** Name the angle that is an exterior angle of both △GIJ and △GKI.

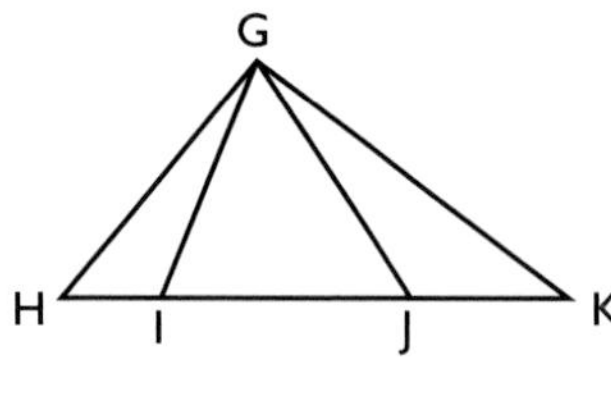

b **i** Name two angles that are exterior angles of both triangles AEB and DEC.

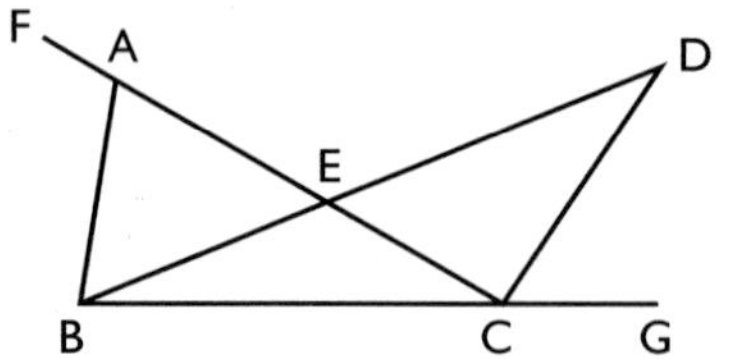

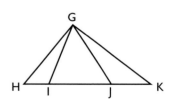

ii Name three angles that are exterior angles of △BEC.

10 What is the size of the exterior angle of $\triangle KLM$?

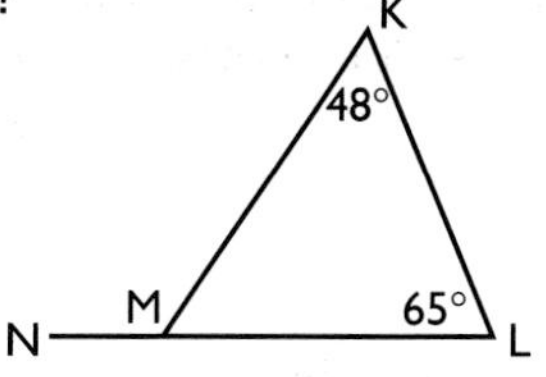

11 Express $\angle PQS$ in terms of x and y.

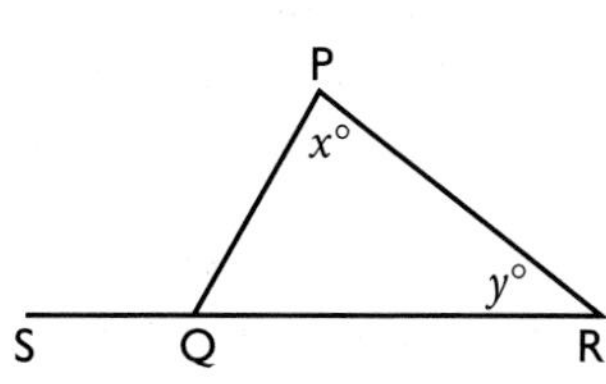

14 Ratio and proportion

The Golden Ratio
When the length of a pentagon is divided by its diagonal the resulting ratio is referred to as the Golden Ratio.

Pythagoras (sixth century BC) thought that the proportions of the human figure involved the Golden Ratio. The height of a man is about 1·618 times the height of his navel. This figure of 1·618 occurs in maths, art, architecture and nature.

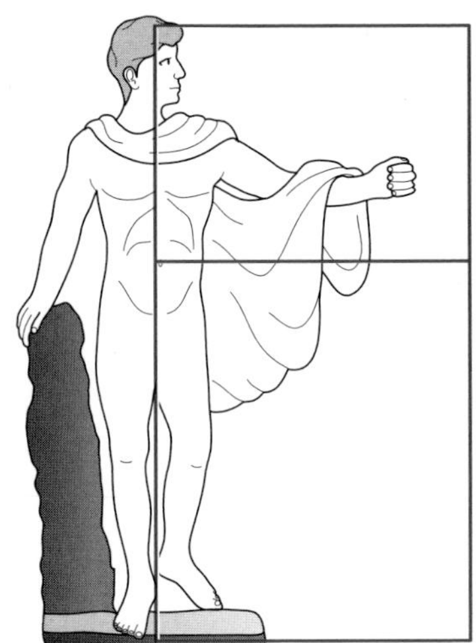

1 Looking back

Exercise 1.1

1 Write each fraction in its simplest form.

a $\frac{2}{4}$ **b** $\frac{3}{9}$ **c** $\frac{2}{8}$ **d** $\frac{6}{9}$ **e** $\frac{6}{8}$ **f** $\frac{10}{12}$ **g** $\frac{12}{16}$ **h** $\frac{12}{15}$

2 Calculate:

a $\frac{1}{2}$ of £14 **b** $\frac{1}{4}$ of 20 kg **c** $\frac{2}{3}$ of 600 ml **d** $\frac{4}{5}$ of 250 m

3 a Change the following volumes into millilitres:
i 3 litres **ii** 0·5 litre **iii** 4·75 litres

b Change the following volumes into litres:
i 2000 ml **ii** 800 ml **iii** 4250 ml

4 a Change the following weights into grams:
i 2 kg **ii** 1·5 kg **iii** 5·6 kg

b Change the following weights into kilograms:
i 4000 g **ii** 50 g **iii** 3250 g

5 In 5 hours Dennis earns £35·00.

a What is his hourly rate of pay?

b How much would he earn in 8 hours at the same rate?

6 Share £360 equally among:

a 3 **b** 8 **c** 10 people

7 What do each of the following measure?

a metres **b** tonnes **c** cm^2

d hectares **e** seconds **f** degrees Celsius

2 Ratio

Ben

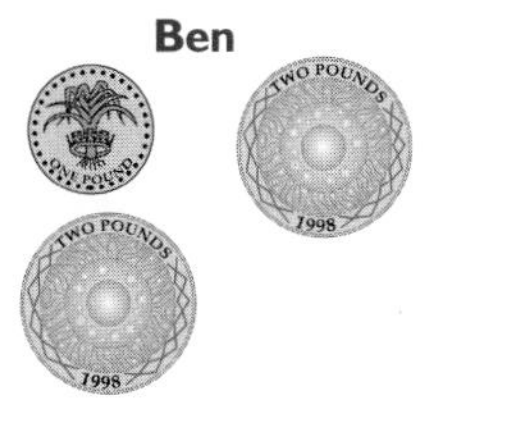

Bee

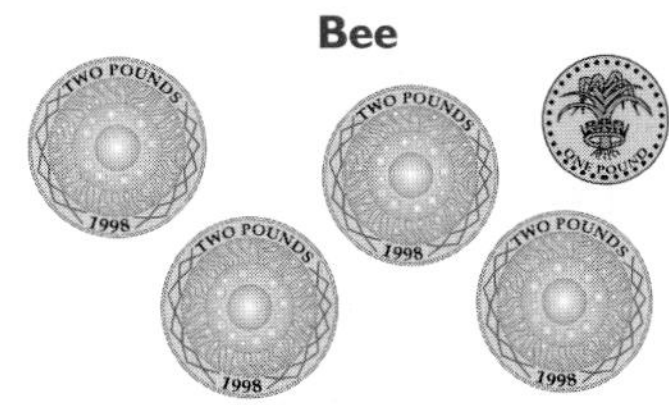

Ben has £5 and Bee has £10.
We say that the ratio of Ben's amount to Bee's is £5 to £10.
This can be expressed as 1 part Ben to 2 parts Bee.
We often write

Ben's amount : Bee's amount = 5 : 10 = 1 : 2

Note that:
- when the units of both sides of the ratio are the same then they can be dropped
- 1 : 2 is called the **simplest form** of the ratio
- we must write 1 : 2 not 2 : 1.

◀◀ E

Exercise 2.1

1 What is the ratio of the heights of these pairs of sunflowers?

a A : B

b C : A

c C : B

A is 1 metre tall.
B is 3 metres tall.
C is 2 metres tall.

2 Write each of these as a ratio in its simplest form:

a 2 : 6 (÷ both numbers by 2) **b** 4 : 10 (÷2) **c** 6 : 9 (÷3)

3 Write each of these as a ratio in its simplest form.

a 4 : 2 **b** 2 : 4 **c** 3 : 6 **d** 6 : 2 **e** 2 : 8

f 8 : 6 **g** 6 : 10 **h** 12 : 8 **i** 20 : 15 **j** 6 : 12

k 12 : 9 **l** 16 : 24 **m** 16 : 10

4 Copy and complete:

a value of P : value of Q = 10 : …

b in its simplest form, value of P : value of Q = 1 : …

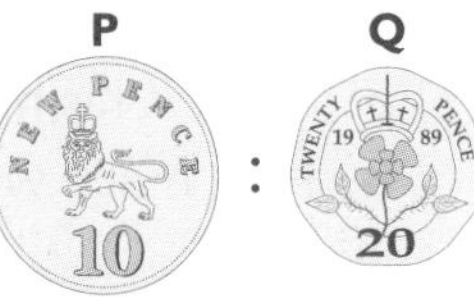

5 Pauline keeps a horse and a pony.
The horse is 18 hands tall and the pony is 14 hands.

a Write down the ratio of the height of the horse to the height of the pony.

b Express this in its simplest form.

6 Maureen gets 25 days' holiday a year. Her brother Maurice gets 40 days off.

a What is the ratio of Maureen's holidays to Maurice's holidays?

b Express this ratio in its simplest form.

7 To bake a potato Iris puts it in the oven for 60 minutes.
In the microwave it only takes 5 minutes.
Write the ratio of time in the oven to time in the microwave in its simplest form.

8 Write the ratio width : height in its simplest form for each picture frame.

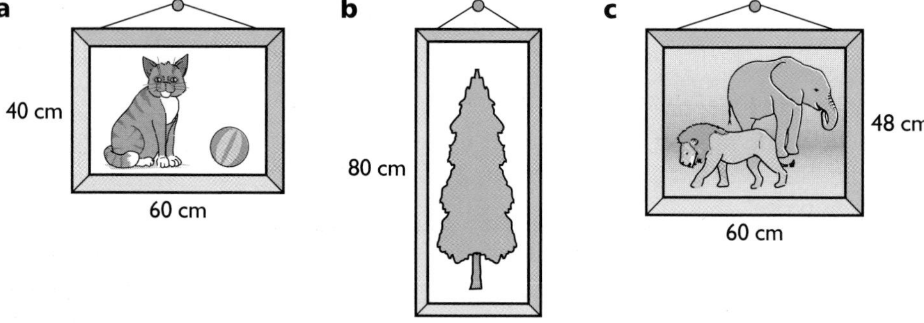

9 Brian's bread machine makes three sizes of loaves. Write these ratios in their simplest form:

a large : small

b medium : large

c small : medium

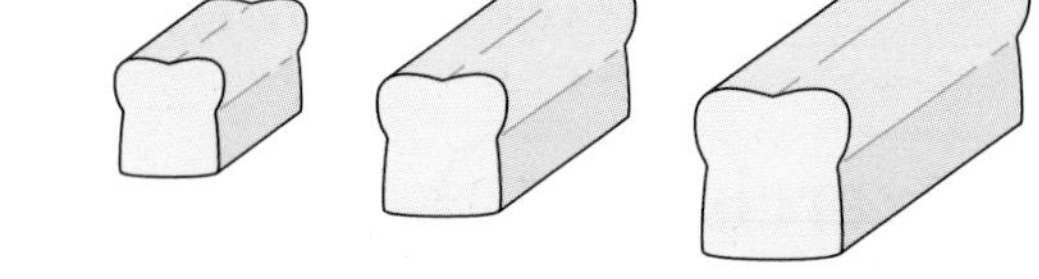

10 Two rectangles are said to be *similar* if the ratio of length to breadth is the same for both.

a Calculate the ratio of length to breadth for each of these rectangles.

b Which rectangles are similar?

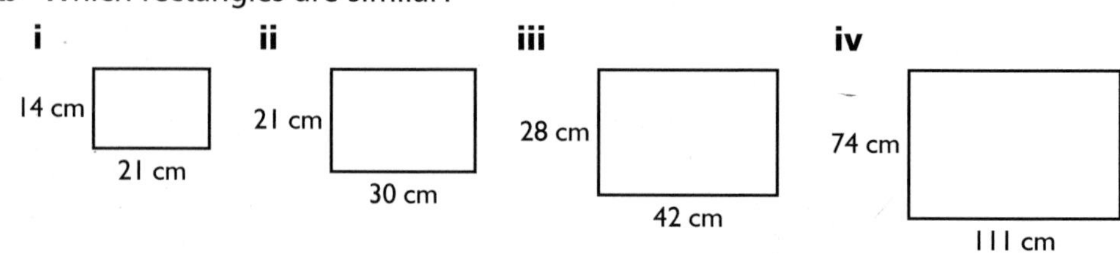

The quantities in the ratio must be the same units.

Example Tania takes 20 minutes to walk to school. Tony takes 1 hour.

Tania's time : Tony's time = 20 min : 1 hour = 20 min : 60 min = 20 : 60 = 1 : 3

Exercise 2.2

1 Copy and complete:
- **a** the ratio of 1 mm : 1 cm = 1 : …
- **b** the ratio of 1 day : 1 week = 1 : …
- **c** the ratio of 1 m : 1 cm = … : 1

2 Copy and complete these ratios in their simplest form:
- **a** the value of 50p : the value of £1 = 50 : … = 1 : …
- **b** the value of 20p : the value of £1 = 20 : … = 1 : …
- **c** the value of 50p : the value of £2 = … : … = … : …

3 Write each of these ratios in its simplest form.
a 1 second : 1 minute **b** 1 g : 1 mg **c** 1p : £1 **d** 1 day : 1 hour

4 To earn some pocket money Harry washes the car and hoovers the carpets.
The car takes 90 minutes and the carpets two and half hours.
He's given 240p for the car and £3·20 for the carpets.
- **a** Write the ratio of
  - **i** time spent on the car : time on the carpets
  - **ii** money earned on the car : money earned on the carpets

  in its simplest form.
- **b** Comment on the two answers.

5 Write the ratio of the cost of a child's ticket : an adult's ticket in its simplest form.

6 Write the ratios, A : B, of the weights and volumes below in their simplest form.

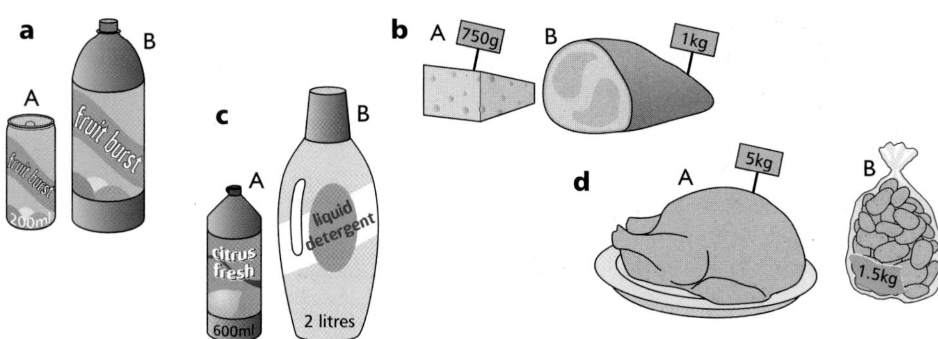

7 Susan and Ian share a paper round. Susan works Monday to Thursday. Ian does Friday to Sunday. Susan gets paid £12·40 and Ian gets £9·30.

a Calculate the ratio of Susan's time to Ian's time.

b Susan gets paid £12·40 and Ian gets £9·30.
Is this fair?

8 At a supermarket, tins of soup were sold at £3·80 for 2 or £9·00 for 5.

a Explain, using ratios, why the second pricing could be considered a bargain.

b What price would you expect to pay for five tins?

3 Using ratios

Example 1 On a computer training course the ratio of staff to students is set at 1 : 5.

a How many students can attend a course when six staff are available?

b How many staff are needed for 45 students?

Answer: a staff : student = 1 : 5
$= 6 \times 1 : 6 \times 5$
$= 6 : 30$
30 students can attend.

Multiply both sides of the ratio by whatever it takes to make the *staff* side equal to 6.

b staff : student = 1 : 5
$= 9 \times 1 : 9 \times 5$
$= 9 : 45$
9 staff are needed.

Multiply both sides of the ratio by whatever it takes to make the *student* side equal to 45.

E

Exercise 3.1

1 Alistair is filling holes in his walls to prepare for wallpapering.
The ratio of water to filler is 1 : 2 (1 cup of water needs 2 cups of filler).

a How much filler is needed for 4 cups of water?

b How much water is needed for 10 cups of filler?

2 Kumar makes lime and lemon juice using a mixture of 1 part lime to 3 parts lemon.

a Write down the ratio lime : lemon.

b How much lemon should be added to 4 litres of lime?

c How much lime should be added to 9 litres of lemon?

3 The scale of a model is the ratio of *model size* to *actual size*.
A boat is 20 m long. A model is made using a scale of 1 : 10.

a How long is the model boat?

b The mast of the model is 1·5 m tall.
How tall is the boat's mast?

4 A museum has a model space shuttle 5 m long. The scale used is 1 : 8.

a How long is the actual space shuttle?

b The actual shuttle is 24 m wide. How wide is the model?

5 To supervise a crowd of spectators at a sporting event, a club has a ratio of stewards to spectators of 1 : 50.

a How many spectators are present when the number of stewards required is 30?

b How many stewards are needed for a crowd of 10 000?

6 The school hockey pitch measures 70 m by 45 m.
A plan of it is drawn using a scale of 1 : 100.
Calculate the dimensions of the plan in

a metres

b centimetres.

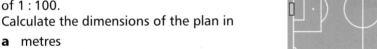

7 A count of the number of words on the pages of a novel gives an approximate ratio of pages to words of 1 : 300.

a About how many words would you expect in a book of 200 pages?

b About how many pages are needed for a chapter of 4500 words?

8 At Glenside High School the headteacher says she will find £4 for every £1 the students raise towards furnishing a common room.

a Write down the ratio of
i student contribution : headteacher's contribution
ii student contribution : total amount raised

b The students raise £1200. How much
i does the headteacher contribute?
ii is the total available amount?

9 The ratio of width to height of TV screens is usually 4 : 3.

a Calculate the height of a screen which is 32 cm long.

b Calculate the width of a screen which is 36 cm high.

c The ratio of width : diagonal is 4 : 5.
When stating the size of a TV screen, the length of the diagonal is usually quoted. Calculate the height and width of a
i 55 cm **ii** 30 cm **iii** 655 mm TV.

Another way

A ratio can also be expressed as a fraction, for example:

$2 : 3 = \frac{2}{3}$

This allows us to compare ratios.

Example 2 Which is bigger, 2 : 3 or 4 : 5?

Answer: Express both as fractions: $\frac{2}{3}$ and $\frac{4}{5}$

$\frac{2}{3} = \frac{10}{15}$ and $\frac{4}{5} = \frac{12}{15}$

So we see that 4 : 5 is the bigger ratio.

It also allows us to write relationships in a more useful form, for example:

A : B = 2 : 3 means either $A = \frac{2}{3}$ of B or $B = \frac{3}{2}$ of A

Example 3 The ratio of John's height to Anne's height is 3 : 2. If John is 1·80 m tall, how tall is Anne?

Answer: John's height : Anne's height = 3 : 2

$\Rightarrow$ Anne's height = $\frac{2}{3}$ of John's height

$\Rightarrow$ Anne's height = $\frac{2}{3} \times 1{\cdot}80 = 1{\cdot}20$ m

Exercise 3.2

1 Express each ratio as a fraction in its simplest form.

a 6 : 9 **b** 25 : 40 **c** 120 : 270 **d** 36 : 12 **e** 52 : 13 **f** 53 : 53

2 Find the bigger ratio in each pair.

a 2 : 3 or 3 : 4 **b** 5 : 9 or 1 : 2 **c** 2 : 5 or 7 : 20

3 The steepness of a hill is given, on road signs, as the ratio *change in height* : *distance along road*.

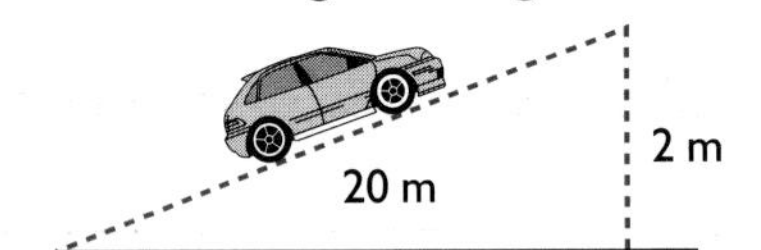

2 : 20 = 1 : 10

a Give the steepness of each hill in a similar manner.

(i) 51 m, 3 m

(ii) 42 m, 1·5 m

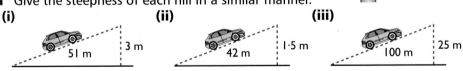

(iii)

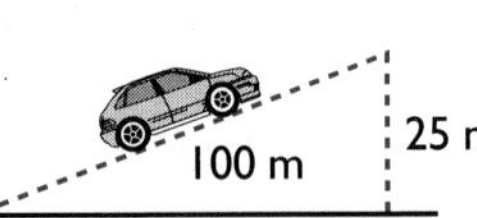

b Going up a hill where the gradient is 1 : 12, how much height do you gain after travelling **i** 12 m **ii** 60 m **iii** 108 m **iv** 9 m?

c If you gain 5 m height when climbing a hill with a slope of 2 : 9, how far along the hill have you travelled?

d Put these hills in order, steepest first. The Hurlet Hill 1 : 10, Summit Crest 7 : 60, Black Bend 1 : 12, Green Ridge 2 : 15.

4 Two types of flour are mixed to provide the batter for fish.
They are blended in the ratio of Grade A : Grade B = 3 : 7.

a How much Grade A is needed if 98 grams of Grade B are used?

b How much Grade B is required if 99 grams of Grade A are used?

c What total weight of flour is used if there are
i 210 g of Grade B
ii 210 g of Grade A

5 A geologist will name igneous rocks by measuring the ratio of quartz to other minerals in the sample.
The table gives a rough guide.

Name	**Ratio of quartz : others**
Granite	between 2 : 3 and 3 : 7
Quartz Diorite	between 3 : 7 and 1 : 9
Diorite	less than 1 : 9

a What name would a geologist give the following rock samples where the ratio of quartz : other minerals is
i 1 : 2 **ii** 1 : 3
iii 1 : 10 **iv** 3 : 29
v 1 : 8 **vi** 9 : 20?

b If a sample of granite contains 2 kg of quartz what is
i the least amount of other minerals
ii the most amount of other minerals it might contain?

6 A scientist does an experiment with coloured spinners.
When the ratio of red to blue on the spinner is
12 : 5 a purple colour is produced.

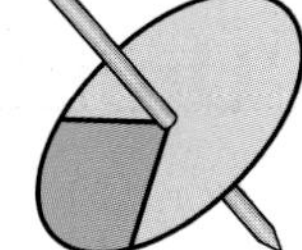

a What area of blue must the spinner have if 72 cm^2 are coloured red?

b What area of red must the spinner have if 100 cm^2 are coloured blue?

c What is the area of such a spinner which has 102 cm^2 coloured red?

7 The table shows the number of hours of daylight on the 21st of each month for a complete year in Stirling.

a For each month work out the ratio daylight hours : night hours in its simplest form.

21st of month	Jan	Feb	Mar	Apr	May	Jun	Jul	Aug	Sep	Oct	Nov	Dec
Hours of daylight	5	8	12	16	19	20	19	16	12	8	5	4

b The 21st of March is called the spring equinox.
i Why might this be?
ii Around what time is the autumn equinox?

c The 21st of June is called the summer solstice.
i Can you guess what this is?
ii In which month is the winter solstice?

E

Investigation

This table shows the frequency of the sound waves for different notes in the musical scale.

Note	Middle C	D	E	F	G	A	B	Top C
Frequency (hertz)	256	288	320	342	384	426	480	512

Pythagoras thought that the notes formed simple ratios,

for example middle C : D = 256 : 288 = 8 : 9.

a If we assume that the figures are only accurate to the nearest whole number, what simple ratio is equal to
i middle C : E **ii** middle C : F
iii middle C : Top C **iv** B : middle C?

b Explore the values of other ratios in the scale.

E

4 Unitary ratios

When one side of a ratio is 1, then it is referred to as a unitary ratio.

Example 1 2 : 5 can be expressed as

i $\frac{1}{2} \times 2 : \frac{1}{2} \times 5 = 1 : 2{\cdot}5$

or **ii** $\frac{1}{5} \times 2 : \frac{1}{5} \times 5 = 0{\cdot}4 : 1$

Example 2 When walking with his father, Duncan compares the number of steps they each take.
For 10 of his father's steps Duncan takes 15.

a Express the ratio of his father's steps : Duncan's steps in the form 1 : *n*.

b How many steps will Duncan need to take when his father takes 24?

Answer: **a** 10 : 15 = 1 : 1·5 (dividing each by 10) so Duncan takes 1·5 steps for 1 of his father's.

b 1·5 × 24 = 36 steps

Note that when wanting to find out about Duncan, we made the other side of the ratio 1.

Exercise 4.1

1 Express the following in the form 1 : n.

a 2 : 10 (÷ both numbers by 2)

b 3 : 6 (÷ by 3)

c 5 : 8 (÷ by 5)

2 Express each of the following in the form 1 : n.

a 2 : 6 b 3 : 12 c 2 : 9 d 5 : 4

3 Debbie counts the number of 2-door cars and 4-door cars on her road. She finds 10 are 2-door and 30 are 4-door.

a Express the ratio of 2-door to 4-door cars in the form 1 : n.

b In a larger survey she finds 50 2-door cars. How many 4-door cars should she expect to find?

4 The ratio of Megan's age to her mother's is 2 : 5.

a Express this in the form 1 : n.

b Megan is 12 years old. How old is her mother?

E

5 A woodland trust has a rule that for every four pines planted they will plant one broad leaf tree.

a Express the ratio of pine trees : broad leaf trees in the form 1 : …

b How many broad leaf trees should they plant in an area where they plant

i 600 ii 10 000 pine trees?

6 In a survey of 100 families there are 210 children.

a Express the ratio of families : children in the form 1 : n.

b How many children would you expect to find in

i 400 ii 6000 families?

7 The ratio of a large bottle of tomato sauce to the medium size is 5 : 3. A large bottle holds 450 g.

a Express 5 : 3 as a unitary ratio.

b Calculate the weight of a medium size bottle.

8 In a survey of his year, Sean finds that 48 dogs and 60 cats are kept as pets.

a Write the ratio of dogs : cats in the form 1 : n.

b Eight dogs are kept as pets by members of his class. How many pet cats might he expect?

Investigations

1 Investigate gear ratios on a mountain bike (the number of turns of a wheel for each turn of the pedals).
What is the ratio on the **a** lowest **b** highest gears?
Typically in a high gear one turn of the pedals rotates the back wheel through 2 revolutions. So the ratio is 1 : 2.

Gear A has 30 teeth and is connected to Gear B which has 10 teeth.

a Express the number of turns of A : the number of turns of B in the form $1 : n$.
b If gear B makes 6 turns, how many turns will gear A make?
c If gear A makes 6 turns, how many turns will gear B make?

2 Unitary ratios are useful when looking for bargains.

Example Which is the better bargain in each case?
a 5 bottles for £7 or 4 bottles for £6·20
b 5 items for £7 or 4 items for £5

Compare the ratio smaller : larger for both *number of items* and *cost*.

a Number of items 4 : 5 = 0·8 : 1
Cost 6·20 : 7 = 0·886 : 1 (3 d.p.)
The cost ratio is larger
so the offer with the larger number of items is the better buy.

b Number of items 4 : 5 = 0·8 : 1
Cost 5 : 7 = 0·714 : 1 (3 d.p.)
The cost ratio is smaller
so the offer with the smaller number of items is the better buy.

Investigate why this works.
What would you say if the cost ratio was the same as the number of items ratio?

3 The Golden Ratio

Start with any two small squares joined … … and complete the rectangle.

Draw another square on the back of the rectangle … forming another rectangle.

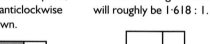

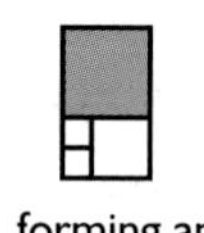

Add another square, going anticlockwise as shown.

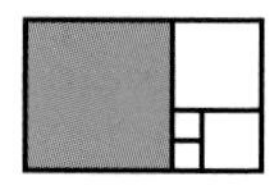

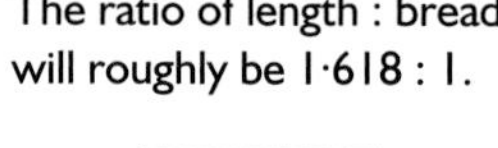
The ratio of length : breadth will roughly be 1·618 : 1.

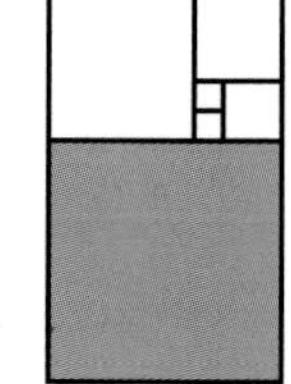

Try this with other starting squares.
If you keep going, the rectangle will be very nearly a **Golden Rectangle**.
Find out what you can about this. Surf the net, if you can.

E

5 Sharing

Example

Zoe spends 2 hours and Zack 3 hours helping to strip wallpaper.
They are given £20 to share for their work.
How much should each get?

To be fair they share it in the ratio 2 : 3 (the same ratio as the times).
Zoe gets 2 shares and Zack 3 shares … a total of 5 shares.
Each share is worth £20 ÷ 5 = £4
So Zoe gets £4 × 2 = £8 and Zack gets £4 × 3 = £12

Exercise 5.1

1 Brian and Barney are paid £15 to dig up potatoes.
Brian fills 2 sacks and Barney 1 sack.

- **a** What is the ratio of Brian's work : Barney's work?
- **b** If they share the payment fairly, how many shares will there be?
- **c** What is one share worth?
- **d** How should they share the £15?

2 Kylie is keen to get the right effect in her garden. She plants red and white carnations in the ratio 2 : 5. She wants a total of 35 plants.

- **a** 2 parts red, 5 parts white … how many parts are involved altogether?
- **b** How many plants are in one part?
- **c** How many plants of each colour should she buy?

3 Denise puts in £13 and her brother £7 to buy the CDs.

SPECIAL OFFER
100 blank CDs
for £20

- **a** How many CDs does £1 buy?
- **b** How many should they each receive?

4 Share:

- **a** £28 in the ratio 3 : 4
- **b** 30 kg in the ratio 1 : 5
- **c** 200 litres in the ratio 3 : 7
- **d** 180 m in the ratio 7 : 5.

5 Pewter is made from tin and lead.
John uses a mixture of tin and lead in the ratio 7 : 1.
What weight of each metal is needed to make 40 kg of pewter?

6 To get the exact shade of green he wants, Dominic mixes blue and yellow in the ratio 5 : 3.
How much of each colour should he use to get 400 ml of paint?

F

7 Gill has applied for a 'sandwich' course lasting 200 days. It means that for every 4 days with her employer she will study at college for 1 day.
How many of the 200 days will she be:

a at college **b** with her employer?

8 The atomic weight of iron is 56. The atomic weight of sulphur is 32.

a Write the ratio of iron : sulphur in its simplest form.

b The ratio is used to make iron sulphide.
Calculate the weight of each needed to make 440 g of iron sulphide.

Brainstormer

At the end of the season the West End soccer team look at their results. They played 24 matches and the ratio of win : draw : lose was 3 : 2 : 1.

At 3 points for a win and 1 for a draw, how many points did they total?

6 Direct proportion

F

Example 1 Abdul buys 2 books of stamps making a total of 12 stamps.
Jolie buys 3 books of stamps containing a total of 18 stamps.
Ratio of books = 2 : 3 Ratio of stamps = 12 : 18 = 2 : 3
The ratios are the same.
We say the number of stamps is **directly proportional** to the number of books.

Example 2 On 8 litres of fuel a car travels 120 km.

a How far will it go on 10 litres?

b How many litres are needed to travel 90 km?

a If we assume that the amount of fuel used is directly proportional to the distance travelled then
on 1 litre the car will go $120 \div 8 = 15$ km.
So on 10 litres it will go $15 \times 10 = 150$ km.

b A 90 km journey needs $90 \div 15 = 6$ litres.

Exercise 6.1

1 A 3 minute phone call costs 12p.
A 5 minute call costs 15p.

a Is the ratio of times equal to the ratio of costs?

b Is the cost of the calls in direct proportion to the time?

2 A flight of 6 steps has a rise of 72 cm.
Another flight of 4 steps rise by 48 cm.

a Is the ratio of steps equal to the ratio of rises?

b Is it reasonable to assume that the rise is in direct proportion to the number of steps?

3 A photocopier produces 75 copies in 5 minutes, then it produces 45 copies in 3 minutes.
Is it reasonable to assume that the number of copies is in direct proportion to the time?

4 Two cans of orange cost 60p.
A six pack costs £1·50.
Is the cost of the cans in direct proportion to the number bought?
Give a reason.

In each of the following assume the quantities are in direct proportion.

5 **a** What is the cost of having one item dry-cleaned?

b How much would it cost for 4 items?

6 A stack of 8 paving flags weigh 80 kg.

a How much would a stack of 6 paving flags weigh?

b How many paving flags are in a stack that weighs 140 kg?

7 For 5 hours' work Angie earns £35.

a How much does she earn when she works 8 hours?

b How many hours does she work on a day when she earns £42?

8 A water tank is filled by a tap. In 6 minutes the level rises by 15 cm.

a How far will it rise in 10 minutes?

b How long does it take to rise 70 cm?

9 A washing machine does 400 spins in 50 seconds.

a How long will it take to do 1000 spins?

b How many spins will it do in 40 seconds?

F

7 Graphing direct proportion

The table shows the number of tiles needed to cover a bathroom wall.

Area (m^2)	0	1	2	3	4	5
Number of tiles	0	20	40	60	80	100

The number of tiles is graphed against the area to be covered.

We see two things:

- a straight line is produced
- the line goes through (0, 0), meaning 0 tiles for 0 area.

This tells us that the number of tiles is directly proportional to the area.

If *either* of these things is not true, then we don't have direct proportion.

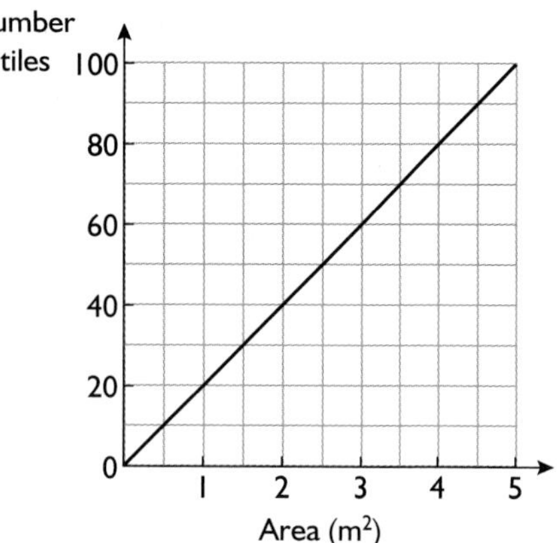

F

Exercise 7.1

1 On a charity walk John travels on average 5 km per hour for 4 hours.

Time (hours)	0	1	2	3	4
Distance (km)	0	5			

a Copy and complete the table.

b Draw a graph to illustrate the table.

c How can you tell the average distance travelled is directly proportional to the time?

d Could the information be used to do calculations for the fifth, sixth, seventh hour?

2 The table shows the distance a screw tightens for each turn.

Number of turns	0	1	2	3	4	5
Distance (cm)	0·0	0·3	0·6	0·9	1·2	1·5

a Draw a graph to illustrate the table.

b Is the graph a straight line, passing through (0, 0)?

c Is the distance directly proportional to the number of turns?

d How far does the screw tighten after 8 turns?

3 Weights are hung on a spring and the stretch of the spring is measured.

Weight (kg)	0	1	2	3	4	5
Stretch (cm)	0·0	0·8	1·6	2·4	3·2	4·0

a Draw a graph to illustrate the table.

b Give two reasons to explain how the graph shows direct proportion.

c How far will the spring stretch when 6 kg is hung on it?

Investigation

Question **3** illustrates a topic in physics called **elasticity**.

- Find out what you can about Hooke's law.
- Find out what is meant by the **limit of proportionality**.

4 Explain why each graph does not show direct proportion.

a Hiring a mountain bike

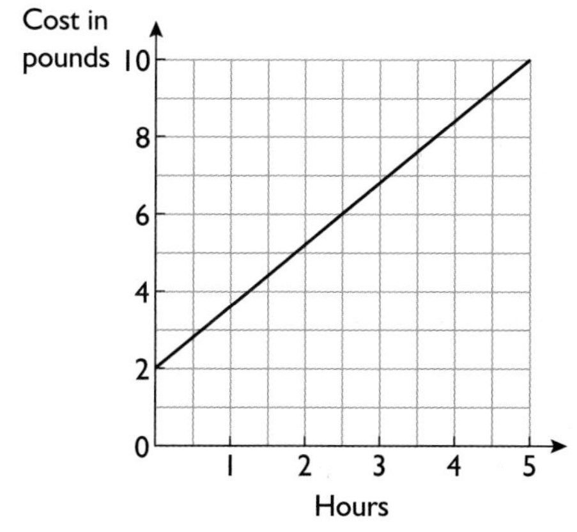

b Gas bill

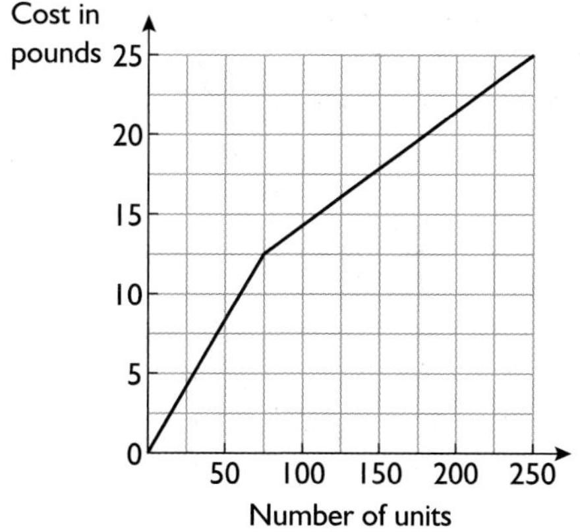

5 The table shows the cost of hiring a rowing boat.

Time (hours)	0	1	2	3	4	5
Cost (£)	0	2·50	5·00	7·50	10·00	12·50

a Draw a graph to illustrate the table.

b Is the cost directly proportional to the time? Explain why.

c How much would it cost to hire the boat for 6 hours?

d How many hours would you get for £20?

F

8 Inverse proportion

If 2 people share a prize of £100 they each receive £50.
If 4 people share the prize they each receive £25.

As the number of people doubles, the share of the prize halves.
This is called **inverse proportion**.

Example Val can record six 30-minute programmes on her video tape. Assuming that the length of the programmes is inversely proportional to the number of programmes she can record, how many 45-minute programmes can she get on the tape?

Length of tape $= 6 \times 30 = 180$ minutes
Number of 45-minute programmes $= 180 \div 45 = 4$ programmes

Exercise 8.1

F

1 Lynn has enough plant food to feed her 8 tomato plants for 6 weeks. She doubles the number of plants to 16. If it is used up at the same rate, how long will the food last?

2 At City High School, end of year reports are posted to parents. It usually takes 4 members of staff 6 hours to organise the letters. How long would it take

a 1 member of staff working alone **b** 8 members of staff?

3 A coffee jug holds enough for 10 cups of 150 ml each.

a What is the volume of the jug?

b How many 250 ml mugs can be filled from the jug?

4 On a scout camping holiday there are enough rations to last 24 people for 10 days. The number of scouts is increased to 30. How long will the rations last, assuming they are eaten at the same rate?

5 A tin of paint will cover 6 walls each with an area of 12 m^2. How many walls with an area of 8 m^2 could be covered with the same tin?

6 There is enough flour in a bag to make 14 loaves each weighing 500 g. How many loaves each weighing 350 g could be made?

7 In a national contest 5 people win £20 000 each.

a Calculate the total prize money.

b If there had been 8 winners sharing the prize how much would each of them have received?

8 A group of friends plan to walk the West Highland Way in 4 days at an average of 25 miles a day.
They change their minds and allow an extra day.
What now should be the average daily mileage?

9 The cost of renting a holiday cottage is shared by 6 friends.
Each of them pays £60.
At the last minute one of them drops out.
How much will it now cost each of the remaining friends?

10 It takes 5 lorries 12 loads each to carry the stone needed for a building job.
  a If 6 lorries were used, how many loads would each have to take?
  b If each lorry were to carry 15 loads, how many lorries would be required?

9 Mixed examples

Example 1 4 pears cost 80p.
If the cost is directly proportional to the number of pears, how much will 6 pears cost?

The more pears, the more cost.

4 pears cost 80p

$\Rightarrow$ 1 pear costs $80 \div 4 = 20$p

$\Rightarrow$ 6 pears cost $20 \times 6 = 120$p

Example 2 Walking at 5 km/h, Bernie takes 24 minutes to get to school.
Assuming that the time taken is inversely proportional to the speed, how long will she take when she cycles at 12 km/h?

The greater the speed, the less time.

5 km/h means it will take 24 minutes

$\Rightarrow$ 1 km/h means it will take $24 \times 5 = 120$ minutes

$\Rightarrow$ 12 km/h means it will take $120 \div 12 = 10$ minutes

Exercise 9.1

1 Say whether each is an example of direct or inverse proportion.
  a The number of boxes of eggs bought and the cost.
  b The number of days and the number of weeks.
  c The share of a lottery win and the number of winners.
  d The time to read a book and the reading speed.
  e The distance walked and the time taken.
  f The time to paint an office block and the number of painters.

F

2 Six scientific calculators cost £54. How much would ten cost?

3 Three friends each get eight sweets when they share a packet.
How many sweets would four friends get if they shared the packet?

4 Four packets of crisps weigh 120 g. How much would five packets weigh?

5 Moira buys enough cat food to last six cats ten days.
How long would the food last if there were five cats to feed?

6 Heather plans to walk the Southern Upland Way.
She aims to average 20 km a day for 16 days.
How many kilometres per day would she need to average to complete the walk in 10 days?

7 When he works a 7-hour day Norman earns £50·40.

- **a** How much does he earn on a day when he works 8 hours?
- **b** How many hours does he work on a day when he is paid £36?

8 Four people share a cash prize. They each receive £6000.

- **a** If five people share the prize how much would each one receive?
- **b** How many people share the prize when each receives £2000?

CHECK-UP

1 Sandy uses 3 kg of cement and 8 kg of sand to make mortar.
Express weight of cement : weight of sand as a ratio in its simplest form.

2 Joe's caravan has a 12 volt battery. His television needs 240 volts.
He buys a transformer to 'step up' the voltage.
Write down the ratio of battery voltage : television voltage in its simplest form.

3 Males are more likely to be colour-blind than females.
The ratio is 20 : 1.

- **a** For every 100 colour-blind females in the population, how many colour-blind males would you expect to find?
- **b** For every 100 colour-blind males in the population, how many colour-blind females would you expect to find?

4 Express each of the following as a unitary ratio (1 : n).

a 2 : 12 **b** 5 : 15 **c** 2 : 7 **d** 4 : 2

5 Sam uses the ratio of water : emulsion = 1 : 4 to thin paint.
What volume of each should he use to make 10 litres of paint?

6 In a survey of 60 pupils the ratio of those who prefer an activity holiday to a beach holiday is 3 : 2.
How many prefer **a** an activity **b** a beach holiday?

7 Sharon reads 500 words in a magazine in 4 minutes.
She reads 400 words in her history textbook in 5 minutes.
Could the number of words read be directly proportional to the time?

8 On a full tank of 120 litres of diesel Trevor can keep going on a motorway for 6 hours without refuelling.
How much fuel is needed for a 5-hour trip at the same rate?

9 Keith retrieves his fishing line by turning the handle of his reel.
The table shows the length of fishing line retrieved.

Turns of handle	0	1	2	3	4	5
Length retrieved (m)	0·0	0·5	1·0	1·5	2·0	2·5

a Draw a graph to illustrate the table.
b How do we know that the length retrieved is directly proportional to the number of turns?
c How much line is retrieved in 10 turns?

10 Paul needs to word-process his essay.
He reckons it would take him 90 minutes to key it in at 20 words per minute.
How long would it take at 30 words per minute?

15 Fractions and percentages

In Greek arithmetic, fractions were thought of as ratios between numbers. In Egypt they were considered part of a number.

The word fraction comes from the Latin *frangere* (to break).

The Romans worked a lot with twelfths, using them in weight, length and currency problems.

Their word for twelfths was *unciae,* from which we get our words inch and ounce.

The Babylonians worked with sixtieths.

In the Middle Ages, hours were broken into sixtieths and called *pars minuta prima,* meaning the first small parts.

These parts were then also broken into sixtieths and called *pars minuta secunda* ... the second small parts.

These names were later shortened to minutes and seconds.

---

1 Looking back ◀◀

Exercise 1.1

1 Out of eight rooms in Hilda's house, five have radiators. What fraction of the rooms have radiators?

2 Thirty-one per cent of the earth's land is covered by forest or woodland. What percentage is not covered by trees?

3 Calculate:

a $\frac{1}{4}$ of £60 **b** $\frac{1}{6}$ of 24 cm **c** $\frac{1}{3}$ of 600 kg **d** $\frac{1}{8}$ of 48 hours

e $\frac{1}{10}$ of 3000 km **f** $\frac{1}{20}$ of 80 litres **g** $\frac{1}{50}$ of 200 m **h** $\frac{1}{100}$ of 800 tonnes

4 Two-fifths of an exhibition of 50 paintings are landscapes.
How many paintings are landscapes?

5 In a 72-hole golf competition, $\frac{5}{8}$ of Monty's drives hit the fairway.
How many drives is this?

6 Which of the following are equivalent to $\frac{1}{4}$?

a $\frac{2}{8}$ **b** $\frac{3}{12}$ **c** $\frac{4}{20}$ **d** $\frac{10}{40}$

7 Write these fractions in their simplest terms:

a $\frac{2}{4}$ **b** $\frac{6}{8}$ **c** $\frac{3}{9}$ **d** $\frac{8}{12}$ **e** $\frac{12}{20}$

8 Express each fraction or mixed number in decimal form.

a $\frac{9}{10}$ **b** $\frac{3}{100}$ **c** $\frac{37}{100}$ **d** $\frac{1}{4}$
e $\frac{3}{5}$ **f** $2\frac{3}{4}$ **g** $4\frac{9}{100}$

9 Write these as common fractions or mixed numbers in their simplest form.

a 0·7 **b** 0·83 **c** 0·09 **d** 0·8
e 0·75 **f** 1·21 **g** 3·01

10 Convert these decimals to percentages.

a 0·5 **b** 0·8 **c** 0·01 **d** 0·25

11 Change these to decimal fractions.

a 10% **b** 40% **c** 75% **d** 3%

12 Thirty per cent of students in a history exam achieved grade A. Write 30% as

a a decimal fraction **b** a common fraction in its simplest form.

13 Mr Grimes found that $\frac{1}{5}$ of his pupils had forgotten to do their homework.
Express $\frac{1}{5}$

a in decimal form **b** as a percentage.

2 Further fraction calculations

Example 1 Calculate $\frac{3}{4}$ of £9.

$\frac{1}{4}$ of £9 = £9 ÷ 4 = £2·25, so $\frac{3}{4}$ of £9 = £2·25 × 3 = £6·75
This can be shortened to $\frac{3}{4}$ of £9 = 9 ÷ 4 × 3 = £6·75

Example 2 Calculate $\frac{3}{100}$ × 8000.

$\frac{3}{100}$ × 8000 = 8000 ÷ 100 × 3 = 240

Remember: 'of' means '×'

Exercise 2.1 

1 Calculate:

a $\frac{1}{2}$ of £7 **b** $\frac{1}{3}$ of £240 **c** $\frac{1}{4}$ of £50
d $\frac{2}{3}$ of £24 **e** $\frac{3}{4}$ of £120 **f** $\frac{2}{5}$ of £3
g $\frac{5}{8}$ of £4 **h** $\frac{9}{10}$ of £6 **i** $\frac{3}{20}$ of £2

2 Calculate:

a $\frac{3}{5} \times 200$ **b** $\frac{7}{8} \times 48$ **c** $\frac{7}{10} \times 6000$
d $\frac{9}{20} \times 160$ **e** $\frac{3}{50} \times 350$ **f** $\frac{9}{100} \times 5000$
g $\frac{11}{12} \times 60$ **h** $\frac{2}{25} \times 200$ **i** $\frac{17}{40} \times 80$

3 In a survey of 60 houses Sheila finds $\frac{3}{5}$ have double glazing.
How many houses have double glazing?

4 A group of 40 pupils select a foreign language to study.
$\frac{5}{8}$ choose German and $\frac{3}{8}$ choose French.
How many choose

a German **b** French?

5 A bus seats 96 passengers. $\frac{5}{12}$ sit downstairs and $\frac{7}{12}$ sit upstairs.
How many passengers sit

a downstairs **b** upstairs?

6 Mr Williams pays $\frac{3}{50}$ of his salary towards a pension scheme.
How much does he pay in a week when he earns

a £400 **b** £350?

7 Calculate the angle that is $\frac{3}{20}$ of a revolution.

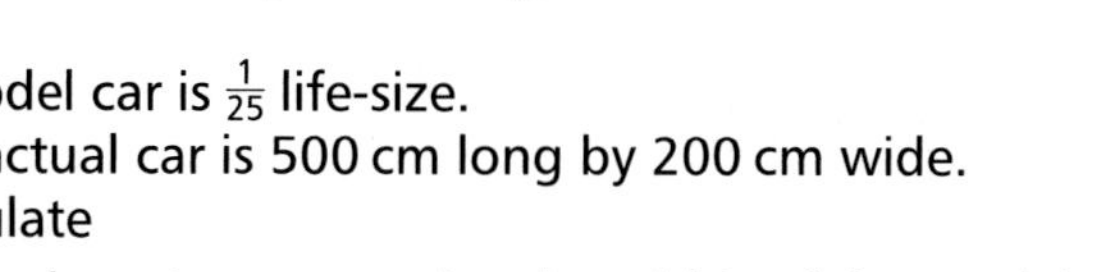

8 A model car is $\frac{1}{25}$ life-size.
The actual car is 500 cm long by 200 cm wide.
Calculate

a the length **b** the width of the model car.

9 Thirteen-twentieths of the 1000 seeds Marcus plants grow into lettuces.
How many lettuces does he get?

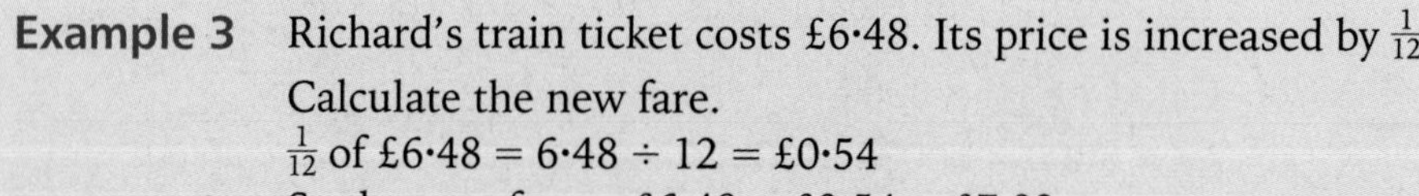

Example 3 Richard's train ticket costs £6·48. Its price is increased by $\frac{1}{12}$.
Calculate the new fare.
$\frac{1}{12}$ of £6·48 = 6·48 ÷ 12 = £0·54
So the new fare = £6·48 + £0·54 = £7·02

Exercise 2.2

1 Calculate:

a $\frac{3}{7}$ of 210 m **b** $\frac{2}{9}$ of 333 g **c** $\frac{7}{15}$ of 135 ml
d $\frac{3}{25}$ of 9500 tonnes **e** $\frac{19}{40}$ of 6600 km **f** $\frac{11}{50}$ of 8500 litres.

2 Mrs Watson retires after teaching for 29 years.
Calculate her yearly pension which is $\frac{29}{80}$ of £31 000.

3 A company gives $\frac{3}{100}$ of its profits to charity.
Calculate the amount donated in months when the profits are:

a £9000 **b** £15 500 **c** £12 350 **d** £40 000.

4 Which is greater?

a $\frac{7}{10} \times 560$ or $\frac{5}{6} \times 450$ **b** $\frac{11}{16} \times 240$ or $\frac{19}{25} \times 250$

5 Tony is paid £20 514 in a year. Calculate:

a $\frac{7}{12}$ of £20 514 (7 months' salary) **b** $\frac{7}{52}$ of £20 514 (7 weeks' salary)

6 Easysell Estate Agents charge $\frac{3}{200}$ of the sale price of a house for their fee.
Calculate the fee for houses which sell for:

a £50 000 **b** £85 000 **c** £172 000 **d** £299 000.

E

7 Calculate **i** the extra volume **ii** the total volume in these offers.

a

b

c

8 The population of Broom Bay was 24 560.
Over the last 10 years it has risen by $\frac{3}{20}$. Calculate

a the increase **b** the size of the population now.

9 An extra charge of $\frac{7}{100}$ is made on these holiday flights.
Calculate **i** the extra charge **ii** the total cost of these flights.

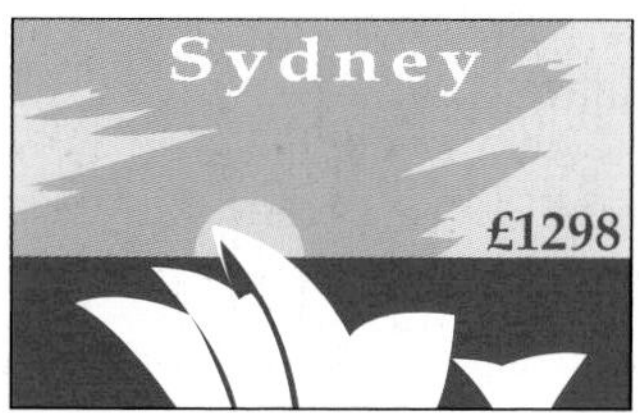

Brainstormer

What unit is a $\frac{1}{365}$ of a year b $\frac{1}{1000}$ of a litre c $\frac{1}{1\,000\,000}$ of a kilometre
d $\frac{1}{3600}$ of an hour e $\frac{1}{1\,000\,000\,000}$ of a tonne?

3 Calculating a percentage of an amount

Example 1 Calculate a 10% b 20% c 5% of £25.

Remember that 10% = $\frac{1}{10}$

a 10% of £25 = $\frac{1}{10}$ × £25 = £2·50
b 20% of £25 = £2·50 × 2 = £5 (20% = 2 × 10%)
c 5% of £25 = £2·50 ÷ 2 = £1·25 (5% = $\frac{1}{2}$ × 10%)

Example 2 Calculate a 1% b 3% c $\frac{1}{2}$% of £70.

Remember that 1% = $\frac{1}{100}$

a 1% of £70 = $\frac{1}{100}$ × £70 = £0·70
b 3% of £70 = £0·70 × 3 = £2·10 (3% = 3 × 1%)
c $\frac{1}{2}$% of £70 = £0·70 × $\frac{1}{2}$ = £0·35 ($\frac{1}{2}$% = $\frac{1}{2}$ × 1%)

E

Exercise 3.1

1 Calculate 10% of:
a £60 **b** £5 **c** £600 **d** £75 **e** £4·20 **f** £0·80.

2 Find 1% of:
a £2 **b** £40 **c** £700 **d** £85 **e** £620 **f** £9000.

3 Calculate:
a 10% **b** 20% **c** 30% **d** 5% **e** 15% of £60.

4 Calculate:
a 1% **b** 2% **c** 3% **d** 7% of £5.

5 Calculate **i** 50% **ii** 25% **iii** 75% of:
a £8 **b** £40 **c** £14 **d** £27 **e** £350.

6 Melanie receives a gift of £300.
She spends 20% on presents, 25% on a mobile phone, 15% on taking her parents out for a meal and she saves the remaining 40%.
How much does she spend on each item?

7 **a** Calculate **i** 10% **ii** 5% **iii** 2·5% of £80.
b Diane's garage bill is £80. The tax on it is 17·5%.
Use your answers to **a** to calculate the tax.

8 Calculate:

a 10% of 1700 tonnes **b** 20% of 460 litres **c** 5% of 90 m
d 15% of 300 g **e** 25% of 8000 km **f** 75% of 120 days.

9 Viv's garden has an area of 80 m^2.
60% of it is lawn, flowers are grown on 25% and 15% is a vegetable patch.
Find the area of each part.

10 **a** Calculate **i** 10% **ii** 5% **iii** 2·5% of £16.
A tax of 17·5% is charged on Hannah's £16 hairdresser's bill.
b Use your answers to **a** to calculate the tax.

Example 3

Calculate 17·5% of £47·60.

17·5 ÷ 100 × 47·60
= £8·33

10% of £47·60 = £4·76
5% of £47·60 = £2·38 (5% = $\frac{1}{2}$ of 10%)
$2\frac{1}{2}$% of £47·60 = £1·19 ($2\frac{1}{2}$% = $\frac{1}{2}$ of 5%)

$17\frac{1}{2}$% of £47·60 = £8·33

Exercise 3.2

1 Colin weighs 72 kg. During a marathon he loses 5% of his weight.
Calculate his weight lost.

2 740 students sit an exam. 55% of them pass.
Calculate the number who **a** pass **b** fail.

3 The label on a jar of marmalade shows 27% fruit and 67% sugar.
Calculate the weight, correct to the nearest gram, of

a fruit
b sugar in a jar weighing 454 g.

E

4 Tax on gas and electricity bills is charged at 5%.
Calculate the tax on these bills, to the nearest whole penny.

a £36·80 **b** £74·44 **c** £85·39 **d** £136·75

5 Calculate the discount on these sports goods.

6 Which is the greater in each pair?

a 50% of £80 or 80% of £50 **b** 75% of £30 or 30% of £75

c 17% of £90 or 90% of £17 **d** 9% of £45 or 45% of £9

7 Darren and Greg practise their basketball shots.
The table shows their results.

a Who scores more baskets?

b By how many?

	No. of shots	Success rate
Darren	80	37·5%
Greg	50	56·0%

8 The table shows how the National Lottery takings are distributed.
Calculate the amount that each receives in a draw when the total to be distributed is

a £8 000 000

b £12 550 000.

Prize money	45%
Money for good causes	28%
Government	12%
Camelot	5%
Retailer	5%
Superdraw, scratchcards	5%

9 The table shows the estimated percentages of the population living in different parts of the United Kingdom in 2000.
The total population is estimated to be 59 755 700.
Calculate the estimated population of each country correct to the nearest 100.

Country	Percentage
England	83·67%
Scotland	8·56%
Wales	4·93%
Northern Ireland	2·84%

Investigation

- Investigate the percentage of fat in different brands of margarine.
- Examine how content is described on different food packets.

E

4 Proper fractions and mixed numbers

A **proper fraction** is one where the numerator is less than the denominator, e.g. $\frac{3}{4}$.
An **improper fraction** has a numerator larger than the denominator, e.g. $\frac{5}{4}$.
A **mixed number** consists of a whole number part and a fractional part, e.g. $3\frac{3}{4}$.

Example 1 Express $4\frac{2}{3}$ as an improper fraction.

There are $4 \times 3 = 12$ *thirds* in 4, plus the 2 *thirds*, which gives $12 + 2 = 14$ *thirds*,
i.e. $4\frac{2}{3} = \frac{4 \times 3 + 2}{3} = \frac{14}{3}$

Example 2 Express $\frac{14}{3}$ as a mixed number.

$14 \div 3 = 4$ remainder 2, that is 4 *wholes* and 2 *thirds*
$\Rightarrow \quad \frac{14}{3} = 4\frac{2}{3}$

Exercise 4.1

1 How many halves are there in **a** 5 **b** $5\frac{1}{2}$?

2 How many quarters are there in **a** 3 **b** $3\frac{3}{4}$?

3 How many thirds are there in **a** 3 **b** $3\frac{2}{3}$?

4 When these mixed numbers are changed to improper fractions what number replaces each *?
a $1\frac{1}{2} = \frac{*}{2}$ **b** $2\frac{1}{2} = \frac{*}{2}$ **c** $3\frac{1}{2} = \frac{*}{2}$ **d** $4\frac{1}{2} = \frac{*}{2}$

5 When these mixed numbers are changed to improper fractions what number replaces each *?
a $1\frac{1}{4} = \frac{*}{4}$ **b** $2\frac{1}{3} = \frac{*}{3}$ **c** $4\frac{3}{4} = \frac{*}{4}$ **d** $2\frac{3}{5} = \frac{*}{5}$ **e** $1\frac{7}{10} = \frac{*}{10}$

6 Write these mixed numbers as improper fractions.
a $8\frac{1}{2}$ **b** $1\frac{4}{5}$ **c** $4\frac{1}{4}$ **d** $5\frac{2}{3}$ **e** $3\frac{9}{10}$
f $2\frac{5}{6}$ **g** $2\frac{1}{8}$ **h** $10\frac{1}{2}$ **i** $6\frac{3}{4}$ **j** $5\frac{2}{5}$

7 Change these improper fractions to mixed numbers by replacing each * with a number.
a $\frac{9}{2} = 4\frac{*}{2}$ **b** $\frac{7}{4} = *\frac{*}{4}$ **c** $\frac{12}{5} = 2\frac{*}{*}$ **d** $\frac{19}{8} = *\frac{*}{*}$

8 Express the following as mixed numbers.
a $\frac{9}{4}$ **b** $\frac{13}{3}$ **c** $\frac{6}{5}$ **d** $\frac{15}{8}$
e $\frac{23}{6}$ **f** $\frac{27}{10}$ **g** $\frac{26}{3}$ **h** $\frac{29}{5}$

E

Investigation

Find out how the fraction keys on a scientific calculator can be used to change mixed numbers to improper fractions and vice versa.

Example 1 Express in decimal form: a $\frac{29}{100}$ b $\frac{9}{1000}$ c $5\frac{73}{1000}$

a $\frac{29}{100} = 0{\cdot}29$ (29 hundredths)
b $\frac{9}{1000} = 0{\cdot}009$ (9 thousandths)
c $5\frac{73}{1000} = 5{\cdot}073$ (5 wholes and 73 thousandths)

Example 2 Change $\frac{7}{8}$ to a decimal.

$\frac{7}{8} = 7 \div 8 = 0{\cdot}875$

$$8 \overline{)7{\cdot}{}^{7}0{}^{6}0{}^{4}0} = 0{\cdot}875$$

Example 3 Convert these decimal fractions to common fractions or mixed numbers expressed in their simplest form.

a 0·28 b 7·025

a $0{\cdot}28 = \frac{28}{100} = \frac{4 \times 7}{4 \times 25} = \frac{7}{25}$

b $7{\cdot}025 = 7\frac{25}{1000} = 7\frac{1 \times 25}{40 \times 25} = 7\frac{1}{40}$

E

Exercise 4.2

1 Write these common fractions as decimal fractions.

a $\frac{1}{10}$ **b** $\frac{1}{100}$ **c** $\frac{1}{1000}$ **d** $\frac{37}{100}$ **e** $\frac{199}{1000}$

2 Express these mixed numbers in decimal form.

a $5\frac{3}{10}$ **b** $2\frac{3}{100}$ **c** $1\frac{13}{100}$ **d** $4\frac{7}{1000}$ **e** $3\frac{41}{1000}$

3 Convert these common fractions to decimals.

a $\frac{4}{5}$ **b** $\frac{3}{4}$ **c** $\frac{1}{8}$ **d** $\frac{3}{8}$ **e** $\frac{5}{8}$

4 Write each of these in decimal form.

a $2\frac{1}{2}$ **b** $6\frac{1}{4}$ **c** $4\frac{2}{5}$ **d** $7\frac{3}{8}$ **e** $1\frac{7}{8}$

5 Change each of these to a common fraction in its simplest form.

a 0·2 **b** 0·57 **c** 0·24 **d** 0·003 **e** 0·004
f 0·85 **g** 0·064 **h** 0·125 **i** 0·486 **j** 0·275

6 Express these decimal fractions as mixed numbers in their simplest form.

a 5·7 **b** 3·02 **c** 1·6 **d** 7·08 **e** 4·35
f 6·007 **g** 8·005 **h** 2·625 **i** 9·32 **j** 3·775

5 Expressing a quantity as a percentage

Example In a class of 25 pupils, 12 are boys.
Write the number of boys as a percentage of the class size.

As a fraction, the boys are $\frac{12}{25}$ of the class.
As a percentage, $\frac{12}{25}$ of 100% = 48%

Exercise 5.1

1 A survey of commuter traffic shows that 4 out of 10 cars contain a driver and no passengers. What percentage of cars are driver only?

2 Twenty office staff order a meal at a restaurant.
Three of them are vegetarians.
Calculate the percentage that are vegetarians.

3 The table shows Ling's test marks.
Write each mark as a percentage.

Subject	Mark
English	13/20
Maths	17/25
Science	22/40
Languages	42/60

4 Sharon has earned £40.
She decides to spend £8 on a sweatshirt, £12 on a birthday present, £9·60 on a new calculator and save the rest.
Calculate the amount she spends on each item as a percentage of the £40.

5 The table shows Jenny's and Saeed's results in chess competitions.

a Calculate the percentage of matches won by each of them

b Who has the better record?

Player	Wins	Played
Jenny	15	24
Saeed	18	30

6 A 500 g margarine tub contains 38 g of fat.
What percentage of the margarine is fat?

7 Jamie goes to the cinema. He's there for 150 minutes.
The film lasts for 125 minutes. The rest is adverts and trailers.
Calculate the percentage of his time spent watching

a the film **b** trailers and adverts, correct to the nearest whole number.

F

8 The average female body contains 4·5 litres of blood.
The average male body contains 5·5 litres.
Express the volume of blood in a female body as a percentage of the volume of blood in a male body, correct to the nearest whole number.

9 The table shows the number of Members of Parliament for each of the main parties in Scotland in 1999.
The total number of MPs is 129.
Make a new table showing the percentage of seats each party holds, correct to 1 decimal place.

Party	Number of MPs
Labour	56
SNP	35
Conservative	18
Liberal Dem.	17
Others	3

Brainstormer

a Calculate the percentage discount of this special offer.
b Calculate the percentage discount if the offer is
i 3 for the price of 2
ii 4 for the price of 3
iii 5 for the price of 4.

F

6 Percentage increase and decrease

Example A bus fare is increased from 40p to 48p.
Calculate the percentage increase.

Increase = 48 − 40 = 8p
Increase as a fraction of the original cost = $\frac{8}{40}$
Percentage increase = $\frac{8}{40} \times 100 = 20\%$

Exercise 6.1

1 Calculate **i** the increase **ii** the new amounts when:
a 60 kg is increased by 20% **b** 300 litres is increased by 25%
c 360 m is increased by 85% **d** 24 hours is increased by 12·5%.

2 Calculate **i** the decrease **ii** the new amount when:
a 80 tonnes is decreased by 30% **b** 600 ml is decreased by 75%
c 6800 hectares is decreased by 12% **d** 4000 km is decreased by 7·5%.

3 The seating capacity of a sports arena is increased from 20 000 by 16%. Calculate:

a the number of extra spectators that can be seated

b the new total capacity.

4 Earl earns £420 a week. He receives a 5% increase. Calculate:

a the increase **b** his new wage.

5 8000 cars drive through Eastbury. A bypass reduces this traffic by 30%. Calculate:

a the reduction in the number of cars

b the number of cars that still drive through the town.

6 The prices in the canteen rise by 8%. Calculate:
i the increase
ii the new price, correct to the nearest penny, for these items:

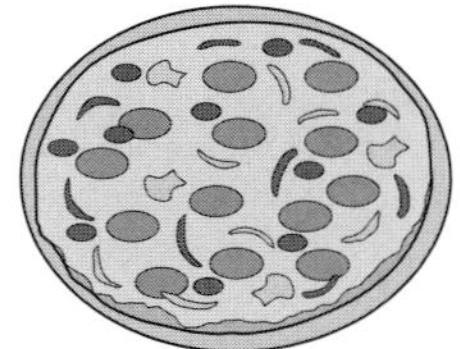

Pizza £1·20

Cheese salad £1·45

Burger £1·69

7 One year ago Terry was 160 cm tall. He calculates that he has grown by 5%. How tall is he now?

8 On her computer Bernie designs a draft front page for her project using a font size of 8. In her final version she increases the size by 150%. What is the font size of her finished front page?

9 1200 people live in Vicarage Hall. The population falls by 10% a year for two years. Calculate:

a **i** the fall in population
ii the total population at the end of the first year

b **i** the fall in population
ii the total population at the end of the second year.

10 Zoe deposits £6000 in a savings account. In the first year it earns 4% interest.

a Calculate the amount of interest earned.

b She leaves the interest in the bank. Add the £6000 to find the total amount in her account.

c In the second year her account pays 4% interest. Calculate the interest earned.

d What is the total amount in her account at the end of the second year?

Brainstormers

1 At Phantastic Photos a standard print measures 6 by 4 inches.
The next size is 7 by 5 inches.
   a Calculate the increase in *area* as a percentage.
   b Is their claim true?

2 To find the original price of the CD player, let its original price = 100%.
10% off so CD is 90% of its original price.
90% of original price = £72
$\Rightarrow$ 1% of original price = £72 ÷ 90
$\Rightarrow$ 100% of original price = £72 ÷ 90 × 100 = £80
In the same way, find the original price of the TV.

7 Switching between forms: fractions, decimals and percentages

F

Reminder

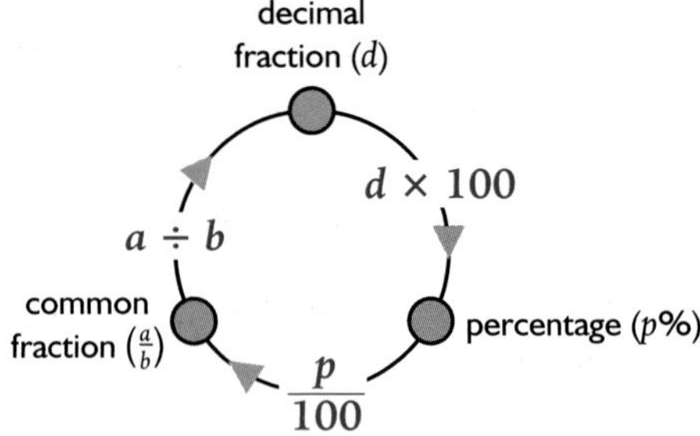

Example 1 Write 0·06 as **a** a percentage
b a common fraction in its simplest form.

a 0·06 = (0·06 × 100)% = 6%

b $6\% = \frac{6}{100} = \frac{2 \times 3}{2 \times 50} = \frac{3}{50}$

Example 2 Change 21% to **a** a common fraction **b** a decimal fraction.

a $21\% = \frac{21}{100}$ **b** $\frac{21}{100} = 21 \div 100 = 0{\cdot}21$

Example 3 Express $\frac{2}{3}$ as a decimal fraction correct to 3 decimal places.

$\frac{2}{3} = 2 \div 3 = 0{\cdot}6666 \ldots = 0{\cdot}667$ (to 3 d.p.)

Note: 0·666 666 … is an example of a **recurring** decimal.

$$\begin{array}{r} 0\cdot\ 6\ \ 6\ \ 6\ldots \\ 3\overline{)\,2\ \cdot{}^{2}0^{2}0^{2}0^{2}} \end{array}$$

Exercise 7.1

1 Change each common fraction to **i** decimal form **ii** a percentage.

a $\frac{1}{10}$ **b** $\frac{1}{2}$ **c** $\frac{3}{4}$ **d** $\frac{2}{5}$
e $\frac{1}{25}$ **f** $\frac{1}{100}$ **g** $\frac{1}{50}$ **h** $\frac{1}{20}$

2 Express each decimal as **i** a percentage
ii a common fraction in its simplest form.

a 0·3 **b** 0·6 **c** 0·09 **d** 0·15 **e** 0·08 **f** 0·39

3 Convert each percentage to **i** a common fraction in its simplest form
ii a decimal.

a 25% **b** 70% **c** 55% **d** 16% **e** 3% **f** 6%

4 Copy and complete the table.
(Write common fractions in their simplest form.)

Fraction	$\frac{9}{10}$			$\frac{7}{20}$			$\frac{13}{50}$		
Decimal	0·9	0·8			0·18			0·48	
Percentage	90%		20%			95%			13%

5 Express each of these in decimal form, correct to 3 decimal places.
a $\frac{2}{3}$ **b** $\frac{1}{9}$ **c** $\frac{5}{9}$ **d** $\frac{1}{6}$ **e** $\frac{5}{6}$ **f** $\frac{1}{7}$ **g** $\frac{6}{7}$

6 Write each part of **5** as a percentage, correct to 1 decimal place.

7 $\frac{1}{9} = 0{\cdot}111\ldots$ Write the following recurring decimals as common fractions.
Check by using your calculator.

a 0·222 … **b** 0·444 … **c** 0·777 … **d** 0·888 …

8 Write these mixed numbers **i** in decimal form
ii as a percentage.

a $2\frac{1}{2}$ **b** $5\frac{3}{4}$ **c** $3\frac{3}{5}$ **d** $7\frac{3}{100}$

9 Express each decimal as
i a mixed number in its simplest form
ii a percentage.

a 1·25 **b** 2·8 **c** 6·12 **d** 8·04

10 Convert these percentages to
i decimal fractions
ii mixed numbers in their simplest form.

a 475% **b** 110% **c** 220% **d** 302%

F

Investigation

Recurring decimals 

1 Each of the following produces a recurring decimal. Can you spot a rule?

a $\frac{2}{9}$ **b** $\frac{5}{9}$ **c** $\frac{11}{99}$ **d** $\frac{28}{99}$ **e** $\frac{7}{99}$ **f** $\frac{127}{999}$ **g** $\frac{751}{999}$

h $\frac{7}{999}$ **i** $\frac{21}{999}$ **j** $\frac{7125}{9999}$

Express 0·436 436 436 … as a common fraction.

2 Each of the following produces a recurring decimal.

a $\frac{2}{9}$ **b** $\frac{2}{90}$ **c** $\frac{2}{900}$ **d** $\frac{5}{9}$ **e** $\frac{5}{990}$ **f** $\frac{5}{9990}$ **g** $\frac{12}{90}$

h $\frac{12}{990}$ **i** $\frac{21}{900}$ **j** $\frac{7125}{9000}$

Can you spot a rule?

3 $\frac{1}{7}$ = 0·142 857 142 857 14 … This means that $\frac{1}{7} = \frac{*}{999999}$. What is * worth?
Investigate the decimal form of $\frac{2}{7}, \frac{3}{7}, \frac{4}{7}$, etc.

4 $\frac{1}{11} = \frac{9}{99}$. What is the decimal equivalent to $\frac{1}{11}$?
Investigate the decimal form of $\frac{2}{11}, \frac{3}{11}, \frac{4}{11}$, etc.

5 Investigate the decimal form of $\frac{1}{13}, \frac{2}{13}, \frac{3}{13}, \frac{4}{13}$, etc.

F

8 Equivalent fractions

Two common fractions are equivalent if they both have the same decimal form.
If $\frac{a}{b}$ is a common fraction then $\frac{a \times k}{b \times k}$ is equivalent to it, where k is any whole number.

Example 1 Find two fractions equivalent to $\frac{3}{5}$.

- Pick any number, say 2, then $\frac{3}{5} = \frac{3 \times 2}{5 \times 2} = \frac{6}{10}$
(Check 6 ÷ 10 = 3 ÷ 5 = 0·6)
- Pick any other number, say 7, then $\frac{3}{5} = \frac{3 \times 7}{5 \times 7} = \frac{21}{35}$
(Check 21 ÷ 35 = 3 ÷ 5 = 0·6)

Example 2 Express $\frac{3}{5}$ and $\frac{4}{7}$ as two fractions with a common denominator. Hence decide which is the bigger fraction.

Note that the denominators 5 and 7 can both easily be *made* 35 by multiplication.

So $\frac{3}{5} = \frac{3 \times 7}{5 \times 7} = \frac{21}{35}$ and $\frac{4}{7} = \frac{4 \times 5}{7 \times 5} = \frac{20}{35}$

Since $\frac{21}{35} > \frac{20}{35}$ then $\frac{3}{5} > \frac{4}{7}$ … by $\frac{1}{35}$

Exercise 8.1

1 Find two equivalent fractions to:

a $\frac{1}{3}$ **b** $\frac{1}{4}$ **c** $\frac{2}{5}$ **d** $\frac{7}{10}$

2 Find the value of * in each case:

a $\frac{1}{2} = \frac{4}{*}$ **b** $\frac{2}{3} = \frac{*}{9}$ **c** $\frac{3}{4} = \frac{15}{*}$ **d** $\frac{5}{8} = \frac{20}{*}$

3 Write each fraction in its simplest form.

a $\frac{3}{6}$ **b** $\frac{3}{9}$ **c** $\frac{8}{12}$ **d** $\frac{6}{12}$ **e** $\frac{12}{16}$ **f** $\frac{20}{25}$ **g** $\frac{30}{50}$ **h** $\frac{24}{32}$

4 **a** Express $\frac{1}{2}$ and $\frac{1}{3}$ with a common denominator of 6.
b Express $\frac{3}{5}$ and $\frac{2}{3}$ with a common denominator of 15.
c Express $\frac{5}{8}$ and $\frac{2}{5}$ with a common denominator of 40.
d Express $\frac{5}{8}$ and $\frac{2}{5}$ with a common denominator of 80.

5 Express each pair of fractions with the denominator shown in brackets.

a $\frac{1}{4}$ and $\frac{1}{5}$ (20) **b** $\frac{1}{3}$ and $\frac{1}{8}$ (24) **c** $\frac{2}{3}$ and $\frac{4}{5}$ (15) **d** $\frac{4}{5}$ and $\frac{1}{2}$ (10)

6 The lowest common denominator of $\frac{1}{4}$ and $\frac{1}{6}$ is twelfths.
a Express $\frac{1}{4}$ and $\frac{1}{6}$ as twelfths.
b Which is bigger, and by how much?
c Name one fraction in-between $\frac{1}{4}$ and $\frac{1}{6}$.

7 Express each pair as fractions with a common denominator and use your results to decide which fraction is bigger.

a $\frac{3}{4}$ and $\frac{2}{3}$ **b** $\frac{2}{5}$ and $\frac{1}{6}$ **c** $\frac{1}{6}$ and $\frac{1}{8}$ **d** $\frac{5}{6}$ and $\frac{2}{9}$

F

Investigation

a By considering equivalent fractions, find a fraction between $\frac{1}{2}$ and $\frac{1}{3}$.
b Repeat your method to find a fraction between
i $\frac{1}{3}$ and $\frac{1}{4}$ **ii** $\frac{1}{4}$ and $\frac{1}{5}$ **iii** $\frac{1}{9}$ and $\frac{1}{10}$.

Brainstormer

Martin finds an old set of spanners measured in inches.
The sizes marked on the spanners are $\frac{7}{16}$, $\frac{1}{4}$, $\frac{3}{8}$, $\frac{5}{16}$ and $\frac{1}{2}$.
Write these sizes in order, smallest first.

9 Adding and subtracting fractions

To add or subtract fractions, first express them as equivalent fractions with a common denominator.

Example 1 Add $\frac{1}{7}$ and $\frac{3}{7}$.

$\frac{1}{7} + \frac{3}{7} = \frac{4}{7}$ ... 1 *seventh* and 3 *sevenths* gives 4 *sevenths*.

Example 2 Calculate $\frac{4}{5} - \frac{3}{5}$.

$\frac{4}{5} - \frac{3}{5} = \frac{1}{5}$ ... 4 *fifths* less 3 *fifths* gives 1 *fifth*.

Example 3 Calculate $\frac{2}{5} + \frac{1}{4}$.

$\frac{2}{5} + \frac{1}{4} = \frac{8}{20} + \frac{5}{20} = \frac{13}{20}$ ... converted to *twentieths* before addition can take place.

Example 4 Calculate $\frac{7}{8} - \frac{3}{4}$.

$\frac{7}{8} - \frac{3}{4} = \frac{7}{8} - \frac{6}{8} = \frac{1}{8}$ ... converted to *eighths* before subtraction can take place.

F

Exercise 9.1

1 Calculate:

a $\frac{2}{5} + \frac{1}{5}$ **b** $\frac{3}{7} + \frac{2}{7}$ **c** $\frac{3}{5} - \frac{1}{5}$ **d** $\frac{7}{9} - \frac{5}{9}$

2 Calculate and simplify:

a $\frac{1}{4} + \frac{1}{4}$ **b** $\frac{3}{8} + \frac{1}{8}$ **c** $\frac{7}{8} - \frac{1}{8}$ **d** $\frac{5}{6} - \frac{1}{6}$

3 Calculate $\frac{1}{3} + \frac{1}{5}$ by first expressing both fractions as fifteenths.

4 Calculate $\frac{1}{3} + \frac{1}{4}$ by first expressing both fractions as twelfths.

5 Calculate:

a $\frac{1}{2} + \frac{1}{3}$ **b** $\frac{1}{6} + \frac{1}{5}$ **c** $\frac{2}{5} + \frac{2}{7}$ **d** $\frac{1}{2} + \frac{1}{4}$

6 Calculate:

a $\frac{2}{3} - \frac{1}{4}$ **b** $\frac{3}{5} - \frac{1}{2}$ **c** $\frac{3}{4} - \frac{1}{6}$ **d** $\frac{1}{2} - \frac{1}{4}$

When mixed numbers are concerned, work with the whole numbers first.

Example 5 $\frac{4}{5} + \frac{5}{6} = \frac{24}{30} + \frac{25}{30} = \frac{49}{30} = 1\frac{19}{30}$

... or you may prefer to leave it as $\frac{49}{30}$.

Example 6 $2\frac{3}{4} + 3\frac{3}{5} = 5 + \frac{15}{20} + \frac{12}{20} = 5\frac{27}{20} = 5 + 1\frac{17}{20} = 6\frac{7}{20}$

Example 7 $4\frac{1}{4} - 1\frac{1}{8} = 3 + \frac{2}{8} - \frac{1}{8} = 3\frac{1}{8}$

... subtract 1 from 4 first then subtract $\frac{1}{8}$.

Example 8 $6\frac{1}{10} - 2\frac{2}{5} = 4 + \frac{1}{10} - \frac{4}{10} = 3 + 1 + \frac{1}{10} - \frac{4}{10} = 3 + \frac{11}{10} - \frac{4}{10} = 3\frac{7}{10}$

... a whole had to be treated as $\frac{10}{10}$ to allow us to subtract the fractions.

Exercise 9.2

1 Calculate:

a $\frac{3}{4} + \frac{1}{2}$ **b** $\frac{7}{8} + \frac{1}{2}$ **c** $\frac{2}{3} + \frac{3}{4}$ **d** $\frac{4}{5} + \frac{2}{3}$

2 Calculate:

a $3\frac{1}{4} + 2\frac{1}{4}$ **b** $1\frac{7}{8} + 4\frac{1}{8}$ **c** $2\frac{3}{4} + 4\frac{1}{4}$ **d** $3\frac{3}{4} + 5\frac{3}{4}$

e $4\frac{7}{8} - 1\frac{1}{8}$ **f** $6\frac{3}{4} - 3\frac{1}{4}$ **g** $5\frac{1}{4} - 2\frac{3}{4}$ **h** $7\frac{1}{4} - 4\frac{3}{4}$

3 Calculate:

a $1\frac{1}{3} + 2\frac{2}{5}$ **b** $4\frac{1}{4} + 3\frac{2}{3}$ **c** $1\frac{7}{8} + 2\frac{3}{4}$ **d** $5\frac{4}{5} + 1\frac{2}{3}$

e $4\frac{3}{4} - 1\frac{1}{3}$ **f** $6\frac{4}{5} - 2\frac{3}{4}$ **g** $3\frac{1}{2} - 1\frac{3}{4}$ **h** $5\frac{1}{8} - 2\frac{5}{6}$

4 Bill waits $1\frac{3}{4}$ hours for his holiday flight.
The flight takes $3\frac{1}{2}$ hours.
What is the total time for his trip?

5 Gill is at work for $8\frac{1}{2}$ hours each day but she has $\frac{3}{4}$ of an hour off for lunch.
Calculate the actual working time.

6 Calculate:

a the total volume

b the difference in volume

of the two containers.

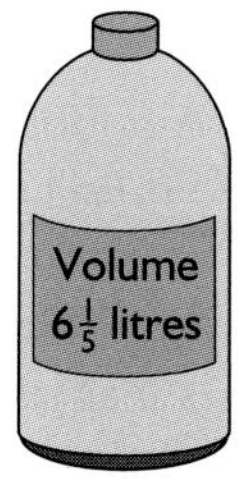

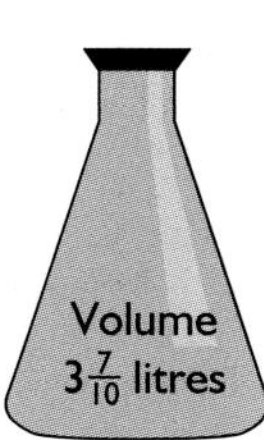

F

10 Multiplying fractions

If the square has an area of 1 unit^2 then, by counting, the shaded part has an area of $\frac{6}{12}$ units^2.

The shaded part is a rectangle of area $\frac{2}{3} \times \frac{3}{4}$ units^2

$\Rightarrow \quad \frac{2}{3} \times \frac{3}{4} = \frac{6}{12}$

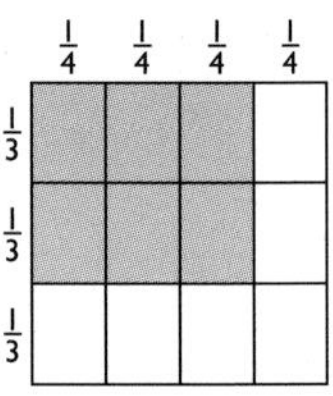

> To multiply fractions, multiply the numerators and the denominators separately.

Example 1 Calculate $\frac{2}{5} \times \frac{5}{8}$ and simplify if possible.

$\frac{2}{5} \times \frac{5}{8} = \frac{2 \times 5}{5 \times 8} = \frac{10}{40} = \frac{1}{4}$

F

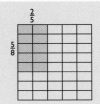

Exercise 10.1

1 Evaluate each product, then draw a square to illustrate the calculation.

a $\frac{1}{2} \times \frac{2}{3}$ **b** $\frac{1}{4} \times \frac{2}{3}$ **c** $\frac{3}{5} \times \frac{1}{3}$ **d** $\frac{3}{4} \times \frac{2}{9}$

2 Calculate:

a $\frac{1}{2} \times \frac{1}{3}$ **b** $\frac{1}{4} \times \frac{3}{5}$ **c** $\frac{2}{5} \times \frac{2}{3}$ **d** $\frac{3}{4} \times \frac{7}{10}$

e $\frac{1}{2} \times \frac{2}{5}$ **f** $\frac{3}{4} \times \frac{1}{6}$ **g** $\frac{3}{10} \times \frac{5}{8}$ **h** $\frac{1}{3} \times \frac{9}{10}$

i $\frac{3}{8} \times \frac{2}{3}$ **j** $\frac{5}{12} \times \frac{3}{5}$ **k** $\frac{5}{6} \times \frac{3}{5}$ **l** $\frac{6}{7} \times \frac{7}{10}$

3 It takes Ruth $\frac{1}{2}$ an hour to walk all the way to school.
What fraction of an hour does it take her to walk $\frac{1}{3}$ of this distance?

4 James and his friend have won the lottery.
James has to get $\frac{4}{7}$ of the prize.
He can collect $\frac{2}{3}$ of this just now and the rest later.
What fraction of the prize can he collect just now?

5 When fully laden, a van carries $\frac{9}{10}$ tonne.
What weight is in the van when it is $\frac{2}{3}$ full?

6 A minute is $\frac{1}{60}$ of an hour. A second is $\frac{1}{60}$ of this.

a What fraction of an hour is a second?

b What fraction of a day is a minute?

Multiplying mixed numbers

When multiplying mixed numbers they must first be expressed as improper fractions.

Example 2 Calculate $\frac{1}{3}$ of $2\frac{1}{4}$.

$\frac{1}{3}$ of $2\frac{1}{4} = \frac{1}{3} \times \frac{9}{4} = \frac{9}{12} = \frac{3}{4}$

Example 3 Evaluate $1\frac{1}{2} \times 2\frac{1}{3}$.

$1\frac{1}{2} \times 2\frac{1}{3} = \frac{3}{2} \times \frac{7}{3} = \frac{21}{6} = \frac{7}{2} = 3\frac{1}{2}$

Exercise 10.2

1 Evaluate:

a $\frac{1}{4}$ of $1\frac{3}{5}$ **b** $\frac{2}{5}$ of $3\frac{1}{3}$ **c** $2\frac{1}{2} \times 1\frac{3}{5}$ **d** $1\frac{2}{3} \times 4\frac{1}{2}$

2 Calculate, simplifying where possible.

a $\frac{1}{2}$ of $1\frac{1}{3}$ **b** $\frac{1}{4}$ of $1\frac{3}{5}$ **c** $\frac{2}{3} \times 1\frac{1}{8}$ **d** $\frac{3}{4} \times 1\frac{1}{9}$

e $2\frac{2}{3} \times 2\frac{1}{4}$ **f** $1\frac{1}{3} \times 1\frac{7}{8}$ **g** $7\frac{1}{2} \times 1\frac{3}{5}$ **h** $1\frac{1}{4} \times 1\frac{4}{5}$

3 One lap of a track is $1\frac{1}{3}$ km. Dianne cycles $2\frac{1}{2}$ laps. How many kilometres has she cycled?

4 Calculate the area of each window.

a

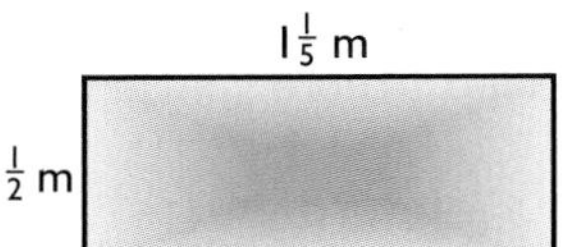

b

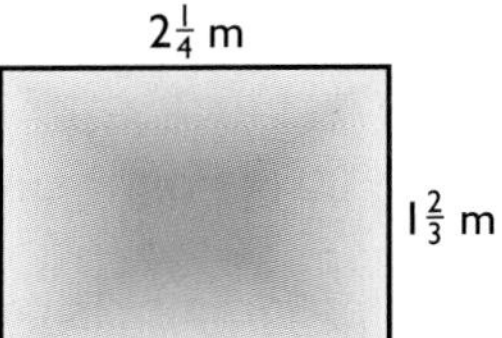

11 Dividing fractions

$12 \times 2 = 24 \Rightarrow 24 \div 2 = 12$ but $24 \times \frac{1}{2} = 12$

Dividing by 2 is the same as multiplying by $\frac{1}{2}$.

$12 \times \frac{3}{4} = 9 \Rightarrow 9 \div \frac{3}{4} = 12$ but $9 \times \frac{4}{3} = 12$

Dividing by $\frac{3}{4}$ is the same as multiplying by $\frac{4}{3}$.

In general, dividing by $\frac{a}{b}$ is the same as multiplying by $\frac{b}{a}$.

F

Example 1 Evaluate $\frac{1}{3} \div \frac{1}{2}$.

$\frac{1}{3} \div \frac{1}{2} = \frac{1}{3} \times \frac{2}{1} = \frac{2}{3}$

Example 2 Calculate $\frac{3}{10} \div \frac{5}{6}$.

$\frac{3}{10} \div \frac{5}{6} = \frac{3}{10} \times \frac{6}{5} = \frac{18}{50} = \frac{9}{25}$

Exercise 11.1

1 Evaluate:

a $\frac{1}{2} \div \frac{3}{4}$ **b** $\frac{2}{3} \div \frac{4}{5}$ **c** $\frac{3}{5} \div \frac{2}{3}$ **d** $\frac{3}{8} \div \frac{2}{5}$

2 Calculate, simplifying where possible:

a $\frac{1}{4} \div \frac{1}{3}$ **b** $\frac{1}{5} \div \frac{1}{4}$ **c** $\frac{2}{3} \div \frac{3}{4}$ **d** $\frac{2}{5} \div \frac{1}{2}$

e $\frac{3}{8} \div \frac{2}{3}$ **f** $\frac{1}{5} \div \frac{2}{7}$ **g** $\frac{4}{9} \div \frac{2}{3}$ **h** $\frac{9}{10} \div \frac{3}{5}$

3 Calculate and simplify where possible.

a $\frac{3}{4} \div \frac{1}{6}$ **b** $\frac{5}{8} \div \frac{1}{4}$ **c** $\frac{9}{10} \div \frac{4}{5}$ **d** $\frac{5}{6} \div \frac{2}{3}$

e $\frac{3}{10} \div \frac{4}{5}$ **f** $\frac{5}{12} \div \frac{1}{3}$ **g** $\frac{6}{7} \div \frac{9}{14}$ **h** $\frac{7}{8} \div \frac{5}{12}$

4 Convert each mixed number to an improper fraction before doing the calculation.

a $2\frac{1}{4} \div 2\frac{1}{2}$ **b** $1\frac{1}{5} \div 3\frac{1}{5}$ **c** $1\frac{7}{8} \div 2\frac{1}{4}$ **d** $3\frac{1}{2} \div 3\frac{1}{3}$

e $1\frac{2}{3} \div 1\frac{1}{9}$ **f** $4\frac{1}{2} \div 1\frac{3}{4}$ **g** $3\frac{3}{4} \div 1\frac{1}{8}$ **h** $1\frac{3}{5} \div 1\frac{1}{10}$

5 A glass contains $\frac{1}{12}$ litre. How many glasses can be filled from a $\frac{3}{4}$ litre jug?

6 How many $\frac{1}{4}$ hour programmes can be recorded on a 3 hour tape?

7 How many $\frac{1}{2}$ kg bags of salt can be filled from a $3\frac{1}{2}$ kg packet?

8 Dave has a part-time job. He works $4\frac{1}{2}$ hours each day.
How many days does he work in a month when his total is 54 hours?

F

CHECK-UP

1 Calculate: **a** $\frac{5}{6}$ of 30 litres **b** $\frac{13}{20}$ of 60 tonnes **c** $\frac{9}{50}$ of 200 km.

2 Calculate: **a** 20% of £22 **b** 5% of £15 **c** 75% of £30.

3 **a** How much is saved on a rug priced at £43·50?

b What is the actual cost?

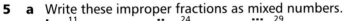

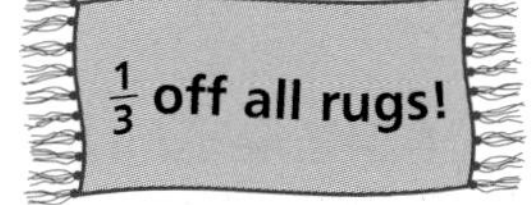

4 Calculate the tax, at 5%, on a £72 gas bill.

5 **a** Write these improper fractions as mixed numbers.

i $\frac{11}{4}$ **ii** $\frac{24}{5}$ **iii** $\frac{29}{8}$ **iv** $\frac{101}{100}$

b Express these mixed numbers as improper fractions.

i $6\frac{1}{2}$ **ii** $5\frac{2}{3}$ **iii** $3\frac{9}{10}$ **iv** $4\frac{7}{20}$

6 **a** Write in decimal form:

i $\frac{8}{1000}$ **ii** $\frac{73}{1000}$ **iii** $2\frac{3}{5}$ **iv** $5\frac{1}{8}$

b Change to a common fraction or a mixed number expressed in its simplest form.

i 0·45 **ii** 0·375 **iii** 3·006 **iv** 8·875

7 In the 1999 election to the Scottish Parliament 48 out of 129 MSPs were female.
Write this as a percentage, correct to 1 decimal place.

8 Jenny changes her bedside light bulb from 40 watts to 60 watts.

a What is the increase in wattage?

b Express the increase as a percentage.

9 In Scotland, the capercaillie population has decreased from 20 000 in 1970 to 4000. Calculate the decrease as a percentage.

10 Convert these to percentages:

a 0·05 **b** 0·625 **c** $\frac{2}{5}$ **d** $\frac{11}{25}$

11 Write 17·5% as **a** a decimal **b** a fraction in its simplest terms.

12 Express as decimals, correct to 3 decimal places.

a $\frac{5}{6}$ **b** $\frac{4}{7}$ **c** $\frac{8}{9}$

13 Calculate, writing the answers in their simplest form.

a $\frac{3}{8}+\frac{3}{8}$ **b** $\frac{3}{5}+\frac{1}{4}$ **c** $2\frac{3}{4}+3\frac{7}{8}$

d $\frac{9}{10}-\frac{3}{10}$ **e** $\frac{5}{6}-\frac{1}{3}$ **f** $4\frac{1}{2}-1\frac{3}{8}$

14 The fraction of school leavers going to university has increased from $\frac{1}{8}$ to $\frac{1}{3}$.
Calculate the difference between these two fractions.

15 Calculate, writing the answers in their simplest form.

a $\frac{1}{8}\times\frac{1}{2}$ **b** $\frac{1}{4}\times\frac{2}{5}$ **c** $1\frac{2}{3}\times 1\frac{1}{5}$

d $\frac{5}{8}\div\frac{1}{2}$ **e** $\frac{3}{4}\div\frac{9}{16}$ **f** $3\frac{1}{8}\div 1\frac{1}{4}$

16 Two-dimensional shapes

The study of 2-dimensional shapes has a long history.
Euclid (300 BC) formalised it in his work known as *The Elements*.

Even today there is much to discover … consider the computer-created images made in the study of *fractals*.

1 Looking back

Exercise 1.1

1 A square has been dissected as shown.

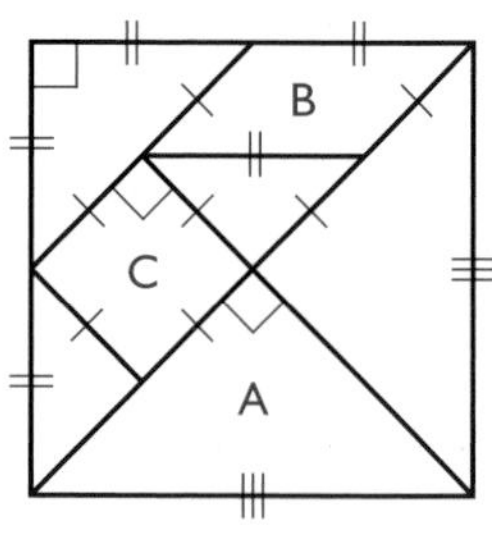

a What do the purple squares indicate?

b What do the small purple markings indicate?

c Give as accurate a name for each of the labelled shapes as you can.

2

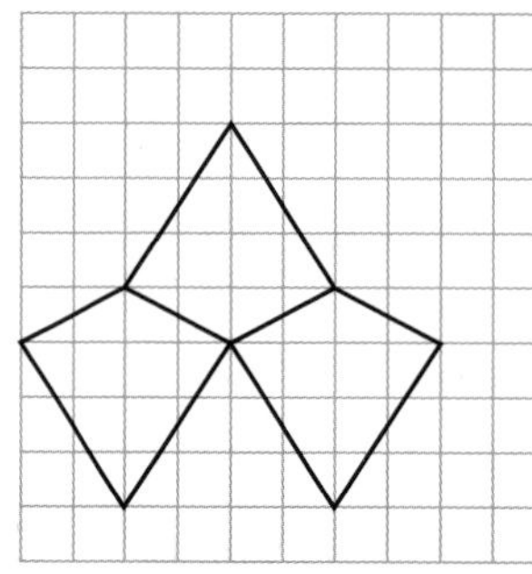

a Copy and continue this tiling.

b What do we mean when we say that a shape tiles?

c What is the name of the shape you have tiled here?

3 **a** Name all the rectangles in this diagram that have A as a vertex.

b How many rectangles are in the diagram?

4 **a** Draw a square, indicating where its four axes of symmetry are.

b Describe all the symmetries of the rectangle.

5 The shape ABCD has been reflected in PQ.

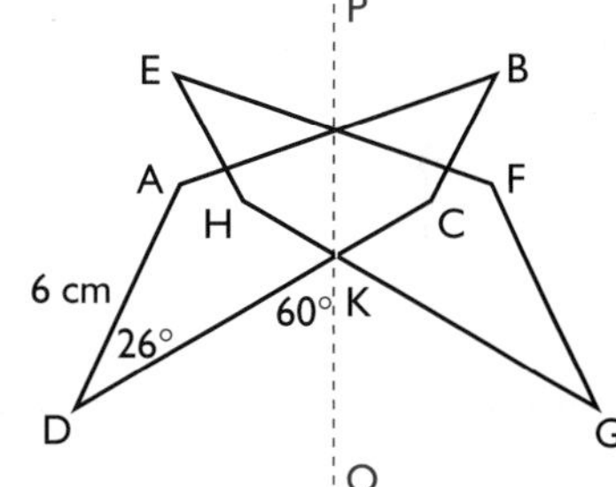

a Name the image of
- **i** the point A
- **ii** the line AB
- **iii** the angle ABC.

b State the size of
- **i** the line FG
- **ii** ∠HGF
- **iii** ∠DKG.

6 Sort the faces of a dice into different groups according to their symmetries. List the set which possesses:

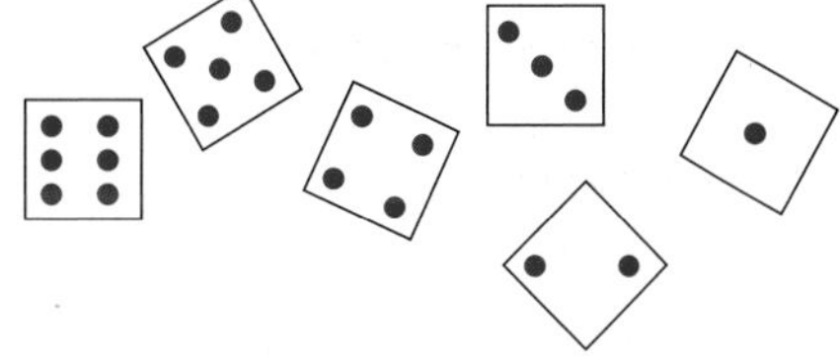

a half-turn symmetry

b rotational symmetry of order 4

c two axes of symmetry

d only one axis of symmetry.

2 The square and rectangle

Definitions

- A square is a quadrilateral with four axes of symmetry
- A rectangle is a quadrilateral with two axes of symmetry which pass through its sides.

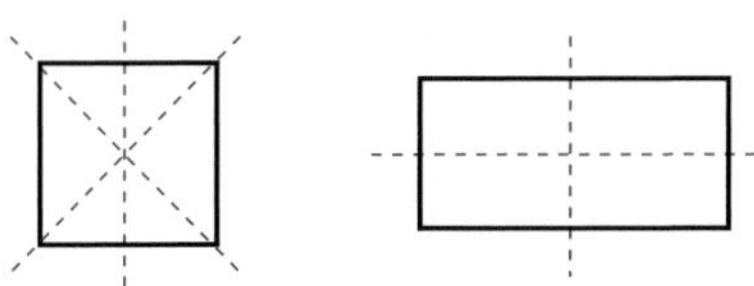

We can use these symmetries to deduce other properties of the shapes.

Example 1

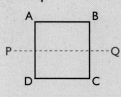

Given that PQ is an axis of symmetry, when the square reflects in PQ:

$A \rightarrow D$ ... read as 'A goes to D'

$B \rightarrow C$ ... 'B goes to C'

$\Rightarrow AB \rightarrow DC$ ... 'AB goes to DC'

$\Rightarrow AB = DC$

Example 2

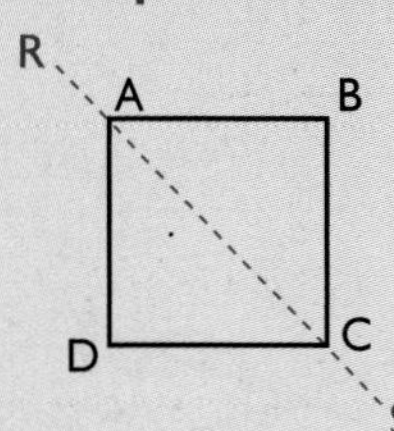

Given that RS is an axis of symmetry, when the square reflects in RS:

$A \rightarrow A$

$B \rightarrow D$

$C \rightarrow C$

$\Rightarrow ABC \rightarrow ADC$ → This also proves that triangles ABC and ADC are congruent.

$\Rightarrow \angle ABC = \angle ADC$

Similarly $\angle BAD = \angle BCD$

$\Rightarrow$ opposite angles of a square are equal.

E

Exercise 2.1

1 **a** Use diagram 1 to prove $\angle BAD = \angle ADC$.

b Together with the findings of Example 2, what does this prove about the four angles of a square?

c Use diagram 2 to prove the four angles of a square add up to 360°.

d What does this prove about the size of one angle of a square?

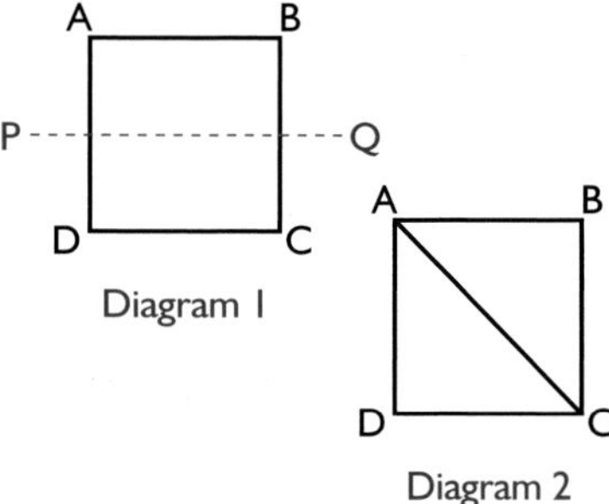

Diagram 1

Diagram 2

2 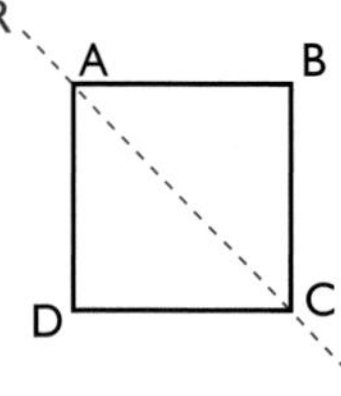

a Prove $AB = AD$.

b Prove all four sides of a square are equal.

c Prove $\angle BAC = \angle CAD$ and state their size.

3 **a** Prove the diagonals of a square are equal (i.e. $AC = DB$).

b Prove

i $AE = EC$ by considering the axis through BD

ii $BE = ED$ by considering the axis through AC

i.e. the diagonals bisect each other.

c Prove $\angle AEB = \angle BEC = \angle CED = \angle DEA$ and state their size.

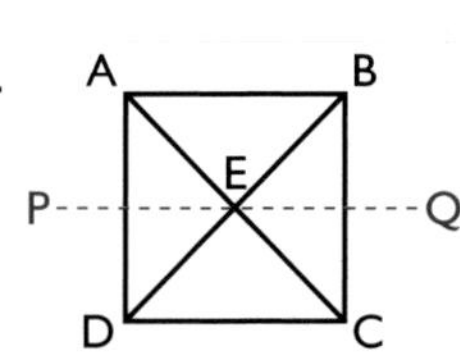

Square summary

Knowing these symmetries

... lets us deduce these properties

A B E D C

• = 45°

4 **a** How many ways can this rectangle of paper fit into the tray?

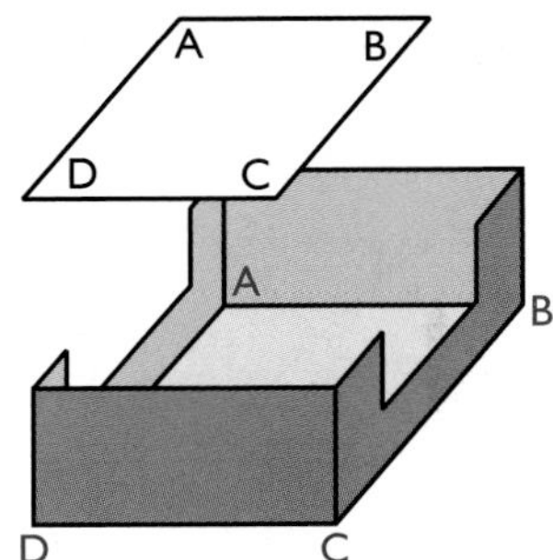

b Use the symmetries of the rectangle to prove

i opposite sides are equal (AB = DC and AD = BC)

ii ∠DAB = ∠CBA and ∠ADC = ∠BCD

iii ∠DAB = ∠ADC and ∠ABC = ∠DCB

iv all angles are right angles.

c Prove

i the diagonals are equal

ii they bisect each other.

5

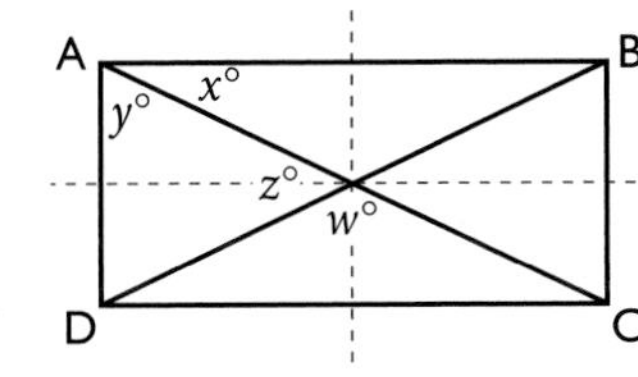

Rectangle ABCD has its axes of symmetry drawn. Make a copy of the rectangle.

a ∠CAB = $x°$. Mark three other angles equal to ∠CAB in your diagram.

b ∠CAD = $y°$.

i Mark three other angles equal to ∠CAD.

ii What is the relation between x and y?

c Mark another angle equal to

i $z°$

ii $w°$.

d What is the relation between

i y and z

ii x and w

iii z and w?

6 Copy each rectangle and fill in the sizes of as many angles as you can.

a

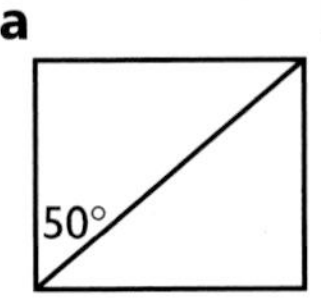

b

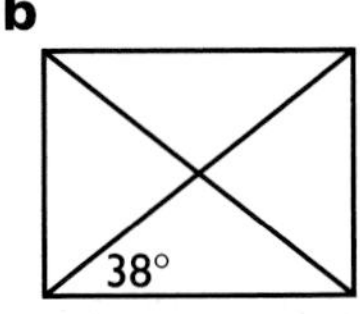

c

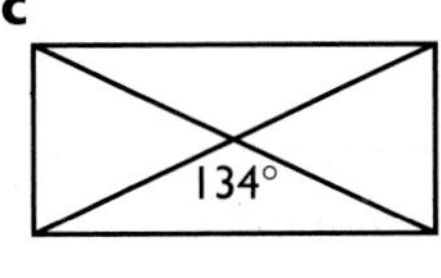

d

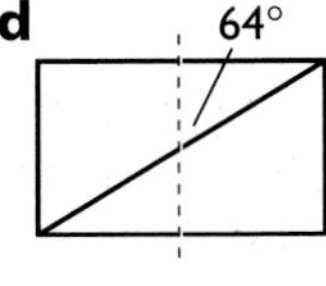

e

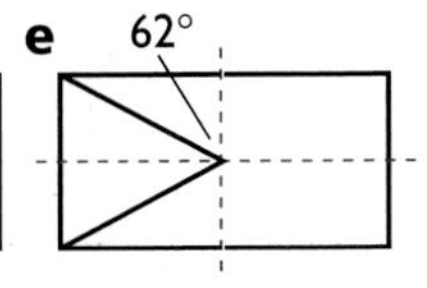

7 A joiner makes shelves. He checks they are true by measuring various angles.
Which of the following definitely need adjusted (i.e. which cannot be rectangles)?

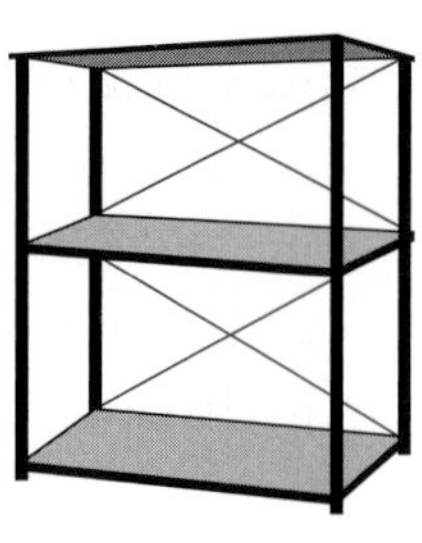

a

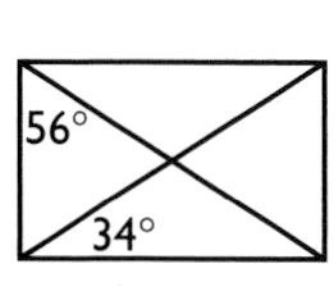

b

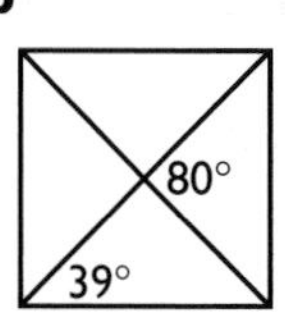

c

d

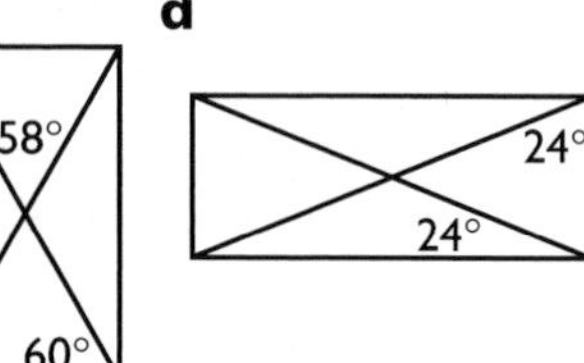

8 Calculate the size of each labelled length in the rectangles below.

a

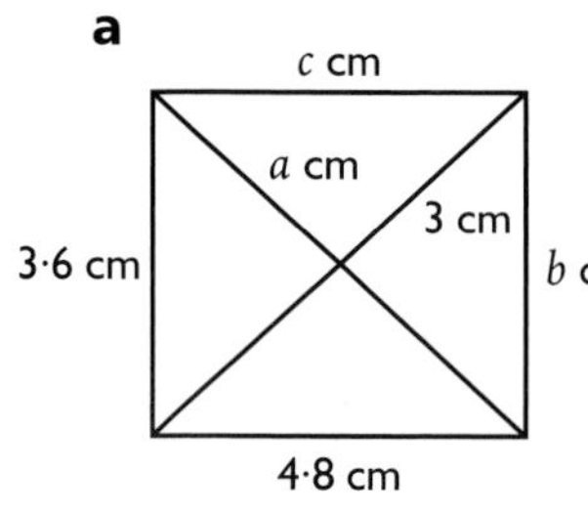

b

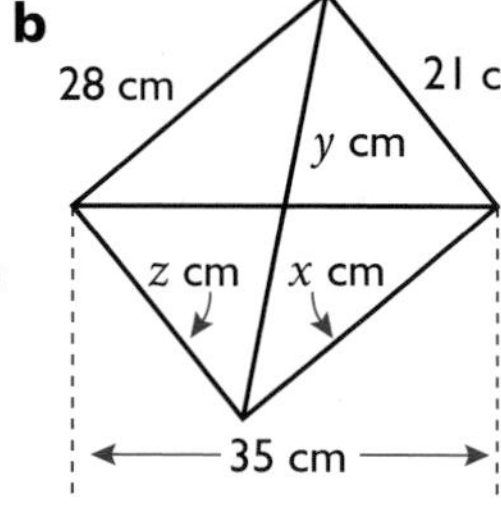

c

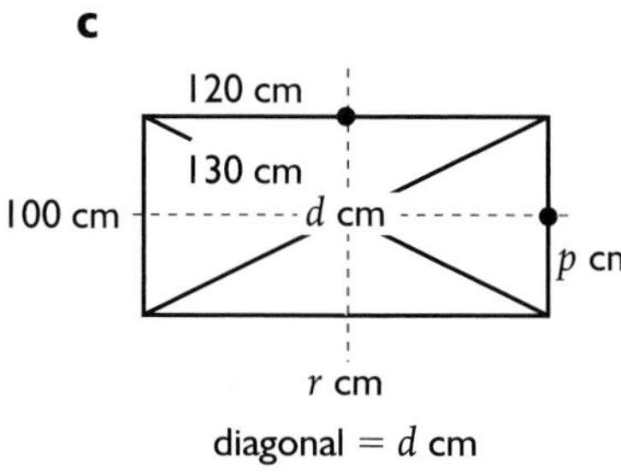

9 A copy of the Brazilian flag is drawn on a grid made of rectangles. Calculate:

a the length and breadth of the rectangle

b the perimeter of the diamond

c the length of each diagonal of the diamond.

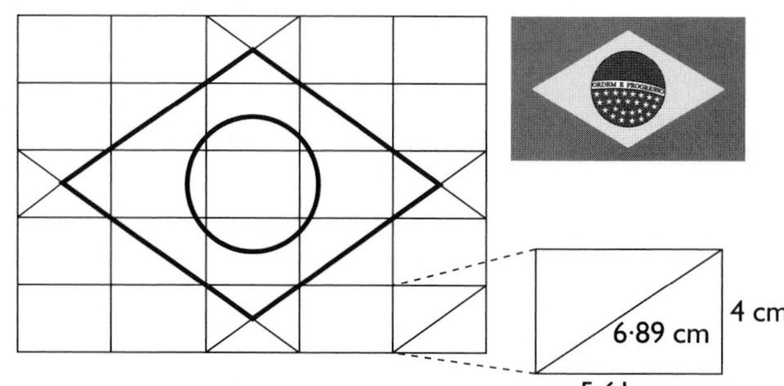

Exercise 2.2

1 The face of a watch is based on two rectangles as shown.
AB = 1·8 cm, AD = 2·4 cm, PQ = 0·3 cm and RS = 0·4 cm.

a Calculate the perimeter of
  i ABCD
  ii the inner rectangle.

b EC = 1·5 cm and GD = 0·5 cm.
Calculate the length of GB.

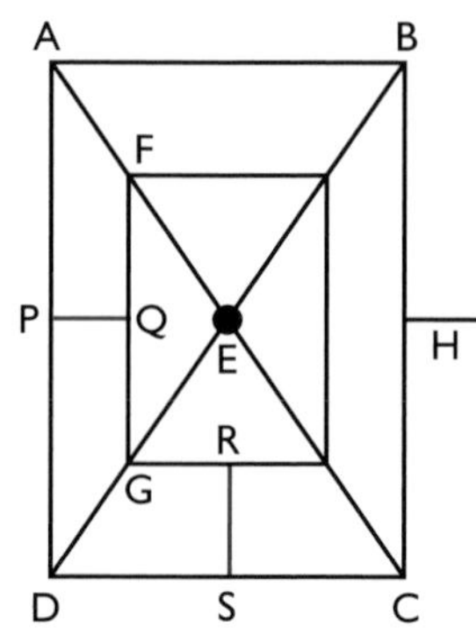

2 A rectangle has vertices A(4, 1), B(1, 5), C and D(−4, −5).

a On a coordinate grid plot A, B and D.

b Find the point C and state its coordinates.

c Find the point E, where the diagonals of the rectangle intersect.

d The perimeter of the rectangle is 30 units.
The length of the rectangle is twice its breadth.
What are the dimensions of the rectangle?

3 **a** Draw the line which passes through the points (1, 5) and (−1, 3).

b Draw a line parallel to this passing through the point (4, 0).

c A third line passes through (4, 4) and (7, 1). Draw it.

d Draw the line which is parallel to this and passes through (0, 4).

e Find the coordinates of the four intersections of the lines.

f These four points define either a square or a rectangle.
By examining the diagonals, decide which.

4 The diagram shows half of a rectangle and its axis of symmetry.

a Copy the diagram.

b Find R, the image of Q, and S, the image of P, under reflection in the axis.

c Where do the diagonals intersect?

d What is the length of PR?

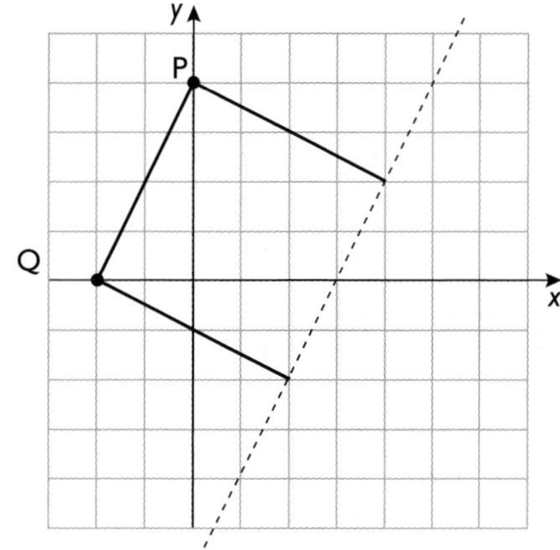

5 The diagram shows two congruent rectangles, one at right angles to the other, whose diagonals intersect at the same point.
Prove that the shape formed by the intersection of the rectangles is a square.

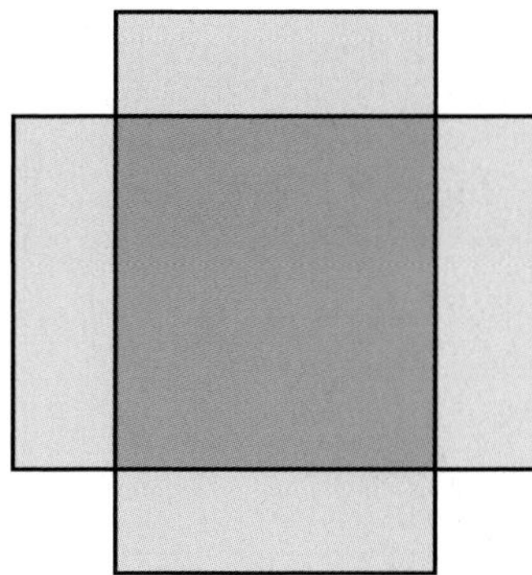

Challenge

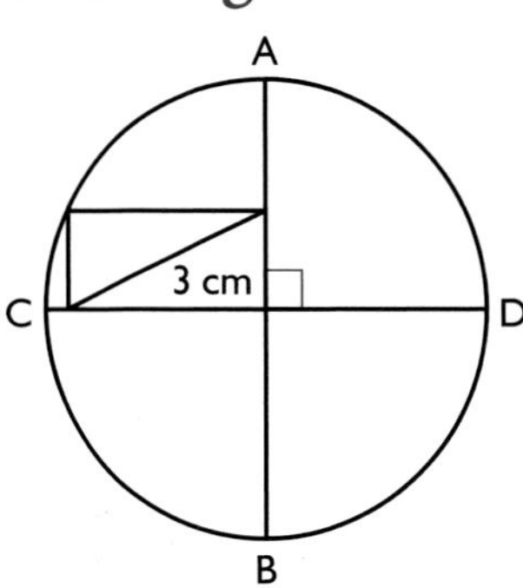

A circle has diameters AB and CD drawn at right angles.

A rectangle is drawn with sides parallel to AB and DC and a diagonal of length 3 cm as shown.

What is the diameter of the circle?

Rectangle summary

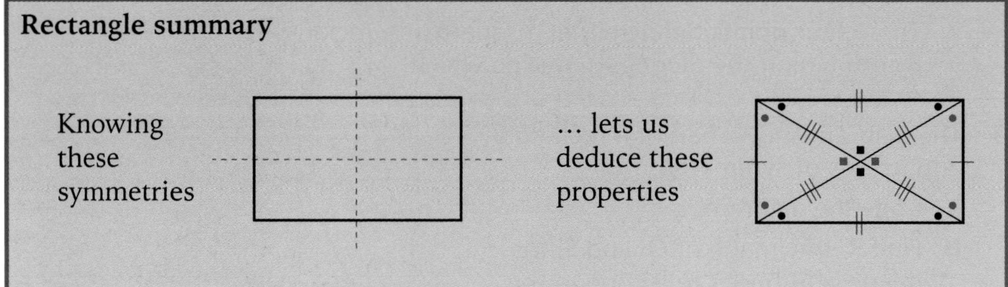

Knowing these symmetries
... lets us deduce these properties

E

3 The rhombus and kite

Definitions

A **rhombus** is a quadrilateral with two axes of symmetry which pass through its vertices.

A **kite** is a quadrilateral with one axis of symmetry which passes through a pair of its vertices.

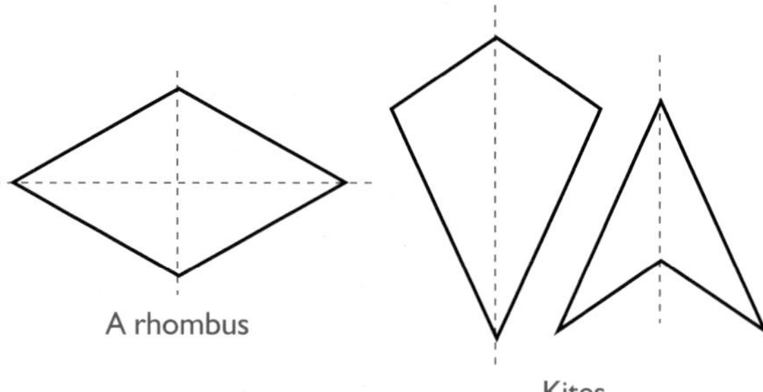

Example Prove the sides of a rhombus are equal.

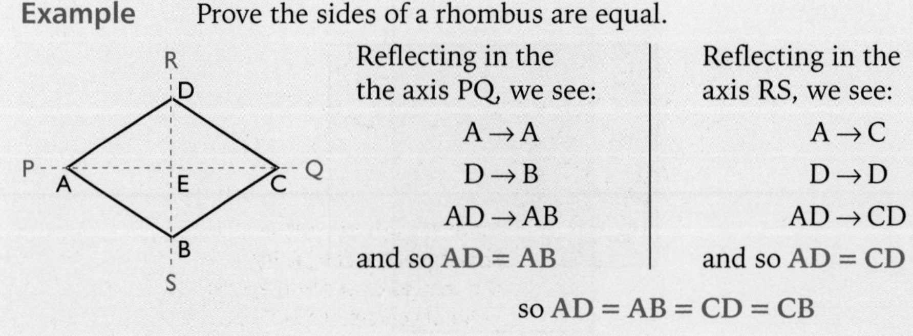

Reflecting in the the axis PQ, we see:	Reflecting in the axis RS, we see:
A → A	A → C
D → B	D → D
AD → AB	AD → CD
and so AD = AB	and so AD = CD

so AD = AB = CD = CB

Exercise 3.1

1 Use the symmetries of the rhombus to prove that:

- **a** opposite angles are equal
- **b** diagonals bisect each other
- **c** the diagonals intersect at right angles.

2 Copy the diagram of the rhombus ABCD.

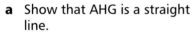

- **a** $\angle DAC = x°$.
  Use symmetries to help you mark up the other angles equal to $x°$.
- **b** By considering alternate angles, prove that opposite sides of a rhombus are parallel.
- **c** Use symmetries to help you find the other angles equal to $y°$.
- **d** How are x and y related?
- **e** Prove that the sum of the angles of a rhombus is 360°.

3 A tiling of four rhombuses produces the shape ABCDEFGH.

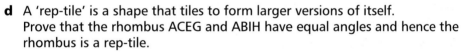

- **a** Show that AHG is a straight line.
- **b** Show that the sum of the angles round I is 360°, and hence there are no gaps or overlapping of tiles.
- **c** Prove ABCDEFGH is a rhombus.
- **d** A 'rep-tile' is a shape that tiles to form larger versions of itself.
  Prove that the rhombus ACEG and ABIH have equal angles and hence the rhombus is a rep-tile.
- **e** What kind of quadrilateral is HBDF?

4 Four coins are arranged as shown.
Prove that the quadrilateral formed by joining their centres is a rhombus.

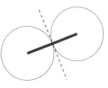

Note: the axis of symmetry shows that the line joining the centres passes through the point of contact of the circles.

E

5 **a** Prove that the diagonals bisect the angles of the rhombus.

b Name four isosceles triangles in the diagram.

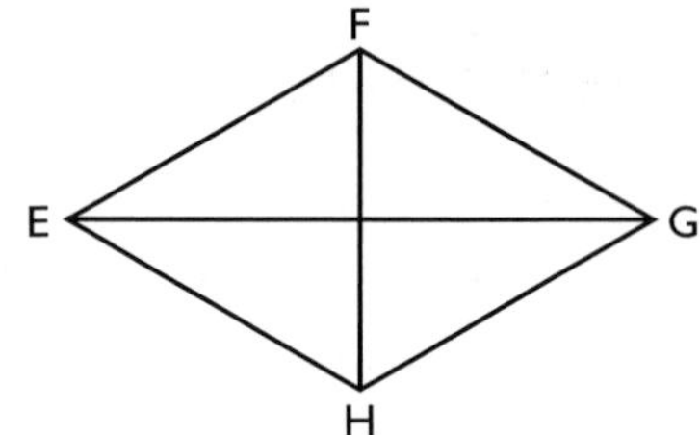

6 Copy each rhombus and then find as many angles as you can.

a

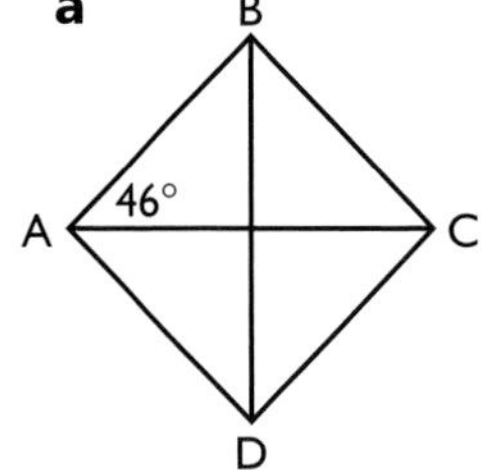

b

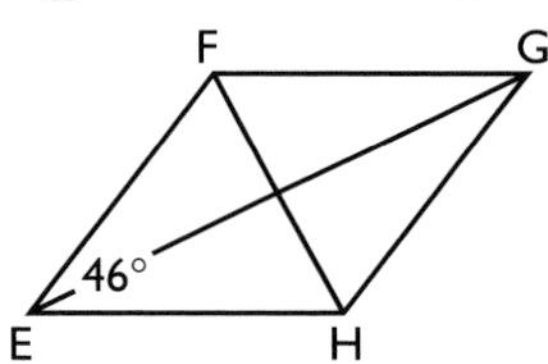

c

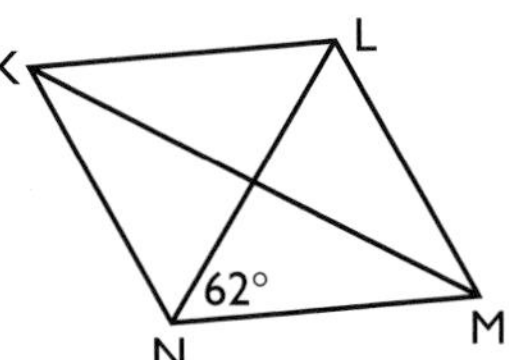

7 Prove that:

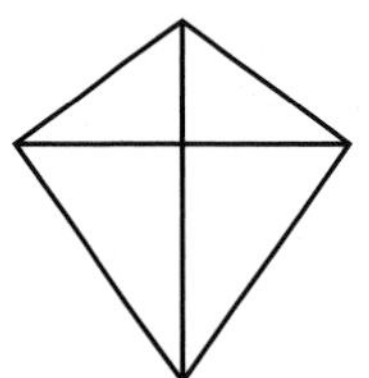

a the diagonals of a kite cross at right angles

b one diagonal bisects the other …

c … and bisects the angles of the kite that it passes through.

8 **a** Explain why ABCD cannot be a rhombus.

b If $\angle AEB = 90°$, what kind of shape is it?

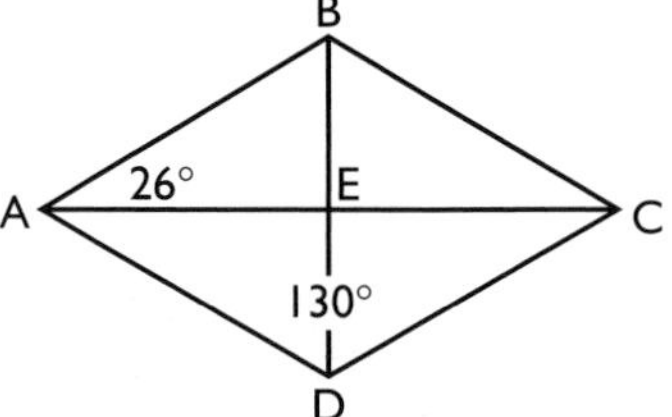

9 Calculate the perimeter of each kite.

a

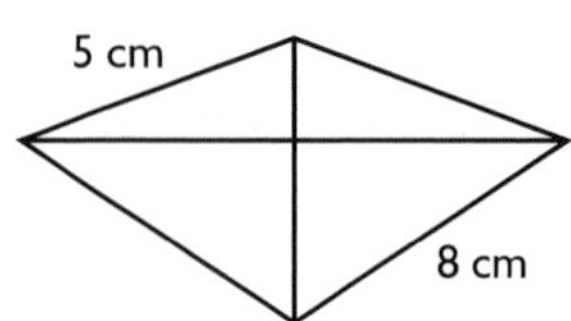

b

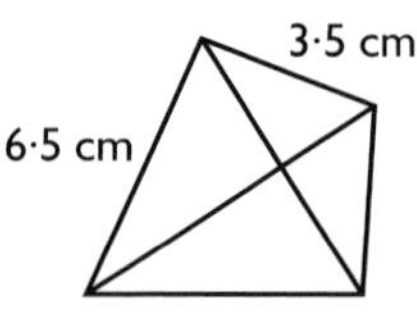

c

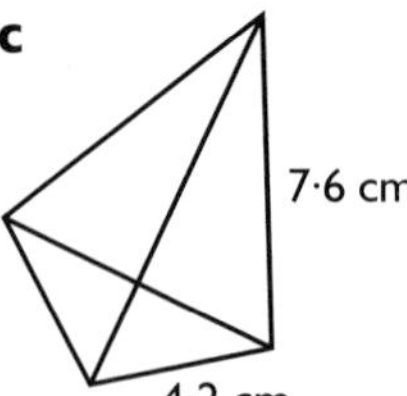

10 Three congruent kites tile to form a triangle.

a Calculate the size of each angle in the diagram, giving reasons.

b If the perimeter of the triangle is 12 cm, what information about the kite can be deduced?

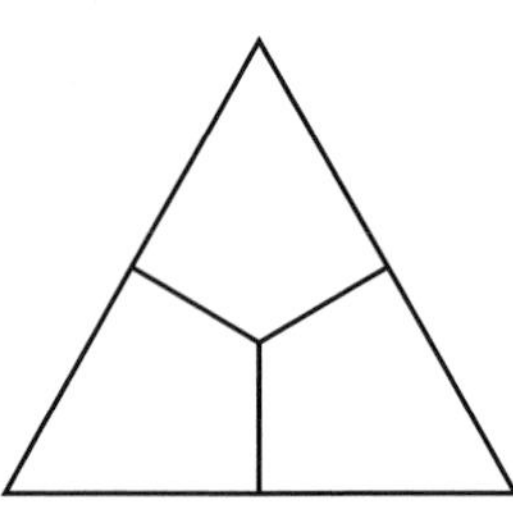

Investigation

Suppose, instead, that the height of the triangle in question **10** is 12 cm.

a Make an accurate drawing of the triangle.

b Break it into kites.

c Measure the sides of a kite. What seems to be the case?

d Try it for different heights.

Exercise 3.2

1 ABDE is a rectangle.
When AC and AD are drawn it is found that they break ∠BAE into three equal angles.
CF is drawn perpendicular to AD.

a What is the size of ∠CAD?

b Prove △CAD is isosceles (and hence AC = CD).

c Prove DF = AC.

d What kind of shape is ACDF?

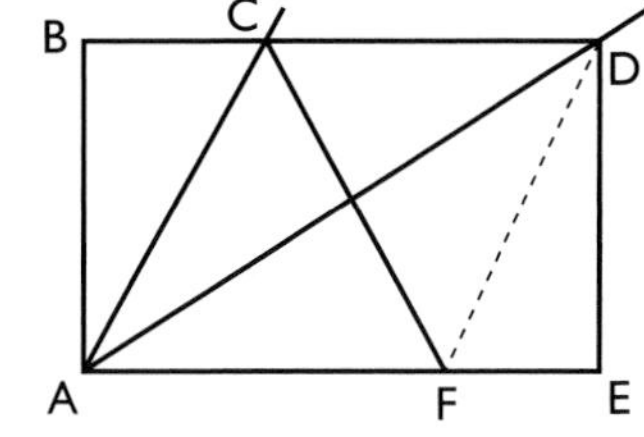

2

A fisherman's record catch can be modelled as a rhombus.
Nature often produces symmetry.

The rhombus has been placed inside a rectangle in two different ways.

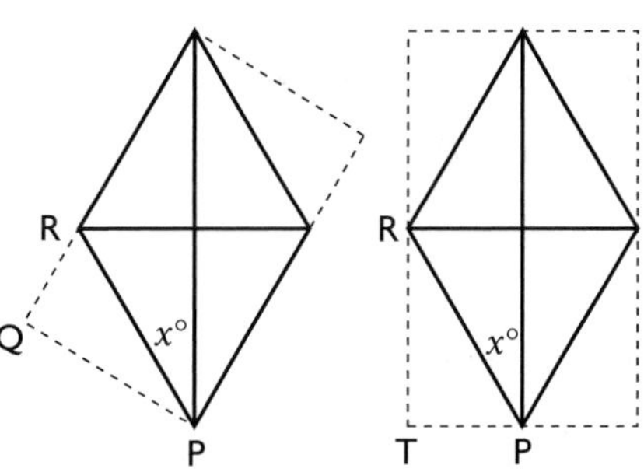

a If $x° = 30°$, copy both diagrams and find as many angles as you can.
Is △PQR = △PTR?

b What is the ratio of the areas of the rectangles?

3 The two-dimensional representation of a cube shown is made of three congruent rhombuses.

Prove that the outline of the representation is a regular hexagon.
(Regular means having equal angles and equal sides.)

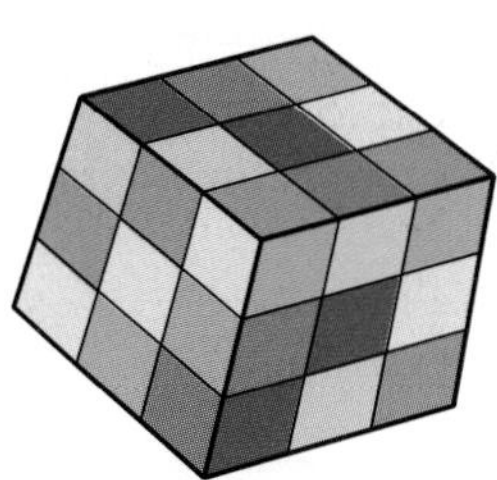

4 A(1, 2), B(4, 4) and C(7, 2) are three vertices of a quadrilateral ABCD.

a What kind of shape is it if D has coordinates:
i (4, −2) **ii** (4, −1) **iii** (4, 0) **iv** (4, 1) **v** (4, 3) **vi** (4, 7)?

b In each case state the point of intersection of the diagonals.

c If D has an x coordinate of 4, what two values can its y coordinate not take?

5 P(2, 3), Q(7, 4), R(6, −1) and S are the vertices of a rhombus.

a What are the coordinates of S?

b What are the coordinates of the point of intersection of the diagonals?

c PTRU is a square whose diagonals lie on the diagonals of the rhombus. Find the coordinates of T and U if T is closer to Q than it is to S.

d Name four kites in a diagram that shows the rhombus and square.

6 The triangle with vertices J(3, 1), K(4, −2) and L(10, 0) is right-angled. It forms one quarter of a rhombus whose diagonals intersect at K.

a Find the coordinates of the other vertices M and N of the rhombus given that JM is a diagonal.

b A second, congruent, rhombus is drawn which shares the side JL with the first.
Find the coordinates of its **i** vertices **ii** centre.

c By considering a suitable rectangle whose sides are parallel to the x and y axes, calculate the area of the rhombus JLMN.

E

Challenges

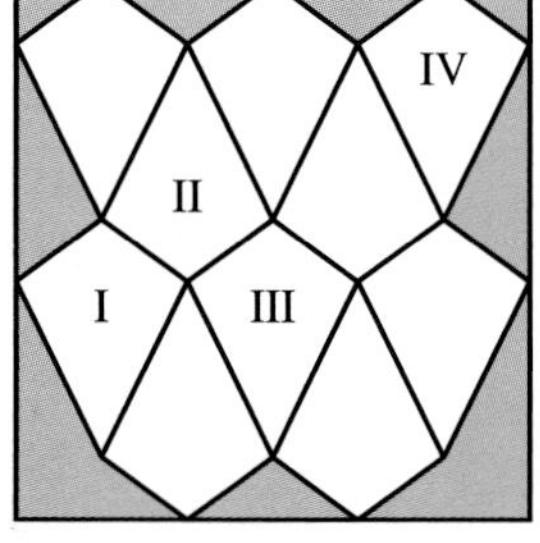

1 A manufacturer of toy kites stamps out the shapes from cloth.
In order to save on wastage these kites are tiled.
The coordinates of the vertices of the kite I are A(−2, −1), B(0, 0), C(2, −1), and D(0, −5).

a Find the coordinates of the vertices of kite
i II ii III iii IV.

b What are the dimensions of the rectangle from which the ten kites are cut?

c Calculate:
i the area of the rectangle
ii the area of the kites
iii the wastage expressed as a percentage of the rectangle.

2 The manufacturers make a V-kite model.
Explore the ways it could be tiled to make savings on wastage.

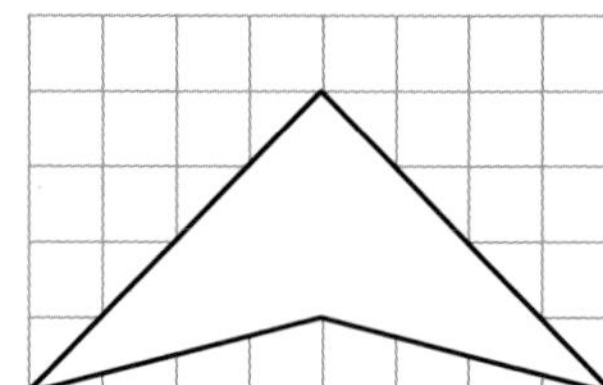

From the symmetries of the rhombus and kite we deduce the following:

Rhombus summary

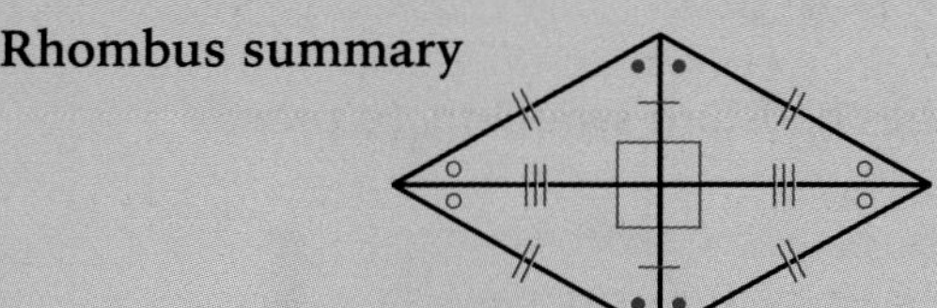

Kite summary

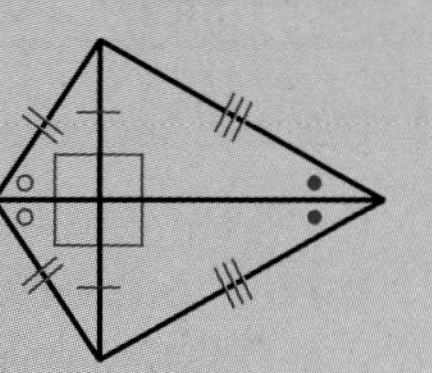

4 The trapezium and parallelogram

Definitions A **trapezium** is a quadrilateral with one pair of parallel sides.
A **parallelogram** is a quadrilateral with two pairs of parallel sides.

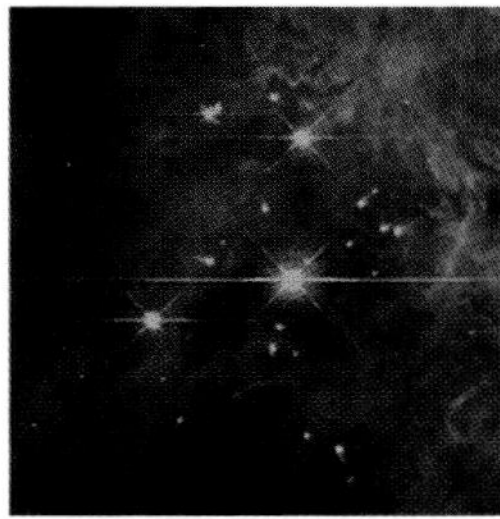

This cluster of stars in the constellation of Orion is called The Trapezium.

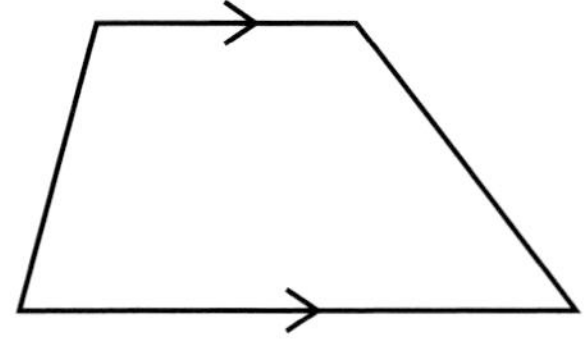

A trapezium

In general, the trapezium has no symmetries.

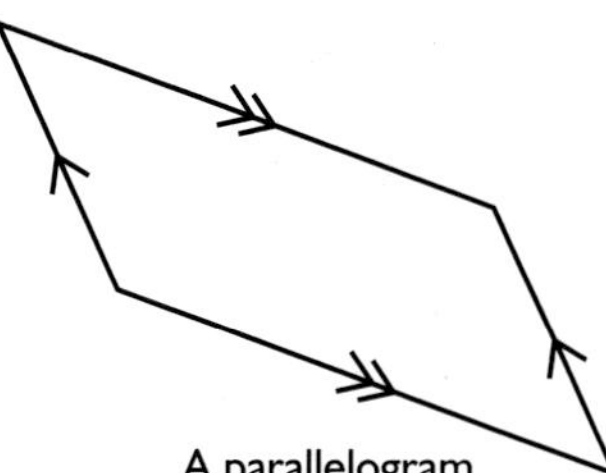

A parallelogram

The parallelogram posseses half-turn symmetry.

Example 1 Calculate the size of ∠BCD.

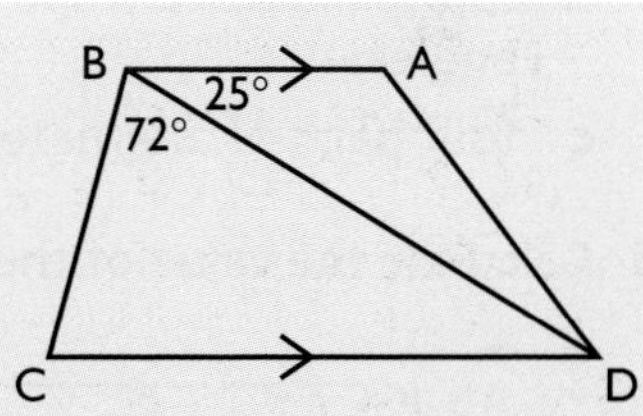

AB is parallel to CD

⇒ ∠BDC = 25° (alternate angles)

⇒ ∠BCD = 83° (third angle in a triangle)

Example 2 Prove opposite sides of a parallelogram are equal.

After a half turn about the centre E,

A → C, B → D, C → A and D → B

⇒ AB → CD ⇒ AB = CD

and AD → CB ⇒ AD = CB

⇒ opposite sides are equal.

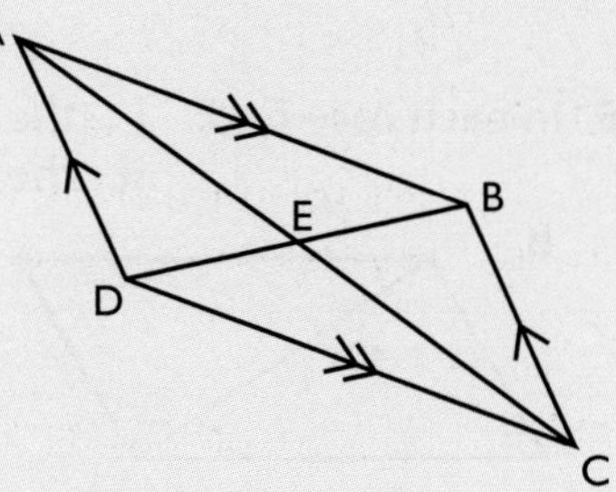

Exercise 4.1

1 Use the fact that the parallelogram has half-turn symmetry to prove:

a opposite angles are equal

b diagonals bisect each other

c a diagonal splits the parallelogram into two congruent triangles.

2 **a** What is the sum of the four angles of the parallelogram?

b Prove it.

c Opposite angles are equal.
What is the relation between adjacent angles (neighbouring angles $x°$ and $y°$)?

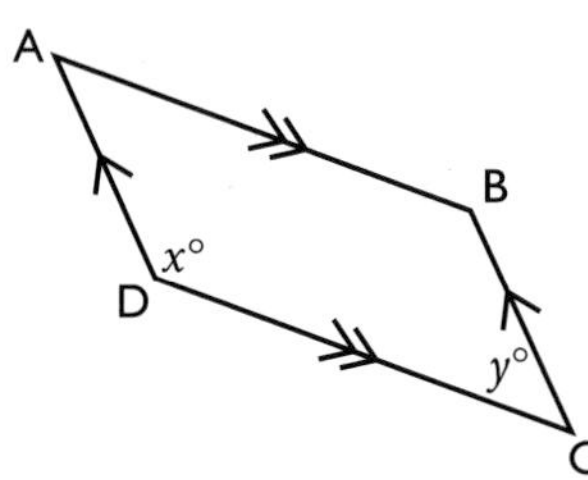

3

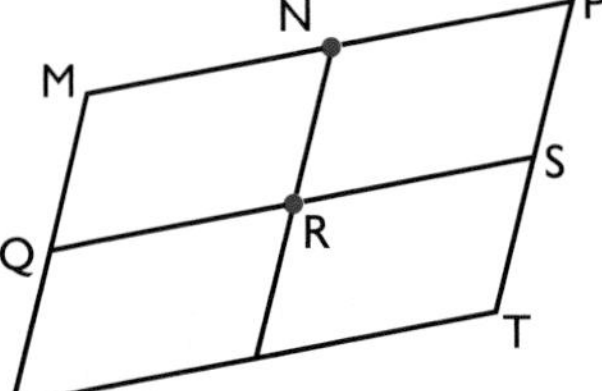

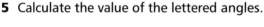

Examine the tiling of these four congruent parallelograms.
Using the above findings, prove:

a there are no overlaps or gaps round R

b MNP is a straight line

c the parallelogram is a rep-tile.

4 ABCD is a parallelogram. Its diagonals intersect at K. Name:

a two pairs of vertically opposite angles

b four pairs of corresponding angles

c four pairs of alternate angles.

H B C G K F A D E

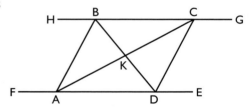

5 Calculate the value of the lettered angles.

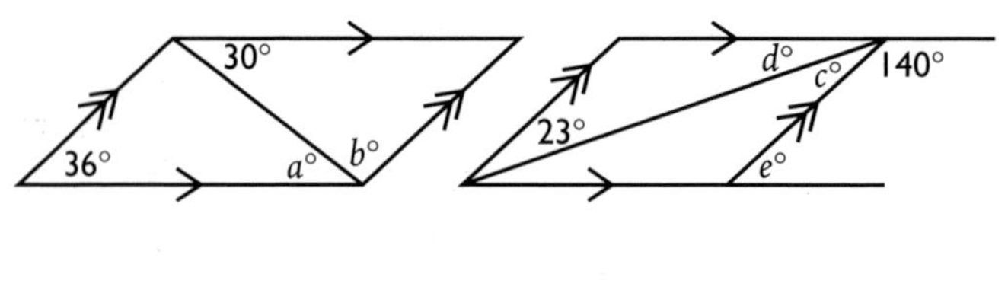

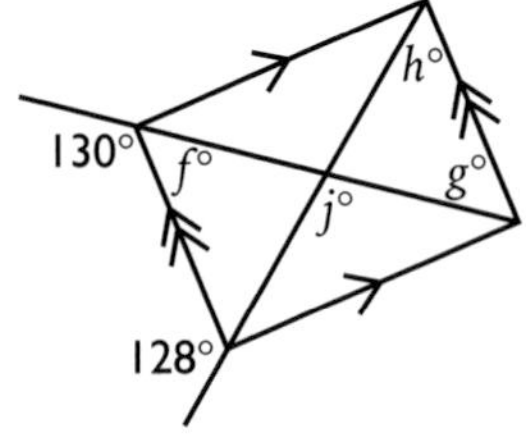

6 In each case find: **i** the value of x

ii the size of the angles of the parallelogram.

a

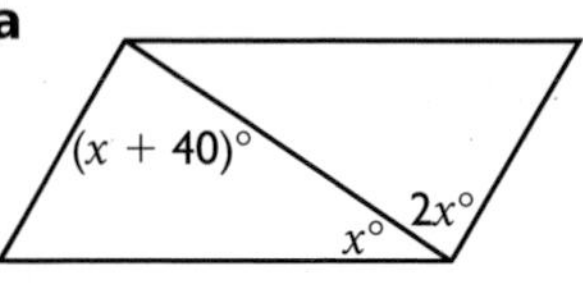

b

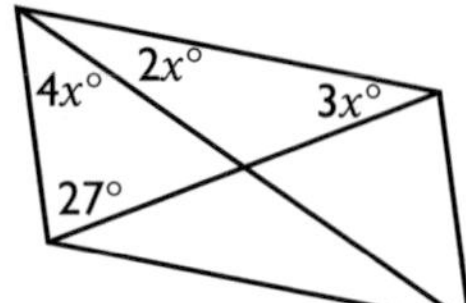

7 The weighing instrument shown has a mechanism based on the parallelogram.
As CB goes down under the weight it remains vertical as it is parallel to AD.

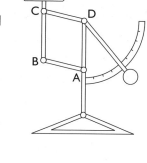

  a Calculate the size of ∠CDA when ∠DAB is
  i 100°
  ii 90°
  iii 47°.

  b As the size of ∠CDA changes, what can be said about:
  i the perimeter of the parallelogram
  ii the length of the diagonal DB?

8 A parallelogram is such that by the addition of two appropriate lines AP and AQ, a kite can be picked out. Prove that the parallelogram has to be a rhombus.

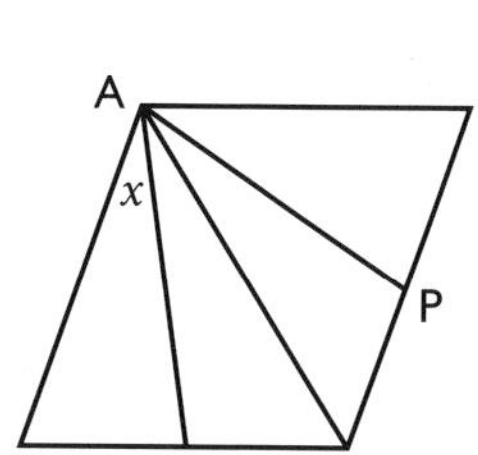

Investigation

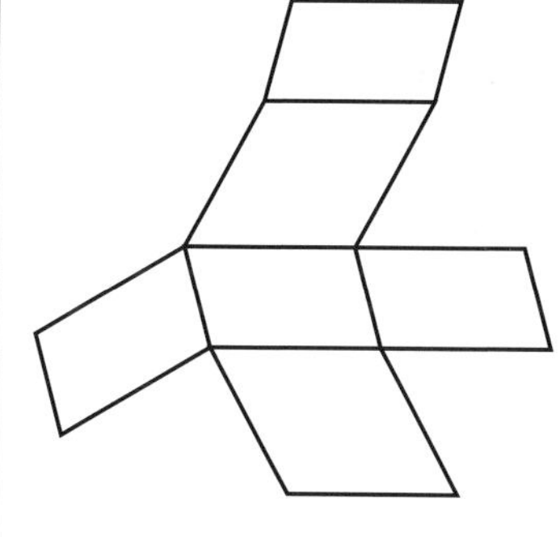

The mineral calcite grows in crystals of six faces, each of which is a parallelogram.

Make an enlargement of this diagram.
Cut it out.
Try and make the model of the calcite crystal.

Such a solid is called a **parallelopiped**.

9 Trapezia tile.

  a Copy the tiling and mark each angle with an a, b, c or d.

  b Match up a, b, c and d as supplementary pairs.

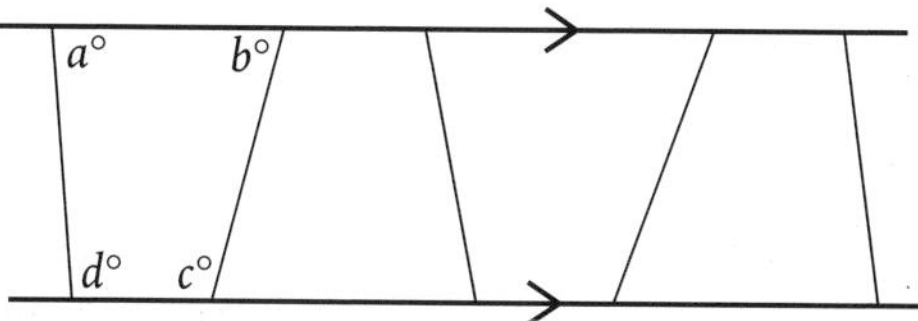

10

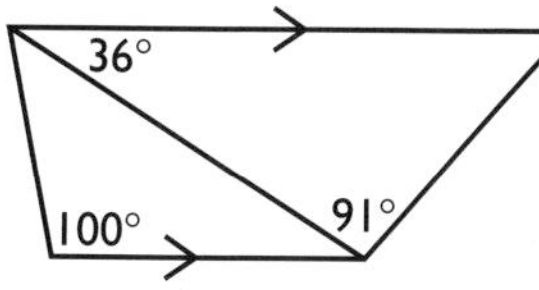

Calculate the size of each unmarked angle.

E

11 A furniture company sells different sets of tables each of which is a symmetrical trapezium.

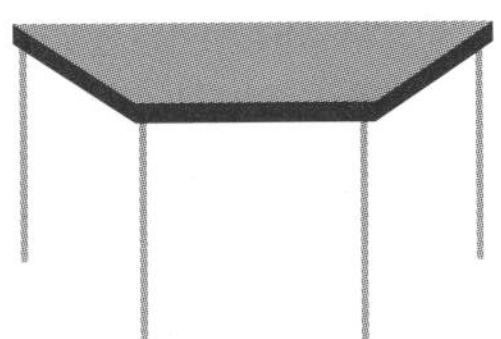

a Model 1 is such that four can be nested to form a square as shown.

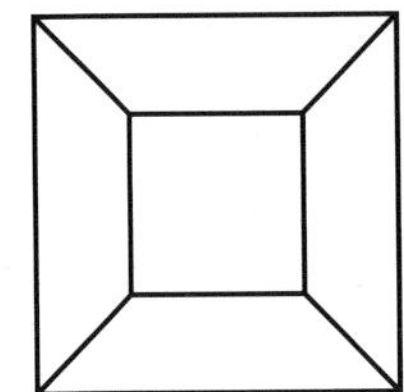

Make a sketch of the table-top and mark on it the size of each angle.

b

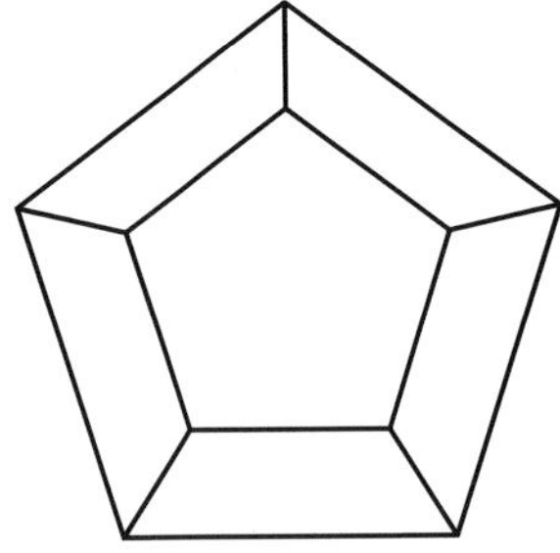

Model 2 in a similar fashion forms a regular pentagon. By considering the joins being extended to the centre, make a sketch of this table-top and mark on it the size of each angle.

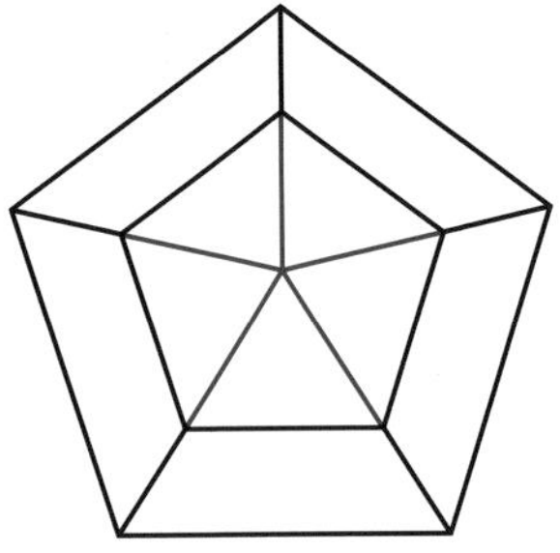

c Model 3 is such that two tables can be arranged to form a regular hexagon. Sketch this table-top.

E

12

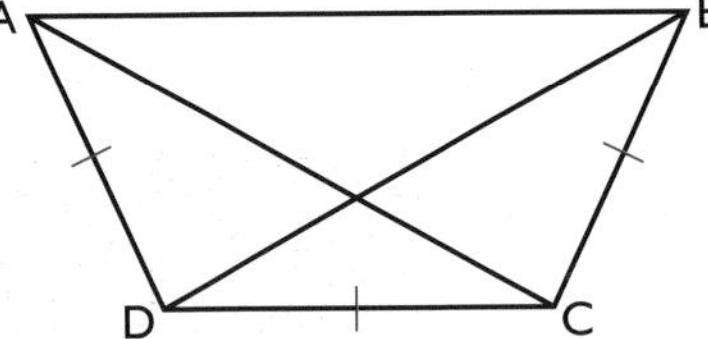

The cross-section of a bridge is a symmetrical trapezium with three sides equal.

a Prove that the diagonals bisect the angles at A and B.

b If $\angle DAC = 15°$, calculate all the angles of the trapezium.

Exercise 4.2

1 Calculate the size of each labelled angle.

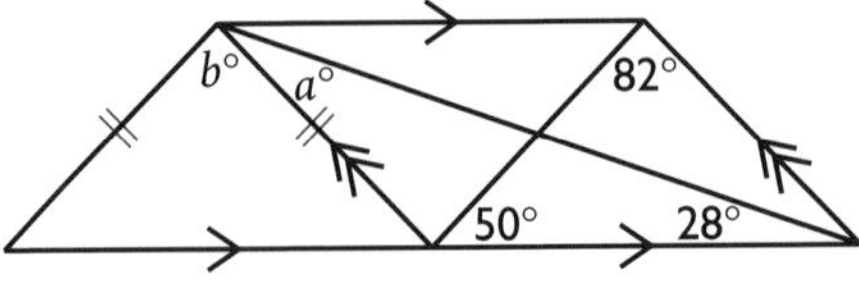

2 The triangle ABC is translated along AF to the position DEF.

a Mark equal angles.

b Name two parallelograms.

c Name two trapezia.

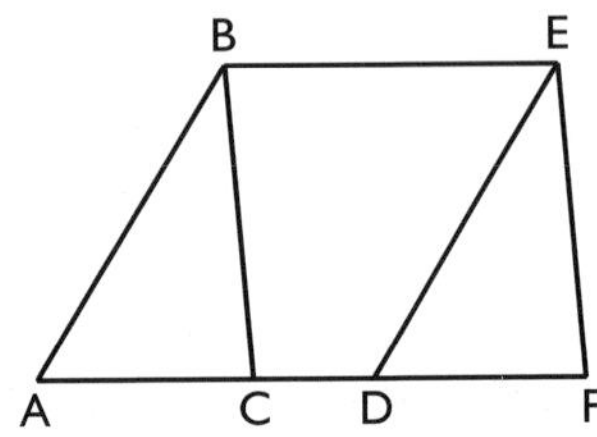

3 A certain symmetrical trapezium is a rep-tile as demonstrated here.

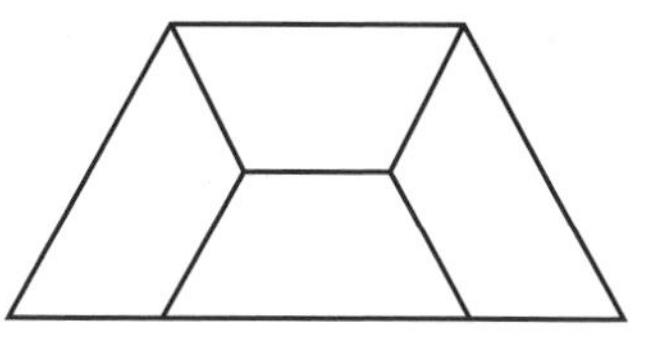

a Calculate the size of each angle.

b What is the ratio of the lengths of the parallel sides of one trapezium?

4 ABCD is a parallelogram.
To go from A to B we take 5 steps in the x-direction and 1 step in the y-direction.

a In a similar manner give instructions to get from
i D to C **ii** D to A **iii** C to B.

b Comment on the instructions for parallel lines.

c Test your conjecture with the parallelogram EFGH.

5 A parallelogram has vertices P(1, 3), Q(8, 5), R(11, 3) and S.

a Find S and give its coordinates.

b Its diagonals cross at the point K. State the coordinates of K.

c Give the instructions to get from
i P to K **ii** P to R **iii** S to K **iv** S to Q.
Comment.

6 The suspension on the Lunar Lander makes use of a parallelogram linkage.

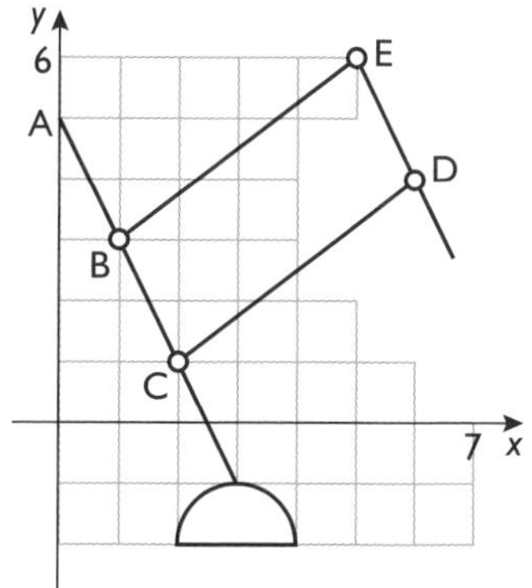

It has been modelled in the grid opposite.

The leg ABC is fixed. The body is attached to the leg by linkages BE and CD.

E and D can move to absorb some of the shock of the landing.

BCDE is a parallelogram.

a State the coordinates of B and C.

b In the position shown, E is the point (5, 6). What is the corresponding position of D?

c What is the position of D when E is at **i** (4, 7) **ii** (6, 3)?

7 The illustration shows a non-symmetric trapezium tiling in such a way that it forms a larger form of itself … another rep-tile.

Calculate the size of each angle in the tile.
Give reasons for each decision.

E

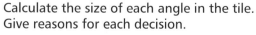

8 The lean-to extension of a house has sides which are trapezia.
The parallel sides have lengths 2·6 m and 2 m.
The base is 1 m wide. The base angles are right angles.

a By considering a right-angle triangle and a rectangle, calculate the area of the trapezium.

b Calculate the missing angles given that $x = 31°$, $y = 38°$ and $z = 21°$ correct to the nearest degree.

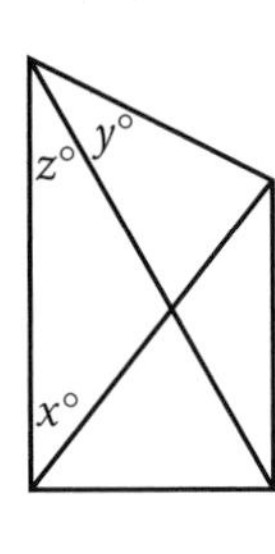

Investigation

a Draw a trapezium ABCD whose smaller parallel side is half the length of the larger.

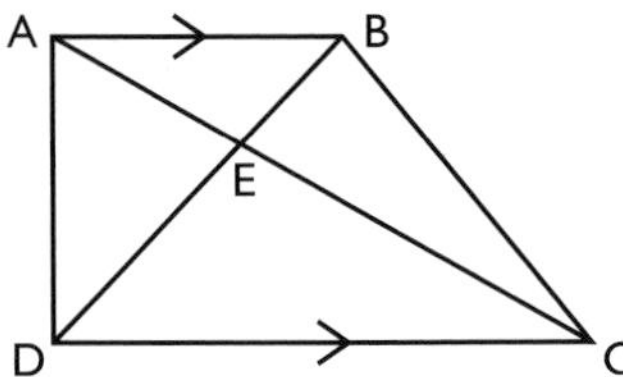

b Its diagonals intersect at E.
  i Measure the length of AE and EC.
  ii What is the ratio of AE : EC?
  iii Measure the length of DE and EB.
  iv What is the ratio of DE : EB?
  Comment.
  Compare your results with those of your friends.

c Repeat these steps with a trapezium whose smaller side is a third of the larger.
  Again compare your results with others.

Write a report on your findings after testing your conjectures on other different trapezia.

Parallelogram summary

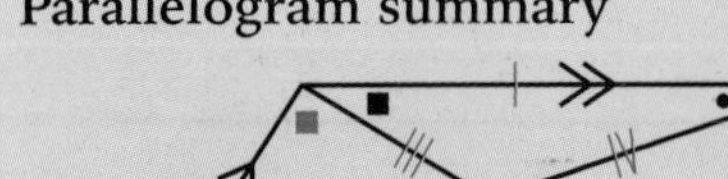

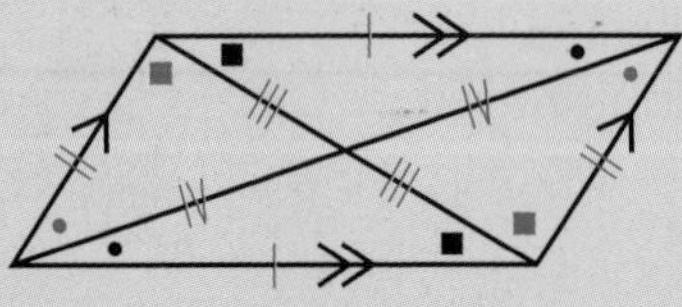

Trapezium summary

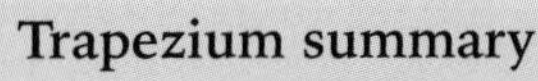

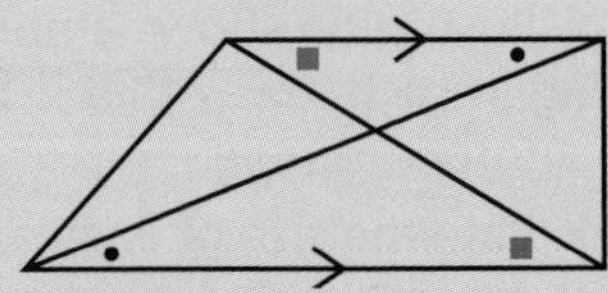

5 Classifying quadrilaterals

We have sorted the family of quadrilaterals into seven basic types:

- square — a quadrilateral with four axes of symmetry.
- rectangle — a quadrilateral with two axes of symmetry passing through sides
- rhombus — a quadrilateral with two axes of symmetry passing through vertices
- kite — a quadrilateral with one axis of symmetry passing through vertices
- parallelogram — a quadrilateral with two pairs of parallel sides
- trapezium — a quadrilateral with one pair of parallel sides
- trapezoid — a quadrilateral with no pairs of parallel sides.

We did not actually examine the trapezoid but, by its inclusion, the list covers all quadrilaterals.

Note that each of the seven is a *special* quadrilateral … it meets the description of a quadrilateral and has extra properties besides.

In the same way, the square is a special kite. It has one axis of symmetry passing through vertices and has extra properties besides, namely three other axes.

The sorting of shapes into different families is called **classification**. Focusing on different properties will produce different classifications.

We can use different diagrams to help us sort.

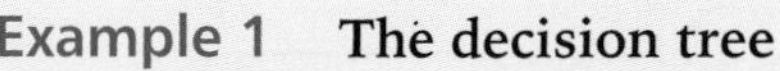

Example 1 **The decision tree**

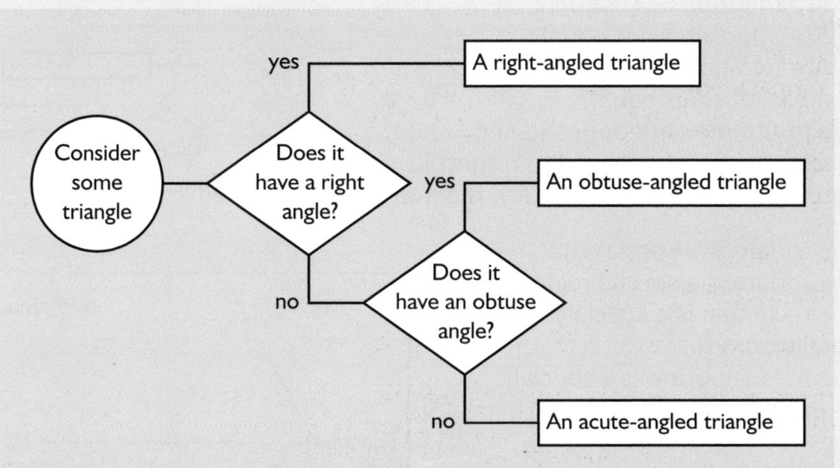

Asking questions that demand the answer 'yes' or 'no' quickly divides a group up.

Example 2 The Carroll diagram

This diagram was named after its inventor, Lewis Carroll, the author of *Alice in Wonderland*.

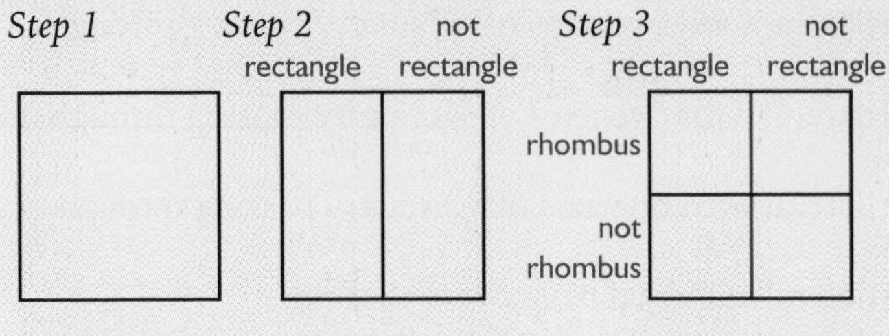

Step 1: The box represents all the quadrilaterals.

Step 2: The left column holds the rectangles; the right column holds the rest.

Step 3: Above the line holds the rhombuses; below the line holds the rest.

Step 4

	rectangle	not rectangle
rhombus	square	rhombus
not rhombus	rectangle	kite parallelogram trapezium trapezoid

Four families are created. The square is a rhombus and also a rectangle.

Exercise 5.1

1 Make a decision tree to help you sort the triangles into types using the questions:
- Are all sides equal?
- Are two sides equal?

Note that a triangle with three sides different is called **scalene**.

2 Make a decision tree to sort the quadrilaterals out using the questions:
- Are its angles right angles?
- Are the four sides equal?
- Are opposite sides equal?
- Are two pairs of adjacent sides equal?

Use the framework opposite and ignore, for the moment, the trapezoid.
Can the order in which you ask the questions be altered?

3 The square is a special kite.
The square is a special rectangle.
The rectangle is a special parallelogram.
The parallelogram is a special trapezium.
These relations are being illustrated in the diagram opposite by the use of arrows.
Copy the diagram and complete it to show all the *special* relations of this sort.

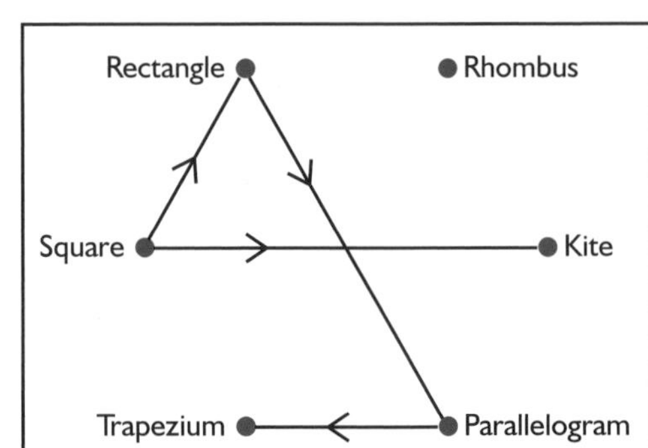

4 Copy each Carroll diagram and complete it by entering the names square, rectangle, rhombus, kite, parallelogram and trapezium into the appropriate boxes.

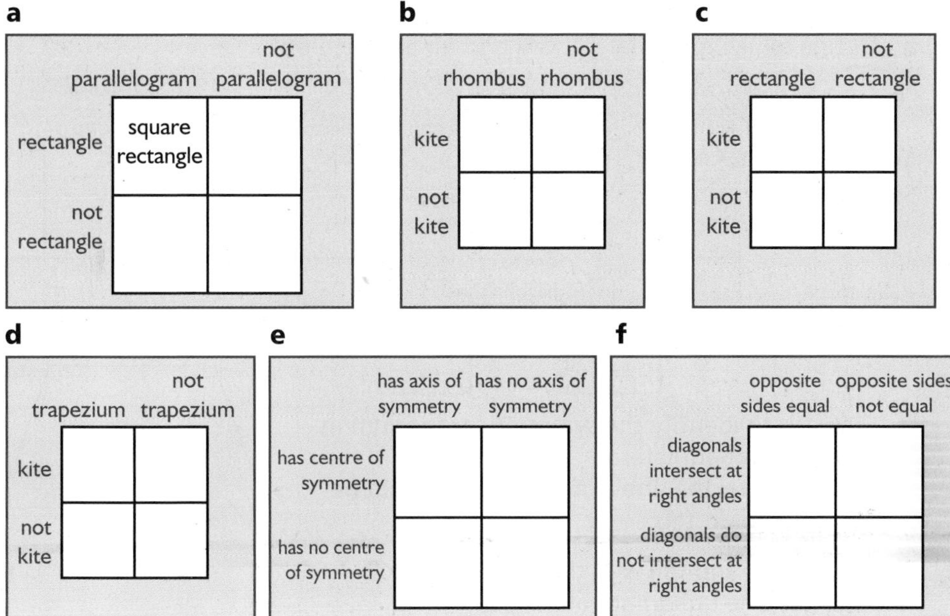

Investigation

By asking the right question we can subdivide a group into two parts.
By asking the right two questions we can subdivide a group into four parts.
By asking the right three questions we can subdivide a group into eight parts.

A panel game on the radio was called '20 questions'.
You could ask up to 20 questions each requiring a yes/no answer before guessing some mystery object.

If you asked the right questions, into how many parts might you subdivide the set of all objects?

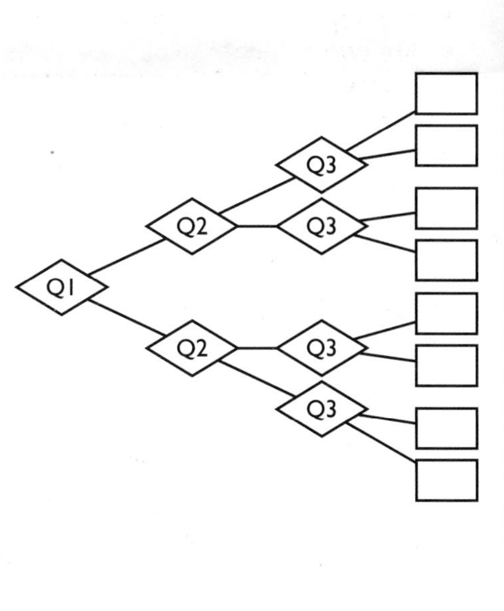

Exercise 5.2

1 This decision tree is based on the symmetries of the quadrilaterals.

a Decide which quadrilateral will end up in which box.

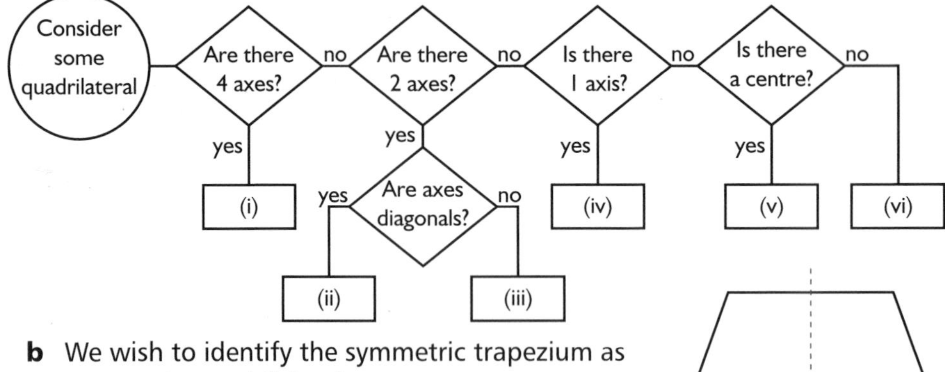

b We wish to identify the symmetric trapezium as a separate quadrilateral.
Describe how the above decision tree could be modified to do this.

Symmetric trapezium

2 The diagonals, and the way that they intersect, helps us tell one quadrilateral from another.

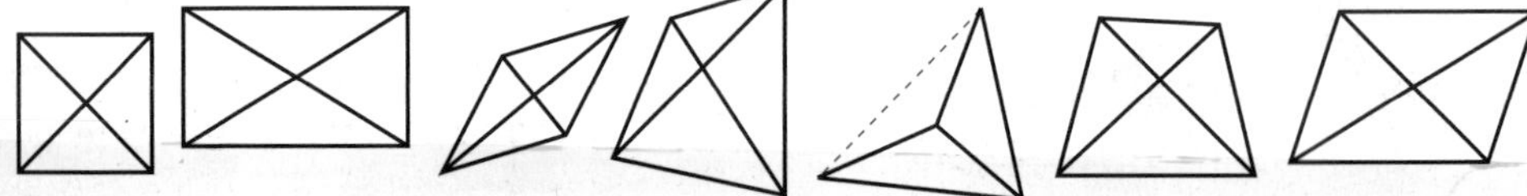

Design a decision tree to classify the quadrilaterals based on questions about the diagonals.

3 Every square is a rectangle but not ever rectangle is a square.

a Is the rectangle a special trapezium or the trapezium a special rectangle?

b Is the kite a special square or the square a special kite?

c Is the parallelogram a special rectangle or the rectangle a special parallelogram?

d Describe the relation between

i the kite and the rhombus **ii** the trapezium and the parallelogram

iii the rhombus and the parallelogram **iv** the square and the rhombus

v the square and the parallelogram.

4 Which of the following statements are true?

a The square is a rhombus which is also a rectangle.

b The square is a kite which is also a rectangle.

c The rectangle is a parallelogram which is also a kite.

d The rhombus is a kite which is also a parallelogram.

e The rhombus is a trapezium which is also a kite.

f The rectangle is a parallelogram which is also a rhombus.

5 Explore how you might use the way that different quadrilaterals tile to classify them.
Consider things like the boundaries formed, the way some have to 'flip' to fit and so on.

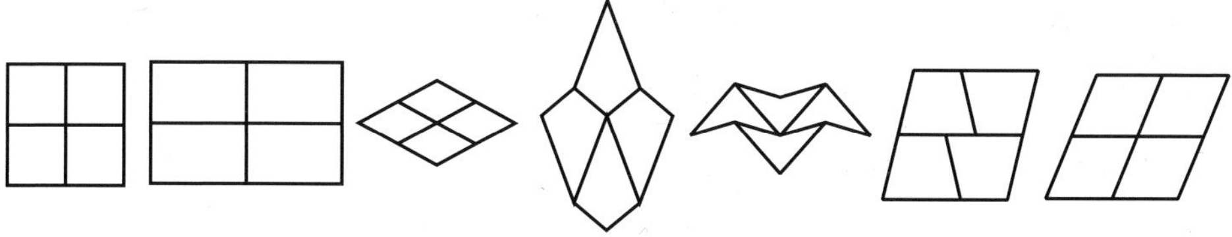

6 Drawing polygons

To draw a polygon we need a ruler, a protractor and a set of compasses.
Drawing a sketch first helps us plan our steps.

Example 1 Draw a quadrilateral with sides QR = 4 cm, PQ = 3 cm, PS = 5 cm, SR = 6 cm and ∠PQR = 65°.

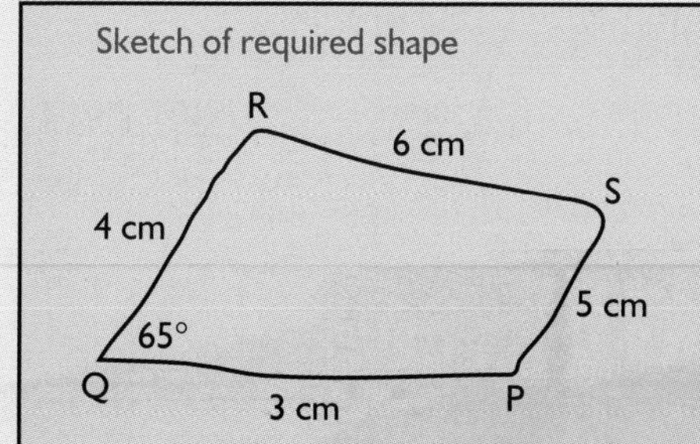

The sketch helps us plan the steps.

- Draw PQ 3 cm long.
- Measure 65° at Q.
- Draw QR 4 cm long.
- Draw an arc, centre R, radius 6 cm.
- Draw an arc, centre P, radius 5 cm.
- Identify the point S and complete the shape.

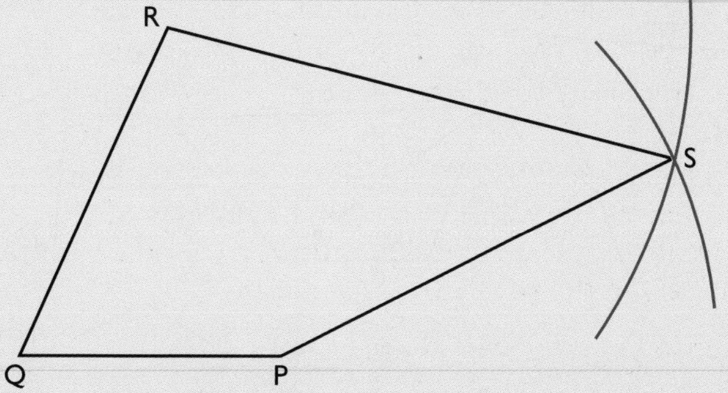

Once the accurate drawing is made, other measurements, which were not given, can be measured.
For example:

the diagonal QS measures 7·8 cm and ∠QPS = 154°.

Example 2 Draw a regular pentagon of side 3 cm.

Remember: a regular polygon is one whose angles are equal and whose sides are equal.

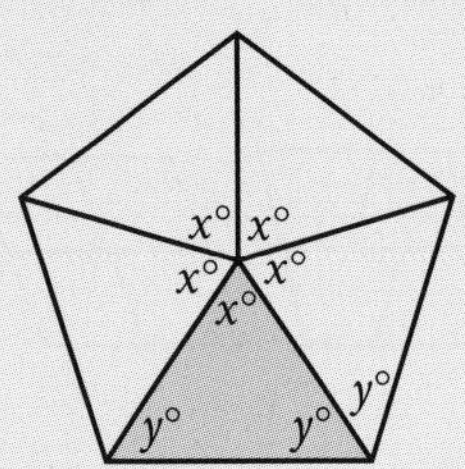

First calculate the size of the angles.

We see that $5x = 360$

$\Rightarrow \quad x = 72.$

From the triangle we see $2y = 180 - x = 108$.

Note that the size of the angles of the pentagon are each $2y$

$\Rightarrow \quad$ angle of the pentagon = 108°.

- Draw AB 3 cm long.
- Draw ∠ABC = 108°.
- Draw BC 3 cm long.
- Continue round the shape.

Once again other measurements can be taken, for example the diagonal AC measures 4·9 cm (to 1 d.p.).

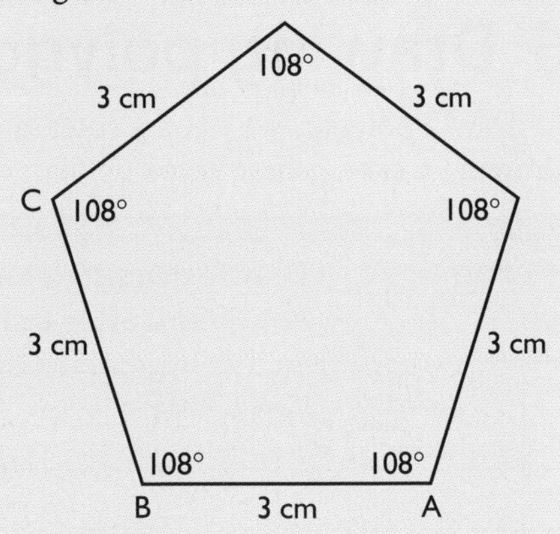

Exercise 6.1

1 **i** Make an accurate drawing of each of the following sketches.
ii Find the value of each length or angle indicated.

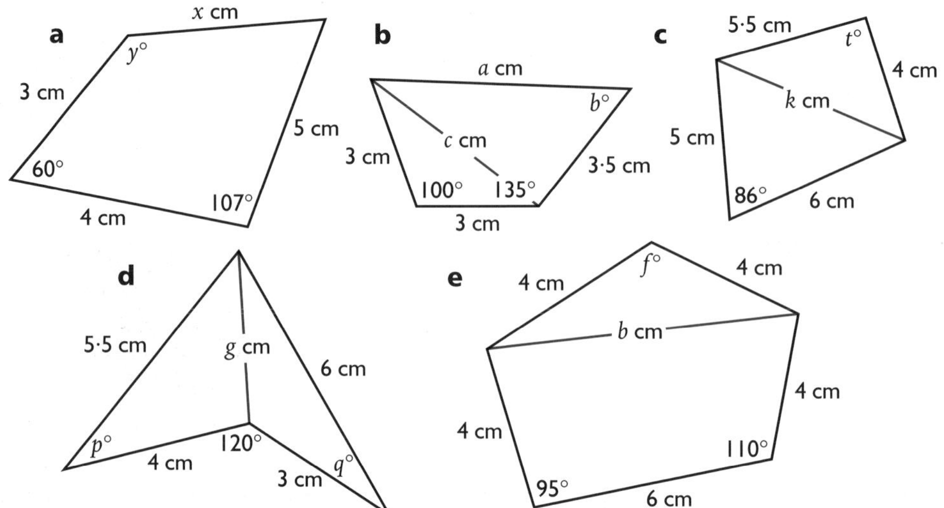

2 

The star is drawn by making a regular pentagon of side 5 cm and then drawing the diagonals.

a Draw a regular pentagon of side 5 cm.

b Measure the length of a diagonal.

c Measure the perimeter of the star.

3 This model is made from symmetrical pieces as shown.

a Make an accurate drawing of the pentagon.

b Measure the size of

i the side marked x

ii the angle marked y.

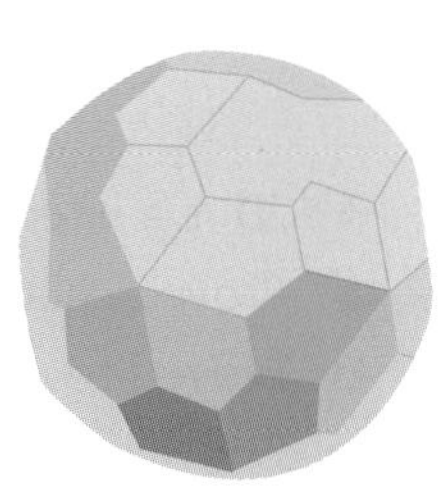

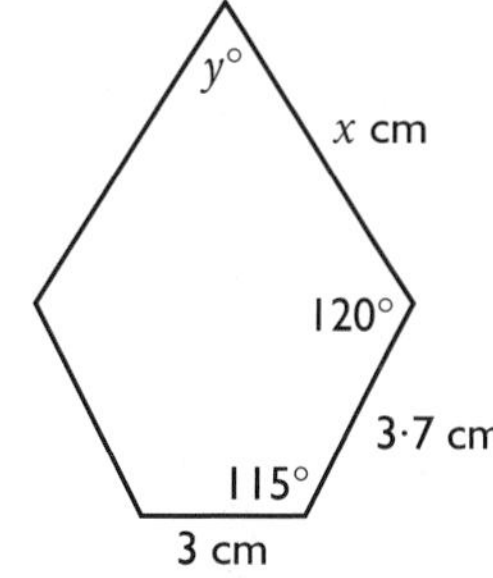

4 

Viewed from above, this greenhouse will look like a regular hexagon.
It has a side of 2 metres.

a Draw a hexagon of side 4 cm to represent the greenhouse.

b What scale is being used?

c There are two sizes of diagonals to a regular hexagon. Measure the length of both of them.

d What actual distances do these lengths represent?

5 The old fashioned threepenny bit which disappeared as currency in 1971 was regular dodecahedron (12 sides).

Draw a regular dodecahedron making use of drawings of regular hexagons of side 5 cm.

Challenge

Study the design of a 50p piece.
Can you make an accurate drawing of its outline twice life-size?

CHECK-UP

1 Here is a square marked up to show its properties.
In a similar way mark up:

a the rectangle

b the kite

c the parallelogram.

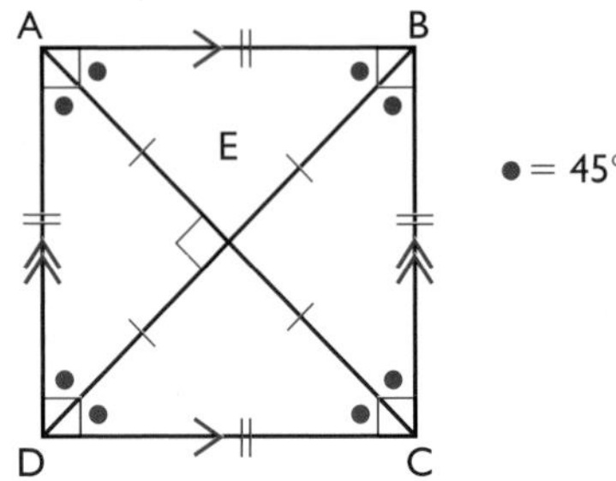

2

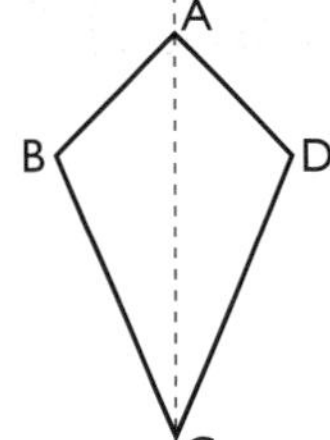

ABCD is a kite.

a Prove ∠ABC = ∠ADC.

b Prove the diagonal BD is bisected at right angles by the diagonal AC.

3 Calculate the size of each unmarked angle.

a

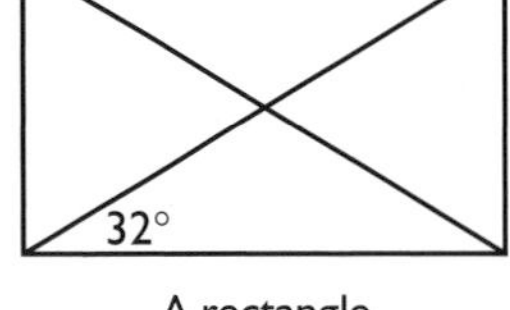

A rectangle

b

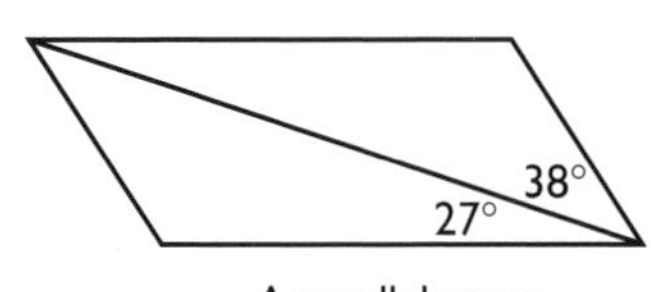

A parallelogram

4 The doorways in an Inca temple are symmetric trapezia.
Copy this sketch of one doorway and calculate all the missing angles.

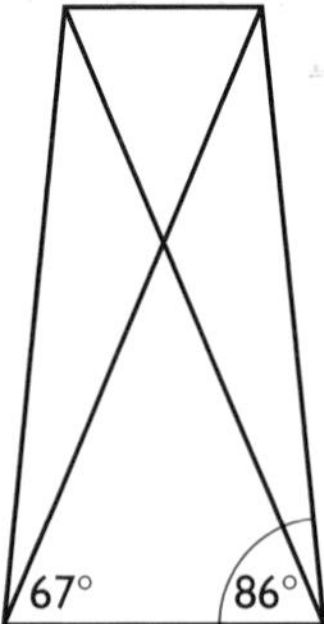

5 Calculate the size of each angle in the diagram.

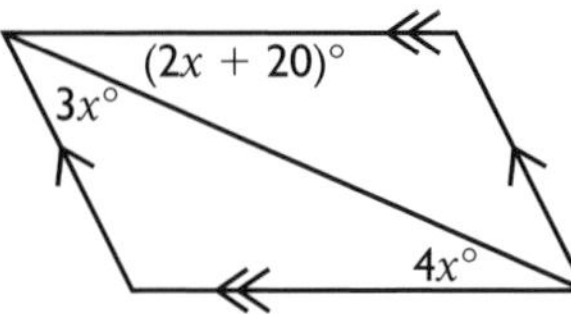

6 Which of the following statements are true?

a The rectangle is a special trapezium.

b The parallelogram is a special rectangle.

c The kite is a special rhombus.

d The rhombus is a special parallelogram.

7 This star is created by drawing a regular heptagon and drawing some of its diagonals.

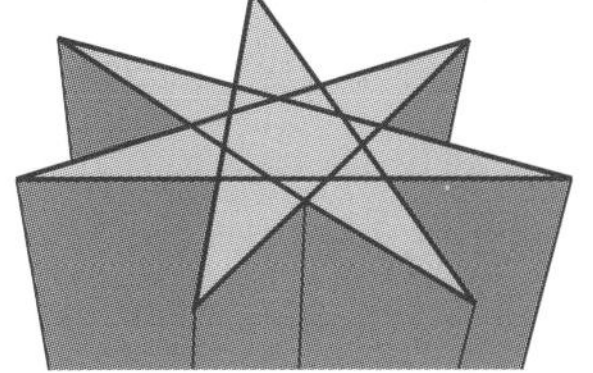

a Draw a heptagon of side 4 cm.

b How long is one of the drawn diagonals?

8 **a** Make an accurate drawing of this quadrilateral.

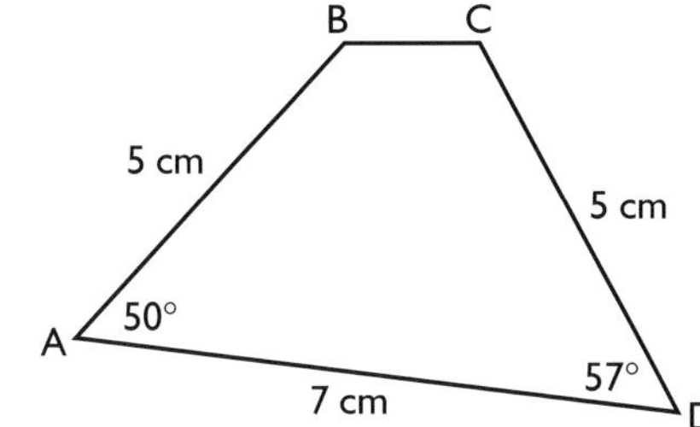

b Measure the length of the longer diagonal.

c Measure the size of the angle at B.

EF

17 Three dimensions

Studying shape and form is an important part of the life of artists, architects and engineers.

Being able to represent 3-D objects on a 2-D surface is very necessary, although full of possible pitfalls. René Magritte, the famous artist, drew a picture of a pipe and called it 'Ceci n'est pas une pipe' ('This is not a pipe') to remind people that there is a big difference between the representation of an object and the object itself.

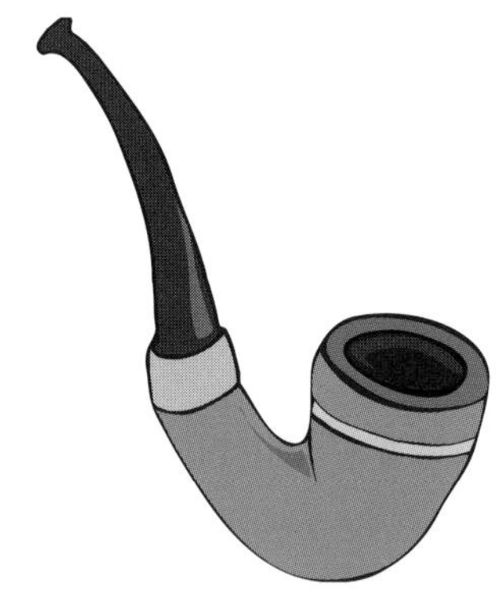

1 Looking back

Exercise 1.1

1 Identify the basic 3-dimensional solid that each of these objects is based on.

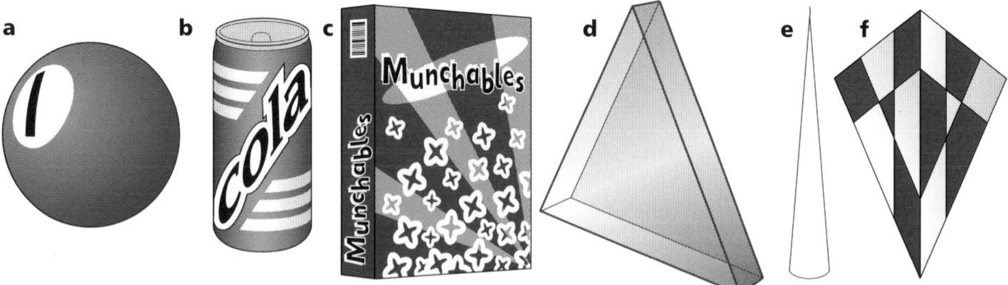

2 This cuboid is made of glass.

a Name **i** the nearest face **ii** the base.

b Which edges meet at the point B?

c Which face is opposite AEHD?

d Name the diagonals of the top face.

e Name the four space diagonals.

f Name three edges equal to AB.

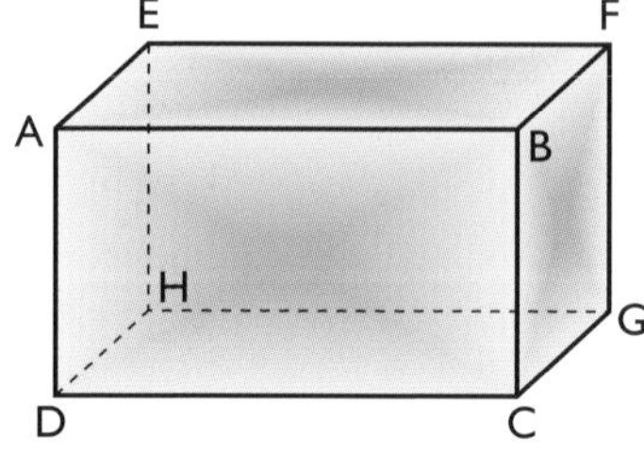

3 Which of the following are not the nets of a cube?

a 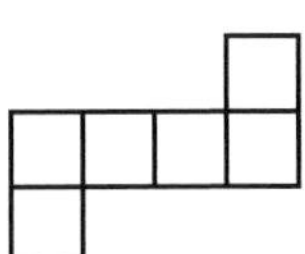

b 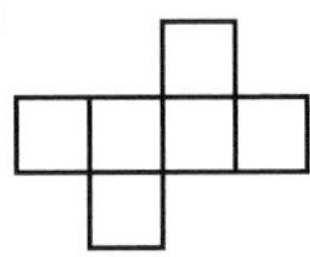

c 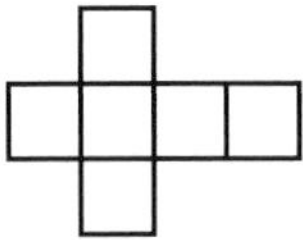

d 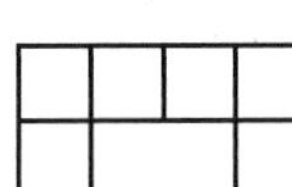

e 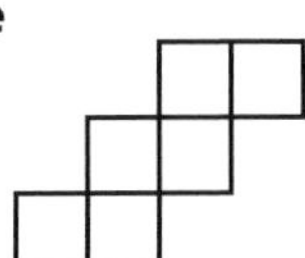

f 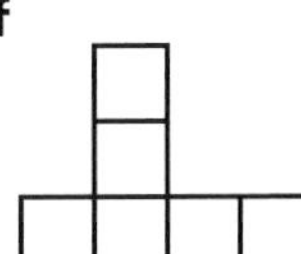

g 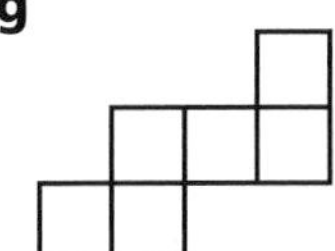

h 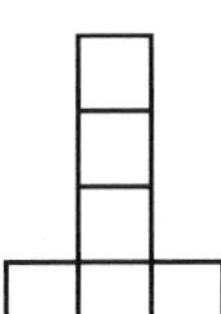

4 A cube has to be made from a set of 5 cm straws, stuck into balls of modelling clay.

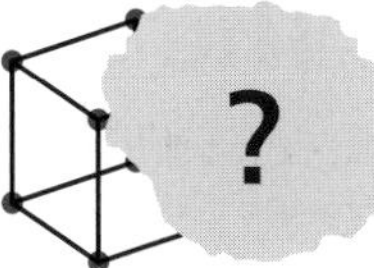

- a How many balls of modelling clay should be made?
- b What total length of straw is required?
- c What name is given to this kind of model?

5
- a How many cubic centimetres make 1 litre?
- b Change the following quantities to litres:
  - i 26 000 ml
  - ii 750 ml.
- c How are the millilitre and the cubic centimetre related?
- d Change the following quantities to millilitres:
  - i 7 litres
  - ii 0·6 litre.
- e How many litres are in a cubic metre?

6 Write down the volume of each cuboid, given that each small cube represents 1 cm^3.

a 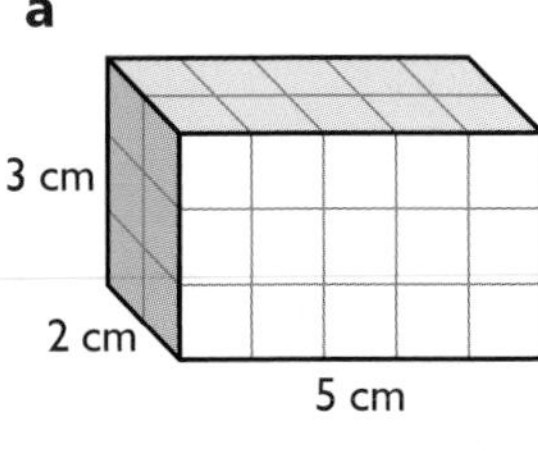

b 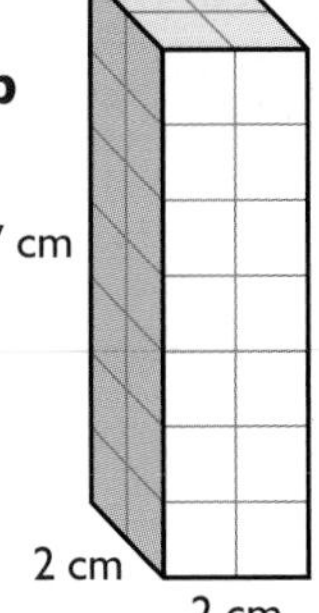

c 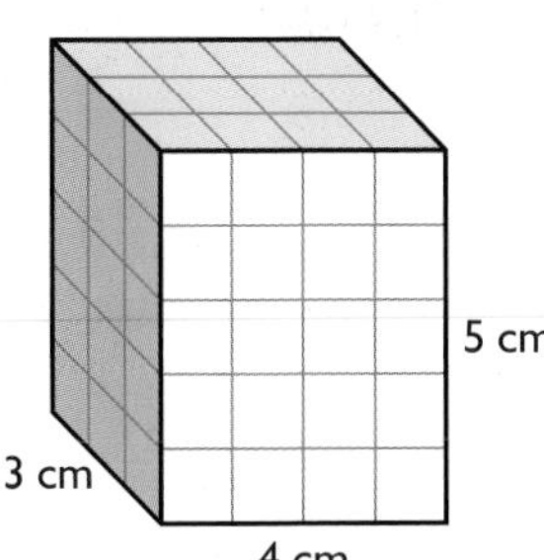

7 A cardboard box is filled with special packs of four tins of beans. The box has dimensions as shown below.

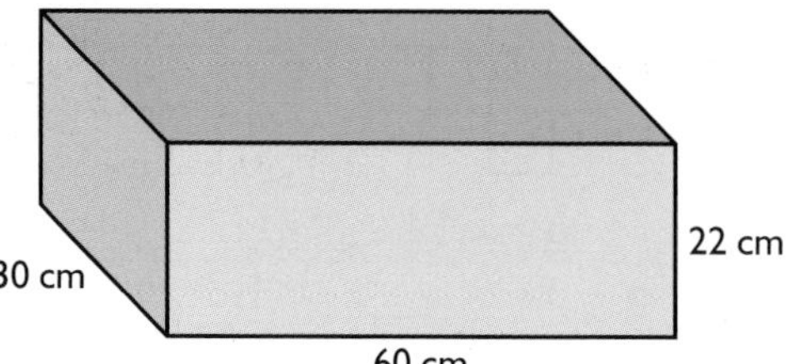

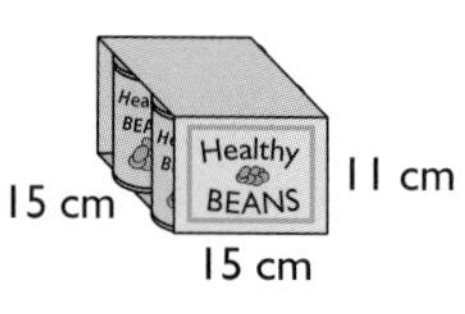

a How many packs fit in the cardboard box?

b How many tins of beans are in the box?

2 The anatomy of a solid

Each solid we study is bounded by **surfaces** or faces.

Where two faces meet, **edges** are formed.

Where edges meet, **vertices** are formed.

The sphere has 1 surface, and no edges.

The cylinder has 3 faces and 2 edges.

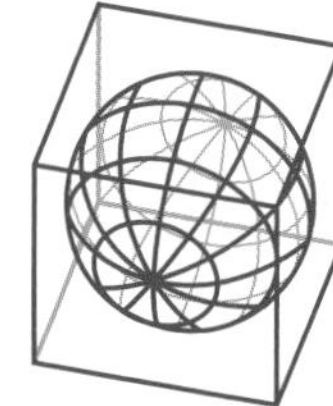

The cube has 6 faces, 12 edges and 8 vertices.

E

Exercise 2.1

1 a Copy and complete the table.

	faces (F)	edges (E)	vertices (V)	$F + V - E$
cube	6	12	8	2
cuboid				
cone				
cylinder				
sphere				
triangular prism				
square-based pyramid				

b A mathematician called Euler discovered that for certain solids, calculating faces + vertices − edges gives the answer 2.
For which of the above solids is this not true?

c The diagram shows a four-faced solid called a **tetrahedron**.
Does Euler's formula work for it?

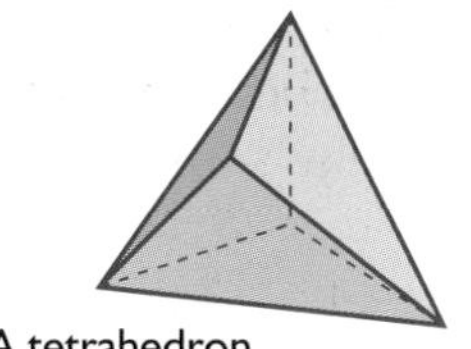
A tetrahedron

2 A cuboid is being transformed. The four top vertices, A, B, C and D, are coming together to form one vertex at P.

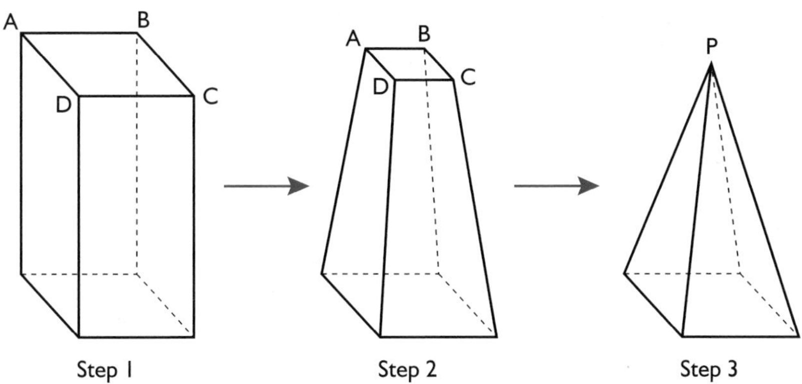

a How many faces go missing in the transformation?

b How many **i** edges **ii** vertices go missing?

c The initial shape obeys Euler's rule. Does the shape at the end?

d Suppose instead that A and D joined to become a single vertex Q.
Repeat parts **a** to **c** and comment.

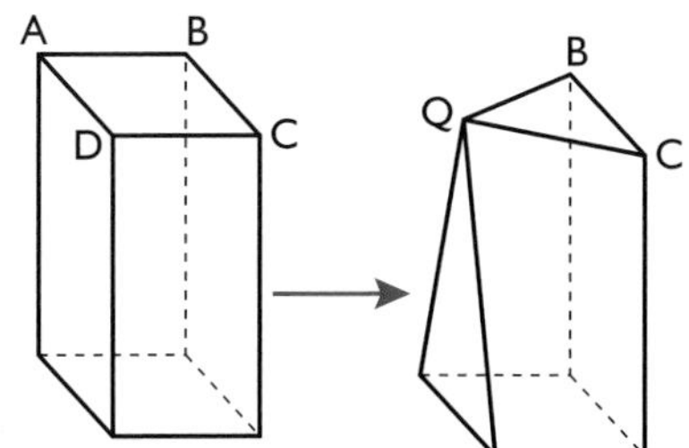

e Test Euler's rule as the solid continues to transform as shown.

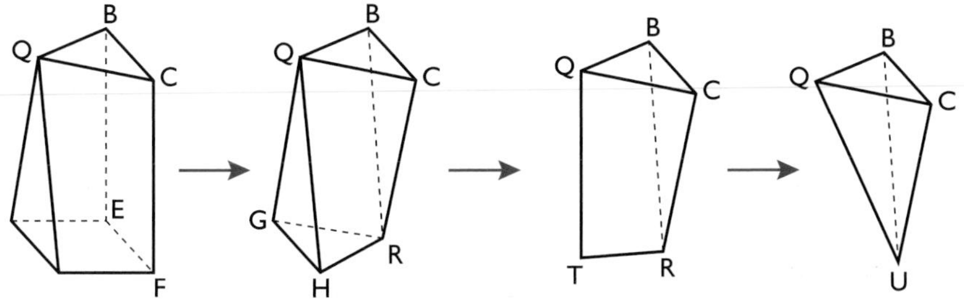

E

3 The sphere has no edges and no vertices.
How many faces would it have if it were to obey Euler's rule?

Brainstormer

A solid with a triangular face obeys Euler's rule. It has f faces, v vertices and e edges.

The three vertices of the triangular face come together, similar to the example above, to form a single vertex.

a How many **i** vertices **ii** faces **iii** edges go missing in the change?
b Show that the new solid obeys Euler's rule.

3 Families of shapes

A The pyramids

The pyramids of Egypt are square-based.

Take any shape and a point V not on the same surface.

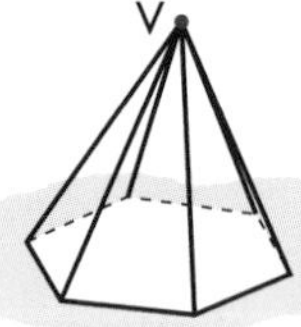

Draw an edge from V to each vertex of the shape.

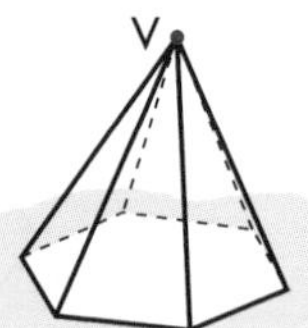

The solid formed is a pyramid. It takes its name from the name of the base.

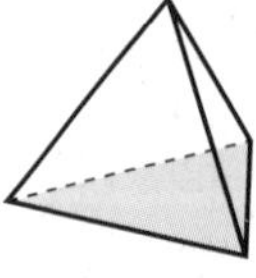

A triangular-based pyramid or **tetrahedron**

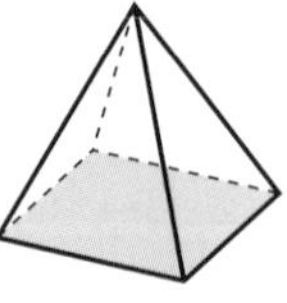

A square-based pyramid

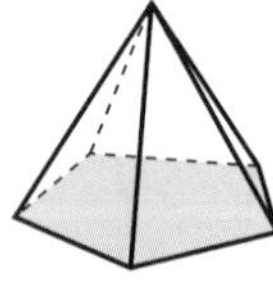

A pentagonal-based pyramid

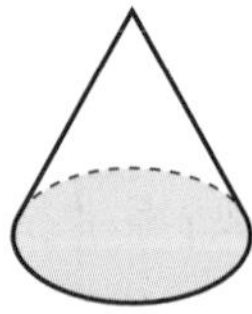

A circular-based pyramid or **cone**

Exercise 3.1

1 Name each of these shapes.
Note the vertex does not need to be above the centre of the base for the shape to be a pyramid.

a

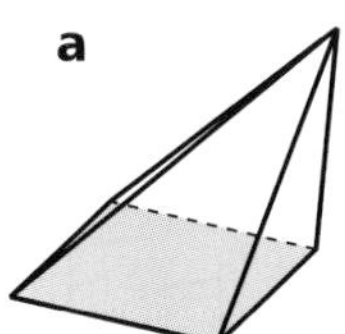

b

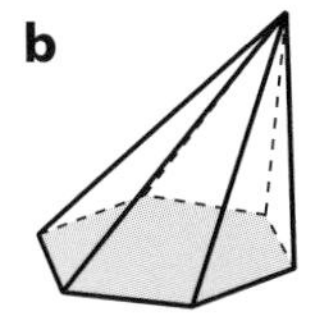

c

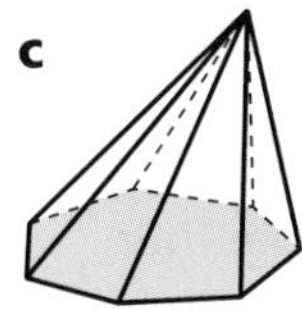

2 **a** Copy and complete the table for the first six rows.

b Use your knowledge of sequences to help you find the nth terms in the last row.

c How many faces, vertices and edges would a pyramid with a base with 20 sides have?

Shape of base	Faces	Edges	Vertices	Euler?
triangle	4	6	4	✓
square				
pentagon				
hexagon				
heptagon				
octagon				
n-gon				

3 A solid with a triangular base has a special name.

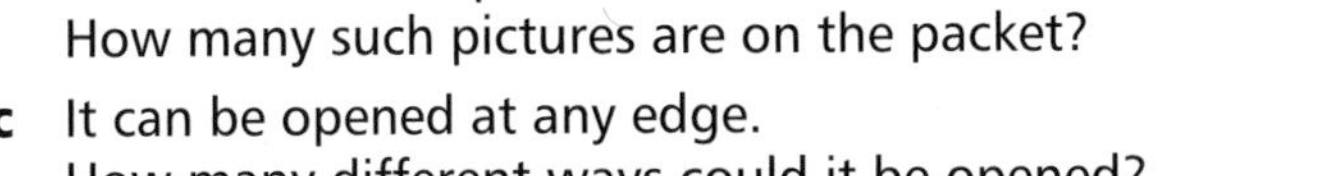

a What is it?

b This solid is used to package sweets.
On each face is a picture of a chocolate tree.
How many such pictures are on the packet?

c It can be opened at any edge.
How many different ways could it be opened?

4 This decoration has 20 faces. It is an icosahedron.

a At its top and bottom is a pyramid.
What kind of pyramid?

b How many edges has the icosahedron?
(Hint: count the vertices and use Euler's theorem.)

c Another decoration is made by putting two identical square-based pyramids back to back.
   i How many faces does the final solid have? Can you guess its name?
   ii How many vertices does it have?
   iii Use Euler's theorem to calculate the number of edges.

5 A toy house has a framework as shown. It is a cube topped by a square-based pyramid. Each face is made of canvas, including a groundsheet, and the faces are stitched together.
   a How many stitched edges are there?
   b How many canvas faces are there?
   c Will a composite shape like this still obey Euler's rule?

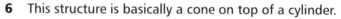

6 This structure is basically a cone on top of a cylinder.
   a How many curved surfaces has it?
   b How many surfaces are there altogether?
   c Check that it obeys Euler's rule.
   d A child's toy is made from a cylinder with a cone either side. Does this obey the rule?

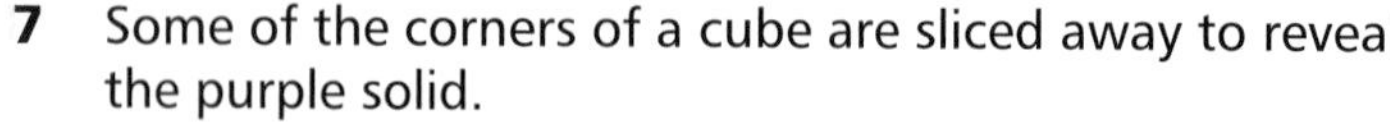

E

7 Some of the corners of a cube are sliced away to reveal the purple solid.
   a i What kind of shapes have been cut away from the corners?
     ii Sketch the faces of one and mark in the sizes of as many angles as you can.
   b i What name is given to the purple solid that is left?
     ii How do you know that the triangles of its faces are equilateral?

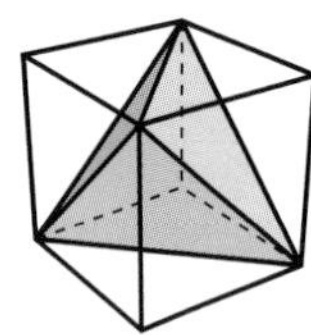

Investigation

Make a poster of different pictures showing where pyramids are used in everyday life. Include in your poster instructions for making a tetrahedron.

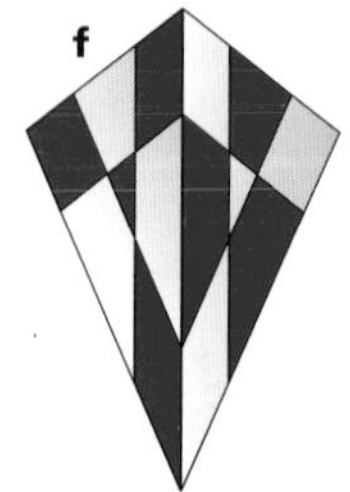

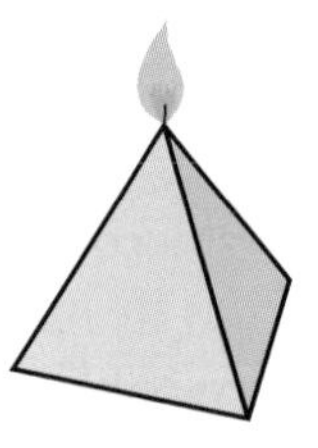

B The prisms

Any shape that has a constant cross-section throughout its length is a prism.

A piece of holiday rock is a prism – wherever you cut through it you read the same lettering.

d

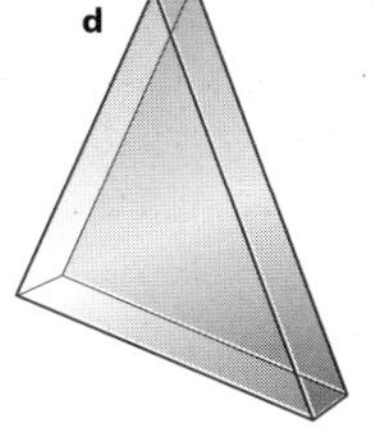

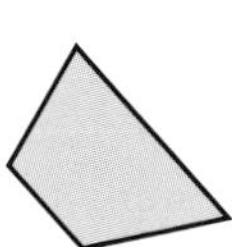

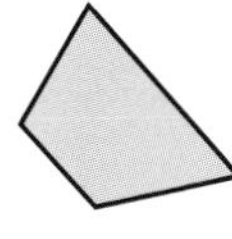

Take any shape, duplicate it and translate …

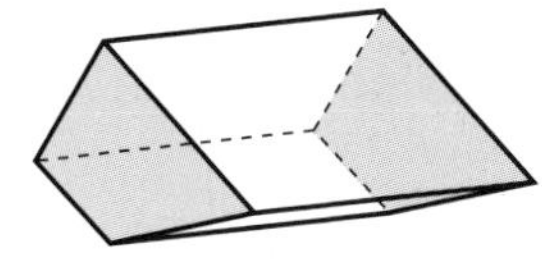

… then join corresponding vertices.

The finished article is a prism. It takes its name from its cross-section, often referred to as its base.

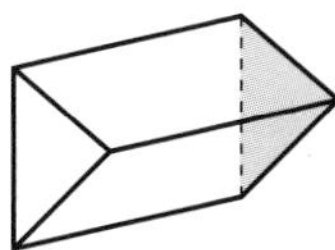

A triangular prism.

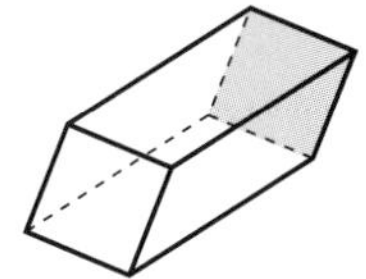

A square-based prism or **cuboid**

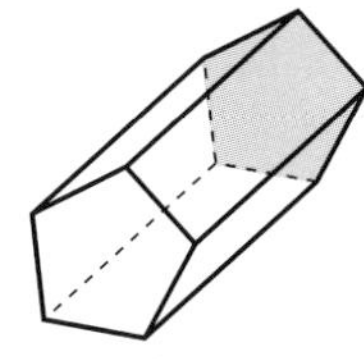

A pentagonal prism

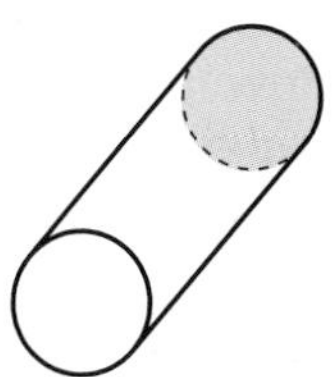

A circular prism or **cylinder**

E

Exercise 3.2

1 Name each prism below.

a

b

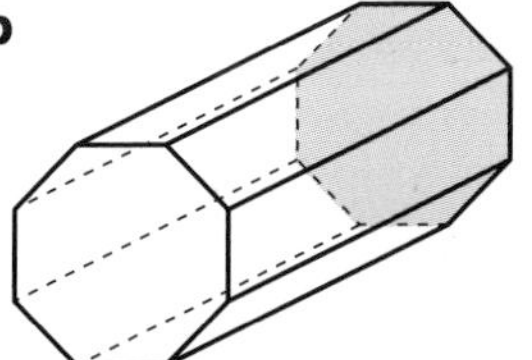

c

2 a Copy and complete the table for the first six rows.

Shape of base	Faces	Edges	Vertices	Euler?
triangle	5	9	6	✓
square				
pentagon				
hexagon				
heptagon				
octagon				
n-gon				

b Use your knowledge of sequences to help you find the nth terms in the last row.

c How many faces, vertices and edges would a prism with a base with 20 sides have?

3 **a** Theresa describes a solid as having 16 faces, 36 edges and 22 vertices.
  i Does this obey Euler's law?
  ii Could it be a prism?

b Simon describes a solid as having 15 faces, 39 edges and 26 vertices.
  i Does this obey Euler's law?
  ii Could it be a prism?

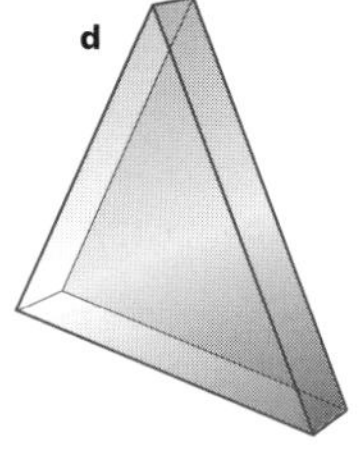

4 A glass paperweight has a base which is an equilateral triangle.

a How many rectangular faces has the paperweight?

b What is the size of
  i ∠BAC **ii** ∠EBC
  iii ∠ADE **iv** ∠BCG?

c The perimeter of triangle ABC = 12 cm.
The total length of AB + BE = 5 cm.
  i What is the length of BE?
  ii What is the total length of all the edges of the prism?

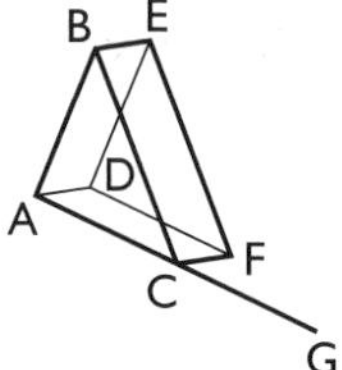

E

5 To make a model of a house, a triangular prism is glued to a cuboid as shown. ABCDE now forms one face.

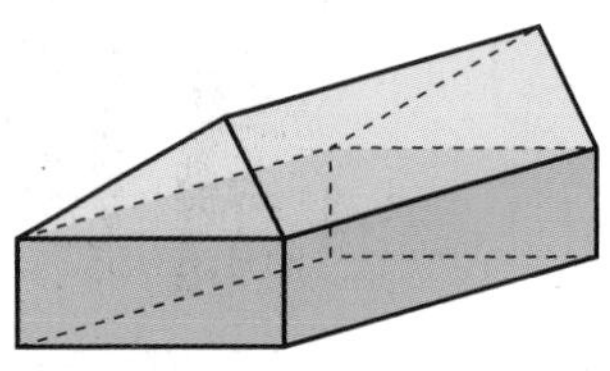

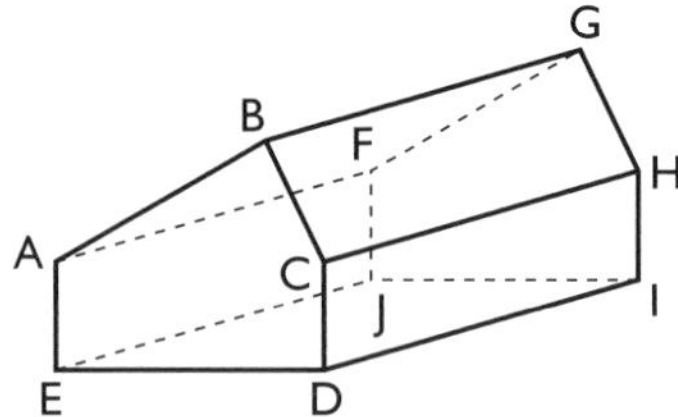

a What is the name of the shape ABCDE?

b What is the name of the solid ABCDEFGHIJ?

c Count the number of **i** faces **ii** vertices.

d Use Euler's law to calculate the number of edges.

6 A hat box is a prism. It has eight faces, six of which are rectangular.

a What is the name of the solid?

b How many vertices does it have?

c If the base is regular, with an edge of 25 cm, and the box is 30 cm high, what is the total length of all the edges of the box?

7 A crystal of nephaline is a hexagonal prism. Its base has an area of $25\,mm^2$. One rectangular face has an area of $15\,mm^2$. Assuming the base is regular, what is

a the area of the top of the crystal

b the total area of all the faces of the crystal?

8 In the Space Agency, different satellites are being built. Both those illustrated are based on prisms.

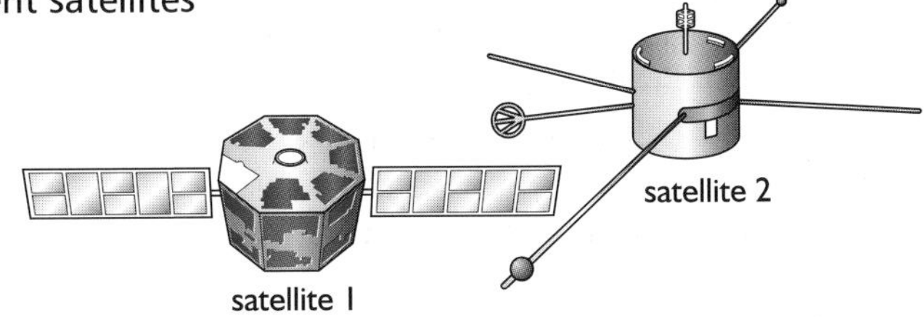

a The base usually has rotational symmetry as balance is important. Name the prism used for **i** satellite 1 **ii** satellite 2.

b Sketch the base of satellite 1 and mark in the size of the angle between two edges.

Brainstormer

The circumference of the base of satellite 2 is 4 m. The satellite is 1·5 m tall. What is the area of the curved surface of the satellite?

Challenge

The pillar box and the cola can are both based on a prism with a circular base.

a What name is usually given to this solid?

b What measurements would you have to make to estimate the area which is red in each case?

Investigation

Investigate the occurrence of prisms in everyday life.

Make a poster to illustrate your findings.

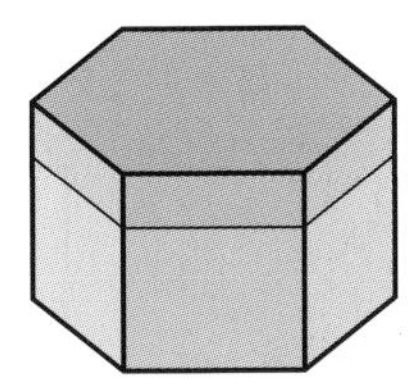

Containers – useful prisms

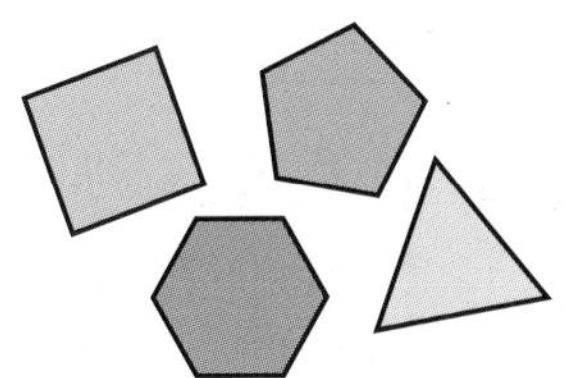

Tiles – very thin prisms

E

4 Skeleton models

When studying solids, we sometimes wish that we could see right through them so that we have a complete picture by seeing hidden edges, vertices and faces.

Paleontologists have learned a lot about dinosaurs by studying their skeletons.

Scientists and mathematicians use framework models to help with their studies.

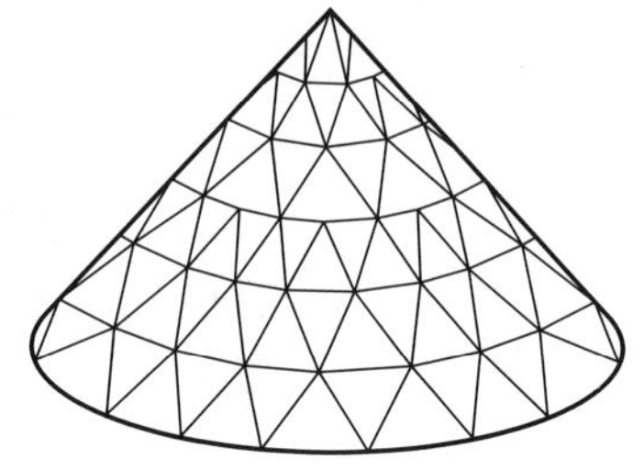

Example

A skeleton model is made of a triangular prism using wire as shown.
What total length of wire is needed?

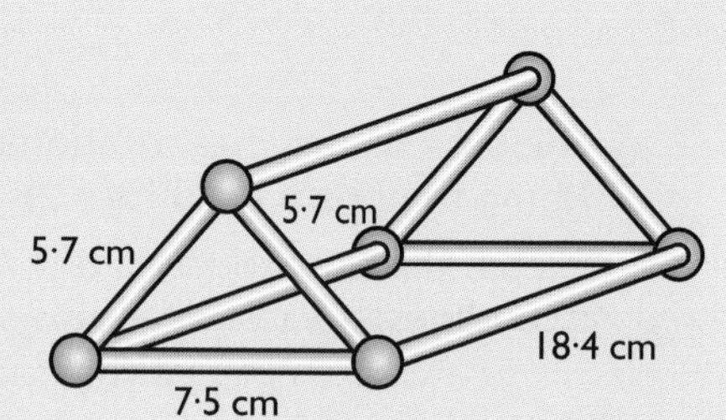

Answer:

4 lengths of 5·7 cm $= 4 \times 5{\cdot}7 = 22{\cdot}8$ cm
2 lengths of 7·5 cm $= 2 \times 7{\cdot}5 = 15{\cdot}0$ cm
3 lengths of 18·4 cm $= 3 \times 18{\cdot}4 = 55{\cdot}2$ cm

total length $= 93$ cm

E

Exercise 4.1

1 Each model is made from straws and modelling clay.
Each vertex requires 2 grams of clay.
For each model calculate
i the total length of straw **ii** the total weight of clay needed.

a

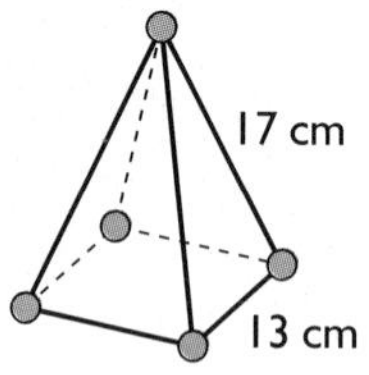

A square-based pyramid

b

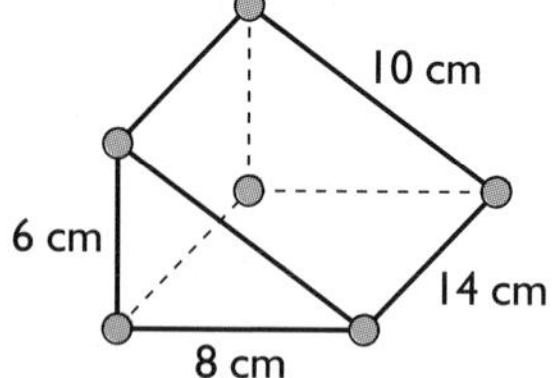

A right-angled triangular prism

c

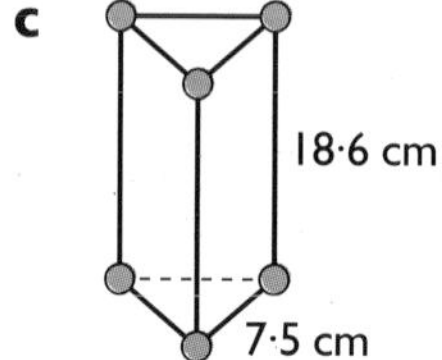

Triangles are equilateral

d

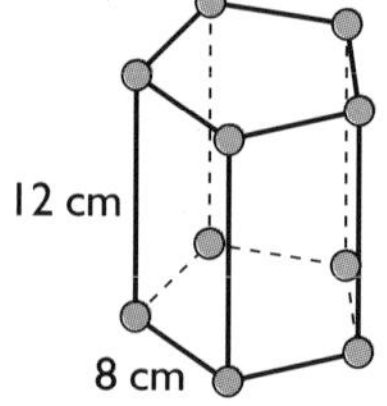

Base is regular

2 Mr McGill is making cloches and a cold frame to protect his plants. He makes frames with strong wire and then covers the frames with polythene. Calculate the total wire needed to make each of these cloches.

a

0·6 m
0·6 m
1·5 m
0·9 m

b

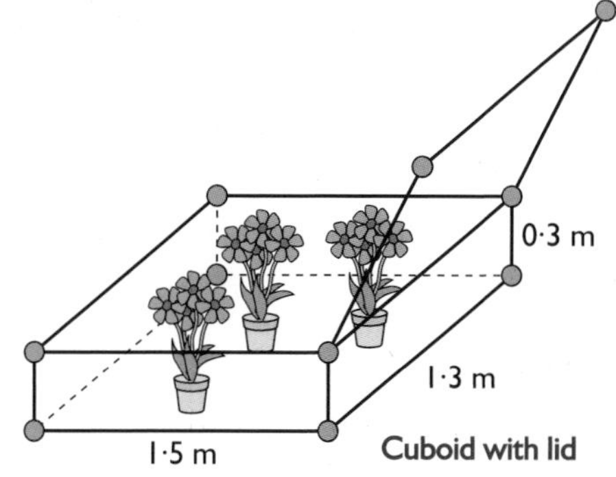

3 A windbreak folded inwards can form a prism with a regular pentagonal base. Wooden rods form the frame and a light cloth covers it.

1·25 m
1·4 m

a Make a sketch of the pentagonal prism.

b Calculate the total length of rod needed.

c When laid flat it forms a rectangle. What area of cloth is needed?

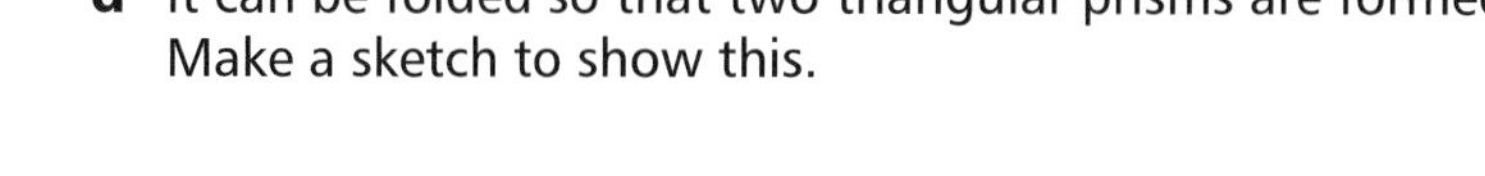

d It can be folded so that two triangular prisms are formed. Make a sketch to show this.

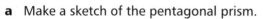

4 A toy house consists of rods held together by corner connectors. Boards of the proper shape are then clipped to the rods. A list of contents is printed on the box in which the house kit comes.

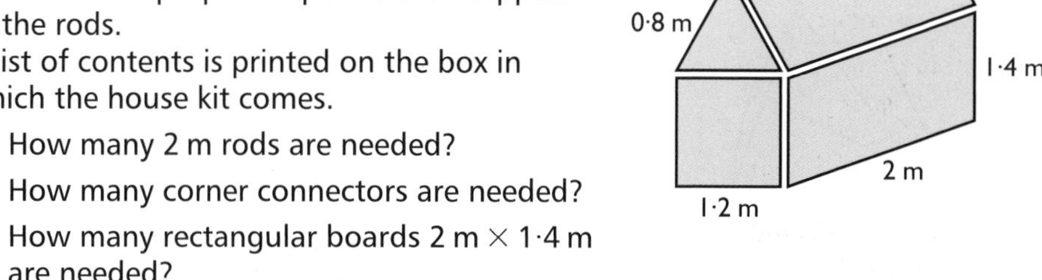

a How many 2 m rods are needed?

b How many corner connectors are needed?

c How many rectangular boards 2 m × 1·4 m are needed?

d Write out the complete contents list.

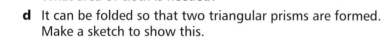

5 The total length of wire needed to make a square-based pyramid is 148 cm. If the sloping edges are equal and each is 25 cm long, how long is an edge of the square base?

Exercise 4.2

1 A tree protector is made from wire welded at each vertex.
All the horizontal edges are 110 mm long.
All the vertical edges are 450 mm long.

a Write down the name of this *solid*.

b Calculate the total length of wire used to make this solid.

c At 3p per centimetre and 5p per weld, what is the total cost of the frame?

2 This model is made of straw with dimensions as shown.

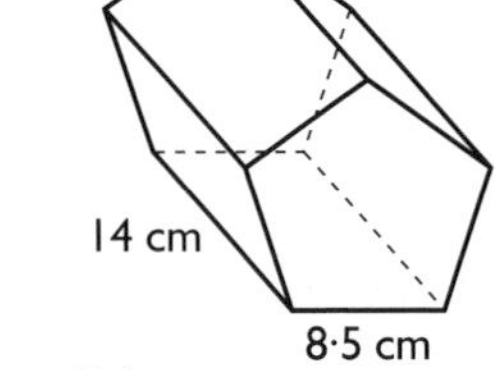

a What is the name of this solid?

b How much straw is needed to make a pentagonal face given that the pentagons are regular?

c How much straw is needed in total to make all the 14 cm edges?

d Calculate the total length of straw used to make this solid.

e What is the area of one rectangular face?

f It costs 0·5p per centimetre for the straw.
How many complete models can be made for £5?

E

3 A school supplier makes skeleton models for use in the maths classroom. They are made from plastic rods (£0·20 per centimetre) and connectors (10p each). Calculate, for each model:

i the total length of plastic rod
ii the number of connectors
iii the total cost.

a

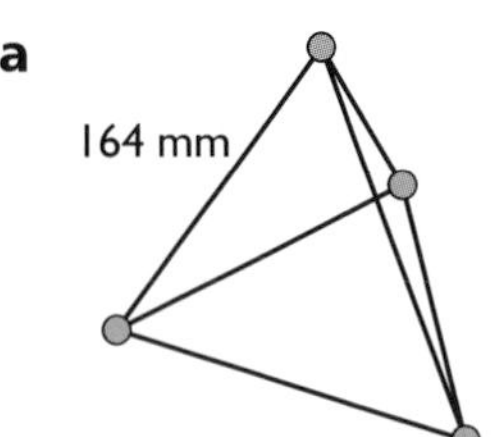

Regular tetrahedron

b

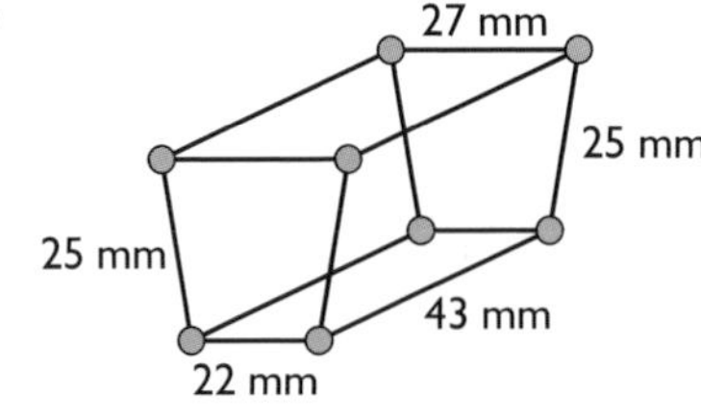

Trapezium cross-section

c

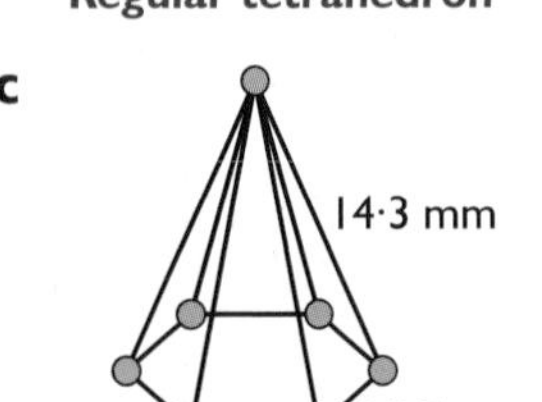

Pyramid with regular hexagonal base

d

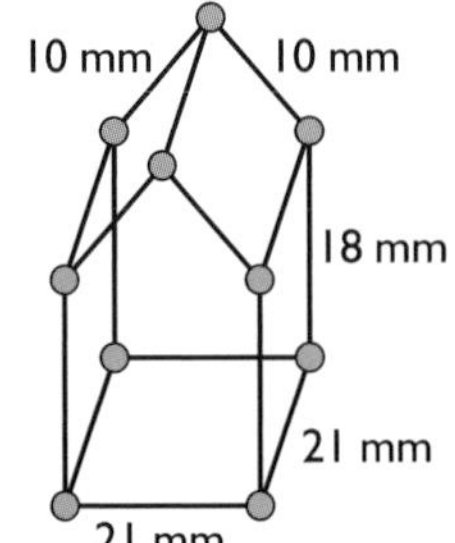

5 Nets of solids

A cereal box is carefully opened along its edges.
Six connected rectangles form the net of the box.

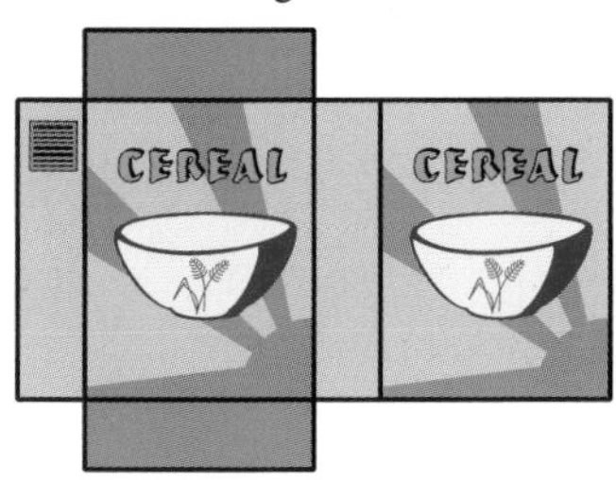

The net can be formed in more than one way.

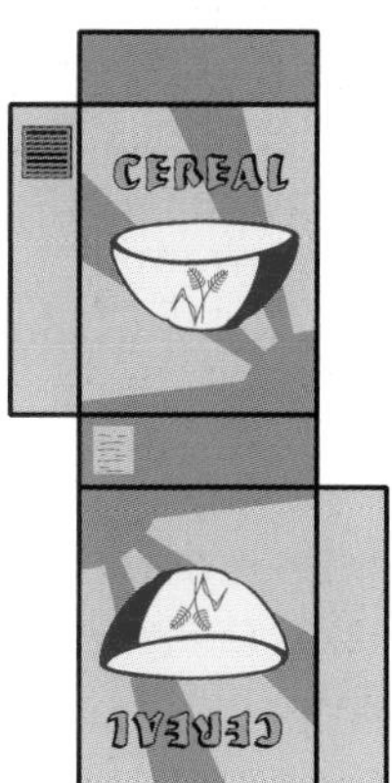

The net is a good way of studying the faces of a solid and how they are connected.
The net provides a pattern for the shape.
When we know one net we can easily find others.

Example The diagram shows the net of a square-based pyramid.
Sketch two other nets.

Answer: Note that when the solid is formed DE will join with DC.
We can take the face FDE away from the edge DF and stick it to the edge CD.
This will produce another net as shown below.

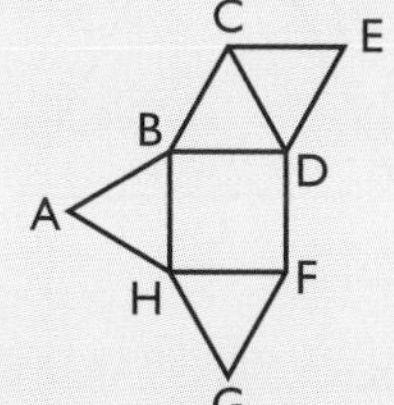

We could move AB to BC

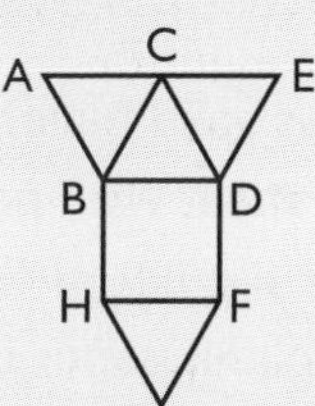

... and produce another net.

Exercise 5.1

1 Can you find yet another net of the square-based pyramid?

2 This is a net of a triangular prism.
Copy the net onto squared paper, cut it out and fold along the dotted lines.

a Count **i** edges **ii** faces **iii** corners in this prism.

b What is special about the triangular faces?

c By considering altering the net, make a sketch of two other nets of the same solid.

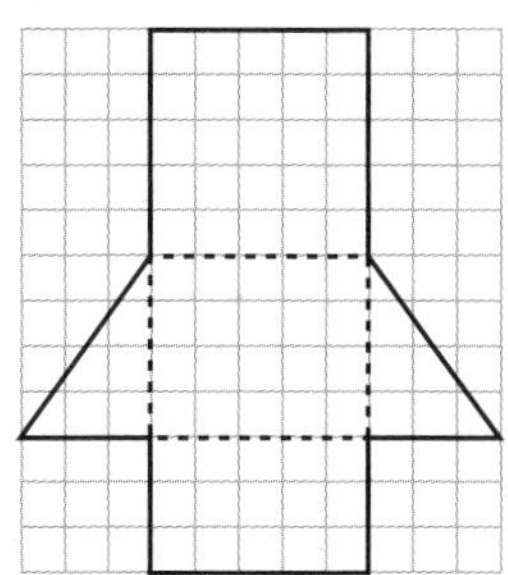

E

3 Copy the net onto squared paper, cut it out and fold along the dotted lines to make a solid.

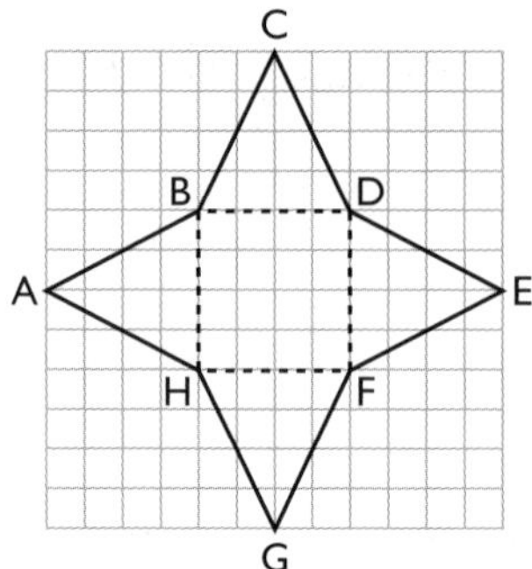

a What is the name of this solid?

b When the solid is made up

i what edge does AB join onto?

ii where does the edge GF go?

iii which letters meet at the apex of the pyramid?

c What kind of triangles make up the triangular faces?

4 Copy this net onto squared paper using the dimensions shown.
Cut it out and fold along the lines to make a solid.

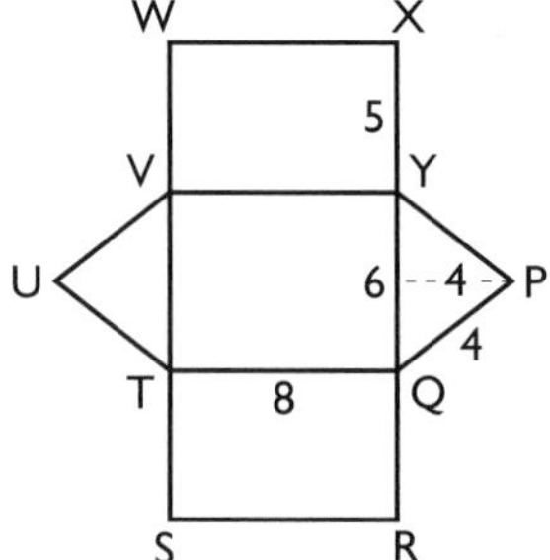

a What is the name of this solid?

b How long is **i** PY **ii** SR **iii** VT?

c How many edges meet at corner P?

d Which edge joins onto **i** SR **ii** PQ **iii** UT?

5 This net is cut out and folded along the dotted lines to form a solid.
The triangles are equilateral.

a What solid is formed?

b How many faces does this solid have?

c Name the corners which meet with point A.

d Draw two other forms of the net of this solid.

A
F
B
E
D
C

To draw the net you need **i** blank paper **ii** compasses.
Draw a base line BC, 8 cm long.
Using compasses set at 8 cm, make arcs from B and C to cross at A.
Join the midpoints of the three sides with dotted lines.
Cut out and fold along the dotted lines.

6 Some of the following shapes are nets of solids.
Identify which are nets and name the solid which is formed when folded.

a

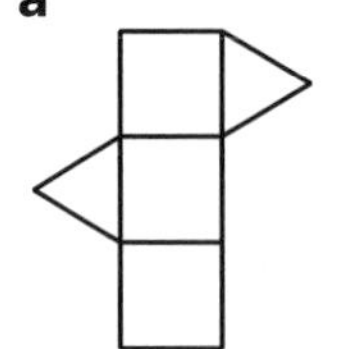

b

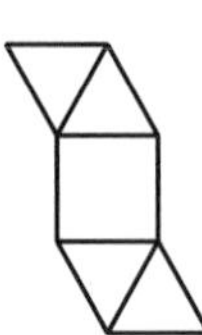

c

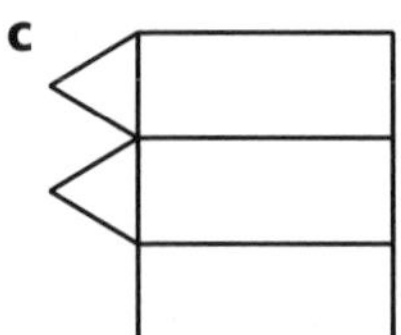

d

e

Investigation

You cannot make the net of a sphere.
Find out what you can about cartographers and why this fact is a problem to them.

Exercise 5.2

1 **a** Of which solid is this the net?

b AB will join to BC. Use this fact to sketch an alternative net.

c Which of the following could not be a net of the solid?

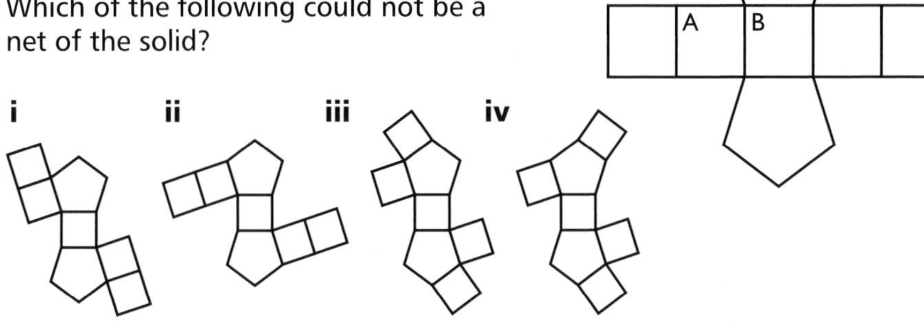

2 Here is the net of the pillar box.

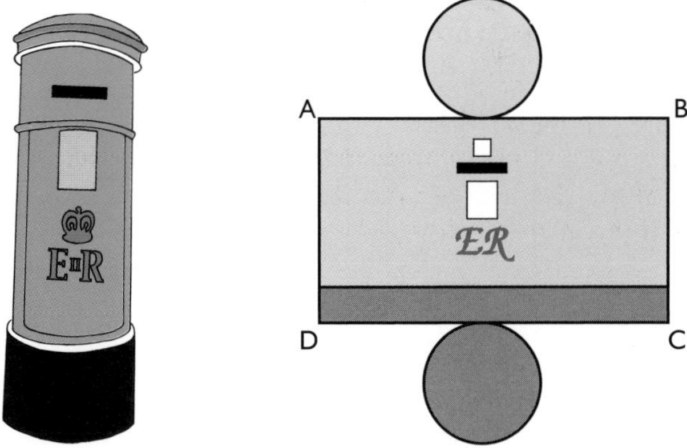

a What is the name of the basic solid?

b What shape is ABCD?

c What is the connection between the length AB and the circle?

d The distance round a circle is roughly three times its diameter. Use this to help you make your own net of the solid.

3 Draw a circle centre Q and radius PQ.
Cut out a sector PQR as shown.
Join PQ to QR to form a solid.

a What is the name of the solid?

b Experiment to find what effect changing the angle PQR has on the final shape.

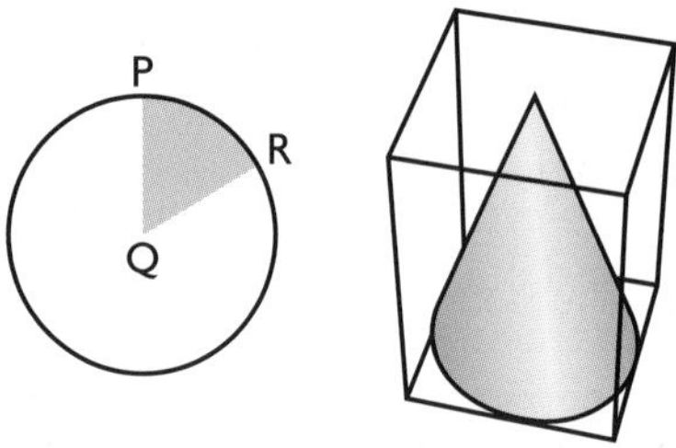

4 A candle-maker makes prism and pyramid shaped candles by pouring wax into prepared moulds.
Draw the net of:

a a hexagonal prism

b an octagonal prism with square faces

c a hexagonal pyramid

which would be suitable as candle moulds.

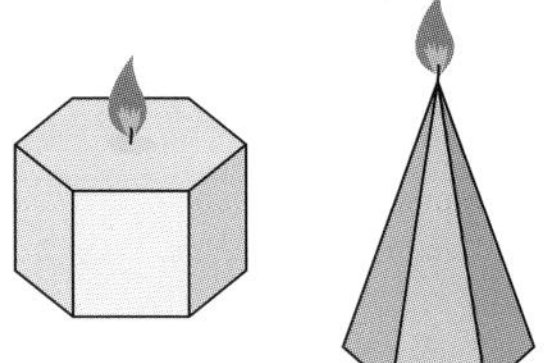

Brainstormer

Can you figure out the net of the icosahedron?

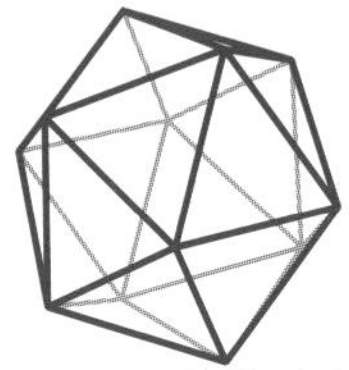

E

6 Surface area and volume

The cube and cuboid

The surface area of a solid is the total area of all the faces of the net.

Example

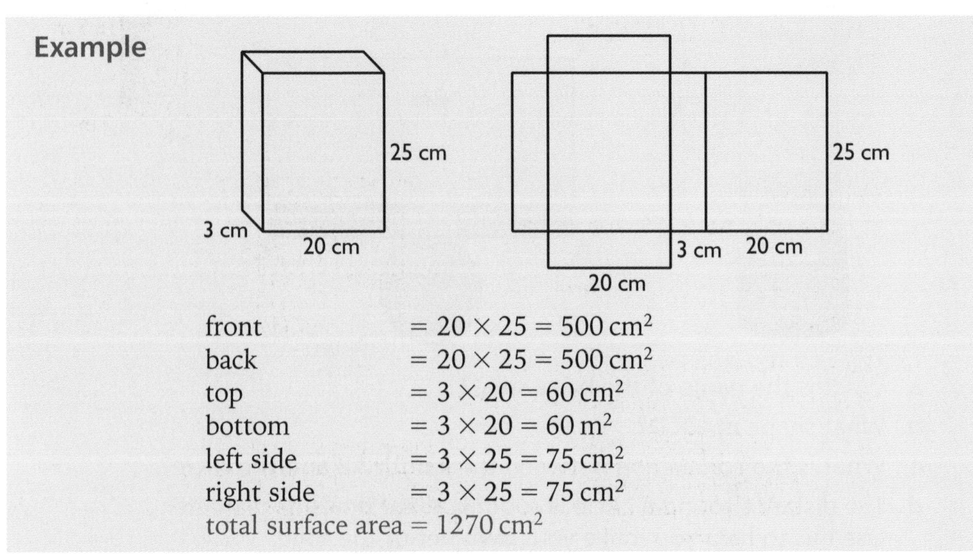

front	$= 20 \times 25 = 500\ \text{cm}^2$
back	$= 20 \times 25 = 500\ \text{cm}^2$
top	$= 3 \times 20 = 60\ \text{cm}^2$
bottom	$= 3 \times 20 = 60\ \text{m}^2$
left side	$= 3 \times 25 = 75\ \text{cm}^2$
right side	$= 3 \times 25 = 75\ \text{cm}^2$
total surface area	$= 1270\ \text{cm}^2$

Exercise 2.1

1 A formula is entered into cell D3 in the spreadsheet.

D3	× √				
	A	B	C	D	E
1	3	4	15		
2	2				
3					
4					

Write down what number will appear in cell D3 when the formula is:

a =A2+10 **b** =A1+A2 **c** =A1*A2

d =C1+A1−B1 **e** =C1/5 **f** =C1/A1

g =(A1+C1)/2 **h** =(A2+B1)/A1 **i** =(A1+B1+C1+A2)/3

j =2*A1+A1*A1−C1

2 In the Commonwealth Games table on the previous page, Scotland is in row 10.

a What formula should be entered in E10 to calculate the total medal count for Scotland?

b What position in the results does Scotland hold?

E

3 A reporter would like to know the mean number of medals per million of population for each country. The population of each country (to the nearest 1 million) is shown in this table.

Country	Australia	Canada	England	India	Scotland
Population (nearest million)	20	32	50	1050	5

a What formula, entered in say column F, would give the mean number of medals per million for

i Australia **ii** England **iii** Scotland?

b Calculate these means.

4 In a shortened medals table only the first four teams appear.
The number 199 appears in B6 in the results table.

a What formula is likely to have been entered in B6?

b What formula could be entered in B7 to give the mean number of gold medals for these four countries?

c If similar formulae are entered in C6 and C7, what values will appear in these cells?

5 Suppose one of Canada's gold medal athletes is later disqualified by the ruling committee.

a Which cell should be changed?

b What is now entered in this cell?

c What effect does this have on cell E5?
(Assume formulae for totals have been entered in column E.)

Some useful formulae

=SUM(A1 : A10) will calculate the sum of the cells from A1 to A10

=AVERAGE(A1 : A10) will calculate the mean of the entries in the cells A1 to A10

=MAX(A1 : A10) will calculate the biggest of the entries in the cells A1 to A10

=MIN(A1 : A10) will calculate the smallest of the entries in the cells A1 to A10

Exercise 2.2

1

	A	B	C
1		1st week	2nd week
2	Sunday	6·7	3·5
3	Monday	5·4	7·8
4	Tuesday	6·3	6·1
5	Wednesday	4·8	5·2
6	Thursday	7·0	5·8
7	Friday	6·8	5·9
8	Saturday	5·7	6·3
9	Total	42·7	
10	Mean	6·1	
11	Maximum	7·0	

In this spreadsheet Theresa has recorded the number of hours of sunshine in her two-week holiday.

a Cells B9, B10 and B11 contain formulae.
Write down the formula in cell
i B9 **ii** B10 **iii** B11.

b Similar formulae have been entered in C9, C10 and C11.
Write down the values which will appear in cell
i C9 **ii** C10 **iii** C11.

c Compare week 1 with week 2, making a comment about
i their means **ii** their maximums.

2 The spreadsheet shows the performance of three darts players over eight visits to the board.

	A	B	C	D	E	F	G	H	I	J	K	L	M
1	Player	Visit 1	Visit 2	Visit 3	Visit 4	Visit 5	Visit 6	Visit 7	Visit 8	Mean	Max.	Min.	Total
2	Sam	59	56	25	26	60	59	26	12	40·4	60	12	323
3	Terence	26	24	11	22	32	19	60	32		60		
4	Helen	33	3	180	56	12	40	100	6			3	430

The cells J2 to L4 contain formulae.

a What formula is in cell **i** J2 **ii** K3 **iii** L4?

b What values will appear in cell **i** J3 **ii** K4 **iii** L3?

c Who is the most inconsistent player?

d On average, who is the highest scorer?

3 The rector of a school wishes to see which of two bus companies is the more reliable. School starts at 9 a.m. and ends at 4 p.m. He records the number of minutes early or late the bus is each day. (−1 means 1 minute late)

	A	B	C	D	E	F	G	H	I
1		Mon	Tue	Wed	Thu	Fri	Mean	Max.	Min.
2	Westway (a.m.)	3	−5	8	−2	9	2·6	9	−5
3	Westway (p.m.)	−2	−1	−3	3	3	0	3	−3
4	Easybus (a.m.)	3	1	0	5	−1	1·6	5	−1
5	Easybus (p.m.)	4	5	−1	5	7			−1

a What formula was entered into cell **i** G3 **ii** H4?

b What entry will appear in cell **i** G5 **ii** H5?

c Write a report for the rector, commenting on average arrivals and dependability using the means, maximums and minimums computed.

If you have access to a computer, try to reproduce these spreadsheets.

3 Displaying data: line graphs

Reminder

Line graphs with straight line segments are good for showing how something changes with time. They make **trends** easier to spot.

Curved line graphs can be used when some underlying law is likely to connect the quantities or when you expect that all changes are gradual and predictable.

Exercise 3.1

1 The chart shows the temperature of a patient during a bout of influenza.

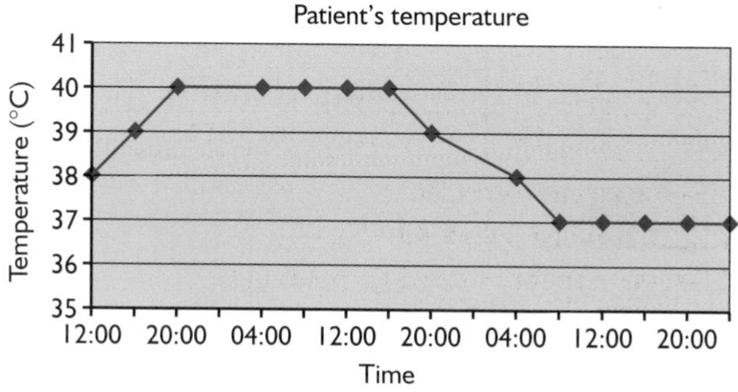

a How high did his recorded temperature go?

b How long did his temperature remain at this highest temperature?

c To reduce his temperature he was given an ice bath. When was this?

d Normal temperature is 37 °C.
For how long was his temperature recorded above normal?

2 Mr Jordan noticed there were some noises he could not hear so he went for a hearing test.
During the hearing test his hearing was measured for various frequencies.
The results are given in the table:

frequency (hertz)	250	500	1000	1500	2000	3000	4000
sound loss (decibels)	20	20	50	69	72	72	72

a Draw a graph, showing the given data, plotting frequency horizontally. Join the points with a smooth curve.

b Was his hearing loss worst for low or high frequencies?

c Above which frequency did his hearing loss start to worsen?

3 Say whether you would use straight lines or a curved line to graph each of the following situations:

a The temperature of a bowl of soup as it sits on a table.

b Weekly collections for a school charity.

c Distance travelled after various stages of a journey.

d The growth of a child over time.

E

4 The population of a Scottish town (to the nearest 1000) over the last few years is shown in the table.

year	1992	1993	1994	1995	1996	1997	1998	1999	2000	2001	2002	2003
population (1000s)	137	138	136	134	132	133	131	128	127	125	122	122

a Show the information in a line graph. (Think about where to start your vertical axis.)

b When did the population first drop below 130 000?

c Describe the trend in these results.

5 The Highway Code gives this information on braking:

Speed mph	Speed m/s	Distance to stop (m)
30	13	13
50	22	36
70	31	73

a Show this information on a graph, plotting miles per hour (mph) horizontally and distance to stop vertically.

b From your graph, estimate the distance to stop at 40 mph.

c Estimate the speed of travel of a car which takes 50 m to stop.

d One car travelling at 60 mph took 70 m to stop. Why might this have been the case?

If you have access to a computer, try to enter the data for questions **4** and **5** into a spreadsheet. Choose the correct sort of graph required from the chart menu. Experiment with different styles if possible.

Comparing data sets

Superimposing one line on another is an effective way of comparing data sets.

Example Two secretaries work for 7 hours. Each hour their work is sampled and the number of typing errors in the sample counted. The **comparative line graph** shows the results.

Over time, secretary 2 seems to be more consistent.

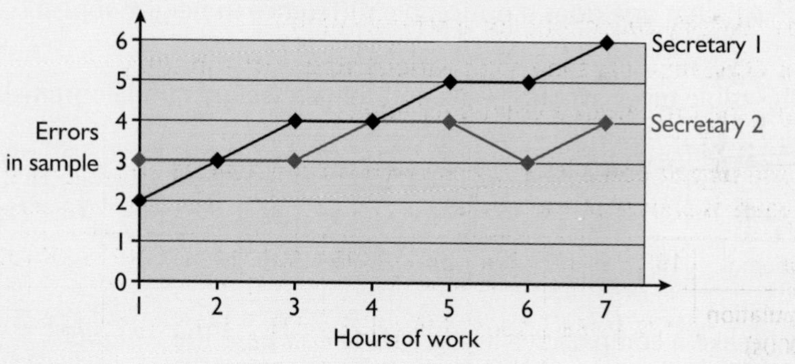

E

Exercise 3.2

1 The absentee figures for classes A1 and A2 are to be compared.

Section	Mon	Tue	Wed	Thu	Fri
A1	3	2	5	5	6
A2	1	2	3	3	2

a Use the figures to help you construct a comparative line graph.

b Write a short sentence comparing the two sections.

2 Over a seven-day spell the number of millimetres of rain is recorded in two towns.

Town	Mon	Tue	Wed	Thu	Fri	Sat	Sun
Tenby	5	6	0	7	1	1	6
Dryton	2	1	4	1	1	0	1

a Illustrate the figures in a comparative line graph.

b Calculate the mean rainfall for each town.

c Compare the two towns, mentioning the mean and any trend.

3 The table shows the average heights in centimetres of boys and girls as they grow up.

Age	0	2	4	6	8	12	16	18
Boys (cm)	50	88	100	120	130	150	175	178
Girls (cm)	50	86	100	118	126	152	165	165

a Make a suitable comparative line graph.

b Over what period are their average heights the same?

c At what age does a noticeable difference in height appear?

E

4 This table gives average male and female weights (in kilograms).

Age	0	1	2	4	6	8	10	12	14	16	18	25	45	65
Male	4	10	13	16	22	27	34	38	53·5	65	72	75	84	80
Female	4	9	12	15	23	25	33	40	54	59	60	62	69	64

a Make a comparative line graph to compare the weights.

b The difference between males and females is more pronounced after the age of 14. Make a graph to compare the difference before the age of 14 with after.

c We wish to examine the weights from ages 4 to 12 in more detail. Make a comparative graph for this range using a bigger vertical scale than before to exaggerate the difference.

If you have access to a computer, try to enter some of the data into a spreadsheet. Comparative line graphs are part of the chart menu. Experiment with different styles if possible.

4 Displaying data: pie charts

Reminder:

Pie charts are good for comparing categories of data or for comparing the size of one category with the whole sample.

The angle at the centre of a sector representing a category is proportional to the frequency of the category.

Example 1 Susan did a survey of the types of birds visiting her garden.

robin	sparrow	starling	crow
10%	30%	50%	10%

Draw a pie chart to illustrate the data.

10% of 360° = 36° ... 36° represents the number of robins.

30% of 360° = 108° ... 108° represents the number of sparrows.

50% of 360° = 180° ... 180° represents the number of starlings.

10% of 360° = 36° ... 36° represents the number of crows.

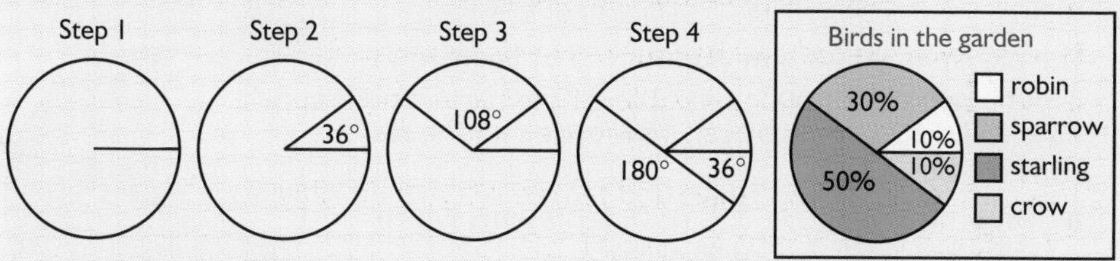

You will find it easier to draw the angles if you make your chart more than 5 cm across.

Exercise 4.1

1 Copy and complete the table to show what angle at the centre of a sector would represent each percentage.

Percentage	5%	10%	20%	25%	30%	33·33%	40%	50%	75%
Angle at centre	5% of 360° = 18°								

2 Graeme surveyed his garden, focusing on land use. He found that 5% of the area was paved, 20% was grassed, 30% was taken over for vegetables and 45% was used for cultivating flowers.
Draw a pie chart to illustrate this.
Use a protractor to measure the angles.

E

3 Eric had a railway line at the bottom of his garden.
He counted the trains as they passed and discovered that 25% of trains were long distance trains, 60% were local trains and the rest were goods trains.
Draw a pie chart to illustrate this data.
Give it a title and label the sectors or make a key.

4 Jamila noticed the fabric composition of her new top was 50% cotton, 45% polyester and 5% elastane.
Show this information in a pie chart.
Don't forget a title and labels or a key.

5 **a** What is the total percentage shown in the pie chart?
b Which type of pop music is most popular?
c What percentage of teenagers like male solo artists?
d 250 teenagers were polled.
How many liked female solo artists?

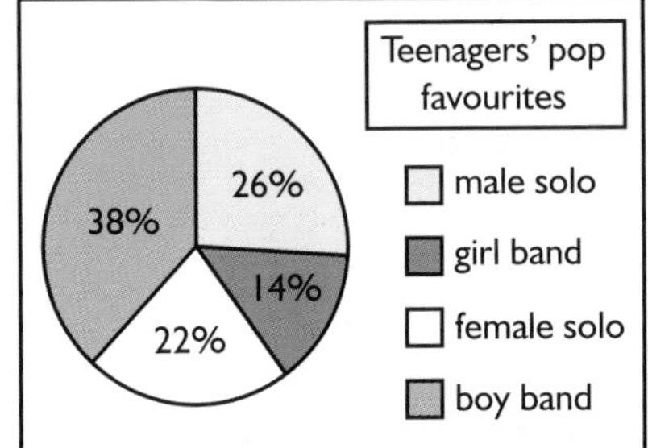

6 The pie chart shows how pupils in S2 at Logie High School come to school:
25% walk, 20% come by car, 10% cycle and the rest come by bus.
a Say which sector, A, B, C or D, represents which category: walk, car, cycle or bus.
b If there are 160 pupils in S2, how many
i walk **ii** come by bus?
c Suggest a title for the pie chart.

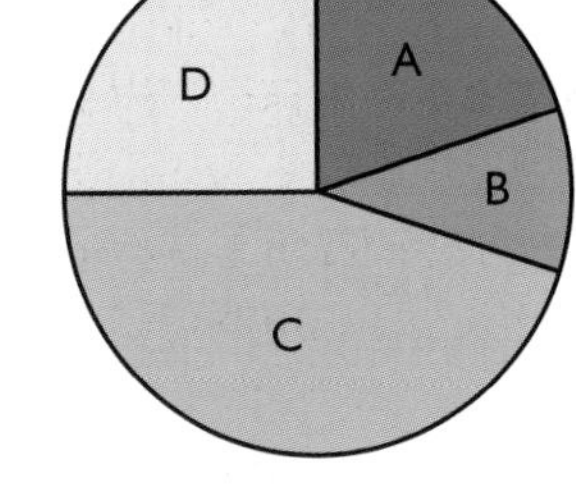

7 In a traffic survey, the number of passengers in each vehicle was recorded:
42% had no passengers, 32% had one passenger, 8% had two passengers and the rest had three or more passengers.
a Say which sector represents which category.
b If 850 cars were surveyed, how many have
i no passengers
ii three or more passengers?
c What percentage of cars had one or more passengers?
d If a car was chosen at random, what would be the most likely number of passengers?

Number of passengers

S R P Q

If you have access to a computer, try to enter the data for questions **3** through to **7** into a spreadsheet. For each question enter the data as numbers in a single row or column.

Choose the pie chart option from the chart menu. Experiment with different styles if possible.

In a pie chart the angle at the centre of a sector is always calculated using a fraction or a percentage of 360°.

When raw data are given, use the total of the frequencies to find the fraction for each category.

Example 2

In a car showroom, five models were family saloons, four were small hatchbacks and there was one four-by-four offroad vehicle.
Draw a pie chart to illustrate the data.

Answer:

The total frequency is 10.
5 out of 10 means $\frac{5}{10} = \frac{1}{2}$ were family saloons.
So the angle that represents family saloons
$= \frac{1}{2} \times 360° = 180°$
4 out of 10 means $\frac{4}{10} = \frac{2}{5}$ were small hatchbacks.
So the angle that represents small hatchbacks
$= \frac{2}{5} \times 360° = 144°$
1 out of 10 means $\frac{1}{10}$ were four-by-fours.
So the angle that represents four-by-fours
$= \frac{1}{10} \times 360° = 36°$

It is not necessary to calculate this last angle but it acts as a good check to see that $180 + 144 + 36 = 360$.

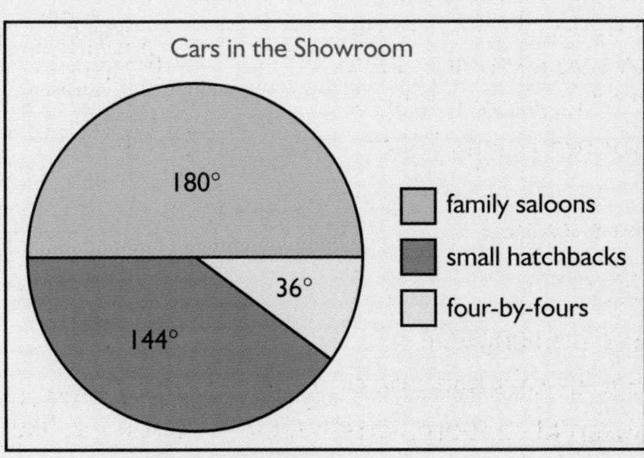

Exercise 4.2

1 Class 2X collected information for a project called 'The way we live today'. One question was 'How far from school do you live?' The responses were recorded to the nearest kilometre.

Distance from school	up to 2	3 to 5	6 to 8	9 or over
Frequency	8	11	5	6

a Copy and complete the table:

Distance	Frequency	Fraction	Angle
up to 2	8		
3 to 5	11	$\frac{11}{30}$	$\frac{11}{30} \times 360° = 132°$
6 to 8			
9 or over			
total		check total	360°

b Draw a pie chart, making the diameter at least 6 cm. Add a key or labels and a title.

F

2 Another question answered in the project was 'How many people live in your household?' The answers are given in the table.

Number in household	2	3	4	5	6 or more
Frequency	4	7	14	3	2

a 360° represent all pupils. How many degrees represent one pupil?

b Copy and complete the table.

Number in household	Frequency	Angle
2	4	$4 \times \ldots = 48°$
3		
4		
5		
6 or more		
	check total	

c Draw the pie chart.

3 'What drinks do you keep in the fridge?'
Each person in Kevin's home economics class recorded the drinks they found in their fridges at home.
Milk was found in 18 fridges, fruit juice in 10, bottled water in 6 and fizzy drinks in 15.

a Calculate the angles required for each category, rounding your answers to the nearest degree. Adjust your answers to make the total 360°.

b Draw the pie chart.

4 Leanne spent a week at her local vet's surgery for her work experience.
In her report she decided to illustrate the type of animals which visited the surgery.
She counted 33 cats, 28 dogs, 12 rabbits, 4 birds and 2 reptiles.
Show this information in a pie chart.

5 Lee High School was proud to support various charities.
The pie chart illustrates how their money was distributed.

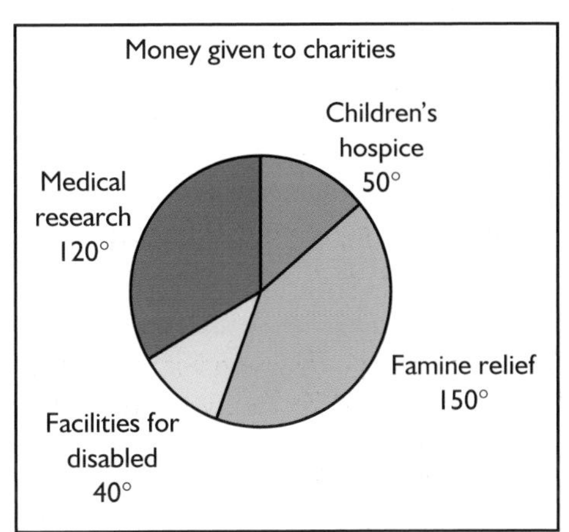

a Which charity received
i most support
ii least support?

b Copy and complete the table.

Charity	Angle	Fraction of 360°

c If £5000 were given to charity in total, work out how much was given to each charity (to the nearest £).

6 **a** Make a table similar to the one in question **5** showing the angle and fraction for each colour of car.

b If there were 450 cars in the car park, work out how many cars there were of each colour.

c Which colour was most popular?

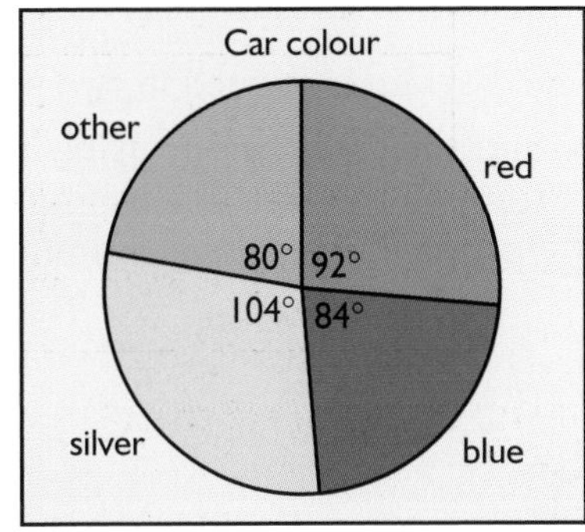

F

7 Use the pie chart to help you answer the following questions.

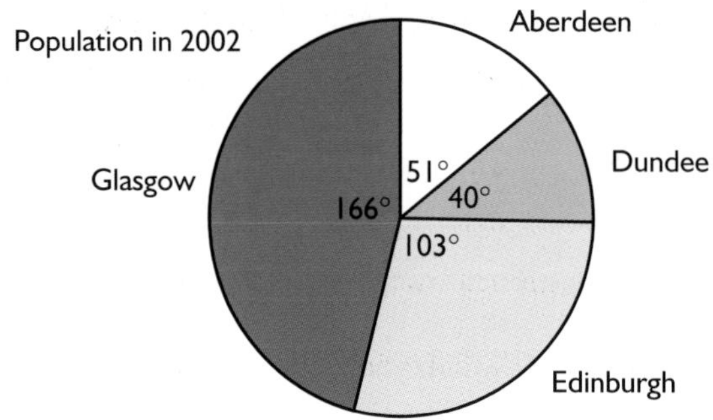

a Which is Scotland's largest city?

b If the total population in these four cities is 1 327 000, how many people does 1° represent?

c Work out the population in each city to the nearest 10 000.

If you have access to a computer, try to enter the data for questions **1** through to **4** into a spreadsheet. For each question enter the data as numbers in a single row or column.

Choose the pie chart option from the chart menu. Experiment with different styles if possible.

F

5 Other data displays: stem and leaf

The statistician John Tukey invented the **stem and leaf** diagram.
The overall shape of the diagram is similar to a horizontal bar graph, but the individual data are all recorded in the diagram.
The diagram is a useful way to organise and order data.

(Most spreadsheets have the facility to sort data into order but do not offer stem and leaf diagrams as an option in their chart menu.)

The diagram is formed in two stages:

- Sort the data roughly using 'stems' by reading through the data line by line.
- Sort the 'leaves' in each stem.

Example The weights, in kilograms, of the luggage of the first 20 families checking in to a summer holiday flight were:.

58,	96,	42,	76,	102,
68,	65,	78,	56,	51,
78,	93,	46,	109,	40,
59,	72,	58,	77,	79.

Make a stem and leaf diagram with the data.

1st stage: You wish to divide your data into six or seven classes.

stems	leaves (unsorted)
4	2 6 0
5	8 6 1 9 8
6	8 5
7	6 8 8 2 7 9
8	
9	6 3
10	2 9

Make the 'stems' by leaving off the *least significant digit*,
e.g. 58 has a stem of 5 and a leaf of 8,
109 has a stem of 10 and a leaf of 9.

2nd stage: Sort the leaves, putting the smallest nearest the stems, and spacing the leaves equally.

Add a key, title and state the sample size.
This is known as an **ordered** stem and leaf diagram.

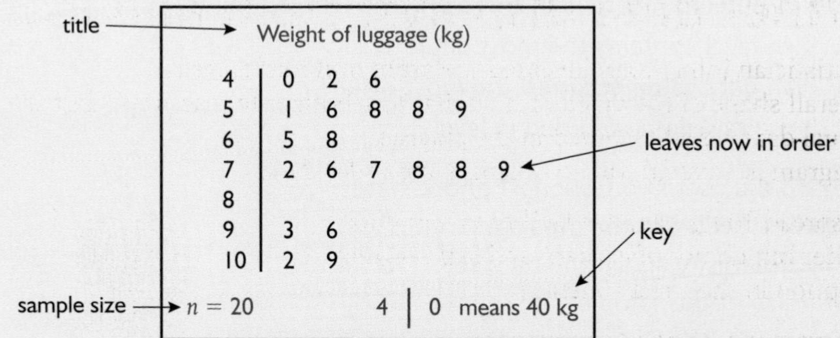

Rows are referred to as **levels**. Each level can be named by giving its stem, e.g. level 6 records the raw data 65 and 68.

F

Exercise 5.1

1 The first row of this stem and leaf diagram, level 6, records the raw data 62, 65, 67.

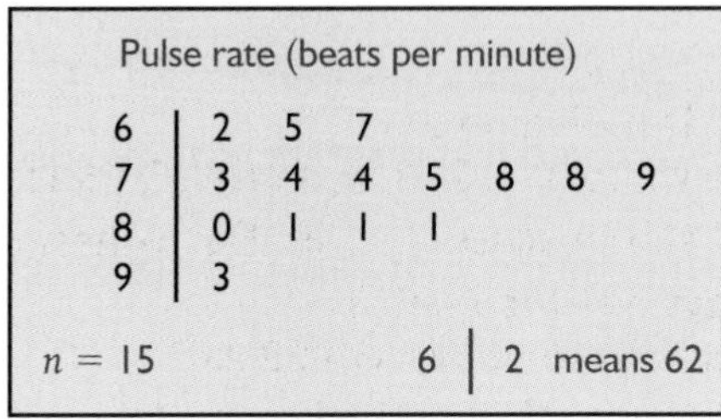
Pulse rate (beats per minute)

Stem	Leaves
6	2 5 7
7	3 4 4 5 8 8 9
8	0 1 1 1
9	3

$n = 15$ 6 | 2 means 62

a What raw data is recorded in level 7?

b How many pieces of data are recorded in level 8?

c The diagram represents a list of data 15 items long.
Which piece of data occupies the middle position in this list?

2

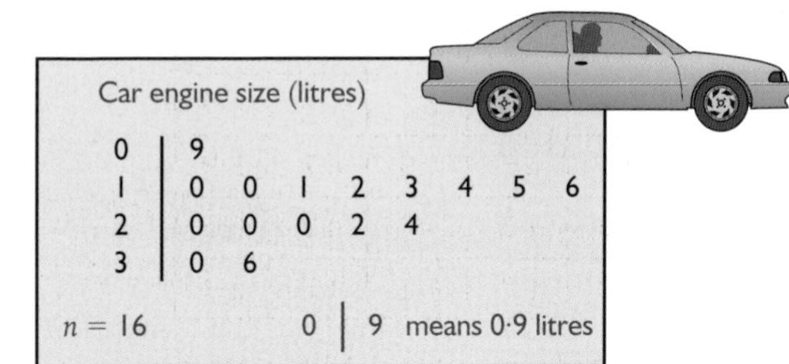
Car engine size (litres)

Stem	Leaves
0	9
1	0 0 1 2 3 4 5 6
2	0 0 0 2 4
3	0 6

$n = 16$ 0 | 9 means 0·9 litres

a What is being recorded in this stem and leaf diagram?

b Which level contains the most data?

c Which data value occurred the most often?

d List the raw data recorded in level 3.

3 For each data set in questions **1** and **2** state:

a the least value in the data set

b the greatest value in the data set

c the size of the sample

d the mode (the value which occurs most frequently).

4 Test marks for Miss Kelly's class were:

81	93	56	62	73	88	90	77	78	85
66	83	85	79	80	69	76	59	63	78

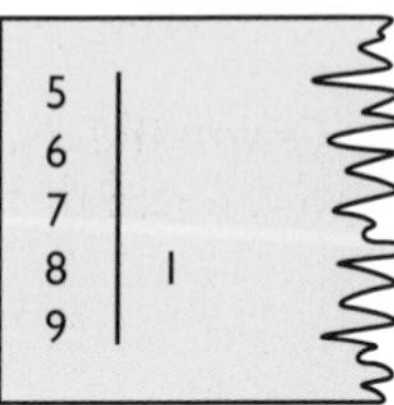

Stem	Leaves
5	
6	
7	
8	1
9	

a Copy and complete the first stage of the stem and leaf diagram.

b Complete the second stage by sorting the leaves, adding a key and title and stating the sample size.

5 The daily rainfall in centimetres was measured each day during one month:

2·2 0·0 2·7 0·0 0·9 0·3 0·8 4·2 4·1 2·3
1·0 3·5 1·4 1·8 0·0 3·0 0·0 0·9 0·7 1·1
0·9 3·6 2·4 3·1 1·5 1·1 1·2 4·2 1·8 2·3

a What is the sample size?

b Make a stem and leaf diagram.
(Hint: let your stems be 0, 1, 2, 3, 4, so that 3 | 5 represents 3·5 cm.)

c What was **i** the smallest **ii** the highest daily rainfall?

d On how many days was the rainfall
i less than 2 cm **ii** more than 3 cm?

e Is the daily rainfall more likely to be less than 1 cm or more than 1 cm?

f What is the modal daily rainfall?

g What is the median daily rainfall?

6 Fifty different toasters were timed to see how long they took to 'pop'. The table below gives the trial times to the nearest tenth of a minute.

2·1	6·5	2·6	5·1	3·7	6·5	5·2	4·6	4·2	2·6
3·3	3·1	1·2	6·4	1·1	1·2	1·6	4·2	1·9	4·5
3·3	4·4	3·5	4·0	4·2	2·6	2·3	1·6	6·7	3·5
5·1	5·0	6·2	6·5	1·9	6·6	2·7	3·6	4·8	5·6
1·2	1·0	5·7	5·2	2·2	4·3	6·8	6·4	1·7	2·3

a Make a stem and leaf diagram to help you sort out the data.

b If it takes more than 4·5 minutes, the toaster needs to be checked.
How many were in this category?

c Which level holds the most pieces of data?

7 Which diagram would you choose to illustrate the following data sets – a pie chart or stem and leaf?

a Scores at the eighteenth hole in a golf tournament:
3, 3, 2, 4, 6, 5, 4, 4, 3, 2, 5, 4, 4, 5, 5.

b Ages of mothers of newborn babies one week in a certain hospital:
29, 21, 16, 35, 24, 42, 25, 33, 28, 30, 18, 26, 29, 31, 36.

c Types of magazine read by a sample of 13-year-olds:
fashion, comic, computer, fashion, fashion, computer, music, fashion, music, fashion, fashion, comic, computer, fashion, fashion.

8 Create the diagrams you chose in question **7**.
Use a computer if appropriate.

6 Other data displays: scatter graphs

Many statistical diagrams illustrate just one quantity (or variable),
e.g. this bar chart shows 'time spent on homework'.

We can see, for example, that six pupils said they spent between 40 minutes and 60 minutes on homework.

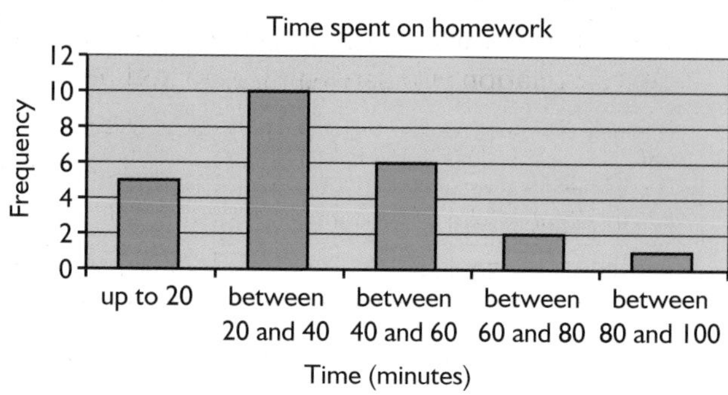

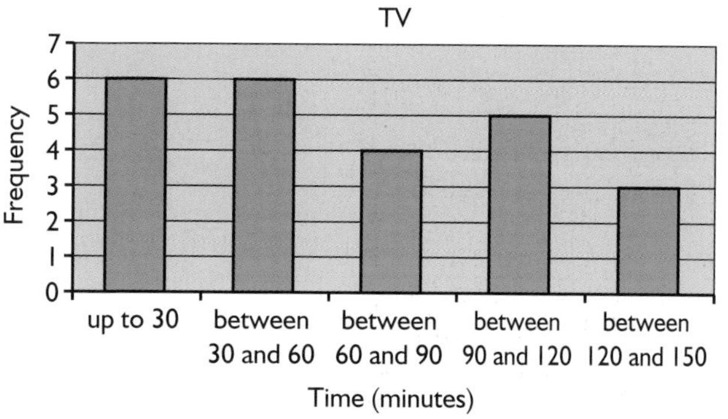

This diagram illustrates 'time spent watching TV'. Again we can read things like 'four pupils watched between 60 and 90 minutes of TV'.

Often, however, it's the relationship between two quantities that is important,
e.g. 'Is there a connection between the time pupils spent watching TV and the time they spent on homework?'.

For each pupil we need to know *both* bits of data.

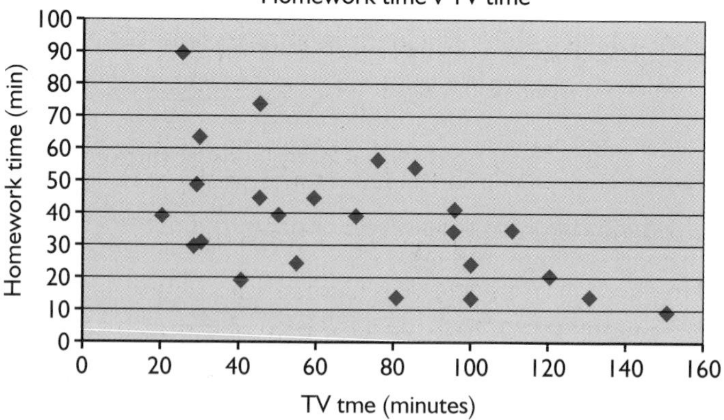

Each pair of data is plotted as a point on a graph with 'Homework time' on one axis and 'TV time' on the other.

This is called a **scatter graph**.

Notice the points are not joined up!

Each point represents a different pupil.

If there is a relationship between time spent watching TV and doing homework, it will be easier to spot on the graph.

Example

The lengths and widths of 12 holly leaves are given in the table.
Is there a relationship between length and width?

leaf	1	2	3	4	5	6	7	8	9	10	11	12
length (mm)	42	38	51	32	45	61	84	76	70	88	95	69
width (mm)	34	28	36	25	35	36	40	41	36	42	45	32

If there is a relationship, it will be easier to spot on a scatter graph.

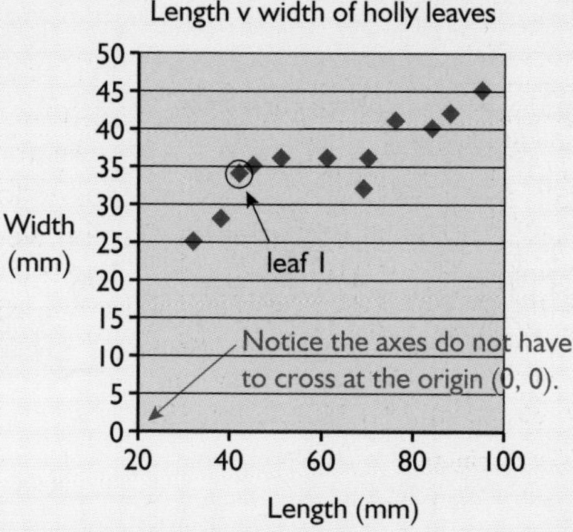

- Plot the length horizontally (on the x axis).
- Plot the width vertically (on the y axis).
  For example, leaf 1 is plotted as (42, 34).

The points certainly do not form a straight line, but there does seem to be a relationship between the length and width of the holly leaves.

The longer the leaf, the wider it tends to be.

This scatter graph shows two quantities which *increase* together.
We say there is a **positive** correlation between the two quantities.

If one quantity tends to *decrease* as the other *increases*, we say there is a **negative** correlation between the two quantities.

Types of data

Discrete data is data that can be counted.
Continuous data is data that is measured.

For example, the *number of names given to babies* is discrete, but the *birthweight of these babies* is continuous.

F

Types of relationships

Relationships between two variables can be strong or weak.

Examples

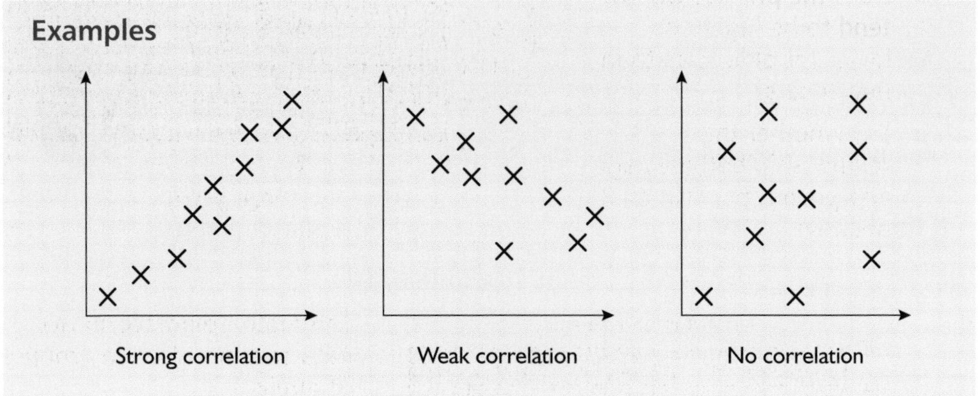

Exercise 6.1

1

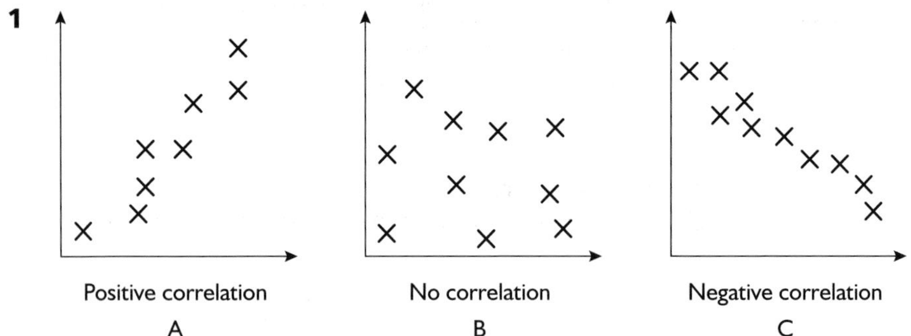

State which diagram, A, B or C, is likely to represent the relationship between:

a	daily rainfall	and	daily sunshine
b	number of letters in first names	and	number of letters in surnames
c	pupil's height	and	number of brothers and sisters
d	distance travelled on a train	and	number of stations stopped at
e	money spent on sweets	and	pocket money
f	pocket money	and	age
g	percentage unemployed	and	holiday sales

2 For the variables in question **1a–d**, say whether data is *discrete* or *continuous*.

3 The scatter diagram shows data collected at a used-car forecourt.

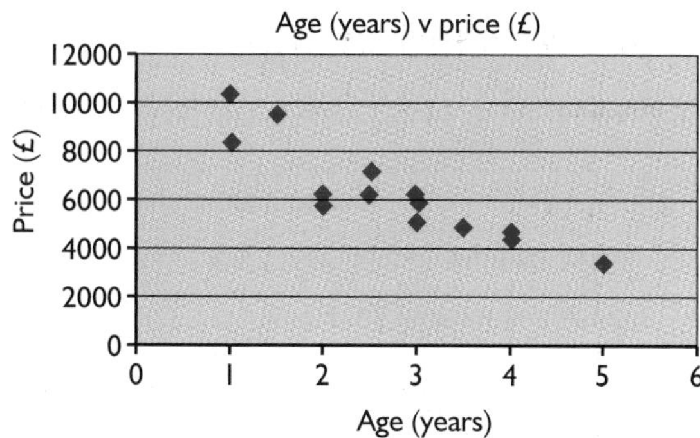

a Does the price of the car tend to be higher or lower for older cars than newer cars?

b Say whether the relationship between age and price is positive or negative.

4

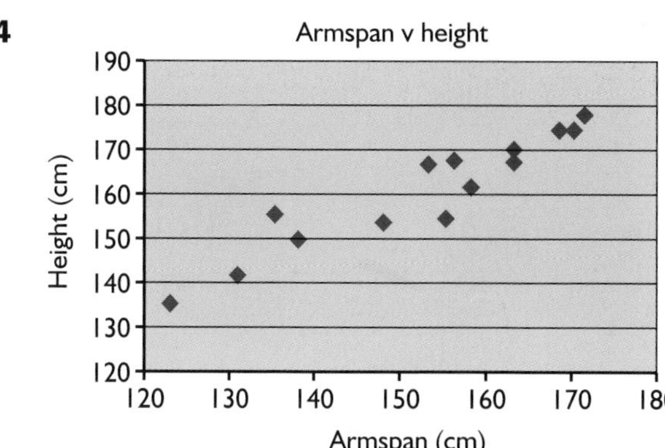

The scatter diagram shows data collected from a group of pupils.

a Copy and complete: 'As armspan increases, height …'

b Say whether the relationship is positive or negative.

5 Describe the relation illustrated in each diagram. Say whether the correlation is positive or negative, weak or strong or non-existent.

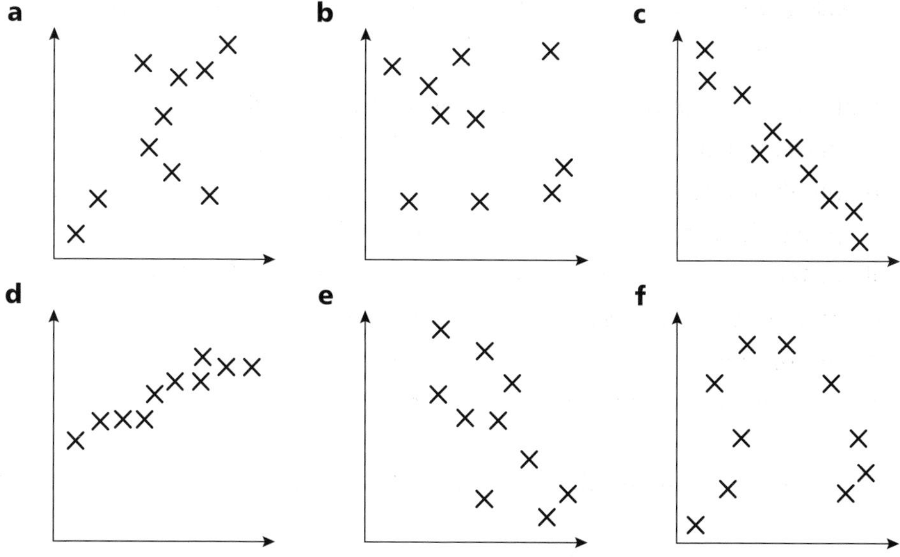

F

6 At a road safety test centre, young car drivers were asked to do an emergency stop. Their instructor noted the speed and timed how long it took them to stop.

	Angus	Bob	Charlie	Dean	Elkie	Fran	Gina	Hugh	Irene	Janis
speed (mph)	25	39	30	27	32	34	26	35	37	28
stopping time (s)	2·5	3·4	2·8	2·8	2.8	3	2·7	3·1	3	2·5

a Draw a scatter graph using the information in the table.
Plot the speed horizontally with a scale from 20 to 40, and stopping time vertically with a scale from 0 to 4.

b From the scatter graph write a sentence describing the relationship between speed and stopping time for this group.

Try to create the scatter diagrams for question **6** using a spreadsheet.

7 Probability

Data is often collected in order to find out how likely something is to happen. We often estimate the **probability** that something will happen in the light of past experience.

For example, if you know how many times your favourite soccer team has won this season, you are in a good position to predict whether they are likely to win their next match.

Insurance companies would definitely like to know how likely you are to have a car crash.

The probability, or chance, that something happens can be described using words such as likely, unlikely, more likely than not, and so on.
Although they offer a guide to likelihood, these words are generally too vague for our purposes.

We usually place events on a scale depending on how likely they are to occur.

- If an event is *certain* to happen, it has a probability of 1.
- If an event is *impossible*, it has a probability of 0.

In situations when all possible outcomes are *equally likely*, we define the probability of an event using this formula:

$$\text{Probability of an event} = \frac{\text{number of ways that the event can occur}}{\text{total number of different possible outcomes}}$$

In other words, given all the things that can happen, we ask the question 'What fraction are favourable?'

We use the symbols
P(event) for the probability that the event will occur
n(event) for the number of ways the event can occur
and T for the total number of possible outcomes.

Example 1

For a fair dice, each face is equally likely to turn up.
What is the probability of a face with a dot right in the middle turning up?

The event 'dot in the middle of a face' can occur in *three* ways:

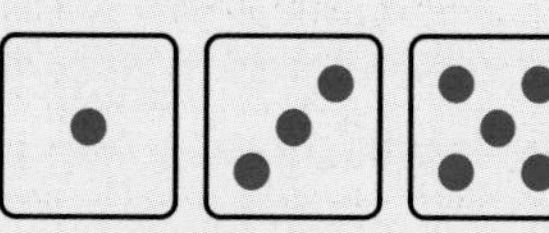

Of course, there are six different faces: so there are six different outcomes.

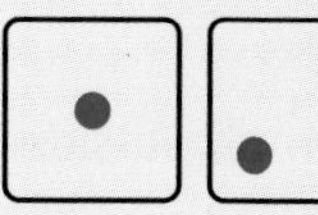
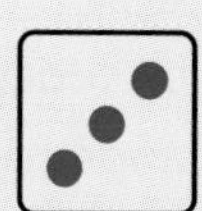

We write $\text{P(dot in the middle of a face)} = \frac{n(\text{dot in the middle of a face})}{T} = \frac{3}{6} = \frac{1}{2}$

Example 2

Given the ten cards shown, what is the probability of picking:

a a prime number **b** 6♥
c a card less than 8 **d** 6♠?

a P(prime) = P(2 or 3 or 5 or 7) = $\frac{4}{10}$ = 0·4
b P(6♥) = $\frac{1}{10}$ = 0·1
c P(card < 8) = $\frac{7}{10}$ = 0·7
d P(6♠) = $\frac{0}{10}$ = 0 … *impossible*.

Probabilities can be represented on a number line:

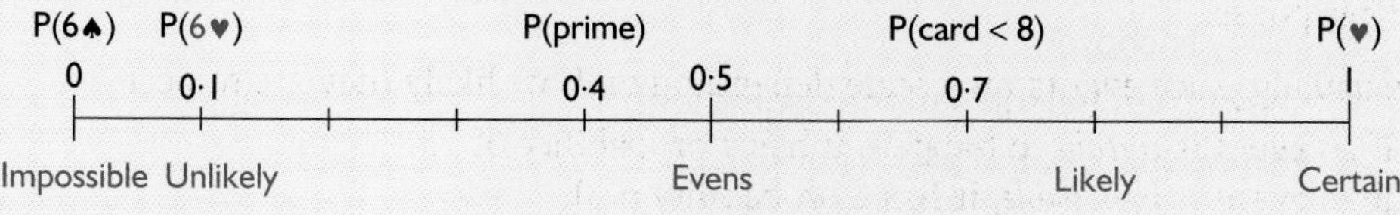

Exercise 7.1

1 When you throw a dice, how would you describe the probability of these events?
(Choose from the words certain, evens or impossible.)

a an even number
b 1, 2, 3, 4, 5 or 6
c 0
d a positive number less than 4

2 You throw two dice together. Say which statements are true and which are false.

a a double 6 is likely
b a total of more than 2 is likely
c a double anything is unlikely
d a total of less than 10 is unlikely
e a total of more than 2 is certain
f a total of 1 is impossible

F

3 Choose words to describe the probability of these events.

a It will snow in August.
b Your coin lands heads up.
c The supermarket is open today.
d The speed limit will change to 20 mph outside all schools.

Show roughly where the probabilities of these events lie on the number line.

4 Find the probability, when rolling a fair dice, of getting:

a a 3
b a 5 or 6
c an odd number
d any number but a 1

giving your answer as a fraction.

5 One of the following is to be chosen to receive a prize: Tina, Stuart, Trudy, Tony, Tristan, Samuel, Tiffany, Stephen, Simon.
They put their names in a bag and one name is chosen at random.
What is the probability that:

a Sam is chosen
b a boy is chosen
c the chosen person's name begins with T
d the winner's name had 5 letters?

6 A card is dealt from a shuffled pack of 52 playing cards. Assuming each card is equally likely to be dealt, find the probability of dealing:

a a red card

b a spade

c a 4

d a face card

e any card but a face card.

The face cards

7 A 12-sided spinner is used to play a game. What is the probability that it lands on:

a 12

b an even number

c a 2-digit number

d a number smaller than 6?

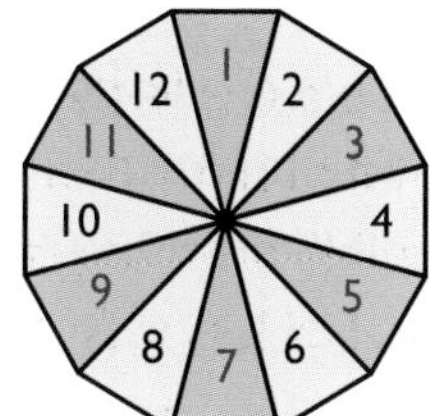

E F

CHECK-UP

1 Daniel drew a pie chart to illustrate a project on his neighbourhood. There were 80 homes altogether.

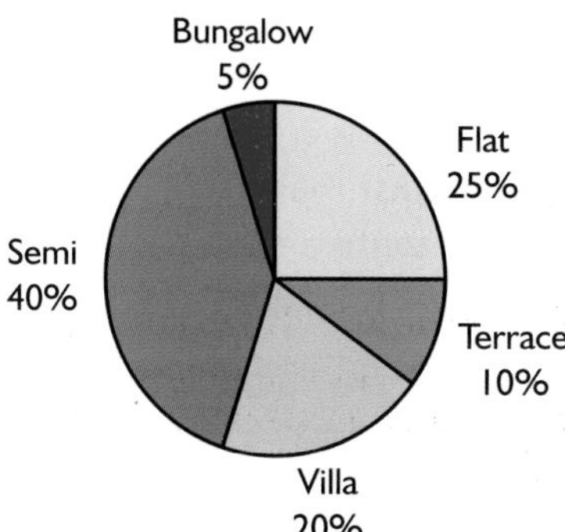

a Use the pie chart to find how many homes were:
i semis **ii** bungalows.

b A builder plans to build 20 more flats in the area.
What percentage of the pie chart will each type of home become?

2 Mrs Fisher's new car should do an average of 12 km/litre for urban driving.

a She buys 30 litres of petrol which half-fills her tank.
Copy and complete the table:

number of litres	1	30
kilometres of urban driving		

b Show this information as a line graph, plotting the number of litres horizontally.

c Say how far she should expect to travel on
i 5 litres **ii** $\frac{1}{2}$ litre **iii** 17 litres **iv** a full tank.

d In fact Mrs Fisher noticed that when her tank was $\frac{1}{4}$ full, she had travelled 220 km. Plot this point on your graph and say whether it is above or below your line.

e Can you give a possible explanation for this point?

3 The ages (in years) of a sample of members at a sports complex are:

22, 24, 16, 18, 33, 52, 28, 29, 35, 36,
46, 23, 40, 41, 31, 36, 27, 60, 35, 38.

a What is the sample size?

b Construct a stem and leaf diagram for this sample.

c How many were in their twenties?

d What percentage of the sample are over 50?

e What is the median age?

f What is the mean age?

g If a member is chosen at random, are they more likely to be in their thirties or forties?

4

pupil	1	2	3	4	5	6	7	8	9	10
maths mark %	65	83	94	76	60	72	69	87	59	80
art mark %	85	67	72	78	75	61	66	59	68	70

a For this group of pupils, draw a scatter graph showing how maths test marks vary with art test marks.

b From the scatter graph, write a sentence about the relation between maths and art marks for this group.

5 a On a bunch of grapes, 63 are edible and 7 are bad and should be thrown away.
You pick a grape without looking.
What is the probability that it will be bad?

b You have eaten 10 good grapes from the bunch without finding any bad grapes.
What is the probability of picking a good grape now?